MOON

MW00461240

Tahiti & French Polynesia

CHANTAE REDEN

TAHITI AND FRENCH POLYNESIA

S O U T H   P A C I F I C

Penrhyn

Cook Islands
Northern Group

Rakahanga

Manihiki

Mataiva
Tikehau
Rangir
Bellingshausen   Leeward Islands
Scilly   Maupiti   Motu-Iti   Makatea
                Bora Bora
Society   Taha'a   Huahine
Maupihaa   Raiatea   Tetiaroa
Islands   Moorea   **Tahiti**
                     Maiao   Mehet
                Windward Islands

Aitutaki
Te Au Ot
Takutea   Mitiaro
Atiu   Mauke
Cook Islands
Southern Group
Rarotonga
Mangaia   Maria

Rimatara   Rurutu
           A u s t r a l   Tubuai
           I s l a n d   Raivava

South Pacific Ocean

MEXICO

MAP AREA

AUSTRALIA   PERU

NEW
ZEALAND   CHILE

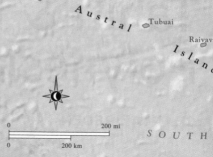

0   200 mi
0   200 km

S O U T H

OCEAN

Eiao • • Hatutaa

Marquesas

Motu Iti •
Nuku Hiva • • Ua Huka
Islands

Fatu Huku •
Ua Pou • Hiva Oa •
Tahuata • • Moho Tani

Fatu Hiva •

Disappointment Islands

Tepoto Nord •
Napuka •

T u a m o t u Manihi •
• Pukapuka

Takapoto • Takaroa •
Tikei •

Apataki • Aratika •
Kaukura • Taiaro •
Fakarava Pass Kauehi •
Toau • Raraka • Katiu •
akarava Raraka • Taenga • Takume •
Faaite • Hiti • Makemo • Raroia •
Tahanea • Tuanake • Nihiru •
Motutunga • Marutea •
Haraiki • Tekokota •
Anaa • Reitoru • Hikueru • Tauere •

I s l a n d s

Fangatau •
Fakahina •

Rekareka •

Tatakoto •

Marokau •
Ravahere • Amanu •
Nengonengo • Hao •

Akiaki •
Vahitahi • Pukarua •
Reao •

Duke of Gloucester Islands

Manuhangi • Paraoa •
Hereheretue • Vairaatea • Nukutavake •
Ahunui • Pinaki •

Amanu–Raro •
Amanu–Runga •
Nukutipipi •

Vanavana • Tureia •

Tematangi • Tenararo • Tenarunga •
Vahanga •
Moruroa • Mature- Marutea •
Fangataufa • Vavao •
Maria •

Morane • **Gambier**
Islands
Mangareva •
Temoe •

PACIFIC OCEAN

P A C I F I C

Rapa •

© MOON.COM

Contents

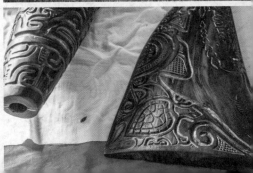

Cook's Bay, Moorea

Tahiti & French Polynesia

French Polynesia is a destination that rewards curiosity. With 118 islands and atolls spread throughout the archipelago, it's impossible to condense Tahiti and its islands into a single experience. Whether you've come to lounge on a beach under the shade of a palm frond, dive into traditional culture at a Tahitian dance performance, or go scuba diving with hundreds of sharks, there's a place for you here.

On these islands, you can connect with a world that cannot be encapsulated in the pages of any book or posted on any website. Make eye contact with a humpback whale as it migrates through tropical waters. Break away from the heat and humidity by cooling off under a waterfall or taking a dip into the sea. Even when you're lounging inside, the outside world finds its way in, with hand-carved wooden sculptures and bouquets of tropical flowers. No matter where you are, windows almost always look out to the calming sea or tropical foliage that refuses to stay shaped and tamed for long.

When it's time for a bit of indulgence, spas, fine dining restaurants, and spacious overwater bungalows welcome those who want to fall in love with one another or with the islands themselves.

In this archipelago where tall volcanic islands intermingle with low-lying atolls that barely peek over the water's edge, a perfect journey consists of surfing, trekking, sailing, exploring, diving, chatting with new friends over a drink, and cuddling up to a loved one under the stars. So stoke your imagination and pack your bags—French Polynesia is singing its siren song to your heart.

the pool at Four Seasons Resort Bora Bora

10 TOP EXPERIENCES

1 Scuba diving alongside hundreds of gray sharks at Fakarava's **Tumakohua Pass** (page 241) and bottlenose dolphins in Rangiroa's **Tiputa Pass** (page 224).

2 Lounging on **Les Sables Roses,** the pink sand beaches of the Tuamotus (page 223).

3 Eating well in Papeete, from the freshest produce at **Papeete Market** (page 45) to the vibrant roulottes (food trucks) of **Place Vaiete** (page 60).

4 Exploring the lagoons of **Bora Bora** (page 152) and **Huahine** (page 176) on a boat tour in search of reef sharks, stingrays, corals, and white sand motu (small islands).

5 Wandering the archaeological sites of the Marquesas: You'll feel a sense of mystery and awe at the overgrown remains of **Hatiheu** (page 272) and **Maʻae lʻipona** (page 288).

6 Making eye contact with a humpback whale, or seeing a calf jump playfully from the water, off the shores of **Moorea** (page 114) or **Rurutu** (page 312).

7 Watching the dramatic wave break at **Teahupoo** from the safety of a boat—there's no greater testament to the raw power of the ocean (page 85).

8 Trundling down Tahiti's **Papenoo Valley** in a four-wheel drive, passing stunning waterfalls and soaring mountains covered in mist and greenery (page 81).

9 Treating yourself to a stay in one of French Polynesia's **one-of-a-kind accommodations,** whether it's a deluxe overwater bungalow or a remote, family-owned pension (page 33).

10 Adjusting to island time in **Taiohae** (page 263) and **Atuona** (page 284), idyllic Marquesan villages where you can dine on fresh seafood, shop for the finest Polynesian crafts, and truly get away from it all.

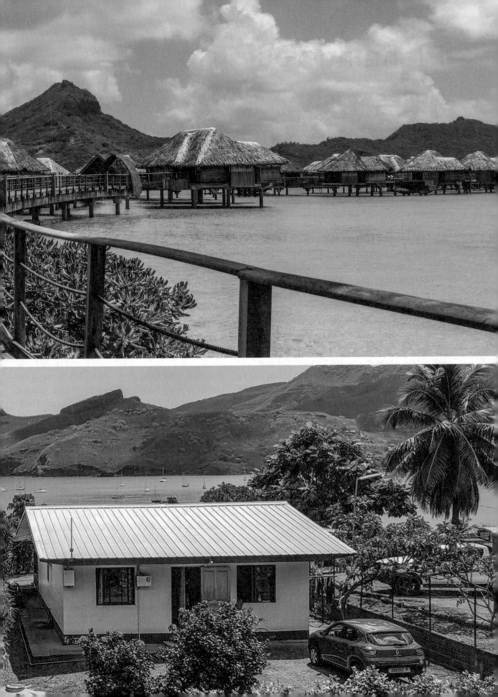

Planning Your Trip

WHERE TO GO

Tahiti

Tahiti is the largest island in French Polynesia, home to the capital city of **Papeete.** Drink, dine, and shop in the city center, where Polynesians from outer islands come to intermingle. Exciting **events, museums,** and **art galleries** call to travelers who are curious to learn more about Tahitian culture. Outside Papeete, dirt roads lead to roaring **waterfalls** and dense **jungle valleys.** Out in the water, one of the world's largest waves barrels just offshore from the tiny town of **Teahupoo.**

Moorea

Adventure awaits on Moorea, which taunts Tahiti from just across the water to the west with its spectacular mountainous skyline and white sand **beaches.** Travelers in search of excitement are bound to find it here: from **trekking** to **kayaking** to **swimming with whales** to bumbling down a dirt road in a 4WD, the island is a natural fit for explorers. When hunger strikes, sample the sweetest **pineapples** in French Polynesia. Accommodations range from five-star overwater bungalows to modest guesthouses, making Moorea accessible to anyone who ventures here.

Bora Bora and the Leeward Islands

The Leeward Islands offer romance, relaxation, and colors a camera can't capture. Sand bottom **lagoons** create an electric blue hue unseen anywhere else. The sweetheart of the region, Bora Bora, is one of the most romantic places in French Polynesia with **overwater bungalows, fine dining venues,** and **spa** services galore. Slow living is the sentiment elsewhere on the Leeward Islands—**archeological sites, fruit plantations, vanilla farms,** and **hiking trails** hide amid untamed forests.

The Tuamotu and Gambier Islands

There's no better place to experience the sea than the Tuamotus, which rise only slightly above sea level and act as sanctuaries for **marine wildlife.** Dolphins, sea turtles, sharks, manta rays, and tiny creatures take refuge within the lagoons. **Pink sand beaches, quiet villages,** and **pearl farms** await in between dives. The dry and hilly Gambier Islands welcome travelers keen to trek unmarked **trails** and listen to the mesmerizing hymns sung inside Catholic **churches** each Sunday.

The Marquesas Islands

The Marquesas Islands have **dramatic landscapes** that defy mainstream stereotypes of French Polynesia: pine tree forests, grassy plateaus, and limestone cliffs. With no outer reef to protect the shoreline, the islands' jagged coastlines are exposed to a moody ocean. Here, generations of Marquesan **wood and stone sculptors** create artwork in a style not found elsewhere. Remnants of ancient Polynesia exists here through stone **tiki, petroglyphs,** and sacred **archeological sites.**

The Austral Islands

While there are no formal hotels on this little-visited archipelago, friendly guesthouse hosts ensure travelers straying this far off the tourist trail feel right at home. Many islands are small enough to circumnavigate by bicycle or even on foot, with trails leading to **hidden caves, swim spots,** and **archeological sites.** Otherwise, tag along for a **fishing trip,** go **whale-watching,** or peer into the treetops to spot rare **Polynesian birds.**

WHEN TO GO

With a tropical climate, French Polynesia is warm and worth visiting all year round, with an average temperature ranging from 21-31°C (71-91°F). With over 100 islands dispersed throughout the South Pacific (and over 1,800 km/1,100 mi in between the most remote islands), each island group is subject to its own weather. There are two seasons in French Polynesia, dry season and wet season.

Dry Season

The dry season takes place **May-October,** when rain showers are less frequent, and temperatures are cooler—hovering around 21-27°C (71-80°F). Most tourists arrive from June to the end of August, coinciding with Northern American and European **summer holidays.** This is when tours, accommodations, flights, and car rental options might be priced higher and in high demand. The **shoulder months** of May, September, and October will bring pleasant

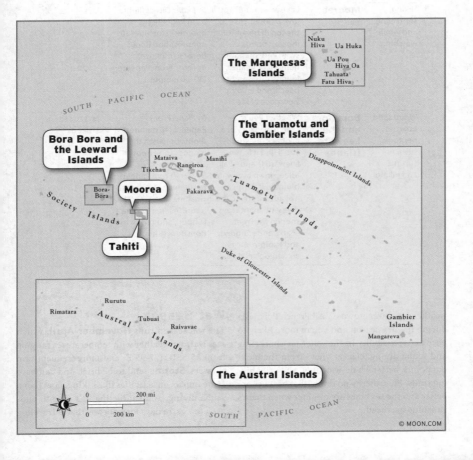

© MOON.COM

The Islands at a Glance

If you like...	Island	Why go?	Getting there	How long to stay
Dining, culture, nightlife, and surfing	**Tahiti**	On the cultural capital of French Polynesia, you can drink and dine in the city of Papeete, explore the Papenoo Valley in search of rivers and waterfalls, and surf (or watch) the incredible wave of Teahupoo.	*By Plane:* All international flights arrive at Faa'a International Airport on Tahiti; direct flights arrive from San Francisco and Los Angeles (8 hours), Honolulu (6 hours), Auckland (5.5 hours), and Tokyo (11 hours).	3 days
Hiking, snorkeling, and whale-watching	**Moorea**	Love adventure? You'll love Moorea. Hike to the top of beautiful lookout points, swim with migrating humpback whales, lounge on a sandy beach, and enjoy a slow pace of life.	*By Plane:* Direct flights from Papeete (15 minutes), Huahine (30 minutes), and Bora Bora (50 minutes). *By Ferry:* From Papeete (30-60 minutes).	3 days
White sand beaches, heritage sites, surfing, and hiking	**Bora Bora and the Leeward Islands**	Whether you're in search of luxury or a laidback guesthouse, you'll find it in the Leeward Islands. Fall asleep in an overwater bungalow, go on a 4x4 adventure, scuba dive with manta rays, snorkel with reef sharks and stingrays, and explore ancient archeological sites.	*By Plane:* From Papeete (40 minutes); flights between the islands range from 10-30 minutes. *By Ferry:* From Papeete to Huahine (3.5 hours), Huahine to Raiatea (1 hour), Raiatea to Taha'a (1 hour), and Taha'a to Bora Bora (1 hour).	8 days to see 2-3 islands

weather and fewer crowds. Visit French Polynesia during the dry season and you're more likely to have better visibility in the water for snorkeling and scuba diving, clearer views from the lookout points, better whale-watching, and drier hiking trails. Plus, there's no doubt that beaches are better and the sea blues are brighter when there's sunshine overhead.

Wet Season

The wet season runs **November-April,** which sees warmer weather with temperatures ranging from 25-35°C (77-95°F) and more frequent rain showers. **Storms** tend to be brief, and can have some impact on activities like hiking, boat tours, scuba diving, and snorkeling. It's wise to budget a few extra days for poor weather if traveling

If you like...	Island	Why go?	Getting there	How long to stay
Sandy beaches, snorkeling, and scuba diving	**The Tuamotu and Gambier Islands**	The lagoons of the Tuamotu atolls are havens for marine life. Scuba dive, snorkel, kayak, stand-up paddle, and explore the thin sandy beach slivers set around the sea. In the Gambiers, 19th-century churches and hilltops beckon offbeat travelers.	*By Plane:* From Papeete to the Tuamotus—Fakarava (1 hour), Makemo (1.5 hours), Rangiroa (1 hour), Mataiva (1 hour), and Tikehau (1 hour). Direct flights between the Tuamotus are between 10-30 minutes. Direct flights connect Papeete to Mangareva (4 hours).	7 days to see 2-3 islands
Culture, art, hiking, and archeology	**The Marquesas Islands**	Feel the spirit of Polynesia in the Marquesas Islands, a magnetic archipelago with striking landscapes and talented artisans. Relics of ancient Polynesia are found all throughout these faraway islands.	*By Plane:* Direct flights from Papeete to Nuku Hiva (3 hours 15 minutes) and Hiva Oa (3 hours 20 minutes). Direct flights connect Hiva Oa and Nuku Hiva (40 minutes). *By Ferry:* The *Aranui 5* supply ship offers a 12-day cruise around the Marquesas.	8 days to see 2-3 islands
Offbeat adventure, whale-watching, and bird-watching	**The Austral Islands**	You're far from the tourist trail here, where you can stay with a local family and go bird-watching, cave-trekking, and whale-watching.	*By Plane:* From Papeete to Raivave (2 hours), Rurutu (1.5 hours), Tubuai (1 hour 40 minutes), and Rimatara (2.5 hours with a stopover). Direct flights between the islands are around 30 minutes.	6 days to see 2-3 islands

during this time. Fortunately, the rain doesn't usually last long, and once it blows over you'll have all the benefits of the dry season without the price hikes and the crowds.

The **Marquesas Islands** are an exception, as their dry season runs from November-April and their wet season is from May-October. The Tuamotus tend to be sunny and warm no matter the time of year and are less subject to long-lasting storms. Still, in the tropics, it's best to keep sun protection and an umbrella on hand on any given day.

BEFORE YOU GO

Passports and Visas

U.S., Canadian, Australia, New Zealand, and **U.K.** citizens must have a passport with a minimum of three months validity from the date of arrival into French Polynesia. No visa is required for stays up to 90 days. **South Africans** need to apply for a short stay visa, which allows stays up to 90 days. All visitors must provide proof of onward travel in the form of a confirmed flight ticket. This can be a flight to your home destination or to any other international destination.

If you are arriving by boat, you must have proof of financial savings that will cover your flight home should you need to be repatriated.

Reservations

It's wise to book your **accommodation, flights,** and **tours** in advance of arrival. During the high travel months (June-August, December, and January), spaces are limited—especially once you leave the Society Islands. Some islands have just one or two accommodation options on the entire island, and the dates rooms are available may not overlap with flight availability.

If you are using any of the **Air Tahiti Air Passes,** it's wise to book your flight itinerary as soon as possible—ideally at least a month before arrival. Then, book your accommodation, prioritizing smaller islands first.

While large hotels and luxury properties tend to have functional websites with online reservation systems available, many of the pensions (guesthouses) do not. It's wise to first call or email requesting availability, and then arrange it with confirmation via email. Most accommodations and services on the Society Islands will have booking staff who speak English. Elsewhere, it might be more convenient to have a French translation of your request attached to your email, as this can save a lot of time and prevent misunderstandings.

When to Go For...

- **Whale-watching:** July-November
- **Scuba diving and snorkeling:** All year long, with better visibility and calm waters more likely April-November
- **Hiking:** May-October, though the Marquesas Islands are best September-April
- **Sailing:** May-October
- **Surfing:** April-October

Transportation
Getting There
PLANE

Nearly all international flights land at **Faa'a International Airport,** on the island of Tahiti. This is the central airport for both domestic and international air travel and can connect you to any major island group in French Polynesia. The most convenient way to get from one island group to another is often by plane with **Air Tahiti.** Typical flight times, including layovers, are:

- U.S. (Los Angeles or San Francisco): 8 hours
- Hawaii (Honolulu): 6 hours
- U.K. (London): 22-25 hours
- Australia (Sydney): 10 hours
- New Zealand (Auckland): 5.5 hours
- South Africa (Cape Town): 35 hours
- France (Paris): 22-25 hours

FERRY AND BOAT

Public ferries connect the Society Islands a few times per week and run between Tahiti and Moorea daily. Some cargo ships connect Tahiti to the outer islands, but these rarely accept non-working passengers, and the vessels that do are often booked out months in advance.

Passenger ferries run between Tahiti to

Adventure on a Budget

French Polynesia is rightfully rarely thought of as a budget destination. Simple meals often cost at least CFP 2,000 (US$20) and the most basic rooms hover around the CFP 7,000 mark (US$70). Despite this, there are ways to stretch your French Pacific francs further than you think.

- **Stay in a pension:** Pensions are family-run guesthouses found all throughout the islands, usually consisting of a room with a bed and access to a shared bathroom. Many pensions include breakfast and dinner with the cost of the stay. Many pensions also allow guests to use the kitchen, slashing restaurant spending substantially.

- **Go camping:** Camping can help cut costs on accommodation and food if the campsite has kitchen access. Expect to pay around CFP 1,500-3,500 (US$15-35) per person per night with your own camping gear.

- **Take ferries or use the Air Tahiti Multi Islands Air Pass:** Even the 15-minute flights in French Polynesia can cost over CFP 10,000 (US$100). Cut the costs of transport by taking the

Apetahi Express ferry in the Society Islands, or traveling with an Air Tahiti Air Pass that'll allow you to see multiple islands for around 30-40 percent cheaper than buying each flight on its own.

- **Shop at the markets:** Supermarkets and convenience stores are often stocked with imported goods, making them expensive places to resupply. Instead, browse the local market for seasonal produce, locally sourced meat, and fish for an affordable price.

- **Stay during the shoulder season:** Prices of accommodations, car rentals, and tours spike during the busy months of June, July, August, and the end of year holidays. Travel during the other months to enjoy a wider selection of services and accommodations for a much lower price.

- **Pack wisely:** Love to snorkel? Buying your own set of snorkel gear (mask, snorkel, and fins) is one of the best investments you can make. It'll be a go-to free activity on almost every island, and you'll save yourself from paying CFP 1,000 (US$10) or more for masks that leak and fins that cause blisters.

Moorea around five times per day, taking 30-40 minutes each way (around CFP 1,300 one-way per person).

The Apetahi Express *Aremiti 5* runs a course from Tahiti to the **Leeward Islands,** taking 3.5 hours to reach Huahine, 1 hour to Raiatea, 45 minutes to Taha'a, and another 1 hour 15 minutes to Maupiti with a 20-minute stop at each island. Monthly passes are CFP 17,900-23,900 for unlimited travel or around CFP 7,400-8,900 one-way for a single leg of the journey.

The *Aranui 5* links Tahiti to the **Marquesas Islands** once or twice per month with the prices starting at CFP 360,500 per person for the full 11-night journey. It takes about 1-2 days to reach the Marquesas from Tahiti, with a half day of travel in between each of the Marquesas Islands.

The **Austral Islands** are reached by the *Tuhaa Pae IV,* a passenger freighter that departs 2-3 times per month from Tahiti to the Austral Islands. The full trip takes around 10 days to complete, with a full day of travel in between islands. Single-leg trips start at CFP 5,500 per person.

Getting Around
PLANE

Plane is often the only practical way to get between most of the islands in French Polynesia. The domestic carrier, **Air Tahiti,** flies to each of the six island groups in French Polynesia. Its hub is in **Papeete** on the island of Tahiti. Flight prices change seasonally and rise with demand. It's wise to book your flights before anything else, as they are often more limited compared to accommodation and tour availability.

If you'll be island-hopping, note that round-trip tickets are about 10 percent cheaper than two one-way flights. To see more than two islands on a budget, opt for an **Air Tahiti Air Pass.** Air Passes are valid for 28 days and allow travelers to stop at each island included in the pass, though you don't have to visit them all. Each pass includes 23 kilograms of baggage allowance. Scuba divers can bring an extra 5 kilograms for their diving equipment. Flight times vary from 15 minutes (Tahiti to Moorea) to over 4 hours (Tahiti to the

Marquesas Islands); expect to pay CFP 7,000-20,000 for flights of up to 2 hours and CFP 30,000-50,000 for flights longer than 2 hours one-way. Passengers can combine one pass and one extension to use within 28 days of travel.

- **Discovery Pass:** Moorea, Huahine, Raiatea (low season €332/adult, €272/child; high season €357/adult, €292/child)

- **Bora Bora Pass:** Moorea, Huahine, Raiatea, Bora Bora, Maupiti (low season €435/adult, €354/child; high season €469/adult, €380/child)

- **Lagoons Pass:** Moorea, Rangiroa, Tikehau, Fakarava (low season €441/adult, €357/child; high season €476/adult, €384/child)

- **Bora-Tuamotu Pass:** Moorea, Huahine, Raiatea, Maupiti, Bora Bora, Rangiroa, Tikehau, Fakarava (low season €584/adult, €472/child; high season €632/adult, €508/child)

- **Austral Pass:** Rurutu, Tubuai, Raivavae, Rimatara (low season €602/adult, €484/child; high season €651/adult, €522/child)

- **Marquesas Pass:** Nuku Hiva, Hiva Oa (low season €780/adult, €610/child; high season €851/adult, €665/child)

- **Austral Extension:** Rurutu, Tubuai, Raivavae, Rimatara (low season €365/adult, €294/child; high season €394/adult, €317/child)

- **Marquesas Extension:** Nuku Hiva, Hiva Oa (low season €582/adult, €460/child; high season €634/adult, €499/child)

Tahiti Air Charter flies between the Leeward Islands of Raiatea, Huahine, Bora Bora, and Maupiti. Prices range from CFP 8,000-9,000 one-way. Aside from their regular routes, Tahiti Air Charter offers private plane charter, scenic flights, and day trips to Maupiti.

BOAT TAXIS AND CHARTER BOATS

Within island groups, boat taxis and charters offer rides to nearby islands, though these usually run as needed rather than on a schedule. Most taxi boats depart at the island or atoll's main wharf or jetty, and if there's a snack (casual restaurant) nearby, they'll likely be able to point you in the right direction. Otherwise, boat rides are best arranged with the help of your accommodation. Costs vary greatly, but expect to pay around CFP 1,000 per kilometer per person, plus CFP 500 per piece of luggage.

CAR AND MOTORBIKE

Having a rental car is the most convenient way to get around most of the larger islands of French Polynesia, especially the Society Islands and the Marquesas. Some islands also have motorbikes for rent. On islands with fewer tourists, pensions can often connect travelers to someone willing to rent out their private vehicle.

Most vehicles for rent have manual transmission. Roads range from newly paved to rutted out dirt tracks. If you'll be driving along the latter, opt for a 4WD. Drivers often pick up hitchhikers, an act that is popular wherever it's possible to get around by wheel. It is not recommended to hitchhike alone.

BICYCLE

Many of the islands are easily covered by bicycle; basic ones will be available for rent at many accommodations. Most islands have one main road looping around the perimeter of the island, which is rarely busy, making for easy cycling. On Tahiti, however, navigating congested traffic around Papeete is best left to experienced cyclists only.

PUBLIC TRANSPORT

Public transport is not common on islands aside from Tahiti, the only island with a well-connected bus system. Buses lap the island of Tahiti and cost CFP 150-450 per trip. On the Society Islands, many restaurants will offer a shuttle bus service to transport patrons to and from their accommodation.

TAXI

When available (typically on the Society Islands), getting around by taxi is one of the most expensive forms of transportation in French Polynesia. Always negotiate the fare in advance or arrange that the meter be turned on. Some drivers charge extra for luggage. Hiring a private driver or vehicle for a full day is oftentimes only slightly more expensive than taking a few taxi rides. Rideshare apps are not commonly used on French Polynesia.

Ships depart for outer islands at the Papeete Ferry Terminal.

BEST OF

Tahiti & French Polynesia

With over 100 islands in French Polynesia—some large, some tiny; some with volcanic peaks soaring above the water, others barely rising above sea level—it's easy to get overwhelmed by which to choose. In this itinerary, you'll see sacred archeological sites, pink sand beaches, and bright blue lagoons, as well as Papeete, the gateway to French Polynesia and Tahiti's version of a tropical metropolis. This itinerary is best for those who don't mind moving at a quick pace. But we won't blame you if you land on an island and decide to spend the rest of your time there. (Stranger things have happened.)

To save on airfare on this itinerary, purchase the **Bora-Tuamotu Air Pass** (www.airtahiti. com; low season €584, high season €632), which includes a stop at each island featured on its itinerary. It's wise to book your flights at least 2-3 months before your trip. To minimize stopovers, follow the route listed below or the itinerary featured on the Air Tahiti website. This itinerary follows the "Four Islands" recommended itinerary from Air Tahiti.

If you prefer to travel by ferry, you can buy the **Apetahi Pass** (www.apetahiexpress.pf; CFP 23,900 for all ferry rides). Fly to Rangiroa and travel to the other islands onboard the *Aremiti 5*, which departs on a route around the Society Islands three times per week. Budget an extra half day of travel to return from Moorea to Tahiti, to venture from Tahiti to Huahine (4 hours), and another half day from Huahine to Bora Bora (4.5 hours).

Moorea
Day 1

After flying into Faa'a International Airport on Tahiti, where most international flights to French Polynesia arrive, head to Moorea by 40-minute ferry or 15-minute flight from Tahiti. Enjoy a relaxed day on the island's sun-soaked beaches. Choose between **Temae Beach,** a stretch of white sand and turquoise waters; **Ta'ahiamanu,** where there's plenty of shade and decent snorkeling; or **Tipaniers Beach** for kayaking and stand-up paddling. Dinner at **Rudy's** stays true to the day's laid-back theme as you adjust to island time.

view from Belvedere Lookout, Moorea

Day 2

Rent a bicycle or car today to explore the island. The trip up to **Belvedere Lookout** is obligatory, with views of Cook's Bay and Opunohu, and you'll pass the **Marae Titiroa** archeological site along the way. Then, head to the **Manutea Tahiti Distillery** for a taste of Tahitian spirits. If you prefer not to drive, 4WD day tours cover these sights and include a rumble along Moorea's gorgeous **Pineapple Road.** For dinner, grab a meal at **Le Lézard Jaune Café** or attend a Polynesian cultural performance at one of the major hotels or Tiki Village Theater.

Day 3

Spend today out on the water, either on a snorkel tour or whale-watching excursion. Some boat trips venture to **Stingray World,** a site with tens of pink whip rays and black tip reef sharks. Keep an eye on the horizon for signs of splashing from humpback whales and dolphins. Once evening arrives, enjoy dinner at **Le Coco D'Isle.**

Huahine
Day 4

Take a 35-minute flight to Huahine and check into an accommodation near **Fare.** (If you're taking the ferry, you will need to backtrack to Tahiti and catch the boat to Huahine, which takes roughly four hours.) Explore the town of Fare on foot or by bicycle, stopping at the **distillery** and

the **waterfront** to admire the Huahine Nui skyline, which looks like a sleeping woman. For dinner, enjoy the social scene at the **Huahine Yacht Club.**

Day 5

Rent a scooter or car to go on a day trip around Huahine. Begin with the archeological remains of **Maeva** and the ancient fish traps, then stop in **Faie** to browse for pearls and see blue-eyed eels. Cross the bridge to **Huahine Iti,** stopping at **Hotel Le Mahana** on Avea Beach for lunch. End the day with a dinner at the roulottes (food trucks) in Fare.

Day 6

Seize the opportunity to venture around Huahine by boat on a **lagoon tour** departing from Fare. These trips often stop at a snorkel spot with black tip reef sharks off Fare, the **Huahine Pearl Farm,** reefs for snorkeling, and a picnic lunch on the white sands of a small island in the lagoon.

Bora Bora
Day 7

Catch a 25-minute direct flight or 2.5-hour ferry ride from Huahine to Bora Bora. If you want to have an all-out luxury experience, check into one of the **overwater bungalows** on Bora Bora's outer motu (islets). If you're on a budget, opt for

Scuba Diving and Snorkeling in French Polynesia

Take the plunge into the blues of French Polynesia to admire a spectacular seascape. Coral reefs rife with hard and soft corals, deep crevasses, sandy sea beds, and reef passes teeming with marine life create plenty of playgrounds for the avid scuba diver or snorkeler. Armed with your own mask and snorkel, any tranquil bay is your oyster to explore.

SCUBA DIVING 101

French Polynesia is a wonderful destination if you're learning how to scuba dive; many scuba centers on the islands of Tahiti offer a discovery dive for first-time divers. And if you want to dive the region's best dive sites, most dive centers offer open water certification courses, which take around three days to complete. You'll want to notify the school in advance if you prefer your course taught in English, as French is the default language for tourists.

DIVING PASSES

Diving passes, which allow you to purchase dives in bulk, are an easy way to save money as you travel and dive.

- **eDivingPass** (edivingpass.com) has packages of 6 dives for €62.85 per dive, €377.10 per pass, valid at nearly 40 dive centers.
- **Te Moana Diving Pass** (temoanadiving.com) offers a pass of 10 dives for CFP 72,000 or CFP 7,200 per dive at 14 dive centers.

BEST SCUBA DIVE SITES

- **La Zélée, Tahiti:** This is a wreck dive at a century-old gunboat now encrusted with corals (page 53).
- **The Rose Garden, Moorea:** The corals here resemble an underwater rose garden, frequented by tiger sharks (page 108).

- **Avapehi Pass, Huahine:** Large schools of barracuda are seen here, plus reef sharks in their natural habitat (page 174).
- **Anau, Bora Bora:** Witness a manta ray ballet at this thriving stretch of reef (page 148).
- **Tiputa Pass, Rangiroa:** In this shark-laden reef pass, you have a chance to dive with the atoll's resident pod of bottlenose dolphins (page 224).
- **Tuheiava Pass, Tikehau:** Thousands of fish, hammerhead sharks, tiger sharks, manta rays, and barracuda cruise regularly through this densely packed pass (page 233).
- **Tumakohua Pass, Fakarava:** Hundreds of gray reef sharks inhabit the southern pass of Fakarava, making it a shark diver's dream (page 241).
- **Hammerhead Guard Rock, Nuku Hiva:** This rarely dived site is your best shot at spotting tens of hammerhead sharks (page 266).

BEST SNORKEL SITES

- **Mahana Park Beach, Tahiti:** Snorkel along this accessible trail of coral reefs marked with informative plaques (page 77).
- **Stingray World, Moorea:** Blow bubbles with tens of black tip reef sharks and pink whip stingrays in the shallows of Tipaniers Beach (page 108).
- **Anau, Bora Bora:** Spot manta rays gliding through the water like acrobats from the surface of the sea (page 148).
- **Aquarium, Rangiroa:** Technicolor reef fish, reef sharks, manta rays, and moray eels hang out off this reef near Tiputa Pass (page 226).

an accommodation near Vaitape Wharf or Matira Point. A free 20-minute shuttle ride connects airport arrivals to Vaitape Wharf, while the more upscale hotels meet travelers at the airport and ferry them directly to the resort. Spend an afternoon lounging on **Matira Beach** before venturing to **Bloody Mary's** for dinner.

Day 8

Spend a full day out on the water, either on a **scuba diving** trip to see coral reefs and manta rays, or on a **snorkeling** trip onboard a motorized outrigger canoe. On snorkel trips, you're likely to see reef sharks and stingrays, with the occasional manta ray or eagle ray gliding beneath. Picnic lunches often consist of raw fish served with coconut milk (poisson cru), served on a white sand beach. For dinner, enjoy a meal at **Restaurant St. James.**

Day 9

Rent a **bicycle** and pedal around Bora Bora, stopping at the naval canons, points, and small settlements. You can circumnavigate the island in about three hours; scooters and cars are also available. If you're feeling extra adventurous, rumble around the island on an **ATV tour**—they stop at hard-to-reach lookout points found on dirt roads and are led by an informative guide. Enjoy fresh seafood, pasta, and crepes doled out from the food trucks and stands near Vaitape Wharf.

Rangiroa
Day 10

Hop on a direct 1-hour-15-minute flight from Bora Bora to Rangiroa. Stay on the main motu (island), near Avatoru, or the tiny town of Tiputa. Take a tour of **Vin de Tahiti,** the archipelago's sole winery, and enjoy a cold glass of wine at **Relais de Josephine,** which overlooks Tiputa Pass; bottlenose dolphin sightings are common.

Day 11

Spend your day scuba diving in **Tiputa Pass** for a chance to spot gray sharks, barracudas, manta rays, sea turtles, and Rangiroa's pod of bottlenose dolphins. If you're not certified for scuba diving, embark on a snorkel tour to the Aquarium snorkel site and through the Tiputa Pass if conditions allow. Spend the rest of the day at the beach. For dinner, head to **Snack Chez Lili.**

Day 12

Book a day tour to the **Blue Lagoon,** a little over 30 kilometers (18 mi) away from Avatoru. White sand islets flanked with palm trees and aquamarine waters await. The lagoon is a nursery for black tip reef sharks, so pack a snorkel. Most tour operators host a lunch of raw fish, grilled fish, coconut bread, and platters of fresh fruit. Sunglasses and sunscreen are a must.

Tahiti
Day 13

Catch the earliest flight you can to Tahiti, a one-hour direct flight from Rangiroa. Spend the day exploring **Papeete,** beginning at the market and strolling through the administrative district, the shops, and the waterfront. If you are in need of an escape, venture to **Point Venus** to swim and enjoy a cold drink near a black sand beach. For dinner, no trip to Papeete is complete without a meal at **Place Vai'ete,** a hub for roulottes (food trucks).

Day 14

If your international flight is departing late into the evening, spend the day on a mini road trip north to see the **blowholes** and **Faarumai Waterfall,** or head south to **Mahana Parc Beach** for prime snorkeling. If you prefer to go inland, book a 4WD excursion into Tahiti's **Papenoo Valley,** where gorges, creeks, and waterfalls await.

Back to Nature: French Polynesia's Best Hikes

Overgrown trails on the islands of French Polynesia lead to volcanic peaks, grassy plateaus, caves, waterfalls, and lookout points with sea views. Pack your hiking shoes, sunscreen, and a hat to explore the islands on foot.

- **Fautaua Valley, Tahiti:** Trek on an all-day trip to Tahiti's tallest waterfall roaring down a moss-cloaked cliff and into a cool pool below (page 79).

- **Three Coconut Trees, Moorea:** This trail through Moorea's cloud-topped interior from Belvedere Lookout leads to views of Opunohu Bay and Cook Bay (page 110).

- **Les Trois Cascades, Raiatea:** A trail of tropical flowers leads to a series of three waterfalls. Cool pools for swimming reward tired legs (page 192).

- **Tetuanui Plateau, Rurutu:** You might spot humpback whales breaching from Rurutu's scenic plateau (page 312).

- **Mount Hiro, Raivave:** The trail to the highest point on Raivave is steep but worth it once you catch the many shades of blue of the lagoon (page 325).

- **Vaipo Waterfall, Nuku Hiva:** Trek from a palm tree bay past archeological sites to a trickling waterfall pouring between the crags of a giant cliff (page 271).

- **Hanatekuua Bay, Hiva Oa:** Wander from the tiny settlement of Hanaiapa to the quiet beach of Hanatekuua, accessible solely by those who come on foot or by boat (page 290).

Love and Luxury

The legendary beauty of French Polynesia has made it an obvious choice for honeymooners and couples looking for a romantic escape, and upscale resorts on the islands deliver on the dream with overwater bungalows, spa services, couples' massages, gourmet dinners, canoe breakfasts, rose petal baths, and imported champagnes. Symbolic and official wedding ceremonies and elopements are available for lovers who want to tie the knot in the tropics. Note that if you plan to stay in four- to five-star properties during your visit, it's often more cost-effective to book your trip with a travel agent or as a package tour.

Moorea
Day 1
After arriving in Papeete, catch the 15-minute flight or 40-minute ferry ride from Papeete to Moorea. Check into one of the properties with overwater bungalows, like **Sofitel Kia Ora Moorea Beach Resort** or **Hilton Moorea Lagoon Resort and Spa.** Enjoy unwinding at the property's white sand beaches before checking in for a couples' spa treatment to ease out any post-travel stress. Dine on-site.

Day 2
Go for a sunrise swim from your bungalow before getting picked up for a **whale- and dolphin-watching excursion.** Some operators stop at snorkel spots replete with shy reef sharks and stingrays. Tonight, dine at one of Moorea's small restaurants around the island such as **Rudy's.**

Day 3
Set out to explore Moorea's wild interior: rent a car and drive to the top of **Belvedere Lookout,** where views of Moorea's emerald mountainous landscape are seen. The **Three Coconut Trees**

Try pineapple brut on Moorea.

Trail makes for a fun few-hour hike. If you prefer to join a tour, book one that ventures to the top of **Magic Mountain** for a spectacular view of Moorea's lagoon. For lunch, head to **Coco Beach Moorea** for a quaint meal on a little motu. In the afternoon, embark on a **sunset cruise** of Moorea's lagoon for a toast to the setting sun.

Bora Bora
Day 4

Fly 50 minutes to the airport of Bora Bora and then catch the private boat to your private motu

the private beach of Four Seasons Resort Bora Bora

resort, like the **Four Seasons Resort Bora Bora, St. Regis Bora Bora,** or **Le Bora Bora.** If you're on a budget, there are basic overwater bungalows to enjoy at **Oa Oa Lodge.** Go for a swim at the resort's pool or in the sea from the comforts of your bungalow's swim deck, then read undisturbed under the shade. If there's a Polynesian dance performance tonight, be sure to enjoy the show!

Day 5

Wake up and order breakfast from room service, delivered by outrigger canoe. Then, venture onto Bora Bora's turquoise **lagoon** on a day cruise—most include spots to snorkel and a private picnic lunch. Or, if you prefer to see the island from above, a scenic **helicopter ride** is in order. The helicopter usually laps the interior of Bora Bora's lagoon, revealing mesmerizing blues of every shade. Enjoy dinner at the resort.

Day 6

Catch the shuttle boat from your resort to the main island of Bora Bora and take a circle island tour, stopping at **Matira Beach,** the naval cannons, and a few scenic lookout points. The island also has boutique black pearl shops worthy of perusing. For dinner, enjoy an intimate dining experience at **Villa Mahana,** which includes transport to the Vaitape Wharf.

Tahiti
Day 7

After a morning swim, catch the 50-minute flight back to Tahiti. If you have a full day, stay at **Intercontinental Tahiti Resort & Spa** to soak in an infinity pool or get a massage with monoï oil at their on-site spa. Or, if you prefer to sightsee, head into the center of Papeete to browse the **Papeete Market** and walk along the waterfront. Make reservations at **Hei** to end your journey with a fine dining experience.

Your Own Slice of Paradise: French Polynesia's Best Accommodations

From family-run pensions hidden on the hillside to overwater bungalows set above sparkling waters, French Polynesia offers a wide range of accommodations no matter your interests or budget. Generally, pensions (family-run guesthouses) offer a more affordable stay, while foreign-owned hotels and luxury resorts will cost a pretty penny. These are some of the best accommodations on the islands.

LUXURY OVERWATER STAYS

- **Sofitel Kia Ora Moorea Beach Resort:** Overwater bungalows look out across the sea from Moorea to Tahiti and are just steps away from a wide alabaster beach (page 124).

- **Four Seasons Resort Bora Bora:** Admire the turquoise lagoon and Bora Bora's Mount Otemanu from this five-star stay with a spa and multiple restaurants (page 164).

- **The St. Regis Bora Bora Resort:** Featuring the most spacious overwater bungalows in French Polynesia, the St. Regis lets you live large with its butler service and private lagoon (page 162).

- **Le Taha'a by Pearl Resorts:** Incredible snorkeling is just a few fin kicks away from your overwater bungalow (page 202).

- **Le Tikehau by Pearl Resorts:** Adventure meets luxury at this diver's dream resort; overwater rooms have their own shaded lounge deck (page 236).

PENSIONS & ECO-FRIENDLY RETREATS

- **Hotel Fenua Mata'i'oa, Moorea:** This quiet waterfront retreat is decorated with Polynesian artwork and antique furniture (page 127).

- **Fare Mahi Mahi, Raiatea:** An infinity pool overlooks the sea at this pension with spacious rooms, plenty of lounge areas, and accommodating hosts (page 188).

- **Vanira Lodge, Tahiti:** Disconnect from the outside world and spend the night in a treehouse bungalow near Tahiti's surf town of Teahupoo (page 89).

- **Tahiti Yacht Charter, Raiatea:** Why not cruise around the Society Islands on a sailing yacht? Skilled sailors can charter a vessel to themselves, while those who prefer to have a stress-free stay can charter a boat with captain and crew (page 135).

- **Ninamu Resort, Tikehau:** This private island resort is powered by solar energy and built from natural materials. Guests can paddle, kitesurf, snorkel, and take a wander through the property's organic garden (page 236).

Tikis and Treks in the Marquesas

The magic of the Marquesas Islands is best experienced firsthand. Within the islands' dramatic valleys, waterfronts, and plateaus, you'll find ancient and sacred archeological sites where the spirit of the island is sure to be felt. Purchase the **Air Tahiti Marquesas Pass** or the **Marquesas Extension** for more affordable flights to Nuku Hiva and Hiva Oa. Alternatively, you could take a 12-day trip through the Marquesas as a passenger onboard the *Aranui 5*, which stops at all inhabited islands in the Marquesas.

Hiva Oa

Day 1

Take a direct 3-hour-20-minute flight from Tahiti to Hiva Oa. Arrange your accommodation somewhere close to **Atuona.** If time allows, take a walk through Atuona to browse through its handicraft market, and admire the town from above from the **Cavalry Cemetery.** Dine at **Relais Moehau** for a pizza or seafood dinner.

Day 2

Rent a car or hire a private driver to explore the highlights of Hiva Oa, first stopping at the **Smiling Tiki** before driving to the seaside town of **Nahoe,** and then the reverent **Ma'ae I'ipona,** an ancient archeological site with tikis. On your way back, stop for a break or picnic at **Puamau.** Dine at your accommodation or **Hotel Hanakee Lodge.**

When in French Polynesia: Doing as Locals Do

Want to experience life like a local in French Polynesia? While there are plenty of activities and accommodations designed with tourists in mind, it's possible to see a more intimate side of the islands, too.

- **Shop at the market:** In the mornings, local markets are abuzz with residents shopping for their weekly produce, meat, fish, and other goods. Papeete Market is the largest of them all, selling everything from food to crafts to clothing to jewelry to cosmetics.

- **Visit a marae:** A marae (Tahitian) or ma'ae (Marquesan) is the site where sacred ceremonies once took place. Sometimes, they're adorned with tikis. Visit the marae at Maeva Village on Huahine, Taputapuatea on Raiatea, or Ma'ae l'ipona on Hiva Oa.

- **Eat from a roulotte or snack:** The roulottes (food trucks) of Place Vai'ete in Tahiti, Fare in Huahine, and Vaitape in Bora Bora dole out easy eats and are popular with locals. "Snacks," little restaurants usually serving seafood, also cater to tourists and locals alike with large portions and a laid-back atmosphere.

- **Stay with a family:** Most pensions, also known as guesthouses, are owned by families who stay on the property with their guests. Lounge areas and kitchens are often communal, offering a glimpse at a daily life in French Polynesia.

- **Take the ferry:** While it's true it's easiest to get around on a plane, taking a ferry to Moorea or elsewhere in the Society Islands will give you enough time to chat with locals onboard. Don't be surprised if you hear the strumming of a ukulele, and if you know the words of the song, feel free to sing along.

the ceremonial ma'ae and tiki on Taiohae's waterfront

Day 3

Venture out on a day trip to the neighboring island of **Tahuata,** an island with sandy beaches and quiet settlements just 30 minutes away by boat. These trips usually stop in **Vaitahu** for a seafood buffet lunch, the **Hapatoni craft market,** and a small beach for swimming. You'll probably return to Atuona just before sunset for an early night in.

Nuku Hiva
Day 4

Catch a direct 40-minute flight to Nuku Hiva, where arrangements for transport from the airport to your accommodation should be made in advance. The drive from the airport to the main town of **Taiohae** takes a little under two hours, and stops at a few lookout points along the way. If you've arrived in Taiohae while the sun is still out, walk along the waterfront to **Tiki Tuhiva.** For dinner, **Moana Nui Pizzeria** features scrumptious dishes.

Day 5

Rent a car or embark on a full-day tour across

Nuku Hiva to **Hatiheu,** where you'll find a large collection of stone tikis and sacred ma'ae (ceremony sites). Stop at the craft market in **Taipivai, Hooumi Bay,** and **Chez Yvonne** for lunch. Enjoy dinner at your accommodation.

Day 6

Take a 30-minute boat ride from Taiohae to **Hakaui** and trek to **Vaipo Waterfall** in the Hakaui Valley. The hike should take around four hours and includes lunch at one of the homes near the Hakaui Bay waterfront. Back in Taiohae, sip cocktails and have dinner at **Le Keikahanui Nuku Hiva Pearl Restaurant.**

Tahiti
Day 7

The two-hour airport transfer from Taiohae plus the 3-hour-15-minute flight from Nuku Hiva to Tahiti is likely to take up most of your day. If time allows in Papeete, head to **Place Vai'ete** for a meal of piping hot crepes, pastas, noodle dishes, or seafood served from the famous roulottes (food trucks).

Tahiti

Depending on who you ask, Tahiti may conjure images of aquamarine waters, perfectly detailed tattoos, dancers who don't miss a beat, densely forested mountain peaks, or one of the world's heaviest waves. It's taken on a mythical reputation, with mana, the sacred Polynesian spirit, cloaking its land and sea. The island of Tahiti is home to French Polynesia's capital city of Papeete, where vibrant markets await. In its interior, hiking trails lead to waterfalls, and small towns welcome travelers to come and snorkel from the shore, pick fruit from the gardens, admire the ancient ceremonial structures called marae, and enjoy life on island time.

This 1,045-square-kilometer (403-square-mi) island was formed more than 1 million years ago by two or three shield volcanoes,

Highlights

Look for ★ to find recommended sights, activities, dining, and lodging.

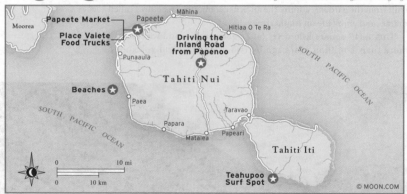

★ **Papeete Market:** Shop for food, pearls, and handcrafted souvenirs at Tahiti's liveliest market (page 45).

★ **Beaches:** Behold the beauty of beaches made from volcanic sand—under full sunlight, they sparkle (page 52).

★ **Place Vaiete Food Trucks:** After sunset, this square comes alive with food trucks (roulottes) doling out some of the city's best dishes (page 60).

★ **Driving the Inland Road from Papenoo:** Mountain peaks, waterfalls, and panoramic views await in the island's interior (page 81).

★ **Teahupoo Surf Spot:** Even if you don't surf, watching one of the world's most powerful waves is a humbling sight (page 85).

and accounts for almost a third of French Polynesia's land area. Two distinct circular sections of the island—Tahiti Nui (the larger, western section) and Tahiti Iti (the smaller eastern section)—are joined at the isthmus of Taravao.

On Tahiti Nui, the rounded, verdant summits of Orohena (2,241 m/7,352 ft) and Aorai (2,066 m/6,778 ft) once stood 3,000 meters (9,842 ft) above the sea, 12,700 meters (41,666 ft) high from the seabed. Deep valleys radiate from these central peaks, and steep slopes drop abruptly from high plateaus to coastal plains. The northeast coast is rugged and rocky, without a barrier reef, and thus exposed to intense pounding surf; villages lie on a narrow strip between mountains and ocean. The south coast is broad and gentle with large gardens and coconut groves; a barrier reef shields it from the sea's fury and forms some tranquil lagoons. A few hundred thousand years younger than Tahiti Nui, Tahiti Iti's heart is Mount Rooniu (1,323 m/4,340 ft), and black beaches of volcanic sand fringe this turtle-shaped island.

Most of French Polynesia's population lives on Tahiti, largely gathered around the city of Papeete and concentrated along the coast; the interior is almost uninhabited. Anthropologists think Polynesian sea voyagers first settled here in 500 BC, arriving in 20-meter (65-ft) outrigger canoes from Pacific Islands found to the west. The intimate connection Tahitians hold with the sea is evident at the fish markets and stands by the roadside, in the ubiquitous canoes gliding across Tahitian waters, and by the care Tahitians have for their land.

ORIENTATION

Almost everyone arrives at **Faa'a International Airport,** 5 kilometers (3 mi) west of **Papeete,** French Polynesia's capital.

To the east are the towns of **Arue** and **Mahina,** with a smattering of hotels and black sand beaches, and the peninsula of **Point Venus.** South of Faa'a lie the commuter communities **Punaauia, Paea,** and **Papara. Papenoo Valley,** the mountainous heart of Tahiti Nui, runs all the way to **Lake Vaihiria,** accessible via an interior road from the settlement of Papenoo on the north coast. At **Taravao,** a refueling stop on your 117-kilometer (72-mi) way around Tahiti Nui, Tahiti Iti is connected to Tahiti Nui by an isthmus. On Tahiti Iti, dead-end roads line the north and south coasts. Road markers begin at Papeete Market, counting around the island in both directions and meeting in Taravao.

PLANNING YOUR TIME

You can see the main sights of Papeete in **a day;** spend at least half a day browsing through the **market** and **art galleries** before venturing to **Point Venus** at sunset. A lap around the island is also a worthwhile way to spend the day, stopping at the small towns of **Paea, Papara,** and **Teahupoo.** If you can afford the time and expense, it's worthwhile to rent a car for three days and explore at your leisure. If you want to see the **Papenoo Valley,** hire a guide to navigate hairpin turns with a 4x4 (book in advance). Trips on the water whale-watching, exploring the Te Pari coast, scuba diving, or cruising make for a fun day out and should also be booked ahead.

A good selection of accommodations is available across the island, but staying within 20 kilometers (12 mi) of **Papeete** is most convenient, as most tours include free transport within this radius. Once you venture outside of Papeete, the pace of life slows dramatically and it's easy to enjoy the natural surroundings. But on weekends, life washes out into the countryside, making the capital a ghost town.

Previous: Papenoo Valley waterfall; Papenoo Valley; the lighthouse at Point Venus.

Tahiti

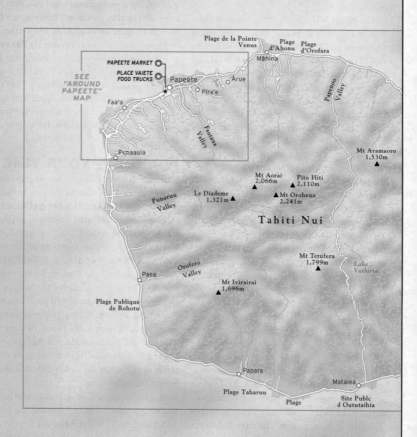

Plage de la Pointe Venus

Plage d'Ahonu

Plage d'Orofara

Māhina

PAPEETE MARKET

PLACE VAIETE FOOD TRUCKS

Papeete

Arue

SEE "AROUND PAPEETE" MAP

Pira'e

Faa'a

Papenoo Valley

Fautaua Valley

Punaauia

Mt Aramaoro 1,530m

Punaruu Valley

Mt Aorai 2,066m

Pito Hiti 2,110m

Le Diademe 1,321m

Mt Orohena 2,241m

Tahiti Nui

Mt Tetufera 1,799m

Lake Vaihiria

Orofero Valley

Mt Ivirairai 1,696m

Paea

Plage Publique de Rohotu

Papara

Mataiea

Plage Taharuu

Plage

Site Publc d Oututaihia

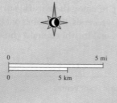

0   5 mi

0   5 km

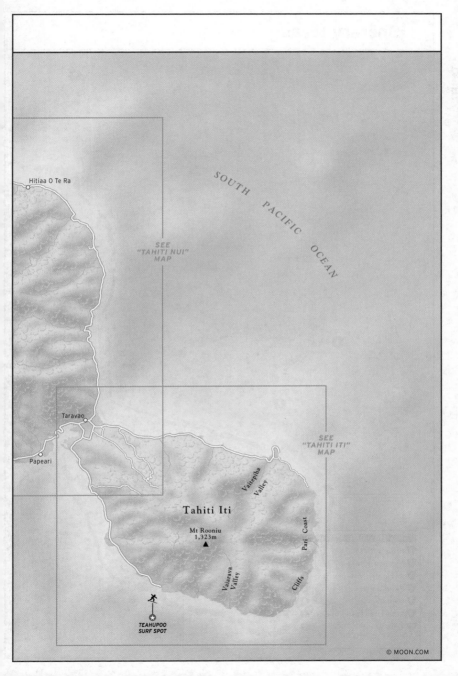

SOUTH PACIFIC OCEAN

Hitiaa O Te Ra

SEE
"TAHITI NUI"
MAP

Taravao

SEE
"TAHITI ITI"
MAP

Papeari

Vaitepiha Valley

Tahiti Iti

Pari Coast

Mt Rooniu
1,323m ▲

Cliffs

Vaiarava Valley

TEAHUPOO
SURF SPOT

© MOON.COM

Itinerary Ideas

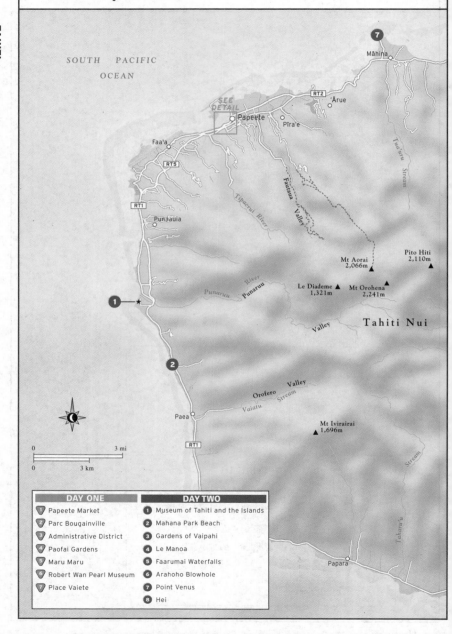

SOUTH   PACIFIC
OCEAN

SEE DETAIL

Papeete

RT2

'Ārue

Pīra'e

Faa'a

RT5

RT1

Punaauia

Tipaerui River

Fautaua Valley

Tuauru Stream

Mt Aorai
2,066m

Pito Hiti
2,110m

Le Diademe ▲
1,321m

Mt Orohena
2,241m

Punaruu River

Punaruu

Valley

Tahiti Nui

Orofero   Valley

Vaiatu   Stream

Paea

Mt Ivirairai
1,696m

RT1

0   3 mi
0   3 km

Taruru Stream

Papara

DAY ONE	DAY TWO
① Papeete Market	❶ Museum of Tahiti and the Islands
② Parc Bougainville	❷ Mahana Park Beach
③ Administrative District	❸ Gardens of Vaipahi
④ Paofai Gardens	❹ Le Manoa
⑤ Maru Maru	❺ Faarumai Waterfalls
⑥ Robert Wan Pearl Museum	❻ Arahoho Blowhole
⑦ Place Vaiete	❼ Point Venus
	❽ Hei

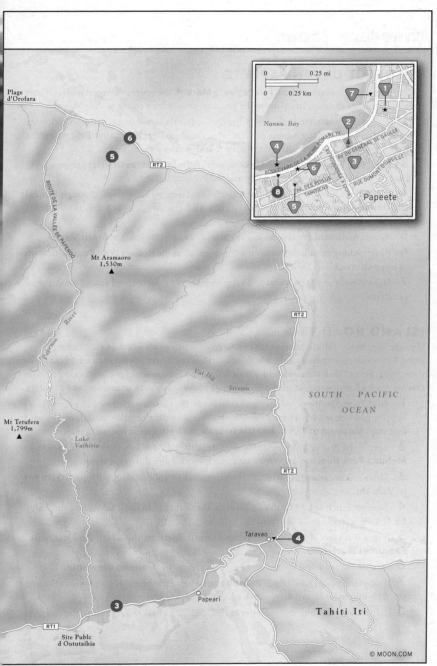

Itinerary Ideas

A PERFECT DAY IN PAPEETE

1 Bring a bag and start your day at **Papeete Market,** the country's largest market. Grab a few fruits for the road from one of the vendors, or stop for a coffee at Café Maeva.

2 Walk three minutes to Cathedral Notre Dame, Tahiti's oldest standing Catholic church, and continue south along Avenue du Général de Gaulle to **Parc Bougainville,** a nice place to enjoy any snacks you've picked up at the market under a shady tree.

3 From Parc Bougainville, you'll find Papeete's **Administrative District** just across the road. Peek at the Territorial Assembly and the Presidential Palace.

4 Walk three minutes back to the waterfront. Then, go for a stroll through **Paofai Gardens,** perusing the handicraft stands and finding a bench for some idyllic people-watching.

5 Across Boulevard Pomare on Rue du Mars 1795, stop for lunch at **Maru Maru.**

6 Backtracking east along Boulevard Pomare, stop at the **Robert Wan Pearl Museum** to learn all about how Tahitian pearls are cultivated.

7 Have dinner at **Place Vaiete,** trying whichever roulotte (food truck) tempts your tastebuds.

ISLAND ROAD TRIP

If you're keen to see Tahiti's interior, it's best to do so with a guide who has a knack for driving along Tahiti's steep, unpaved roads. For this day trip, hire a driver or your own rental car to see these sights along Tahiti's coastal road. Plan a full eight-hour day to enjoy each stop featured on this list. Pack a bathing suit, snorkel, towel, change of clothes, snacks, sunscreen, and a camera.

1 Grab breakfast from your accommodation or the closest patisserie and plan to leave Papeete just before 9am. Drive 15 kilometers (9 mi) south along the coastal road to your first stop, **Museum of Tahiti and the Islands,** for a glimpse at the archipelago's past.

2 Spend the rest of your morning seaside, driving 20 kilometers (12 mi) south to **Mahana Park Beach,** a great spot for a quick snorkel and dip in the water.

3 Drive 35 kilometers (21 mi) south from the beach to walk around the tropical **Gardens of Vaipahi.**

4 Stop for lunch at **Le Manoa** in Taravao, the point connecting Tahiti Nui and Tahiti Iti, 11 kilometers (6 mi) away from the gardens.

5 From Taravao, drive 30 kilometers (18 mi) north to the admire the cascading **Faarumai Waterfalls.**

6 Across the road, feel the sea spray shooting from the **Arahoho Blowhole.**

7 End your coastal road trip at **Point Venus,** one of the best places to witness the sunset, a 13-kilometer (8-mi) drive north of Arahao Blowhole.

8 After a long day out, enjoy dinner at **Hei,** one of the best restaurants in Papeete.

Papeete

Papeete (pa-pay-EH-tay) means "water basket." The most likely explanation for this name is that islanders originally used calabashes enclosed in baskets to fetch water at a spring behind the present Territorial Assembly. Papeete was founded as a mission station by the Reverend William Crook in 1818, and whalers began frequenting Papeete's port in the 1820s, as it offered better shelter than Matavai Bay, a bay 10 kilometers (6 mi) to the east. It became the seat of government when young Queen Pomare IV settled here in 1827.

Today Papeete is the political, cultural, and economic hub of French Polynesia. Since the opening of Faa'a International Airport in 1961, Papeete has blossomed, with large hotels, swanky restaurants, sunset bars, cultural events, and a thriving arts scene. It's one of the few places in French Polynesia prone to traffic jams, with automobiles, trucks, and buses rumbling through Papeete's roads.

Yet along the waterfront the yachts rock luxuriously in their moorings. There's no need to "tour Papeete"—instead, simply wander around without any set goal. Visit the pearl shops, boutiques, cafés, and cluttered no-name shops that seem to sell everything. In the morning, grab the best produce of the day from the markets. At night, eat with the locals at Place Vaiete, where roulottes (food trucks) offer everything from Asian cuisine to french fries to the catch of the day. Though many see Papeete as only the starting or ending point of their French Polynesian journey, it's worth exploring.

Orientation

Papeete is on the northwest coast of Tahiti Nui, 5 kilometers (3 mi) north of the **Faa'a International Airport.** Greater Papeete extends for 32 kilometers (20 mi) from **Paea** to **Mahina,** including the surrounding towns of **Faa'a, Pirae,** and **Arue.** More than 130,000 people live in this cosmopolitan city, crowded between mountains and sea. The main coastal road of Tahiti runs along the waterfront of Papeete, here called **Boulevard de la Reine Pomare IV**—though most people simply call it **Boulevard Pomare.** The 1-kilometer (0.6-mi) stretch from Papeete Port and Ferry Terminal in the north and the Office du Tourisme and Papeete Market to the south is where you'll find most of Papeete's sights and restaurants, from Paofai Gardens to Place Vaiete.

SIGHTS
Central Papeete
MAIRIE DE PAPEETE
Rue Paul Gauguin; tel. 40 41 57 00; www. ville-papeete.pf; 7:30am-3:30pm Mon.-Thurs., 7:30am-2:30pm Fri.; free
Mairie de Papeete is the city's town hall, an elegant building with a red roof, central spire, and pastel yellow walls. If there's no event or major meeting going on, tourists are welcome to wander around the grounds.

TOP EXPERIENCE

★ PAPEETE MARKET
Rue Francois Cardella; 5:30am-4pm Mon.-Fri., 5:30am-1pm Sat., 4:30am-11am Sun.; free to enter
If there's one thing you won't want to miss in Papeete, it's a visit to the Papeete Market. The teeming central market, a block away from the waterfront, has been a city mainstay for decades. It's divided into sections, each with their own color palette and aromas. In the morning, one of the busiest areas is the seafood section, where last night's catch is sold to early risers. In another section you'll find perfectly stacked piles of produce, like mangoes, papayas, bananas, root crops, breadfruit, tomatoes, cucumbers, heads of lettuce, and whatever else is thriving in season. Some stands dole out pineapple lollipops and slices

Papeete

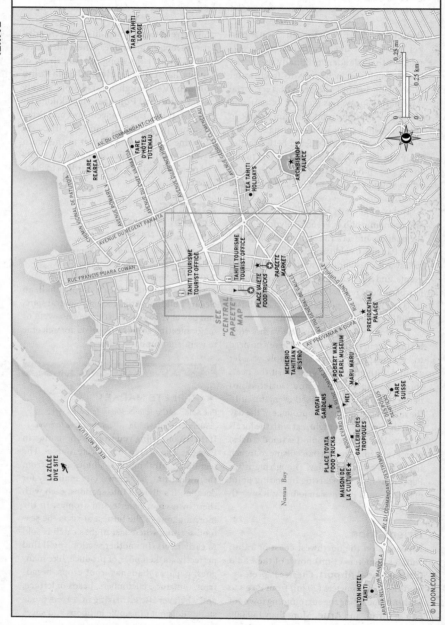

TARA TAHITI LODGE

AV. DU COMMANDANT CHESSÉ

FARE D'HÔTES TUTEHAU

FARE REAREA

AVENUE ROMARE V

AVENUE DU CHEF VAIRAATOA

AVENUE DU PRINCE HINOI

AVENUE GEORGES CLEMENCEAU

ARCHBISHOP'S PALACE

TEA TAHITI HOLIDAYS

CHEMIN VICINAL DE PATUTOA

AVENUE DU REGENT PARAITA

RUE FRANCIS PUARA COWAN

TAHITI TOURISME TOURIST OFFICE

TAHITI TOURISME TOURIST OFFICE

PAPEETE MARKET

PLACE VAIETE FOOD TRUCKS

RUE DU MAR

RUE DUMONT DURVILLE

PRESIDENTIAL PALACE

AT POUVANAA A OOPA

SEE "CENTRAL PAPEETE" MAP

MERIO TAHITIAN BISTRO

ROBERT WAN PEARL MUSEUM

MARU MARU

RUE DE LA REINE POMARE IV

PAOFAI GARDENS

HEI

FARE SUISSE

GALLERIE DES TROPIQUES

BOULEVARD DE LA REINE POMARE IV

AV. DES RUUS

AV DES RUUS

RUE DE MOU'UTA

LA ZÉLÉE DIVE SITE

PLACE TO'ATA FOOD TRUCKS

MAISON DE LA CULTURE

Nunua Bay

AV. DU COMMANDANT DESTREMAU

HILTON HOTEL TAHITI

ARATIA NELSON MANDELA

0.25 mi

0.25 km

© MOON.COM

of fresh watermelon, the perfect treat to enjoy as you browse. Stalls with fresh bread, desserts, and fast food flank the perimeter.

The territory's largest handicrafts market is also here with pareu (sarongs with bright floral prints), colorful tifaifai quilts, Marquesan wood carvings (including weapons, statues, tiki, and home goods), shell necklaces, lower-quality pearl jewelry, monoï oil, woven goods, and just about every other kind of curio you can find on the islands. Surprisingly, it's often cheaper to buy handicrafts here than on the outer islands where they are made. There's also a large cafeteria upstairs where you can get a self-service meal and listen to local musicians at lunchtime. Floral crowns, bouquets, and necklaces can be bought here.

CATHEDRAL NOTRE DAME

Place Notre Dame; tel. 50 30 00; www.
cathedraledepapeete.com; mass at 5:50am
Mon.-Sat., 6pm Sat., 8am Sun., noon Wed.; free to
enter

In the middle of one of Papeete's busiest intersections is the quaint Cathedral Notre Dame, a small cathedral with three church bells inside. Built between 1867-1875, it's the oldest standing Catholic church on Tahiti. Inside, you'll find a blend of biblical tales told through Tahitian artwork. The stained-glass windows make it worth a wander through the front doors.

PAPEETE ADMINISTRATIVE DISTRICT

Place Tarahoi

Papeete's Administrative District is where you'll find most of French Polynesia's government buildings, with a few public parks tucked in between. **The Territorial Assembly** (Avenue du Général de Gaulle; tel. 40 41 63 00; www.assemblee.pf; 8am-5pm Mon.-Fri.; free) is the main government building, where the assembly and president meet. It occupies the site of a former Pomare royal palace, demolished in 1966 to make room for the building you see today.

The Pomare dynasty ruled Tahiti for nearly a century, from 1788 until 1880; their reach extended to the Society Islands, the Austral Islands, and the Tuamotusl. Their reign ended with the occupation of France in 1880. Visitors can wander around freely and see the inside of the assembly on an hour-long guided tour (English available), which takes place hourly from 8am-3pm Monday-Friday, and must be booked at least two days in advance through the website.

Behind the compound is a tranquil botanical garden with a lily pond separating the gardens from the French high commissioner's residence (closed to visitors). The **Bassin de la Reine,** the royal bathing pond of Queen Pomare IV, is a calm pool set beneath a giant banyan tree at the back of the gardens. Throughout the gardens are symbols representing the major island groups in French Polynesia.

In 2006, Papeete renamed its administrative center to honor Tetuaaupua Pouvanaa a Oopa (1895-1977), deemed the Metua, or father of Polynesians. He was an advocate for Tahitian independence and represented Tahiti in the French Senate until his death. There is a **Pouvanaa a Oopa monument** in his honor, where Tahitian residents gather to protest. Well-kept gardens, leafy marumaru trees, and fountains make the area feel distinctly formal with the chaos of the city just a few blocks away.

Further along Avenue Pouvanaa a Oopa is the **Presidential Palace** (tel. 40 47 20 00; www.presidence.pf), the official residence of the president of French Polynesia. From a glance, it's obvious that the Presidential Palace is more grandiose than the French high commissioner's residence—some say this was intentional to act as a symbol of Tahitians' loyalty to Tahiti over France.

ARCHBISHOP'S PALACE

Rue Monseigneur Michel Coppenrath; 9am-3pm
Mon.-Fri.; free to enter grounds

The Catholic Archbishop's Palace (1869) is a lonely remnant of Papeete's colonial era,

Central Papeete

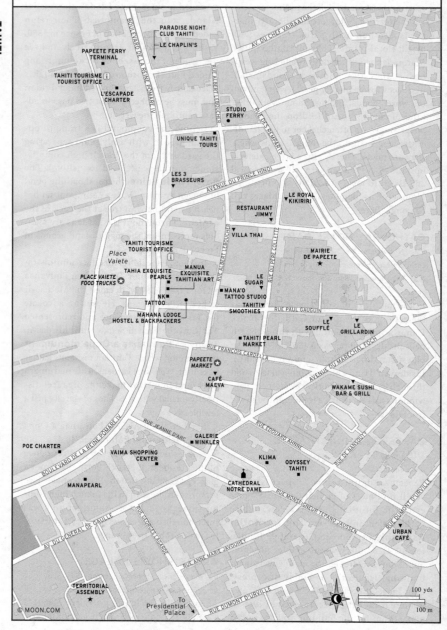

PARADISE NIGHT CLUB TAHITI
LE CHAPLIN'S
PAPEETE FERRY TERMINAL
TAHITI TOURISME TOURIST OFFICE
L'ESCAPADE CHARTER
STUDIO FERRY
UNIQUE TAHITI TOURS
LES 3 BRASSEURS
LE ROYAL KIKIRIRI
RESTAURANT JIMMY
VILLA THAI
TAHITI TOURISME TOURIST OFFICE
Place Vaiete
MAIRIE DE PAPEETE
TAHIA EXQUISITE PEARLS
MANUA EXQUISITE TAHITIAN ART
LE SUGAR
PLACE VAIETE FOOD TRUCKS
MANA'O TATTOO STUDIO
NK TATTOO
TAHITI SMOOTHIES
MAHANA LODGE HOSTEL & BACKPACKERS
LE SOUFFLÉ
LE GRILLARDIN
TAHITI PEARL MARKET
PAPEETE MARKET
CAFÉ MAEVA
WAKAME SUSHI BAR & GRILL
POE CHARTER
GALERIE WINKLER
VAIMA SHOPPING CENTER
KLIMA
ODYSSEY TAHITI
MANAPEARL
CATHEDRAL NOTRE DAME
URBAN CAFÉ
TERRITORIAL ASSEMBLY
To Presidential Palace

AV. DU CHEF VAIRAATOA
BOULEVARD DE LA REINE POMARE IV
RUE ALBERT LEBOUCHER
RUE DES REMPARTS
AVENUE DU PRINCE HINOI
RUE ALBERT LEBOUCHER
RUE DU PERE COLLETTE
RUE PAUL GAUGUIN
RUE FRANÇOIS CARDELLA
AVENUE DU MARECHAL FOCH
RUE JEANNE D'ARC
RUE EDOUARD AHNNE
RUE DE NANSOUTY
BOULEVARD DE LA REINE POMARE IV
RUE MONSEIGNEUR TEPANO JAUSSEN
RUE DUMONT D'URVILLE
AV. DU GENERAL DE GAULLE
RUE GEORGES LAGARDE
RUE ANNE MARIE JAVOUHEY
RUE DUMONT D'URVILLE

0   100 yds
0   100 m

© MOON.COM

French Polynesia's Best Souvenirs

- **Monoï oil:** This oil is made from Tahitian tiare flowers and coconut oil, and is used as a perfume or moisturizer to protect the skin from salt water.

- **Sculptures:** Craftsmen create intricate figurines and utilitarian items from tou wood and stone. Each island group is known for their unique style and specialty, though the Marquesas group is world famous for the quality of their sculptures.

- **Pearls:** Tahiti's rare black pearls are world-renowned, and also come in iridescent shades of cream, pink, silver, blue, and orange.

- **Tifaifai quilts:** A room is instantly made brighter with these handwoven quilts, often made with colorful fabrics and patterns inspired by nature. Many are passed down from generation to generation as heirlooms, and it is customary to gift one to newlywed couples.

- **Floral arrangements:** Floral crowns (hei upo'o) and necklaces (hei) are used to mark special occasions and ceremonies. They are typically made with fresh flowers, though synthetic versions will pass through customs and last for years.

- **Tapa:** A paper-like cloth crafted from bark painted or dyed with natural inks, tapa is sold as tablecloths, tapestries, or place mats.

- **Pareu:** These sarongs made from cotton or rayon can be worn as a skirt, dress, or top, or used as a beach blanket. Some are hand painted.

- **Woven goods:** Palm and pandanus leaves are woven to create mats, baskets, hats, bracelets, bags, and more. The tighter the weave and more intricate the design, the more you can expect to pay. Many resorts offer weaving lessons.

built shortly after Tahiti was colonized by the French. To get there, take Rue Jaussen behind the Catholic cathedral, keep straight, and ask for the Archevêché Catholique. The park grounds, planted with citrus, and the modern open-air church nearby (to the right) also merit a look. The huge mango trees here were planted in 1855 by Tahiti's first bishop, Monseigneur Tepano Jaussen.

ROBERT WAN PEARL MUSEUM
Blvd. de la Reine Pomare IV; tel. 40 54 86 40; www. robertwan.com; 9am-5pm Mon.-Sat.; free
This is a small museum with elegant exhibits on the famous Tahitian pearl. Learn about the history of pearl diving and cultivating techniques and admire some of the most intriguing pearls ever collected. If you're visiting at the start of your journey through the islands, this is a great primer on learning how

to choose a pearl wisely. Displays have English descriptions, and staff members are happy to answer even the most obscure pearl questions. There's an adjoining pearl shop with high-ticket pearls for sale that are high quality, but are valued with pearl farming pioneer Robert Wan's name in mind—so expect a little padding on the price tag.

PAOFAI GARDENS
Blvd. de la Reine Pomare IV; open 24/7; free
Along Papeete's waterfront is a marked walking path that weaves through grassy areas and trees. Locals head to the gardens to play ball games on the soccer field, little ones swarm the playgrounds, and paddlers practice and race their outrigger canoes from here. If you pack a picnic, there are plenty of leafy trees, tables, benches, and gazebo areas for a snack in the shade.

MAISON DE LA CULTURE

Blvd. de la Reine Pomare IV; tel. 40 54 45 44;
www.maisondelaculture.pf; 8am-5pm Mon.-Thurs.;
8am-4pm Fri.; price depends on event

Maison de la Culture, the Te Fare Tahiti Nui in Tahitian, is an octagonal building that hosts many of Tahiti's largest cultural events, with a small library inside. Throughout the year, the center holds a variety of workshops, dance and music performances, film festivals, and **Heiva I Tahiti** (heiva.org), a traditional Tahitian song and dance festival that has been taking place for over 140 years. The Maison de la Culture website has a handful of educational videos that highlights Polynesian craft and culture.

Around Papeete
JAMES NORMAN HALL MUSEUM

PK 5.5; tel. 40 50 01 60; 9am-4pm Tues.-Sat.; CFP 600/person

James Norman Hall achieved fame in the 1930s as coauthor of the *Bounty Trilogy* with Charles Nordhoff. He moved from America to Tahiti in the early 1920s, building his home here—now the museum—shortly after arriving. The museum is filled with photos and memorabilia from his life, and has a small section on his previous career as a military pilot. There's signage in English, French, and Tahitian. About 3,000 books from Hall's personal library are on display, with a comfortable lounge you can sit and read in.

BELVEDERE DE TAHARAA

PK 8, off of Col du Taharaa; sunrise-sunset daily; free

A lookout point that offers views of Papeete and the ocean spanning to Moorea on a clear day. There are a few spots to sit under the shade. During whale migration season, bring along a pair of binoculars and look for a gray fin or tuft of white water in the distance.

TOMB OF ROI POMARE V

PK 4.7; free

At PK 4.7, Arue, is the Tomb of King Pomare V. The mausoleum, surmounted by a Grecian urn, was built in 1879 for Queen Pomare IV, but her remains were subsequently removed to make room for her son, Pomare V, who died of alcoholism in 1891 at the age of 52. A century earlier, on February 13, 1791, his grandfather, Pomare II, then age nine, was made first king of Tahiti on the great marae that once stood on this spot. Pomare II was also the first Christian convert and built a 215-meter-long (705-ft-long) version of King Solomon's Temple here, but nothing remains of either temple.

BEACHES

All the beaches near Papeete are of the volcanic sand variety, which sparkles under full sunlight, and are often paired with emerald mountains in the distance. Even on the busiest days, you should be able to find a spot in the sand.

PLAGE LAFAYETTE

PK 7; free

The black sands of Plage Lafayette at Matavai Bay are a welcoming place to settle in for a few hours as a convenient break from the city. You can almost always find a spot to yourself, even on weekends. A gentle slope leads to the water, making it a calm place to swim, though there aren't too many coral patches for good snorkeling. Families will find it ideal for wading and sandcastle building.

PLAGE DE TAAONE

Rue de Taaone

This is one of the best beaches for families, with a playground, outdoor gym, shade shelters on a spacious grassy area, bathrooms, and snack stand near its ashy shores. The water is often calm here, making it a good place to take kids who aren't the most confident swimmers.

1: Cathedral Notre Dame 2: the Territorial Assembly of French Polynesia 3: Papeete Market is the largest market in French Polynesia.

☆ Tahiti's Best Beaches

Tautira Beach

Tahiti's sparkling black and gray sand beaches are distinct from the sugar sands found elsewhere on the Society Islands; what makes them unique is their access to ocean activities. You can surf, snorkel, paddle, swim, and bodysurf directly from shore at many of these understated beaches.

- **Best for families:** Kids will be in heaven at **Plage de Taaone,** a calm beach with a playground not far from central Papeete (page 51).

- **Best for snorkeling: Mahana Park Beach** truly shines underwater, where you can spot sea turtles, anemones, and more (page 77).

- **Best for photos:** The dark gray sand of **Taharuu Beach** turns black in the sun, a striking place to photograph (page 77).

- **Best for surfing: Papenoo Beach** has friendly waves and a welcoming surf scene (page 77).

- **Best for history buffs:** Captain Cook camped at **Point Venus,** which is also a good place to paddle and lounge on the sand (page 71).

- **Best for escaping the crowds:** Journey to Tahiti Iti to find your own slice of paradise on **Tautira Beach** (page 84).

SURFING
Surf Spots
ARUE SURF SPOT
Paddle out at Plage Lafayette

There's a left-hander that breaks over shallow reef at Plage Lafayette, as well as dumpy beach breaks that bodyboarders love. You'll want a northerly swell and southeasterly winds.

Surf Schools
MO'O SURF SCHOOL
InterContinental Resort; tel. 87 36 94 28; https:// moosurfschool.com; 6am-7pm daily; CFP 5,000/ two-hour lesson

There are few surf spots around Tahiti for beginners, but if you're keen to learn, surf and bodyboard lessons are taught by Cyril, who has over 15 years of teaching experience.

Small classes, maxing out at six surfers, take place at one of Tahiti's friendliest beaches. Private surf lessons are also available for individuals, families, and groups of up to eight. Each two-hour lesson includes equipment and transportation within Punaauia and Mahina. Lessons are geared toward beginners and intermediates aged four and up.

SCUBA DIVING

Tahiti doesn't exactly have an international reputation for diving, but there are tens of dive sites on the island—and they're rarely crowded, even in the high season. On the boat ride out you'll have a shot at spotting whales and dolphins. Underwater, there are volcanic seascapes to explore. Tiger sharks, reef sharks, sea turtles, and manta rays are regular sights in Tahitian waters. If you wish to snorkel, it's best to go straight from shore at **Mahana Park Beach** in Puna'auia (page 77).

Dive Spots
ARUE FAULT
Off of Arue
A stunning seascape awaits at Arue Fault, a beginner-friendly dive site with a coral-encrusted wall at 5 meters (16 ft) and undersea caves at 30-meter (98-foot) depth (advanced open water divers only). A vast variety of reef fish live within the coral crags. It's a great spot to see tiger sharks.

LA ZÉLÉE
Off of Motu Uta
The remnants of *La Zélée*, a gunboat that was bombarded in 1914, is now a healthy home for corals and juvenile reef fish. The wreck is found around 10-meter (32-foot) to 20-meter (65-foot) depth, and rests in multiple pieces. Black corals, pink corals, and large gorgonian fans accent this dive site. Currents tend to be mild here, and it's suitable for all levels.

WHITE VALLEY
Off of Faa'a
The White Valley, or La Vallée Blanche, is a drift dive site starting in the Faa'a Lagoon, a lagoon just 1 kilometer (0.6 mi) south from the airport. On a slow day, you'll spot technicolor corals, reef sharks, and schools of reef fish. Dive here during whale migration season and you might spot humpback whales cruising through the blue—it's one of the few spots you can see them with a tank.

AQUARIUM
Off of Faa'a
An ideal spot for beginners and divers in need of a refresher. The dive takes place at a coral reef with the wrecks of two small fishing boats and a Cessna plane nearby. It's common to see juvenile reef fish, manini, giant anemones, pufferfish, angelfish, and lionfish. Some snorkeling tours feed the critters here against conservation best practices, so the fish can be a little *too* friendly at times.

PAPA WHISKEY
Off of Faa'a
With most of the site around 25-meter (82-foot) depth, this is a dive site best suited for more experienced divers. The reef is home to sea turtles, schools of reef fish, reef sharks, eels, and pelagic fish who cruise in the deeper waters.

Dive Shops and Schools
SCUBATEK TAHITI
Next to Yacht Club de Tahiti; tel. 89 40 04 99; scubatektahiti.com; around CFP 7,000 per dive including equipment
Scubatek Tahiti has been a diving mainstay on the island since 1981 and offers a range of whale excursions, SSI scuba dive courses, and fun dives, with up to four fun excursions taking place throughout the day. If your dream is to swim alongside humpback whales, the dive center leads guided whale swims and whale-watching tours from August-late October (4 hours; CFP 8,500 per adult, CFP 6,500 children ages 6-12; maximum capacity 12 people). Book direct for the cheapest rate.

Around Papeete

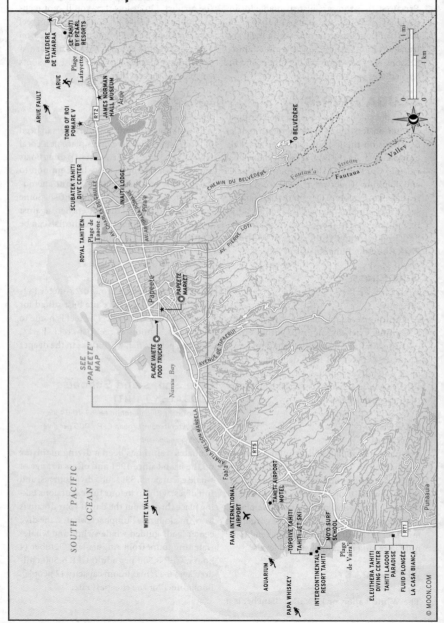

SOUTH PACIFIC OCEAN

BELVEDERE DE TAHARA

LE TAHITI BY PEARL RESORTS

Plage Lafayette

ARUE

ARUE FAULT

TOMB OF ROI POMARE V

JAMES NORMAN HALL MUSEUM

Arue

RT2

BELVÉDÈRE

SCUBATEK TAHITI DIVE CENTER

INAITI LODGE

AV. ARIIPAEA POMARE

AV. CHARLES DE GAULLE

Pirae

CHEMIN DU BELVÉDÈRE

Fautau'a Stream

Fautaua Valley

ROYAL TAHITIEN

Plage de Taaone

AV. PIERRE LOTI

Papeete

PAPEETE MARKET

SEE "PAPEETE" MAP

PLACE VAIETE FOOD TRUCKS

Nanuu Bay

AVENUE DE TIPAERUI

RT5

ARATIA NELSON MANDELA

TAHITI AIRPORT MOTEL

Faa'a

WHITE VALLEY

FAAA INTERNATIONAL AIRPORT

TOPDIVE TAHITI

TAHITI JET SKI

MO'O SURF SCHOOL

Plage de Vaira'i

Punaauia

RT1

AQUARIUM

PAPA WHISKEY

INTERCONTINENTAL RESORT TAHITI

ELEUTHERA TAHITI DIVING CENTER

TAHITI LAGOON PARADISE

FLUID PLONGÉE

LA CASA BIANCA

0   1 km
0   1 mi

© MOON.COM

TOPDIVE TAHITI

InterContinental Resort; tel. 40 53 34 96; www.
topdive.fr; around 10,000 CFP per dive including
equipment

Topdive is one of the most popular and well-run dive chains throughout the region, with a center at the InterContinental Resort (you do not need to be a guest to use dive center facilities). They offer discovery dives for first-time divers and rescue courses for divers who hold their advanced open water certificate. Specialized certs are available upon request. Free Nitrox is included in each dive—if you don't have your certification, you can take a test that will let you use Nitrox at the other Topdive centers in French Polynesia.

ELEUTHERA TAHITI DIVING CENTER

Marina Taina; tel. 40 42 49 29; www.eleutheratahiti.
com; around CFP 7,500 per dive including equipment

Eleuthera Tahiti Diving Center offers fun dives, dive courses (discovery to rescue), and non-diving ocean excursions, like snorkel trips (CFP 7,900-14,000) and lagoon cruises (CFP 15,000). Staff are friendly and the equipment is well-maintained. Transport can be arranged for divers staying nearby.

FLUID PLONGÉE

Marina Taina (PK 8.5); tel. 40 85 41 46; www.
fluid-tahiti.com; around CFP 5,500-7,000 per dive

This SSI dive center at Marina Taina offers a range of courses from discover to dive master, with specialty courses available upon request. A free transport service is also available for divers staying near the property. The dive center has a casual but still professional atmosphere and is a short boat ride away from some of Tahiti's best dive sites. Snorkel trips (CFP 9,000 and up) are available for non-divers. They also offer a full day dive trip (three tanks/CFP 30,000) to see tiger sharks for more experienced divers.

GUIDED HIKES AND EXCURSIONS

The best way to see Tahiti's interior is with a guide. Trails are largely unmarked and roads are rough, steep, and often only wide enough for one vehicle. Almost all excursions shuttle tourists around via the back of a 4WD pickup truck. Sometimes, there is space inside of the cab, which makes for a more comfortable ride. Pack a bathing suit and towel, as most tours offer a stop at a swim spot.

IAORANA TAHITI EXPEDITIONS

tel. 87 75 88 07; www.iaoranatahitiexpeditions.com;
CFP 10,000 /day hike

Teuai Lenoir leads hiking and sightseeing tours around Tahiti's interior, largely through Papenoo Valley and Fataua Valley. Tours are highly personalized to guests' abilities and interests, and go into detail about local culture, legends, plants, and geography. There are multiple tour options available—you'll want to get in touch as early as possible if you have your heart set on a particular trip. Pickup services are offered.

TAHITI SAFARI EXPEDITION

tel. 40 42 14 15; www.tahiti-safari.com; CFP 7,500/
day tour

Venture to Tahiti's interior with Tahiti Safari Expedition. Full-day tours include a drive through Papenoo Valley with multiple river crossings, a stop to swim in a river, and trip through the Urufau Tunnel, which runs through the mountainside near Lake Vaihiria. Lunch is served at a restaurant overlooking the cloud-topped forest. While tours are offered in English, descriptions will largely be given in French unless there is a large (four or more) group of English speakers.

SMILE WITH LILI

tel. 89 31 77 30; liligaulier@gmail.com; www.
facebook.com/Smilewithlilitahiti; from CFP
1,500-6,000/guided hike

If you love hiking, Smile with Lili is your best bet for discovering Tahiti's incredible hiking trails. Guides Lili and Willy offer treks ranging from easy, flat hikes suitable for inexperienced hikers to treks that are steep, slick, and long. Some trails require crossing shallow rivers. Most hikes range from 2-6 hours, though there are outliers, and no two trips are exactly alike, with tens offered each month. The Facebook page publishes the scheduled hikes for the next quarter. Children ages three and up are welcome to join depending on the hike.

MARAMA TOURS

tel. 40 50 74 74; maramatours.com; CFP 12,500/ day tour

Marama Tours offers multiple types of excursions ranging from guided hikes through Tahiti's lava tubes (CFP 8,000) to circle island tours that cover the main coastal sights (CFP 11,400/full, CFP 6,500/half). Excursions through the interior of Tahiti (CFP 12,500) venture through Papenoo Valley on a covered 4WD. Marama Tours can also help arrange accommodation packages, and they offer pickup service.

WATER SPORTS AND BOAT TOURS
TAHITI LAGOON PARADISE

Marina Taina; tel. 87 22 66 06; www.whale-dolphin- turtle.com; CFP 17,000/three-hour tour

With over 10 different tours to choose from, Tahiti Lagoon Paradise really leans into a D.I.Y.-style adventure, as each trip is private and customizable. Activities range from snorkeling wrecks or reefs, whale- and dolphin- watching, searching for sea turtles, and taking sunset cruises on the lagoon. The tour can accommodate up to five people and includes snorkeling gear, pictures, and drinking water. The captain, Benoit, is an expert on Tahiti's surrounding reefs and can tailor a trip depending on interests and skill level.

POE CHARTER

Papeete Ferry Terminal; tel. 87 71 55 55; poecharter. pf; CFP 18,000/day tour

Poe Charter offers a catamaran charter service for overnight trips around French Polynesia

with a handful of catamarans to choose from. Or, opt for the day-trip excursion to Tetiaroa, an idyllic island around three hours away by boat. The day starts just after sunrise and includes breakfast, lunch, snacks, tea and coffee, snorkel equipment, Tahitian dance lessons, and a guide who is happy to point out resident bird life on the island. The boat returns just before sunset and can pick up or drop off on Moorea or Tahiti.

L'ESCAPADE CHARTER TAHITI

Papeete Ferry Terminal; tel. 87 72 85 31; tahiti- charter-catamaran.com; CFP 17,000/day tour

L'Escapade Charter Tahiti has two catamarans in its fleet, each with four double cabins with bathrooms onboard. For a full day out on the water, join their sailing trip to Tetiaroa for bird-watching, relaxing, and snorkeling. The day trip includes lunch, breakfast, and snorkeling equipment. They can also arrange custom trips with scuba diving to any major island group in French Polynesia.

TAHITI JETSKI

InterContinental Resort; tel. 87 29 01 60; www. tahiti-jetski.pf; 8am-5pm daily; CFP 10,000/30 minutes, CFP 28,000/two hours

Tahiti Jetski hosts a few guided Jet Ski tours around the lagoon ranging from 30 minutes to two hours. Book the earliest morning tour you can for your best chance at seeing dolphins. Longer tours include a visit to nearby surf spots and a snorkel stop. Customized tours can also be arranged. Kids ages six and up can ride with an adult.

ENTERTAINMENT AND EVENTS
ROYAL TAHITIEN

Servitude Marcel Sachet; tel. 40 50 40 40; www. royaltahitien.com; entertainment starting from 5pm Thurs.-Sat.; free with drinks or dinner

The Royal Tahitien has been famous for its evening entertainment since it first opened in the late 1960s. On Thursdays, Fridays, and Saturdays, musicians come to perform for guests, starting from around 5pm (happy hour starts at 5:30pm). Your greatest chance for seeing a dance performance is on Fridays and Saturdays at the bar.

INTERCONTINENTAL RESORT TAHITI

Seaside at PK 7; tel. 40 86 51 50; tahiti. intercontinental.com; dinner starting 6:30pm, shows from 8:30pm Wed. and Fri. (call to confirm); CFP 8,400-9,400/person

Enjoy a buffet dinner of Polynesian fare along with a cultural performance during the resort's theme nights. The Te U'i Tapairu show features song and dance from the archipelago. The perfectly synced hips, pops of color, drumming, and singing make it one of the most exciting nights out on Tahiti. There's also a show that highlights Marquesan culture through dance, art, and storytelling. Show dates are irregular, but typically take place on Wednesdays and Fridays.

SHOPPING

Papeete has the largest variety of shops in French Polynesia. Think handicrafts, pearls, art, and perhaps a tattoo or two.

Art and Souvenirs

The best handicraft shopping is in Papeete Market. Surprisingly, handicrafts are often cheaper here than on their island of origin.

GALERIE WINKLER

17 Rue Jeanne d'Arc; tel. 40 42 81 77; www. galeriewinkler.net; 9am-12:30pm and 1:30pm-5pm Mon.-Fri., 8:30am-noon Sat.

Galerie Winkler has been a Papeete mainstay since the 1960s, a place for local artists to exhibit their work when there were few spots for them to do so at the time. Today, it's a contemporary art gallery with rotating exhibits and workshops. For a simple souvenir, pick up a postcard with a print designed by a local artist.

MANUA EXQUISITE TAHITIAN ART

Blvd. de la Reine Pomare IV; tel. 40 85 39 53; www. manuatahitianart.com; 9am-5pm Mon.-Sat.

At this upscale boutique with artwork from throughout the archipelago, you'll find Marquesan wood carvings, hand-painted pareu and tapa, and mixed-media sculptures crafted from shell, stone, and bone. While beauty is in the eye of the beholder, higher quality carvings tend to be smooth with few jagged lines and edges. Even if you won't be reaching for your wallet, the gallery is worth browsing to learn about each island group's famous forms of art. If you can't find what you like in the shop, the gallery can arrange a commissioned work with an artist. The gallery offers a shipping service via DHL or FedEx should you purchase something you're unable to carry on the plane.

VAIMA SHOPPING CENTER

Av. du Maréchal Foch; tel. 89 48 90 00; centrevaima. com; 5am-8pm Mon.-Fri., 7am-noon Sat.

The largest shopping mall in Papeete, Vaima Shopping Mall caters largely to the cruise ships coming into port. You'll find a mix of pearl, souvenir, tech, and surf shops. If you're looking for clothing and shoes, you'll also find that here. **Ganesha Gallery** (tel. 40 43 04 18; www.ganeshatahiti.com; 1:30pm-6pm Mon., 9:30am-6pm Tues.-Fri., 9:30am-5pm Sat.) is one of the standout shops. Collecting works from all over Polynesia and Melanesia, you'll find jewelry from the Society Islands, weavings from the Austral Islands, and sculptures hailing from the Marquesas, Easter Island, Fiji, and New Zealand.

Pearls

There are many pearl shops in Papeete selling Polynesia's famous black pearl, and it's wise to visit several before making your decision. While aggressive haggling is not recommended, you can usually get a better deal by asking for around 10-20 percent less than the advertised price, especially if you're planning to buy more than one pearl.

1

2

TAHIA EXQUISITE TAHITIAN PEARLS

Blvd. de la Reine Pomare IV; tel. 40 54 06 00;
tahiapearls.com; 9am-5pm Mon.-Sat.

This pearl shop was founded by 1994's Miss Moorea, Tahia Haring, who left to the United States to study pearl design before returning to French Polynesia and establishing her own company. Designs tend to be elegant and minimalistic, with organic shapes and colors. This shop is known for its colorful and iridescent pearls—if you want something unique, you might find it here.

MANAPEARL

Fare Tony Building; tel. 89 71 76 17; www.manapearl.
com; 9am-5pm Mon.-Sat.

Manapearl pearls are grown and cultivated in the Tuamotu atolls, with pieces at the mid-range price point compared to other pearl shops on the island. Their baroque, asymmetrical pearl jewelry is especially beautiful.

TAHITI PEARL MARKET

25 Rue du Père Collette; tel. 40 54 30 60; www.
tahitipearlmarket.com; 10am-4pm Mon.-Fri.

Tahiti Pearl Market is a luxury pearl retailer with higher quality pearls in stock. Jewelry ranges from pieces ideal for casual wear to simple and elegant to uniquely Polynesian, like pearls paired with a manta ray or tiki pendant. This shop has one of the widest variety of styles and pearls to choose from. Pearls are sourced from seven pearl farms in the Tuamotu atolls.

Tattoo Shops

In some parts of French Polynesia, it'll be harder to spot someone *without* a tattoo than with one. Tattooing is one of the most common forms of art on the islands, and it's hard not to be drawn to their allure. You can find a tattoo artist's work by looking through their social media accounts and leafing through their portfolio at the shop, though you'll likely want to create your own custom piece. Inquire about sanitary precautions, including clean razors and disposable needles—a listing here is no guarantee. It's best to get your tattoo near the end of your journey, as too much sun and saltwater lead to infection or distortion.

MANA'O TATTOO STUDIO

43 Rue Albert Leboucher; tel. 40 42 45 00;
manaotattoo.com; 9:30am-5:30pm Mon.-Sat.

This shop hosts a handful of tattoo artists known for a more modern take on traditional Polynesian patterns. The founder, Manu, has over 30 years of tattooing experience. The shop is clean, well-organized, and professional. All tattoos are by appointment only.

NK TATTOO

Blvd. de la Reine Pomare IV; tel. 87 75 53 55;
nk-tattoo-tahiti.com; 9am-5pm Mon.-Fri., 8am-noon
Sat.

If you're looking to leave Tahiti with a tattoo, NK Tattoo is used to developing a highly personalized tattoo idea from scratch. Tattoo artists at NK Tattoo are very familiar with designs and styles hailing from all throughout the Polynesian triangle.

Bookstores

KLIMA

Pl. Notre Dame; tel. 40 42 00 63; librairieklima.
blogspot.com; 7:30am-5:15pm Mon.-Fri.,
7:30am-noon Sat.

Most books in Klima are written in French or Tahitian, but there are usually a few in English tucked beneath the shelves. The shop regularly has author readings and workshops, with their upcoming events posted on the Klima Facebook page.

ODYSSEY

Pl. Notre Dame; tel. 40 54 25 25; www.odyssey.pf;
8am-5pm Mon.-Fri., 8:30am-4pm Sat.

Odyssey is a bookstore selling books by local authors as well as games, art supplies, and stationery. Readings, art workshops, and cultural activities often take place on the weekends.

1: shops in Papeete 2: InterContinental Resort pool

Polynesian Tattoos

Tattooing likely first began in Polynesia over 2,000 years ago; the word "tattoo" originates from Polynesia, stemming from "tatatau" in Marquesan or "tatau" in Tahitianto. Traditionally, tattoos were crafted through tools like bone, shells, and turtle shells strapped to a whittled piece of wood. They communicated legends, genealogy, social ranking, and the islands' history. Tattoos took on new meanings as the art form spread throughout the Pacific, seen in places like the Marquesas, Cook Islands, Tahiti, Niue, Hawaii, Samoa, and Aotearoa (New Zealand). A tattoo is often linked to the ancestral heritage of the person who adorns it; rarely is it purely decorative.

Christian missionaries banned tattooing shortly after arriving in the early 1800s, erasing one of the region's most prominent forms of storytelling. However, non-missionary European sailors continued to get tattooed by Polynesians, returning to their homeland with patterns that many Polynesians could not have. It wasn't until the 1980s that tattooing was allowed to resume in French Polynesia, and the sacred artform has seen a recent revival.

If you are planning to get a tattoo, it's worth consulting with members of the community about the meaning, history, and cultural elements of the tattoo pattern you plan to get. Some members of the community might find it disrespectful to get a tattoo without understanding the significance behind it—what can happen when tourists treat tattoos like a simple souvenir. Ultimately, getting a tattoo is a highly personal decision that should be made in conjunction with a Polynesian tattoo artist who can create a piece that is meaningful for you and respectful of the culture.

FOOD
Food Trucks

TOP EXPERIENCE

★ PLACE VAIETE
369 Boulevard de la Reine Pomare IV; 6pm-2am nightly; CFP 1,000-2,500

Come sunset, you're bound to hear the sizzle of oil on a hot pan and the clamoring of kitchenware as the food trucks, called les roulottes, set up shop over the 1,200 square meters (12,900 square feet) of concrete that is Place Vaiete, next to the ferry terminal. You'll find everything from pizza, crepes, waffles, noodles, and grilled meats alongside a sky-high pile of french fries (pommes frites) served from the windows of a few dozen trucks. Poisson cru, raw fish in coconut milk, is also a mainstay here. Each truck has its own assortment of chairs, stools, and tables. The trucks are popular with tourists and locals alike, and even the pickiest of eaters are bound to find something. If a cruise ship is in town, this is the place to be in the evening. Musicians and dancers perform here regularly, and artisans set up shop in the walkways in between the food trucks and tables. It's not fancy, but it sure is fun.

PLACE TO'ATA
Blvd. de la Reine Pomare IV near Paofai Gardens; 6pm-2am nightly; CFP 1,000-2,500

Near Paofai Gardens is another hotspot for les roulottes, food trucks doling out crepes, pizza, and grilled meats. This is also one of the most popular areas to hear live music, and you may catch a dance troupe performance if you wander around. The plaza is also surrounded by some restaurants with open terraces that provide similar types of food, but in a slightly more formal atmosphere.

Snacks
TAHITI SMOOTHIES
Rue Paul Gauguin; tel. 40 53 35 22; www.facebook. com/tahitismoothies; 8am-4pm Mon.-Sat.

This little snack shop serves healthy eats like bowls of fish and vegetables, salads, and sandwiches, as well as treats like cookies, brownies, and ice cream. Smoothies and juices are also on offer as an antidote to humidity and heat. During weekend nights, the snack is open until late and often has DJs and live music playing from 8pm-1pm.

French Polynesian
LE SOUFFLÉ
Rue Paul Gauguin; tel. 40 57 00 17; www. restaurantlesouffle.com; 11am-2pm and 7pm-10pm Mon.-Sat.; CFP 2,500

Aptly named Le Souffle is a quaint French restaurant with Parisian-inspired decor. Their dishes offer a new take on French traditional cuisine. Local favorites include lobster soufflé, escargot gratin, seafood ratatouille, and a leek with taro and cheese soufflé. After main plates are put away, enjoy a soufflé of the sweet variety—like vanilla or guava. For a kick of caffeine, order an Irish coffee.

★ MARU MARU
1797 Rue de 5 Mars; tel. 40 45 20 20; 11:30am-1:30pm and 6:30pm-9pm Mon.-Sat.; CFP 3,000

Maru Maru is reminiscent of a French bistro with its terrace and simple dining room. But don't let its unassuming exterior fool you— each gourmet plate is thoughtfully made and almost always features local ingredients, like croquettes made from cassava, beef tenderloin encrusted with autera'a (a local nut), and ravioli stuffed with crab.

MEHERIO TAHITIAN BISTRO
Blvd. de la Reine Pomare IV; tel. 40 41 01 10; www. meheriotahitianbistro.com; 10am-10pm Mon.-Sat., 10am-3pm Sun.; CFP 3,500

Surrounded by palm trees at Papeete's waterfront, this bistro serves European and Tahitian dishes. Happy hour runs 5pm-7pm daily, and their wine list is worthwhile on its own. For food, try the mushroom risotto, lamb shanks, smoked tuna, or marinated eggplant, or nibble on the cheese charcuterie board. Musicians and DJs perform on Thursdays, Fridays, and Saturdays.

★ LE GRILLARDIN
60 Rue Paul Gauguin; tel. 40 43 09 90; restaurantlegrillardin@yahoo.fr; noon-2pm and 7pm-10pm Tues.-Sat.; CFP 4,500

At Le Grillardin, each dish is thoughtfully plated with garnishes and small details that make a meal here feel special. It's known for the rack of lamb, though the mahi-mahi in puff pastry, trio of duck, and scallops are all worth an order as well. Plant-based diners might struggle to find an option, however. Their French wine list is one of the best in town. Reservations are recommended.

O BELVÉDÈRE
Rue de Belvedere; tel. 89 40 34 03; www.o-belvedere. com; 4pm-10pm Thurs., 10am-10pm Fri.-Sat., 10am-4pm Sun.; CFP 5,000

At 600 meters (1,968 ft) above sea level, indulgent O Belvédère is the highest restaurant on the island. The French influence is there, with cheese dishes galore—baked camembert, truffle-infused cheese fondue, morbier cheese raclette, and of course, cheesecake. There's also broth fondue, burgers, and salads. Pack your bathing suit to enjoy the on-site pool after your meal is done, and drink to theater and music performances taking place throughout the year. Reservations are recommended and best booked over the phone.

★ HEI
Blvd. de la Reine Pomare IV; tel. 40 43 77 14; www. heirestaurant.com; 7pm-10pm Tues.-Wed. and Sat., noon-10pm Thurs., noon-7pm Fri.; CFP 5,000/ three-course meal

For fine dining, Hei is one of the best. With only a handful of tables in the intimate restaurant, it's often a challenge to nab a reservation. If you're feeling adventurous, come hungry and order the degustation menu— dishes change about every month depending on what's in season. Wear your finest outfit and take your time savoring each bite. For dessert, unique offerings like pistachio and raspberry pie make it worthwhile to save room for something sweet.

Fruits of French Polynesia

Market stalls throughout French Polynesia display boun-
ties of nature's treats: usually sweet, sometimes sour, and
occassionally tangy fruit. While you'll undoubtedly want
to enjoy all the mangoes, pineapples, coconuts, bananas,
and grapefruits you can get your hands on, there are a
few tropical fruits to try that you might not have sampled
before. If in season, all of these can be enjoyed at the
Papeete Market.

papaya

- **Soursop:** Soursop is a prickly green fruit with a
  cream-colored center and large dark seeds. As its
  name implies, soursop is a little tangy and sour, a bit
  creamy, and almost tastes like a blend between straw-
  berry and pineapple.

- **Breadfruit:** Breadfruit was brought to Polynesia
  from voyagers hailing from the Malay Archipelago,
  and many species of the fruit are found on French
  Polynesia today. This large green fruit has a fluffy,
  starchy center. When cooked, it tastes similar to fresh
  bread or baked potatoes.

- **Papaya:** If you see a skinny tree with round green fruits clustered at the top, it's probably
  papaya. The inside of a papaya is juicy and sweet, though you'll want to eat it before it gets
  too mushy. Drizzle it with lime juice.

- **Noni:** This yellow and seedy fruit is famed for its health benefits; many Tahitians drink noni
  juice as a holistic preventative for many types of diseases. The smell is pretty pungent, so few
  people consume noni for its taste.

- **Rambutan:** Small red balls with fluffy spikes, rambutans have a translucent, sweet center.

- **Passionfruit:** Grown on vines from the society islands to the most remote atolls, these
  perfectly smooth spheres yield a sour yet sweet scoop of fruity jam.

Asian
WAKAME SUSHI BAR & GRILL
*Rue Charles Viénot; tel. 40 57 68 78; wakame.tahiti@
gmail.com; 11:30am-2:00pm and 6:30pm-9:00pm
Tues.-Sat.; CFP 1,500*

This Japanese restaurant serves fresh sushi
and sashimi in a casual atmosphere. Pick a
plate from the conveyor belt (plates are tal-
lied at the end) or order from the menu. Maki,
salmon rolls, dragon rolls, and bento boxes
with chicken and beef teriyaki are all on order.

VILLA THAI
*Rue Albert Leboucher; tel. 40 85 60 80; 6pm-11pm
Mon. and Sat., 11am-2pm and 6pm-10pm Tues.-Fri.;
CFP 2,000*

Villa Thai serves Southeast Asian cuisine in
a casual setting. Take a seat on a floor pillow
and enjoy hot stacks of Vietnamese banh xeo
pancakes, crispy salad with shrimp, or a pile
of pad thai. They also have vegetarian offerings like lemongrass soup and green curry
with tofu.

RESTAURANT JIMMY
*31 Rue des Ecoles; tel. 40 43 63 32; restaurantjimmy.
com; 11am-2pm and 6pm-9:30pm Mon.-Sat.; CFP
2,000-3,000*

Restaurant Jimmy is a lovely little oasis from
the sensory overload of Papeete thanks to its
calm ambiance. They have extensive Asian offerings with salads, soups, vegetarian dishes,

meats, and seafood. Many of their best dishes are found on the Chinese section of the menu. From 6pm onward Monday-Thursday, Restaurant Jimmy hosts a Chinese fondue dinner, tapenlou, with beef, chicken, fish, seafood, and vegetables cut and cooked in pots of broth. Meals can also be ordered as takeaway.

Italian
LA CASA BIANCA

Marina Taina; tel. 40 43 91 35; www.
casabianca-tahiti.com; 10am-10pm daily; CFP 2,000
La Casa Bianca is a casual al fresco restaurant on the waterfront. Enjoy Italian and French dishes while watching yachts cruising in and out of the marina. Their menu features salad, pasta, carpaccio, tartare, and pizza. If you're on the fence between offerings, go for the pizza. Chocolate mousse, tiramisu, and a selection of ice cream are there if you're keen for something sweet. Every day 5pm-6pm is happy hour. Some form of entertainment (usually live music) takes place multiple times per week from around 5pm onward.

Pub Food
LES 3 BRASSEURS

Blvd. de la Reine Pomare IV; tel. 40 50 60 25;
www.3brasseurs-pacific.com; 9am-1am Mon.-Sat.,
9am-midnight Sun.; CFP 2,500
At one of the few microbreweries in French Polynesia, you'll want to order a chilled glass of white, blonde, amber, IPA, or experimental beer to complement your meal. Dine on salads, flammkuchens, burgers, cheese plates, carpaccios, grilled meats, or wraps. Items on the menu have a recommended beer accompaniment. For the spontaneous traveler, order the chef's daily pick for both food and drink.

Cafés
★ CAFÉ MAEVA

Upstairs Papeete Market; tel. 87 24 16 46; 7am-5pm
Mon.-Fri., 7am-3:30pm Sat.; CFP 1,500-3,000
Located in Papeete Market, Café Maeva is a popular brunch spot serving plates of waffles, bacon, sausages, fried potatoes, and eggs. A smoothie made from fruit sourced from the market pairs well with just about anything. Come around noon to dine on a sampler plate of Tahitian dishes like poisson cru with coconut milk and taro leaves, roti parcels, fried tuna, ham, and cheese. If football or rugby is on, you'll find a crowd here to cheer with.

★ URBAN CAFÉ

29 Rue Dumont D'Urville; tel. 40 83 39 99; www.
urbancafetahiti.com; 6am-2pm Mon.-Tues. and Sat.,
6am-9:30pm Wed.-Fri.; CFP 2,500
Urban Café has a jungle-meets-warehouse feel to it. The outside area hosts an overgrown garden. Inside, you'll find an industrial feel with vintage furniture. Come hungry for breakfast to enjoy dishes like eggs benedict, pastry plates, pancakes, and French toast. The lunch menu features seafood, salads, packed-to-the-brim burgers, and pasta, with a handful of vegan options available, like a vegan poke bowl. The drinks menu is extensive, with coffee iced and hot, cocktails, beer, wine, and juices.

BARS AND NIGHTLIFE

Tahiti isn't exactly a nightlife destination, but there's still fun to be had after dark. If there's a microphone being passed around a bar, just know Tahitians can sing. They might take pity on an off-key tourist for a song or two, but if a local gestures for the mic in your hand mid-ballad, it's a sign that you're not quite in tune. Many of bars charge a CFP 1,000 cover, which includes one drink.

Bars
LE CHAPLIN'S

Blvd. de la Reine Pomare IV; tel. 40 42 73 05;
11am-1am daily
Chaplin's is a place to sing, dance, and drink. From 9pm onward, every night is karaoke night, and you can sing your heart out with a cocktail or beer in hand. There's often a live DJ in house to keep spirits up. Pizza, sandwiches, and burgers are on the menu. Free WiFi is available for singers who want to double check the lyrics before belting their tune.

Hinano Beer

Hinano Beer is ubiquitous in French Polynesia, the main beer served at every bar and sitting on the shelves of every liquor store. The girl depicted on the Hinano beer label has become an icon of Tahiti, with stickers, T-shirts, and towels of her being slung at many souvenir shops. Flowers in her hair, a red pareu wrapped around her chest, and looking out at a starry sky and motu, she appears not to have a care in the world. She's the symbol of an idyllic Tahitian vacation.

Hinano Beer

The Brasserie de Tahiti was launched in 1914, and over the next 39 years locals quenched their thirst with a brew known as Aorai. The operation underwent a major modernization in 1955, and the hearty Hinano of today was born, much to the delight of beer drinkers. Since 1976 the brewery has received technical support from the Dutch brewer Heineken, whose beer is bottled on Tahiti under license. The cannery that opened at Punaruu on Tahiti in 1986 was expanded in 1991, making it possible to export canned Hinano—lager, amber, gold, and white—to beer connoisseurs around the world.

Some great places to enjoy a Hinano on Tahiti:

- Overlooking the water with your toes in the sand at **L'Escale du France** (page 88).

- At a cultural dance show at the **InterContinental Resort Tahiti** (page 66).

- From the safety of a boat while watching surfer's charge **Teahupoo,** Tahiti's most intense wave (page 85).

- In between karaoke songs at **Chaplin's** (page 63).

LE ROYAL KIKIRIRI

64 Rue du Collette; tel. 40 43 58 64; facebook.com/ LeRoyalKikiriri; 11am-2pm Tues.-Thurs., 11am-9:30pm Fri. (music from 1pm), 5pm-9:30pm Sat., 11am-2pm Sun.; CFP 1,000 entry and includes drink

To experience the more traditional side of Polynesian party culture, come here on a Friday evening. Come to waltz, two-step, and witness ote'a, Tahitian dancing. On Sundays there's a buffet lunch with Tahitian seafood, roasted root vegetables, and grilled meats.

Nightclubs
LE SUGAR

Rue du Pere Collette; tel. 89 72 26 55; www.facebook. com/sugarbartahiti; 9pm-4am Thurs.-Sat.

Le Sugar is one of Papeete's few holdouts for night owls. Sip a cocktail or a cold beer and enjoy the live sets by local DJs. House, trap, reggaeton, hip-hop—it's all here. Check the Facebook page the day of to see who's playing.

PARADISE NIGHT CLUB TAHITI

Blvd. de la Reine Pomare IV; tel. 40 42 73 05; www. facebook.com/ParadiseNightTahiti; 11pm-4am Mon.-Thurs., 7pm-4am Fri.-Sun.

Open every day, this nightclub has regular karaoke nights, beer and cocktails, and basic finger foods. Entry is first-come, first-served (there may be an entry fee depending on the DJ). They often host themed nights (costumes welcome); check out the Facebook page.

ACCOMMODATIONS
US$50-100
MAHANA LODGE HOSTEL & BACKPACKERS

5 Rue Paul Gauguin; tel. 89 50 49 04; mahana-lodge-tahiti.mydirectstay.com; US$30/dorm bed; US$80 private room

A convenient place for travelers on a budget, with a 24-hour reception area that sells snacks and offers information, this hostel also has a communal kitchen, where a basic breakfast of bread, spreads, and fruit is served each morning. Bathrooms are small but clean. If you can, book the four- or six-bed dorms or the private room. The bunk beds in the 12-bed dorm are a little rickety and close together. Because this is not known for being a party hostel, your dormmate is just as likely to be a twentysomething backpacker as they are to be a gray-haired local.

STUDIO FERRY

17 bis Rue Clappier; tel. 87 30 13 56; studio-ferry-papeete.com; US$80-90/room

A great spot if you're taking an early morning ferry to Moorea. Each room has air-conditioning and WiFi access; some have a kitchenette with microwave. Some rooms have shared bathroom access. Rooms are clean and relatively quiet, and staff are helpful when it comes to arranging schedules. Finding the property is no easy feat—you'll want to call in advance to have the owner meet you out front.

FARE REAREA

70 Av. Pomare V; tel. 87 77 15 81; farerearea@gmail.com; US$90/room

A cozy homestay with tropical vibes and pool area. Rooms range from single occupancy with a twin bed and shared bathroom to suites that sleep 2-4. Rooms are set around a tropical garden and pool area. All rooms have air-conditioning, internet access, and a coffee machine. Guests have access to a full kitchen. Luc, the host, is happy to offer tips for traveling around Tahiti.

INAITI LODGE

Seaside at PK 3.2; tel. 87 71 67 40; inaiti-lodge.com; US$70-100/room

Inaiti Lodge is a bed and breakfast hosted in a family home in one of the residential neighborhoods of Papeete. Each room has an uplifting ambiance with tropical decor, fresh flowers, and friendly hosts. It's not fancy, but it's comfortable. There are two room types, one that sleeps three with a single bed and double bed, and another that sleeps four with a double bed and bunk bed. Both types have hot water en suite bathrooms, a television, and a desk. There is also free parking, WiFi, breakfast, and fridge access.

US$100-150
★ FARE SUISSE

Av. des Poilus tahitiens; tel. 40 42 00 30; www.fare-suisse.com; US$110/room

Bright and airy rooms await at Fare Suisse, a welcoming homestay that has been a Papeete mainstay. All rooms have air-conditioning, a private bathroom, and reliable internet access. Rooms can sleep 2-4 people. Guests have access to a full kitchen. The property is close enough to the city—a 10-minute walk away—for convenience, but still away from the noise. There's a spacious terrace and tropical gardens to relax in between sightseeing stops. Free transport to and from the ferry terminal and airport is included.

FARE D'HÔTES TUTEHAU

184 Av. du Ch ef Vairaatoa; tel. 87 31 19 84; www.faredhotestutehau.com; US$90-130/room

A quaint and comfortable family-run guesthouse around 10 minutes' walking distance from Papeete city center. Decor made from shells, sculpted wood, and stone add a Polynesian feel—as does the thatched roof lounge area in the garden. There's a two-bedroom unit with double beds and a shared bathroom; one double room with a king-size bed; and a family room with private bathroom, sofa bed, and single bed that can sleep up to five people. Guests have access to bicycles, a kitchen, and laundry facilities (extra charge).

TARA TAHITI LODGE

50 Chemin Afareii 3; tel. 89 45 64 56; tara-tahiti-lodge.com; US$120/room

Tara Tahiti Lodge is a family-friendly guesthouse with rooms that are modern, clean, and spacious. Each comes with air-conditioning, a mosquito net, and internet, and some rooms have a private bathroom. There are also two multi-bedroom units that can sleep up to nine guests with a living room and full kitchen. All guests have access to bicycles to use in Papeete. The host, Fred, is happy to help guests arrange tours and transport. Breakfast of tropical fruit and pastries is included.

TEA TAHITI HOLIDAYS

Off Av. Georges Clemenceau; tel. 32 87 32 66; tea.tahiti.holidays@gmail.com; US$120/room

Tea Tahiti Holidays is a quirky guesthouse about a five-minute walk away from Papeete city center. Rooms are small, clean, and come with a mini fridge, microwave, kettle, internet access, and TV. Some double rooms share a bathroom, while others have one en suite; family rooms sleep up to four. There's also a plunge pool and lounge area outside that offers a place to unwind after a big day out.

TAHITI AIRPORT MOTEL

Across from Faa'a International Airport; tel. 40 50 40 00; tahitiairportmotel.com; US$130/room

If you're looking for a convenient and clean place to spend the night near the international airport, Tahiti Airport Motel is a popular pick. While *technically* just across the road from the airport, the short hill leading up to the front desk is extremely steep when you're schlepping a heavy suitcase. Rooms are basic but clean, with private bathrooms, WiFi, air-conditioning, and a small TV. Family rooms sleep up to four people; wheelchair accessible rooms are also available on request.

US$150-250

★ FARE ANAPA

Servitude Muriavai; tel. 89 71 08 13; fareanapa.com; US$240/bungalow

If you're after your own private space with modern amenities, check out Fare Anapa. This bungalow suits long-term stays (or travelers who are burned out from hotel-hopping). These two-bedroom bungalows have double beds, air-conditioning, a full kitchen, washing machine, access to a Jacuzzi and sun loungers, outdoor dining area, and parking. The property can also arrange car rentals.

US$250 and Up

HILTON HOTEL TAHITI

Off PK 2; tel. 40 86 48 48; hilton.com; US$320/room

The Hilton Hotel Tahiti is one of the newest resorts on the island—it opened at the end of 2021 after a 10-year hiatus—but it has a retro, 1960s-style feel. The highlight is the massive outdoor lagoon-style pool with poolside cabanas and views to Moorea. There are three restaurants on-site as well as a spa, fitness center, and ballroom. Each of the 200 rooms are spacious and light-flooded with large windows and modern fixtures. All have air-conditioning, a workspace, mini bar, kettle, TV, and internet access.

★ INTERCONTINENTAL RESORT TAHITI

Seaside at PK 7; tel. 40 86 51 50; tahiti.intercontinental.com; US$350/room

With two infinity pools overlooking the water, tropical gardens, views of Moorea, a spa, and a handful of restaurants and bars, the InterContinental Resort Tahiti caters to travelers who want to spend most of their holiday lounging seaside. The pick of the 250 rooms are the overwater bungalows: they're spacious, tastefully decorated, equipped with modern amenities, and have large decks with water access starting at around US$500 per night. The property also has a range of rooms, suites, and villas for those who prefer to stay on terra firma.

LE TAHITI BY PEARL RESORTS

Lafayette Beach at PK 7; tel. 40 48 88 00; www.
letahiti.com; US$250-450/room

One of the few properties on Tahiti with access to the volcanic sands of Lafayette Beach. The surrounding scenery of Matavai Bay makes it one of the most stunning stays on the island. The resort has an outdoor pool, restaurant, bar, spa, and activity center. Live music and cultural performances take place regularly at the restaurant. The 91 rooms range from ocean view double rooms, suites, and duplexes, some equipped with kitchens. For the ultimate chill spot, opt for a room with a hot tub overlooking the ocean.

INFORMATION AND SERVICES

Papeete is the administrative center of French Polynesia, and the best place to obtain any form of supplies or services. It has the best healthcare facilities in the region, and is where you should go should anything serious happen. Most of French Polynesia's embassies, consulates, government buildings, and schools are found in Papeete. There are public toilets located in the ferry terminal.

Visitors Centers

Tahiti Tourisme (tahititourisme.org) runs two tourist offices around Papeete:

- Ferry Terminal; tel. 40 50 40 30; 7:30am-5:30pm Mon.-Fri., 8am-4pm Sat., 8am-noon Sun.
- Blvd. de la Reine Pomare IV; tel. 40 50 40 30; 8am-5:30pm Mon.-Fri., 8am-4pm Sat., 8am-noon Sun.

Post Offices

Below are two of Papeete's most centrally located **Post and Telecommunications (OPT) offices.**

- 8 Blvd. de la Reine Pomare IV; tel. 40 41 42 42; opt.pf; 7:30am-5pm Mon.-Fri.
- Near Faa'a Airport; tel. 40 41 42 73; opt.

pf; 7:30am-11am and 11:45am-2:30pm Mon.-Fri.

Health and Safety

- **Police Aux Frontières:** Faa'a Airport; tel. 40 80 06 00; www.polynesie-francaise. pref.gouv.fr; 7:30am-noon and 1:30pm-5pm Mon.-Fri.
- **Centre Hospitalier de la Polynésie Française:** Av. Général de Gaulle; tel. 40 48 62 62; www.chpf.pf; open 24/7
- **Clinique Cardella:** 11 Rue Anne-Marie Javouhey; tel. 40 46 04 00; cardella.pf; open 24/7
- **Pharmacie Paofai:** Rue de Lieutenant Varney; tel. 40 43 93 93; 7am-7pm Mon.-Fri., 7am-1pm Sat.
- **Prince Hinoi Medical Center:** Av. Prince Hinoi; tel. 87 77 20 35; www.centre-medical-prince-hinoi.com; 8am-noon and 2pm-5pm Mon.-Fri., 8:30am-noon Sun.

Consulates

- **U.S. Consulate:** Tamanu Iti Center, 1st floor; tel. 40 42 65 35; usembassy.gov; 10am-noon Tues. or by appointment
- **Australian Consulate:** Av. du Prince Hīnoi; tel. 40 46 38 99; dfat.gov.au; consulate.papeete@dfat.gov.au; 9am-4pm Mon.-Fri.
- **New Zealand Consulate:** Bureau 88, Vaima Centre; tel. 40 50 02 95; mfat.govt. nz; nzhonconsulate@mail.pf; 8am-3:30pm Mon.-Fri.

Launderettes

- **Laverie Pont de l'Est:** 64 Rue Paul Gauguin; tel. 40 43 71 59; 7am-4pm Mon.-Fri., 7am-noon Sat.
- **Mamao Cleaners:** Danielle Livine Building; tel. 40 42 68 21; www.mamao-cleaners.com; 7:30am-5pm Mon.-Fri., 8am-11am Sat.

Yachting Facilities

- **Directorate of Maritime Affairs:** Fate Ute; tel. 40 54 45 00; www.maritime.gov.pf; 7:30am-3:30pm Mon.-Thurs., 7:30am-2:30pm Fri.

- **Marina Taina:** PK 9; tel. 40 41 02 25; www.marina-taina.com

- **Yacht Club of Tahiti:** PK 4; tel. 40 42 78 03; www.yctahiti.org

GETTING THERE

Tahiti is the travel hub for all other islands in French Polynesia, home to the international airport and the Port of Papeete. To get almost anywhere further afield in French Polynesia, you'll have to touch down here first.

Air

FAA'A INTERNATIONAL AIRPORT

PK 5 in Faa'a; tel. 40 86 60 61; tahiti-aeroport.pf

Faa'a International Airport is 5 kilometers (3 mi) west of Papeete and is the largest airport in French Polynesia, the main hub for **Air Tahiti Nui** (www.airtahitinui.com), the international airline, and **Air Tahiti** (www.airtahiti.com), the domestic airline. The airport has a handful of boutiques, cafés, banking services, phone and internet services, and transport desks.

Flights come into Papeete from Auckland (5 hours), New Caledonia (6.5 hours), Japan (11 hours), San Francisco (8.5 hours), Los Angeles (8.5 hours), and Santiago (11 hours). There are also flights from Europe (major cities being London, Paris, and Madrid) with short refueling stops in Canada or the United States, taking around 22 hours total. While airlines used to stick to set schedules before the pandemic, these have recently been more variable due to changes in demand and travel restrictions.

Papeete is a 10-minute drive from Faa'a International Airport. A steep taxi fare from the airport is a rite of passage for many travelers; the ride to the center of Papeete runs around CFP 2,000, with an extra CFP 100 per piece of luggage or CFP 500 per bulky item, like a surfboard. There is a taxi stand outside of the airport. Buses run from the airport to Papeete city center (30 minutes, CFP 200/one-way). The bus stand is across from the airport parking lot on the main road, marked by a shade shelter and blue sign.

There are multiple car rental counters in the airport, as well as a few companies nearby which tend to be cheaper.

Faa'a International Airport

- **Eco Car** (ecocar-tahiti.com; tel. 40 54 20 09; 7:30am-7:30pm daily; scooters from CFP 3,500/day, cars from CFP 5,800/day, 4WDs from CFP 15,000/day) is a budget car rental company located just across the road from Faa'a International Airport. They offer a free transport service between the airport and their building.

- **Avis** (avis.com) is generally reliable and has a counter in the terminal building at Faa'a International Airport (tel. 40 85 02 84; 5am-7pm daily; cars from CFP 6,500/day).

- **Europcar** (Europcar-tahiti.com; tel. 40 86 61 96; 5am-11pm daily; cars from CFP 7,000/day) has a car rental counter inside the airport.

Ferry
PAPEETE FERRY TERMINAL
Blvd. de la Reine Pomare IV; tel. 40 47 48 00; www.portdepapeete.pf; office hours 7am-3pm Mon.-Thurs., 7am-2pm Fri.

Ferries and cruise ships arrive at Papeete's waterfront; taxis await at the entrance of the terminal. Otherwise, there is a bus stop marked with a blue sign with multiple stops along Boulevard de la Reine Pomare IV.

GETTING AROUND

Papeete's waterfront is largely walkable, but you'll want a set of wheels to see the rest of the island. Paved roads like the coastal road that wraps around Tahiti are easy to navigate by car, but you'll need a 4x4—and ideally a good guide—to explore the interior.

Hitchhiking is common on Tahiti, especially outside of Papeete. If you hitch a ride, it's wise to not to go alone and use discretion before you get in a vehicle. While not expected, giving the driver the amount you'd pay for an equivalent bus fare is appreciated.

Bus
You can reach most of the main points on the island by bus. Buses are white, air-conditioned coaches with the end of the route displayed out front. Riding the bus could even be considered a worthwhile experience to tick off the list while in Tahiti. It's a great way to meet Tahitians, who are happy to chat with and offer tips to travelers willing to get around like a local. You can download route maps from the **Tere Tahiti** website (teretahiti.pf), and there's even a bus route app available on Android and iPhone called Tere Tahiti—though note that these are not always very reliable. Some bus drivers will stop if you wave, though many will drive on through and pick up only at designated bus stops, marked by a blue sign ("arrêt le bus").

Bus fares around Papeete cost CFP 200 per trip, maxing out at CFP 450 to Tahiti Iti. Buses throughout Papeete and coastal towns within a 30-kilometer (18-mi) radius depart every 20-30 minutes from 4am-6pm, with just a few routes operating later. Buses to Teahupoo and Tautira run around every hour or so from 5am-5pm. On Sundays, bus service is very limited; it's worth calling for the latest schedule. Major bus routes depart from the Mairie de Papeete (the town hall) and the Ferry Terminal.

Taxis
No matter how far you go by taxi in Tahiti, it always seems shockingly expensive. Standard taxi fares cost CFP 1,000 as a base fare plus CFP 130 per kilometer from 6am-8pm. From 8pm-6am, rates increase to CFP 230 per kilometer. To estimate the fare between two points, multiply the distance in kilometers by 130 or 230, then add 1,000. It won't be completely accurate, but it shouldn't be too far off either. Current fare prices can be confirmed at Tahititaxi.com.

You'll find taxis buzzing through Papeete along Boulevard Pomare. There are taxi stands at Vaima (tel. 40 43 72 47), Place Vaiete (tel. 40 41 23 42), and Papeete Market (tel. 40 42 97 91). Outside of Papeete, taxis are very challenging to come by.

Car and Scooter
Outside of Papeete, a car or scooter is by far the most convenient way to get around. A 117-kilometer (72-mi) coastal road wraps

around the island, pronging out to Tahiti Iti (stretching 15 kilometers (9 mi) on Tahiti Iti's southern coast and 18 kilometers (11 mi) on the northern coast). If there's no traffic, you can drive all of Tahiti Nui within three hours. Add an extra 1-1.5 hours to see Tahiti Iti. The road gets busy in the early mornings and evenings around Papeete, easing up after Arue to the north and Faa'a to the south. Car rental facilities in Papeete include:

- **Avis:** 56 Rue des Remparts; tel. 40 54 10 10; www.avis-tahiti.com; 7:30am-5pm Mon.-Fri., 7:30am-4pm Sat., 7:30am-noon Sun.
- **Hertz:** Rue des Remparts; tel. 40 42 04 71; www.hertz-tahiti.com; 7:30am-5:30pm Mon.-Fri.

Most car rental companies forbid taking their vehicles on Tahiti's unpaved roads (truthfully, that's probably for the best). Roads in the interior are poorly marked, often washed out, and narrow—it's better to see those sights on a tour or with a guide.

For all car rental companies, you'll want to reserve an automatic well in advance; most last-minute rentals will be manual. Small cars start at around CFP 5,500 per day. Typically, a second driver, unlimited milage, local transport service, and limited insurance are covered, though you'll want to comb through the rental agreement to be sure. Tire damage is not usually covered.

You can also see the island by scooter (from CFP 3,500 per day)—a popular option among locals. Pack a rain jacket if you're out for more than a few hours just in case it gets drizzly on the road.

Parking in Papeete is scarce and chaotic, with sidewalk parking and double-parking commonplace. Most street parking is metered 8am-5pm Mondays-Saturdays (CFP 100/hour). There are a parking lots at Park Bougainville, Paofai Gardens, and the Ferry Terminal.

Local Tours
YOTA TAHITI TOURS
Pickup service within Papeete; tel. 87 79 55 11; yotatahiti.com; 8am-6pm daily; CFP 14,500/day tour
If you want a thorough primer for Tahiti, book a tour with Yota. Yota is a charismatic multilingual guide who is happy to share all that he knows (and it's a lot) about Tahiti—from botany to pearl picking to Polynesian trivia to history to Tahitian dance. Tours are given in an air-conditioned van and move at the pace of the group.

UNIQUE TAHITI TOURS
Rue Clappier; tel. 89 23 69 32; uniquetahiti.com; 8am-5pm daily; CFP 16,000/full-day tour, CFP 10,000/half-day tour, CFP 3,000/Papeete walking tour
Unique Tahiti tours is a boutique tour company with tour options to cover just about every paved part of the island, spanning to Tahiti Iti. The West Coast tour is the most comprehensive, covering Tahiti Nui's western sights like the Marae of Arahuruhu, Caves of Maraa, the Gardens of Vaipahi, and Vaima. Tours take place from an air-conditioned van. If you have a day in Papeete, join the walking tour—it's a great way to learn about the history of local sights from an insider's perspective. Special interest tours centered around religion, culture, government, food, and art are also available upon request.

Tahiti Nui

Tahiti Nui is a land of legends. Outside of Papeete, the largest city in French Polynesia, the island's interior is essentially untouched. Drive around its coastline for cultural sights, glimmering black sand beaches, sleepy towns, and restaurants cooking up the catch of the day. Tahiti Nui is home to most the archipelago's population, so exploring here offers a glimpse at how Tahitians live. Then take a trail inland and discover a land that's largely been left to the wilderness.

Orientation

A paved coastal road wraps around Tahiti Nui, the larger part of the hourglass-shaped island. For orientation, you'll see red and white kilometer stones, called **PK markers,** all along the inland side of the road. These are numbered in each direction from Papeete Market, meeting in **Taravao** (where an isthmus connects Tahiti Nui and Tahiti Iti). A few roads of varying conditions sprawl into its interior. An interior dirt road connects the **Papenoo Valley,** which delves into the island's northern coast, and the small town of **Mataiea** on the southern coast, though this section of road is often closed for construction.

SIGHTS

The PK address markers on Tahiti start at Papeete Market; for all addresses listed below, the PK marker signals the distance from Papeete in kilometers.

Northeast Coast
POINT VENUS

PK 10; free

At the tip of a peninsula on Tahiti's northern coast, you'll find Point Venus. Captain Cook camped on this point between the river and the lagoon during his visit to observe the transit of the planet Venus across the sun on June 3, 1769. Captain Bligh also occupied Point Venus for two months in 1788 while collecting breadfruit shoots for transportation to the Caribbean. And on March 5, 1797, the first members of the London Missionary Society landed here, spreading Protestantism from Tahiti throughout Polynesia and as far as Vanuatu.

Today there's a park on the point, with a 25-meter-high (82-ft-high) lighthouse (1867) among the palms and ironwood trees. A souvenir shop and stands selling snacks are found next to the lighthouse. Across from the monument to Captain Cook, with a large ball behind an iron railing, is a newer monument to the *Bounty* mutineers, erected by their descendants in 2006. Yet another monument in the park recalls the landing of the first missionaries.

The view of Tahiti across Matavai Bay from Point Venus is superb, and twin-humped Orohena, the highest peak on the island, is in view. Weekdays, the beaches of Point Venus are a peaceful place with waters idyllic for wading or even surfing a few waves, the perfect choice if you'd like to get away from Papeete and spend some time at the beach. Weekends draw a crowd. Any bus heading toward Mahina will bring you here.

PAPENOO VALLEY

Entrance road starts near PK 18 just before the Papenoo River; free

The Papenoo Valley is the caldera of Tahiti Nui's great extinct volcano, considered by ancient Tahitians to be the realm of the gods. The valley runs from the town of Papenoo inland 10 kilometers (6 mi) along the Papenoo River toward the slopes of Mount Orohena. The jagged ridgelines of the valley can be seen on the shores of Papenoo Beach. While anyone can drive through the valley up to a certain point, it's best to come here as part of a tour—a 4WD is needed to navigate the steep roads with hairpin turns, and most car rental agencies prohibit driving here. In the valley,

Tahiti Nui

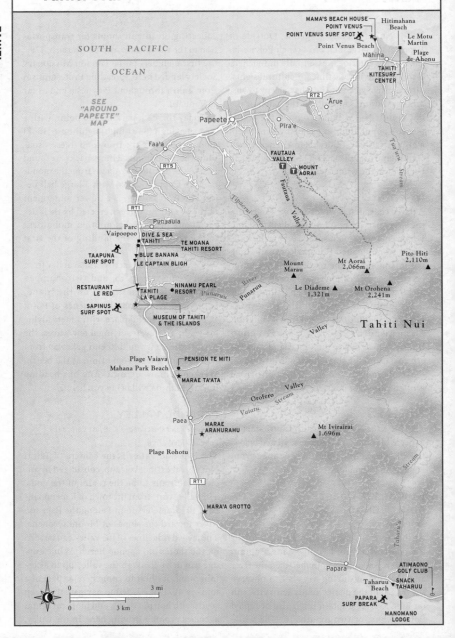

SOUTH PACIFIC

OCEAN

SEE
"AROUND
PAPEETE"
MAP

MAMA'S BEACH HOUSE
POINT VENUS
POINT VENUS SURF SPOT
Point Venus Beach
Hitimahana Beach
Le Motu Martin
Plage de Ahonu
Māhina
TAHITI KITESURF CENTER

RT2

'Ārue

Papeete
Pīra'e

Faa'a

RT5

FAUTAUA VALLEY
MOUNT AORAI

RT1

Punaauia

Parc Vaipoopoo
DIVE & SEA TAHITI
TE MOANA TAHITI RESORT
TAAPUNA SURF SPOT
BLUE BANANA
LE CAPTAIN BLIGH
RESTAURANT LE RED
NINAMU PEARL RESORT
TAHITI LA PLAGE
SAPINUS SURF SPOT
MUSEUM OF TAHITI & THE ISLANDS

Mount Marau
Mt Aorai 2,066m
Pito Hiti 2,110m
Le Diademe 1,321m
Mt Orohena 2,241m

Punaruu
Punaruu River
Valley

Tahiti Nui

Plage Vaiava
Mahana Park Beach
PENSION TE MITI
MARAE TA'ATA

Orofero Valley
Vaiatu Stream

Paea
MARAE ARAHURAHU
Mt Ivirairai 1,696m

Plage Rohotu

RT1

MARA'A GROTTO

Papara
ATIMAONO GOLF CLUB
SNACK TAHARUU
Taharuu Beach
PAPARA SURF BREAK
MANOMANO LODGE

0   3 mi
0   3 km

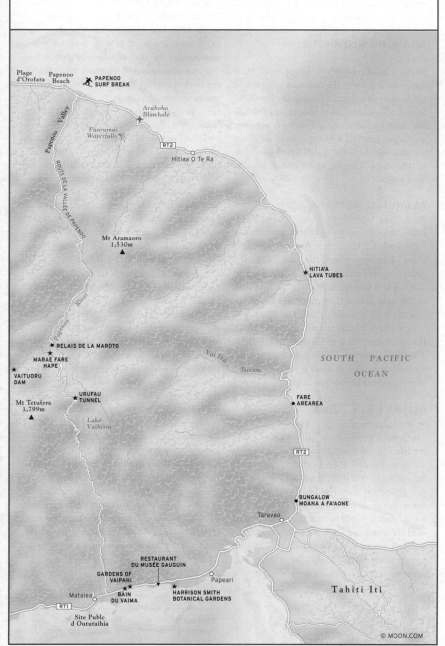

waterfalls, ancient ceremonial sites, creek beds ideal for swimming, and vistas await.

ARAHOHO BLOWHOLE

PK 22; free

At the Arahoho Blowhole, jets of water shoot up through holes in the lava rock at high tide. It's dangerous to get too close to the blowhole, as a sudden surge could toss you out to sea, but there's a sectioned-off viewing area you where you can feel a strong puff of air as the waves surge through. A cute beach is tucked next to the parking lot, and it's a nice place to have a picnic.

FAARUMAI WATERFALLS

PK 22.2; free

Just a little beyond the blowhole, a road to the right leads 1.3 kilometers (0.8 mi) up to the three Faarumai Waterfalls, also called the Tefa'aurumai Falls. Vaimahuta Falls is accessible on foot five minutes along the easy path to the right across the bridge and is a wispy cascade with a wading pool. The 30-minute trail to the left leads to two more waterfalls, Haamaremare Iti and Haamaremare Rahi. The farthest waterfall has a pool deep enough for swimming. Bring insect repellent and lock your rental car before heading off.

HITIA'A LAVA TUBES

PK 36, Hitia'a; free

The jagged corridors of Hitia'a's lava tubes are some of the most geologically interesting sights on Tahiti. Lava tubes form when channels of lava crust over, creating a tunnel for soft pahoehoe, a type of lava, to flow. When the eruption settles, the lava flows downward, leaving tubes in its wake. On the coast of Hitia'a, you can walk inside of a lava tube. While it's possible to visit solo, it's best seen as part of a day trip around Tahiti. Many day tours include a stop here depending on the weather conditions.

Southwest Coast
MUSEUM OF TAHITI AND THE ISLANDS

PK 14.7, Puna'auia; tel. 40 54 84 35; www. museetahiti.pf; 9am-5pm Tues.-Sat.; CFP 600/person

The recently renovated Museum of Tahiti and the Islands first opened in 1977. In a large air-conditioned complex on Punaauia Bay, this museum has multiple halls devoted to the history, natural environment, and settlement of Tahiti, as well as Polynesian material culture and social and religious life. The collections include almost 1,700 seashells, some 13,000 plant specimens dating back as far as 1847, and around 1,300 carvings from pre-European times to the present day. Several hours can be spent studying the exhibits, although a much faster walkthrough will also be educational and entertaining. Outside is an anchor Captain Cook lost at Tautira in 1773. Only some of the captions are in English, and many of those are abbreviated from the French version.

When the waves are right, you can sit on the seawall in the park behind the museum and watch the Tahitian surfers bob and ride, with the outline of Moorea beyond. It's a nice picnic spot. Many of the trees in the park are labeled. On your way back to the main highway from the museum, look up to the top of the hill at an "old fort" used by the French to subjugate the Tahitians in the 1840s.

The museum makes an excellent half-day excursion from Papeete by public bus. Any of the Paea or Papara buses on Rue du Maréchal Foch near Papeete Market will bring you to the turnoff in 30 minutes. The 600-meter (1,968-ft) road to the museum begins around PK 14.7 beside a Total gas station, 100 meters (328 ft) south of the large bridge over the Punaruu River just beyond a major traffic circle.

1: the lighthouse at Point Venus **2:** Arahoho Blowhole **3:** Papenoo Valley tunnel **4:** Papenoo Valley

MARAE TAATA AND MARAE ARAHURAHU

PK 19; free

Marae Taata and nearby Marae Arahurahu are easily the island's most beautiful archaeological sites. They're found up the road inland from Magasin Laut—take care, because the sign faces Papeete, and it's not visible if you're traveling clockwise. These marae lie in a tranquil verdant spot under high cliffs. The ancient open altars built from thousands of cut stones and tiki were carefully restored in 1954, the first such restoration in French Polynesia. At Marae Arahurahu a well-kept path leads to the anthropomorphic tiki or ti'i, to a terrace, the foundation of a former home (called a pote'e), and finally the marae, the site of sacred ceremonies built from volcanic stones. Marae Arahurahu is used during Tahiti's Heiva Nui festivities, connecting today's festivities to rituals of the past. In 1980, archeologists found remnants of pig bones and reliefs within the marae, leading them to believe that the marae was once used as a site for animal sacrifice.

MARA'A GROTTO

PK 28.5; free

This grotto cloaked in ferns is the stuff of fairy tales. Hidden between banyan trees with a well-kept walking path leading from grotto to grotto, it's a good place to grab a fresh coconut from the souvenir stand and dip your toes in the water.

BAIN DU VAIMA

PK 49; free

A few hundred meters west of Vaipahi is the Bain du Vaima, a strong freshwater spring with several deep swimming pools fed by trickling waterfalls. This is one of the favorite free picnic spots on the island, and on weekends it's crowded with locals.

GARDENS OF VAIPAHI

PK 49; 8am-5pm daily; free

Within a short walk from the Bain du Vaima are the Gardens of Vaipahi, a botanical garden with lotus flower ponds, papaya trees, breadfruit trees, ginger, tiny waterfalls, and giant banyan trees. Bright tropical flowers rarely seen outside of these gardens also accent the grounds. A lookout point makes for a tranquil meditation spot with views of the sea. Information plaques in English and French highlight some of the most common plants seen with a little background on their history and use.

HARRISON SMITH BOTANICAL GARDENS

Turn at the sign for Jardin Botanique H. Smith, PK 51; tel. 40 57 10 58; 7am-6pm daily; free

This 137-hectare (338-acre) garden was created from 1919-1921 by the American botanist Harrison Smith (1872-1947), who introduced more than 200 new species to the island, among them the sweet grapefruit (pomelo), mangosteen, rambutan, and durian. Unfortunately, few native Tahitian plants are to be seen here. Yachts can enter the lagoon through Temarauri Pass and anchor just west of the point here.

Inland Tahiti Nui

MOUNT MARAU

At the end of Route de Saint-Hilarie; free

The road inland directly opposite Faa'a Airport goes under the RDO (Route de Dégagement Ouest) bypass road and up the side of the island to an excellent viewpoint over northwestern Tahiti. It's a rough 10-kilometer (6-mi) drive, which should be attempted only by 4WD in dry weather. From the TV tower at the end of the track it's only 30 minutes on foot to the summit of Mount Marau (1,493 m/4,898 ft), with another incredible view up the Fautaua Valley to the north and along the ridge to Mount Aorai to the east. Several tour companies offer half-day 4WD trips here, which is the easiest way to go.

BEACHES

Northeast Coast

POINT VENUS BEACH

PK 10; free

The beach around Point Venus is a popular spot for paddlers who launch their va'a from its black sands. The beach on the southerly side of the lighthouse offers a nice place to swim and lounge.

HITIMAHANA BEACH
PK 11; free
A quiet black sand beach popular with kite-surfers, windsurfers, and wing foilers once the wind is up. It's rarely crowded and has a view of Motu Martin just offshore.

PAPENOO BEACH
PK 17; free
As soon as school is out, kids and teens with surfboards underarm flock to the ashy shoreline of Papenoo Beach. Stretching nearly a kilometer long, it's an easy place to find parking and a patch of sand to yourself even among the crowds. Kids will love bodysurfing and boogie boarding in the whitewash, and competent surfers can paddle out to the outside sets. The town of Papenoo is within walking distance from the beach, with a few convenience stores selling snacks along the main road.

Southwest Coast
PARC VAIPOOPOO
PK 9; free
Parc Vaipoopoo is still off the main tourist radar. While the beach has always been there, a park opened in 2019 to cater to families in the area. The beach has a bathroom, shaded picnic areas, a garden, generally calm water, multiple playgrounds, a lawn bowling area, and a fitness area. There are usually a few roulottes parked here as well.

PLAGE VAIAVA
PK 18; free
Commonly called "Plage PK 18," this beach is one of the few lighter-sand beaches on Tahiti (it's more golden than white). At mid to high tide, it's a great spot to swim and snorkel—though it's wise to keep an eye on the tide as there's little water between sky and reef once

it drops. There's also a decently clean bathroom block.

MAHANA PARK BEACH
PK 18.5; free
Right next to Plage Vaiava is Mahana Park Beach, one of the best places to snorkel in Tahiti. The beach itself is a little rocky and cramped, but it's the coral education program here that makes it worth a visit. In the gin-clear water, you'll see multiple markers with numbers on them. Swim to each marker with a mask, snorkel, and fins to find an informational plaque that features facts about the native marine life. Sea turtles, reef sharks, anemones, starfish, parrotfish, and other reef fish are regularly seen here.

PLAGE ROHOTU
PK 22.5; free
A small beach with beige sand and public bathrooms. You'll rarely see this spot crowded, and it's a nice place to get a quick dip in while circling around the island.

TAHARUU BEACH
PK 38; free
Taharuu Beach is an interesting stretch of dark gray, soft sand that turns jet black once the water hits it. There are a few leafy trees to seek shade underneath, but otherwise it's a pretty hot place to be midday.

SURFING
Northeast Coast
POINT VENUS SURF SPOT
PK 10
There's a wave at Point Venus that works solely in specific conditions—look for a northeasterly swell and southerly winds. It breaks right and can get scarily shallow.

PAPENOO SURF BREAK
PK 18; paddle out at Papenoo Rivermouth
If there's even the slightest pulse in the water, you'll see surfers of all experience levels in the waters of Papenoo. There are a few shifty peaks around the river mouth. Avoid surfing

after heavy rains as the water can get a bit murky. Works best with a northerly swell and southerly winds.

MOANA SURF SCHOOL

tel. 87 78 10 90; moanasurfschooltahiti.com; hours dependent on ocean conditions; CFP 4,500/two-hour lesson

Moana Surf School hosts beginner-friendly surf lessons at Papenoo Beach, usually in the mornings, afternoons, and at sunset. Yoan, the instructor, is patient and has a way of making even the most timid of surfers feel comfortable. Bodyboarding, shortboarding, and longboarding lessons are all available. Groups are kept to a maximum of five; kids must be at least five years old to join.

Southwest Coast

TAAPUNA SURF SPOT

3-minute boat ride from Punaauia; CFP 250/one-way bus fare to Punaauia

Hollow, fast, shallow, and crowded with local surfers who have no qualms about sitting deep, this left-hander is one of the best on the island—but best suited for those who can handle heated conditions. It works best with a southwest swell and easterly winds.

SAPINUS SURF SPOT

PK 14; free

There are a few waves around Sapinus, the water off the point of the Museum of Tahiti and the Islands. You'll find a few unremarkable peaks near the beach, popular with kids and beginners. A 10-minute paddle offshore is the wave of Sapinus Reef, a left-hander that breaks fast and shallow. You'll want a southwesterly swell, easterly winds, and anything above low tide.

PAPARA SURF BREAK

PK 38

Beginner surfers looking for a wave will find it here, known as Papara Surf Break. Small

1: underwater trail at Mahana Park 2: Mahana Park coral garden 3: Point Venus Beach

peaks break left and right in the bay, with a few larger waves farther out on a bigger day (southwesterly swell, northerly winds).

TAIE FA'AHE'E SURF SCHOOL

PK 18; tel. 87 35 20 64; tfsurfschooltahiti.com; sunrise and sunset sessions; CFP 4,500/two-hour lesson including gear rental

Learn to surf, bodyboard, or stand-up paddleboard at Taie Fa'ahe'e Surf School. Classes take place every morning, depending on the tide and weather conditions, and students can be ages five and up. Beginners will enjoy group lessons (maximum of eight students) around Papenoo. More experienced surfers can get private coaching at a reef break, tailor-made to students' skill level and interest. Rental equipment is CFP 1,500 per hour or CFP 5,000 per day.

HIKING

For experienced hikers, Tahiti is one of the best islands in French Polynesia to explore on foot. The lush, mountainous interior is home to trails that are untamed and scarcely marked (if at all). Expect sections to be steep and slippery, especially if you've veered from trails shared with vehicles. For those willing to take up the challenge, waterfalls and vistas rarely found on maps await. Because of the wild nature of hiking on Tahiti, it's best not to venture out alone; almost all trails are best done with a guide.

FAUTAUA VALLEY

Distance: *15 kilometers (9 mi)*
Time: *6 hours*
Trailhead: *Av. Pierre Loti, Papeete*
Information and maps: *www.alltrails.com/ explore/recording/fautaua-valley-and-fachauda-waterfall*

Hike through Fautaua Valley to discover Tahiti's tallest waterfall—if you measure by height, that is. A bridal veil of white water flows down a moss-covered cliff into a cool pool below. It's best to come with a guide who knows the trail well, as much of it is poorly marked. If you venture out solo, you'll need to acquire a permit at Mairie de Papeete for CFP 600—it's hit or miss whether security will be there to collect it at the trailhead. The trail leads through shallow stream crossings, with rock cairns and ribbons marking waypoints.

MOUNT AORAI

Distance: *15.3 kilometers (9.5 mi)*
Time: *9 hours*
Trailhead: *Route de Belvedere*
Information and maps: *www.alltrails.com/trail/france/windward-islands/aorai*

The trail to Mount Aorai (2,066 m/6,778 ft) is best done on a dry day and by experienced trekkers only: it's steep, slippery, and easily eroded after a few days of heavy rain. There are two refuges, one at 1,400 meters (4,593 ft) called Fare Mato and another at 1,800 meters (5,905 ft) called Fare Ata, that can accommodate a handful of hikers and their sleeping bags. The trail starts at the end of Route de Belvédère and takes around nine hours to complete start to finish. You can catch a ride to the trailhead from the trucks that offer a trip to O Belvédère restaurant from Papeete's city center—though you'll be required to pay for a meal here to use this service. It's best to go with a guide like Jimmy Leyral from Aito

Rando (tel. 87 76 20 25; aitorando.com; from CFP 13,900/adult for two-day trip).

OTHER RECREATION
Northeast Coast
TAHITI KITESURF CENTER
PK 11 Quartier Socredo; tel. 87 34 34 35; www.tahitikitesurfcenter.com; 9:30am-5pm daily, lessons dependent on wind

When the wind is up, Tahiti's northeast coast is accented by colorful kites in the sky. Tahiti Kitesurf Center teaches kitesurfing and wing foiling lessons (CFP 12,000/two-hour lesson with a discount offered for bulk lesson packages). Or, learn how to foil from behind a boat (CFP 20,000/1.5-hour lesson). Students must be at least 10 years old for kite lessons and 8 years old for tow foil lessons.

Southwest Coast
DIVE AND SEA TAHITI
PK 9, 3 Pontoons; tel. 87 73 64 66; diveandsea-tahiti.com; 7am-6pm daily; from CFP 7,000/fun dive

Dive and Sea Tahiti is a well-run dive center in Puna'auia offering fun dives, courses ranging from discover scuba to divemaster, whale-watching (CFP 8,500/half-day trip), and stand-up paddleboard rentals (CFP 1,000/hour). Most courses are given in French, so

foiling

☆ Driving the Inland Road from Papenoo

There's no better way to get a sense of the natural environment of Tahiti than to visit its interior; following the dirt track across the center of Tahiti through the Papenoo Valley, which begins at the bridge over the Papenoo River at PK 17.9, is a great way to do so. In the dry season, you can drive a rental car 15 kilometers (9 mi) up the track to a suspension bridge across the Vaitamanu River and to the Vaituoru Dam. Beyond that, you need a 4WD. From coast to coast, it's a four-hour, 40-kilometer (25-mi) trip across Tahiti Nui's center. Most day tours of Tahiti's Papenoo Valley use this route.

A few kilometers past the Vaituoru Dam is the **Marae Fare Hape,** a restored archeological site with a rectangular marae and outlines of former residences and grounds. The marae is free to visit and tended to by those who live nearby, who take care to protect it from being reclaimed by plants and tree roots. Being so close to the center of the island, this marae is believed to be especially sacred thanks to its proximity to the deities thought to reside in Tahiti Nui's volcanic center. Noni, breadfruit, macadamia, and grapefruit trees surround the grounds. Many Tahitians believe this marae was once a ceremonial site and feel the mana, a spiritual connection with the land, here.

Most tour groups stop at **Relais de la Maroto** (tel. 87 24 08 46; relaismaroto@hotmail. fr; US$90/night), the only major accommodation in Papenoo Valley. They serve simple lunches on a large deck tucked in between mountain peaks. Hikers often spend the night here on their two-day trek across the island. Rooms are basic but clean—opt for the bungalows over the main house rooms if you stay.

South of the Relais de la Maroto, the track climbs 5 kilometers (3 mi) to 780 meters (2,559 ft) elevation, where the 110-meter-long (360-ft-long) **Urufau Tunnel** (opened in 1989) cuts through to the south coast watershed. The track then winds down to **Lake Vaihiria,** Tahiti's only lake, at 473 meters (1,551 ft) elevation. Sheer cliffs and waterfalls squeeze in around this spring-fed lake. Native floppy-eared eels, known as puhi taria, can grow up to 1.8 meters (6 ft) long and live in the cold waters, as do prawns and trout. With its luxuriant vegetation, this rain-drenched spot is one of the most scenic on the island.

South of the lake, a concrete track drops down to two dams and power stations. After a few more kilometers, adventurers are spat out onto PK 47.6 on the south coastal road near Mataiea.

you'll want to call them well in advance to arrange for English instruction.

ATIMAONO GOLF COURSE

Allée des Mombins PK 41; tel. 87 27 19 39; golfdetahiti.com; 7am-5:30pm daily; CFP 4,000/ nine holes

Atimaono Golf Course has two courses, an 18-hole par 72 course and a 9-hole par 32 course, as well as a driving range, shop, and clubhouse. It's suitable for beginners and experienced golfers alike.

FOOD
Northeast Coast
MAMA'S BEACH HOUSE

PK 10 at Point Venus; tel. 89 40 00 78; 11am-3pm Tues.-Sun.; CFP 2,000

Mama's Beach House is a little snack shack at Point Venus serving salads, grilled seafood and meat, tuna sashimi and tartare, burgers, and a range of desserts. Service is on island time, but you hardly notice it given the relaxed atmosphere.

Southwest Coast
SNACK TAHARUU

PK 38.7; tel. 40 57 66 17; 8am-3pm Tues.-Sun.; CFP 2,000

Come when the waves are pumping and you'll be sharing table space with surfers stopping in for a refuel before paddling out again. Snack Taharuu serves basic snack fare like grilled fish and fries, poisson cru, and side salads. It's a scenic stop on a trip around the island, with access to Taharuu Beach. Plant-based eaters might struggle to find a full meal.

★ TAHITI LA PLAGE

PK 13; tel. 40 58 21 08; tahitilaplage.com; 11:30am-9:30pm Tues.-Sat., 11:30am-2pm Sun.; CFP 2,500

Tahiti La Plage is one of the best restaurants on the south coast. Set on a black sand beach, dishes change regularly depending on what's available locally and in season. Try the breaded shrimp and chicken, heaping bowls of vegetables and noodles, burgers, pasta, and grilled seafood. If you have a sweet tooth, wait the extra 15 minutes for their French toast drizzled in caramel sauce.

RESTAURANT LE RED

PK 13; tel. 40 43 75 00; leredrestaurant.com; 11am-9pm Mon.-Thurs., 11am-10pm Fri.-Sat.; CFP 2,000-3,500

Restaurant Le Red is a Chinese Japanese fusion restaurant with friendly staff. Opinions are split as to whether their Japanese or Chinese offerings are better, but their menu features extensive offerings of both cuisines. Menu highlights include pork served with taro, sauteed fish with ginger, sushi rolls, and stuffed eggplant. Takeout and delivery options are also available.

★ BLUE BANANA

PK 11; tel. 40 41 22 24; bluebanana.in-tahiti.com; 10am-10pm Mon.-Fri.; CFP 3,000

The Blue Banana is one of the most popular lunch and dinner spots on the island. If the weather is nice, reserve a table out on their pontoon to enjoy views of Moorea while you dine. The menu is typical of French Polynesia, where you'll find dishes like pan seared mahi-mahi, shrimp skewers, and some of the best pizzas on Tahiti. Save room for dessert and try their pies, cream puffs, or lava cake.

LE CAPTAIN BLIGH

PK 11.4; tel. 40 43 62 90; captainbligh@mail.pf; 10am-1pm and 6pm-10pm Tues.-Sun.; CFP 3,000

Le Captain Blight is a casual open-air restaurant set over the water with rays and reef sharks swimming underneath. Enjoy fish served all ways, french fries, pizza, sandwiches, and burgers. The service can be hit or miss depending on who's working, so budget extra time for your meal here just in case. They host a Chinese buffet on Sundays. After sunset, the bar area can get a little rambunctious. Live music and dancing kicks off on Friday nights.

RESTAURANT DU MUSÉE GAUGUIN

PK 50.5; tel. 40 57 13 80; restaurantgauguin.com; 11:30am-2:30pm Tues.-Sun.; CFP 3,000

Restaurant du Musée Gauguin stands alone from the (now defunct) Paul Gauguin Museum. A spacious overwater restaurant with woven bamboo walls and tropical decor, it's a relaxing lunch spot—though you'll want to get there around noon or so to enjoy their full menu, as dishes run out around 2pm. Most of the menu is seafood heavy, with a few salads, beef, and chicken dishes as well.

ACCOMMODATIONS
Northeast Coast
FARE AREAREA

Fa'aone; tel. 87 78 19 20; US$150/night

Just steps away from a black sand beach, Fare Arearea is a beachy guesthouse with a handful of standalone thatched-roof bungalows set among a well-kept grassy area. Each room has a balcony, TV, air-conditioning, kitchenette with coffee machine, microwave, and fridge. Guests are also free to use the kayaks to cruise along the shoreline. The hosts are also happy to arrange day trips around the island, including Tahiti's interior.

BUNGALOW MOANA A FA'AONE

Fa'aone; tel. 89 70 63 11; US$150/night

Bungalow Moana a Fa'aone is a family-run guesthouse with recently renovated rooms, set just steps away from a small black sand beach. A peaceful place, it's easy to spend a few days relaxing here on a seaside hammock with a book in hand. Guests have access to kayaks, and owners are happy to arrange day trips to a nearby motu. Rooms have WiFi, kitchen access, and a balcony.

Southwest Coast
PENSION TE MITI

Paea PK 18.6; tel. 40 58 48 61; www.pensiontemiti. com; US$35/dorm bed, US$80/room

This relaxed guesthouse draws an adventurous crowd with private rooms and four-bed dorm rooms available. It's within walking distance of Mahana Beach, a prime place to snorkel. A small grocery store and bus stop are also within a five-minute walk. Rooms are simple and clean with kitchen access, WiFi, and breakfast included with each stay. Private rooms share a bathroom.

★ MANOMANO LODGE

PK 39.8; tel. 87 76 60 03; manomanolodge.com; US$130/room

Set on the edge of a coral reef, Manomano Lodge is a beach bum's paradise. There are a few room configurations available, most sleeping up to four, that have full kitchens, private bathrooms, garden or ocean views, WiFi, and a barbecue area. The rooms aren't fancy, but they're clean and comfortable enough. Snorkeling, kayaking, paddleboarding, and swimming are all accessible from the beach—surf trips can be arranged for an extra cost. This is a great pick for families with active little ones.

TE MOANA TAHITI RESORT

Seaside at PK 10.5; tel. 40 47 31 00; www. temoanatahitiresort.pf; US$150-300/room

Te Moana Tahiti Resort (formerly the Manava) is a seaside retreat with a spacious infinity pool offering views out to Moorea, two restaurants, a beach bar on an artificial white sand island, and a spa. There are 120 rooms on the property. The furniture is a little dated and scuffed, but the balcony, kitchenette, and spaciousness of the rooms help make up for it. It's easy to spend evenings at the Taapuna Bar ordering tapas and cocktails. Grab a lounge chair and watch talented foilers, wakeboarders, and paddlers cruise on by.

★ NINAMU PEARL

Inland from Puna'auia; tel. 87 73 36 57; www.ninamu-pearl-tahiti.com; US$180/room

Ninamu Pearl Resort is a cliff-top luxury guesthouse with modern bedrooms available to rent. The property has a spacious terrace with sunset views, and each room has a TV, WiFi access, and en suite bathroom; some have a balcony plunge pool and outdoor shower. The guesthouse has a restaurant on the communal terrace that serves pizzas, grilled meats, stir fries, and French wines. Note that this property is found atop a steep hill, so it's best to have transport arranged ahead of time.

GETTING THERE AND AROUND

The northern coastline's major sights can be visited on a day trip from Papeete, or accessed by the bus running to Taravao, which stops on request and at major towns along the coastal road (from CFP 400 one-way).

Getting to Tahiti Nui's southwest coast is easy if you have your own vehicle: just follow the coastal road west from Papeete. The Tere Tahiti bus to Tautira stops at all towns along the coastline, and usually as requested (cost is CFP 400 one-way).

For most of Tahiti Nui's interior sights, hiring a private guide for the day or a 4WD is a wise idea. Most trailheads for hikes in the area begin at the end of a steep and bumpy road.

Taxis are hard to come by outside of the vicinity of Papeete. It's easier to arrange transportation through your accommodation.

Tahiti Iti

Tahiti Iti is the smaller section of Tahiti, a sleepy and serene place to visit for travelers with extra time to spare. A small village on the southern coastline, Teahupoo, is home to one of the world's most iconic waves and attracts the surfers who want to take it on—or simply want to feel the power of its presence. To the north, you'll find solitude and a sense of adventure on the road stretching to the laid-back town of Tautira.

Orientation

At the isthmus connecting Tahiti Iti with Tahiti Nui, you'll find the town of **Taravao** (PK 53), where there is an old fort built by the French in 1844 to cut off Tahitians who had retreated to Tahiti Iti after a battle with the French. Germans were interned here during World War II. Today, it's less tumultuous and is a convenient place to live for its residents. The assortment of supermarkets, banks, a post office, petrol stations, and restaurants make Taravao a good place to stop on a circle-island tour.

Tahiti Iti does not have a belt road around its coastline but rather has two short roads stretching north and south along the coast from Taravao. Drive along the north road to reach **Tautira**. The south road connects to **Teahupoo**. Hiking the section between Tautira and Teahupoo is reserved for intrepid travelers—almost everyone backtracks through Taravao or crosses this section by motorboat.

SIGHTS
Belvédère de Taravao

Follow the main road inland near the Hospital of Taravao; a sign will point to "Belvédère de Taravao"; free

On a sunny day, the view from Belvédère de Taravao offers breathtaking views of both Tahitis, spanning over pastoral hills and jagged mountain peaks to a cobalt sea. The road leading here is only wide enough for one vehicle, so take care watching for oncoming traffic. Horses, cattle, and sheep graze among the meadows. A gazebo and wooden tables make it an idyllic place to stop for a picnic. A narrow side road near the viewpoint cuts to rejoin the Tautira road near the PK 3 marker.

Te Pari Cliffs

Off Tahiti Iti

The coastline of Tahiti Iti is the wildest on the island and looks like a lost world. Take a boat ride to Te Pari, dramatic cliffs topped with fluffy palm trees. The dark rock contrasting against the bright blue water is a sight to behold. It's possible to hike along these cliffs, but it is best done with a guide. Expect steep, slippery sections where both hands are needed. To enjoy the cliffs without the risk, take a boat tour along the Tahiti Iti coast. Some surf tour providers, like Teahupoo Adventures (tel. 89 78 23 53; teahupooadventures.com; CFP 26,000/person) and Tahiti Surfari (tel. 89 77 72 26; tahitisurfari.com; CFP 15,000/adult, CFP 7,500/child), offer full-day tours to the Te Pari Cliffs.

BEACHES
TAUTIRA BEACH

PK 18 (east of Taravao); free

The skyline of Tahiti Nui cuts through the sky like emeralds from the dark sands of Tautira Beach. Rarely crowded and an idyllic spot for swimming, this beach offers some of the most mesmerizing views of the island. At high tide, the sand is little more than a sliver, but it's still worth walking along if only for the photo op.

Tahiti Iti

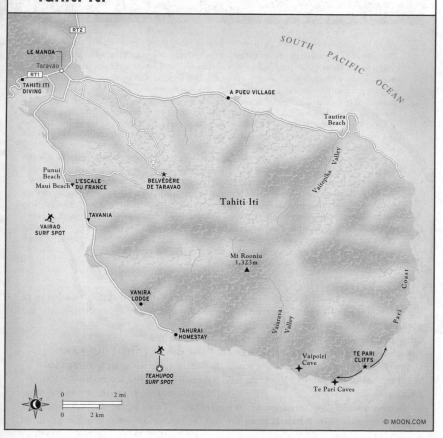

SURFING
Surf Spots

★ TEAHUPOO SURF SPOT

Boat ride from Teahupoo

There are few waves in the world as iconic as Teahupoo. For decades, this wave spun off Tahiti Iti's peninsula without the greater surf world knowing of its existence. Few humans marked its face. It's relatively young as a wave on the surf scene, with the first known

surfer taking off at its peak in 1985. By the late 1990s, it was still just a small blip on the surf scene radar. Then, in 2000, a photo of big wave surfer Laird Hamilton surfing a monster of a wave hit the surf media world—surfers couldn't get enough. Hamilton looked like a speck against the gargantuan wave, its lip seemingly a few meters thick. Professionals poured in from all over the world to take on the challenge of one of the world's heaviest waves.

When a big swell rolls through, witnessing Teahupoo break is a once-in-a-lifetime

The Science Behind Teahupoo's Incredible Wave

When big wave surfers see a swell heading toward Tahiti, they're often on the next flight over. These swells are brewed by storms in the Southern Ocean and the South Indian Ocean, and are predicted to arrive in Tahiti by surf forecasters, then published on surf forecast websites. Teahupoo is one of the heaviest waves in the world, with a lip that can measure nearly the same as its face; put another way, the part of the wave rising up from the ocean can be nearly as thick as the wall of the wave itself. The power of Teahupoo begins thousands of kilometers away, when storms form southeast of the archipelago. Waves in the open sea are formed by wind from the storms. These waves travel uninterrupted by any land mass, sustaining energy underneath the sea's surface. Once the wave reaches Tahiti, the full power of the wave releases onto coral reef, in what's known as the breaking zone.

Teahupoo's reef is very steep. Just half a kilometer (a third of a mile) offshore from the reef, the sea plunges over 300 meters (984 ft) in depth. This means there is nothing to dissapate the wave before it reaches the reef. Once the wave roars toward the reef, it pulls water from the reef into the wave. The wave walls up with most of the power behind the wave, creating its signature thick lip. When it crests, this is the point where surfers take off and surf along the face—actually surfing below sea level. The face of Teahupoo is known to reach heights of over 12 meters (40 ft). The swell direction, the angle that the wave will be hitting the reef, also plays a massive role in how the wave of Teahupoo acts and breaks. The best waves tend to happen from April-September, as its when the southern hemisphere brews up the largest storms during its winter months.

experience. You can see the raw power of the ocean in the thick curl of the wave as it peels over the sky and plummets like a guillotine into the water. Once the wave breaks, the whitewater rushes toward land like a stampede of white horses. From the water, the sharp peaks of Tahiti look anything but friendly.

Even on a small day, Teahupoo is not a beginner-friendly wave. It barrels along the shallows of coral reef and can reach sizes not relevant for the surf forecasting radars. It likes a southwesterly swell and northeasterly winds.

If you don't surf, take a wave-watching tour to Teahupoo. It'll either scare you out of surfing, or inspire you to book a lesson.

VAIRAO SURF SPOT

Boat ride from Vairao Marina

Vairao is a hollow, fast, and shallow left-hand barrel that's not quite as intense as Teahupoo. It likes a southerly swell and northerly winds to really work. The same surf boat companies offering rides to Teahupoo will also take surfers to Vairao, but you may have to have a

minimum number of surfers wanting to go here to turn the tour in this direction.

Surf Tours

TEAHUPOO TAHITI SURFARI

Meet at Teahupoo Marina; tel. 87 77 72 26; www. tahitisurfari.com; CFP 8,500/day tour

If you're looking for a ride out to the wave, Teahupoo Tahiti Surfari shuttles surfers out to Teahupoo (CFP 3,000/hour), or groups of up to five surfers to other spots of Tahiti Iti for CFP 35,000/boat half day or CFP 60,000/boat full day. Coaching and in-water cameramen can be arranged on a trip-by-trip basis.

TEAHUPOO EXCURSION

Meet at Teahupoo Marina; tel. 89 75 11 98; www. teahupooexcursion.com; CFP 10,000/day tour

Teahupoo Excursion is a surf charter on the more comfortable end of adventure with a freshwater shower, sunshade, and cushioned seats onboard. Michael, the captain, has been

---

1: Teahupoo 2: Teahupoo is home to one of the heaviest waves in the world.

surfing Teahupoo for over 25 years and is happy to offer personalized tips for paddling in. If the surf is flat (or too big for your liking), you can venture around the area on a snorkel tour, sunset tour, or sightseeing tour to spot grottos and lava tubes along the Tahiti Iti coastline.

TEAHUPOO ADVENTURE TOURS

Meet at Teahupoo Marina; tel. 89 78 23 53; www. teahupooadventure.com; from CFP 20,000/half-day trip

Teahupoo Adventure Tours arranges surf tours, wave-watching, and tours of the Tahiti Iti coastline (private and group options available). If it's pumping, it's worth venturing out for an hour just to watch the Teahupoo break (CFP 3,000/hour). Groups of up to four surfers can book a custom tour to eaves in the region—the captain is happy to share the best spots to go depending on surfers' skill levels and ocean conditions.

SCUBA DIVING
TAHITI ITI DIVING

PK 58; tel. 87 71 80 77; tahitiitidiving.com; 8am-5:30pm daily; CFP 7,900/fun dive

Tahiti Iti Diving is one of the few dive centers on Tahiti teaching both scuba and freediving courses. If you're keen to dive with a tank, dives take place twice per day along the fringing reef. Courses range from discover scuba to divemaster certification. Learn to dive on one breath with a freediving course. Beginners can learn from CFP 8,500 for a half-day intro course and CFP 39,000 for AIDA 2 certification. There are also specialty courses for surfers to help conquer longer breath holds in stressful situations. Whale-watching trips also take place, with peak months being August-November (CFP 9,900/adult, CFP 7,900/child under 12).

FOOD
★ LE MANOA

PK 53 Taravao; tel. 40 57 71 01; 11am-2pm and 6pm-9pm Tues.-Sat., 11am-2pm Sun.; CFP 1,500

Le Moana is a worthwhile stop for lunch or dinner in Taravao, next to an old fort. Each dish is freshly made from local ingredients, with giant salads and seafood platters, excellent poisson cru, beef carpaccio, and gourmet dishes like oysters glazed in champagne and crumbed burrata served on a bed of pesto. The atmosphere is casual, upbeat, and friendly, with plenty of outdoor seating.

TAVANIA

Route de Teahupoo; tel. 40 57 72 35; 11am-3pm Mon.-Thurs., 11am-3pm and 6pm-9pm Fri.-Sat.; CFP 1,500

Found on the mountain side of the road, this unassuming snack offers plates of fresh-caught fish served many ways, grilled meats, fries, and simple salads. Portions are on the larger side. The place can get pretty popular among locals come lunchtime.

L'ESCALE DU FRANCE

Route de Teahupoo; tel. 87 74 71 99; 11am-4pm daily; CFP 2,500

This beachy seaside restaurant is a fun stop to grab a cold Hinano and heaping plate of seafood. You have the mainstays of poisson cru, tuna tartare, grilled fish, and french fries, and a few local favorites like mahi-mahi cooked in a creamy shallot sauce. There are also coconut curries with goat, chicken, or shrimp. Kick your shoes off to feel the sand in your toes and pick a table next to the water to watch fish search for stray morsels dropped from the tables.

ACCOMMODATIONS
TAHURAI HOMESTAY

Route de Teahupoo; tel. 87 75 15 30; facebook.com/ tahuraihomestay; US$60/dorm, US$100/private room

This is a popular place with surfers who want to be as close to Teahupoo as possible, with a mix of dorm rooms and private rooms just a few minutes' walking distance from the beach of Teahupoo. Bedrooms are quirky—they're shaped like pyramids, painted pastel blue, and fit just a bed inside. Guests share bathrooms, a kitchen, a dining room, and beach bikes.

★ VANIRA LODGE

Route de Teahupoo; tel. 40 57 70 18; www.
vaniralodge.com; US$250/night

This is one of the most novel accommodations
on the island, with two bungalows set on stilts,
giving guests the feeling of sleeping in a treehouse. The other bungalows are all made of
wood and woven bamboo, and have thatched
roofing, making the property feel embedded
into its environment. No two bungalows are
alike; the largest one sleeps up to five people.
WiFi only works well in the restaurant.

A PUEU VILLAGE

PK 9.8 Route de Tautira; tel. 87 74 71 99; www.
pueuvillage.com; US$300/night

For silence and solitude, check into A Pueu
Village. This four-bungalow guesthouse is just
a few steps away from the water (though expect a lawn in lieu of a sandy beach). Rooms
are simple and beachy with bamboo woven
walls, a private terrace, sun loungers, and a
fan (none have air-conditioning). The internet
connection is virtually nonexistent, making it
a great place to completely disconnect.

GETTING THERE AND AROUND

Tahiti Iti is reachable via the paved road that
wraps around Tahiti. It takes about an hour
to reach Tahiti Iti from Papeete via either the
north (54 km/33 mi) or south (59 km/36 mi)
coastal road. On the Tere Tahiti buses, take
the Taravao line up Tahiti's northern coast
and change to the Tautira line at Taravao. Or,
take the line to Teahupoo along the southwest coast. A one-way trip from Papeete to
Tahiti Iti is CFP 400-450 and takes around
two hours. Transport can also be arranged
through your accommodation.

Moorea

The island of Moorea looks as if a photographer bumped up the saturation and clarity on its landscape. Dramatic mountain peaks emerge from its center like uncut emeralds. Long, deep bays feature every shade of blue. And adventure is found at every turn.

Rumble along a dirt path on foot or with a sturdy 4WD to vantage points overlooking Moorea's incredible landscape. Snorkel with curious stingrays and black tip reef sharks in the shallows of the lagoon. Plunge underwater to aquarium-clear waters on a scuba dive. You'll never forget the feeling of swimming alongside a humpback whale, the gentlest of giants.

When it's time relax, you'll find a patch of shade under a palm tree on a beach worthy of being featured in a travel brochure. A population

Highlights

Look for ★ to find recommended sights, activities, dining, and lodging.

★ **Cook's Bay:** This quiet three-kilometer (1.8-mi) bay is the perfect place to admire views of Mount Rotui (page 96).

★ **Manutea Tahiti Distillery:** Sip juices, teas, and spirits made from Moorea's sweetest fruits (page 97).

★ **Belvedere Lookout:** Enjoy mesmerizing views of Cook's Bay and Opunohu Bay from one of Moorea's most accessible lookout points (page 99).

★ **Tiki Village:** Feast on traditional Polynesian fare as performers dance in sync with the beat of Tahitian drums (page 101).

★ **Ta'ahiamanu Beach:** Composed of white sand, palm trees, clear water, and a reef made of bright corals, this is one of Moorea's most scenic beaches (page 103).

★ **Snorkeling at Stingray World:** Hang out with the fever of stingrays and shiver of black tip reef sharks as they cruise through the sandy shallows off Tipaniers Beach (page 108).

★ **Swimming with Humpback Whales:** Let the song of a bull humpback whale reverberate through your heart and watch as a calf practices the art of fin-slapping under the watchful eye of its mother—no two experiences are alike (page 114).

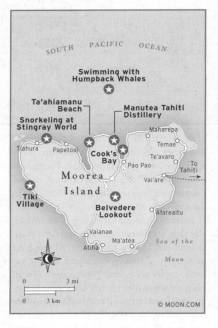

Moorea

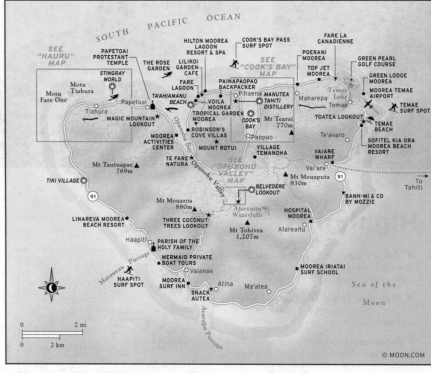

SOUTH PACIFIC OCEAN

© MOON.COM

of around 16,000 lives in vegetation-draped dwellings, alternating with coconut, pineapple, and vanilla plantations. Tourism is concentrated along the north coast around Paopao and Hauru; many of the locals live in the more spaced-out south.

Moorea's interior valley slopes are unusually rich, with large fruit and vegetable plantations and human habitation. At one time or another, coconuts, sugarcane, cotton, vanilla, coffee, rice, and pineapples have all been grown in the rich soil of Moorea's plantations. Stock farming and fishing are other occupations. Vegetables such as taro, cucumbers, pumpkins, and lettuce, along with fruits

such as grapefruit, papaya, starfruit, avocados, mangoes, and breadfruit, make Moorea a veritable Garden of Eden.

Accommodations range from five-star overwater bungalows to modest guesthouses, making Moorea accessible to anyone who ventures here. Visit Moorea for its striking scenery, its unlimited adventure opportunities, and a laid-back way of living that allows you to appreciate Moorea's one-of-a-kind natural surroundings.

ORIENTATION

This triangular 125-square-kilometer (48-square-mi) island is the surviving southern

---

Previous: Cook's Bay; sculpture near Tiki Village; view from Belvedere Lookout.

rim of a shield volcano once 3,000 meters (9,842 ft) high. Twice as old as its Windward partner, Tahiti, Moorea's weathering is noticeably advanced. Shark-tooth-shaped **Mount Mouaroa** (880 m/2,887 ft)) on Moorea's eastern side is the most striking, but **Mount Tohivea** (1,207 m/3,960 ft), south of Mount Mouaroa, is higher and visible from Moorea's eastern coast. Two spectacular bays cut into the north coast on each side of **Mount Rotui** (899 m/2,950 ft): **Cook's Bay** and **Opunohu Bay,** with **Belvedere Lookout** overlooking both bays at once. The peaks protect the north and northwest coasts from the rain-bearing southeast trades; the drier climate and scenic beauty explain the profusion of hotels along this side of the island.

Moorea is surrounded by a coral ring that acts as a barrier between the deep ocean and Moorea, creating a lagoon. Twelve passes in the reef are formed by freshwater runoff from Moorea's valleys, creating an environment where corals can't grow. These passes act as channels in the reef, linking the deep sea to the lagoon. Three small islands, called motu, enhance the lagoon: one off Afareaitu in the south and two off Hauru in the northwest.

The PKs (kilometer stones) on Moorea are measured in both directions from PK 0 at the access road to Temae Airport. They're numbered up to PK 35 along the north coast via Hauru and up to PK 24 along the south coast via Afareaitu, meeting at Haapiti halfway around the island (PK 35/24). The 59-kilometer (36-mi) main road around Moorea is well paved and rarely crowded, and takes roughly over 1.5 hours to drive around. A rough 4-kilometer (2.4-mi) dirt road up to the paved Belvedere viewpoint road, locally known as the "Rue des Ananas" or "Pineapple Road," begins just west of the bridge at Paopao (PK 9.6), and is a good shortcut to the Opunohu Valley, though most car rental companies forbid driving down this route.

Northeast Moorea

Moorea Temae Airport (PK 0) is on the northeast corner of Moorea, and **Vaiare Wharf** (PK 4) is 4 kilometers (2.4 mi) south. Heading west, there's a cluster of pearl, souvenir, and clothing shops in **Maharepa.** This is also where you'll find banks (Bank Socredo and Banque de Polynesie), a medical center, a dentist, and a handful of cafés.

Cook's Bay

The start of Cook's Bay begins 7 kilometers (4.3 mi) west of the airport along Moorea's northern coastline. It's a quiet area, with just a few restaurants and accommodations spread along its palm-tree-lined coastline. On the shores of Cook's Bay, **Paopao** (PK 9) is the capital of Moorea, with a gendarmerie, supermarket, and handful of restaurants serving the community. It's a waypoint for heading east toward Opunohu Bay, inland along Rue des Ananas, (also called Pineapple Road) to Belvedere, and west toward Temae Beach. From point to point, the road around Cook's Bay is about 6 kilometers (3.7 mi) long.

Opunohu Bay

Moving west from Cook's Bay, the coastal road wraps around Mount Rotui, a mountain dissecting the waters of Opunohu Bay and Cook's Bay. The quiet settlement of **Faimano Village** (PK 15) is at the water's edge. Ta'ahiamanu Beach is at the bay's eastern end. At the most inland point of the bay, a paved road leads directly to Belvedere. The road around the bay is about 8 kilometers (5 mi) long, and on its western end you'll find the road to Magic Mountain.

Hauru Point

The scenic road from Opunohu Bay toward Moorea's western coastline has more accommodations and restaurants than the two bays. From **Tipaniers Beach** (PK 26), you can access two small islets via kayak or boat, and snorkel at Stingray World. A few kilometers farther, the town of **Hauru** (PK 29) has a handful of shops but no major attractions. Tiki Village is found at PK 30, just before the settlement of **Haapiti,** a haven for surfers.

Southern Moorea

There are very few sights, restaurants, and accommodations on Moorea's southern coast. While a drive along here is nice for the lush landscape, the few properties here are residential. Only the town of **Afareaitu** (PK 10) has choices when it comes to accommodations and restaurants, and it's also where you'll find Moorea's hospital.

PLANNING YOUR TIME

You'll need a minimum of **two nights** to see the best of Moorea: one day for a trip around the island with a side trip to the **Belvedere Lookout**, and another for a **lagoon trip**, where you'll spend a day snorkeling, whale-watching, or scuba diving around Moorea's lagoon. While it's possible to see Moorea as a day trip from Tahiti, you'll have a better experience if you pencil in plenty of time to relax. With so many types of accommodations available, weekly and monthly rentals make even extended stays possible. In terms of where to stay, the hotels in **Paopao** enjoy better scenery, but the beaches are better near **Hauru.** If you don't want to hire a car or taxi and instead plan to get around via day tours, **Maharepa** is an ideal home base with a variety of shops, restaurants, and cafés within a 10-minute walk.

Save your **beach relaxation** days for the end of your stay on Moorea. If you plan to **swim with whales, surf, scuba dive,** or enjoy other weather-dependent activities, book these for the beginning of your trip. That way if you strike out on seeing whales or catching waves, you'll have a spare day to try again.

Itinerary Ideas

Three days on the island allows you spend one day exploring Moorea's lagoon, one day venturing through the island's interior, and one day cruising along the coastline like a local.

DAY ONE: OCEAN ADVENTURE

1 Spend your morning swimming with humpback whales and learning about the latest research with **Dr. Michael Poole Dolphins and Whales.**

2 Catch the shuttle boat to **Coco Beach Moorea** and hang out with stingrays and reef sharks while you wait for your lunch.

3 Ask the shuttle boat to drop you off at **Tipaniers Beach** and spend the afternoon relaxing in the white sand until sunset.

4 Spend the evening enjoying Polynesian food and entertainment at **Tiki Village;** shows take place on Tuesdays and Fridays.

DAY TWO: MOOREA'S INTERIOR

You will need to rent a car or hire a driver to enjoy Moorea's interior. Many of the sights featured below are also covered on day tours offered by **Franckyfranck Moorea Tours.**

1 Drive along Rue du Belvedere to **Marae Titiroa** and Marae Afareaito, Polynesian ruins that are believed to have been temples and palaces.

2 Continue driving inland for 1 kilometer (0.6 mi) to **Belvedere Lookout** and admire Moorea's northern coastline with views that stretch out to Cook's Bay and Opunohu Bay.

3 If you're up for it, hike the 6-kilometer (3.7-mi) **Three Coconut Trees Trail,** which starts at the Belvedere Lookout parking lot.

Itinerary Ideas

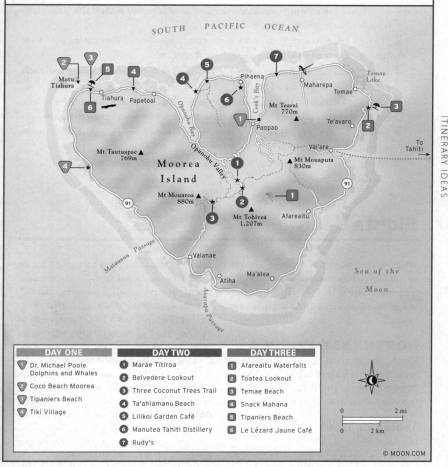

DAY ONE
1. Dr. Michael Poole Dolphins and Whales
2. Coco Beach Moorea
3. Tipaniers Beach
4. Tiki Village

DAY TWO
1. Marae Titiroa
2. Belvedere Lookout
3. Three Coconut Trees Trail
4. Ta'ahiamanu Beach
5. Lilikoi Garden Café
6. Manutea Tahiti Distillery
7. Rudy's

DAY THREE
1. Afareaitu Waterfalls
2. Toatea Lookout
3. Temae Beach
4. Snack Mahana
5. Tipaniers Beach
6. Le Lézard Jaune Café

0   2 mi
0   2 km

© MOON.COM

4   Drive back to Opunohu Bay and west along the coastline to **Ta'ahiamanu Beach** for a dip in the clear water or relaxation under a palm tree.

5   Drive or walk 700 meters (2,300 ft) to **Lilikoi Garden Café** for a hearty and healthy lunch made from ingredients sourced from the island.

6   Just 2.6 kilometers (1.6 mi) east is **Manutea Tahiti Distillery,** a fine place to sample unique beverages like pineapple brut, rum, tea, juice, and liqueur.

7   Stroll through the shops of Maharepa (7 km/4.3 mi east) in search of a black pearl, stopping at **Rudy's** when it's time for dinner.

DAY THREE: MOOREA LIKE A LOCAL

You'll need a rental vehicle or driver for this itinerary.

1 Start your morning in Moorea's interior and visit **Afareaitu Waterfalls,** a shimmering cascade that pours over sheer rock.

2 Drive 9 kilometers (5.5 mi) north to get a bird's-eye view of aquamarine waters and Tahiti from **Toatea Lookout,** perched above the Sofitel.

3 Just 1 kilometer (0.6 mi) down the road, you'll find palm-tree-speckled **Temae Beach,** one of the locals' most beloved beaches.

4 Drive 23 kilometers (14 mi) west along the coastal road to **Snack Mahana** for poisson cru or breaded mahi-mahi in coconut milk. Get there before noon to beat the lunch rush.

5 Spend the rest of the afternoon exploring the lagoon from a kayak. Kayaks can be rented from **Tipaniers Beach.**

6 After sunset, make your way to **Le Lézard Jaune Café** for a casual and delicious Polynesian dinner.

Sights

With mesmerizing viewpoints, emerald mountains, sandy beaches, and waters that span from electric blue to deep cobalt, most of Moorea's best sights are made by mother nature.

NORTHEAST MOOREA

You'll probably arrive on Moorea's northeast coast, either at **Vaiare Wharf** or **Moorea Tamae Airport.** This part of the island offers views of Tahiti on a clear day.

Toatea Lookout

PK 1

Toatea Lookout is a viewpoint on the ocean side of the main road. You'll find views of the deep passage, romantically named the Sea of the Moon, between Tahiti and Moorea. A handful of benches make this an easy place to stop for as little or long as you like. Admire the bright blue water off Temae Beach and the bird's-eye view of Sofitel Kia Ora Moorea's overwater bungalows.

★ COOK'S BAY

PK 6-10

Ironically, Captain James Cook did not arrive in the bay that today bears his name. Captain Cook first anchored in 1777 at Opunohu Bay to the west, which is considered sacred, and thus renaming it would've been sacrilegious. Today, Cook's Bay is easily one of Moorea's most scenic highlights, offering an unobstructed view into the island's interior. Rectangular **Mount Tohivea** overlooks the south end of the bay, and as you approach the capital of Paopao, **Mouaroa,** or "Shark Tooth," pierces the sky. To the west, **Mount Rotui** towers over the bay. While there's no public beach to be found, there are a few wooden benches around the bay that make for decent places to enjoy the view.

On the shores of Cook's Bay, Paopao's **fish market** (PK 9.3) is worth a peek if you want to get a look at what may end up on your dinner plate later this evening.

Te Pu Atiti'a

PK 11.5; tel. 89 75 65 46; 8am-6pm Mon.-Fri., 8am-noon Sat.; cost varies per event

Te Pu Atiti'a Cultural Center, standing on the hillside at PK 11.5, features a garden with medicinal plants, canoe-building exhibitions, and a thatched fare pote'e, or traditional

Cook's Bay

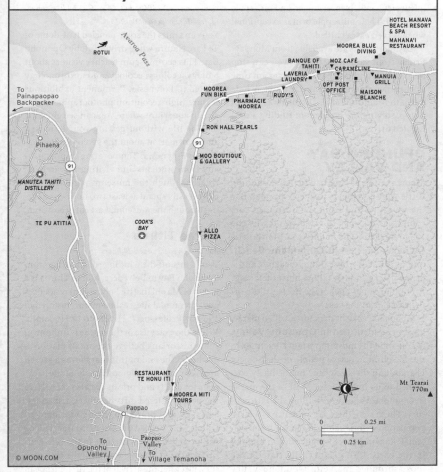

meeting house. The center hosts folkloric Polynesian performance groups in its open-air amphitheater on special occasions. It's part-nered with the University of Berkeley Gump Station, a research station that examines sus-tainable development. Researchers here work in conjunction with the community to com-bine both modern and traditional knowledge with the goal of preserving Moorea's natural environment.

★ Manutea Tahiti Distillery

PK 12; tel. 40 55 20 00; www.rhum-manutea.com; 9am-5pm Mon.-Fri., 8am-noon Sat.; free

What's island living without a dash of rum? Manutea Tahiti Distillery is a worthwhile stop hillside from the main road. In addition to the excellent papaya, grapefruit, soursop, guava, and pineapple juices made from local fruits at the on-site Rotui Tahiti juice plantation, they make an excellent range of fruit-flavored teas.

Beeline it to the bar area of the distillery to sample 40- to 60-proof rums and 25-proof liqueurs (coconut, lychee, ginger, and pineapple varieties). Their pineapple brut is exceptional when served extra chilled.

Distillery visits are available from Monday-Friday from 9am-4pm, though you can stop by to sample and purchase beverages anytime the distillery is open. Many day tours include a trip to Manutea Tahiti Distillery as part of a stop, solving the problem of finding a designated driver.

OPUNOHU BAY AND VALLEY

Moorea residents have had to fight a running battle with developers to keep Opunohu Bay the way it is, and from the unspoiled surroundings it's easy to understand why the 1984 remake of *The Bounty* was filmed here. Opunohu Bay hosts **Ta'ahiamanu Beach,** one of Moorea's best public beaches and a prime place to watch sailors hoist their sails. A popular yacht anchorage hosts sailors off the east side of the beach.

About 500 ancient structures, called marae, have been identified in **Opunohu Valley.** Marae were the most important structures to the Ma'ohi, the native people of the Society Islands, and the size of the marae likely correlated to its importance. Most of the marae in Opunohu Valley were built in the 14th century. These structures are evidence of a large population with a highly developed social system. Following the acceptance of Christianity in the early 19th century, the state of the moss-shrouded marae in Opunohu Valley declined sharply. Marae Titiroa, listed below, is one of the most accessible marae sites. Park along Rue du Belvedere and walk down the trail leading from Marae Titiroa to a network of other trails that venture to similar marae. Today, plenty of side trails lead nowhere in particular, but you'll discover many crumbling walls, and naturalists will enjoy the vegetation.

Te Fare Natura

PK 18; tel. 87 70 60 61; farenatura.org; 9am-4pm Wed.-Sun.; CFP 2,100/adult, CFP 400/children under 18, free for children under 10

You can't miss the solar-paneled half-dome of Te Fare Natura while driving along Opunohu Bay. This eco-museum teaches visitors about biology, geology, ecology, and anthropology related to Polynesia. Permanent exhibitions feature high-resolution photographs of corals, an aquarium where you can see endemic marine life without getting your hair wet, and information about the geological formation of Polynesia. Temporary exhibits, usually from students and visiting researchers, rotate through the museum regularly. You could easily spend at least two hours wandering through the museum. Last entry is at 3pm.

Marae Titiroa

Rue du Belvedere; open 24 hours; free

Found just off the winding road leading from Opunohu Bay to Belvedere, Marae Titiroa is a group of Ma'ohi (native Polynesian) residences and ceremonial sites, called marae, restored in 1969 by Professor Y. H. Sinoto of Honolulu. While the exact use of the marae is unknown, some historians believe the small platform, or ahu, at the end of this marae was a sacred area reserved for religious rituals. Stone backrests for chiefs and priests are also seen. Here the people offered gifts of tubers, fish, dogs, and pigs, and prayed to their gods, many of whom were deified ancestors. Marae Titiroa was probably built sometime in the 14th century and used in some way until the 19th century, just after the arrival of the first European missionaries.

Continue up the main road from Marae Titiroa about 200 meters (656 ft) and watch for some stone archery platforms on the left. Here kneeling nobles once competed to see who could shoot an arrow the farthest. The bows and arrows employed in these contests were likely never used in warfare. Up on the left is access to another archery platform and **Marae Afareaito.** The stone slabs you see

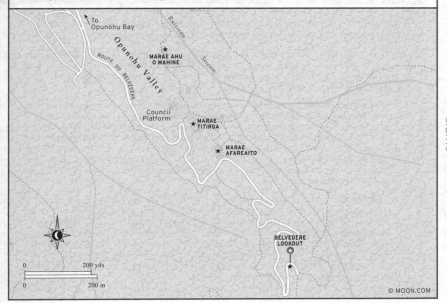

Opunohu Valley

sticking up in the middle of the marae were backrests for participants of honor.

Near the water tanks just 50 meters (164 ft) northwest of Marae Titiroa is a long council platform, and 50 meters (164 ft) farther are two smaller marae surrounded by towering Tahitian chestnut trees (mape). The most evocative of the group is four-tiered **Marae Ahu o Mahine,** about 250 meters (820 ft) down the trail. The stones of this marae are stacked with such precision and care, showing how tedious it must have been to build such great structures solely with nearby materials.

★ Belvedere Lookout

End of Rue du Belvedere; open 24 hours; free

At the end of Rue du Belvedere, a steep and winding but well-paved road leads to one of the best panoramic viewpoints on Moorea. Belvedere, or **Roto Nui,** overlooks Cook's Bay and Opunohu Bay, with Mount Rotui in the center. According to Polynesian legend, an octopus used to live on Mount Rotui and

split the island to create the two bays. From this lookout point, you can see the silhouette of the octopus and its arms reaching north around the bays. This is one of the most accessible viewpoints on Moorea, and one of the few interior lookouts reachable by paved road. Behind the viewpoint's small parking lot are trailheads to some of Moorea's most trod hiking trails. Most day tours and ATV tours feature Belvedere as a stop on their trip, giving you a chance to see it even if you don't hire a car. You can also access Rue de Belvedere from an unpaved road, Rue des Ananas (Pineapple Road), which starts at Paopao.

Rue des Ananas ("Pineapple Road")

Road runs between Rue du Belvedere and Paopao; free

Head inland from Paopao and veer west onto a dirt road that links Paopao to Rue du Belvedere, 2 kilometers (1.2 mi) inland from Opunohu Bay. This 3-kilometer (1.8-mi) road

Moorea's Myths and Legends

There are as many myths and legends about Moorea as there are grains of sand on Temae Beach. While interpretations vary, these are some of the most commonly told stories:

- **Oro:** Oro, the god of war, is one of the greatest gods in Polynesian mythology and the main god of Moorea. Archeological sites like that of **Marae Afareaito** (page 98) and Marae Nuurau near Haapiti once served as places to honor Oro, often through human and animal sacrifice. During eras of peace, Oro is the god of arts.

- **The yellow lizard:** The name Mo'orea is a nod to one of its legends: *mo'o* means "lizard" and *rea* means "yellow" in Tahitian. The story goes that a husband and wife were living on an island near Tahiti. When the wife became pregnant, she dreamed her son would be born yellow. She gave birth to an egg, which was hidden in a cave. When the egg hatched, they were shocked to see a yellow lizard, Moorea, emerge. They cared for Moorea in a cave until he grew so large they feared him. The parents escaped on a canoe and Moorea swam after them, perishing in the open ocean. His body drifted back to the island, where a group of people found him and named the island Moorea.

- **The octopus:** Much of Moorea's mythology revolves around an octopus. From the northern edge of the lagoon, the ridgeline of Moorea resembles an octopus with outstretched arms sweeping around Opunohu Bay and Cook's Bay. Prior to European settlement, Mooreans worshipped an octopus deity and built a temple to honor him on the edge of Opunohu Bay. When Protestant missionaries arrived in the early 1800s, they destroyed the marae and erected a protestant temple in its place. Superstitious about angering the deity, the missionaries built the **Papetoai Temple** (page 100) in the shape of an octagon. The building is the oldest European church still standing in the South Pacific.

winds around pineapple plantations, which is how it earned its name. Most of the pineapples here are grown for the Rotui fruit juice company, and it takes over a year for each pineapple to mature. Many car rental companies prohibit driving along this stretch, so it's best to go on a guided 4WD or quad tour.

Magic Mountain Lookout

PK 21; open 24 hours; CFP 200/person

Jutting over the western side of Opunohu Bay, the top of Magic Mountain reveals views of Moorea's interior, the bay, and the village of Pihaena. Much of northern Moorea is visible from the viewpoint, and it's easy to visualize the great volcano that once existed here. Mount Rotui (899 m/2,950 ft) in front of you was once the central core of an island, more than three times as high as the present.

Magic Mountain is on private property, and visitors can enter by 4WD, ATV, or on foot by paying an entrance fee of CFP 200 per person. The road leading up to the mountain is steep,

narrow, and windy—driving without a guide is not recommended. If you're hiking, start early, bring plenty of water, and plan around 45 minutes to trek the 2 kilometers (1.2 mi) each way. There's a small parking lot near the top of the mountain, and a narrow 100-meter (328-ft) trail leads to a fenced lookout platform. Ice cream and fresh fruit are sold from a stand at the base of Magic Mountain for refreshing treats after the journey.

Papetoai Protestant Temple

PK 23

The Papetoai Protestant Temple is the oldest remaining European church in the South Pacific. When Protestant missionaries came to Moorea in 1822, they set out building a Protestant temple (completed 1827) over the site of a sacred marae. As Polynesian legend states that an octopus was sent by the gods to watch over Moorea, the superstitious missionaries built the temple with eight sides over the marae they demolished as a nod to the deity.

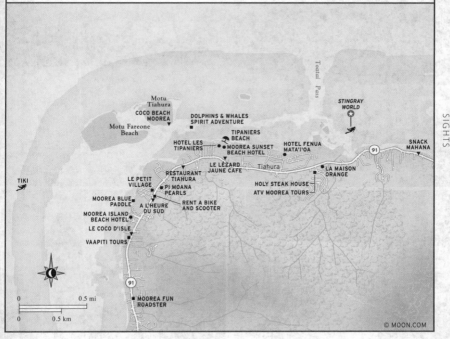

Access to the temple is usually reserved for churchgoers on Sundays, but you can see its pastel yellow exterior and maroon roof from the gate and from the top of Magic Mountain.

HAURU POINT AND AROUND
★ Tiki Village

PK 31; tel. 40 55 02 50; www.tikivillage.pf; 11am-3pm Tues.-Sat., shows take place on Tues. and Fri. from 6pm-10pm; CFP 10,950

Since 1986 Moorea has had its own instant culture village, the Tiki Village Theater. During the day, workshops centered around Polynesian art, cooking, dancing, and music take place. Learn how to weave from coconut fibers or pandanus leaves, paint bright patterns on pareu (fabric sarong), assemble the island's famous raw fish dish of poisson cru, and shake your hips to the sound of beating drums. Workshops cost CFP 3,000 per person per workshop or CFP 6,000 for a bundle of three.

On Tuesday and Friday evenings, there's a **sunset show** with dancing and drumming accompanied by an underground oven buffet (CFP 10,950, reservations required). And if you've got up to CFP 195,000 to spare, a wedding can be arranged at the village (BYO lover). The ceremony lasts two hours. The bridegroom arrives by canoe and the newlyweds are carried around in a procession by four strong men. There's also a less extravagant wedding for CFP 120,000, photos included. (Such weddings are not legally binding.)

SOUTHERN MOOREA

Most of Moorea's main sights, accommodations, good beaches, and restaurants are found

on Moorea's northern coast, but there's an air of magic to the island's quiet south. You'll drive for kilometers through coconut plantations past quiet villages and scenic vistas. PK markers for Southern Moorea move clockwise from Moorea's airport.

Parish of the Holy Family

PK 23.5; tel. 40 57 72 31; diocesedepapeete.com

Built in 1891, this twin-towered Catholic church was once the mission headquarters on the island. Under moody skies, it makes for an interesting stop, and doors are usually unlocked during daylight hours for travelers keen to take a peek inside.

Beaches

The handful of public beaches on Moorea are of the island paradise variety, with white sand and palm trees.

NORTHEAST MOOREA
TEMAE BEACH

PK 1; free parking

Temae Beach is the picturesque beach that the name "French Polynesia" evokes. A half-mile stretch of sand and coconut trees spans from the Sofitel Kia Ora Moorea to the Temae Beach parking lot, found off Moorea's main road. The smell of barbecue smoke, melodies from impromptu music circles, and mesmerizing sight of turquoise water lapping the shoreline make it easy to relax and lose track of time. Thanks to its proximity to the ferry terminal, it's a popular spot for weekenders escaping the chaos of Papeete. It can get crowded, but you'll find a spot to yourself if you walk toward the Sofitel—most people tend to cluster near the large parking lot. There are public bathrooms in the parking area. **Snorkeling:** There's a shallow reef just off the shoreline where you can see triggerfish, trumpetfish, parrotfish, giant clams, anemonefish, and the occasional eel—the calm water makes it a great spot for kids.

OPUNOHU BAY
★ TA'AHIAMANU BEACH

PK 15; free parking

Time slows down at Ta'ahiamanu Beach, a white sand beach with picnic benches welcoming travelers on the grassy areas between palm trees. A thin strip of white sand beckons those with towels and beach umbrellas. During sailing season, it's common to see a handful of yachts anchored here. Wade out into the water and you'll have a view of clear aquamarine waters stretching out into Opunohu Bay with a jade mountain skyline ahead. There are few other sights in French Polynesia quite like it. On this family-friendly beach with calm water, kids can swim, dig holes, and build sandcastles to their hearts' content. There's a free parking lot across the road with public bathrooms, change rooms, and the occasional food truck. **Snorkeling:** The colorful reef off this beach is just a few fin kicks from the shoreline—sea turtles, eels, and rays are frequently spotted.

HAURU POINT AND AROUND
TIPANIERS BEACH

PK 26; free parking across from Tipaniers Hotel until 5:30pm

The public beach at Tipaniers is one of Moorea's best for those who love adventure and wildlife. Walk along the path that cuts across Les Tipaniers Hotel and you'll find a tiny cove with palm trees, a grassy area, and a small wooden pier. This is where many of the island's ocean excursions depart from. A small stand on Tipaniers Beach, **Tip Nautic** (tel. 87 78 76 73; tipnautic.com), rents kayaks (CFP

1: Opunohu Bay 2: Manutea Tahiti Distillery 3: Parish of the Holy Family 4: Tiki Village Theater

Moorea's Conservationists

The Keep Moorea Wild movement advocates for the conservation of Moorea.

Many of Moorea's residents have a passion for preserving the culture, wildlife, and land of Moorea as issues like sea-level rise, climate change, foreign-owned development, and overfishing threaten to change its natural landscape. If you want to get involved or support local conservation movements on Moorea, these are three to consider.

KEEP MOOREA WILD

@keepmooreawild on Instagram

Linger on Moorea long enough and you'll likely hear about Keep Moorea Wild, a movement led by a group of environmental conservationists and activists. The group is protesting the widespread development of the island, stating that building these luxury villas and apartments could cause damage to Moorea's green spaces, lagoon, and cultural heritage. In late 2021, hundreds of locals and tourists gathered on Temae Beach to show solidarity with the Keep Moorea Wild movement, and support has only grown since then. More information can be found on Instagram.

CORAL GARDENERS

coralgardeners.org

Coral Gardeners was founded in 2017 by a group of local environmentalists passionate about protecting Moorea's lagoon. They surveyed the reefs of Moorea after a bleaching event to see which corals were still thriving, and deeming them the most resistant to sea temperature change, cut fragments of these corals and relocated them to a coral nursery. Once the coral fragments grow large enough to thrive on their own, they're embedded into a damaged section of the natural reef. Travelers can support the project by donating directly to the organization or by sponsoring a coral (from CFP 2,500).

TE MANA O TE MOANA

temanaotemoana.org

Te Mana o Te Moana is a sea turtle sanctuary operating from the InterContinental Moorea Resort & Spa (PK 28.5). The clinic rehabilitates injured sea turtles with the goal of releasing them into the wild. So far, the center has assisted nearly 600 sea turtles. The center also hosts education sessions, tracks and documents wild sea turtles, and cares for sea turtles deemed too injured to be released. Visitors can come to the center and learn more every Wednesday and Saturday at 10am. Reservations are mandatory (tel. 40 56 40 11; info@temanaotemoana.org).

500/hour single; CFP 1,000/hour double), paddleboards (CFP 1,000/hour), and snorkeling gear (CFP 500/half-day). **Snorkeling:** If you're a strong swimmer, venture west along the coastline until you reach the channel in between Motu Tiahura and Les Tipaniers Beach, where there are tens of coral bommies teeming with reef fish. Kayakers can also access the Stingray World snorkel and dive site, a spot to swim with pink whip stingrays and black tip reef sharks.

MOTU FAREONE AND MOTU TIAHURA
Off Hauru

Motu Fareone and Motu Tiahura are neighboring motu off Tipaniers Beach. Free transport to Motu Tiahura is included with a lunch at **Coco Beach,** the excellent restaurant on the motu, but it's also possible to get here with your own might via 20-minute kayak (you can rent one from **Tip Nautic** on Tipaniers Beach) in calm conditions. These sleepy islands have small white sand beaches, palm trees, and a channel populated with coral bommies, sea turtles, reef sharks, and stingrays. Paddling between the two motu takes just a few minutes.

Surfing

Twelve passes in the reef that surrounds the island also make Moorea one of the best surf destinations in the Society Islands. Because coral cannot grow in freshwater, the river mouths of Moorea have created deep channels in the reef, offering prime conditions for waves to break. All decent waves around Moorea break at the reef, so you'll need to hire a boat or kayak to get to them. These are challenging to come by if you're not staying at an accommodation catered to surfers. You'll want to arrange boat hire in advance with the help of your accommodation, or by booking a trip with one of the surf schools listed below. Almost all breaks featured require a 20- to 40-minute paddle from the shoreline, making them best suited for intermediate surfers only.

Waves are best from **March-October,** when southerly swells roll in. Water temperatures hover around 26°C (78°F) all year long, so there's no need to pack a wetsuit. A rash guard paired with a thick layer of reef-safe sunscreen on exposed skin is the only way to escape a sunburn.

SURF SPOTS
Northeast Moorea
TEMAE SURF SPOT
Boat ride from Temae Beach

Temae is an inconsistent right-hander that works best with southerly swells large enough to squeeze through the channel. It's shallow, fast, and fickle. When it is working, you'll have a tough time getting onto the wave before a local does. Experienced surfers only.

Cook's Bay
COOK'S BAY PASS SURF SPOT
Boat ride from Cook's Bay

Cook's Bay Pass works when a northerly swell rolls in (usually from November-late February). Most surfers stick to the left-hander, though it's rarely crowded. There's also a shallower and sketchier right-hander on the other side of the pass.

Hauru Point and Around
HAURU REEF
Boat ride from Tipaniers Beach Pier

A short boat ride from the pier of Tipaniers Beach is a pass in the reef where waves break on either side. On a small day, the left-hander is mellow and popular with kids and beginner surfers, though it can get quite sharp and shallow at low tide. If you've booked a beginner surf lesson, there's a large chance it'll be taught here. Once there's some size in the swell, the waves at Hauru Reef have quite a bit more muscle. You'll want a northwest swell rolling through to really see the potential of the pass.

Southern Moorea
HAAPITI SURF SPOT
Boat ride from Haapiti

Haapiti is a swell magnet and best reserved for intermediate to experienced surfers, especially if there's any pulse in the water. The takeoff is cruisey compared to other waves of this caliber, and it can barrel once it gets overhead. Because this break is one of the most popular among tourists on Moorea, it tends to have a friendlier crowd than the lesser-known spots.

SURF SCHOOLS
MOANA SURF COACHING
Boat pickup and drop-off dependent on ocean conditions; tel. 89 54 38 05; domenechmoana@ gmail.com; CFP 6,000/two-hour lesson

Moana is a friendly, patient, and skilled surf guide who offers both group and private surf

coaching. Lessons include surfboard rental, boat ride to and from the wave, water, and fresh-cut fruit. Students should bring their own sunscreen, and more experienced surfers will likely want their own board as his range is limited. Moana grew up surfing the waves of Moorea, and he has a teaching style that's informative without being overwhelming.

MOOREA IRIATAI SURF SCHOOL
PK 12; tel. 89 52 90 38; mooreairiataisurfschool@ gmail.com; lesson times dependent on weather, Wed.-Sun.; CFP 12,000/three hours

Moorea Iriatai Surf School is owned by former pro-surfer Prisca Amaru, who runs group and private surf lessons on the breaks around Hauru. Group classes are typically divided by age and ability: all beginners spend an hour bodyboarding before progressing to a surfboard, which can be unexpected for those who have just one day to surf or want to attempt a pop up from day one. Intermediate surfers should be able to catch waves without assistance. Lessons must be scheduled in advance by phone, Facebook (search for Moorea Iriatai Surf School), or email. Lessons include surfboard rental and transportation to and from the wave.

Snorkeling and Scuba Diving

There are countless snorkel spots around Moorea, and you can usually explore on your own wherever you spot a reef. The public beaches of **Temae, Ta'ahiamanu,** and **Tipaniers** offer decent snorkeling right offshore if you have your own equipment. You might spot sea turtles, reef sharks, stingrays, and hundreds of species of reef fish roaming around the waters of the island. If you want a guided experience of the most pristine spots,

it's best to go on a snorkel tour—which ventures to snorkel sites only reachable by boat.

For scuba diving, Moorea is underrated. Honeymooning dive-buddy duos tend to flock to Bora Bora, and divers with libraries of dive logs flock to the Tuamotus. Other ocean-obsessed travelers spend their days whale-watching. This means Moorea's best dive sites are rarely crowded, despite there being so much seascape to explore.

1: the friendly stingrays at Stingray World **2:** Coral reefs are found just a few fin kicks away from the shore.

SNORKELING AND DIVE SPOTS

Cook's Bay and Around

ROTUI DIVE SITE

Off Cook's Bay

The dive site of Rotui is a beginner-friendly reef dive with just 15-meter (49-ft) depth. It's a popular spot to see black tip reef sharks, lemon sharks, nurse sharks, and the occasional sea turtle. Manta rays and eagle rays cruise through occasionally. You could snorkel here, but the hit-or-miss visibility makes it a site best reserved for scuba divers.

Opunohu Bay

THE ROSE GARDEN DIVE SITE

Off of Opunohu Bay

The Rose Garden earned its name from the garden of Montipora corals that grow on the reef. The coral grows flat, irregular plates that resemble rose petals and leaves when seen from a distance. This dive site is typically reserved for advanced divers due to its depths of 30-45 meters (98-147 ft). This is also a popular spot to see a variety of sharks, including the rare tiger shark.

RAY'S CORRIDOR DRIFT DIVE SITE

Off of Opunohu Bay

Drift divers, this one is for you. The currents along a 2-kilometer (1.2-mi) stretch of reef makes for interesting drift diving, where you might spot a group of eagle rays. White and black tip reef sharks, gray sharks, nurse sharks, manta rays, and dolphins are often seen here. Depths drop to 30 meters (98 ft), so it's a site best suited for experienced divers only.

Hauru Point and Around

★ STINGRAY WORLD

PK 26; 500 meters (1,640 ft) off Tipaniers Beach

Around 500 meters (1,640 ft) off Tipaniers Beach is a snorkel spot with water so clear, it often looks like glass. You're bound to see pink whiprays and black tip reef sharks who fearlessly approach snorkelers in hopes of receiving a piece of fish. For years, fishermen cleaned their catch at this spot, and sharks and rays gathered in hopes of picking up a stray morsel. While fish-feeding is banned on Moorea, enough people still do it to keep the scavengers around. Touching any type of marine life is not recommended—though the rays haven't gotten the memo and have no qualms against gliding against you. Ramon, the biggest ray regularly seen at Stingray World, regularly approaches swimmers unprompted. Some of the black tip reef sharks of Stingray World have been here for nearly a decade as they live up to 12 years and rarely stray far from their home territory. Some boat tours offer a stop at this snorkel spot, and confident paddlers can kayak here.

If you want a souvenir you won't have to stow in a suitcase, book an underwater photo shoot at Stingray World with photographer Greg Fleurentin (tel. 89 58 55 26; en.gregfleurentin-photography.com; CFP 35,000/hour) who takes his clients to the snorkel site just after sunrise, beating the crowds from all other tour companies. His friendly demeanor puts timid swimmers at ease.

TIKI DIVE SITE

Off of Hauru

Tiki is one of the most popular dive sites on Moorea and earned its moniker from the stone tiki within the site. Sharks, eels, sea turtles, barracuda, and even humpback whales are common. The max depth of this site is 35 meters, and it's suitable for open water divers.

SNORKELING TOURS

MOOREA MITI TOURS

PK 9; tel. 87 23 43 02; www.mooreamititours.com; 8am-3:30pm daily

At Moorea Miti Tours, cruise through Moorea's lagoon onboard a 35-foot traditional outrigger canoe—which is quite a comfortable ride thanks to a shade canopy, ladder, and sun deck. Their three-hour snorkeling tour (€67/adult, €33/child) visits spots where you'll snorkel over coral reefs, plus a spot to see reef sharks and stingrays up close. The six-hour tour (€83/adult, €41/child) stops at similar snorkel spots and includes a lunch and cooking demonstration on a motu. All tours include hotel transport, towels, and snorkeling equipment, though bringing your own is recommended. Each tour can accommodate up to 12 passengers, and private two-hour sunset cruises can be arranged from €420 for up to eight people.

MOOREA WATER GAMES

tel. 87 33 77 67; www.mooreawatergames.com; 7:30am-4pm daily; €92/four-hour tour/person, €53/ two-hour tour/person

If you're not a strong swimmer or simply want a unique snorkel experience, book a snorkel tour with Moorea Water Games. Their tour accommodates up to eight guests, who are given an underwater scooter that can cruise at speeds of up to 7 kilometers/hour (4 mph), snorkeling equipment, and life jacket to explore the reefs of Moorea. Guests must be ages seven and up to participate. Transportation is available from €40 per trip.

DIVE SHOPS AND SCHOOLS

MOOREA BLUE DIVING

PK 5.5 Manava Beach Resort and Spa; tel. 87 74 59 99; www.mooreabluediving.com; 7am-5pm Mon.-Sat., 7am-1pm Sun.; 8,500 CFP/fun dive

If you love sharks, Moorea Blue Diving has a knack for finding the best shark-diving spots around Moorea. It's possible to see lemon sharks, reef sharks, and if you're lucky, tiger sharks at some of the dive center's most frequented dive sites. Free transport is included between Vaianar and the Hilton Hotel. Dive courses range from introductory (CFP 9,000) to Advanced Adventurer SSI (CFP 50,000). An Open Water SSI course is CFP 60,000. Packages of up to 12 dives (CFP 75,000) drop the per-dive price considerably and can be split among two people. Moorea Blue Diving is included in the Te Moana Dive Pass.

MOOREA FUN DIVE

PK 26.6; tel. 40 56 40 38; moorea-fundive.com; 8am-5pm daily; CFP 7,000/fun dive

Moorea Fun Dive is an independent dive center set on a white sand beach near Moorea's western coastline. Two tank dives take place at 8:30am and one tank dive takes place at 2:30pm daily, depending on booking numbers. Book a fun dive for CFP 7,000 per dive or a package (CFP 36,000/6 dives, CFP 57,000/10 dives). The center offers PADI Open Water (CFP 60,000) and PADI Advanced Open Water (CFP 50,000) courses, with more advanced training available on request. Moorea Fun Dive is included in the Te Moana Dive Pass.

Hiking

Moorea is one of the best islands in French Polynesia for hikers of all abilities. From ancient marae hidden between gargantuan trees to open grasslands to tucked-away pineapple plantations, the terrain is varied enough to make every hike interesting. No matter what trail you choose, venture out early in the daytime to escape the heat and humidity, and ensure you have plenty of water. Some of the best-marked hiking trails begin at Belvedere, just behind the parking lot. Those trails are easy to hike on your own, but you'll want a guide for unmarked excursions. Magic Mountain, featured in the Sights section of this chapter, is also possible to reach on foot. The website Alltrails (alltrails.com) has decent coverage of the popular hiking routes on Moorea.

HIKES
Opunohu Bay
MOUNT ROTUI

Distance: *7 km (4.3mi) out-and-back*
Time: *6 hours*

Trailhead: *Faimano Village (PK 15), in between Opunohu Bay and Cook's Bay*
Information and maps: *www.alltrails.com/ trail/french-polynesia/tahiti/mount-rotui-depuis-faimano*

A trail up Mount Rotui (899 m/2,950 ft), Moorea's second-highest peak after Mount Tohiea (1207 m/3,960 ft), begins in Faimano Village, the town between Opunohu Bay and Cook's Bay, across from where most accommodations are clustered. Go down the road opposite Faimano Village and turn right before the house on the hill. A red arrow painted on a coconut tree points the way, but you may have to contend with the local dogs as you start up. Once up behind the house, the trail swings right and onto the ridge, which you follow to the summit. The land at the trailhead belongs to the Faimano Village's owner, and he doesn't mind climbers, but you should ask permission to proceed from anyone you happen to meet near the house. From the top, you'll have a sweeping view of the entire north coast. It's better not to go alone, as there are vertical drops from the narrow ridgeline. In wet conditions this trail is dangerous. While not as challenging as Mount Mouaputa, this is not a climb to be undertaken lightly.

THREE COCONUT TREES (Col des Trois Cocotiers)
Distance: *6 km/3.7 mi*
Time: *3 hours*
Trailhead: *Belvedere parking lot*
Information and maps: *www.alltrails.com/ trail/french-polynesia/moorea/col-des-trois-cocotiers*

The Three Coconut Trees trail begins behind the Belvedere parking lot and trickles into a forest where out-of-place chickens cluck around, making the trail feel less remote than it initially seems. The trail leads over creek beds and through a small tunnel of bamboo trees. Steep switchbacks lead to a lookout point (beware of the steep cliff drop) at 336 meters (1,102 ft) where you'll spot views of Opunohu Bay, Cook's Bay, Moorea's interior, and glimpses of the western coastline. Though the trek is named after a trio of coconut trees,

they were wiped out in a cyclone and no longer feature as part of the trail. Plan around three hours to complete this 6-kilometer (3.7-mi) trail. Follow the blue trail markings to stay on course.

Southern Moorea
MOUNT MOUAPUTA
Distance: *5 km (3.1 mi) out-and-back*
Time: *5-6 hours*
Trailhead: *At the end of Cascade Road in Afareaitu*
Information and maps: *www.alltrails.com/ trail/french-polynesia/moorea/mou-aputa*

Mount Mouaputa (830 m/2,723 ft) is one of the most striking mountains in all of French Polynesia. Its silhouette looks like a woman's face turned up toward the sky, with a hole piercing through the face's nose near the summit. Polynesian legend states that the hole through Mount Mouaputa was created by Pai, a deity who threw a spear through the mountain to stop thieves from stealing nearby Mount Rotui.

The hike up Mount Mouaputa is best suited for experienced hikers, as it's one of the hardest on the island. There are plenty of unstable, steep, and slippery sections that require holding onto ropes to navigate, and crossing through streams, making it best in dry conditions. The view from the top offers a 360-degree view of the island. Plan for at least 5-6 hours to complete the journey.

AFAREAITU WATERFALLS
Distance: *1.5 km (0.9 mi) out-and-back*
Time: *1 hour*
Trailhead: *Afareaitu*
Information and maps: *www.alltrails.com/ trail/french-polynesia/moorea/cascade-d-afareaitu*

From opposite the old Protestant church (1912) in Afareaitu (PK 9), a one-hour walk on the road between Magasin Ah Sing and a school leads up the Afareaitu Valley to a high waterfall, which cascades down a sheer cliff

1: Trails into Moorea's lush interior weave from Belvedere Lookout. **2:** a waterfall on a hike in Moorea

into a pool. You can cut your walking time in half by driving a car two-thirds of the way up the valley. Park at the point where a normal car would have problems and hike on up the road to the right. When this road begins to climb steeply, look for a well-beaten footpath on the right, which will take you directly to the falls.

You'll get a good view of Mount Mouaputa, the peak pierced by Pai's spear, from the hospital just north of Afareaitu. The first road inland north of the hospital leads to a different waterfall, Atiraa Falls. The access road is rough, so park just before a small concrete bridge and continue the 30-minute hike on foot.

GUIDED HIKES

HIRO HIKING MOOREA

tel. 79 41 54; hirohikingmoorea.blogspot.com; hours dependent on weather; CFP 5,250/half day, CFP 7,350/full day

Hiro Damide has been guiding hiking trips around the island for over 10 years, and commonly leads guests along the popular Three Coconut Trees trail. He is happy to share about the history, geology, and biology of the island. You must have at least two guests to book.

MOOREA TREK

tel. 87 25 74 74; www.facebook.com/ MooreaTrekTeheiaruaRando2016; 7:30am-4pm Mon.-Sat.; CFP 6,000/person/half day

Led by Val Urarii, hikes with Moorea Trek range from beginner-friendly to experienced hikers only. While Moorea Trek can certainly help you wander down the main well-marked trails stemming from Belvedere, more intrepid (and skilled) hikers will enjoy the guide's ability to lead them to lesser-known paths, like that up to Mount Mouaputa. Transport to and from your accommodation to the trailhead is included with each trip.

Water Sports and Boat Tours

Moorea's lagoon, the ring of water in between land and an outer barrier reef, is where you'll find thriving populations of reef sharks, stingrays, eagle rays, and tropical fish that can be seen underwater as a snorkeler or scuba diver. Or, admire Moorea's technicolor reefs from the comfort of a boat. Among Moorea's frequent visitors are hundreds of humpback whales, who migrate along the island's outer reefs. Making eye contact with one of these gentle giants on a whale swim tour will reveal a mysterious realm of the animal kingdom, an experience that will linger with you throughout life. Venturing out on a themed boat tour is the easiest way to explore the lagoon; choose one that suits your main interest. Some accommodations have kayaks, canoes, and stand-up paddleboards for rent. Otherwise, the most convenient stand renting them is found at Les Tipaniers Beach.

MOOREA ACTIVITIES CENTER

PK 21; tel. 87 77 09 71; www.mooreaactivitiescenter. com; 7:30am-6pm daily

Moorea Activities Center is a one-stop shop for all things adrenaline on Moorea. Cruise through the waters on a Jet Ski tour (CFP 15,000/one hour, CFP 19,000/two hours, CFP 23,000/three hours for two people) to see Opunohu Bay. Tours include a swim stop with stingrays and sharks. Quad tours (CFP 18,000-23,000/two people) through the Opunohu Valley can include stops at Belvedere, pineapple plantations, and Magic Mountain. The center also arranges four-hour boat tours of the lagoon (CFP 10,000/ adult, CFP 5,000/child) to both bays, coral gardens, and stingray and reef shark snorkel spots. Private tours can be arranged for CFP 65,000/12 people. Four-hour whale-watching excursions are available for CFP 12,000/adult and CFP 6,000/child.

TOP JET MOOREA

PK 3.3; tel. 87 73 63 83; topjetmoorea.com;
7:30am-6pm daily

Cruise in the calm waters of Moorea's lagoon on a roaring Jet Ski. Top Jet Moorea offers Jet Ski rentals by the hour (CFP 15,000/Jet Ski) as well as guided tours. Jet Skis seat two, and the three-hour discovery tour (CFP 22,000/Jet Ski) ventures to Cook's Bay, Opunohu Bay, and stingray and shark snorkeling spots, and may offer a chance to see humpback whales depending on the season. For a more off-beat adventure, take a lap around the island (29,000 CFP/Jet Ski) and stop at a motu for a snack. Top Jet Moorea also offers boat tours (CFP 10,000/four-hour tour/adult, CFP 6,000/child), whale-watching and swimming (CFP 10,000/four-hours/adult, CFP 6,000/child), and Jet Ski plus quad tour packages from CFP 37,000 per vehicle for a 6.5-hour tour. A driver's license isn't required for Jet Ski rental, but you'll need one to drive a quad.

MERMAID PRIVATE BOAT TOURS

tel. 87 36 17 17; mermaidprivateboattours.com;
7:30am-sunset daily; CFP 35,000-45,000/
three-hour tour

For a fully customized lagoon tour, Mermaid Private Boat Tours offers three-hour trips for up to four guests. Spend it whale-watching, snorkeling, or cruising from motu to motu, or create a mix-and-match experience. Each trip includes fresh fruits, juice, snorkeling equipment, hotel transport, and photos (including underwater) from your excursion.

MOOREA BLUE PADDLE

tel. 89 51 11 11; www.mooreabluepaddle.com;
7:30am-3pm daily; CFP 6,000-14,000/adult, children
under 8 half price

Explore around the clear waters of Moorea on a transparent kayak or stand-up paddleboard. While you're bound to see more with a mask and snorkel, the feeling of being immersed in the water as you paddle is a novelty ocean-obsessed travelers won't want to miss. Moorea Blue Paddle offers morning, afternoon, and full-day tours. Guests can create a DIY full-day excursion by combining kayaking or electric bike with an electric scooter or paddle tour—it's a more sustainable version of the popular Jet Ski and quad tours of the island.

VAAPITI

tel. 87 21 29 95; vaapiti.com; 8am-6pm daily

For a tour that combines innovation, culture, and adventure, spend half a day sailing on *Vaapiti*. This 26-foot double sailing canoe

stand-up paddleboarding off Moorea

was built by owner Raphaël Labaysse, who is passionate about sharing his knowledge of Polynesian navigation. On a half-day tour (CFP 8,000/adult, CFP 5,000/child), you'll learn the basics of sailing Vaapiti, like hoisting the sails and navigating the lagoon. Private tours (five hours) are available from CFP 45,000 for two adults plus CFP 2,500 per adult afterward, seating up to eight passengers.

VOILA MOOREA

tel. 87 30 43 33; voilamoorea.com; 8am-sunset daily
The cherry red hulls of *Taboo,* a 30-foot sailing catamaran, stand out against the turquoise water of the lagoon as it sails from snorkel spot to snorkel spot. Viola Moorea offers trips for up to eight people onboard and includes snorkeling equipment. Spend your time swimming, learning sailing tips, or lounging on the trampoline. Each tour is around four hours long with morning, afternoon, and sunset excursions available. Shared tours cost CFP 8,500 CFP per adult and CFP 4,300 for children under 10. Private tours are available for CFP 57,000 for up to four people, or CFP 62,000 for up to eight people.

★ Dolphin- and Whale-Watching

TOP EXPERIENCE

Every year, thousands of **humpback whales** migrate along the waters of Moorea from Antarctica, arriving in Polynesian waters in **late July-mid-November.** First, pods of strong bulls lead the way of the migration, with whales traveling solo and juvenile whales shortly behind. Mother whales and their calves, occasionally accompanied by a bull escort, trail toward the end of migration. Peak season is from **July-late August.**

Coming eye to eye with one of the most intelligent animals on the planet is an experience that may make you see the world in a new way. It's not uncommon for whales to interact with humans. Juvenile whales often twirl and slap their tail, as if they're putting on a performance. Curious calves swim up for a peek at you while their mother keeps a watchful eye from below. The sound of a bull singing underwater is haunting, and if it's close enough, the tune will reverberate through your body. For your best chance at a life-changing interaction, swim slowly and avoid splashing.

DR. MICHAEL POOLE
DOLPHINS AND WHALES

tel. 87 77 50 07; www.drmichaelpoole.com; 8am-5pm daily; US$110/half day/person
Dr. Michael Poole has been researching the whales and dolphins of Moorea's waters since the late 1970s and started his whale-watching and swimming company in 1992. Most whale swim companies in Moorea do not provide extensive information on the marine mammals spotted on the tour—and if they do, it's often solely in French. On a trip led by Dr. Michael Poole, you'll learn about the dolphins and whales of Moorea from an expert perspective.

MOOREA MOANA TOURS

tel. 89 78 68 70; www.mooreaoceantours.com; 8am-sunset daily; US$120/half day
Moorea Moana Tours offers a range of tour experiences like guided whale-watching and swimming (U$120/person/half day), guided spearfishing trips (US$600/three people/half day), and private personalized tours (US$600/ eight people/half day). They are also one of the only operators that leads guests to swim with majestic tiger sharks on Moorea (US$1,500/six people). Moorea Moana Tours also runs the Mao Mana Foundation, a mission centered around shark preservation and education.

DOLPHINS & WHALES
SPIRIT ADVENTURE

tel. 87 36 59 91; www.dolphinsandwhalesspiritadventu re.com; 8am-sunset daily; US$100/half day

Tips for Ethical Whale-Watching

humpback whales

While boats are required to keep 100 meters (about 328 ft) from a whale, and diving after them is forbidden, there is currently little regulation when it comes to whale swimming tours. During high season, tens of swimmers may be in the water around a single whale at once like a swarm of mosquitoes, clamoring after whales who have no interest in interacting. There is a push for stricter regulations to decrease human-caused stress on humpback whales, but regulations have yet to take hold. If you notice your tour operator is chasing or allowing other guests to harass whales, say something, request a refund, and leave a public review. Here are some tips to have the best experience:

· **Choose smaller boats and tour groups:** It might be a little more expensive, but it's best to book a tour that limits their group size to 10 swimmers or less.

· **Keep clear from breaching whales:** It's common to see whales sleeping or resting underwater, especially when they're traveling with a calf. Give the whales plenty of space to come up and breathe; don't swim to where they're likely to ascend.

· **Allow for extra days in the water:** Book a whale swim during the beginning of your stay to leave an opportunity to go again should you not see a whale during your first attempt. This allows tour guides to feel less pressure from their guests and might prevent them from chasing a whale that's not interested in interacting.

· **Stay still:** Calm, slow movements around the whales will allow them to swim in peace, without the fear of being chased.

Dolphins & Whales Spirit Adventure has been hosting whale and dolphin excursions for over 25 years, making it one of the first operators in business. Tours accommodate up to 12 guests and take place on an aluminum boat with plenty of shade. Their whale swim guides tend to be more respectful toward the whales than many other operators. The reservation system isn't reliable, so be sure to confirm your booking with them the day before (and morning of) your trip.

MOOREA OCEAN ADVENTURES

tel. 87 34 29 99; moorea-ocean-adventures.com;
7am-5pm daily; US$550/two people/four hours,
US$650/six people/four hours, US$990/six people/
eight hours

Moorea Ocean Adventures caters solely to private groups, leading a customized excursion based on the group's interests. Each trip can include swimming with whales, dolphins, sharks, sea turtles, or stingrays, depending on the season. Tours are led by a marine biologist or naturalist and include a free video of the day. The boat has an underwater tow board for guests who want to feel like they're flying over the reef.

Other Recreation

DEEP-SEA FISHING
MOOREA FISHING ADVENTURES

tel. 87 71 85 32; mooreafishingadventures.com;
sunrise-sunset daily; US$250/person/half day

Catch your dinner with Moorea Fishing Adventures, where a 23-foot aluminum boat and experienced captain brings guests beyond the lagoon to fish for the likes of skipjack tuna, yellowfin tuna, mahi-mahi, wahoo, and the occasional marlin. Four-hour trips accommodate six people onboard for US$250 per person. A private charter is available for US$800 for four hours, US$1,200 for seven hours.

GOLF
GREEN PEARL GOLF COURSE

PK 1.5; tel. 40 56 27 32; greenpearl.golf; 7am-5pm
daily; CFP 4,650-5,650/9 holes, CFP 6,700-9,300/18
holes

The 18-hole, par-70 Jack Nicklaus Moorea Green Pearl Golf Course wraps around the west end of Temae Lake near the inter-island airport. There's a pro shop below the large restaurant at the entrance. Greens fees are cheaper on weekdays than weekends. You can purchase packages that include greens fees, cart rental, and club rental (CFP 9,500/person for 9 holes, CFP 9,900-15,000/ person for 18 holes). Practice on the putting and chipping green for CFP 750.

The Temae course is the first major golf course to be built in French Polynesia in 35 years (the Olivier Breaud golf course on the south side of Tahiti was laid out in 1970). Golf course and resort development is a controversial issue in French Polynesia. A 1991 attempt to construct an 18-hole golf course and Sheraton resort in Moorea's Opunohu Valley was defeated by referendum voters.

Shopping

NORTHEAST MOOREA
Clothing and Accessories
BAMBOU SHOP MOOREA

PK 5.2; facebook.com/bamboushopmoorea;
9am-6pm Mon.-Sat., 9am-noon Sun.

This small boutique shop sells clothing both plain and patterned for kids and adults. It's a decent place to pick up something appropriate for the islands if you've left home without it. There is also a small selection of pareu.

Pearls
PEARL ROMANCE

PK 5.8; tel. 87 70 92 70; pearlromance.fr;
8:30am-6pm Mon.-Sat.

Pearl Romance is an upscale pearl shop selling handmade jewelry made from Tahitian black pearls grown primarily on Ahe atoll in the Tuamotus. There is also a shop inside the Sofitel Kia Ora Beach Resort.

Shopping for the Best Souvenirs

MONOÏ OIL

Monoï oil, ubiquitous throughout French Polynesia, is produced by squeezing coconut pulp to liberate the oil, which is then allowed to cure for several weeks. Blossoms of the tiare Tahiti, a white-petaled flower often used as a symbol of Tahiti, are added to the oil to give it a special fragrance. Monoï is judged by its fluidity and purity, and it's primarily a skin conditioner used as a **moisturizer** after showers or in **traditional Polynesian massage.** Monoï is also a sure **remedy for dry hair.** It doesn't prevent sunburn and can even magnify the sun's rays, but it does provide instant **relief for sunburned skin.** On Tahiti, newborn babies are bathed in monoï rather than water during their first month of life. Some say it works as a mosquito repellent, though you might want to pack a more potent backup.

black pearls

Throughout the islands you'll likely see small bottles of monoï oil being sold at roadside market stands and supermarkets alike, along with bars of soap made by Monoi Tiare Tahiti and Royal Monoi. Homemade soaps and oils exist as well, and are sold at shops like **Made in Moorea, La Maison Blanche,** and **Tropical Garden Moorea.**

BLACK PEARLS

Black pearls (Tahitian pearls) are pearls grown from a black lip oyster. Despite their name, their color can range from white to dark charcoal, with hues of pink, blue, green, silver, and yellow in between. You can get lower-quality black pearls for as little as US$100, mid-range pearls from US$1,000, and the sky is the limit when it comes to pearls of a higher caliber.

They say beauty is in the eye of the beholder, and this is true when it comes to buying pearls. If you want to judge a pearl somewhat objectively, these are the six features to consider:

- **Color:** The darker the pearl, the more valuable it tends to be. Darker pearls may have hints of iridescent pink, blue, yellow, and green.

- **Luster:** Luster is the pearl's shine quality. Pearls with a shiny, silky luster are worth more than pearls with a matte or chalky appearance.

- **Nacre thickness:** Nacre is the outer layer of the pearl and is key to determining the pearl's luster. The thicker the nacre, the shinier it tends to be.

- **Size:** A black pearl is typically between 5mm-20mm, and larger pearls are worth more. Most large pearls are crafted using a nucleus that the nacre adheres to, meaning a larger pearl doesn't always equal a thicker layer of nacre.

- **Surface:** The smoother the pearl, the more valuable it is.

- **Shape:** Perfectly spherical pearls are rare and highly prized. They can also be shaped like ovals, raindrops, or buttons, and can have rings and lumps.

Shops may offer a discount, especially if you've come without a guide who would have earned a commission. Higher quality pearls are found at specialized shops rather than souvenir stalls. A reputable dealer will give you an invoice or certificate verifying the authenticity of your pearl. If you've made an expensive choice, ask the dealer to take an x-ray right in front of you to check the quality. Check out the black pearl selection at **Pearl Romance, Ron Hall Pearls,** and **Pai Moana Pearls.**

Souvenirs
MADE IN MOOREA

*PK 6; tel. 87 24 38 25; moorea.south.pacific.island@
gmail.com; 9am-5pm Wed.-Sat.*

One of the best souvenir shops on Moorea.
As the name implies, most items are designed
and made locally. Their wares include an
array of pareu, postcards, printed art, home
decor, and clothing. The shop is found on the
second story above the Banque de Polynesie.

COOK'S BAY
Clothing and Accessories
MAISON BLANCHE

PK 5.4; tel. 56 13 26; 8:30-5pm Mon.-Sat.

La Maison Blanche is a popular shop that
sells pareu, jewelry, woven bags, faux flower
crowns, and souvenirs.

Pearls
RON HALL PEARLS

PK 6.9; tel. 40 56 11 06; 9am-5pm Mon.-Sat.

Ron Hall Pearls is one of the most popular
pearl shops on Moorea, known for its elegant
designs. A visit to the shop includes a short
educational session on pearl growing and
harvesting (if desired). Staff tend to be helpful without being pushy. A free shuttle is available to and from major hotels.

Souvenirs
MOO BOUTIQUE & GALLERY

*PK 7.1; tel. 87 37 18 73; 9am-5pm Mon.-Fri., 9am-noon
Sat.*

Moo Boutique & Gallery sells goods made primarily in Polynesia, including wooden sculptures made in the Marquesas Islands, prints
from Tahitian artists, woven goods, hand-
painted pareu, and shell crafts.

HAURU BAY AND AROUND
Souvenirs
LE PETIT VILLAGE

PK 26; 9am-5pm daily

Le Petit Village shopping mall has a bank,
grocery store, snack bar, gas station, and lots
of expensive little souvenir shops patronized
by people on circle-island bus tours.

Pearls
PAI MOANA PEARLS

*PK 27; tel. 40 56 25 25; 9am-5pm Mon.-Fri.,
9am-noon Sat.*

Pai Moana Pearls is a family-owned pearl
shop selling jewelry made with pearls grown
at Manihi. Free pickup and drop-off for travelers on Moorea is available (call to request).
There is a second shop in Cook's Bay (PK
7.7; tel. 40 56 50 73) with a slightly different
selection.

Food

Most restaurants are found on Moorea's
northern coast, with few options once you
wrap around the southern edge of the island.
Most snacks and restaurants are closed on
Sundays, and your best option for finding
food will be at your accommodation (or a
large hotel), or cooking it yourself. Many restaurants include transportation for guests;
you'll want to call in advance to confirm.

NORTHEAST MOOREA
European
PURE

*Sofitel Kia Ora Moorea Beach Resort; tel. 40 55 12
25; www.sofitel-moorea-kiaora.com; 6:30am-9pm
daily; CFP 2,500-4,000*

Pure at Sofitel Kia Ora Moorea Beach Resort
offers mostly European fare like pizzas,
pastas, grilled meats, and seafood served
in its thatched-roof oceanfront dining
hall. The wine list is extensive, with many

options imported from mainland France. Reservations are recommended if you want to dine during the twice-weekly dance performance (inquire in advance as the schedule changes seasonally).

Quick Bites
FARE LA CANADIENNE
PK 2.5; tel. 87 73 45 78; 11am-8:30pm Mon. and Sat.; 11am-1:30pm and 6pm-8pm Sun. and Wed.-Fri.; CFP 2,000-4,000

Come hungry to Fare La Canadienne, a casual burger joint serving burgers, fries, and salads in hefty proportions without skimping on quality. Their poutine (french fries smothered in marinara sauce and topped with mozzarella) might confuse true connoisseurs, but the friendly French-Canadian owners and maple-syrup drizzled desserts help the restaurant earn its name.

COOK'S BAY
Tahitian
MANUIA GRILL
Manava Resort; tel. 40 56 26 64; 6pm-10pm daily; CFP 2,500-4,000

Come evening, this is one of the most popular restaurants among locals. Dine on seasoned and grilled beef, seafood, and chicken in a casual open-air dining hall. Portion sizes are huge and usually come with a side of french fries, salad, or vegetables, plus a choice of sauce. Vegetarian and vegan travelers will have to stick to the side dishes, as there are no plant-based proteins on the menu.

European
MAHANAI RESTAURANT
Manava Beach Resort; tel. 40 55 17 69; www.manavamoorearesort.com; 7am-8:30am and 5:30pm-8:30pm daily; CFP 2,900-4,100

This thatched-roof restaurant inside Manava Beach Resort has a small menu with mostly European dishes on offer, like tagliatelle, risotto, grilled fish, lamb shank, and soups. Book a table for around sunset to enjoy bubblegum pink skies over desserts like tiramisu and cheesecake. On Saturdays, the restaurant

hosts a Polynesian dance show and buffet—reservations are recommended.

Quick Bites
CARAMELINE
PK 5.5; tel. 87 33 03 61; www.allocara.com; 6:30am-8pm Mon.-Fri.; CFP 900-2,000

Carmeline is a casual restaurant known around the island for its pastries and vast selection of ice cream. The breakfast menu features bowls of granola with berries and homemade yogurt or toast served with bacon, eggs, and hash browns. For a meal, you'll find burgers, sandwiches, seafood, salads, and fajitas. You can dine in, have your food delivered for an extra fee, or pick it up as a takeaway order.

ALLO PIZZA
PK 7.8; tel. 40 56 18 22; www.facebook.com/ AlloPizzaMoorea; 11am-2pm and 5pm-8:30pm daily; CFP 1,500-2,500

Allo Pizza is a laid-back pizza stand with outdoor seating along a bar bench—takeaway and delivery are also available. Choose from over 20 variations of piping-hot thin-crust pizzas, or try a DIY variation of your own. They also offer salads, barbecue steak, and tuna carpaccio. Grab a salad to share. Most dishes can be amended on request, making it one of the few decent spots for plant-based diners on the island. For dessert, their banana pizza made with fresh cream, bananas, and brown sugar is worth a try.

Seafood
RESTAURANT TE HONU ITI
PK 9; tel. 40 56 19 84; www.facebook.com/ restaurantTehonuiti; 11am-2:30pm and 6pm-9:30pm daily; CFP 1,700-2,800

A meal at Restaurant Te Honu Iti is never boring, thanks to the local stingrays and reef sharks cruising around beneath the overwater deck. Enjoy dishes like lobster-filled ravioli, grilled mahi-mahi, seared tuna, and roasted duck, followed by apple pie for dessert. Service moves at a relaxed pace, so request a table near the water for ocean entertainment to pass the time. Transport to and from the restaurant can be arranged if booked in advance.

RUDY'S

PK 6; tel. 40 56 58 00; 5:30pm-10pm daily; CFP 2,000-4,500

Rudy's has been s dinnertime mainstay on Moorea for over a decade. Most nights, Rudy, the owner, can be found chatting with guests behind the bar or making his way from table to table. The menu leans toward the meat and seafood side, with parrotfish stuffed with crab being the dish the restaurant is most known for. The lobster, wahoo, and grilled garlic shrimp are also popular picks. Save room for the gooey chocolate lava cake served with vanilla ice cream. There's a free transport service available for diners who book in advance.

Breakfast
MOZ CAFÉ

PK 5.5; tel. 40 56 38 12; 7am-3pm Mon.-Fri.; CFP 1,500-2,500

Moz Café is a cozy and friendly café tucked above Banque de Polynesie that's open for breakfast and lunch. Eggs, French toast, crepes, pastries, and fruit salad are found on their breakfast menu. Enjoy sandwiches, burgers, salads, poisson cru, and tuna tartare

for lunch. While the menu highlights a handful of vegan-friendly items, the chef is usually happy to offer more options on request. Grab one of the outside patio tables for views of the sea.

OPUNOHU BAY
Quick Bites
TROPICAL GARDEN MOOREA

Inland of PK 15.5; tel. 87 70 53 63; 8am-4pm Mon.-Sat., 8am-2pm Sun.; CFP 500-1,000

It's easy to laze the day away from a picnic table at Tropical Garden Moorea, a fresh fruit garden and snack shop perched above Opunohu Bay. The property is dotted with fruit trees including passionfruit, noni, banana, mango, papaya, and breadfruit, and it houses a vanilla farm. Try their homemade jams, sorbets, gelato, smoothies, and fruit platters. The taro gelato is a highlight.

LILIKOI GARDEN CAFÉ

PK 14; tel. 87 29 61 41; lilikoimoorea.com; noon-2:30pm Mon.-Sat.; CFP 1,200-1,800

Set among tropical gardens, Lilikoi Garden Café is a casual lunch spot serving fresh juices and smoothies, coffee, salads, seafood, chicken, and their signature dessert, grilled pineapple with rosemary. Hearty eggplant

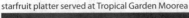

starfruit platter served at Tropical Garden Moorea

curries make it one of the best spots for plant-based travelers. Foodies can also sign up for the café's food tour (CFP 9,000), a six-hour activity that includes visits to vanilla and pineapple plantations, a talk with a fisherman, fruit tastings, a cooking class, and a buffet lunch.

TOATEA CREPERIE & BAR

Hilton Hotel; tel. 40 55 11 11; www.hilton.com; 6pm-9:30pm daily; CFP 1,200-2,500

Enjoy crepes of the sweet and savory variety at Hilton Hotel's Toatea Creperie & Bar, a perfect spot for a meal after a grand adventure. The thatched-roof dining area is set overwater, with the occasional eagle ray, sea turtle, shark, or stingray cruising underfoot. The savory crepes are generous enough to be a meal on their own, with a shared sweet one being ideal for dessert.

HAURU POINT AND AROUND

Fine Dining
HOLY STEAK HOUSE

PK 24.5; tel. 40 55 15 14; www.holysteakhouse.com; noon-10pm daily; CFP 1,700-3,600

Holy Steak House is one of the more upscale restaurants on Moorea—though you'll be welcomed even in casual attire. You'll find comfort food classics like macaroni and cheese, mashed potatoes, and casseroles. Pizzas, burgers (including a vegetarian option), salads, and grilled meats imported from New Zealand make up most of the menu. Their bar is one of the best stocked on Moorea outside of the major resorts. Book a table for sunset to enjoy dinner under tangerine skies.

Quick Bites
COCO ET BANANA

PK 24.5; tel. 40 56 45 43; 7:30am-2pm Thurs.-Sun.; CFP 300-1,300

Coco et Banana is where you can get your croissant cravings satisfied. This small patisserie serves fresh-baked breads, pastries, cakes, donuts, and a range of spreads like hummus, jam, and marmalade.

A L'HEURE DU SUD

PK 26; tel. 87 70 03 12; 10:30am-4pm Thurs.-Tues.; CFP 1,000

This colorful sandwich shack channels Moorea's laid-back beach culture. Generous burgers, baguettes, and club sandwiches are served with a side of crispy fries. Grilled fish skewers, sashimi, and salads are also available. Check the chalkboard for daily specials.

★ SNACK MAHANA

PK 23; tel. 40 56 41 70; 11am-3pm Tues.-Sat.; CFP 1,800-2,500

This open-air beach restaurant is one of the most popular lunch spots on the island, so much so that their food often runs out before noon. Get there early to enjoy their full menu and a picnic table over the water. Portion sizes are hefty; you can't go wrong with the breaded mahi-mahi cooked in coconut milk, shrimp curry, or seared tuna. Note there's not much here for plant-based diners.

★ COCO BEACH MOOREA

Motu off Les Tipaniers Beach; tel. 87 72 57 26; www.facebook.com/cocobeachmoz; 10am-2pm Wed., Thurs., Sat., and Sun.; CFP 2,500

You'll want to bring your snorkel gear when you dine at Coco Beach Moorea. The café is set on the beach of a nearby motu, and patrons are shuttled back and forth from mainland Moorea about every half hour. Reservations must be made by phone. The menu is simple but delicious, featuring fresh-caught fish, salads, burgers, and grilled meats. Stingrays and reef sharks gather around the shallows in front of the restaurant once they hear the hum of the restaurant boat coming over, like a lunch bell. It's a fun experience to wade in the water with them while you wait for your meal. Credit cards are accepted.

Seafood
LE LÉZARD JAUNE CAFÉ

PK 27.3; tel. 89 56 58 64; www.facebook.com/lelezardjaunecafe; 6:30pm-10pm Wed.-Sun.; CFP 1,800-3,000

Reservations are recommended at Le Lézard

Jaune Café, a spot that's become well known for its exceptional poisson cru made with freshly sliced ginger and cucumber. The atmosphere of the restaurant is lively, and the owners usually come over to explain the specials. Regular favorites include grilled mahi-mahi served with a tangy coconut curry sauce, shrimp skewers, and tuna tartare.

LE COCO D'ISLE

PK 27; tel. 87 21 22 94; www.facebook.com/ SnackCocoDIsle; 6pm-9pm Mon.-Sat.; CFP 2,000-3,000

Le Coco d'Isle has an island flair, with its bamboo walls and sand floors. Each dish is artfully plated, which makes it worth dining in rather than getting your order takeaway. Seafood is its specialty, with poisson cru served three ways, tuna both raw and grilled, shrimp, and platters ideal for groups. There's a free shuttle service available if booked in advance.

RESTAURANT TIAHURA

PK 25.5; tel. 87 23 34 89; 10am-2pm and 5:30pm-8pm Tues.-Sat.; CFP 2,200-3,500

Restaurant Tiahura is a casual seafood restaurant decorated with Polynesian artwork and decor. Try their shrimp curry with coconut milk or plate of tuna served three ways. If you're traveling as a duo, your best bet is to split the tuna platter for two served with warm coconut bread. While their menu features beef and chicken, it is best to stick to the seafood side.

SOUTHERN MOOREA
Quick Bites
BANH-MI & CO BY MOZZIE

PK 2; tel. 87 35 48 79; facebook.com/poihere.pf; 10:30am-1:30pm Mon.-Fri.; CFP 600

This vibrant yellow food truck doles out scrumptious sandwiches stuffed with fish, tofu, or beef. You can also get a pile of noodles topped with vegetables and beef or tofu, lemon chicken served with rice, and a range of desserts like waffles drizzled in chocolate sauce. The owners are cheerful and happy to modify any sandwich with ingredients they have on hand.

SNACK AUTEA

PK 18; tel. 89 76 90 40; 11am-1:30pm and 5:30pm-8:30pm Mon.-Sat., 11am-1:30pm Sun.; CFP 1,500

Snack Autea is a popular lunch spot with locals that serves fresh seafood—white and red tuna being mainstays on the menu. You can get poisson cru, spring rolls and samosas stuffed with fish, smoked tuna, and fries and simple salads.

Accommodations

NORTHEAST MOOREA
Under CFP 30,000
FARE LAGOON

PK 6; tel. 87 74 47 37; farelagoon@gmail.com; CFP 10,000/room

If you're after seaside tranquility, you'll find it at Fare Lagoon. This quiet pension has three double rooms, available for rent on a per-room basis or as a full villa. Guests have access to a kitchen, lounge area, terrace, TV, internet, and kayaks. Each room has a fan. Above-par reefs for snorkeling are found just in front of the property, and are rarely crowded with other guests. The host, Myriam, is helpful and attentive without being overbearing.

HAERE MAI I TE FARE

PK 3.5; tel. 87 71 48 25; CFP 10,000-13,000/room

Haere Mai I Te Fare is a family-owned and -managed guesthouse in a neighborhood near the ferry terminal. Chickens and friendly dogs putter around the property. A large open-air dining room on the ground floor welcomes

Pineapple Paradise

One of the best ways to explore unpaved Pineapple Road is on a day tour.

Moorea is French Polynesia's pineapple paradise: around 80 percent of all cultivated land on the island is dedicated to growing this fragrant fruit. The rich volcanic soil and humid climate creates the ideal environment for pineapple perfection. Throughout Moorea, you'll spot rows of spiky plants with pineapples plopped in their centers, growing until they're large enough to harvest. Because pineapples take around 1-2 years to mature, farmers plant them in monthly phases.

During the colonial era, pineapples were seen as the ultimate status symbol—a fruit from a faraway land too perishable to grow at scale in a greenhouse. Only the richest members of society could afford to eat them, and serving a pineapple to a guest was seen as an honor. Pineapple motifs exploded throughout Europe and North America as a symbol of wealth and hospitality.

On today's Moorea, you don't have to be a member of the elite to enjoy pineapple in all its wonderful forms, such as:

- chilled pineapple bubbly from **Manutea Tahiti Distillery** (page 97).

- a drive along **Rue des Ananas,** called "Pineapple Road," to see the pineapple plantations (page 99).

- pineapple salad with fresh vegetables and pesto at **Lilikoi Garden Café** (page 120).

- pineapple sorbet and homemade pineapple jam from **Tropical Garden Moorea** (page 120).

- and of course, slices of freshly picked pineapple sold at produce stands along the coastal road.

guests during mealtimes, and it's worth spending at least a dinner here. A large family room on the second floor can sleep up to four people, and a large balcony makes you feel like you're staying inside a treehouse. Double rooms are also available. Finding the property can be an initial challenge—it's at the end of a dirt road near the small bridge next to the large green building in Teavaro.

CFP 30,000-60,000
GREEN LODGE MOOREA

PK 3; tel. 40 56 31 00; greenlodgemoorea.com; CFP 20,000-40,000/room

A seaside guesthouse near the airport, Green Lodge Moorea's five thatched-roof bungalows and main lodge offer a quiet retreat (in between plane landings). Hang out at the pool, play billiards, and down ice-cold Hinano beers at the bar in between outings. Each room is outfitted with air-conditioning, a fan, internet, a safe, mini-fridge, and kettle. Only kids over age seven are allowed to stay.

POERANI MOOREA ✗

PK 5; tel. 87 37 38 39; www.poerani-moorea.com; CFP 45,000/room

Book your room directly with Poerani Moorea, a guesthouse with dated but spotless bungalows set among immaculately kept gardens, for the best price. Accommodation options range from two- to six-person villas and double rooms with a shared bathroom and kitchen. Each has a full kitchen, air-conditioning, and terrace. Some of Moorea's best snorkeling is found in front of the property. The shops of Maharepa are about a 10-minute walk away. Rates can be negotiated for long stays.

Over CFP 60,000
★ SOFITEL KIA ORA MOOREA BEACH RESORT

PK 1.3; tel. 40 55 12 12; www.sofitel-moorea-kiaora. com; CFP 60,000/room

Sofitel Kia Ora Moorea Beach Resort is a luxury retreat set on a white sand beach with over 120 overwater bungalows perched above turquoise water. Wooden walls, thatched roofing, and swim decks on each bungalow make it a home base for relaxation and adventure. Inside, each room is minimally decorated and spacious. Groups might prefer the beachside villa with a Jacuzzi, two bedrooms, and a living room that can sleep up to eight people. Two on-site restaurants, beach bars, a spa, a pool, and a sports center make it easy to check in without seeing much else of Moorea during your stay.

COOK'S BAY
Under CFP 30,000
PAINAPAOPAO BACKPACKER

PK 13.1; tel. 87 22 86 24; www.painapaopao.com; 3,000 CFP/dorm bed; 8,000 CFP/room

Solo travelers and those looking to make adventure buddies should check into Painapaopao Backpacker, a spacious hostel with two private double rooms and a six-bed dormitory. Each private room has a double bed, fan, private bathroom with hot water shower, and covered terrace. Every bed in the dormitory has a lamp, power socket, fan, and safe. All guests have access to WiFi, a shared kitchen, and shared bathroom. Because French Polynesia is primarily visited by traveling couples, it's one of the few places on the island to meet friend groups and solo travelers.

★ VILLAGE TEMANOHA

Inland from Super U Are near PK 10; tel. 87 21 55 92; villagetemanoha.com; CFP 14,000/room

While most of Moorea's accommodations are found along its coastline, Village Temanoha is a forest retreat hidden inland in Paopao Valley and best accessed with a personal car. The property is surrounded by fruit trees, tropical foliage, and bamboo. Each bungalow can sleep up to five people and has a private kitchen, bathroom, terrace, and elevated views of the valley—none are equipped with air-conditioning. A pool and lounge deck makes it easy to relax after a big day out. The family who owns the property is usually on-site, happy to help arrange tours and transport for those who need it.

CFP 30,000-60,000
★ HOTEL MANAVA BEACH RESORT AND SPA

PK 5.5; tel. 40 55 17 50; www.manavamoorearesort. com; CFP 46,000-82,000/room

Hotel Manava Beach Resort and Spa is a four-star resort within walking distance of the main shops of Maharepa. If you're set on

---

1: Hotel Manava Beach Resort and Spa **2:** Sofitel Kia Ora Moorea Beach Resort

ing over the water, the overwater bun- are on the more affordable end com- other resorts in the region. Guests greeted with a spacious lobby that leads to a dining room and poolside bar, where staff often host activities like flower-crown-making and palm-leaf weaving. Spend your day soaking in the pool, lounging under a beach umbrella, or paddling the calm waters surrounding the resort. Unlike most resorts with overwater bungalows in French Polynesia, there's worthwhile snorkeling around Manava. Overwater bungalows feature a glass-bottom table looking through to the reef below, a deck, couch, and mini-bar.

OPUNOHU BAY
CFP 30,000-60,000
ROBINSON'S COVE VILLAS

PK 16.5; www.robinsoncove.villas; CFP 40,000/room
Escape from the big city and become a castaway on a desert island—that's the dream, isn't it? At Robinson's Cove Villas, you can live your real Robinson Crusoe fantasies without any of the inconveniences that come with being left to fend for yourself. The ocean-front villas at this beach resort are equipped with hot water showers (outdoor and indoor), air-conditioning, kitchen and laundry facilities, and WiFi, and some have entertainment systems. Guests have access to a sandy beach, snorkel spots, and views across Opunohu Bay from the front of the property. All villas have ocean access.

Over CFP 60,000
HILTON MOOREA LAGOON RESORT AND SPA

PK 14; tel. 40 55 11 11; www.hilton.com; CFP 60,000/room
The Hilton Moorea Lagoon Resort and Spa has a triton of overwater bungalows jutting out into Moorea's lagoon, with garden bungalows set near a white sand beach. The 104 rooms vary in size and view, with some having private plunge pools. Of the overwater bungalows, those at the end of each path offer the most privacy, while those facing Moorea

have striking views of the island's skyline. The resort also has an overwater restaurant and bar, pool, spa, tennis court, and hosted recreational activities. Kids up to age 11 can stay free in their parents' room.

HAURU POINT AND AROUND
Under CFP 30,000
LA MAISON ORANGE

PK 24.5; tel. 87 37 72 72; locationmaison@gmail.com; CFP 12,000/room
La Maison Orange is a guesthouse owned and managed by one of the most entrepreneurial families on Moorea who have a range of electric bikes, scooters, and cars to rent as well as an on-site pearl shop. Rooms are equipped with WiFi and air-conditioning. Some have en suite bathrooms, and there are a few family-friendly rooms available that can sleep up to four people. All guests have access to a spacious sun deck, kitchen, and lounge area with an entertainment system. The orange house is not in the most central or scenic location, but it's clean and ideal for travelers who plan to be out on excursions for most of the day.

HOTEL LES TIPANIERS

PK 26; tel. 40 56 12 67; lestipaniers.com; CFP 19,000-27,000/bungalow, CFP 10,000/room
An obvious hub for ocean adventures, Hotel Les Tipaniers is a mid-range resort found on its namesake beach. The hotel has a mix-and-match situation when it comes to bungalow amenities and sleeping arrangements. The newer bungalows, called Vanilla Api, have two bedrooms that can sleep up to six guests, air-conditioning, and a miniature kitchen (CFP 25,000-27,000/bungalow). Standard bungalows can sleep up to four guests and have a fan and fridge only (CFP 19,000-23,000/bungalow). Others have a kitchen but no air-conditioning (CFP 19,000-23,000/bungalow). Rooms attached to the main building have a fan, fridge, and private balcony starting from CFP 10,000 per room. It's best to book directly with the hotel to avoid any confusion. The property has two on-site restaurants, and

access to an activity rental center, dive shop, and the Les Tipaniers Beach pier.

MOOREA ISLAND BEACH HOTEL

PK 27.5; tel. 87 74 33 07; mooreaislandbeach.com; CFP 25,000-40,000/room

Set on a thin strip of cookie-crumb sand, Moorea Island Beach Hotel is a boutique hotel with 12 two-person bungalows and a two-room family bungalow. All have a private bathroom, air-conditioning, and internet access. The property also has a handful of kayaks for exploring nearby motu. Bikes are available for guest use. There's also a communal lounge terrace that serves breakfast each morning (CFP 2,500 extra), with a kitchen that is open for guest use during lunch and dinner.

CFP 30,000-60,000
HOTEL FENUA MATA'I'OA

PK 25.5; tel. 40 55 00 25; www.fenua-mataioa.com; CFP 30,000/room

Hidden on a quiet beach, Hotel Fenua Mata'i'oa is a boutique hotel with five spacious rooms decorated with Polynesian artwork and antique furnishings, a nice change from chain hotel decor. No two rooms are alike; some are set in a garden with tropical flowers while others are directly on the water's edge. Small touches like a welcome cocktail and flower necklace help set the scene for relaxation. Meals are priced higher than average here, so be sure to request a quote before you reserve a table.

MOOREA SUNSET BEACH HOTEL

PK 26; tel. 40 55 00 00; mooreasunsetbeach.com; CFP 30,000/room

Moorea Sunset Beach Hotel is one of the best resorts for groups, as all bungalows and suites can sleep a minimum of four people and maximum of six people. Both bungalows and suites are set on manicured gardens with a grass lawn separating the front door from the lagoon. Each unit comes with a kitchen, lounge area, terrace, laundry facilities, air-conditioning, and private bathroom.

SOUTHERN MOOREA
Under CFP 30,000
MOOREA SURF INN

PK 20; tel. 87 70 80 29; www.facebook.com/mooreasurfinn; CFP 15,000/room

Moorea Surf Inn is one of the few accommodations with easy access to Haapiti surf spot, which is why most of its guests usually check in with a surfboard underarm. Guests can rent a surfboard (CFP 5,000) and catch a ride to the wave with Tama, the owner. Or, borrow a kayak to paddle out. Bungalows are simply furnished with a bed, wardrobe, and fan. All have internet access. The kitchen and bathrooms are shared with other guests. Come evening, most guests gather on the lounge deck, where there's a small take-one leave-one library and TV. If the surf is flat, the inn also has mountain bikes, cruiser bikes, snorkeling gear, and stand-up paddleboards for rent.

★ LINAREVA MOOREA BEACH RESORT

PK 32; tel. 40 55 05 65; linareva.com; CFP 17,500-27,500/room

Linareva Moorea Beach Resort is ideal for travelers who prefer rustic, remote accommodation and surfers who want easy access to the wave of Haapiti. The resort is made up of bungalows that can sleep up to two people, studios for up to four people, and villas that can sleep up to six people. All are within a short walk to the ocean, with a few having direct beach access. Each option has air-conditioning, TV, and a safe. Most rooms have access to a full kitchen or a kitchenette in the room.

Information and Services

VISITORS CENTERS

Tourist Office: PK 9 (Cook's Bay); tel. 40 56 50 55; mooreatourism.com; 8am-4pm Mon.-Fri. This tourism office is well-stocked with brochures and friendly staff who are happy to assist with tour bookings and provide transportation information.

SERVICES

- **OPT Post Office:** PK 5.5 (Maharepa); tel. 40 56 27 00; 8am-4pm Mon.-Fri.

- **Laveria Laundry:** PK 6 (Maharepa, light blue house with "Laveria" sign); tel. 70 44 65; 10am-3pm Mon.-Fri.

BANKS

- **Banque de Tahiti:** PK 6 (Maharepa); tel. 40 55 00 55; www.banque-tahiti.pf; 8am-noon and 1pm-4pm Mon.-Fri.

- **Banque de Polynesie:** PK 6 (Maharepa); tel. 40 55 05 08; www.sg-bdp.pf; 7:45am-noon and 1pm-4:30pm Mon.-Fri.

- **Banque Socredo:** PK 6 (Maharepa); tel. 40 47 00 00; socredo.pf; 7:45am-11:45am and 1pm-3:30pm Mon.-Fri.

HEALTH AND SAFETY

- **Pharmacie Moorea:** PK 6.5 (Maharepa); tel. 40 55 20 75; 7am-12:15pm and 2pm-6pm daily

- **Pharmacie Haapiti:** PK 27 (Haapiti); tel. 40 56 41 16; 8am-12:30pm and 3pm-6pm Mon.-Sat., 9am-11am Sun.

- **Pharmacie Afareaitu:** PK 8.7 (Afareaitu); tel. 40 56 35 47; 6:30am-6:30pm Mon.-Fri., 7:30am-1:30pm Sat., 7:30am-11:30am Sun.

- **Hospital Moorea:** PK 9 (Afareaitu); tel. 40 55 22 22; annuaire.moorea-actu.com; 24 hours daily

- **Gendarmerie (Police Station):** PK 10 (Paopao); tel. 89 55 25 05; lannuaire.service-public.fr; 7am-noon and 2pm-6pm Mon.-Sat., 9am-noon and 3pm-6pm Sun.

Transportation

GETTING THERE

You can reach Moorea by sky and sea, and it's the closest major island to Tahiti. When you account for the check-in time at the airport, venturing to Moorea by plane is only slightly faster than getting there by ferry, but is usually twice as expensive. Take the plane if you want to see Moorea from above; otherwise, the ferry offers a more relaxed experience.

Air

Air Tahiti (tel. 40 55 06 00; www.airtahiti.com; reservation@airtahiti.pf) has direct flights between Moorea and Papeete (15 minutes, CFP 8,039/one-way), Bora Bora (50 minutes, CFP 26,639/one-way), Raiatea (45 minutes, CFP 19,039/one-way), and Huahine (35 minutes, CFP 19,039/one-way). A stop in Moorea is included in the following Air Tahiti Multi-Islands Passes: Discovery Pass, Bora Bora Pass, Lagoons Pass, and Bora-Tuamotu Pass. For the best views, sit on the left side of the aircraft on the way to Moorea from Papeete. Flights to Moorea are open seating.

MOOREA TEMAE AIRPORT

PK 0; tel. 40 55 06 00

Moorea Temae Airport (MOZ) is in the northeast corner of the island. Shuttle service from the airport should be arranged in advance through your accommodation or day tour. Taxi drivers wait at the arrivals area to pick up stray travelers, though they may not be there for every flight. Avis and Albert Transport have counters for car hire, but vehicles are limited and it's essential to reserve beforehand. There are two small souvenir shops and a café inside the airport.

Ferry
VAIARE WHARF
PK 4

The convenient ferry ride between Moorea and Tahiti is a scenic and economical way to get between the islands. If you're lucky, you may spot whales and dolphins during your journey. Two types of ferries complete this trip: fast ferries carrying mostly walk-on commuters (30 minutes) and large car ferries with capacity for foot-passengers and vehicles (45 minutes). Ferries to Moorea depart from the Papeete Ferry Terminal and arrive at Vaiare Wharf (PK 4) on the eastern side of Moorea.

Aremiti (tel. 40 56 31 10; www.aremiti. pf) has offices at the Papeete Ferry Terminal (5am-5:30pm Mon.-Thurs., 5am-5:45pm Fri., 6am-12:30pm, 1:30pm-2:15pm, 4:45pm-5:30pm Sat., 6am-9am, 1:45pm-2:30pm, 2pm-6pm Sun.) and Vaiare Wharf (4:30am-5pm Mon.-Thurs., 4:30am-6:45pm Fri., 5:30am-12:30pm, 3:30pm-5:30pm Sat., 5:30am-7:45am, 12:30pm-6:45pm Sun.). Current timetables are posted on their website, where you can also reserve tickets. Ferries run regularly between 5:50am-5pm on weekdays, and between 7am-6:45pm on weekends. While you can typically buy tickets to walk onto the ferry at the terminal, it's recommended to book vehicle space in advance, especially on weekends. Trips cost CFP 1,500 each way for adults, 950 CFP for children, 1,000 CFP for passengers over age 60, and children under two years old ride for free. Bicycles cost 250 CFP, motorbikes cost 1,000 CFP, and vehicles cost between CFP 4,330-9,800 depending on the size. A round-trip ticket for a family of two adults, two children, and one vehicle is available from CFP 12,990-14,990.

Terevau (tel. 40 50 03 59; www.terevau. pf) offers six departures between Papeete and Moorea from 5:50am-5:45pm on weekdays, and five departures from 6am-6pm on weekends, with current schedules posted on the Terevau website. The ferry can carry up to 360 passengers and 10 vehicles, with vehicle space selling out quickly on weekends. A one-way ticket costs CFP 1,160 per adult, CFP 580 per child, and CFP 950 for passengers over 60. Motorbikes cost CFP 1,100, bicycles cost CFP 250, and vehicles cost between CFP 4,350-9,850 depending on the size.

GETTING AROUND

To get around Moorea, it's best to rent a car, scooter, or bicycle, or take a bus tour. The public buses serving Moorea are unreliable, and hitchhiking is less common than it used to be due to the pandemic. Few parts of the road have sidewalks, and the cars roaring around the island make walking an unpleasant experience.

That said, many land and lagoon tour operators offer transportation to and from your accommodation, and restaurants also offer rides by private shuttle van to and from their venue, so you can still sightsee without renting a car. If you want to see all the major sights with added commentary and little stress, it's best to book a day tour.

Public Transport

Buses await the ferries from Tahiti at Vaiare Wharf. Although they don't go around the entire island, the **northern and southern bus routes** meet at Le Petit Village (Small Village Bus Station; 5am-4:45pm daily; CFP 300/adult; CFP 150/child), so you could theoretically lap Moorea by changing buses there, catching the last service back to Vaiare from Le Petit Village. You should have no problem finding a seat when you arrive on Moorea from Tahiti by ferry, but be quick to jump aboard. Buses are timed around the Aremiti ferry departure and arrivals. Buses marked "uta ra a tamarii" are for schoolchildren only.

Car

Having your own set of wheels is the best way to get around Moorea and can be more economical than taking taxis. There are a handful of car rental companies on the island, though you might want to weigh the costs of bringing a vehicle over from Papeete onboard the ferry, as it can often be much cheaper than renting on Moorea. If you prefer automatic transmission, it's best to book well in advance. **Avis** (tel. 89 40 10 75; avis-tahiti.com; 6:30am-5pm Mon.-Fri., 7:30am-4pm Sat.-Sun.; from CFP 12,000/day) has a main office at Vaiare Wharf and offers a pickup service from Moorea Temae Airport. **Europcar** (tel. 40 56 28 64; europcar.com; 6am-6pm daily; from CFP 12,000/day) also has an office at Vaiare Wharf. **Albert Transport** (tel. 40 55 21 10; albert-transport.net; 7:30am-5pm daily; from CFP 10,000/day) rents cars and scooters, and offers a shuttle service.

There are five **gasoline stations** around Moorea: Mobil is beside Champion one kilometer (0.6 mi) south of Vaiare Wharf, Shell is opposite Vaiare Wharf, Total is at the airport access road, another Mobil is near Paopao,

and another Total is at Le Petit Village. The maximum speed limit on Moorea is 60 kilometers per hour (about 37 mph).

Taxi

Taxis can be arranged through your accommodation, and there is a stand at the airport (6am-6pm daily), but they're one of the most expensive forms of transport on the island. Fares start at CFP 800 and cost around CFP 200 per mile. A 30-minute ride from the airport will cost around CFP 4,000. Taxis are marked by a letter T inside a circle. For a reliable driver, contact **Mareva Jamie** (tel. 87 28 65 54; mareva.jamie@gmail.com).

Scooter, Bicycle, and Roadster

Because the main road circling Moorea's coastline is well-maintained and rarely crowded, it's fun and affordable to get around by scooter, roadster, or bicycle, but only if the weather is clear. On rainy days, the roads get slippery. **Moorea Fun Roadster** (PK 26; tel. 87 25 60 70; www.mooreafunroadster.com; CFP 15,000/4 hours, CFP 19,500/8

The easiest way to get around Moorea is with your own car.

hours, CFP 25,000/24 hours) rents open-air two-seater buggies that are fun to drive under blue skies. **Moorea Fun Bike** (PK 6.7 Kikipa Center; tel. 87 70 96 95; moorea-fun-bike@ hotmail.fr; CFP 5,000/day) rents a range of 50- to 125-cc motorbikes. **Rent a Bike and Scooter** (Haapiti; tel. 87 71 11 09; rent-a-bike-moorea.e-monsite.com) has mountain bikes (CFP 2,000/day), e-bikes (CFP 4,500/8 hours), and scooters for rent (CFP 5,500/day), with free delivery to and pickup from your accommodation.

Local Tours
ATV MOOREA TOURS
PK 24.6; tel. 87 70 73 45; www.atvmooreatours.com; 7am-5pm daily; CFP 15,000-22,000/tour

Drive around the island long enough and you're bound to spot a caravan of brightly painted ATVs roaring down the road. And while having your own rental car is comfortable on the tarmac, some of Moorea's best sights, like Magic Mountain and Rue des Ananas, also known as "Pineapple Road," require more heft to get to. ATV Moorea Tours offers half-day tours (CFP 15,000) to Belvedere and Opunohu Valley via off-road trails. A full-day tour (CFP 22,000) extends to Papetoai and Magic Mountain. All drivers must have a driver's license and be 18 years old. If you're a solo traveler without a license, ask if you can sit behind the guide.

FRANCKYFRANCK MOOREA TOURS
tel. 87 76 40 28; www.franckyfranck-mooreatours. com; 7am-4pm daily; CFP 5,000/adult, CFP 2,500/ child

Franck, owner of Franckyfranck Moorea Tours, is one of the most entertaining tour guides in French Polynesia. He has a way of weaving in information about the island between jokes that are bit risqué—so he may not be the best choice for bashful travelers. On his 3.5-hour tour, admire Moorea from Belvedere and visit a vanilla plantation and fruit garden where you can sample local fruits, marmalades, sorbet, and ice cream. He'll be your designated driver at Manutea Tahiti Distillery, Magic Mountain, and the bumpy pineapple road. Tours are done in the back of a 4WD truck, and transport to and from your accommodation is included.

Bora Bora and the Leeward Islands

The Leeward Islands, the western cluster of the Society Islands, is made up of a handful of islands often connected by sandy lagoons and coral reefs. Each of the islets offers a sense of discovery and relaxation, and the region hosts vivid color palettes that a camera can't capture. Sand-bottom lagoons create an electric blue hue that connects to a deep cobalt sea. Sunrises and sunsets only add to the islands' allure.

The sweetheart of the Leeward Islands, Bora Bora is undoubtedly one of the most romantic places in French Polynesia. With thatched-roof bungalows lingering over the water, private white sand beaches, and a developed tourism scene dedicated to making worries disappear, it's easy to fall in love on—and with—Bora Bora. Activities like snorkeling, scuba

Highlights

Look for ★ to find recommended sights, activities, dining, and lodging.

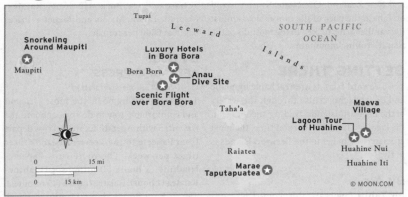

★ **Anau Dive Site:** Scuba dive with manta rays and watch them glide and twirl like underwater acrobats at this dive and snorkel site inside Bora Bora's lagoon (page 148).

★ **Scenic flight over Bora Bora:** Discover blue hues you've never seen before on a tour over Bora Bora's iconic lagoon (page 153).

★ **Luxury hotels in Bora Bora:** Enjoy spa treatments, beachside cocktails, and sunbathing on the deck of your private overwater bungalow (page 160).

★ **Maeva Village:** This archeological village on Huahine with sacred ceremonial sites and ancient fish traps provides a look at Polynesia's past (page 170).

★ **Lagoon tour of Huahine:** Swim with stingrays and reef sharks, visit a pearl farm, and then relax for a picnic lunch on a white sand motu (page 176).

★ **Marae Taputapuatea:** Raiatea's UNESCO World Heritage site is an archeological wonder (page 191).

★ **Snorkeling around Maupiti:** Explore the vibrant lagoon around Maupiti, taking breaks on its sandy motu (page 207).

diving, hiking, and cycling excursions ensure that the relationship never hits a lull. Though there are luxury resorts, spa treatments, and fine dining venues in spades, an uptick in guesthouses and affordable adventure activities means that it's no longer impossible to visit Bora Bora on a budget.

Slow living is the sentiment elsewhere on the Leeward Islands, where you can catch a glimpse of what life was like before French Polynesia's islands became the go-to image for computer screensavers. On Huahine, travelers are privy to one of French Polynesia's most underrated secrets as a land rich with archeology sites. And if that isn't enough, Raiatea is home to a UNESCO World Heritage Site, the Taputapuatea marae. Raiatea is hailed as the most sacred island in the region, as it was the first place Polynesian explorers touched land before moving further afield to Hawaii and New Zealand. On Raiatea's sister island of Taha'a, the pace of life moves slow amidst the vanilla farms tucked in the foothills of the island's rolling mountains.

GETTING THERE

The Leeward Islands are reachable by plane and boat. Yachts cruise through the waters of the Leeward Islands, finding anchorage in the lagoons. If you're short on time, the most efficient way to get to the Leeward Islands is to fly.

By Air

Air Tahiti (www.airtahiti.com) flies non-stop from Papeete and Moorea to Huahine, Raiatea, and Bora Bora, and from Papeete, Raiatea, and Bora Bora to Maupiti. The longest flight, from Papeete to Maupiti with a stop in Raiatea, is under two hours. Most flights are under 45 minutes.

You can island-hop throughout the Leeward Islands on the Air Tahiti Airpass:

• **Discovery Pass:** Tahiti to Moorea, Huahine, and Raiatea (€332 low season/€357 high season)

• **Bora Bora Pass:** Tahiti to Moorea, Huahine, Taiatea, Bora Bora, and Maupiti (€435 low season/€469 high season)

• **Bora-Tuamotu Pass:** Tahiti to Moorea, Huahine, Raiatea, Maupiti, Bora Bora, Rangiroa, Tikehau, and Fakarava (€584 low season/€632 high season)

High season runs from June 1-October 31 and December 11-January 10.

Tahiti Air Charter (tel. 40 50 54 86; tac.pf) flies to Raiatea, Maupiti, and Bora Bora in Cessna 208 aircraft that can seat up to seven passengers. Prices range CFP 15,800-17,900 one-way.

Tahiti Nui Helicopters (tel. 87 77 72 56; www.tahitinuihelicopters.com) runs inter-island transfers between Tahiti, Moorea, Tetiaroa, Bora Bora, Huahine, Raiatea, Maupiti, Taha'a, Maiao, and Mehetia. Prices begin at €800 per transfer.

By Boat
APETAHI EXPRESS

tel. 40 50 54 59; apetahiexpress.pf

To get around by boat, the most efficient and comfortable way to do so is onboard the *Aremiti 5* with Apetahi Express. Trips depart from Papeete to the Leeward Islands three times per week. The route runs Papeete-Huahine (3 hours 50 minutes), Huahine-Raiatea (1 hour), Raiatea-Taha'a (45 minutes), Taha'a-Bora Bora (1 hour 15 minutes) with a 20-minute stop on each island. The catamaran runs from **Tahiti to Bora Bora** on Wednesdays, Fridays, and Sundays. The **Bora Bora to Tahiti** route runs on Mondays, Thursdays, and Saturdays. Find the latest schedule on their website.

An unlimited 31-day pass to all six islands is CFP 23,900 per person. A pass for four islands (Huahine, Raiatea, Taha'a, and Bora Bora) is CFP 17,900 per person. Each passenger

---

Previous: The clear waters of Taha'a have some of the Society Islands' best snorkeling; handmade pareu in Huahine; Bora Bora Airport.

is entitled to two bags of up to 23 kilograms (about 50 lbs) each plus a 10-kilogram (about 22-lb) carry-on. Surfboards, additional baggage, bikes, pets, and canoes can also come onboard for extra cost (CFP 1,000-2,000 per item).

CARGO SHIPS
There are also two older cargo ships that venture to the Leeward Islands, the **MV Taporo VII** and the **MV Hawaiki-Nui** from Papeete (Motu Uta wharf). Northbound, the *MV Taporo VII* leaves Papeete Tuesday and Thursday; southbound it leaves Bora Bora Wednesday and Friday. The *MV Hawaiki-Nui* also departs Papeete for Huahine, Raiatea, and Bora Bora on Tuesday and Thursday. Southbound, the *Hawaiki-Nui* leaves Bora Bora Wednesday and Friday. The *Aremiti 5* is more comfortable and reliable than either of these options.

TAHITI YACHT CHARTER
Apooiti Marina, Raiatea; tel. 40 66 28 80;
tahitiyachtcharter.com
Tahiti Yacht Charter is a yacht charter company based in Raiatea with a range of catamaran sailing yachts. Experienced sailors can bareboat charter or charter a yacht with a full crew and skipper. A week-long sailing trip starts at €4,000 (without skipper) or €5,500 (with skipper) for a 36-foot catamaran sleeping 6-8 people. Trips venture all around the Leeward Islands.

MAUPITI EXPRESS 2
The 20-meter fast ferry *Maupiti Express 2* shuttles between Bora Bora and Maupiti, Taha 'a, and Raiatea three or four times a week. The boat leaves Bora Bora for Taha'a (80 minutes) and Raiatea (95 minutes) Monday, Wednesday, Friday, and Sunday. The ferry leaves Bora Bora for Maupiti Tuesday, Thursday, and Saturday. The 140 passengers have a choice of sitting in an air-conditioned salon or standing on the open upper deck.

GETTING AROUND
Four-wheel-drive tours are offered on all the main islands, and these are cheaper than renting a car. There are also sightseeing tours by outrigger canoe or motorboat with snorkeling included.

Car
Renting a car will give you the largest sense of freedom on some of the larger islands like

Luxury resorts offer a pickup service from Bora Bora Airport.

Bora Bora and the Leeward Islands

Tupai

Leeward

SEE
"MAUPITI"
MAP

SNORKELING
AROUND MAUPITI

Maupiti

SEE
"BORA BORA"
MAP

LUXURY HOTELS
IN BORA BORA

Bora Bora

ANAU
DIVE SITE

Vaitape

SCENIC FLIGHT
OVER BORA BORA

SOUTH PACIFIC OCEAN

0   10 mi

0   10 km

SOUTH PACIFIC OCEAN

Islands

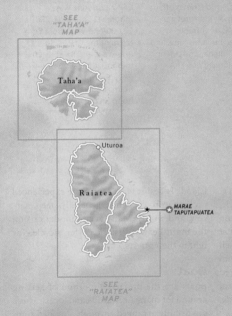

SEE
"TAHA'A"
MAP

Taha'a

○ Uturoa

Raiatea

★ ⊕ *MARAE
TAPUTAPUATEA*

SEE
"RAIATEA"
MAP

*MAEVA
VILLAGE* ⊕

*LAGOON TOUR
OF HUAHINE* ⊕ ○ Fare

Huahine Nui

Huahine Iti

SEE
"HUAHINE"
MAP

© MOON.COM

Bora Bora and the Leeward Islands at a Glance

Island	Why Go	How to Get There
Bora Bora (page 143)	Experience paradisical luxury in overwater bungalows, watch manta rays glide around the lagoon, and lounge on palm-fringed beaches on this famous island.	*Air:* From Tahiti (45 minutes, CFP 25,800/one-way), Moorea (45 minutes, CFP 26,000/one-way), Huahine (25 minutes, 11,700/one-way), Maupiti (20 minutes, CFP 9,7000), Raiatea (20 minutes, CFP 9,500/one-way), and Rangiroa (1 hour 15 minutes, CFP 37,000/one-way). *Ferry:* From Tahiti, Huahine, Raiatea, Taha'a on the *Aremiti 5* and from Maupiti, Taha'a, and Raiatea on the *Maupiti Express 2.*
Huahine (page 166)	Huahine stands out for its lagoon, which shows off the island's lush greenery, as well as its vibrant underwater landscape, and Maeva Village, a fascinating archeological site.	*Air:* From Tahiti (40 minutes, CFP 21,300/one way), Moorea (35 minutes, CFP 22,000/one-way), Bora Bora (25 minutes, CFP 14,500/one-way), and Raiatea (20 minutes, CFP 9,500/one-way). *Ferry:* From Tahiti (4 hours) and Raiatea (1 hour) on the *Aremiti 5.*

Huahine, Raiatea, Bora Bora, and Taha'a. Maupiti can be covered on foot or by bicycle. The larger islands all have cars for rent—if you prefer an automatic, you'll want to book it at least a month in advance as they tend to sell out quickly. Almost all vehicles are manual and come with insurance. Roads are paved and well-maintained for the most part. Expect to pay at least CFP 10,000 per day for a vehicle.

Bike

You can bring your own bicycle over to the Leeward Islands onboard the *Aremiti 5.* Otherwise, it's usually easy to rent a bike from a stand or from your accommodation to get around. Long-distance cycling around the

islands is best reserved for more experienced cyclists, as roads can be generally steep, narrow, and windy. Many accommodations on the main Leeward Islands offer bicycles for rent to their guests.

Boat

Boats are the preferred method of getting around for many Leeward Island locals. These are usually arranged through a guided tour, with your accommodation, or as part of an informal charter with a resident boat owner.

ORIENTATION

The Leeward Islands are 80 kilometers (50 mi) northwest of Tahiti, starting with the closest

Island	Why Go	How to Get There
Raiatea (page 183)	Untouched dive sites, waters perfect for paddling, and an archeological UNESCO World Heritage site are among the attractions that draw intrepid travelers to Raiatea, though it's not a great island for beaches.	*Air:* From Tahiti (45 minutes), CFP 23,000/one-way), Bora Bora (20 minutes, CFP 10,000/one-way), Huahine (20 minutes, CFP 9,000/one-way, and Maupiti (25 minutes, CFP 12,000 one-way) *Ferry:* From Bora Bora (1 hour and 15 minutes) on *the Aremiti 5* or *Mauipiti Express 2*, Huahine (1 hour) via the *Aremiti 5*, and Taha'a (45 minutes) via the *Aremiti 5* and Enota Transport Maritime.
Taha'a (page 196)	Learn about vanilla growing on "vanilla island" where 70 percent of French Polynesia's Tahitian vanilla is produced. Sip vanilla spiced rum on the island and shop for prized Tahitian black pearls.	*Ferry:* From Bora Bora on the *Aremiti 5* and *Mauipiti Express 2* and from Raiatea via *Aremiti 5, Maupiti Express 2,* and Enota Transport Maritime.
Maupiti (page 204)	The least visited of the accessible Society islands, Maupiti enjoys quiet beaches, fresh fruits, and spectacularly clear waters that make for technicolor snorkeling.	*Air:* From Tahiti (50 minutes, CFP 25,000/one-way, Bora Bora (20 minutes, CFP 10,000/one-way), and Raiatea (25 minutes, CFP 10,900/one-way) *Ferry:* From Bora Bora on the *Maupiti Express 2*.

island of **Huahine. Raiatea** is 16 kilometers (10 mi) west of Huahine, with **Taha'a** 4 kilometers (2.5 mi) north of Raiatea, sharing Raiatea's lagoon. **Bora Bora** is 16 kilometers (10 mi) northwest of Taha'a, and the last main Leeward Island, **Maupiti,** is an outlier at 50 kilometers (31 mi) west of Bora Bora.

Two other Leeward Islands are not well-frequented by travelers. **Tupai,** or Motu Iti, which has no permanent residents or accommodations, is 16 kilometers (10 mi) north of Bora Bora. Tiny 360-hectare (889-acre) **Maupihaa** (Mopelia), 185 kilometers (115 mi) southeast of Maupiti, is the only Society Islands atoll that can be entered by yachts, but to attempt to do so in stormy weather is

dangerous. About 50 people from Maupiti live on Maupihaa.

PLANNING YOUR TIME

When to go? May through October is the cooler, less humid time, although prolonged rainfall is possible year-round. An optimum time to be there is for the **Heiva festival** on Huahine and Bora Bora in early July.

Most travelers choose one or two of the islands to spend most of their time, often with a few days on Tahiti or an island from another group, like the Tuamotus. If you can, it's worth trying to visit several of the islands, as they are all very different. Bora Bora and Maupiti have similar environments, but the former is three decades ahead of the latter in tourism development. Huahine has good facilities without the crowds often encountered on Bora Bora. Raiatea and Taha'a have larger local populations and are less dependent on tourism. Raiatea's craggy coastline is not the place to go for a beach vacation, but those interested in offbeat travel, culture, archeology, and diving will find plenty to do.

Three nights on **Bora Bora** gives you enough time for a trip around the island and a lagoon tour to see the sharks and rays. Every visitor should attend at least one **cultural show** at a fancy Bora Bora resort for the exciting tamure dancing and drumming. These happen several times a week, and it's often possible to avoid the high cost of the buffet by settling for a drink at the bar. If you have the time, make a two-night side trip from Bora Bora to unspoiled **Maupiti.**

Raiatea is worth a couple of nights to explore the island by rental car and to do a day trip to **Taha'a** by boat. The *Aremiti 5* ferry between Bora Bora and Raiatea makes it practical to do this leg by boat as well. **Huahine,** another jewel of the Leeward Islands, is worth at least a two-night trip as it has an interesting archeological site in Maeva Village, an easygoing main town, pearl farm, botanical garden, hiking trails, and beaches with prime snorkeling.

If you want to go to all five of the main Leeward Islands, about 10 days is enough to see the best of these islands, even if you decide to do part of your inter-island traveling by ferry. On all islands, **opening times** are often irregular. While some shops have hours posted on their doors, shopkeepers admit that they're merely guidelines—and you'll want to call ahead if obtaining an item is urgent.

Budgeting

There's no getting around the fact that travel here is expensive. Bora Bora is easily the most upscale tourist destination in French Polynesia, with over a dozen resorts charging more than US$400/double per night without meals. You can greatly reduce your costs if you book your top-end hotel rooms as part of a package tour or visit during the off-season. Another option is to stay in small, locally operated pensions. Bora Bora has hostels and pensions in the US$50-100 range; some allow camping. The other islands have fewer swanky resorts and more family-run pensions. Most visitors get around the islands by air, and you can save money by purchasing one of Air Tahiti's Multi Islands Air Pass or a monthly ticket on the *Aremiti 5* with Apetahi Express.

Itinerary Ideas

Most islands can be broken up into three days of activities: one day on the lagoon, one day exploring the island, and one day for lounging on a sandy beach. Plan your hikes, scuba diving and snorkeling trips, lagoon excursions, and any other activities that are weather-dependent at the beginning of your stay.

ONE DAY ON BORA BORA

It's easy to see the best of Bora Bora on a lagoon tour or quad tour, which will cover the main highlights on both land and sea. The following itinerary works best for a free day and allows for some time lounging under the sun.

1 Rent a vehicle to enjoy a day out on Bora Bora. Spend the morning shopping for pearls and clothing at the boutiques of Vaitape, and handicrafts at the **Centre Artisanal.**

2 Drive 7 kilometers (4.3 mi) south to Matira Beach and have lunch at **Bora Bora Beach Club,** a restaurant overlooking the vivid waters off Matira Beach.

3 For the second half of the day, stake out a space in the sand at **Matira Beach.** Swim, wade, and laze until you get thirsty.

4 Enjoy a therapeutic spa treatment at your resort or **InterContinental Le Moana Bora Bora,** found just next to Matira Beach. Then, head back to your room and relax until dinnertime.

5 For dinner, request pick-up service from **Restaurant Saint James** and enjoy an evening of impeccably mixed cocktails and French-Polynesian cuisine.

ONE-DAY ROAD TRIP ON HUAHINE

For this itinerary, you'll need your own set of wheels. Pack comfortable clothes and swimming attire.

1 Start your journey in **Maeva Village,** 7 kilometers (4.3 mi) east of Fare, and stop in at the Fare Pote'e Maeva Museum to learn about the many marae on Huahine, as well as the island's history.

2 Drive or walk 700 meters (0.4 mi) east along the road to see the ancient **fish traps** near the bridge of Maeva Village made from rock canals, a fishing technique still in use today.

3 Cross the bridge and drive 500 meters (0.3 mi) to **Marae Manunu,** a ceremonial space likely dedicated to the sea.

4 Venture 5 kilometers (3.1 mi) south along Huahine's eastern road to the town of Faie. In its river you'll find **sacred blue-eyed eels.**

5 Drive 17 kilometers (10.5 mi) south, stopping at a **viewpoint** overlooking **Maroe Bay** and crossing the bridge to Huahine Iti.

6 Dine on sandwiches and fresh coconut water at Hotel Le Mahana. The best beach on Huahine Iti, **Avea Beach,** is just a few steps away. Spend an hour or two snorkeling, swimming, or lounging before heading 18 kilometers (11 mi) north to Fare.

7 Arrive in Fare just before sunset to enjoy pink-hued skies. For dinner, walk to the **Huahine Yacht Club** for fresh seafood, cold drinks, and a lively atmosphere.

ONE DAY ON RAIATEA

1 Rent a vehicle the night before to embark on an early-morning road trip to **Marae Taputapuatea,** one of the most sacred archeological sites in all of Polynesia. Wear comfortable walking shoes and sun protection. If you'd like to see the marae from an elevated perspective, walk along the 1.5-kilometer (0.9-mi) out-and-back trail leading from the marae to a lookout platform; blue views of the lagoon await.

2 Drive 16 kilometers (10 mi) north to Faaroa Bay for a short stroll through the **Faaroa Botanical Garden,** a great place to stop for a drink and snack if you've brought them.

3 Venture 15 kilometers (9.3 mi) north by car to Raiatea's main town, Uturoa. Shop for souvenirs, fresh fruit, and perfectly baked pastries along the wharf at **Patisserie Bon Apetahi.**

4 Before sunset, drive 9 kilometers (5.5 mi) west to **Fish & Blue,** a seaside restaurant with a jetty idyllic for ending the day with a cold drink in hand. Their hearty dinners are some of the best on the island.

Itinerary Ideas

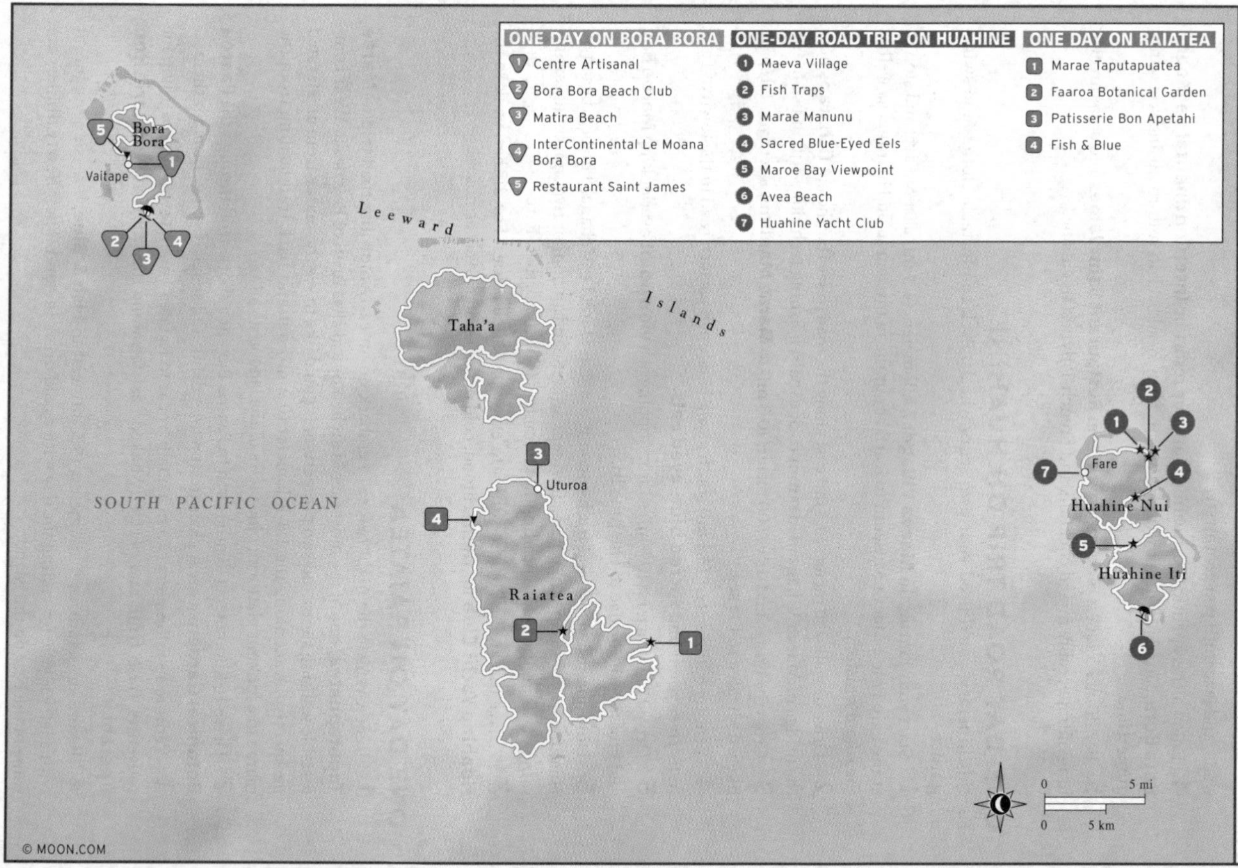

ONE DAY ON BORA BORA
1. Centre Artisanal
2. Bora Bora Beach Club
3. Matira Beach
4. InterContinental Le Moana Bora Bora
5. Restaurant Saint James

ONE-DAY ROAD TRIP ON HUAHINE
1. Maeva Village
2. Fish Traps
3. Marae Manunu
4. Sacred Blue-Eyed Eels
5. Maroe Bay Viewpoint
6. Avea Beach
7. Huahine Yacht Club

ONE DAY ON RAIATEA
1. Marae Taputapuatea
2. Faaroa Botanical Garden
3. Patisserie Bon Apetahi
4. Fish & Blue

Huahine Nui
Huahine Iti
Fare

Leeward Islands

Taha'a

Raiatea
Uturoa

Bora Bora
Vaitape

SOUTH PACIFIC OCEAN

5 mi
5 km

© MOON.COM

Bora Bora

There's no blue quite like the hue found in Bora Bora's lagoon. From the sky, it looks pastel. On the water, it's electric, changing like a chameleon depending on the sky overhead. Bora Bora has just Teavanui Pass linking the lagoon to the ocean, its barrier reef ringing around the emerald isle like a halo. Dramatic basalt peaks soar 700 meters (2,300 ft) into the sky; slopes and valleys blossom with hibiscus. Some of the most perfect beaches you'll ever see are found on its outer motu (islands), as well as the shores of the mainland. Beyond the beaches, there's no shortage of things to see and do. Scuba dive with sharks and manta rays, snorkel in the shallows, rumble along a dirt road in a quad, and grab cocktails at some of Polynesia's liveliest bars. Tourism is Bora Bora's main form of business, so if you've come to simply lounge on the deck of your overwater bungalow, only getting up to attend a spa appointment, there are plenty of resorts here for that, too. The sound "b" doesn't exist in Tahitian, so Bora Bora is pronounced Pora Pora, meaning "first born," as it was the first island created after Raiatea.

Orientation

Seven-million-year-old Bora Bora is made up of a 10-kilometer-long (6.2-mi-long) main island, a few smaller higher islands in the lagoon, and a long ring of motu on the barrier reef. **Pofai Bay** marks the center of the island's collapsed crater. Mount Pahia's gray basalt mass rises 649 meters (2,129 ft) behind Vaitape, and above it soar the sheer cliffs of Mount Otemanu's mighty volcanic plug (727 m/2,385 ft). Teavanui Pass, the sole pass in Bora Bora's barrier reef, is found on the western side of Bora Bora.

Flights arrive at Motu Mute airport, a small motu on the northern end of Bora Bora. A public ferry links the airport motu to the mainland, arriving in the small town of **Vaitape,** the capital of Bora Bora, on the west coast. If you need to obtain groceries or pharmacy items, it's best to do so in Vaitape before being whisked away elsewhere. Many of Bora Bora's five-star stays are on private islands ringing the island and require a resort shuttle to reach Bora Bora's mainland. Most of the stores, banks, and offices are near Vaitape Wharf. Moving clockwise, the village of **Faanui** on the north coast is mostly residential and was developed by Americans during WWII; many locals call it "American Bay." The northern coastline has a few naval gun sites and a naval museum. The quiet village **Anau** is on the eastern coast of the island. Venturing around the southern point of the island are more tourism services, restaurants, and lookout points. **Matira Beach** is a major hub, where many accommodations are clustered. **Mount Otemanu** and **Mount Pahia** rise in the island's center.

SIGHTS
Vaitape

Vaitape is where tourists come to shop for handmade goods at the Centre Artisanal, browse the pearl shops strung along the main road, grab a crepe from a roulotte (food truck), pick the freshest papaya from the tiny produce stands that pop up along the main road, and await accommodation pickup from the Vaitape Wharf, which is the locus of activity that also spills onto the main road of Vaitape. While it might seem charmless to some, a stroll along the road is bound to be met with smiles and striking views of Bora Bora's interior peeking out from inland roads.

Northern Bora Bora

Bora Bora's northern end is largely quiet and residential. Five kilometers (3.1 mi) north of Vaitape is the quiet town of Faanui. In between are a cluster of restaurants, the Bora Bora Yacht Club, and the trailhead to Mount Pahia. Naval gun stations, and the Naval

Bora Bora

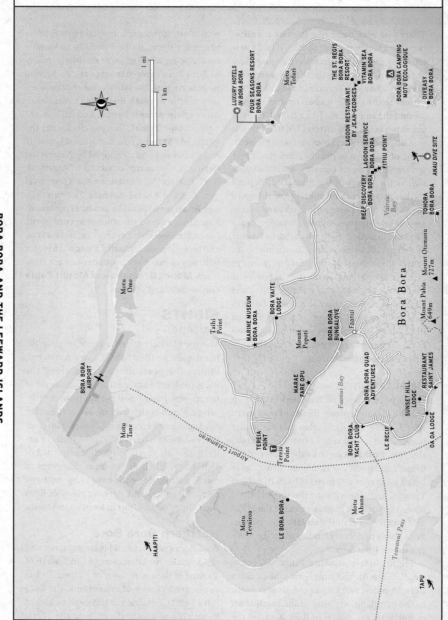

0   1 mi

0   1 km

LUXURY HOTELS IN BORA BORA

FOUR SEASONS RESORT BORA BORA

Motu Tofari

THE ST. REGIS BORA BORA RESORT

VITAMIN SEA BORA BORA

BORA BORA CAMPING MOTU ECOLOGIQUE

DIVEASY BORA BORA

LAGOON RESTAURANT BY JEAN-GEORGES

LAGOON SERVICE BORA BORA

FITIIU POINT

REEF DISCOVERY BORA BORA

ANAU DIVE SITE

Vairou Bay

TOHORA BORA BORA

Motu One

Taihi Point

MARINE MUSEUM BORA BORA

BORA VAITE LODGE

Mount Popoti

BORA BORA BUNGALOVE

Faanui

Mount Otemanu 727m

Mount Pahia 649m

Bora Bora

Bora Bora Airport

Motu Tane

MARAE FARE OPU

Faanui Bay

BORA BORA QUAD ADVENTURES

RESTAURANT SAINT JAMES

SUNSET HILL LODGE

Airport Catamaran

TEREIA POINT

Tereia Point

BORA BORA YACHT CLUB

LE RECIF

OA OA LODGE

Motu Tevairoa

LE BORA BORA

Motu Ahuna

Teavanui Pass

HAAPITI

TAPU

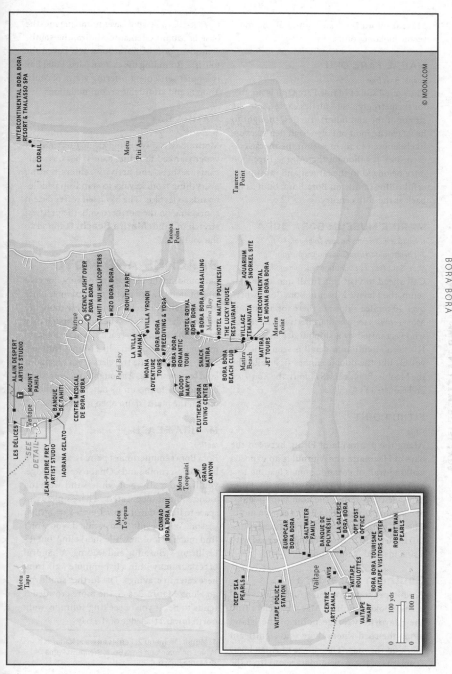

© MOON.COM

INTERCONTINENTAL BORA BORA RESORT & THALASSO SPA

LE CORAIL

Motu Piti Aau

Taurere Point

Paaoaa Point

AQUARIUM SNORKEL SITE

INTERCONTINENTAL LE MOANA BORA BORA

Matira Point

BORA BORA PARASAILING

HOTEL MAITAI POLYNESIA

THE LUCKY HOUSE RESTAURANT

VILLAGE TEMANUATA

Matira Beach

MATIRA JET TOURS

BORA BORA BEACH CLUB

Matira Bay

HOTEL ROYAL BORA BORA

SNACK MATIRA

BORA BORA ROMANTIC TOUR

BORA BORA FREEDIVING & YOGA

VILLA YRONDI

ROHUTU FARE

H2O BORA BORA

SCENIC FLIGHT OVER BORA BORA

TAHITI NUI HELICOPTERS

Nurue

LA VILLA MAHANA

MOANA ADVENTURE TOURS

BLOODY MARY'S

ELEUTHERA BORA DIVING CENTER

Povai Bay

MOUNT PAHIA

ALAIN DESPERT ARTIST STUDIO

CENTRE MEDICAL DE BORA BORA

BANQUE DE TAHITI

Vaitape

SEE DETAIL

LES DÉLICES

JEAN-PIERRE FREY ARTIST STUDIO

IAORANA GELATO

Motu Tooputaiti

GRAND CANYON

Motu To'opua

CONRAD BORA BORA NUI

Motu Tapu

DEEP SEA PEARLS

VAITAPE POLICE STATION

CENTRE ARTISANAL

VAITAPE WHARF

Vaitape

AVIS

VAITAPE ROULOTTES

EUROPCAR BORA BORA

SALTWATER FAMILY

BANQUE DE POLYNÉSIE

LA GALERIE BORA BORA

OPT POST OFFICE

BORA BORA TOURISME VAITAPE VISITORS CENTER

ROBERT WAN PEARLS

0   100 yds
0   100 m

Museum Bora Bora, are found at the most scenic lookout points.

MARAE FARE OPU

Faanui Bay; free

The sacred site of Marae Fare Opu is notable for the petroglyphs of turtles carved into the stones of the ahu (altar). Turtles, thought to be a favorite food of Polynesian deities, were likely offered to them within the marae (sacred site). It's thought that Marae Fare Opu once belonged to the largest and most powerful ruling family on Bora Bora, built as far back as the 15th century.

MARINE MUSEUM BORA BORA

11 km (6.8 mi) from Vaitape, Taihi; tel. 40 67 75 24; bertranddarrasse@hotmail.com; 9am-6pm Mon.-Sat.; free, but donation recommended

Call ahead to visit this small maritime museum, the Marine Museum Bora Bora, where over 40 replica ships are there for admiring. Most replicas were built by Bertrand Darrasse, who was raised by a shipbuilder in Tangier. His keen attention to detail is seen in iconic vessels like the double canoes first sailed by the Maohis, Bligh's *HMS Bounty*, the *Kon Tiki*, and Cousteau's *Calypso*.

FITIIU POINT

Fitiiu

Along the peninsula of Fitiiu, between the bays of Haamaire and Vairou, is an exposed walking trail of volcanic stones leading to a lookout point and WWII naval canons. From here, views span over the pom-pom treetops of coconut palms to Bora Bora's eastern motu. The end of the point is about 600 meters (0.3 mi) from the main road. Follow the road with a sign marked "canon" on it.

Southern Bora Bora

Bora Bora's southern end has no shortage of scenic lookout points. Many travelers find their favorite vantage point of the island along the road where there's no significant mark on the map. The village of Anau hosts remnants of the ancient marae, and from the town itself, you'll spot caves tunneling into the base of Mount Otemanu. Matira, the southernmost point of Bora Bora, is a haven for tourists. Rounding the eastern edge, Pofai Bay is a quiet settlement offering views of Motu Toopua and affordable accommodations.

MATIRA BAY

Matira

Matira Bay is a sweeping stretch of tranquil water flanked by white sands, bars, restaurants, resorts, and activity centers renting everything from kayaks to stand-up paddleboards to Jet Skis. The bay itself offers decent snorkeling on the northern end; the prettiest stretch of sand, **Matira Beach,** is found to the south.

BEACHES AND MOTU

Surrounding the main island of Bora Bora is a ring of atolls, called motu, that resemble parts of the Tuamotu archipelago. These motu are home to the island's best beaches, though they can be challenging to reach if you're not staying on them. Taxi boats, like **Manu Taxi** (tel. 87 79 11 62), shuttle travelers from the mainland to outer motu. Although Bora Bora's best beaches are found on its outer motu, there's one on the main island open to everyone.

MATIRA BEACH

Matira

Bora Bora's southernmost point is surrounded by cookie-crumb sands. On the western edge, you'll find a sliver of white sand weaving along vibrant blue waters. There's plenty of space to throw down a towel, even during high season. With a soft sandy seabed, you won't find much to look at while snorkeling, but it's idyllic for swimming and wading. A handful of restaurants within a five-minute walk from here cater to cravings. The further south you go along Matira Beach, the more crowded it tends to be. If you're seeking solitude, walk north toward the edge of the bay.

1: Mount Otemanu **2:** Ferries arrive at Vaitape Wharf on mainland Bora Bora. **3:** Mount Pahia **4:** Matira Beach

MOTU PITI AAU

Southeast Bora Bora, 1.5 km (0.9 mi) offshore

Slender Motu Piti Aau is the largest motu in Bora Bora, stretching over 12 kilometers (7.4 mi) long along Bora Bora's east side. It's home to a few five-star resorts, but most of it is inhabited solely by palm trees. Head to the southern end of the island for alabaster beaches and waters ideal for wading.

Snorkeling: A sandy seabed makes for lackluster snorkeling along most of Motu Piti Aau, but you might see an occasional shark or ray. There is some decent snorkeling found in between the St. Regis Bora Bora Resort and Le Meridien Bora Bora, but few boats venture here.

MOTU TEVAIROA

Northwest Bora Bora, 700 m (0.4 mi) offshore

The circular 2-kilometer (1.2-mi) motu of Motu Tevairoa is where to find those signature blue waters you've come for. Many full-day lagoon excursions stop at Motu Tevairoa's southernmost beach to play volleyball, lounge in the sand, and enjoy a picnic of fresh seafood. A wispy white sand beach on the northern end is a great spot to lounge, and is the entrance for a flatwater spot for kitesurfers who've come with their own gear.

Snorkeling: If you wish to snorkel, the channel on the northern coast is rife with colorful corals and reef fish.

MOTU TO'OPUA

Southwest Bora Bora, 1.8 km (1.1 mi) offshore

Unlike the more atoll-like motu of Bora Bora, 2.5-kilometer-long (1.5-mi-long) Motu To'opua is formed by rolling hills, and its coastline's sole sandy beach is reserved for resort guests at the Conrad Bora Bora Nui.

Snorkeling: On the island-facing side of the motu, sandy beaches are scarce, but it's a goldmine for snorkeling and intrepid exploring. Exciting reef life like angelfish, surgeonfish, bannerfish, trumpetfish, parrotfish, eels, and octopi live among the corals.

SCUBA DIVING AND SNORKELING

Bora Bora's waters are unique. With just one reef pass allowing seawater to flow into Bora Bora's expansive lagoon, the waters within its barrier reef are relatively calm and idyllic for snorkelers and beginner scuba divers to gain confidence. Snorkeling is possible off some motu beaches. Meanwhile, out on the open ocean, outside the reef, experienced divers have plenty of coral crags to explore.

Scuba Dive and Snorkel Sites

★ ANAU

East Bora Bora Lagoon, Fitiiu Point

Watch as graceful manta rays perform a ballet inside Bora Bora's lagoon. Most scuba diving and lagoon tour operators take their clients to a site called Anau, where huge manta rays are on patrol. Depths reach 20 meters (65 ft), making it an ideal dive site for beginner divers, and snorkelers can see the manta rays from the surface. The animals use this sandy pass to commute between their feeding areas, and as many as a dozen manta rays up to 3 meters (almost 10 ft) across appear at a time. Aside from the mantas, black tip reef sharks, barracuda, remora, Napoleons, and other fish cruise between the sand flats and the reef. The visibility is variable. Access is by boat; it's too far to swim from shore.

AQUARIUM

Off Motu Pitiuuia

Just 5 meters (16 ft) deep, Aquarium is a tranquil snorkel site—and an easy spot for first-time scuba divers. Small schools of damselfish, sergeant major fish, butterflyfish, angelfish, and bannerfish linger around the coral bommies. Most snorkeling trips will make a quick stop here. If you head to the eastern side of the reef, the words "Love Bora Bora" have been spelled out in the sand from rocks and broken corals. You could also paddle for 1.5 kilometers (about a mile, 45 minutes) from Matira Beach with your own kayak if waters are calm.

TAPU
Teavanui Pass

Just south of Bora Bora's sole reef pass is a haven for various sharks, corals, and reef fish. Snorkeling tours usually spot black tip reef sharks and lemon sharks from the surface. Venturing deeper, around 20 meters (65 ft), scuba divers fin alongside gray reef sharks, lemon sharks, manta rays, barracudas, and reef fish swimming around the coral seascape. Lionfish, crustaceans, and moray eels hide within the crags. There's a swim-through for intermediate scuba divers.

GRAND CANYON
Between Motu Toopua and mainland Bora Bora

A current brings life into the channel between a motu and Bora Bora's southern end. A spot mostly suitable for scuba divers, around 20 meters deep (65 ft), here it's common to see spotted eagle rays, white and black tip reef sharks, humphead wrasse, and lemon sharks. The topography of the reef is rife with caverns and tunnels.

HAAPITI
Outer reef nothern Bora Bora

On ultra-calm days, dive operators venture outside the reef to Bora Bora's northern end, diving along 10-meter (32-ft) craters in the seabed. Black tip, white tip, gray, and lemon sharks are frequently seen. Within the reef, you'll find butterflyfish, damselfish, bannerfish, octopus, eels, and starfish throughout.

Scuba Diving and Snorkeling Operators

Snorkel and scuba diving tours often venture to the same dive sites, like Anau for manta ray spotting and Tapu to see sharks. Snorkel tours tend to venture to the shallower sections of the site, while scuba tours drop off their divers over deeper waters. Dive operators select sites depending on the ocean conditions and divers' certification level, but many are happy to arrange trips to specific sites if requested well in advance. Most operators include all equipment in the price of their tour, though quality and size selection varies. It's worth confirming before booking. Most operators can accommodate groups of at least 12 divers plus their guides.

REEF DISCOVERY BORA BORA
tel. 87 76 43 43; reefdiscovery.com; 8am-5pm daily; from 13,000/person for a half-day tour

See Bora Bora's underwater world in style with Reef Discovery Bora Bora, a tour company

Black tip reef sharks are a frequent sight in Bora Bora.

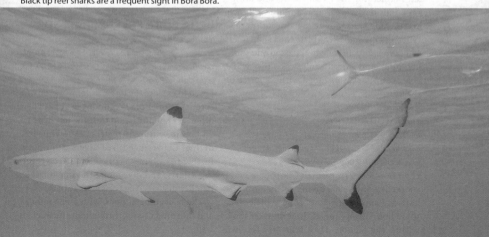

with standard snorkeling tours venturing to manta ray, stingray, and reef shark snorkel sites. Full-day tours include a motu lunch, where you'll dine on fresh seafood at picnic tables set in ankle-deep water. Private tours are also available for around CFP 70,000 for a half day for two people. Kids love the treasure hunt tour where they can search for clues underwater.

ELEUTHERA BORA DIVING CENTER
Matira Beach; tel. 87 77 67 46; www.
eleutheraboradiving.com; 8am-7pm daily; CFP 9,700/
fun dive, CFP 82,000/10 fun dives
Eleuthera Bora Diving Center is a PADI five-star operator running fun dives and scuba courses from Discover Scuba to PADI Advanced Open Water. Dives run twice in the morning, once in the afternoon, and at night on request. Private trips can also be arranged from CFP 90,000 for two people for a half-day trip. Transport and gear rental are included with each trip.

LAGOON SERVICE BORA BORA
tel. 87 75 69 57; www.lagoonservice.com; 8am-6pm daily; from CFP 11,500/person per half-day tour
Explore the Bora Bora Lagoon onboard a motorized outrigger canoe. Half-day tours usually stop at multiple snorkel spots, including sites famed for their reef sharks and stingrays. Full-day trips stop at a motu for lunch and include a coconut demonstration, pareu-tying lessons, and a leaf-plate workshop (CFP 16,000/person). Private tours, quad and snorkel tours, and sunset cruises are also available. Transport is included with the price of the tour.

H2O BORA BORA
tel. 87 72 90 52; www.boraborah2o.com; 8am-5pm daily; snorkeling CFP 11,000/person half-day group tour, scuba CFP 9,000/fun dive
H2O Bora Bora runs small (six people max) snorkeling and scuba diving excursions. The half-day snorkeling tour runs a little over three hours, stopping at three snorkel spots within the lagoon. Dive trips are for two

tanks. Private trips are also available (CFP 120,000 for six guests), stopping at a motu for a traditional Polynesian lunch, included in the price. Accommodation transport is included.

DIVEASY BORA BORA
tel. 87 79 22 55; www.diveasyborabora.com; 8am-4pm daily; scuba CFP 9,000/fun dive, snorkel CFP 11,000/person half-day tour
A highly personalized scuba and snorkel operator, Diveasy Bora Bora runs fun dives for scuba divers, snorkeling excursions, boat tours, and combination trips. They also have a "snukah" experience, where swimmers are connected to an air supply at the surface of the water—a blend of snorkeling and scuba diving. Scuba courses are available on request.

TOHORA BORA BORA
tel. 87 79 53 83; www.tohoraborabora.com; 8am-4pm daily; whale-watching CFP 14,000/person half-day, snorkel CFP 10,000/person half-day
Tohora Bora Bora snorkel trips also venture to Bora Bora's lagoon snorkel sites, and in calm conditions, venture just beyond the barrier reef for a chance to see dolphins and technicolor corals. Tohora Bora Bora operates **whale watching** and swimming in Bora Bora from July to November, usually led by a guide with over a decade of experience. Transport is included.

BORA BORA FREEDIVING & YOGA
Matira; tel. 87 21 78 23; www.boraborafreedivingyoga.com; 9am-5pm daily; AIDA1 certification CFP 15,000, training session CFP 5,000, yoga class CFP 1,500
Learn to explore the underwater world on one breath at Bora Bora Freediving & Yoga. Their discovery and initiation training teaches divers how to venture 10 meters (32 ft) while free diving. Experienced free divers can obtain further free diving certifications, go on training safaris, and dive along the line to reach new depth goals. Yoga classes take place every weekday evening at 6pm, with a few midday and morning classes throughout the week as well.

Eco-Friendly Snorkeling Tips

The marine ecosystems in French Polynesia are fragile, sensitive to pollutants, loud noises, human interaction, and destruction. On islands that see a large influx of tourists, like the Society Islands, tour operators don't always act in the best interests of the environment. Here are a few choices you can make to minimize your impact:

- **Wear reef-friendly sunscreen:** Common sunscreen ingredients like oxybenzone and avobenzone are known to damage coral polyps. Opt for a mineral-based sunscreen made from non-nano zinc and titanium oxide particles instead. Wearing a rashguard and swim leggings will also help cut down the amount of harmful chemicals that leach from your skin into the water.

- **Avoid fish feeding:** Feeding marine wildlife like reef sharks and stingrays disrupts their natural feeding behaviors. But, it's often a challenge to find which snorkel tour operators in French Polynesia do this and which ones don't. Most of the sharks and stingrays at the popular snorkel sites come when they hear a boat engine as if it's a dinner bell. If you're offered a fish to feed to the sharks and rays, it's best to decline and admire them without petting or grabbing onto them. **Moana Adventure Tours** (page 152) is one tour operator that does not feed marine wildlife.

- **Look but don't touch:** Coral reefs are sensitive to touch and slow-growing. Avoid touching, kicking, or walking on the reef. Wait until the tide rises to snorkel in shallow snorkel sites.

- **Pick up debris:** Take a small bag with you to pick up any rubbish stuck on the reef. Many marine animals mistake plastic bags for food and get caught in fishing lines. While most snorkel spots in French Polynesia are quite clean, there's bound to be a few pieces of trash on the shoreline or stuck between coral crags.

OTHER SPORTS AND RECREATION
Hiking
MOUNT PAHIA
Distance: *3.4 km (2.1 mi) out-and-back*
Time: *4 hours*
Trailhead: *Trailhead begins in Pofai Bay on inland road on the north side of the bay*
Information and maps: www.alltrails.com

This very steep and slippery trail leads to the summit of Mount Ohue (620 m/2,034 ft) and Mount Pahia (661 m/2,168 ft). It's best to do this trail with a guide; many hikers who embark on their own turn around at the halfway point due to the steepness, and most of the trail is unmarked. The trailhead begins in Pofai Bay. The trail starts in a dense forest and quickly climbs in altitude; some sections have ropes for assistance and you'll want both hands free for balancing. The summit of Mount Ohue reveals panoramic views of Bora Bora's western end, and it's striking to

see the lagoon from such an angle. Trek in the morning to beat the heat and skip it if it's just rained. A local guide is recommended for this hike due to its difficulty. Contact **Polynesia Island Tours** (tel. 87 29 66 60; polynesiaislandtours@mail.pf) for guided trips starting at CFP 13,000 per person.

TEREIA POINT
Distance: *5 km (3.1 mi) out-and-back*
Time: *2 hours*
Trailhead: *North Faanui (8 km/5 mi north of Vaitape)*
Information and maps: www.alltrails.com

An easy walking trail leads from the northern end of Faanui to Tereia Point, where you'll find abandoned WWII naval guns and views overlooking bright blues of the lagoon. The dirt trail starts steep but levels out, and is too rough to drive in a rental vehicle—it's best to walk (bring water and wear sun protection) or stop here as part of a day tour. The point itself is reachable by quad or 4WD, but no rental companies allow it. It's best to park at the trailhead and continue on foot.

Local Tours

All lagoon excursions typically have at least one stop for snorkeling, usually at a site to see reef sharks and stingrays. Snorkeling gear is provided, but size selection and quality can be hit-or-miss, so it's best to bring your own.

BORA BORA QUAD ADVENTURES

tel. 89 75 54 58; www.boraboraquadadventures.com; 8am-5pm daily; CFP 25,000/two-person quad or Jet Ski for a half-day tour

Bora Bora Quad Adventures hosts day tours for travelers in search of a more thrilling experience than your typical 4WD excursion. On powerful quads, rumble along dirt roads to Mount Popoti, Matira Beach, or the naval canons of Faanui, with a stop for drinks. The lagoon excursion is just as exciting, with trips to Teavanui Pass, a stop at a white sand motu, and peek at Bora Bora's lagoons. Both trips are around three hours long, and are possible to combine in one day. Accommodation transport is included.

MOANA ADVENTURE TOURS

tel. 87 78 27 37; moanaadventuretours.com; 8am-5pm daily; from CFP 10,000/person for a half-day tour

Moana Adventure Tours is one of the few operators that does not feed marine wildlife. Venture around the lagoon on a Jet Ski or boat tour, stopping at multiple snorkel sites, a white sand motu, and for lunch at Bloody Mary's. Almost all lagoon excursions run around three hours long. Combination trips with Jet Skis, 4WD land excursions, and a sunset boat trip are also easily arranged. Transport to and from your accommodation is included.

BORA BORA EXPLORER

tel. 89 45 45 45; boraboraexplorer.com; 8am-5pm daily; from CFP 90,000/person for a half-day tour

Bora Bora Explorer runs six themed tours depending on your budget and interest. The cultural tour ventures to most of Bora Bora's land sights in a 4WD, revealing the history of marae. Their boat tour stops at multiple snorkel spots around the lagoon. Land-and-sea combination trips are also available. If you like stargazing, book their sunset cruise, which starts on the water and ends with a guided tour of the night sky. Pickup service is available.

MATIRA JET TOURS

Matira Beach; tel. 87 77 63 63; www.matirajettours. com; 8am-5pm daily; Jet Ski CFP 30,000/two people, quad CFP 28,000/two people

Matira Jet Tours runs Jet Ski trips, quad tours, combination trips, and stand-up paddleboard rentals from Matira Beach. Half-day Jet Ski tours venture to a motu for refreshments and relaxation. Quad trips explore Bora Bora's main island. If you prefer to explore on your own, this is one of the few non-accommodation rental stands offering stand-up paddleboards.

Water Sports and Boat Tours

Bora Bora's lagoon is a prime place for a variety of water sports like stand-up paddling, kayaking, and canoeing—all of which are typically rented through your accommodation or included as part of a local tour, as there are no major rental spots around Bora Bora outside of Matira Beach. Kitesurfers and wing foilers will find the shallow flatwater of Bora Bora's lagoon a prime place for catching wind, but will need to arrive with their own gear as no rental stands exist on the island.

BORA BORA PARASAILING

Matira Beach; tel. 87 70 56 62; boraboraparasailing. com; 8am-4pm daily; CFP 30,000-48,000/two people

Catch the bright blues of the lagoon from the height of a parasail ride, where you'll be towed behind a boat and lifted into the air. Peek into the shallows to search for the silhouettes of stingrays and reef sharks, and spot Bora Bora's peaks from a unique perspective. Trips last around 15-25 minutes and venture along the eastern side of Bora Bora's lagoon. Two people can ride at a time; the price increases with duration and rope length. Transport is not included in the rate.

VITAMIN SEA BORA BORA

tel. 87 37 77 27; www.sailingborabora.com; 8am-7pm daily; from CFP 21,000/person for half-day tour

Sail through Bora Bora's lagoon onboard a racing catamaran, traversing over the blues with solely the wind as power. Trips range from half-day sails that include snorkeling (CFP 26,000/person), sunset sails with live music and drinks (CFP 21,000), or customized private tours (CFP 100,000). The catamaran hosts up to eight passengers.

BORA BORA ROMANTIC TOUR

tel. 87 78 27 37; www.boraboraromantic.com; 8am-7pm daily; from CFP 22,000/person for six-hour tour

Targeted to honeymooners and couples looking to celebrate, Bora Bora Romantic Tour runs snorkeling excursions, sunset cruises, and private island picnics to enjoy a bottle of champagne from its motorized outrigger canoe or speedboat. Guides can also arrange proposals and elopement ceremonies, as well as private tours.

★ Scenic Flights
TAHITI NUI HELICOPTERS

tel. 87 77 72 56; www.tahitinuihelicopters.com; 8am-5pm daily; 10 min €126, 20 min €243, 30 min €360

One of the best ways to enjoy Bora Bora's misty emerald peaks and turquoise lagoon is from above. Tahiti Nui Helicopters runs scenic flights over the lagoon, ranging from 10-30 minutes long. The best of the bunch is the full "Heart of Tupai" tour, which includes a buzz over Bora Bora as well as Tupai, a heart-shaped desert atoll.

ENTERTAINMENT AND EVENTS

Many of the large resorts put on a **cultural performance** complete with dancing, music, and art demonstrations a few times per week.

Festivals and Events
HEIVA I BORA BORA

The Heiva I Bora Bora festivities are celebrated in Bora Bora with special fervor during July. While the sun is out, there are canoe races by sail and paddle, javelin throwing,

the view of Bora Bora from above

coconut husking, and other sports (foot races, volleyball, tennis, Ping-Pong, etc). The Maohi Triathlon involves a canoe race, fruit carrying, and coconut milk preparation. One evening is devoted to a floral carriage contest, and traditional singing and dancing competitions run for 10 nights from 8pm. Most events are free to attend and don't require a ticket. Accommodations tend to book out well in advance during this festival, so reserve early if you'd like to take part in this celebration of life. The Tahiti Tourisme website (tahititourisme.pf) hosts a calendar with Heiva I Bora Bora event times, location, and prices.

HAWAIKI NUI VA'A

The largest canoe race in French Polynesia typically takes place in October or November, starting at the sacred Marae Taputapuatea in Huahine and ending at Bora Bora's Matira Beach. The region's best paddlers venture on a 129-kilometer (80-mi) course from Huahine to Raiatea and Taha'a before crossing the channel to Bora Bora. It's a feat that honors the ancestral seafarers of Polynesia. Visitors are welcome to take part in the festivities surrounding the event, which typically involves music, dancing, floral creations, and scrumptious feasts. Check the Tahiti Tourisme website (tahititourisme.pf) for the event times and information.

SHOPPING

Bora Bora is one of the only islands in French Polynesia with an established shopping scene. Plenty of small boutiques along Vaitape's main road sell handmade jewelry, pearls, pareu (sarongs), art, and resort wear. All pearl shops on Bora Bora sell Tahitian pearls, also known as black pearls.

CENTRE ARTISANAL

Vaitape Wharf; 8am-4pm Mon.-Fri., 8am-noon Sat.
This market found just behind the Vaitape Wharf is the best place to get handmade goods on Bora Bora. Shop for hand-painted pareu, wooden sculptures, woven hats, handmade jewelry, and other souvenirs. If you're seeking a custom item, this is a great place to start.

ALAIN DESPERT ARTIST STUDIO

Vaitape; tel. 87 71 78 06; www.despert.com;
10am-6pm Mon.-Sat. by appointment only
Alain Despert is a contemporary artist whose bright, bold paintings often feature elements of the Society Islands. His work has been commissioned by companies, organizations, and private collectors interested in capturing the bold colors of Polynesia on canvas. Visits to his studio are by appointment only; exhibitions are regularly hosted at Four Seasons Resort Bora Bora and St. Regis Bora Bora.

DEEP SEA PEARLS

Vaitape; tel. 40 67 61 76; 9am-5:30pm Mon.-Sat.
Deep Sea Pearls sells elegant pearl jewelry without pressure. Custom pieces typically have a short turnaround, sometimes as quickly as a few hours. Discounts are usually offered to those purchasing more than one piece, but you'll likely have to ask.

ROBERT WAN PEARLS

Vaitape; tel. 40 67 50 27; robertwan.com; 9am-5pm Mon.-Sat.
Robert Wan Pearls are some of the most famous in French Polynesia, selling pearls for over four decades. Their designs tend to err on the simpler side, letting the pearls themselves stand out. Custom pieces are made upon request.

LA GALERIE BORA BORA

Vaitape; tel. 40 67 55 00; www.pearla.fr; 9am-5pm Mon.-Sat.
La Galerie Bora Bora is a women's clothing boutique selling Pearla clothing, resort wear with a pearl embedded into the ensemble. Pareu, art, home goods, and jewelry are also for sale.

JEAN-PIERRE FREY ARTIST STUDIO

Vaitape; tel. 87 38 12 58; www.jeanpierrefrey.com; 9am-5pm Mon.-Sat.

Spa Day

Four Seasons Resort Bora Bora

Nothing says tropical paradise vacation quite like a spa treatment with sea salt scrubs, fragrant oils, and the sound of palm fronds rustling outside the treatment room. Bora Bora's best spas are found within impeccably kept luxury resort grounds. A popular spot for honeymooners, couples' massages are often the most economical (and romantic) way to enjoy a spa treatment for two.

- **InterContinental Bora Bora Resort & Thalasso Spa:** Lean into nature at this ocean-centered spa, where treatments take place in a glass-bottom treatment room overlooking blue waters of the lagoon. Thalassotherapy, treatments that incoporate sea water, are their specialty. A full body massage with scrub and body wrap starts at CFP 26,700 for 80 minutes. The property has a fitness center, steam baths, tea lounge, and boutique. Accommodation and treatment packages exist for those who wish to get more than one treatment.

- **Te Mahana Spa at Four Seasons Resort Bora Bora:** Massage tables here overlook aquamarine waters and tropical gardens. Signature massage and facial treatments often incorporate ingredients like Tahitian black pearl powder, coconut sugar, and locally sourced essential oils. Massages and facials start at CFP 33,500 for 80 minutes.

- **Hina Spa at Conrad Bora Bora Nui:** Seashells and rattan decor accent the wooden and spacious Hina Spa. Guests have access to baths, a sauna and steam room, a lounge, and a choice of indoor or outdoor treatment rooms. Their signature massage is a slow deep-relaxation treatment, available for CFP 25,000 for 90 minutes.

Jean-Pierre Frey's artwork has a nostalgic feel to it, almost as if looking at postcards from the past. His mixed-media style using maps, calligraphy, watercolor paints, and travel paraphernalia makes his pieces distinctly unique.

SALTWATER FAMILY

Vaitape; saltwater-family.com; 9am-4:30pm Mon.-Fri., 9am-noon Sat.

A cheerful shop selling casual clothes for men, women, and kids with tropical prints: think tie-dye tanks, floral-print shirts, vibrant beach towels, and basic accessories.

FOOD

If you're staying on an island resort, you'll likely eat most of your meals at your accommodation. If you're on the mainland, the area around Vaitape hosts the lion's share of Bora Bora's restaurants. Larger restaurants often have a have a shuttle bus service for patrons. Like most islands elsewhere, plant-based eaters and those with food allergies are not particularly well catered for on Bora Bora.

Vaitape
VAITAPE ROULOTTES
Vaitape Wharf; 6pm-10pm nightly; CFP 2,000
The most affordable food is found just behind the Vaitape Wharf each evening, where food trucks serve pizzas, pastas, barbecued meats, crepes, and snacks. Each roulette has a handful of tables to dine at.

LES DÉLICES
Vaitape; tel. 89 40 08 48; 7:30am-11am and 6pm-10pm Tues.-Sat.; CPF 3,000
Come to Les Délices for fresh seafood platters, salads, traditional Polynesian fare, lamb, and steak; few plant-based options are available. The highlight of their menu for many is the raclette, a meal of meats and cheese cooked on the table's own grill (24 hours advance notice, CFP 3,900/person). The dining room has a jovial atmosphere, with regular live music performances and karaoke nights.

★ RESTAURANT SAINT JAMES
North Vaitape; tel. 40 67 64 62; saintjamesborabora. com; 6:30am-10pm Mon.-Sat.; CFP 4,000
Overlooking the water, Restaurant Saint James is one of the most popular sundowner spots. Head to the bar area for cheese platters and cocktails, or come for a full meal in their upscale dining room. Main dishes feature roasted mahi-mahi with coconut crust, seared ahi tuna, grilled lamb, beef tenderloin, and a vegetable risotto. Shuttle bus service starts at 5:45pm each evening.

IAORANA GELATO
Vaitape; tel. 89 50 42 52; 8:30am-4:30pm and 5:30pm-9:30pm Mon.-Fri., 5:30pm-9:30pm Sat.
Scoops of handmade gelato are doled out from Iaorana Gelato's shop, 500 meters (0.3 mile) south from Vaitape Wharf. Occasionally, their ice cream cart is seen parked at a busy beach. Crepes, tiramisu, smoothies, macarons, and custom cakes also delight travelers with a sweet tooth.

Northern Bora Bora
★ BORA BORA YACHT CLUB
South Faanui; tel. 40 67 60 47; www. boraborayachtclub.org; 10:30am-11pm daily (lunch 11:30am-2pm, dinner 5:30pm-9:30pm); CFP 3,000

Shop for pareu, woven goods, and jewelry in the Centre Artisanal.

Pull up a chair on the overwater deck at Bora Bora Yacht Club, a social hub for yachties anchored just offshore. Their bar comes alive just before sunset, serving beers, cocktails, and select wines. For dinner, starters include beef carpaccio, roasted scallops, and shrimp skewers. Heartier plates feature pastas, grilled fish, duck, beef, and steak. Pickup service begins at 5pm each night.

Southern Bora Bora
SNACK MATIRA
Matira; tel. 40 67 77 32; 10am-4pm daily; CFP 1,500
If you're spending the day at Matira Beach, head to Snack Materia on the southern end of the sand. Your typical snack fare is offered here: grilled fish and steak served with rice or fries. Pizza is available as well. Service can take a little longer than expected, but it's no matter, as views from the dining area look out to turquoise waters.

★ BORA BORA BEACH CLUB
Matira; tel. 40 67 52 50; www.borabora-beachclub. com; 10am-11pm daily; CFP 3,500
Boutique beach house vibes set the scene at Bora Bora Beach Club, a pleasant restaurant on the shores of Matira Beach. Pull up a seat at the bar, or head to the terrace area to feel the sea breeze while dining on hearty plates of fish served many ways, racks of lamb, lobster, burgers, and pasta. If you've come just to enjoy a scoop of ice cream or a drink, you're in good company.

THE LUCKY HOUSE RESTAURANT
Matira; tel. 40 67 68 08; 11:30am-11pm daily; CFP 3,500
The Lucky House Restaurant at Fare Manuia is a casual eatery with salads, wood-fired pizzas, steaks, and seafood served raw, grilled, and fried. For a holiday feel, bring your bathing suit and go for a dip in their outdoor pool while you wait for your meal. Their bar is well-stocked, and they sell imported cigars. The pavlova served with pineapple and passionfruit puree is delightful.

LA VILLA MAHANA
Pofai Bay; tel. 40 67 50 63; www.villamahana.com; damien@villamahana.com; 6pm-11pm Mon.-Sat.; CFP 14,000
Perhaps the most intimate restaurant on the island, La Villa Mahana serves just seven tables for dinner each evening, spread around a Mediterranean-style villa. Chef Damien Rinaldi-Dovio was trained in France, and his background comes through in the plates featured on his à la carte and degustation menus. Top dishes include lobster served on creamy risotto and curried mahi-mahi served with banana. The personalized wine pairings are impeccably matched. Tables at La Villa Mahana book out months in advance, so it's wise to reserve a space as soon as possible.

Motu
Some resorts on Bora Bora's outer motu accept guests just for lunch or dinner. You'll likely have to pay extra for boat shuttle service if coming from the mainland. Try to time your meal with the resort's cultural performance night, if they have one. Many resorts have not returned to a set schedule when it comes to cultural performance nights. It's wise to call ahead and find the latest schedule before making your reservation.

LAGOON RESTAURANT BY JEAN-GEORGES
St. Regis Bora Bora; tel. 40 60 31 70; www.marriott. com; 6pm-9:30pm Mon.-Tues. and Thurs.-Sun.; CFP 9,000
Head to the Lagoon Restaurant by Jean-Georges at the St. Regis just before sunset to watch the sky turn shades of pink over the silhouette of Mount Otemanu. This Asian-fusion restaurant is upscale but not pretentious, and many come solely for the tasting menu. Favorite menu items are crumbed tuna, quinoa-crusted squid, grilled mackerel, and truffle mashed potatoes. They are happy to adapt dishes to suit vegans and vegetarians. The service is attentive, and the wine list extensive.

LE CORAIL
Intercontinental Bora Bora Resort & Thalasso Spa; tel. 40 60 76 00; thalasso.intercontinental.com; 6:30pm-9:30pm Tues.-Thurs. and Sat.-Sun.; CFP 17,000/person tasting menu

The restaurant at Le Corail is spacious and chic, with white tablecloths illuminated by dim lights and candles. Their menu is one of the most diverse of the five-star stays, and guests can choose from a series of three-course tasting menus, including one that's fully vegetarian. À la carte options feature roasted mahi-mahi in a black garlic crust, beef filet marinated in a spiced whisky sauce, and marinated octopus with watermelon. For dessert, opt for the coconut surprise—coconut foam with a white chocolate shell.

BARS AND NIGHTLIFE
BLOODY MARY'S
South Pofai Bay; tel. 40 67 69 10; www.bloodymarys. com; 11:30am-2:30pm and 5:30pm to 9pm Tues.-Sat.; CFP 3,000/meal

Having a drink at Bloody Mary's is a rite of passage for travelers coming through Bora Bora. Built in 1979 from bamboo and palm leaves, Bloody Mary's is iconic. It's a place where shoes are quickly abandoned, and dancing on their sand floors is encouraged whenever the music comes on. Over 200 names of A- to D-list celebrities appear on the restaurant's de facto hall of fame. Cocktails, beer, wine, burgers, sandwiches, seafood, steak, and a few plant-based dishes make up the menu. Bloody Mary's is open for lunch and dinner.

LE RECIF
Faanui; tel. 40 67 73 87; 8pm-late Wed.-Sat.; CFP 1,000-1,500 cover charge

Those who say Bora Bora's social scene is "boring boring" haven't spent a big night out at Le Recif, the island's only nightclub. The bar hosts karaoke, live music, DJs usually playing EDM or house music, and themed nights. It's a jovial place, often packed with locals and travelers alike.

ACCOMMODATIONS
Bora Bora's upscale accommodations are mostly found on outer motu, though there are a few five-star stays on the main island as well. If you're trying to visit Bora Bora on a budget, check into a pension on the main island to save on your nightly rate, meals, and transport. Some accommodations require a two- to three-night minimum stay; inquire when booking.

Vaitape
OA OA LODGE
Vaitape; tel. 87 72 45 49; www.oaoalodge.com; CFP 11,500/room

Wake up on the water at Oa Oa Lodge, a hotel with three semi-overwater bungalows. A swim deck provides direct ocean access. Behind the overwater bungalows are a handful of garden rooms, equipped with a kitchen and terrace. Most rooms sleep three people. On-site, there's a small restaurant and bar. All guests are free to use the bicycles. Furniture in the rooms could do with a refresh, and the scarcity of decor makes the rooms feel a little lackluster.

SUNSET HILL LODGE
Vaitape; tel. 87 79 26 48; www.sunsethilllodge.com; CFP 12,800/room

Sunset Hill Lodge is a family-run guesthouse with two properties: one, Sunset Hill Lodge, tucked on the mountain side of the main road, and another, Villa Moana, on the water. At Sunset Hill Lodge, there are seven studio options sleeping from 2-6 people, each equipped with air-conditioning. Some have showers, a private kitchen, and terraces. The rooms at Villa Moana are similarly equipped but come with the perk of stunning sea views. The owners are happy to help arrange tours and provide pickup and drop-off to the Vaitape Wharf. Breakfast is not included in the nightly rate.

1: Restaurant Saint James **2:** fruits at a market near Vaitape Wharf **3:** Bloody Mary's serves some of the best cocktails in Bora Bora. **4:** Bora Bora Yacht Club

☆ Bora Bora's Luxury Hotels

While the island of Raiatea holds the claim of being the first island to host the world's first over-water bungalows for tourists, built in 1967, Bora Bora quickly eclipsed its neighbor in terms of quality and quantity. Yes, the price tag can be shocking, but there's nowhere else quite like Bora Bora when it comes to a laidback yet luxe retreat. Where else can you open your door to a private deck set above aquamarine waters? Where views span over a lagoon to an emerald island? Small touches like fresh-baked pastries delivered in an outrigger canoe, above-water spa treatments, private plunge pools, and white sand beaches being just steps away make Bora Bora's luxury resorts well worth their hype.

THE BEST OF THE BEST

- **Best for pampering:** InterContinental Bora Bora Resort & Thalasso Spa has divine spa treatments and above-par cuisine (page 162).

- **Best for luxury and adventure:** Four Seasons Resort Bora Bora features tranquil rooms and a well-equipped activity center (page 164).

- **Best location:** InterContinental Le Moana Bora Bora next to Bora Bora's Matira Beach is a convenient hub for exploring (page 161).

- **Best for solitude:** The St. Regis Bora Bora Resort hosts rooms so spacious, you won't want to leave (page 162).

- **Best for a unique experience:** Rohutu Fare is a jungle retreat where no two accommodations are quite alike (page 160).

Northern Bora Bora
BORA VAITE LODGE

Faanui; tel. 40 67 55 69; boravaite@mail.pf; CFP 13,000/room

Bora Vaite Lodge feels like you're staying at a distant relative's house with helpful Alain and Vaite as hosts. Guests stay inside the main home; rooms sleep 2-3 people and have a fan, internet access, and shared bathroom. All guests have access to a large kitchen stocked with basic spices and cookware. Breakfasts of fresh bread, homemade jams, and tropical fruits are included with each stay. The hosts are happy to transport guests around the island for a modest price (around CFP 700 per trip), and these drives usually double as a mini-tour as Alain shares travel tips and history about the island.

★ BORA BORA BUNGALOVE

Faanui; tel. 40 67 73 58; airbnb.com; CFP 15,000/double

The most cheerful place to stay on the island, Bora Bora Bungalove hosts bungalows where no surface has been left without a splash of paint, artwork, or beachy decor. The bungalows are set among tropical gardens, complete with a lily pond. Guests have access to a kitchen, bicycles, small library, kayaks, internet, and a nice reef for snorkeling just in front of the property. One of the bungalows is stilted above the water. Hammocks, a reading nook with books, and dock make it a tranquil place to lounge.

Southern Bora Bora
★ ROHUTU FARE

Pofai Bay; tel. 87 70 77 99; www.rohotufarelodge.com; €300/room

If you're in search of a tropical escape, Rohutu Fare is a jungle retreat hidden in the hills above Pafoi Bay. Tens of fruit and hardwood trees surround the property, and quiet cobblestone paths weave throughout. Bungalows are spacious and furnished with four-post beds, and decorated with antique wooden furniture, paintings of Polynesia, and textiles. The owners have paid keen attention to detail, and it shows in each room. Each lagoon-view bungalow has air-conditioning, an outdoor shower, and a large terrace looking out to Pofai Bay. For families, there's also a four-person suite complete with a kitchen, bathroom, private garden area, and living room. Bicycles and transport to Matira Beach or Vaitape are included with each stay.

VILLA YRONDI

Pofai Bay; tel. 89 52 32 99; www.villayrondi.com; CFP 15,700-35,000/room

The pink statue of a fish woman, *Vahine e'ia*, is one of the first things travelers see when they fly into Bora Bora. This statue was crafted by artist Garrick Yrondi, owner of Villa Yrondi. His colorful paintings are inspired by the brightness of Polynesia and are placed throughout this welcoming Mediterranean villa. No two rooms at the villa are alike, though all have air-conditioning, internet access, and a bathroom. Some have a kitchen, library, lounge room, and direct access to the villa's pool. Hosts are happy to show you around the on-site Garrick Yrondi gallery and assist with arranging activities.

INTERCONTINENTAL LE MOANA BORA BORA

Matira; tel. 40 60 49 00; www.ihg.com; CFP 90,000/room

The Intercontinental Le Moana Bora Bora is an ideal option if you want all the facilities and perks of a private motu resort, complete with overwater bungalows, but the convenience of staying on Bora Bora's main island. A white sand beach leads to a few dozen overwater bungalows, each with swim decks and decorated with Polynesian artwork. The lagoon-view bungalows arguably have the best view; the ocean-view rooms feel more private. Beach bungalows are just steps away from the water, opening to a white sand beach. Enjoy relaxing at the resort's spa, grabbing a drink at the bar, and dining on Polynesian buffets while watching a cultural performance (Tuesdays and Saturdays).

HOTEL MAITAI POLYNESIA

Matira; tel. 40 60 30 00; www.hotelmaitai.com; CFP 25,000/room

Hotel Maitai Polynesia is a large seaside resort with accommodation options ranging from rooms in a lodge to standalone bungalows in the gardens to overwater bungalows. Dark wood, woven bamboo walls, thatched roofs, and seashell chandeliers create a tropical holiday atmosphere. Rooms have air-conditioning, a fan, a private bathroom, coffee-making facilities, a desk, and a minibar. Most have a day bed as well. Decent snorkeling is found just offshore from the property. A Polynesian dance show takes place at their Haere Mai Restaurant once per week, schedule depending.

VILLAGE TEMANUATA

Matira; tel. 40 67 75 61; www.temanuata.com; CFP 27,000/room

Village Temanuata is a quiet family-owned hotel with 11 bungalows set behind a white sand beach—two of them are directly on the sand; some have ocean views. All sleep two people and have a mini-fridge, microwave, kettle, fan, bathroom, and terrace. Tapa (painted cloth) decorate the walls. Two bungalows can sleep up to five people and come with a full kitchen. There's no restaurant on-site, but the property is within walking distance of a few restaurants, other hotels, and convenience stores. Discounts are offered to those staying longer than 10 days.

HOTEL ROYAL BORA BORA

Matira; tel. 40 60 86 86; www.royalborabora.com; CFP 30,000/room

Hotel Royal Bora Bora has an air of old Polynesian charm, and feels less sterile than many of the more modern resorts. There are 80 hotel rooms, some wheelchair accessible. All have a TV, minibar, terrace, air-conditioning, and en suite bathroom. Meals are served in a spacious restaurant built from dark hardwood, bamboo, and pandanus leaves, doling out seafood and hosting live music performances a few times a week. All guests have access to their infinity pool with ocean views. Kayaks and bikes are available for rent.

Motu

Most new developments around Bora Bora are on the long sandy motu surrounding the main island. These offshore resorts usually have sugar-sand beaches and striking views of Bora Bora's mountainous interior. They're where you'll find the romantic overwater bungalows featured on any advertisement with "Bora Bora" printed on it. Unless you take a shuttle boat to the main island, meals are limited to your accommodation. Overwater bungalows at the end of the pontoon (facing Bora Bora's main island) tend to feel more intimate and secluded—though they'll be farther away from the resort's main communal spaces.

THE ST. REGIS BORA BORA RESORT

Motu Piti Aau; tel. 40 60 78 88; www.marriott.com; CFP 98,000/room

The St. Regis Bora Bora Resort holds onto the accolade of having the most spacious overwater bungalows in Bora Bora—their smallest is over 1,500 square feet. There are a few room types on offer: garden or beachside bungalows and villas, and overwater bungalows and villas. All are tastefully decorated with ample lounge space, situated further apart from one another than most comparable properties. When you're not hanging out on deck, head to the spa, restaurants, swim-up bar, pools, lagoon, or activity center to borrow a stand-up paddleboard, kayak, or canoe.

LE BORA BORA

Motu Tevairoa; tel. 40 60 52 00; www.leborabora. com; CFP 110,000/room

While many of Bora Bora's overwater bungalows have an ultra-modern feel, those found at Le Bora Bora have a local flair. Woven walls, rattan furniture, wooden sculptures, and thatched roofs add to the rustic atmosphere. Room types vary from garden and beach bungalows, many with private pools, to bungalows perched on the water. Multi-bedroom villas accommodate families and groups. Elsewhere in the resort, visit the spa, large beachside pool, fitness center, gift shops, bars, and restaurants. Discounts are available for stays four nights and longer.

CONRAD BORA BORA NUI

Motu To'opua; tel. 40 60 33 00; conradboraboranuiresort.com; CFP 125,000/room

Modern overwater bungalows jut out from Motu To'opua, most facing the open ocean; those on the eastern end face tiny Motu To'opuaiti and peek at Bora Bora's main island. There are around a dozen room types, some with private plunge pools and overwater hammocks. All have a private terrace, lounge area, minibar, and Bluetooth sound system. The pick of the property is their two-story, two-bedroom villa with three terraces and an infinity pool. The property hosts a handful of restaurants, a spa, a fitness center, a kids' club, and a large pool with a swim-up bar. **Polynesian cultural shows** usually take place on Thursday evenings.

★ INTERCONTINENTAL BORA BORA RESORT & THALASSO SPA

Motu Piti Aau; tel. 40 60 76 00; www.ihg.com; CFP 155,000/room

With views looking out to Bora Bora's mainland, Intercontinental Bora Bora & Thalasso Spa is a serene resort made even more so with its on-site spa. Enjoy services at the Deep Ocean Spa, where thalassotherapy—the use of sea water in wellness treatments—is featured in many treatments; glass-bottom overwater rooms add to its appeal. Overwater bungalows are modern, each with a deck, outdoor shower, and access to the water. Some have plunge

1: the overwater bungalows at Four Seasons Resort Bora Bora **2:** Oa Oa Lodge

pools on deck. Dining options range from laid-back to upscale, with enough bar space to linger at in between meals. **Polynesian cultural shows** take place regularly, usually twice per week, with schedules available for those who call and inquire about a month in advance. The resort also has many features catered to honeymooners—like canoe breakfasts, elopement ceremonies, and couples' spa treatments.

★ FOUR SEASONS RESORT BORA BORA

Motu Piti Aau; tel. 40 60 31 30; www.fourseasons. com; CFP 200,000/room

Elegant overwater bungalows await at the Four Seasons Resort Bora Bora, a resort where everything seems super-saturated with blues and greens. Two pontoons of overwater bungalows look out to Bora Bora's main island, and a white sand beach flanks its waterfront. Each room has a lounge area, private deck, entertainment system, and butler service upon request. The activity center has kayaks, stand-up paddleboards, and Jet Skis for rent. Four restaurants cater to all cravings. When you're not enjoying your room, head to the lagoon frequented by eagle rays, or grab a cocktail in a cabana next to the beachside infinity pool. **Polynesian cultural shows** usually take place once per week on Mondays, ending the evening with a fire dance (CFP 12,900 including buffet meal).

CAMPING

★ BORA BORA CAMPING MOTU ECOLOGIQUE

Motu Tupe; tel. 87 77 91 80; boraboracampingmotuecologique@gmail.com; CFP 4,000/two-person tent, CFP 3,100/campsite space for personal tent

Campsites on Bora Bora have largely gone the way of the dinosaur as resorts prioritize high-priced bungalows in lieu of tent sites. On the tiny island of Motu Tupe, Tahianui and Tihoti welcome campers to enjoy a quiet night under the stars that feels worlds away from the big Bora Bora resorts. Meals are vegetarian, largely made from the fruits and vegetables grown on the motu's garden (optional meal plan of CFP 6,000/person for three meals per day). There's no internet, or electricity, to distract from the scenery. Campers can bring their own camping gear, or use the property's for extra cost (CFP 4,900 for a small two-person tent, CFP 11,500 for a four-person tent). Transport is not included.

INFORMATION AND SERVICES

Vaitape is your best bet for finding goods and services on Bora Bora.

Visitor Information

- **Bora Bora Tourisme:** Vaitape; tahititourisme.com; 8:30am-12:30pm and 1:30pm-4:30pm Mon.-Fri., 8:30am-12:30pm Sat. They'll help with booking tours and transport.

Other Services

- **OPT Post Office:** Vaitape; tel. 40 67 70 24; 7:30am-3:30pm Mon.-Fri., 7:30am-11:30am Sat.
- **Banque de Tahiti:** Vaitape; tel. 40 60 59 99; www.banque-tahiti.pf; 8am-noon and 1pm-4pm Mon.-Fri.
- **Banque de Polynésie:** Vaitape; tel. 40 60 57 57; www.sg-bdp.pf; 7:45am-11:45am and 12:45pm-4:15pm Mon.-Thurs., 7:45am-11:45am and 12:45pm-3:15pm Fri.

Health and Safety

- **Centre Medical de Bora Bora:** Vaitape; tel. 40 67 63 66; 7:30am-12:30pm Mon.-Fri.
- **Vaitape Police Station:** Vaitape; tel. 40 60 59 85
- **Pharmacie Lafayette:** Vaitape; tel. 40 67 70 30; www.pharmacielafayettepf.com; 7am-6pm Mon.-Fri., 8am-6pm Sat., 9am-11am Sun.

GETTING THERE

Getting to Bora Bora is easy by plane, ferry, or private yacht.

Air

Bora Bora's airport (BOB) on Motu Mute is on a motu north of the main island. A 30-minute ferry ride brings arriving air passengers to Vaitape Wharf (free for all travelers). Make sure your luggage is loaded on or off the boat at the airport. Returning to the airport, you must board the ferry 1 hour 15 minutes before your flight time. Most motu resorts offer a boat pickup service directly from the airport.

Bora Bora is an included stop on the Air Tahiti Multi Islands Pass (Bora Bora Pass, Bora-Tuamotu Pass). **Air Tahiti** (www.air-tahiti.com) runs direct flights between Bora Bora and:

- Tahiti: 45 minutes, CFP 25,800/one-way
- Moorea: 45 minutes, CFP 26,000/one-way
- Huahine: 25 minutes, CFP 11,700/one-way
- Maupiti: 20 minutes, CFP 9,700/one-way
- Raiatea: 20 minutes, CFP 9,500/one-way
- Rangiroa: 1 hour 15 minutes, CFP 37,000/one-way

Because Bora Bora is such a popular island, flight prices change dramatically based on demand. If you're flying from Papeete to Bora Bora, sit on the left side of the aircraft for spectacular views.

Boat

VAITAPE WHARF

Most boats arrive at Vaitape Wharf on Bora Bora's western coastline. A fast passenger ferry, the *Maupiti Express II* (tel. 40 67 66 69 or 87 78 27 22) departs Vaitape Wharf for Maupiti, Taha'a, and Raiatea. It leaves for Maupiti on Tuesdays and Thursdays. It leaves for Taha'a and Raiatea on Mondays and Fridays. Tickets can be purchased at the Vaitape Wharf or onboard.

The *Aremiti V* from **Apetahi Express** (tel. 40 50 54 59; apetahiexpress.pf) runs between Tahiti, Huahine, Raiatea, Taha'a, and Bora Bora three times per week, with the most recent rates and schedules updated regularly on their website.

GETTING AROUND

Getting around Bora Bora is easier than many of the other Society Islands, and with a little planning you can do so without your own car. Almost all large restaurants and tours include transport with their services, and are usually happy to pick you up at one point and drop you off at another if you request this in advance. You can see most of Bora Bora's main sights on a quad or 4WD tour; the town of Vaitape is walkable, with most shops and restaurants clustered within 1 kilometer (0.6 mi) from the Vaitape Wharf. For the most freedom, rent a car, bicycle, or roadster (a small two-person buggy).

Public trucks usually meet the boats at Vaitape Wharf, but many of the trucks you see around town are for guests of the luxury hotels. If you do find one willing to take you, the fare between Vaitape and Matira is CFP 500, plus CFP 100 for luggage. Taxi fares for the same route are double.

Boat

Most accommodations on the outer motu have a private shuttle boat service for their guests. If you'd like to visit one of the properties for an event or dinner, it's best to arrange it with them directly. Boat shuttles typically start at CFP 2,000 per person. **Manu Taxi** (tel. 87 79 11 62) offers a taxi boat service to the motu.

Car

The easiest way to get around is with your own car. Most car rental facilities are at the Vaitape Wharf, a convenient location if you've come from the airport ferry. If you rent a car and drive at night, watch out for scooters and bicycles without lights.

CAR RENTAL COMPANIES

- **Europcar** (Vaitape; tel. 40 67 69 60; www.europcar-tahiti.com; 8am-5pm daily; CFP 12,000/day compact car): Has GS Moon Buggies (two people), compact cars, scooters, and SUVs for rent. Price includes pickup and drop-off to accommodation.

- **Avis** (Vaitape; tel. 40 67 70 15; www.avis-borabora.com; 8am-5pm daily; CFP 11,900/day compact car): Rents compact cars, SUVs, minibuses, 4WDs, roadsters, and scooters. Price includes pickup and drop-off to accommodation.

Bike

One of the best ways to explore the main island of Bora Bora is on a bicycle, and many accommodations offer them to their guests. There's an excellent paved road right around the island, with only one steep incline (at Fitiiu Point), almost no hills, and lots of scenic bays to shelter you from the wind. You could cover all of Bora Bora's 32-kilometer (20-mi) coastal road in a full day. The 7-kilometer (4.3-mi) stretch between Vaitape and Matira Point has an array of shops, restaurants, and beautiful Matira Beach, which makes for a nice bike route. However, traffic moves fast in this area, so take extra caution.

Huahine

Huahine, the closest Leeward Island to Tahiti, is a friendly, mountainous island (74 square km/28 square mi) cloaked in vegetation. A drive around the island reveals views accented by tropical flowers, quiet beaches, deep bays, archaeological remains, and an inviting main town where everyone knows everyone. Huahine is also an idyllic surfing locale, with consistent lefts and rights in the two passes off Fare. Schools of dolphins sometimes greet ships arriving through Avapeihi Pass, and you're sure to meet Huahine's large mosquito population as well.

It's claimed the island got its name because, when viewed from the sea, Huahine has the shape of a reclining woman—appropriate for such a fertile place. *Hua* means "phallus" (from a rock on Huahine Iti) while *hine* comes from *vahine* (woman). A narrow channel crossed by a concrete bridge slices Huahine into Huahine Nui and Huahine Iti (Great and Little Huahine, respectively). The story goes that the demigod Hiro's canoe cut this strait.

The almost entirely Polynesian population numbers only 6,000, yet some of the greatest leaders in the struggle for the independence of Polynesia, Pouvanaa a Oopa among them, have come from this quiet island. The artist Bobby Holcomb and the poet Henri Hiro are also well remembered.

In recent years Huahine has been discovered by international tourism, and small pensions and bungalow-style developments are now found in different parts of the island. Luckily Huahine has been able to absorb this influx painlessly, as it's a much larger island than Bora Bora, and the resorts are well scattered and constructed in the traditional Tahitian style. It's an oasis of peace after Papeete. The island has also become a major port of call for the yachts that rock at anchor off Fare. Tourism began in 1973 with the building of the airstrip. Today, the accommodations on Huahine are mostly in small pensions, with only a few proper hotels.

Orientation and Planning

The island of Huahine is in the shape of a figure eight with the larger section, **Huahine Nui,** connected to the smaller section, **Huahine Iti,** by a small bridge.

HUAHINE NUI

Located on the west coast of Huahine Nui, just 3 kilometers (1.8 mi) south of the airport, **Fare** is the main town of Huahine, with a

Huahine

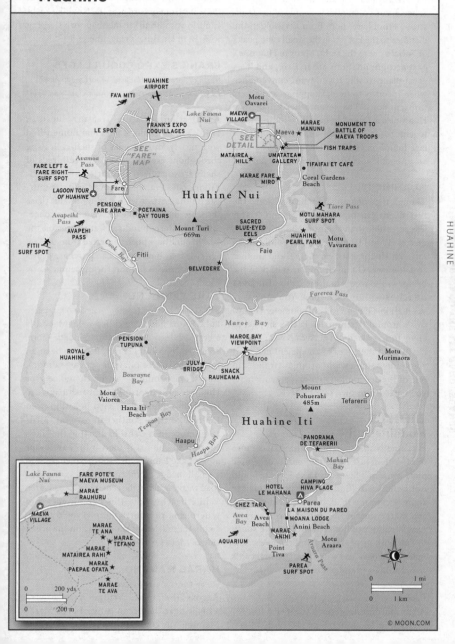

© MOON.COM

tree-lined boulevard along the waterfront, and it is joyfully peaceful after the roar of Papeete. A beach runs along the west side of the main street. From here, Bora Bora is visible in the distance to the left while the small twin peaks of **Taha'a** are to the right. Many of Huahine's best accommodations are in Fare, and it's a great place to stay if you want convenience when it comes to food, shopping, and access to excursions. The seven other villages on Huahine are linked to Fare by winding, photogenic roads. One of these is **Faie,** a quiet village found on Huahine Nui's east coast with an accessible spot to see sacred blue-eyed eels.

HUAHINE ITI

Though the concrete "July Bridge" joins the two islands, Huahine Iti (Little Huahine) is far less accessible than Huahine Nui. It's 24 kilometers (15 mi) from Fare to **Parea,** the main town on Huahine Iti, via Haapu, and another 16 kilometers (10 mi) from Parea back to the bridge via Maroe. Huahine Iti has the **best beaches** within the lagoon. You can easily see it all in a day on the 30-kilometer (18 mi) drive around Huahine Iti. Pack a snorkel to enjoy the corals found at Avea Bay, and wander around the edges of an ancient marae. If you want to stay a while, arrange a transfer to one of the accommodations. If staying here, you'll need your own set of wheels.

SIGHTS
Huahine Nui

Huahine Nui, or Great Huahine, has more to offer than just Fare. The marae, or temple platforms, of Maeva on Lake Fauna should not be missed. Many of the platforms are right next to the road, but the most intriguing marae are on the hillside up a narrow jungle path. You'll also want to drive south to Faie with its pearl farm and river eels. The many deep bays and winding roads make this mountainous island picturesque.

FARE

A handful of restaurants, a yacht club (the social hub of Huahine), a market, a distillery, and a cluster of boutique clothing shops are found within the small town of Fare. From the waterfront of Fare near the Huahine Yacht Club, look south to see the shape of a sleeping woman in Huahine's ridgeline.

FRANK'S EXPO COQUILLAGES

North of Fare on the Huahine Airport road; tel. 87 23 03 23; motutresor@mail.pf; 10am-5pm Mon.-Fri.; free

A collection of natural treasures await in Frank's Shell Expo, a personal home filled with nearly four decades of shell-collecting throughout French Polynesia. Hundreds of shells are organized and sorted into classifications, and Frank is happy to educate tourists on the critters who used to inhabit these intricate shelters—like the venomous conch. All shells were found sans-creatures on the beach; none have been harvested from the sea. Entry is free, but visitors can purchase pearls and souvenirs to support the museum.

LAKE FAUNA NUI

2 km (1.2 mi) north of Fare near Huahine Airport; free

Lake Fauna Nui, also called Lake Maeva, is a brackish lagoon on Huahine's north shore, enclosed by Motu Ovarei. It's long been an important source of ava (a type of salmon), clams, crabs, mullet, sea snails, and eels for Huahine's residents. Ancient fish traps are found throughout, best seen in action from the bridge at its southernmost end. Birds take refuge in the shrubs skirting the lake's shoreline. The main road from Fare loops along Lake Fauna Nui's southern coast, and a small bridge connects it to a less-traveled road weaving along the center of Motu Ovarei. White beaches line this cantaloupe- and watermelon-rich north shore. If you'd care to swim, there's decent snorkeling on the ocean side of Motu Ovarei.

MARAE MANUNU

Ocean side of Maeva Village; free

Across the small bridge near Maeva Village near the ocean is two-tiered Marae Manunu, the community marae of Huahine

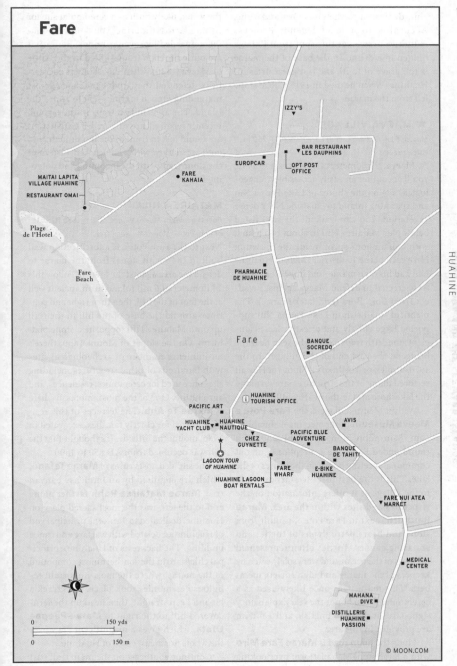

Fare

MAITAI LAPITA
VILLAGE HUAHINE

RESTAURANT OMAI

Plage
de l'Hotel

Fare
Beach

FARE
KAHAIA

EUROPCAR

IZZY'S

BAR RESTAURANT
LES DAUPHINS

OPT POST
OFFICE

PHARMACIE
DE HUAHINE

Fare

BANQUE
SOCREDO

HUAHINE
TOURISM OFFICE

PACIFIC ART

HUAHINE
YACHT CLUB

HUAHINE
NAUTIQUE

CHEZ
GUYNETTE

LAGOON TOUR
OF HUAHINE

FARE
WHARF

HUAHINE LAGOON
BOAT RENTALS

PACIFIC BLUE
ADVENTURE

AVIS

BANQUE
DE TAHITI

E-BIKE
HUAHINE

FARE NUI ATEA
MARKET

MEDICAL
CENTER

MAHANA
DIVE

DISTILLERIE
HUAHINE
PASSION

0   150 yds

0   150 m

© MOON.COM

Nui, dedicated to the gods Oro and Tane. According to a local legend, Princess Hutuhiva arrived at this spot from Raiatea hidden in a drum. In the base of the marae is the grave of Raiti, the last great priest of Huahine. When he died in 1915 a huge stone fell from the marae.

★ MAEVA VILLAGE

Maeva; 6 km (3.7 mi) east of Fare; free (CFP 250 to visit museum)

At Maeva, 6 kilometers (3.7 mi) east of Fare, you'll encounter an easily accessible archaeological site on the shores of Lake Fauna Nui and spanning inland to Huahine Nui's dense vegetation. You can walk all the sites listed below plus Matairea Hill in about two hours, with half an hour spent inside the museum. Here each of the 10 district chiefs of Huahine Nui had his own marae, and huge stone walls were erected to defend Maeva against invaders from Bora Bora (and later France). The plentiful small fish in Lake Fauna Nui supported large chiefly and priestly classes (ancient stone fish traps can still be seen near the bridge at the east end of the village). In the 1970s Professor Yosihiko H. Sinoto of Hawaii restored many of the structures strewn along the lakeshore and in the nearby hills.

Within Maeva Village is the **Fare Pote'e Maeva Museum** (farepotee-maevahuahine. com; 8am-noon Mon.-Fri.; CFP 250) in a round-ended Fare Pote'e, a replica of an old communal meeting house on the shores of the lake. This is the best place to start on a trip to the village as it offers information on the structures and sites within the area. **Marae Rauhuru,** next to Fare Pote'e, is built from stone and bears petroglyphs of turtles and seafaring canoes. Turtles often represented the gods of the ocean, and were solely eaten by keepers of the marae and high society members. This marae was once likely used as a ceremonial site to honor the sea. Explanatory signboards in French, English, and Tahitian are provided in this area.

Along the main road is **Marae Fare Miro** with a large stone slab platform overlooking the water, likely built as a ceremonial site for fishing. Across the bridge you'll find a monument guarded by seven cannons. Beneath it are buried French troops killed in the Battle of Maeva (1846), when the islanders successfully defended their independence against marauding French marines sent to annex the island. The ancient fish traps in the lagoon, recently repaired, are still used. The fish traps are found just in front of the monument, and both are marked with a French sign. Fish enter the stone traps with the incoming and outgoing tides.

MATAIREA HILL

Access begins at Maeva Village, 200 m (656 ft) west of Fare Pote'e Maeva Museum; free

Next to the Fare Pote'e is a fortification wall built in 1846 with stones from the marae to defend the area against the French. Follow this 1 kilometer (0.6 mi) inland to an ancient well at the foot of the hill, then turn right and continue around the base of the hill to the trail up onto Matairea Hill (opposite a stone platform). On the slopes of Mount Tapu, there's an immense number of archeological sites with hundreds of lithic structures including sites once used for ceremonies, residences, and agriculture. One of the most impressive here is **Marae Te Ana.** The terraces of this residential area for chiefly families, excavated in 1986, mount the hillside. It's thought that the hill was occupied from AD 850 to 1800.

The site also hosts ruins of **Marae Tefano,** which are engulfed by an immense banyan tree. **Marae Matairea Rahi,** farther along and to the left, was the most sacred place on Huahine, dedicated to Tane, the principal god of Huahine associated with warfare and canoe building. The backrests of Huahine's principal chiefs are in the southernmost compound of the marae, where the most important religious ceremonies took place. Backtrack a bit and keep straight, then head up the fern-covered hill to the right to **Marae Paepae Ofata,** which gives a magnificent view over the whole northeast coast of Huahine.

Continue southeast on the main trail past

Huahine's Fish Traps

ancient fish traps near Maeva Village

Huahine is one of the few places in Polynesia where ancient fish traps are still in use today. To create these fish traps, fishermen stacked rocks and blocks of coral into V-shaped channels in tidal waters. During incoming tides, fish funnel in from the seaward side and are trapped behind the walled channels as the tide recedes. With only a small entrance and exit in the funnel at low tide, many of the fish stay within the trap. The fish are then easily netted and captured, and those that aren't needed are freed back into the sea. Fish traps in Huahine exist at Lake Fauna Nui and in the waters of Maeva Village. Fish traps similar to those found on Huahine are seen throughout Polynesia, commonly on Hawaii. Today, fishermen on Huahine use the fish traps in a near similar way as their ancestors once did. Most fish is eaten within the community, but you'll see stands selling the day's freshest catch on display along the road early in the morning.

several more marae and you'll eventually cross another fortification wall and meet a dirt road down to the main highway near **Marae Te Ava.** Throughout this easy 2.5-kilometer (1.5-mi) path, watch for stakes planted with vanilla by the residents.

SACRED BLUE-EYED EELS
Faie, East Huahine Nui

In Faie, at the inlet just off the main road, there's a small kiosk selling fish to feed Faie's sacred porcelain-blue-eyed eels. Legend holds that it was huge eels that brought fresh water to the village, and it's considered bad luck to capture them. The eels can grow up to two meters (6.5 ft) long and put on quite an acrobatic performance when tour groups come to

feed them. While blue-eyed eels exist on other Polynesian islands, this is one of the most accessible places to see them.

HUAHINE PEARL FARM
Offshore Faie; tel. 87 78 30 20; www. huahine-pearlfarm.com; 9:30am-4pm Mon.-Sat., 9:30am-noon Sun.

The Huahine Pearl Farm sells pearl jewelry and ceramic pieces just offshore of Faie, with free outrigger boat rides and tours leaving regularly throughout the day. Learn about how pearls are created and shop for a variety of jewelry pieces—simple pearl earrings start at CFP 10,000. The shop also sells handmade pottery crafted by families from a nearby village. If times are slow, you'll often see staff

members glazing the pottery in front of the shop. Tahitian black pearls ranging from hues of pinks, blues, yellows, and greens are found here.

BELVEDERE
Near Maroe Bay

Drive along Huahine Nui's main road south toward Huahine Iti and you'll find a lookout point on the oceanside of the road with views spanning over Maroe Bay. Greens and blues make up the scene, and swaths of vegetation reveal just how fertile Huahine is.

Huahine Iti

Locals will proudly point to the bridge that connects Huahine Iti and Huahine Nui and inform travelers of its ranking as the longest bridge in French Polynesia. Like the rest of Huahine outside of the towns, the landscape is fertile with rolling hills.

MAROE BAY
Bay between Huahine Nui and Huahine Iti

Maroe Bay is where the two islands nearly touch. It's said that the demigod Hiro split the island in half with his canoe after a strong wind blew him through the island. From the middle of the bay, there's a cliff with an indentation resembling the paddle of Hiro's oar. Coming from Faie to Maroe Bay, there's a **viewpoint** on the oceanside of the road with a small turnoff overlooking the blue hues of the bay, spanning across to Huahine Iti.

MARAE ANINI
Southernmost point of Huahine Iti, dirt road access; free

On a white beach on the east side of Point Tiva, 1 kilometer (0.6 mi) south of Parea, is Marae Anini, the community marae of Huahine Iti. It was built by an ancestor of Hiro sometime between 1325 and 1400 as an offshoot of Marae Taputapuatea on Raiatea.

1: the town of Fare in Huahine 2: Learn how Tahitian pearls are made at the Huahine Pearl Farm. 3: the traditional Fare Pote'e Maeva Museum 4: Marae Manunu, a sacred site on Huahine Nui

Look for petroglyphs on this two-tiered structure, dedicated to the god of war Oro, where human sacrifices are thought to have once taken place.

PANORAMA DE TEFARERII
Tefarerii, along Huahine main road; free

A roadside parking lot beckons every driver to stop and enjoy a view of Huahine Iti's greenery and the blues of the lagoon. This lookout point reveals reef, a dark channel, and turquoise hues from the outer sandspit before finally giving way to the open ocean. If you're self-driving around the island, this makes for a well-timed BYO snack spot.

BEACHES

The best beaches are on Huahine Iti.

Huahine Nui

Sandy beaches are surprisingly challenging to come by on Huahine Nui. The lagoon usually backs up into mangroves or coastal vegetation.

FARE BEACH
Fare

Walk north of the Huahine Yacht Club to find a thin crescent of white sand that cedes to aquamarine waters. During school hours, yachties anchored offshore take to the sands. After that, it's a spot beloved by the little ones. **Snorkeling:** The snorkeling isn't the nicest in Huahine, but it's great for a main town spot. Black tip reef sharks frequent the shallows, and there are a few coral bommies to explore.

CORAL GARDENS BEACH
Maeva

Drive along the bridge crossing Lake Fauna Nui to Motu Ovarei and head south along the road until it ends. Park just outside of the defunct resort, and walk past its overgrown paths and concrete blocks (the whole area feels a bit eerie) until you reach a spit of white sand and palm trees. There's a reef to explore between here and Motu Mahare. The beach is quite coarse, and if you're just looking to lounge, it's best to skip this spot. **Snorkeling:** The whole oceanside stretch of Motu Ovarei is flanked by coarse coral beaches, but the best snorkel spot is found at its southernmost point. The current can get quite strong here and it's wise to start at one end of the beach and pop out at the other.

Huahine Iti
HANA ITI BEACH
1 km (0.6 mi) north of Haapu, 1-km dirt trail leads toward the beach

While Hana Iti Beach is most easily accessed by boat or kayak, you can drive and park to the turn-off for a dirt path leading toward the beach—asking the homeowner for permission to walk along the trail. An easy, 20-minute walk through a bamboo forest leads to a castaway cove tucked in between clear waters and palm trees. If you're keen for an offbeat adventure, this beach is the one to visit. **Snorkeling:** Small patches of coral rife with reef fish like parrotfish, angelfish, and butterflyfish are found in the shallows on both the northern and southern ends of the beach.

ANINI BEACH
Southernmost point of Huahine Iti, dirt road access; free

The beach in front of Marae Anini is one of white sand and gin-clear water. Follow the same road you'd take to the Anini Marae, then walk north or south along the beach to enjoy a spot to yourself. **Snorkeling:** If snorkeling here, beware of strong currents in the pass. It's common to spot black tip reef sharks, stingrays, spotted eagle rays, sergeant fish, angelfish, parrotfish, and the occasional coral grouper.

AVEA BEACH
3 km (1.8 mi) from Parea

Perhaps Huahine's most beautiful beach, Avea has a shoreline of soft white sand overlooking Avea Bay. The beach is accessible from Hotel La Mahana, and you can park on their property if you buy a snack or drink at their seaside restaurant. Walk south to escape any crowds. **Snorkeling:** While most of the bottom of the bay is sand, there are coral patches to be found with moray eels, reef sharks, and reef fish cruising about.

SCUBA DIVING
Scuba Dive Sites
Huahine's lagoon is rife with clearwater dive sites that'll impress even the most seasoned divers. These are just a few to get excited about.

FA'A MITI
One of the closest dive sites to Fare, this gentle sloping reef is a haven for reef sharks, giant Napoleon wrasse, eels, and barracudas, and is carpeted in hard and soft corals. Reaching depths of 25 meters (82 ft), it's also one of the most accessible dive sites for new divers.

AVAPEHI PASS
One of the best dive sites in the Leeward Islands, Avapehi Pass is a hotspot for gray reef sharks, white and black tip reef sharks, eagle rays, barracudas, dog-tooth tunas, and schools of pelagic predators. Currents can be quite strong depending on the tides, making it a site best for intermediate divers and up.

AQUARIUM
True to its name, the Aquarium is a clearwater site with plenty of corals to admire. Parrotfish, triggerfish, butterflyfish, and reef sharks galore patrol the site. The site is ideal for snorkel-scuba combination groups, as the depth maxes out around 10 meters (32 ft), making it idyllic for long dives, underwater photographers, and beginners.

Scuba Diving Operators
PACIFIC BLUE ADVENTURE
Fare; tel. 87 26 28 15; www.divehuahine.com; dives depart at 9am and 11am daily; CFP 7,300/fun dive, CFP 40,000/six fun dives

---

1: Avea Beach **2:** Spend a day exploring the lagoon on a motorized canoe. **3:** the hard and soft corals found in Huahine's lagoon

Pacific Blue Adventure has been running dive trips around Huahine for over three decades departing from the center of Fare. Dive sites vary depending on the ocean conditions and group skill level, but usually end up being near one of the reefs on the western side of the lagoon. Dives take place from a 24-foot aluminum boat with shade. Equipment is included with the cost of the dive. Pickup from your accommodation costs CFP 1,500-2,500 for up to four people. This dive center is a member of the Te Moana Diving Pass.

MAHANA DIVE

Fare; tel. 87 73 07 17; www.mahanadive.com; 9am-4pm daily; CFP 7,000/fun dive

Dives depart from Fare on trips with Mahana Dive. Annie, the owner and guide, has a contagious passion for the water and knows which spots work best under the day's ocean conditions. Dives usually take place twice per day, with private dive trips and snorkel tours also available.

SURFING

There are no surf schools or rental stands on Huahine. If you wish to paddle out, you'll need to bring along your own board. Localism is rife on Huahine, and it's best to stick to the inside sets or shoulder until you're welcomed up to the peak. Buying a round of beers for the local surfers can help bump you up the lineup, but only slightly. The incredible waves of Huahine make it worth the trouble, but more beginner surfers will likely want to leave their board behind.

Huahine Nui
FARE LEFT & FARE RIGHT SURF SPOT

Fare

The reef pass at Fare hosts two of Huahine's most popular surf spots. The right loves a northwesterly swell, southeasterly winds, and works decently in all tides. It's long, peeling, and has a playful open face on bigger days. Beginners will enjoy surfing the inside sets.

The left-hand break prefers a westerly swell,

easterly winds, and can barrel under the right conditions. The crowd here can be intense, and set waves aren't handed out easily to new arrivals. On smaller days, the crowd mellows out and good manners will get you far.

MOTU MAHARA SURF SPOT

Motu Mahara, boat ride from Faie

A not-so-crowded surf spot is found offshore from Faie in the pass between Motu Mahara and Motu Vavaratea. Look for northeasterly swells and southwesterly winds for your best chance at a decent wave. It breaks left and is a little friendlier than the one in Fare—but it's still fast.

FITII SURF SPOT

Boat ride or paddle out from Fitii

Fitii can be challenging to get to, requiring a five-minute boat ride or 1-kilometer (0.6-mi) paddle out from Huahine's mainland. Once you're out, a classic right-hand barrel awaits under idyllic conditions. Look for a southwesterly swell.

Huahine Iti
PAREA SURF SPOT

Paddle out at Anini Beach

Strong paddlers can head out to the pass between Motu Araara and Anini Marae to Parea, where the pass breaks right and left. The crowd tends to be more mellow here compared to the spots on Huahini Nui's passes, and the wave is usually friendly. It often gets wrecked by southerly winds—look for northerly winds and southeasterly swells in the forecast. There are no rental facilities here. If the surf is mediocre, the crowd is typically friendly. However, if the waves are going off, it's best to wait your turn and stick to the smaller waves of the sets.

OTHER RECREATION

TOP EXPERIENCE

★ Lagoon Tours

Huahine's lagoon tour operators go above and

beyond the operators found in the Society Islands' more popular islands. So, if you're going to do just one lagoon tour on your journey through these islands, choose one on Huahine. Witness the lush landscape of the island itself, snorkel with rays and sharks, admire rainbow-hued corals, stop at a pearl farm, and dine on a fresh Polynesian lunch with your toes sunk into the white sands of a palm-tree motu.

HUAHINE NAUTIQUE

Fare; tel. 87 78 59 05; www.huahinenautique.com; 8am-4pm daily; CFP 9,500/adult, CFP 4,700/child for a full-day tour

Huahine Nautique offers one of the best lagoon trips in all of French Polynesia—especially compared to those that run in neighboring Bora Bora's lagoon. The lagoon tour starts with a snorkel off Fare, where swimmers fin alongside tens of black tip reef sharks before stopping at a white sand motu for a seafood lunch and pareu-tying demonstration. The trip also ventures to the Huahine Pearl Farm, a second snorkel spot, and between the two islands. Land excursions include stops at Maeva Village, a vanilla plantation, the sacred blue-eyed eels, and picnic on the motu. If you only have two days in Huahine, you could spend one day on land and the other on the lagoon with Huahine Nautique. Combo tours feature half a day on land, half a day on the water.

POETAINA DAY TOURS

tel. 28 92 13; www.poeislandtour.com; 9am-4pm daily; CFP 7,000/person for half-day tour

Poe, the main guide of Poetaina Day Tours, comes from a lineage of charismatic tourism professionals—her parents founded the tour company with boats and 4X4s on Huahine and Bora Bora, plus they have a pension. The lagoon tour runs to the pearl farm, snorkeling sites, and a white sand motu where coconut and poisson cru demonstrations take place. The land tour covers Huahine's main land sights with stops at the sacred eels, a vanilla plantation, panoramic viewpoints, and a fruit farm. It's possible to do both in one day. For those who prefer to stay landside all day, there's a cultural tour where lunch is served at Poe's house with weaving, pareu tying, and Tahitian dance lessons.

Local Tours

With so many archeological sites to uncover, it's best to venture around Huahine with an informative guide. Many tours are done in French unless English is requested in advance, so send a request when making your booking. Lagoon tour operators like **Huahine Nautique** and **Poetaina Day Tours** also offer local tours beyond their main lagoon tour offerings.

GREEN TOURS

tel. 40 68 84 35; greentourshuahine.com; 9am-4pm daily; CFP 6,000/person for half-day tour, CFP 50,000 for a full-day tour (up to eight people)

Green Tours runs themed tours of Huahine centered around the island's culture and natural habitats. On the cultural tour, guides take guests to see the sacred eels, Maeva Village, a vanilla plantation, and the Huahine Pearl Farm. The nature-themed tour includes an easy two-hour walk through Huahine's interior, where guides point out different plant species and share more about Huahine's history. Both tours can be combined for a full-day excursion.

FESTIVALS
HEIVA FESTIVAL

Fare

In July, Huahine has a Heiva Festival similar to the better-known ones on Tahiti and Bora Bora, with an artisans village, fishing tournaments, canoe races, a parade, pétanque competitions, fruit-bearer races, and dance and song contests between Huahine's villages. If you plan to come during this time, book your accommodation well in advance—some pension owners take this time off. Check the Tahiti Tourisme website (tahititourisme.pf) for event times, prices, and locations.

SHOPPING

Huahine Nui

UMATATEA GALLERY

Motu Ovarei; tel. 87 27 27 17; melanie.artiste@free.fr; 9am-3pm Mon.-Fri. (call ahead)

Melanie Shook Dupre at Galerie Umatatea sells prints and original paintings of Polynesian scenes. Her paintings capture the vibrancy and movement of everyday life on Huahine.

PACIFIC ART

Fare; tel. 40 68 70 09; 9am-4pm Mon.-Fri., 9am-noon Sat.-Sun.

This small souvenir and art shop next to the Huahine Yacht Club sells postcards, pareu, clothing, crafts, jewelry, and paintings of Polynesia. Shop hours can be hit or miss, so call ahead if you're going out of your way to stop in here.

DISTILLERIE HUAHINE PASSION

Fare; tel. 87 31 81 35; 9:30am-noon and 2pm-4pm Mon.-Fri.; around CFP 2,000/bottle

If you want to sample fruity liqueur, head to the Distillerie Huahine Passion found on the main road south of Fare. Citrus, banana, coconut, and mixed tropical fruit spirits await, and visitors are welcome to sample them. Note that the coconut-based liqueurs harden into a creamy texture when taken into cooler climates—it's best to enjoy those on-island and save the more fruity concoctions as a souvenir.

Huahine Iti

LA MAISON DU PAREO

Parea; tel. 87 72 01 66; miricolombani@gmail.com; 8:30am-noon and 1:30pm-5pm daily

Sheets of freshly painted pareu dry in the sun at La Maison du Pareo, an art workshop and shop selling hand-painted pareu made by Miri Colombani. Prints range from traditional tiare flowers to scenes of sunsets and sailing yachts.

FOOD

Most pensions include a breakfast and allow guests to access a communal kitchen. There's one supermarket on the island, found in the center of Fare. If you're not staying in a hotel, you'll likely need to find your own lunch or dinner outside of your accommodation.

Huahine Nui

IZZY'S

Fare; tel. 40 68 79 65; 10am-3pm Mon.-Sat.; CFP 1,200

Isabelle opened her namesake restaurant in mid-2017, and it's been a favorite lunch spot among locals ever since. Dishes are served on the open-air terrace with plenty of wooden stools and tables to accommodate the lunchtime rush. Burgers are the main menu item, served 10 ways and with an option for vegans. Chicken nuggets, salads, and hot dogs are also available. All meals are served with a heaping pile of french fries and go well with a cold Hinano.

FARE NUI ATEA MARKET

Fare; open for lunch and dinner; CFP 1,800

Dine like a local at Fare's square of roulotte trucks and snack stands. Come mealtime, locals flock here for affordable plates of fish, barbecued meats, crepes, sandwiches, wraps, and salads.

CHEZ GUYNETTE

Fare; tel. 40 68 83 75; www.pension-guynette-huahine.net; 11am-2pm daily; CFP 1,900

The pension of Chez Guynette also hosts a casual lunchtime spot to enjoy salads, tuna steak, grilled meats, or a hearty burger served with a side of fries. Travelers are welcome just for a cold beer or smoothie. The dining room overlooks the water.

BAR RESTAURANT LES DAUPHINS

Fare; tel. 40 68 89 01; 11:30am-2pm and 6:30pm-8:30pm Tues.-Sun.; CFP 2,200

Bar Restaurant Les Dauphins, beside the post office north of town, is decorated with

---

1: the restaurant at Hotel Le Mahana 2: Shop for handmade pareu at La Maison du Pareo. 3: Izzy's, a spot for the island's best burger 4: waterfront bungalows of Royal Huahine

an array of fishing nets and buoys and serves plates of seafood fare—their mahi-mahi cooked in a creamy vanilla sauce is a popular pick. Crème brûlée and coconut tarts tempt for dessert. On Friday and Saturday nights, it's busy with locals who come to dance to Tahitian music.

★ HUAHINE YACHT CLUB

Fare; tel. 40 68 70 81; 9am-10pm daily; CFP 2,200

Like a magnet, the Huahine Yacht Club attracts whoever is around once the sun starts to sink below the horizon. The jetty out front gets cluttered with dinghies from the yachts anchored just offshore, and locals tend to take over the inside seating areas (with plenty of space to welcome newcomers). True to South Pacific yacht club culture, cats prowl around begging for scraps. Drinks are served ice cold, with happy hour taking place from 5pm-6pm daily. Enjoy dishes of fresh fish (cooked or raw), grilled meats, and vegetables, all usually served with a heaping pile of fries or rice. If you're keen to try a traditional dish, order farafu, fish fermented in sea water. There's usually a jar of it near the cashier.

RESTAURANT OMAI

Fare; tel. 68 80 80; www.huahine.hotelmaitai.com; 11:45am-2pm and 6:45am-9pm daily; CFP 2,500

Surrounded by ponds with lily pads near Fare's waterfront, the restaurant at Hotel Mai Tai is a calm place to enjoy lunch or dinner. The menu has a range of small dishes like salads, wraps, and sandwiches, with heartier dishes of steak, grilled chicken, or fish. Dinnertime features special plates like roasted duck with sweet potato gratin or spiced lamb with cumin. Plant-based diners don't have many options, but the chef is usually happy to create a meal with ingredients they have on hand.

Huahine Iti
SNACK RAUHEAMA

Maroe; tel. 87 78 74 40; 11am-2pm Mon.-Fri.

Snack Rauheama is next to a dock on Maroe Bay. There's a quaint outside dining area with potted plants and picnic tables. Meals are simple snack fare like grilled fish or meat served with grilled vegetables and rice, with cucumber salad and mahi-mahi cooked in vanilla sauce also on offer. The family who owns the snack is quite the entrepreneurial bunch, and have attached a souvenir shop and tattoo parlor to the restaurant building.

CHEZ TARA

Next to Hotel Le Mahana, 3 km (1.8 mi) from Parea; tel. 40 68 78 45; 11:20am-2pm Tues.-Sun.; CFP 1,500

Dine on fresh-caught seafood with your toes in the sand at Chez Tara, a seaside snack serving some of the best tuna with vanilla sauce on Huahine. The service is friendly and laid-back, with the strumming of a ukulele setting the scene. On Sundays, the restaurant hosts a Polynesian buffet—reservations are recommended.

ACCOMMODATIONS

Huahine is low-key when it comes to accommodations. Most stays are family-run pensions, where you're likely to be welcomed as one of their own shortly after the plane touches down. Rooms tend to be clean, with a mosquito net, fan, and internet access. There are a few hotels with spas and restaurants on-site, but they're not nearly as luxurious as those found on Bora Bora.

Huahine Nui
★ PENSION FARE ARA

1 km (0.6 mi) south of Fare; tel. 87 74 96 09; www.fare-ara.com; from CFP 7,000/double room

A 10-minute walk south of Fare is Pension Fare Ara, a pension with multiple accommodation options to choose from: basic rooms in the main house (CFP 7,000/two people), studio apartments (CFP 8,500/two people), and two-bedroom apartments with a living room (CFP 13,500/two people plus CFP 2,000 per additional person). All guests have access to a kitchen, covered terrace, a small gym, and WiFi. Tinau, the host, makes guests feel well cared for with glasses of chilled lemonade and samplings of homemade jam. He's happy to arrange car rental, bike rental, kayak rental, and laundry services for extra cost.

TIFAIFAI ET CAFÉ
Motu Ovarei; tel. 87 77 07 74; tifaifai-et-cafe.com; from CFP 7,000/double room

A little dirt road weaving through a grove of palm tree leads to Tifaifai et Café, a colorful pension on the waterfront of Motu Ovarei. Seashells, fresh flowers, and tifaifai (colorful Tahitian quilts) make the rooms at the pension upbeat and joyful. Two of the three rooms face a garden, while one is set on the waterfront. Rooms sleep from 3-4 people and have an en suite bathroom. Fresh fruits grown on the property are often served to guests. Coral Gardens Beach is a two-minute walk away.

LE SPOT
Fare; tel. 89 09 87 92; www.lespothuahine.com; CFP 10,000/double room

With its own little chalk sand beach, Le Spot is a tranquil place to spend a few days in between the airport and Fare. There are two accommodation options available: rooms in the main block and a two-bedroom villa with full kitchen and living room, ideal for groups. All guests have access to WiFi and cooking facilities. You'll probably want your own set of wheels staying here, as the center of Fare is five minutes away by car.

FARE KAHAIA
Fare; tel. 87 73 64 63; CFP 12,000/two-bedroom home

Fare Kahaia is a cozy two-bedroom home within a five-minute walk from Fare and a one-minute walk from the beach. The property is minimally decorated, clean, and equipped with air-conditioning, a small kitchen, laundry facilities, and living room. One room has a queen bed and the other has two twin beds; petite travelers can squeeze onto the sofa bed. Bernard, the host, is happy to arrange excursions, car rentals, and transport from the airport. It's an ideal spot for groups or families traveling on a budget.

★ PENSION TUPUNA
South Huahine Nui, 2 km (1.2 mi) from the bridge; tel. 40 68 70 36; www.pensiontupuna.com; from CFP 12,500/bungalow

If you have your own transport, staying at Pension Tupuna is a wise choice. The property overlooks the Bay of Port Bourayne, where Huahine's islands split. The pension has five thatched-roof bungalows on its impeccably kept grounds ripe with fruit trees, with options for sleeping up to five people. Driftwood art pieces and furniture made from local wood create a sense of staying in a jungle retreat treehouse. Their features vary (some have hot-water showers and ocean views), but all guests have access to snorkel and kayak equipment. A simple breakfast of bread and fruit is served each morning, and dinner is available for CFP 4,000 per person.

★ MAITAI LAPITA VILLAGE HUAHINE
Fare; tel. 68 80 80; www.huahine.hotelmaitai.com; CFP 30,000/double room

Thirty spacious wooden bungalows are set behind a white sand beach at Maitai Lapita Village, one of the few hotels found on Huahine. Half of the bungalows overlook a lily pond frequented by eels, the rest open out to tropical gardens. All rooms are equipped with private bathrooms and hot-water showers, air-conditioning, a terrace, seating area, and minibar. Some rooms have an extra bed to sleep a total of three guests. The on-site restaurant is one of the best on the island. Guests can easily laze the day away by the seaside pool or little beach (it gets a bit crowded midday when the property is fully booked), strolling the five-minute walk into Fare when it suits. Decent snorkeling is found just offshore. In the evenings, musicians come over to sing and strum as the tides come and go.

ROYAL HUAHINE
South Huahine Nui, 5 km (3 mi) from Fitii; tel. 40 60 60 50; www.royal-huahine.com; CFP 40,000/ double room

On a lonely peninsula on Huahine Nui's south

end, Royal Huahine brings a sense of relaxation from the comforts of its overwater bungalows. It has a real 1960s Tahitian flair to it, with wooden art pieces, tropical prints, and wooden furnishings throughout the property. Some rooms are set on the water—great snorkeling is accessible from the bungalows directly—while the rest are on a white sand beach or garden. All face west with terraces to enjoy sunset. Games tables, a lagoon-style pool, kayaks, and snorkeling equipment help pass the time. Meals are served in a breezy and spacious dining hall. At the time of research, the resort closed for renovation purposes, to refresh the rooms and make them on-par with the overwater bungalows found on Bora Bora.

Huahine Iti

You'll need your own set of wheels while staying on Huahine Iti.

MOANA LODGE

Parea; tel. 87 35 60 98; moanalodge.jimdofree.com; CFP 16,000/bungalow

Moana Lodge is a traditionally Polynesian pension with thatched-roof bungalows set next to a calm bay. A large lawn and sliver of white sand gives kids enough room to run around. Each of the bungalows has a private bathroom with hot-water showers, mosquito nets, fan, and terrace. All can sleep three people. Meals are served in the fare pote'e, usually fresh fruit and bread for breakfast and the catch of the day for dinner. Bikes and kayaks are available for guests.

★ HOTEL LE MAHANA

3 km (1.8 mi) from Parea; tel. 40 45 04 00; www. lemahanahotel.com; CFP 26,500-41,500/bungalow

Hotel Le Mahana is set on arguably the best beach of Huahine, a long wisp of sugar-cookie sand that cedes to bright blue water. The property itself has garden bungalows that can sleep up to two adults, and waterfront bungalows that sleep up to four. Each spacious room is decorated with fresh flowers and painted pareu. The beachside restaurant serves meals all throughout the day

(many accommodations serve just breakfast and dinner), usually sandwiches, wraps, seafood, salads, and steak. Enjoy a cocktail while dangling your feet off the jetty. Guests can use the kayaks, SUPs, and snorkeling gear to explore Avea Bay.

CAMPING
Huahine Iti
CAMPING HIVA PLAGE

Parea; campinghivaplage.over-blog.com; tel. 87 78 19 10; CFP 5,000/double room, CFP 2,600/campsite

Get back to the basics at Camping Hiva Plage, a campsite on a rocky beach of Parea. There's a dedicated spot for campers who have their own equipment, a communal kitchen with worn-down cutlery, a bathroom block, and a handful of bare-bone rooms for rent. The communal area has lounge space and outlets for charging devices.

INFORMATION AND SERVICES

Fare is the main place to find services on Huahine.

- **Huahine Tourism Office:** Fare; tel. 87 68 78 81; 8am-noon Mon.-Sat.

- **Banque de Tahiti:** Fare; tel. 68 82 46; 8am-noon and 1pm-4pm Mon.-Fri.

- **Banque Socredo:** Fare; tel. 40 47 00 00; 7:30am-11:30am and 1pm-3:30pm Mon.-Fri.

- **OPT Post Office:** Fare Inner Road; tel. 68 86 35; 7:15am-1:15pm Mon.-Fri., 7:15am-2:15pm Sat.

- **Pharmacie de Huahine:** Fare; tel. 40 60 61 41; 7:30am-noon and 2:30pm-5pm Mon.-Fri., 8am-noon Sat.-Sun.

- **Medical Center:** Fare; tel. 40 68 82 48; 7:30am-5pm Mon.-Fri., call ahead on weekends

GETTING THERE
Air

Air Tahiti (airtahiti.com) flights arrive at **Huahine Airport** (HUH), just 3 kilometers

(1.8 mi) north of Fare. There is an Air Tahiti office at the airport and in Fare town center. Direct flights connect Huahine to:

- Bora Bora: 25 minutes, CFP 14,500/one-way
- Raiatea: 20 minutes, CFP 9,500/one-way
- Tahiti: 40 minutes, CFP 21,300/one-way
- Moorea: 35 minutes, CFP 22,000/one-way

Most accommodations offer transport from the airport to your accommodation.

Boat

Most yachts arrive at Huahine at the Avamoa Pass or Avapehi Pass near Fare, and there are mooring areas along the west coast.

Passenger ferries tie up at the **wharf** at Fare. The **Apetahi Express** *Aremiti 5* (apetahiexpress.pf) has direct connections to Raiatea (1 hour) and Tahiti (3 hours 50 minutes) three times per week. Huahine is included as part of the Raromatai (CFP 17,900) and Apetahi (CFP 23,900) passes.

GETTING AROUND

Getting around Huahine is not easy unless you rent a car, which most accommodations are happy to help arrange for around CFP 7,000 per day. You will need a car if spending a lot of time on Huahine Iti. Many pensions have bicycles for rent, and it's possible to cover Huahine by bike if you can handle unpredictable weather and hills. Otherwise, locals are usually happy to offer lifts. If you prefer not to drive, take a 4X4 excursion, which will cover most of Huahine's main sights. There are only two gas stations on the island, both in Fare.

- **Avis:** Fare, next to Mobil gas station; tel. 40 68 73 34; 8am-4pm daily; vehicles start at CFP 7,000/day
- **Europcar:** Fare, next to post office; tel. 40 68 82 59; 7am-5:30pm daily; vehicles start at CFP 6,500/day, also have two-wheelers

HUAHINE LAGOON BOAT RENTALS

Fare; tel. 68 70 00; from CFP 10,000/day

Huahine Lagoon, next to New Te Marara Snack Bar at the north end of the Fare waterfront, rents small aluminum boats with an outboard engine for two, four, or eight hours (gas not included) for proficient boat drivers. Masks, snorkels, life jackets, an anchor, oars, and an ice chest come with the boat. Bicycles and kayaks are also for rent for around CFP 1,500.

E-BIKE HUAHINE

Fare; tel. 87 29 90 69; ebikehuahine@gmail.com; 8am-5pm daily; bikes from CFP 5,000/day

Being one of the hillier islands, renting an e-bike isn't a bad choice. Romain, the owner, leads guided e-bike tours of the island and rents his e-bikes for self-guided trips.

Raiatea

Raiatea is traditionally the ancient Havai'i, the "sacred isle" from which all of eastern Polynesia was colonized. It may at one time have been reached by migrants from the west, as the ancient name for Taha'a, Uporu, corresponds to Upolu, just as Havai'i relates to Savai'i, the largest islands of the Samoan chain. A legend tells how Raiatea's first king, Hiro, built a great canoe he used to sail from the deep bay of Faaroa to Rarotonga. With few sandy beaches around its shoreline to tempt sunseekers (these are relegated to Raiatea's motu), Raiatea attracts an intrepid type of traveler. Surfers chase swells at unmapped reef breaks and sailors come for the safe anchorage. Hikers explore the various peaks and valleys often leading through taro plantations, along riverbeds, and through groves of swaying palms. It's the only island where the dainty tiare apetahi grows, and this white flower with petals that look like a crown is often used as the symbol of Raiatea.

Raiatea

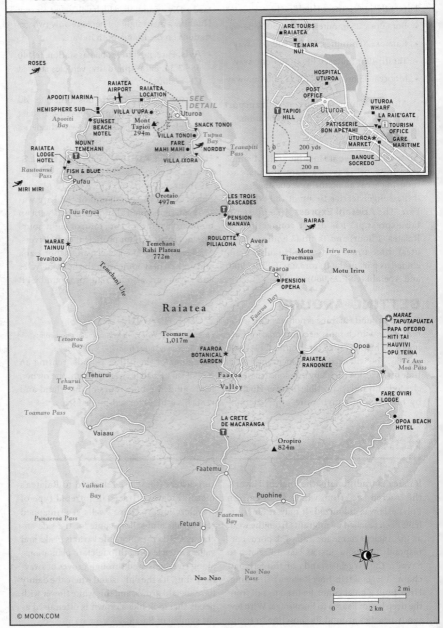

ROSES

APOOITI MARINA
HEMISPHERE SUB

Apooiti Bay

RAIATEA AIRPORT
RAIATEA LOCATION

SEE DETAIL

VILLA U'UPA
Uturoa

SUNSET BEACH MOTEL
Mont Tapioi 294m

SNACK TONOI

Tupua Bay

MOUNT TEMEHANI
VILLA TONOI
FARE MAHI MAHI
NORDBY

Teavapiti Pass

RAIATEA LODGE HOTEL

VILLA IXORA

Rautvanui Pass

FISH & BLUE
Pufau

MIRI MIRI

Tuu Fenua

Orotaio 497m

LES TROIS CASCADES

PENSION MANAVA

RAIRAS

Iriru Pass

MARAE TAINUU
Tevaitoa

Temehani Ute

Temehani Rahi Plateau 772m

ROULOTTE PILIALOHA
Avera

Motu Tipaemaua

Motu Iriru

Tetooroa Bay

Faaroa
PENSION OPEHA

Raiatea

Faaroa Bay

Toomaru 1,017m

FAAROA BOTANICAL GARDEN

RAIATEA RANDONEE

Opoa

Te Ava Moa Pass

MARAE TAPUTAPUATEA
– PAPA OFEORO
– HITI TAI
– HAUVIVI
– OPU TEINA

Tehurui Bay
Tehurui

Faaroa Valley

Toamaro Pass

Vaiaau

LA CRETE DE MACARANGA

FARE OVIRI LODGE

OPOA BEACH HOTEL

Oropiro 824m

Vaihuti Bay

Faatemu

Punaeroa Pass

Faatemu Bay

Fetuna
Puohine

Nao Nao

Nao Nao Pass

Detail inset (Uturoa):

ARE TOURS RAIATEA
TE MARA NUI

HOSPITAL UTUROA

POST OFFICE

TAPIOI HILL

Uturoa

UTUROA WHARF
LA RAIE'GATE

PATISSERIE BON APETAHI

TOURISM OFFICE

UTUROA MARKET
GARE MARITIME

BANQUE SOCREDO

0   200 yds
0   200 m

0   2 mi
0   2 km

© MOON.COM

Orientation

Practically speaking, **Uturoa** is the main town of Raiatea and the business, educational, and administrative center of the Leeward Islands. Uturoa, on the northeastern corner of the island, is an easy place to find your way around, with a row of Chinese stores along a main drag opening onto the **Gare Maritime,** a shopping center on the wharf of Uturoa. The island's airport is 3 kilometers (1.8 mi) west of town, with the main yacht charter base, Marina Apooiti, 1 kilometer (0.6 mi) beyond that. Most travelers stay within a 5-kilometer (3-mi) radius of Uturoa—other accommodations are somewhat isolated from shops, restaurants, and other services.

The balance of Raiatea's population of about 12,000 lives in eight flower-filled villages around the island. Moving clockwise from Uturoa, the villages are Avera, Opoa, Puohine, Fetuna, Vaiaau, Tehurui, Tevaitoa, and Tuu Fenua. The west coast of Raiatea south of Tevaitoa is old Polynesia through and through. Being such a large island—the second largest in the Society Islands—spending a few days here is a must if you want to see it all.

UTUROA

Uturoa (pop. 4,000) is the territory's second city and the first stop on any exploration of the island. The Uturoa waterfront has a cruise ship terminal, information offices, restaurants, and shops, plus a traditional-style market selling fresh produce and handicrafts. The ferry plying between Tahiti and Bora Bora calls here, and there's a frequent shuttle to Taha'a.

Large cruise ships call here several times a week, flooding the little town with visitors. If you'd like to be able to sit at a waterfront café in peace or have the undivided attention of shop clerks, try to find out when love boats will be in port and avoid Uturoa those days. Rental cars will be in high demand, so reserve well ahead. If you're a cruise ship passenger yourself, you'll probably save money on excursions by dealing directly with the tour operators inside the Gare Maritime right on the wharf, although you could also miss out on the excursion if it's already fully booked.

Sights

UTUROA MARKET

Uturoa; 5:30am-4pm Mon.-Sat., 5:30am-noon Sun.

A little after sunrise, Uturoa Market is alive with shoppers who've come to gather fresh fish, meat, and produce for the day. Stands selling vanilla, oils, handicrafts, and hand-painted pareu crowd the second floor. The market is found directly across the road from Gare Maritime.

Scuba Diving and Snorkeling

There's no shortage of untouched dive sites around Raiatea and Taha'a's expansive lagoon—dive shops venture to over a dozen regularly. All dive centers listed can also arrange snorkeling excursions to coral reefs in Raiatea's shallows. **Humpback whales** cruise past Raiatea and Taha'a's coastline from September to December, and are often spotted from the boat in between dives. Most sites listed in this section are suited primarily for scuba divers. Scuba dive operators tend to choose dive sites catered to the ocean conditions and divers' abilities, but are often happy to arrange trips to specific dive sites if requested in advance.

NORDBY DIVE SITE

Uturoa

In 1990, *The Nordby* sunk off Raiatea's east coast. This three-mast ship still has its rigging and hull intact, and it's had just enough time to build a solid base of corals. Surgeonfish, lionfish, anemonefish, reef sharks, eels, angelfish, and other creatures have moved in. Dive it during the day, then come back at night to enjoy its eerie atmosphere.

MIRI MIRI DIVE SITE

Raiatea West Coast

Beginner and experienced divers alike will enjoy the ultra-clear waters of this fish-dense dive site found off Raiatea's western coastline. Black tip reef sharks roam the shallows of the water column, while lemon sharks, Napoleon wrasses, schools of snappers, and the occasional striped barracuda linger in the depths.

ROSES DIVE SITE
Raiatea West Coast

At 35 meters (115 ft) deep, Roses is a dive site reserved for experienced divers only. On the seabed, a garden of rose-shaped corals with flat plates resembling flower petals gives the site its deserved name. Swordfish, various shark species, barracudas, rays, and pelagic fish cruise through the dark blue surrounds.

RAIRAS DIVE SITE
Raiatea East Coast

While gray sharks are the stars of the show at Rairas, black tip reef sharks, white tip reef sharks, and lemon sharks also often make their appearance here. This dive site is suitable for all levels, and is a hot spot for jacks and tunas.

HEMISPHERE SUB
Uturoa; tel. 40 66 12 49; www.hemispheresub. com; 7:30am-9pm daily; CFP 7,500/fun dive, CFP 64,000/10 fun dives

Hemisphere Sub runs fun dives to over 20 sites around Raiatea and Taha'a, tailoring each trip to the skills and interests of the group. They also offer courses from discover scuba to divemaster. If you're in a group, it could be worth chartering their boat for a snorkeling excursion of up to six people (CFP 55,000/day). Four dives take place each day, with the last one departing around 7:30pm. Night divers, take note.

TE MARA NUI
Uturoa; tel. 87 72 60 19; www.te-mara-nui.com; 7:30am-5pm daily; CFP 7,200/fun dive, CFP 5,000/ half-day snorkel trip

Te Mara Nui runs scuba, snorkel, and day trips around the lagoon. Scuba divers can go on fun dives and get their advanced open water training with Te Mara Nui. Snorkel trips usually stop at spots popular with reef sharks, also stopping at a motu for lunch on full-day

excursions. Snorkel and sightseeing tours to Taha'a are also available, stopping at some of Taha'a's main sights (CPF 9,000/day).

Day Tours

Day tours depart from Uturoa on trips around the island or lagoon excursions that stop for a lunch on one of the motu, with many trips also venturing to Taha'a. If you're short on time (or means of transportation), a day tour is the best way to get a primer of the two islands within the lagoon.

ARE TOURS RAIATEA
Uturoa; tel. 87 79 01 98; aretours-raiateatahaa.com; 7:30am-5pm daily; CFP 10,000/adult, CFP 5,000/ child under 12 for full-day tour

The captain drives, the guide plays the ukulele as Are Tours Raiatea's red motorboat cruises over the lagoon. Are Tours Raiatea leads groups on snorkel trips, trips to Taha'a, up the Faaroa River to the Taputapuatea Marae, and more. It's usually a long day out—from morning until near sunset, and the excursions tend to move at a fast pace. Their lagoon trip to Taha'a is one of the best offered.

Hiking

Most hiking guides are based in Uturoa and offer transport between your accommodation and the trailhead. Trails on Raiatea are typically unmarked, steep, slippery, and susceptible to inclement weather—bring a rain shell and sturdy shoes. Hiking guides and day trips are usually best arranged through your accommodation.

TAPIOI HILL
Distance: *3 km (1.8 mi) out-and-back*
Time: *2 hours*
Trailhead: *Uturoa, inland from the Uturoa Hospital*
Information and maps: *www.alltrails.com*

For a spectacular view of four islands (Raiatea, Taha'a, Huahine, and Bora Bora), climb Tapioi Hill (294 m/964 ft), the peak topped by a television relay antenna behind Uturoa. As you stand on the rocky hilltop facing Taha'a, Bora

Bora will be at 10 o'clock on your left and Huahine directly right. There are rope handles to help during the steeper sections. It's one of the easiest and most satisfying climbs in French Polynesia, and an excellent free activity if you're traveling with children.

Take the road beside the gendarmerie and you'll reach the foot of the hill in a few minutes. This is private property, and although the owners allow visitors to climb Tapioi on foot, they've posted a sign just before the cattle grid at the bottom of the hill asking that private cars not be used. During the high season, the trail often closes during the weekends or to allow the trail owners some privacy. It's best to allow two or three hours to hike up and down. Take sufficient water along with you and wear comfortable shoes; the trail can get slippery if it's just rained.

KIAM MARTI

tel. 87 27 23 00; kiam.marti@gmail.com; CFP 10,000/person for a full-day hike

With Kiam as your guide, virtually no trail on Raiatea is off-limits. He's happy to lead short beginner-friendly excursions as well as full-day affairs through the island's interior, like to Mount Temehani to search for the rare tiare apetahi flower, shuffle down lava tubes, and trek through creek beds leading to waterfalls. Lunch and snacks are usually included on full-day trips. Half-day hikes are also possible to arrange on request.

RAIATEA RANDONEE

tel. 40 66 20 32; raiatearando@mail.pf; CFP 10,000/person for a full-day hike

Hiking guide Thierry Laroche has experience exploring Raiatea's most remote regions, and is happy to lead guided hikes along Raiatea's main trekking trails.

Food

Uturoa is home to the lion's share of Raiatea's restaurants, which usually serve traditional Polynesian or French fare.

PATISSERIE BON APETAHI

Uturoa Wharf; tel. 40 66 40 00; 6:30am-4pm daily; pastries around CFP 500

The delightful pastry shop of Patisserie Bon Apetahi doles out typical French pastries and sweets embellished with tropical fruits. Eclairs, glazed fruit tarts, pain au chocolat, almond croissants dusted with powdered sugar… all can be enjoyed in a shaded outdoor dining area on the Uturoa Wharf.

★ SNACK TONOI

Uturoa PK1; tel. 40 66 32 56; 11:30am-1:30pm Mon.-Wed., 11:30am-1:30pm and 6pm-8:30pm Thurs., Fri., and Sun.; CFP 2,000

For a true French Polynesian culinary experience, head to Snack Tonoi, where plates of fresh fish, root vegetables, and side salads test the weight limit of each plate they're served on. The trio of tuna is a popular pick, as is their lobster. Come for dinner for a good chance of seeing locals dance to the live music played regularly. Or, head here while the sun is out to dine on the sand with views of Raiatea blues—tables are on the beach.

LA RAIE'GATE

Uturoa Wharf; tel. 40 66 34 24; 6:30am-9pm Mon.-Fri.; CFP 2,500

La Raie'gate has an earthy-meets-industrial ambiance about it with dangling lightbulbs, a bamboo bar, and furniture crafted from wood and steel. Fresh-baked breads and egg dishes tempt for breakfast, with burgers, pizzas, seafood, and salads for dinner. Their drinks menu is one of the most comprehensive on Raiatea, with craft beers, wines, and cocktails.

VILLA IXORA

Uturoa PK 2.7; tel. 40 66 33 00; www.villa-ixora.com; 11:30am-1:15pm and 6pm-8:15pm Tues.-Sat.; CFP 2,700

The Villa Ixora pension restaurant is open to non-guests for lunch and dinner, and it'd be a shame not to experience Terence's home cooking. Grilled meat and fish often sourced from local farmers and fishermen is served with sides of seasonal produce. A small wine list

BORA BORA AND THE LEEWARD ISLANDS
RAIATEA

of imported French wine completes the meal. The setting is simple; the dining room is next to the pension pool and garden.

Accommodations
FARE MAHI MAHI

Inland Uturoa PK 2; tel. 87 27 80 76; CFP 13,000/ double room

Hammocks on the patio and a small infinity pool welcome travelers to Fare Mahi Mahi, a laid-back accommodation found outside of Uturoa. The road leading to the property is steep, so you'll want your own vehicle to get here (easily arranged through the pension owner, who is also happy to offer occasional rides). Rooms are clean and modern, furnished with plenty of loungers, a private bathroom, and tea kettle. Owners Lauren and Sandrine are happy to suggest Raiatea itineraries and arrange excursions.

VILLA U'UPA

Uturoa, 700 meters (0.4 mi) inland from Total station; tel. 87 72 34 43; CFP 13,000/double room

Villa U'upa, named after the green-feathered dove often spotted around the property, is a wooden villa decorated with seashells and driftwood just outside of central Uturoa—about a 15-minute walk from the pension to the wharf. The villa is set up as a homestay; rooms are a mix of private and shared bathrooms. Two beds are set up in the villa's mezzanine and lack privacy. All guests have use of the kitchen, pool, and patio area. Christine, the host, goes out of her way to ensure tours, car rentals, and hikes are arranged for her guests.

VILLA TONOI

Uturoa PK1; tel. 40 66 44 55; www.villatonoi.com; CFP 15,000/double room

Up on a steep hill overlooking the water, Villa Tonoi is a tranquil pension with a pool, deck, communal lounge area, and a handful of standalone bungalows. Each bungalow has two double beds (standard room rate includes two guests with CFP 2,000 per additional

guest), a microwave, fridge, private bathroom, minibar, WiFi access, fan, and TV. Breakfast is not included, but can be ordered for an extra CFP 1,500 per person. If the humpback whales are around, you can watch them breathe and breach from your room. The hill to the property makes it inconvenient for walking to town, so having your own transport or arranging it in advance is recommended.

Information and Services

- **Tourism Office:** Central Uturoa; tel. 40 66 07 77; raiateainfo@tahiti-tourisme.pf
- **Hospital Uturoa:** Central Uturoa; tel. 40 60 08 00 non-emergency number, tel. 40 60 08 01 emergency
- **Post Office:** Central Uturoa; tel. 40 66 35 50; opt.pf; 7am-3pm Mon.-Thurs., 7am-2pm Fri., 8am-10am Sat.
- **Banque Socredo:** Central Uturoa; tel. 40 47 00 00; socredo.pf; 7:30am-11:30am and 1pm-3:30pm Mon.-Fri.

Getting There

As French Polynesia's second-largest city, the administrative nature of Uturoa makes it easy to reach by plane or boat.

RAIATEA AIRPORT

Uturoa

Raiatea Airport (RFP) is 3 kilometers (1.8 mi) northwest of Uturoa, with a café and car rental stands on its grounds. The Air Tahiti office is at the airport in a separate building adjacent to the main terminal. **Air Tahiti** (air-tahiti.com) has direct flights between Raiatea and Tahiti (45 minutes, CFP 23,000/one-way) multiple times per day. There are also direct flights between Raiatea and Bora Bora (20 minutes, CFP 10,000), Huahine (20 minutes, CFP 9,000), and Maupiti (25 minutes, CFP 12,000). Fares and schedules change seasonally. Raiatea is included in multiple Air Tahiti Multi Islands Air Passes. Tahiti Air Charter (tac.pf) also flies between Raiatea and Maupiti and Bora Bora.

UTUROA WHARF
Uturoa

The Uturoa Wharf is in the center of Uturoa, and is where most ferries and day tours depart from. To arrive by ferry, take the **Apetahi Express** (www.apetahiexpress.pf) *Aremiti 5* ferry, which runs between Uturoa and Huahine (1 hour), Taha'a (45 minutes), and Bora Bora (1 hour 15 minutes) three times per week. The current schedule is posted on their website.

The yellow and blue *Maupiti Express 2* (tel. 40 67 66 69), a fast ferry with 140 airline-type seats, runs one-way/round-trip between Raiatea and Bora Bora, departing Uturoa for Bora Bora Monday, Friday, and Sunday afternoons. It's not possible to go directly from Raiatea to Maupiti on this vessel—you must overnight on Bora Bora.

The fast ferries (navettes) of **Enota Transport Maritime** (tel. 87 72 76 47 or 87 75 73 16) shuttle between Raiatea and Taha'a. The fleet consists of two 57-seat ferries, the *Tehaere Maru IV* and *Tehaere Maru V*. The 66-passenger ferry *Tamarii Taha'a I* also leaves Uturoa for the west coast of Taha'a (Poutoru, Tiva, Tapuamu, Patio). Posted schedules are unreliable, so it's best to call.

Getting Around

Uturoa is walkable, with the main stretch of road along the waterfront being less than 2 kilometers (1.2 mi) long. The 98-kilometer (60-mi) road around Raiatea is well paved, and PK markers begin at Uturoa Wharf. An 11-kilometer (6.8-mi) cross-island road links Faaroa on the east coast and Faatemu on the south coast. There is no reliable form of public transportation, as most locals get around with their own set of wheels. For complete freedom, it's best to rent a car.

LE TRUCK

Getting around by the local minibus, colloquially called "le truck," isn't easy. At around 5:45am, it departs from Opoa near Marae Taputapuatea and drives north along the eastern coast, reaching Uturoa around 7:30am.

It then departs at 10am to loop around the island. You should be able to use it to get into town in the morning, and it's best to check exact times with your accommodation. In Uturoa the trucks usually park between Hotel Hinano and the waterfront, and there are no marked signs. The drivers themselves are the only reliable source of departure information. Budget around CFP 300 per trip, paid in cash to the driver.

RAIATEA LOCATION

Uturoa; tel. 40 66 34 06; www.raiatealocation.com; car rental from CFP 6,500 per day

Raiatea Location rents out a range of small cars like Fiat Pandas and Hyundai I10s as well as larger sedans like Fiat 500s. If you want a 4WD, they have Dacia Dusters and Nissan Navarras for around CFP 15,000 per day. Scooters cost from CFP 3,800-4,300 per day. Boats are also available; a small skiff with a 30hp two-stroke engine goes for CFP 7,500 per day.

APOOITI MARINA

Uturoa; tel. 40 66 12 20

This public marina half a kilometer (a third of a mile) west of the Raiatea Airport has 80 slip spaces, accommodating vessels up to 55 feet long. Vessels have access to water, electricity, and internet.

EAST COAST

The road down Raiatea's east coast circles fjord-like Faaroa Bay. From the coastline, there's a view of Toomaru, the highest peak in the Leeward Islands. French Polynesia's only navigable river, the Apoomau, trains into the verdant Faaroa Valley. Yellow hibiscus flourishes along the riverbanks. On the southern point of Raiatea's east coast is Marae Taputapuapea, one of the most sacred sites in all Polynesia.

Sights and Beaches
FAAROA BAY
PK 12
Twelve kilometers (7.5 mi) south of Uturoa

the road curves inland at Faaroa Bay. Small houses with perfectly trimmed tropical gardens dot the shoreline, and there are a few pullouts along the road to pull over and admire the views.

FAAROA BOTANICAL GARDEN
PK 14; 7am-7pm daily; free
On the edge of Faaroa Bay is the Faaroa Botanical Garden. A path leads through a garden of tropical flowers, fruit trees, picnic areas, and mape trees (Tahitian chestnut trees). A handful of picnic benches beckon those in need of a break, and there are grassy areas for kids to run around. There's rarely a crowd, and some parts of the garden path veer around the inlets of Faaroa Bay.

★ MARAE TAPUTAPUATEA
PK 42; free
From Faaroa Bay, follow the coast south around to a point of land just beyond Opoa, 32 kilometers (20 mi) from Uturoa. Here stands Marae Taputapuatea, one of the largest and best-preserved temples in Polynesia, its mighty ahu (altar) measuring 43 meters long, 7.3 meters wide, and 2-3 meters high (141 ft long, 24 ft wide, and 6.5-10 ft high). Before the altar is a rectangular courtyard paved with black volcanic rocks. A small platform in the middle of the ahu once bore the image of Oro, god of fertility and war (now represented by a reproduction); backrests still mark the seats of high chiefs on the courtyard. Marae Taputapuatea is opposite Te Ava Moa Pass, and fires on the marae may once have been beacons to ancient navigators.

Several of the temple platforms have been restored. **Hauvivi,** on the waterfront of the archeological area, was the welcoming marae (ceremonial site), where guests would have been received as they disembarked from their canoes. They would then have proceeded to Marae Taputapuatea, the main ceremony platform, which gives its name to the whole site

and is where rituals were performed. Meals were served on **Hiti Tai,** a platform on the north side of the complex. Next to Hiti Tai, **Papa Ofeoro** was the place of sacrifice (about 5,000 skulls were discovered during excavations at the site). **Opu Teina** near the beach was the sacred platform where visitors would say their farewells. Departing chiefs would often take a stone from this marae to be planted in new marae elsewhere, which would also receive the name Marae Taputapuatea.

Locals have recently created a well-marked 1.5-kilometer (1-mi) out-and-back walking trail through the marae to a terrace overlooking the site of the marae. The whole walk should take around an hour; wooden stairs and walkways ensure you won't get lost. There is no visitor's center or booth, but the walk is easy to enjoy on your own.

Marae Taputapuatea is one of the most important cultural sites for Polynesian seafarers, and is often the site of modern ceremony. In 2022, Hawaii's voyaging canoes Hōkūle'a and Hikianalia gathered at the marae with Raiatea elders to seek their blessing in crossing long distances in Polynesian waters. This tradition spans decades, with one of the largest expeditions taking place in 1995, when a fleet of traditional Polynesian voyaging canoes gathered at Taputapuatea to pay tribute to their ancient seafaring ancestors. It was also thought this voyage would lift a 650-year-old curse and rededicate the marae. The seven canoes left for the Marquesas, navigating by the stars and swells. Some carried on to Hawaii and the west coast of the United States in an amazing demonstration of the current revival of this aspect of traditional culture. In recent years, communities like the Polynesian Voyaging Society have kept this tradition alive.

MOTU IRIRU AND MOTU TIPAEMAUA
1.5 km (0.9 mi) from Taputapuapea; free
The main island of Raiatea lacks the sandy beaches envisioned on travel brochures. The best beaches are found on the motu, tiny islands at the edge of Raiatea's barrier reef. Just

---

1: the waterfront of Uturoa **2:** Raiatea Airport **3:** Faaroa Botanical Garden **4:** view of Faaroa Valley

off the settlement of Taputapuapea are the two motu of Motu Tipaemaua and Motu Iriru. Both are idyllic as a snorkel stop on a lagoon tour, with Motu Iriru flanked by a white sand shoreline.

Hiking
LES TROIS CASCADES
Distance: 5 km (3.1 mi) out-and-back
Time: 3 hours
Trailhead: Trailhead begins at PK 6.8; follow the road leading to "Pension des Trois Cascades"
Information and maps: www.alltrails.com
Les Trois Cascades trail is steep and slippery with a few stream crossings, so dress accordingly. The dirt path leads through a forest of mape trees with wide roots that were once beaten with rocks like drums to communicate across vast distances. The first waterfall is a series of trickling pools along moss-covered rock steps, reached after around 45 minutes of brisk hiking. The second waterfall is a wide bridal veil roaring off a craggy rock face. The trail to the final waterfall is slippery and narrow, and most hikers will grab onto ropes set up along the trail for assistance. Fortunately, your effort is rewarded with a 35-meter (115-ft) cascade, the most striking of the trio. Depending on the water level, it's possible to wade in the pool below. It's best to complete this trek with a guide like Thierry (tel. 87 77 91 23; raiatearando@mail.pf) or Kiam (tel. 87 27 23 00; kiam.marti@gmail.com). A trip costs around CFP 5,500 per person.

LA CRETE DE MACARANGA
Distance: 1.3 km (0.8 mi) out-and-back
Time: 1 hour
Trailhead: Trailhead begins at the Raiatea cross-island road near Faaroa College; the trailhead is signed
Information and maps: www.alltrails.com
A steep but well-marked trail leads along Macaranga Ridge, with impromptu steps made from tree roots and rope hand-holds for assistance. On a clear day, the view from the top spans to neighboring ridgelines and Raiatea's azure lagoon. Wild berry bushes,

ferns, vines, and tropical flowers accent the trail. There's a large parking area at the trailhead, as well as a sign. This is one of the few trails on Raiatea easily done without a guide.

Food and Accommodations
ROULOTTE PILIALOHA
PK 8; tel. 87 25 29 19; 5:30pm-8:30pm Mon.-Sat.; CFP 1,500
This cheerful snack sells fresh-caught fish dishes like sashimi, tuna many ways, and poisson cru. Chicken, steak, and Chinese rice dishes are also available with sides of salad, fries, or rice. It's one of the few casual restaurants with vegetarian options on Raiatea, offering tofu carpaccio and vegetable chow mein. Don't miss their milkshakes.

★ PENSION MANAVA
PK 7; tel. 40 66 28 26; CFP 11,500/bungalow
Five spacious bungalows are set among a well-kept garden at Pension Manava. Each one has a kitchen, terrace, internet access, and en suite bathroom with hot-water shower. All can sleep up to four guests, making it an ideal pick for families and friend groups on a budget. A breakfast of fresh fruit, bread, juice, and coffee is extra for CFP 1,000 per person. A swimming pool with shaded lounge chairs beckons after a long day of sightseeing. The hosts, Roselyne and Andrew, are exceptionally helpful and happy to arrange lagoon tours onboard their boat with shaded seating, rental cars, and day trips.

PENSION OPEHA
PK 11; tel. 40 66 19 48; CFP 15,000/bungalow
Wake up near the waterfront at Pension Opeha, a pension on the edge of Faaroa Bay. Each of the newly renovated bungalows are equipped with air-conditioning, a kitchen, a bathroom with hot-water shower, and a small terrace—all are just a few steps away from the swim dock jutting from the edge of the property. It's a tranquil space where guests can kayak, go for walks along the bay, and take half-day trips to Motu Tipamaua, the small

motu (island) just a little over a kilometer offshore.

FARE OVIRI LODGE

PK 35; tel. 87 79 63 96; ovirilodge.com; from CFP 19,000/bungalow, CFP 14,000/room

Perched on a hill overlooking the water is a quaint lodge with the ambiance of a tropical treehouse. Two stilted bungalows are built from bamboo and wood sourced on the island, with wide windows that let in the sea breeze. In the main lodge, four private rooms connect to the communal area. All accommodation options have a private bathroom with hot water, desk, and mosquito net. The bungalows are equipped with a kitchenette, and guests in the main lodge have access to the home's kitchen. Fruit trees growing papaya, grapefruit, breadfruit, and soursop are spread throughout the property; a tidy trail leads down to a white sand shoreline, where a handful of beach chairs await.

OPOA BEACH HOTEL

PK 37; tel. 40 60 05 10; opoabeach.com; CFP 40,000

Opoa Beach Hotel hosts nine charming bungalows near the water, each painted white with bright and airy decor inside. It's a peaceful place, where a long pier retreats over a decent snorkeling spot, and guests can explore the coastline by kayak. Each of the rooms has a four-poster bed, air-conditioning, a safe, a lounge area with a TV and minibar, a bathroom with hot-water showers, and a terrace with hammocks strewn about. Rotate between the pool and the sea. Seafood lunches and candlelit dinners (both extra cost) are served at the on-site seaside restaurant.

Getting There and Around

The best way to get around Raiatea's eastern coastline is with a rental car. All accommodations are too far from sights to be convenient to stay in without a vehicle. If you prefer not to rent a car, choose an accommodation with on-site all-day dining or kitchen access.

LE TRUCK

Route begins at 5:30am; from CFP 200 per trip

The le trucks, open-air buses, run from Opoa village at PK 32 starting around 5:30am each morning to Uturoa, reaching Uturoa around 7-7:30am. Their schedules are not regular, and it's wise not to rely on them completely.

WEST COAST

Raiatea's west coast is largely unpopulated; colorful homes line the road sporadically, with the settlements of Fetuna and Vaiaau being the few places to pick up convenience goods.

Sights
MARAE TAINUU

PK 13

Marae Tainuu is dedicated to the Polynesian deity Taaroa, who is thought to be the divine creator. According to legend, Taaroa's existence started as an egg in the void of the universe. He broke from his shell, using the pieces to create the landscape of earth and parts of himself to create earth's creatures. After this was complete, he formed other deities. Petroglyphs on a broken stone by the road at the entrance to the church show a turtle and an oval figure. The site features giant stone slabs built to protect the marae and a large ahu (altar) within the complex. The marae is behind Church Tevaitoa, built intentionally next to the marae by Protestant Missionaries. Within Tevaitoa, Tevaitoa Chief Teraupo and his people fought their last battles against the French invaders in early 1897.

Hiking
MOUNT TEMEHANI

Distance: *15 km (9 mi) out-and-back*
Time: *8 hours*
Trailhead: *Trailhead begins at PK 7.5, near Pharmacie Temehani*
Information and maps: *www.alltrails.com*

When you first set foot on the slopes of Mount Temehani, you might be surprised to be walking among forests of trees that look distinctly out of place. These Caribbean pine trees are the unfortunate result of a failed furniture-making venture. While the business went bust, the trees took over. The trail is steep from the get-go, and as you climb in altitude, forests cede to shrubs and ferns. A rope assists climbers to the summit. Views stretch to Taha'a and Maupiti. It's here that you'll find the symbol of Raiatea, the crown-shaped tiare apetahi, a white five-petal flower which grows nowhere else in the world. The myth of this flower stems from a tragic love story, when a young girl named Tiaitau fell in love with King Tamatoa. After King Tamatoa was lost at sea, heartbroken Tiaitau threw herself from the top of Mount Temehani, and the tiare apetahi grew in remembrance of her love; many tell the story as the flower being a symbol of Tiaitau's hand. The trail up Mount Temehani is not well-trod (or marked), so you'll want to go with a guide like Tierry (tel. 87 77 91 23; raiatearando@mail.pf) or Kiam (tel. 87 27 23 00; kiam.marti@gmail.com). This trek costs around CFP 10,000 per person, including transport and snacks.

Food and Accommodations
★ FISH & BLUE

PK 8.8; tel. 40 66 49 25; CFP 3,500

The owner of Fish & Blue has mastered the art of shabby-chic decor and unpretentious dining. Step onto the property and you'll find an array of driftwood furniture, twinkle lights, throw pillows, candles, and soft textiles set among the white sand dining area. Some guests take their cocktails to the quiet jetty, while a bar in the back of the property welcomes a more rambunctious crowd. A boutique selling cozy resortwear and jewlery is there for those who want to take some of this aesthetic home in their suitcase.

As for the food, enjoy a rotating menu crafted from the catch of the day and imported ingredients. Jocko, the owner, frequently comes around to explain each dish in depth—offering her personal recommendations as needed. Seafood cooked in a creamy vanilla sauce, beef tenderloin, duck served

with pineapple chutney, and burgers regularly feature on the small menu. Reservations are recommended.

SUNSET BEACH MOTEL

PK 5; tel. 40 66 33 47; www.sunset-raiatea.pf; CFP 2,500/person per night for campsite use, from CFP 14,950/double bungalow

Sunset Beach Motel is set on a large seaside property near the Apooti Marina. Travelers with their own camping gear can pitch a tent on a large lawn, where shade structures have been set up to protect tents against the elements. Picnic tables are strewn throughout, and all campers have access to a communal kitchen and bathroom block with cold-water showers. Children are CFP 1,000 per night.

If sleeping indoors is more your style, there are basic bungalows with garden and ocean views. The bungalows are spacious, sleeping up to four or five people; each has a kitchen, lounge area, bathroom, barbecue, and parking space. For groups and families, there's also a two-bedroom villa sleeping up to 10 people (from CFP 30,000 per night). There is no restaurant on-site at the property, but guests can cook for themselves and use barbecue facilities. Airport pickup is included for all stays.

RAIATEA LODGE HOTEL

PK 8.6; tel. 40 66 20 00; raiatea-lodge-hotel.com; from CFP 25,000/double room

A large palm-lined lawn separates the sea and Hotel Raiatea Lodge, a boutique lodge with colonial architecture. At the center of the lodge is a large pool and dining area, where dinners are enjoyed with sunset views. The lodge hosts a few room types, all recently renovated and equipped with a private balcony, air-conditioning, safe, fridge, WiFi, and TV. There are also a handful of standalone bungalows with the same amenities plus a shaded outdoor terrace. Rattan furniture, woven decor, large windows, and tropical colors make the hotel feel cheerful and modern.

1: Fish & Blue seaside restaurant 2: Raiatea island home

Getting There and Around

The only convenient way to explore Raiatea's western coastline is with a rental car. Most accommodations offer free transport to and from the airport, and it's worth requesting a stop at the grocery store in Uturoa as dining options are limited in this region.

Taha'a

Raiatea's 90-square-kilometer (34-square-mi) lagoon mate, Taha'a, is shaped like a hibiscus flower with four long bays cutting into its rugged south side. Mount Ohiri (590 m/1,935 ft), the highest point on the island, got its name from Hiro, god of the underworld, who was born here. Taha'a is known as the "vanilla island" for its plantations that produce 70 percent of the territory's prized crop.

It's a quiet island, with little traffic and few tourists. Most of Taha'a's 5,220 residents use speedboats to commute to their gardens on the reef islets or to fishing spots, or to zip over to Raiatea on shopping trips, so cars are largely unnecessary. Beaches are scarce on the main island, but the string of motu off the northeast side of Taha'a has fine white sand. The pension owners and tour operators arrange picnics on a few of these, and pearl farms have been established on some. This is the only Society Island you can sail a yacht or cruise ship right around inside the barrier reef, and the many anchorages and central location between Raiatea, Huahine, and Bora Bora make Taha'a a favorite of both cruisers and charterers.

There aren't many specific attractions on Taha'a, and a dearth of inexpensive places to stay and lack of public transportation has kept this island off the beaten track. The easy way to visit Taha'a is on a boat tour from Raiatea.

Orientation

The administrative center of Taha'a is at **Patio** (or Iripau) on the north coast, where the post office and mairie (town hall) share a compound. A second post office and the gendarmerie are at **Haamene,** the center of Taha'a where four roads meet. Ships tie up to a wharf at **Tapuamu** on the west coast.

The 67-kilometer (41-mi) coral road around the main part of the island passes six of the eight villages; the other two are south of Haamene. A scenic road goes over the 141-meter (462-ft) Col Taira between Haamene and Tiva. There are ferries from Raiatea to Tapuamu and Haamene, but no regular public transportation.

SIGHTS
Vallee de la Vanille
East Coast, 3 km (1.8 mi) north of Faaaha; tel. 40 65 74 89; 10am-5pm Mon.-Fri.; free

Witness each stage of the vanilla-growing process at Vallee de la Vanille, a family-owned vanilla plantation on the northern edge of Faaaha Bay. A guide reveals how each orchid is pollinated, growing a vanilla pod to be harvested and dried. Premium pods of vanilla are sold at the on-site shop, perfect for putting into a bottle of rum. Cosmetics, oils, and other vanilla goods are also available for purchase.

Haamene Bay Lookout
Between Haamene Bay and Hurepiti Bay; free

The mountain pass between Haamene and Tiva offers excellent views of Hurepiti and Haamene Bays, two of the four deep fjords cutting into the southern side of the island. The views are found when driving in either direction, with a small space to pull off the road to make the stop.

Pari Pari Distillerie
Taha'a west coast in Tapuamu; tel. 40 65 61

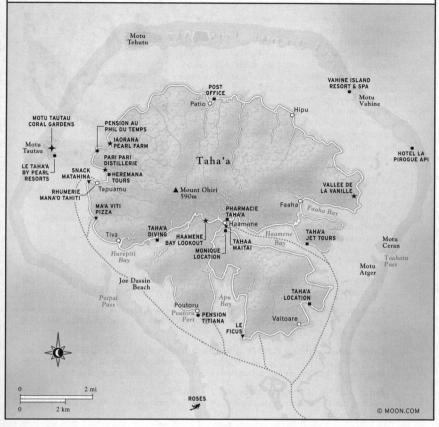

74; domaineparipari.com; 9am-5pm Mon.-Sat., 9am-noon Sun.; free

The rum distillery of Pari Pari Distillerie is often an included stop on a day tour of Taha'a, either by boat or car. The plantation surrounding the distillery grows six species of sugarcane, which are then used to craft a wide variety of Tahitian rums. A tour of the distillery gives an inside look at how the sugarcane is processed, fermented, and distilled. Don't go without trying their Rum Passion, made with rum and passionfruit juice. Vanilla rum remains their classic.

Rhumerie Mana'o Tahiti

Tapuamu; tel. 40 65 66 11; manao.pf; 8:30am-5:30pm Mon.-Sat., 9am-noon Sun.; free

This unpretentious rum distillery is a fun place to stop and linger on your own or as a part of a day tour, when having a designated driver is guaranteed. Each batch of rum is made in small batches, and a visit here will offer insight into the harvesting, grinding, fermenting, and distilling process with a complimentary tasting once the tour is done.

Vanilla

Vanilla, a spice derived from the slender pods of the vanilla orchid, is surprisingly challenging to grow. The crop that was brought to Tahiti from Manila in 1848, the aromatic Vanilla tahitiensis type, which has a worldwide reputation, originated from a mutation of Vanilla fragrans. Each vanilla pod must be hand-pollinated, as the only bees who pollinate the vanilla orchid don't survive in French Polynesia. Plantation workers must massage each pod by hand regularly to prevent it from cracking and drying out. Once the pods are harvested, they're put out to dry for a few months—an exceptionally time-consuming process. Vanilla is used in cooking, perfumes, and cosmetics, and is one of the most expensive spices. In fact, most vanilla used today is synthetic. Between 1915 and 1933, Tahiti produced 50-150 tonnes of real vanilla per year, peaking in 1949 at 200 tonnes. Production remained high until 1966, when a steady decline began because the producers were leaving for paid employment in Papeete related to nuclear testing. By 1990 production had fallen to only 39 tonnes, and in 2008 just 9 tonnes were exported. Today, most vanilla plantations are family owned.

vanilla drying out in the sunshine

How to enjoy Tahitian vanilla:

- **Visit a vanilla plantation:** At Taha'a's Vallee de la Vanille (page 196), learn how vanilla is grown and harvested, then take your pick of some of the best beans from the on-site shop.

- **Dine on grilled fish smothered in vanilla sauce:** A French Polynesian classic dish is made from shrimp or mahi-mahi cooked with sweet vanilla. Get it at Fish & Blue (page 194) on Taha'a or Snack Mahana (page 121) on Moorea.

- **Drink vanilla spiced rum:** DIY your own bottle of vanilla rum by placing three beans in a bottle of your favorite rum and letting it sit for a month. Or, sip vanilla rum from Pari Pari Distillerie on Taha'a (page 196) or Distillerie Huahine Passion on Huahine (page 178).

- **Enjoy vanilla cosmetics:** Monoï oil mixed with vanilla is one of Polynesia's sweetest-smelling skin oils. Shop for soaps, lotions, oils, and other cosmetics at the Papeete Market on Tahiti (page 45).

Iaorana Pearl Farm

Taha'a west coast in Tapuamu; 9am-4:30pm
Mon.-Sat., 9am-1pm Sun.; free

Learn about the art of pearl farming at Iaorana Pearl Farm. Presentations are given in French and English walking you through the cultivating, harvesting, and jewelry-making process of crafting a black pearl. It's one of the few pearl shops where they carve designs in the iridescent pearl nacre, making this shop a great place to find one-of-a-kind pieces. Their shop is small, and salespeople are more relaxed than pushy about making a sale.

BEACHES AND SNORKELING

Taha'a's best beaches and snorkel spots are found on the outer motu perched on the northern edge of Taha'a's barrier reef, resembling the atolls of the Tuamotus. Most boat trips will stop for a picnic lunch on one of these motu, and you'll likely dine on fresh fish with your feet in the sand.

JOE DASSIN BEACH

Tiva

In the 1970s famed French singer Joe Dassin came to Taha'a and fell in love with its quiet natural beauty, investing in a plot of land next to a sliver of white sand. One of the few accessible beaches on Taha'a, it can be reached by boat or a 10-minute walk from the road. Enjoy lounging in the shade of a palm frond. **Snorkeling:** If you've brought your snorkeling gear, a thriving cluster of coral bommies is found just offshore.

MOTU TAUTAU CORAL GARDENS

1.5 km (1 mi) offshore of Tapuamu

In the channel between Motu Tautau and its neighboring motu is one of the Leeward Island's most spectacular snorkeling spots. **Snorkeling:** On Motu Tautau, start at the oceanside end of the channel and drift slowly toward the lagoon to pass over a shallow reef teeming with coral bommies, angelfish, anemonefish, butterflyfish, and parrotfish. Moray eels and octopi often hide in the crags. Some Taha'a day tours stop here to snorkel; travelers staying at Le Taha'a by Pearl Resorts have direct access.

MOTU CERAN AND MOTU ATGER

1.8 km (1.1 mi) offshore of Haamene Bay

The two small motu at the reef pass before Haamene Bay are surrounded by tranquil turquoise waters prime for swimming and snorkeling. Motu Ceran, the smaller of the duo, is pocked with pom-pom palm trees and has a white sand beach. Motu Atger, more rugged, welcomes day-trippers to its namesake pension and restaurant for those in search of sandy beaches and seafood—call ahead (tel. 87 28 26 81). A trip here is best arranged through your accommodation, or with the help of Pension Motu Atger. **Snorkeling:** Snorkel around shallow water coral bommies teeming with anemonefish, damselfish, butterfly fish, eels, octopuses, rays, and reef sharks.

SCUBA DIVING

TAHA'A DIVING

Hurepiti Bay; tel. 87 24 80 69; www.tahaa-diving. com; 8am-5pm daily; CFP 8,000/fun dive, CFP 70,000/10 fun dives

Taha'a Diving runs two fun dives per day for certified divers, one at 8:30am and the second at 1pm, in its eight-person dive boat. Most dives venture to the outer edge of Taha'a's western reef, where you're likely to see striped barracuda, manta rays, multiple shark species, and walls of hard and soft coral. Divers can be picked up at Tapuamu or at accommodations found along the west coast of Taha'a.

LOCAL TOURS

L'EXCURSION BLEUE

tel. 87 78 33 28; www.tahaa.net; 8:30am-5pm daily; CFP 12,000/day tour

Tours of Taha'a with L'Excursion Bleue depart from Uturoa on Raiatea daily at 8:30am, and free transport on Raiatea's north coastline is included with each tour. The trip covers a full day in Taha'a, stopping at a vanilla farm, a motu for a picnic lunch, a pearl farm, the Pari Pari Distillerie, and multiple snorkel spots, like the Coral Gardens off Motu Tautau. It's a full day out, and you'll return to your room with a taste of Taha'a's best sights. If you're staying on Taha'a, you could potentially get picked up at one stop and dropped off at another. The tour takes place from a comfortable motorized outrigger canoe.

HEREMANA TOURS

tel. 87 26 15 60; www.excursiontahaaraiatea.com; 8am-4pm daily; CFP 6,000/person half-day, CFP 10,000/person full-day

Heremana Tours arranges multiple types of tours around Taha'a. Embark on a half-day lagoon safari to three snorkel spots to swim with corals, stingrays, and reef sharks before a fresh fruit snack on Motu Tautau. They also have land-based tours from the bed of a 4X4 truck to a tropical garden, pearl farm, and vanilla plantation. Full-day tours combine the best of both. Sunset lagoon rides depart around 4:30pm on clear evenings from

Tapuamu, where you'll watch the sunset with a cocktail in hand.

TAHA'A JET TOURS

Haamene Bay; tel. 89 79 80 81; www.tahaajetski. com; 9am-4pm daily; CFP 21,500/Jet Ski for two people, two-hour tour

Buzz about Taha'a's lagoon on your own Jet Ski, stopping at snorkel spots, a pearl farm, or a vanilla plantation on a guided tour. Each tour includes a life jacket, waterproof bag, snorkeling gear, and drinks. If you'd rather not go on a tour, Jet Skis are available for rent for CFP 6,000 per hour.

FOOD

Village stores are at Tapuamu, Tiva, Haamene, and Patio. Most accommodations serve meals, though your best bet for finding snacks outside of where you're staying is in Haamene. You won't want to leave Taha'a without trying some variation of vanilla sauce, found at most restaurants.

MA'A VITI PIZZA

North Tiva; tel. 87 73 57 11; www.maavitipizza.com; 11:30am-2pm and 5:30pm-9pm Wed.-Sun.; CFP 1,000/large pizza

A quaint pizza joint, Ma'a Viti Pizza serves around 30 pizza variations with tomato or cream sauce, fries, burgers, cookies, and brownies. The Taha'a pizza comes with tuna, vanilla, parmesan, mozzarella, oregano, and olives. Find this pizzeria at the bridge of Utuone.

SNACK MATAHINA

Tapuamu; tel. 87 73 96 54; 9:30am-1pm and 6pm-10pm Tues.-Sat.; CFP 1,500

This casual snack doles out grilled fish and meats served with a side of fries, salad, or rice. Look for the large wooden "Matahina" sign and its thatched-roof dining area.

★ **TAHAA MAITAI**

Haamene; tel. 40 65 70 85; 9am-2pm and 6:30pm-10pm Tues.-Sat., 11:30am-2:30pm Sun.; CFP 3,000

Tahaa Maitai is a favorite restaurant on Taha'a among sailors and locals, serving a mix of Polynesian and European specialties. Their signature dish is a filet of mahi-mahi served with creamy vanilla sauce, a side of quiche, and rice. Poisson cru, mussels, burgers, and steak are also popular picks, and the cheese platter is worth ordering as a starter. Bruno, the owner, has a massive collection of whiskeys to sample, adding a personal touch. The dining room is set on the seaside.

LE FICUS

Apu Bay; tel. 87 34 98 38; 7pm-10pm daily; CFP 6,000

Pull up a stool and dig your toes into the sand at Le Ficus, a casual seaside restaurant on the south side of Apu Bay. The traditional thatched-roof fare (house) coincides with the authentic Polynesian food typically served buffet-style and includes a bottle of wine. Dine on locally sourced seafood, root crops, and other vegetables—often cooked in coconut cream and vanilla. On Wednesdays and Fridays, there's singing, ukulele playing, and dancing from 7:30pm until late.

ACCOMMODATIONS

PENSION TITIANA

Poutoro; tel. 87 27 56 00; www.hotellapirogueapi.net; from CFP 13,500/bungalow for two people, add CFP 5,500/adult, CFP 2,500/child for half-board

Three spacious bungalows at Pension Titiana are decorated with Tahitian artwork and tifaifai, traditional floral quilts. The largest bungalow has two bedrooms and a lounge area with two single beds, easily accommodating four people. It also has a washing machine, full kitchen, and two bathrooms. The smaller bungalows sleep up to three people and have hot-water showers, a minibar, and fan. Dinners at the pension usually revolve around mahi-mahi, tuna, and salmon, with desserts like Taha'a vanilla crème brûlée.

1: the palm-lined shores of Taha'a **2:** the shallow snorkel site off Le Taha'a by Pearl Resorts

Airport transfer costs CFP 7,900 each way for two people.

PENSION AU PHIL DU TEMPS

Tapuamu; tel. 40 65 64 19; www.auphildutempstahaa. com; CFP 15,000/double room

Pension Au Phil du Temps is a quiet pension on the shores of Taha'a's western coastline. The pension hosts two bungalows and a private room inside a main home, surrounded by a garden of tiare flowers. The bungalows are clean and quiet, and the private room creates a true homestay experience. All rooms sleep up to three people and have a bathroom with hot-water shower, fan, TV, mini fridge, and WiFi access. Muriel cooks hearty three-course dinners each night (CFP 4,000), and Franck runs both boating and land trips (CFP 7,000/person). The half-board option is a wise choice for CFP 16,500 per person, which includes accommodation, breakfast, and dinner, as there is no communal kitchen on-site.

★ HOTEL LA PIROGUE API

Motu Moute; tel. 87 27 56 00; www. hotellapirogueapi.net; from CFP 50,000/bungalow for two people

Escape to your own tiny private motu at Hotel La Pirogue Api, a little resort with a handful of beach bungalows (that nearly take up the entire island). Each bungalow sleeps 3-4 people, featuring a private lounge deck (many with ocean access), hammock, TV, fan, and safe. Clear water idyllic for snorkeling is never more than a few steps away, and the shore of the motu is lined with coarse sand. Sea turtles, rays, and reef sharks lap the motu in minutes. While it is remote, you won't go hungry thanks to an on-site bar and restaurant (half-board is CFP 10,500 per person). Guests can venture out on day trips, arranged through the hotel.

VAHINE ISLAND RESORT AND SPA

Motu Vahine; tel. 40 65 67 38; www.vahine-island. com; from CFP 60,000/double bungalow

Spend your evenings looking over the water to Bora Bora at Vahine Island Resort and Spa, a private island resort on a motu on Taha'a's northeastern end. Accommodations include a trio of luxury overwater bungalows, plus bungalows set in the palm tree grounds of the motu itself. All are airy, cheerful, and decorated with local furniture and art pieces. The three-course dinners served at the restaurant each night are made mostly from local ingredients, and taste divine. A few fin kicks from the shoreline is great snorkeling, though the resort hosts regular trips to a nearby motu for a change of pace. Don't skip the spa.

★ LE TAHA'A BY PEARL RESORTS

Motu Tautau; tel. 40 60 84 00; www.letahaa.com; from CFP 100,000/double bungalow

Le Taha'a by Pearl Resorts is the only five-star resort on Taha'a, and one of the best private island resorts in the Leeward Islands for snorkeling around the property. Around 60 overwater bungalows, villas, and suites are set on the tiny island, each with a natural feel. Thatched roofing, bamboo walls, easy ocean access, and stone mosaics add a rustic feel, but the amenities remain upscale with WiFi, air-conditioning, coffee-making facilities, a satellite TV, private deck, and turndown service with each option. Some overwater bungalows face Bora Bora, and a few beach villas come with a private plunge pool. A communal lagoon-style pool, spa, three restaurants, two bars, gym, tennis court, and activity center make the island feel larger than it is.

INFORMATION AND SERVICES

Most of Taha'a's services are found in Haamene and Patio.

- **Post Office:** Patio and Haamene; opt.pf; 7am-3pm Mon.-Thurs., 7am-2pm Fri., 8am-10am Sat.

- **Banque de Tahiti:** Haamene; tel. 40 65 63 14; www.banque-tahiti.pf; 8am-noon and 1pm-4pm Mon.-Fri.

1: Sample vanilla rum at Taha'a's distillery.
2: Le Taha'a by Pearl Resorts

- **Pharmacie Taha'a:** Haamene; tel. 40 60 86 08; 7:30am-4:30pm Mon.-Fri., 7:30am-noon Sat.

GETTING THERE

There's no airport on Taha'a. Large ships and ferries call at Tapuamu Port on the west side of Taha'a just behind the Total service station. Vessels also call at a port in Haamene and Poutoru.

Maupiti Express II (tel. 40 67 66 69; CFP 4,000-5,000/person) departs from Poutoru on Taha'a in the morning on Mondays and Fridays for Bora Bora and Raiatea. It returns in the evening after 4pm. **Enota Transport** (tel. 87 72 76 47, 87 75 73 16; CFP 2,000/person) runs trips between Raiatea and Taha'a; it takes about 40 minutes each way.

The **Aremiti V** from **Apetahi Express** (tel. 87 39 37 75; apetahiexpress.pf; has an office at Tapuamu Port and runs a boat shuttle service to Raiatea (45 minutes, CFP 1,600/person) and Bora Bora (1 hour 15 minutes, CFP 4,100/person) every day except Tuesday. Month-long passes range from CFP 17,000-23,900.

GETTING AROUND

Trucks on Taha'a are for transporting schoolchildren only, so you may have to hitch to get around. It's not that hard to hitch a ride down the west coast from Patio to Haamene, but there's little traffic along the east coast. If you really want the freedom to see Taha'a, it's best to book a private tour or rental car.

Car rental companies:

- **Monique Location:** Haamene; tel. 40 65 62 48; moniquelocationtahaa@gmail.com; vehicles from CFP 10,500/day, boat transport also arranged
- **Taha'a Location:** Faaaha; tel. 40 65 69 95; tahaalocations@mail.pf; vehicles from CFP 13,000/day, scooters from CFP 8,500/day, also offers day trips upon request

Maupiti

Majestic Maupiti (Maurua), 52 kilometers (32 mi) west of Bora Bora, is the least known of the accessible Society Islands. Maupiti's mighty volcanic plug soars above a sapphire lagoon, and the vegetation-draped cliffs complement the magnificent motu beaches. Two peaks, Mount Hotu Paraoa (250 m/820 ft) and Mount Teurafaatiu (380 m/1,246 ft), punctuate its center. Almost every bit of level land on the main island is taken up by fruit trees, while watermelons thrive on the surrounding motu. Maupiti abounds in native seabirds, including frigate birds and terns. The absence of Indian mynahs allows you to see native land birds that are almost extinct elsewhere.

The population of 1,200 live in the adjacent villages of Vai'ea, Farauru, and Pauma. Vai'ea, while small, is the main hub. Tourism is not promoted because there aren't any regular hotels, which is a big advantage for travelers who prefer a slower pace of travel and glimpse at what the Society Islands were like before the advent of package tours. Ditch your watch and enjoy the quiet beaches, fresh fruits, spectacularly clear waters, and friendly faces that'll look familiar even after a day or two. Maupiti has no ATM, so come with cash in hand.

SIGHTS

Nearly all Maupiti's sights revolve around the island's natural beauty.

VAI'EA
Eastern coast of Maupiti

Stroll along Vai'ea, Maupiti's main town, for a look at how most of Maupiti's residents spend their time. Houses stretch along the main road, their impeccably kept gardens replete with tropical flowers and fruit trees. Driftwood produce stands sell seasonal fruits. Here's where you'll find a few convenience stores selling nonperishable goods. Shop

Maupiti

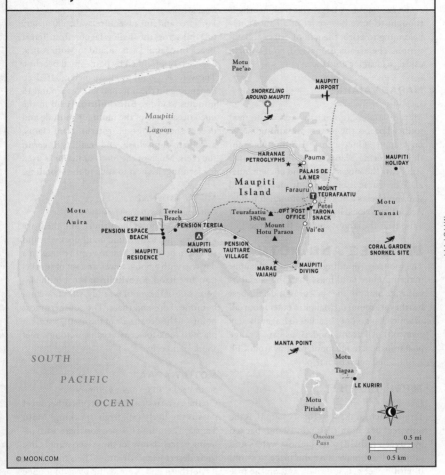

Motu
Pae'ao

**SNORKELING
AROUND MAUPITI**

**MAUPITI
AIRPORT**

*Maupiti
Lagoon*

**HARANAE
PETROGLYPHS** — Pauma

**PALAIS DE
LA MER**

**MAUPITI
HOLIDAY**

*Maupiti
Island*

Farauru

**MOUNT
TEURAFAATIU**

Teurafaatiu
380m

Petei

**OPT POST
OFFICE**

**TARONA
SNACK**

*Motu
Tuanai*

*Motu
Auira*

Tereia
Beach

CHEZ MIMI

PENSION TEREIA

Mount
Hotu Paraoa

Vai'ea

**PENSION ESPACE
BEACH**

**MAUPITI
CAMPING**

**PENSION
TAUTIARE
VILLAGE**

**MAUPITI
RESIDENCE**

**CORAL GARDEN
SNORKEL SITE**

**MARAE
VAIAHU**

**MAUPITI
DIVING**

MANTA POINT

*Motu
Tiapaa*

LE KURIRI

SOUTH

PACIFIC

OCEAN

*Motu
Pitiahe*

*Onoiau
Pass*

0   0.5 mi

0   0.5 km

© MOON.COM

BORA BORA AND THE LEEWARD ISLANDS

MAUPITI

hours are irregular and supplies are limited, so if you see something you like it's best to buy it while you can.

PALAIS DE LA MER

Northeast coast of Maupiti, Pauma; tel. 87 21 74 40; ahkyfiruu@outlook.com; 9am-11am and 2pm-3:30pm daily; CFP 2,000/adult, CFP 1,000/child

A fantastical place built from seashells, driftwood, corals, and cement, Ahky Firuu, aka "The Prince of the Sea," has built himself a

seaside palace. Statues of mermaids, starfish-studded spires, and tritons create an unmistakable under-the-sea feel. Ahky, the charismatic owner, entertains guests with his music, stories, jokes—and glasses of homemade sparkling wine. Hours are irregular, so call before arriving.

HARANAE PETROGLYPHS

Northeast coast of Maupiti, Pauma; free

Hidden behind the Mormon Church is a

stream leading to the Haranae Petroglyphs, where moss-covered etchings of turtles and crabs are found. A large, flat rock nearby is thought to have been part of a canoe once belonging to Hiro, the god of celestial navigation. The area is unmarked, so it's worth asking a local for guidance.

MARAE VAIAHU
South Maupiti; free

Marae Vaiahu, an ancient sacred site next to the shore, is the largest remaining marae on Maupiti. Once a royal landing place for those entering Maupiti's lagoon, the marae still bears the king's throne and ancient burials. The marae itself is built from large coral slabs and hosts a box with a stonefish inside. According to local legend, it's bad luck to light a fire near the largest stone in the marae.

BEACHES AND MOTU

The motu surrounding the island of Maupiti make up more land mass than the island itself. Like many of the Society Islands, the best beaches are found on Maupiti's outer motu (all of which have empty beaches to linger the day away on). All accommodations can arrange boat transport to the motu, ranging from CFP 1,500-2,500 per return trip.

TEREIA BEACH
Main island

Tereia Beach, at the west tip of Maupiti, is the only real beach on the main island, backed by rugged red cliffs. Its shallow waters and sandy bottom make it a calm place to swim. It hardly ever gets crowded, and on the rare occasions it does, the atmosphere is exceptionally friendly. At low tide you can wade across from Tereia's white sands to Motu Auira in waist-deep water. **Snorkeling:** The southern end of Tereia Beach is shallow and sandy, making visibility for snorkeling poor. But, a few fin kicks northwest from the tip of the beach, you'll find coral reefs rife with colorful creatures like parrotfish, bannerfish, wrasses, angelfish, eels, rays, and the occasional reef shark.

MOTU AUIRA
Across from Tereia Beach, 600 m (0.3 mi) from Maupiti Island

For a free and fun adventure, walk 600 meters (0.3 mi) across the shallow lagoon from Tereia Beach on Maupiti's mainland to Motu Auira, a large motu flanked by palm-lined beaches. The water is usually around a meter (3 ft) deep depending on the tide, and it takes around 15 minutes to cross. **Snorkeling:** Head to the open ocean side of the motu for solitude and decent snorkeling—parrotfish, giant clams, angelfish, damselfish, and fusiliers linger in the reefs. Much of the motu's interior is used for farming; it's best to stick to the shoreline.

MOTU TUANAI
East Maupiti, 1 km (0.6 mi) from Maupiti Island

Motu Tuanai hosts the airport, and there are quiet beaches to be found on its northern and southern points. It's best to venture here on a day trip with a book, towel, and set of snorkel gear in a hand. **Snorkeling:** Most of the lagoon side of the motu is sandy, with few coral bommies here and there. The southernmost point, on the ocean side of the motu, is a great place to look for crustaceans, octopus, reef sharks, and eels.

MOTU TIAPAA
South Maupiti, 1.5 km (0.9 mi) offshore

On the eastern side of Maupiti's southern reef pass is the lively (relatively speaking) Motu Tiapaa. There are a few pensions here, each offering peaceful stays for those who want to live their desert island dreams. The sandspit on its northern end is an idyllic place to lounge in the sun. Inland, there's little but palm tree groves. **Snorkeling:** Decent snorkeling is found all along its oceanside edge. Pufferfish, parrotfish, black tip reef sharks, spotted eagle rays, stingrays, and shoals of other colorful reef fish are often spotted.

MOTU PITIAHE
South Maupiti, 2 km (1.2 mi) offshore

Across from Motu Tiapaa is lonely little Motu Pitiahe, where day trips come to set up picnics on its white sands. This motu is the only place where the Tiare de Hina, a smaller flower than the Tiare Tahiti, is grown. **Snorkeling:** The current can be incredibly strong between Motu Pitiahe and Motu Tiapaa, so it's best to snorkel off the northern or western side of the motu, where small coral bommies hide anemones and juvenile reef fish.

HIKING
MOUNT TEURAFAATIU
Distance: 2.5 km (1.5 mi) out-and-back
Time: 2 hours
Trailhead: Farauru
Information and maps: www.alltrails.com
Venture to the summit of Mount Teurafaatiu (380 m/1,246 ft) for an unsurpassed view of Maupiti's lagoon. On a clear day, the silhouette of Bora Bora sits on the horizon. The trail starts opposite of Snack Tarona in Farauru village. Follow the trail until you reach an antenna, then turn at the sign marking the trail for Mount Teurafaatiu. There's a moderate incline throughout the trek, with a few steeper sections once you near the top—ropes assist in these sections. From the summit, enjoy shades of every blue. To the south, you'll see the emeraldlike peaks and Maupiti's cobalt blue reef pass.

SCUBA DIVING
Scuba Dive Sites
MANTA POINT DIVE SITE
South Maupiti
Manta rays glide through Maupiti's waters all year long, though the best time to see them is from March to October. At Manta Point, scuba divers and snorkelers can watch these graceful creatures at their cleaning station. Small cleaner wrasse tend to the scrumptious parasites on the manta rays' skin, forming quite the symbiotic relationship! The dive site is about 10 meters (32 ft) deep and usually has little current; scuba divers often simply relax and enjoy the show from below. If you only snorkel, it's still worth coming out as well. These manta rays are easily admired from above.

Scuba Diving Operators
MAUPITI DIVING
South Maupiti; tel. 40 67 83 80; www.maupitidiving. com; CFP 7,000/fun dive including equipment, CFP 6,000/fun dive excluding equipment, CFP 60,000/10 fun dives
Maupiti Diving hosts small dive groups of just six people on their modified fishing boat. Most scuba dive trips venture to Manta Point, a spot where tens of mantas can be seen at one time. On calm days, guides venture through Maupiti's turbulent reef pass to dive along the ocean edge of Maupiti's barrier reef. Scuba divers with kids can opt for the dive center's babysitting service while they dive, at CFP 3,000 per child. Courses from discover to rescue diver are available on request. Prices include transport.

★ SNORKELING
If the island of Maupiti is underrated, its underwater world is even less so. With so few tourists venturing into Maupiti's aquamarine waters, it's a haven for juvenile reef fish who take refuge in Maupiti's shallows. Rays, reef sharks, and technicolor fish are regularly seen all throughout the lagoon, with anemones carpeting the reef like shag rugs. It's wise to come with your own mask, fins, and snorkel to Maupiti. While most accommodations host lagoon tours, few have snorkeling equipment to accommodate every size. Armed with a set of your own, you'll be ready to explore any calm, clear stretch of reef.

Snorkel Sites
CORAL GARDEN SNORKEL SITE
South of Motu Tuanai
The Coral Gardens south of Motu Tuanai are alive with reef fish. Spot anemones and anemonefish, giant clams with electric colors, butterflyfish, damselfish, eels, octopus, and an array of corals.

Snorkeling Operators
SAMMY MAUPITI TOURS
tel. 87 76 99 28; www.sammy-maupiti.fr; 8am-5pm daily; CFP 8,000/person full-day, CFP 4,000/person half-day

Lagoon tours with Sammy start around 8am. Guests are picked up from their accommodation and taken to snorkel at Manta Point and the Coral Gardens. Afterward, the boat ventures to a motu for a buffet lunch of poisson cru, grilled fish, fried breadfruit, barbecue chicken, coconut bread, and cold Hinano beers. Stingrays often cruise the shallows of the motu in search of fish scraps. All throughout the day, Sammy stops to share stories and songs on the ukulele.

FOOD
Almost all pensions offer half-board (breakfast and dinner) or full-board (three meals) options, which is a wise choice as food options are limited on the island—and pension owners tend to be remarkably skilled chefs.

If you want a souvenir from your time in Maupiti, ask your host to guide you to a local sculptor. A penu, a pestle made from basalt, is used to crush spices, breadfruit, and seeds. You'll see it as a symbol on many of Maupiti's small business logos.

CHEZ MIMI
Tereia Beach; 8am-3:30pm daily; CFP 1,000

Foot-long sandwiches made with fluffy fresh baguettes are the main item on offer at Chez Mimi, a casual beach shack built from bamboo on the shores of Tereia Beach. Get your sandwich stuffed with french fries and egg, grilled meat and fries, ham and vegetables, or a combination of everything. Plates of grilled fish, poisson cru, and rice also come in generous portions.

★ TARONA SNACK
Vai'ea; tel. 40 67 82 46; 11am-3pm Mon.-Sat.; CFP 1,600

Escape to the shaded seaside tables of Tarona Snack for hearty plates of fish all ways (grilled, raw, fried), barbecued meats, salads, and stir-fried noodles. There are a few options to tempt vegans and vegetarians. Most dishes are served with a whopping stack of french fries or rice. Come before 1:30pm for the full menu; favorite items often sell out before then.

ACCOMMODATIONS
There are no formal hotels on Maupiti; all travelers come to stay in family-owned pensions. Most rooms will come with a fan, linens, and access to a private or shared bathroom. Hot-water showers and air-conditioning units are rare. Very few pensions take card payments, so come with enough cash to cover your stay.

PENSION TAUTIARE VILLAGE
Southwest Maupiti; tel. 40 60 15 90; www.pension-tautiarevillage.com; CFP 6,500/double room, CFP 9,000/half-board

A charming pension on the southwestern side of Maupiti, Pension Tautiare Village has a handful of single and double rooms available. Each is simply furnished with a private bathroom and terrace, and additional beds can be added for CFP 2,500 per person. The hosts are exceptionally friendly and happy to arrange lagoon tours. Meals are served in their cozy dining room, and the scrumptious three-course dinners make opting for the half-board package worth it. A long jetty in front of the property leads to a decent snorkeling site.

★ MAUPITI RESIDENCE
Tereia Beach; tel. 40 67 82 61; www.maupitiresidence. info; CFP 12,800/double room

Palm trees and a tidy row of lounge chairs and kayaks front the property of Maupiti Residence, a modern yet personable pension. There are two bungalows overlooking the water, both able to sleep up to five people, equipped with air-conditioning, a hot-water shower, kitchen lounge room, and internet access. Tucked behind the property is also a spacious villa with air-conditioning, kitchen, terrace, washing machine, and lounge room. Conveniently located and with access to a white sand beach, this is the best choice for those in search of accommodation with Bora Bora amenities but on a less touristic island.

PENSION ESPACE BEACH

Tereia Beach; tel. 40 67 80 29; www. pensionespacebeachmaupiti.com; CFP 19,760/double room in guesthouse, CFP 26,020/double room in bungalow

Fruit trees and well-loved plants decorate the exterior of Pension Espace Beach, a guesthouse near Tereia Beach. It's a cozy place to stay, with four rooms inside of a main home and bungalows available. In the guesthouse, all guests share a living room and bathroom. Each room has a double bed, fan, and wardrobe. The bungalows are more like beach glamping, built from palm leaves, each equipped with a private bathroom, minifridge, and fan—all have sand floors. Rates include breakfast, dinner, bicycle rental, kayak rental, and WiFi. A two-night minimum stay is required.

PENSION TEREIA

Tereia Beach; tel. 40 67 82 02; www.pensiontereia. sitew.com; CFP 10,000/person for half-board

Bold, colorful prints and fabrics all throughout Pension Tereia signal the feeling of being on a tropical holiday. The pension is around a five-minute walk away from Tereia Beach, and all rooms are connected to a main guesthouse. Each room has a double bed, air-conditioning (CFP 1,500/day extra charge), private bathroom with hot-water shower, WiFi, and access to a full shared kitchen. Sandra, the host, is an exceptional cook and always happy to help book a tour, offer travel tips, and share a clever joke.

MAUPITI HOLIDAY

Motu Tuanai; tel. 87 70 56 09; www.maupitiholiday. com; CFP 9,500/person for half-board

Maupiti Holiday is ideal for adventure lovers, a hub for snorkeling, kitesurfing (if you have your own equipment), paddling the vaa'a (outrigger canoe), and going on motu outings. The bungalows are basic, each able to sleep four with mosquito nets, and private bathrooms

with limited hot-water showers. However, the elements have taken their toll in the form of rusted metal and tattered curtains, and the rooms could use a refresh. Rates include a delicious breakfast and dinner. Children are half price (under 14).

LE KURIRI

Motu Tiapaa; tel. 87 74 54 54; www.maupiti-kuriri. com; CFP 13,650/person for half-board

Wake up on the tiny islet of Motu Tiapaa at Le Kuriri, where wooden bungalows open out to a grove of palm trees and white sands. No two of the four bungalows are quite alike, though all have a rustic charm to them. Each is built from wood and bamboo, featuring a semi-outdoor bathroom with hot-water shower. Rattan furniture, a communal library, and cheerful decor add to a sense of being at an island escape. Solar panels power the property, and hosts rely on locally sourced ingredients for most meals.

CAMPING

MAUPITI CAMPING

Southwest Maupiti; tel. 87 26 66 60; maupiticamping@gmail.com; CFP 3,000/campsite

Roughing it on Maupiti is not *that* rough if you pitch a tent at Maupiti Camping, a campsite on Maupiti's southwestern stretch of coastline. All guests have access to a newly built restroom block, kitchen, dining room, and the water. If you don't have a tent or sleeping equipment, Maupiti Camping offers it for rent. The hosts run day trips around the lagoon and outer motu depending on the weather, and can arrange guided hikes upon request.

INFORMATION AND SERVICES

Most shops and services are in the town of Vai'ea. Note there are no ATMs on the island; you'll need to bring enough cash to cover your stay plus any incidentals. The water on Maupiti is not potable, but most pensions provide filtered water on request.

- **OPT Post Office:** Vai'ea; 7:30am-3pm Mon.-Thurs., 7am-2pm Fri.; the only place to recharge Vini phone SIM cards and data packages
- **Health Center:** Vai'ea; tel. 40 67 80 18

GETTING THERE AND AROUND

If Maupiti is on your must-see list, prioritize planning your trip around it as most of the other Society Islands are better connected. Flights and boats to Maupiti are limited, so whatever form of transport you choose, book it as soon as possible. Official car rental companies are not available, but you may be able to rent a vehicle from your accommodation.

Air

Air Tahiti (airtahiti.com) has direct flights between Maupiti and Tahiti (50 minutes, CFP 25,000/one-way), Bora Bora (20 minutes, CFP 10,000/one-way), and Raiatea (25 minutes, CFP 10,900/one-way). Maupiti is included on two Air Tahiti Multi Islands Air Passes: the Bora Bora Pass and the Bora-Tuamotu Pass. Flights arrive at Maupiti Airport (MAU) on Motu Tuanai, and you must take a 25-minute shuttle boat ride (CFP 500/person, CFP 100/luggage) to reach the main island. From there, your accommodation usually picks you up. Some accommodations pick up directly from the airport, especially if you're staying on a motu.

Boat

The *Maupiti Express II* departs from Bora Bora to Maupiti on Tuesdays and returns to Bora Bora on Thursdays. Trips usually take around 2.5 hours depending on ocean conditions. Maupiti's Onoiau reef pass is notoriously challenging to cruise through, and there are times when ocean conditions impact this schedule. Tickets are sold onboard or at Bora Bora's Vaitape Wharf. Within Maupiti, pension owners arrange trips to the outer motu for around CFP 1,500-2,500 per person return.

Bike

Maupiti's 10-kilometer (6-mi) road is easily covered on foot or with a bicycle. Some accommodations include bike rental with the price of your stay, or rent them for around CFP 1,200 per day.

The Tuamotu and Gambier Islands

From the sky, the 76 atolls of the Tuamotus resemble pearl necklaces flung across a cobalt sea. The sight is fitting given all the pearl farming that's done here—black pearls grown in the Tuamotus are coveted around the world. In an atoll's center, the lagoon is a haven for marine life big and small, making the Tuamotus a dream destination for scuba divers and snorkelers. Lagoon trips to white and pink sand beaches are prime for relaxing and contemplating, easily done thanks to the lack of internet connection. At night, the lack of light pollution turns the Tuamotus into a dark sky reserve, where thousands of stars can be seen with the naked eye.

The region is home to pods of bottlenose dolphins, solitary tiger sharks, a large concentration of gray sharks, and a reef Jacques Cousteau

Highlights

Look for ★ to find recommended sights, activities, dining, and lodging.

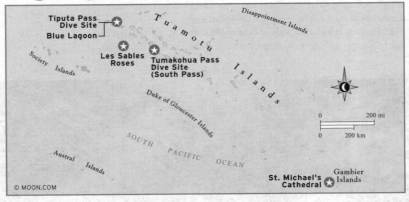

Tiputa Pass Dive Site
Blue Lagoon
Les Sables Roses
Tumakohua Pass Dive Site (South Pass)
Disappointment Islands
T u a m o t u   I s l a n d s
Society Islands
Duke of Gloucester Islands
SOUTH   PACIFIC   OCEAN
Austral Islands
St. Michael's Cathedral
Gambier Islands
0   200 mi
0   200 km
© MOON.COM

★ **Blue Lagoon:** Admire blues of every hue in this sandy lagoon surrounded by palm-tree-covered motu, a sanctuary for reef sharks and rays (page 222).

★ **Les Sables Roses:** The Tuamotus boast a number of paradisical rose-tinted beaches, a photographer's dream (page 223).

★ **Tiputa Pass Dive Site:** Resident bottle-nose dolphins play in this pass, often zipping close to divers (page 224).

★ **Tumakohua Pass Dive Site (South Pass):** The highest concentration of gray reef sharks in the world cruise through Fakarava's incredible southern pass (page 241).

★ **St. Michael's Cathedral:** Visit this 19th-century cathedral on a Sunday to be awed by the sound of melodic hymns (page 251).

once claimed to be the most densely populated with fish in the world. Seafaring birds have taken a liking to the atolls too, using uninhabited motu as breeding and resting grounds.

In contrast to the thriving lagoon life, the islets of the Tuamotus are largely inhospitable. There's little land suitable for farming, though coconut palms, hibiscus, plumeria, and bougainvillea trees grow in abundance. Most residents (around 17,000 across 50 inhabited atolls) live off the lagoon, coconuts, and produce that arrives on ships from elsewhere in French Polynesia. Fresh water and reliable electricity are challenging to come by. There are resorts on Rangiroa, Tikehau, Manihi, and Fakarava, and homestay accommodations are available on most of the others. If you're looking for superlative luxury stays and five-star spa treatments, you'll find that elsewhere in French Polynesia. The Tuamotus are an antidote to overdeveloped tropical islands.

A few hundred kilometers southeast of the Tuamotus, the jagged Gambier Islands live in relative isolation. Within a large barrier reef, four lonely islands are home to just a few thousand residents. Getting here isn't always easy—flights are infrequent and often booked-out—but once you're here, you'll share the experience of wandering around islands so few others ever have before.

GETTING THERE
Air
Air Tahiti (airtahiti.com) has flights from Tahiti to:

- Ahe: 1 hour 55 minutes, CFP 30,000/one-way
- Arutua: 1 hour, CFP 25,000/one-way
- Fakarava: 1 hour 10 minutes, CFP 31,000/one-way
- Hao: 2 hours 10 minutes, CFP 36,000/one-way

- Makemo: 3 hours 40 minutes, CFP 31,000/one-way
- Mangareva: 3 hours 45 minutes, CFP 45,000/one-way
- Manihi: 2.5 hours, CFP 30,000/one-way
- Mataiva: 1 hour, CFP 24,000/one-way
- Rangiroa: 1 hour, CFP 27,000/one-way
- Takapoto: 1 hour 20 minutes, CFP 29,000/one-way
- Takaroa: 1 hour 55 minutes, CFP 30,500/one-way
- Tikehau: 1 hour, CFP 27,000/one-way

Prices are estimates and vary based on demand.

The best way to see multiple islands in the Tuamotus for a (relatively) affordable price is through the Air Tahiti Multi-Islands Pass. There are a few passes that cover the most popular atolls. Prices for passes are based on seasonal rates (low season is from Apr. 1-May 31, Nov. 1-Dec. 10, and Jan. 11-Mar. 31; high season is from June 1-Oct. 31 and Dec. 11-Jan. 10). All passes must be completed within 28 days of travel, and at least two islands must be visited.

- **Lagoons Pass:** Flies to Moorea, Rangiroa, Tikehau, and Fakarava (low season €441/adult, €357/child; high season €476/adult, €384/child).

- **Bora-Tuamotu Pass:** Flies to the Society Islands and Tuamotu Islands including Moorea, Huahine, Raiatea, Maupiti, Bora Bora, Rangiroa, Tikehau, and Fakarava (low season €584/adult, €472/child; high season €632/adult, €508/child).

Ferry
Inter-island boats call at most of the Tuamotu atolls about once a week, bringing imported foods and other goods and returning to Papeete with fish. Aside from the *Aranui 5*,

Yachting in the Tuamotus

The Tuamotus are some of the most beloved atolls for yachties, as their calm lagoons provide shelter from the open ocean. **Svsoggypaws.com** has a free 180-page compendium about sailing the Tuamotus.

VOLUNTEERING

You can often sail from the Society Islands to the Tuamotus by volunteering as crew through websites like **Crewseekers.com** or the **"Find Crew Be Crew" Facebook group,** though it's best to travel with another person and seek references from former crewmates before hopping onboard. If you have little sailing experience, you'll be expected to help with cooking, cleaning, and maintaining the vessel. Usually, these vessels are captained by the owner, and privately owned. Fellow crew may be travelers, professional crew doing a boat transfer, or friends of the captain. Transit times between the islands varies depending on the wind and the vessel, and relying on ideal sailing conditions makes crewing best for travelers who aren't on a tight schedule.

ROUTES

The usual route is to sail either between **Rangiroa** and **Arutua** after a stop at **Ahe,** or through the **Fakarava Pass** between **Toau** and **Fakarava.** Winds are generally from the east, varying to northeast November-May and southeast June-October. Variable currents, sudden storms, and poor charts mean cruising this group is for experienced sailors only—the Tuamotus are popularly known as the Labyrinth, and wrecks litter the reefs of many atolls.

space onboard is not guaranteed and is not bookable in advance.

- The *Aranui 5* (www.aranui.com) stops briefly at Fakarava and Rangiroa or Kauehi and Makatea on its way to an 11-night loop around the Marquesas. It takes about a day of travel to reach the Tuamotus from Tahiti and again from the Marquesas (beds from CFP 340,400/11 nights including food). Pitcairn Islands itineraries stop at Anaa and Amanu (beds from (CFP 409,800/11 nights including food).

- The *Cobia III* (tel. 40 43 36 43; cobia@mail.pf) runs to the Tuamotus, departing Monday and connecting Kaukura-Apataki-Arutua-Aratika-Fakarava, staying one night at each stop. The *Cobia III* has three four-bed cabins at CFP 6,300 one-way. Meals are sold onboard. The office is on the Tuamotu Wharf at Motu Uta, Papeete. Call at least a week in advance to confirm the schedule and cabin availability.

- The *Saint-Xavier Maris Stella* (tel. 40 42 23 58) leaves Papeete every two weeks on a 10-day voyage to the Tuamotus. The journey takes around two days to venture from Papeete to Rangiroa. Their office is on Papeete's Tuamotu wharf. It costs CFP 7,000/one-way, including meals. Call at least one week ahead to confirm the schedule and availability.

Many other copra boats, boats used to transport dried coconut around the archipelago, also serve the Tuamotus. Ask about ships of this kind at the large warehouses west of Papeete's Motu Uta inter-island wharf. The *Nuku Hau* and *Taporo VIII* go as far as the Gambier Islands; the *Nuku Hau* sails from Papeete to Hao, Tureia, Tenania, Marutea, Rikitea, Tematangi, Nukutepipi, and Hereheretui once a month. Tickets are available at the Hawaiki-Nui office (tel. 40 54 99 54) at Motu Uta.

GETTING AROUND

Once you're on an island in the Tuamotus, it's usually easy to get around on foot or with a bicycle. Accommodations, restaurants, shops, and activities tend to be clustered on just one or two small motu at each of the atolls. To get between the atolls, you'll need to fly or take a boat.

Air

Island-hopping in the Tuamotus is easiest by plane. Air Tahiti routes and timetables change depending on the time of year. Flights range from 10 minutes to one hour, not including stopovers. Most flights will cost from CFP 70,000-12,000 one-way during the high season. Rangiroa, Tikehau, Mataiva, and Fakarava are the best connected. For the latest information, contact the airline directly or look at their timetable online.

Boat

Local boats and sailing yachts cruise through the archipelago, often taking travelers onboard. If you have access to a kayak, you can paddle from boat to boat around the anchorage sites in the Tuamotus (usually off the lagoon near the largest villages), making inquiries and leaving your contact information and list of skills (cleaning, cooking, crewing, etc.) behind. Usually, word gets around and you may be able to find a ride between the atolls. Inter-island boat transfers are best arranged through your accommodation. The cargo ships occasionally have space for passengers as well. Time between islands by boat varies, often requiring a full day at sea before reaching the next targeted atoll.

ORIENTATION

Arrayed in two parallel northwest-southeast chains scattered across an area of ocean 600 kilometers (372 mi) wide and 1,500 kilometers (932 mi) long, the Tuamotus are the largest group of coral atolls in the world. **Atolls** are low-lying ring-shaped islands that encircle a lagoon. The closest atolls are around 330 kilometers (205 mi) northeast of the island of Tahiti. Of the 78 atolls in the group, 21 have one pass in the reef connecting the open ocean to the lagoon, 10 have two passes, and 47 have no pass at all. Some have an unbroken ring of

reef around the lagoon, while others appear as a necklace of islets separated by channels. Although the land area of the Tuamotus is only 726 square kilometers (280 square mi), the lagoons of the atolls total some 6,000 square kilometers (2,316 square mi) of sheltered water. Moving from west to east, the most popular atolls are **Mataiva,** which is 40 kilometers (24 mi) from Tikehau; **Tikehau** is 8 kilometers (5 mi) from Rangiroa; and **Rangiroa** is 170 kilometers (105 mi) from Fakarava. **Fakarava** is the center of the Tuamotus, with lesser visited atolls surrounding it. The lonely **Gambier Islands** are over 1,560 kilometers (969 mi) southwest from Tahiti, nearly 440 kilometers (273 mi) southwest from the closest atoll in the Tuamotus (Fakamaru).

PLANNING YOUR TIME

The Tuamotu Islands are meant for travelers who feel as at home underwater as on land. What the atolls lack in mountains and archeological sites, they make up for in undersea adventures. With swirls of white and pink sandbanks, lagoons with water as clear as glass, and coral reefs rife with marine life, a trip here means packing your snorkeling gear and swimwear. Soaking in more sunshine than any other archipelago, the best time to head here is **April-November.**

Two to three nights on each atoll is enough time to relax and enjoy the many dive sites and snorkel tours. **Rangiroa, Tikehau,** and **Fakarava** have the largest selection of hotels, restaurants, and tours. The advantage of the other atolls is that you're bound to have an even more offbeat adventure, negotiating rides with the locals across to le secteur (uninhabited motu) as they go to cut copra or tend the pearl farms. Just don't expect many facilities on these tiny specks of sand scattered in a solitary sea. Once you're on an atoll, you'll likely stick to the motu your accommodation is found on—your hosts or hotel concierge will help arrange any transport and tours while on the atoll.

If you're purchasing an Air Tahiti

The Tuamotu and Gambier Islands

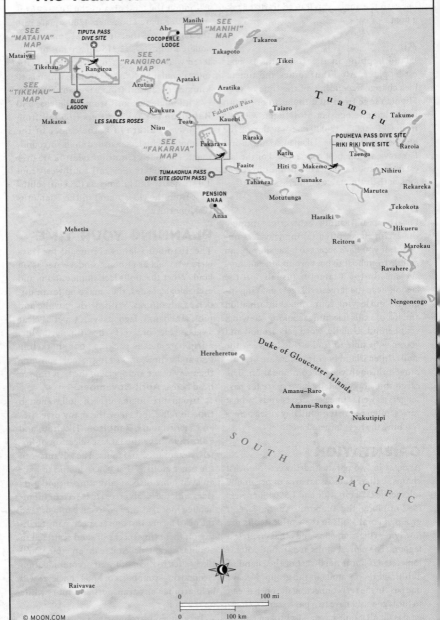

SEE "MATAIVA" MAP

SEE "TIKEHAU" MAP

TIPUTA PASS DIVE SITE

Mataiva

Tikehau

Rangiroa

BLUE LAGOON

LES SABLES ROSES

Makatea

Ahe

Manihi

COOPERLE LODGE

SEE "MANIHI" MAP

Takaroa

Takapoto

Tikei

SEE "RANGIROA" MAP

Apataki

Arutua

Aratika

Kaukura

Toau

Niau

Kauehi

Fakarava Pass

Taiaro

Taro

Takume

SEE "FAKARAVA" MAP

Fakarava

Raraka

Raroia

POUHEVA PASS DIVE SITE

RIKI RIKI DIVE SITE

TUMAKOHUA PASS DIVE SITE (SOUTH PASS)

Faaite

Katiu

Hiti

Makemo

Taenga

Nihiru

Tahanea

Tuanake

Marutea

Rekareka

PENSION ANAA

Anaa

Motutunga

Haraiki

Tekokota

Hikueru

Mehetia

Reitoru

Marokau

Ravahere

Nengonengo

Duke of Gloucester Islands

Hereheretue

Amanu-Raro

Amanu-Runga

Nukutipipi

SOUTH PACIFIC

Tuamotu

Raivavae

0   100 mi

0   100 km

© MOON.COM

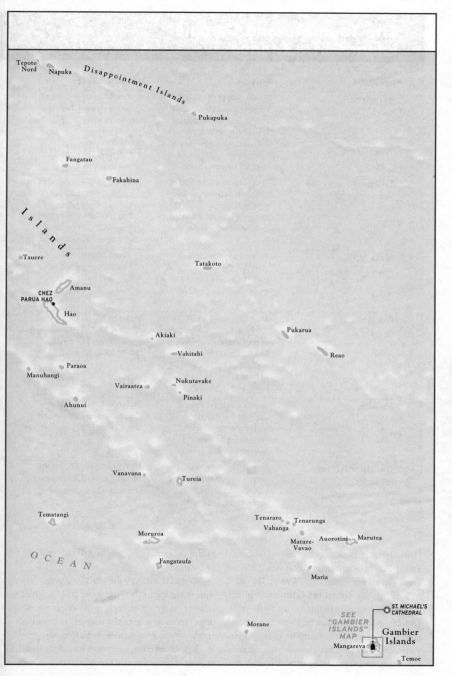

Tepoto Nord

Napuka

Disappointment Islands

Pukapuka

Fangatau

Fakahina

Islands

Tauere

Tatakoto

CHEZ PARUA HAO

Amanu

Hao

Akiaki

Pukarua

Vahitahi

Reao

Paraoa

Manuhangi

Vairaatea

Nukutavake

Pinaki

Ahunui

Vanavana

Tureia

Tematangi

Tenararo

Tenarunga

Vahanga

Moruroa

Mature-Vavao

Aurotini

Marutea

Fangataufa

Maria

O C E A N

SEE "GAMBIER ISLANDS" MAP

☆ ST. MICHAEL'S CATHEDRAL

Gambier Islands

Morane

Mangareva

Temoe

The Tuamotu and Gambier Islands at a Glance

Island	Why Go	How to Get There
Rangiroa (page 221)	Scuba dive in the Tiputa Pass, a haven for dolphins, sharks, and barracudas. Sip wine from French Polynesia's sole winery. Visit a bright blue lagoon, home to black tip reef sharks.	*Air:* From Tahiti (1 hour, CFP 28,000/one-way), Tikehau (20 minutes, CFP 10,000/one-way), Fakarava (45 minutes, CFP 11,000/one-way), and Mataiva (30 minutes, CFP 10,000/one-way).
Tikehau (page 231)	Snorkel and scuba dive in a lagoon densely packed with fish, visit a manta ray cleaning station, and lounge on pink sand beaches.	*Air:* From Tahiti (55 minutes, CFP 27,000/one-way), Rangiroa (20 minutes, CFP 10,000/one-way), Bora Bora (2 hours, CFP 32,000/one-way), stopping in Rangiroa.
Mataiva (page 237)	An atoll of serenity and solitude. Cycle in between palm trees and admire the mosaic blue hues of the closed lagoon.	*Air:* From Tahiti (1 hour, CFP 23,900/one-way).
Fakarava (page 239)	Scuba dive and snorkel with the highest concentration of reef sharks in the world. Kitesurf over calm, flat water. The main town of Rotoava is the most lively in the Tuamotus.	*Air:* From Tahiti (1 hour 15 minutes, CFP 27,000/one-way) and Rangiroa (45 minutes, CFP 10,100/one-way).
Manihi (page 246)	One of the least-visited atolls in the Tuamotus with accommodation. Guaranteed private beaches and clear waters.	*Air:* From Tahiti (2.5 hours including stops in Arutua and Ahe, CFP 29,500/one-way).
Gambier Islands (page 248)	Rugged remote islands with hiking, old churches, welcoming settlements, and raw adventure.	*Air:* From Tahiti (3 hours 45 minutes, CFP 44,900/one-way) around twice per week.

Multi-Islands Pass, a potential itinerary is Tahiti-Tikehau-Rangiroa-Fakarava-Tahiti or Tahiti-Fakarava-Rangiroa-Tikehau-Tahiti.

Visiting the **Gambier Islands** is much more challenging, as flights are somewhat rare and can book out quickly. Expect to spend around five days in the Gambier Islands. Plan a minimum of two full days on Mangareva for hiking and sightseeing plus two day trips to the other islands, one to Aukena and one to Taravai.

Note that it's very difficult to change foreign currency in the Tuamotus and Gambier Islands, so bring enough cash. There are no large stores on any of the islands, so pack everything you might need including sun protection, snorkeling gear, and water shoes to protect your feet against rough sand.

Itinerary Ideas

With little land coverage in the Tuamotus, most days are spent exploring the lagoon or diving at the entrance of an atoll pass. For all itineraries, you'll want to wear plenty of sun protection and bring along snorkel gear, water, and reef-safe sunscreen.

ONE DAY IN RANGIROA

For this itinerary, arrange a guided boat tour through your accommodation in advance. A full-day boat tour will cost around CFP 9,000 per person. You do not need to be an experienced snorkeler to participate, but you do need to know how to swim. Some boat tours can provide a life vest; confirm in advance.

1 Enjoy an early breakfast at your accommodation before getting ready and venturing to the **Tiputa Pier,** where your boat and guide await.

2 Ride approximately one hour to Rangiroa's **Blue Lagoon,** a tranquil lagoon surrounded by tiny motu. Swim and snorkel with the resident black tip reef sharks. You'll dine on a picnic lunch on the motu, usually of poisson cru and coconut bread.

3 After lunch, the boat will depart to the Tiputa Pass for snorkeling at the **Aquarium dive site,** where hundreds of reef fish gather. Look for bottlenose dolphins playing in the current.

4 Return to your accommodation and dress for dinner at **Relais de Josephine,** pairing your meal with a glass of wine from Vin de Tahiti—French Polynesia's sole winery.

ONE DAY IN TIKEHAU

Certified scuba divers should spend their day scuba diving at Tikehau's sole pass (CFP 6,900 per dive). Otherwise, arrange a boat and guide for a day out on the lagoon for around CFP 7,000 per person.

1 Have a hearty breakfast at your accommodation before being picked up by your boat guide. Ask to stop for a snorkel at the **Manta Cleaning Station dive site,** where majestic manta rays glide through the waters below an old pearl farm. Your lunch is likely to be fresh-caught fish under the shade of a palm tree; try your hand at basket weaving from found palm fronds.

2 Next, ask your guide to head to **Les Sables Roses,** pink sand beaches formed by powdered red corals. Take plenty of pictures from all angles—no filter is needed to bring out those rosy tints.

3 Return to your accommodation for a mellow evening of seaside relaxation. If you're staying on Tikehau's main motu, **La Cloche de Hina** beach makes for a tranquil sunset spot.

Itinerary Ideas

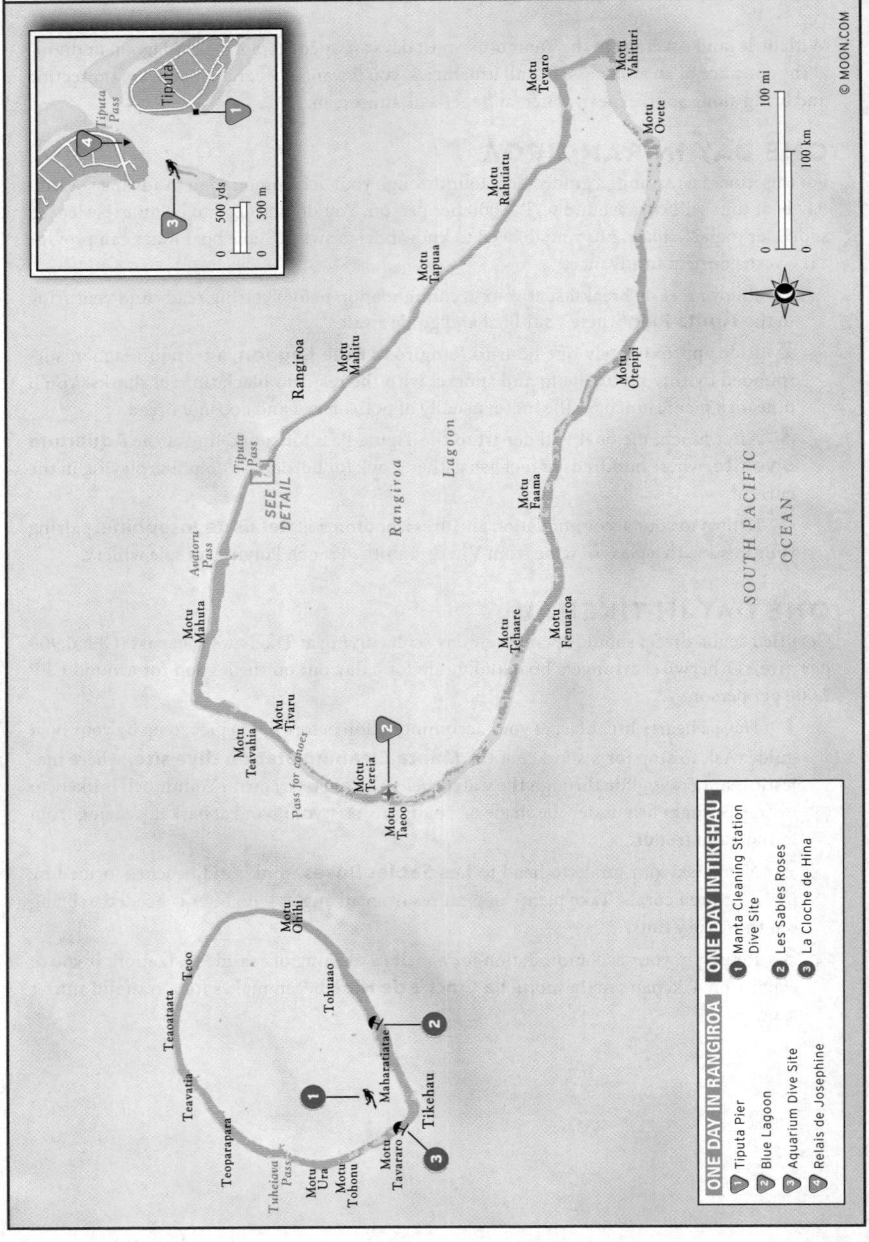

© MOON.COM

Motu Tevaro
Motu Vahituri
Motu Ovete
Motu Rahuiatu
Motu Tapuaa
Motu Otepipi

Rangiroa
Motu Mahitu

Tiputa Pass
SEE DETAIL
Avatoru Pass

Rangiroa Lagoon

SOUTH PACIFIC OCEAN

Motu Mahuta

Motu Faama

Motu Tehuere
Motu Femuaroa

Pass for captivo

Motu Teavahia
Motu Tivaru
Motu Tereia
Motu Taevo

Motu Ohihi
Tcoo
Teaoataata

Teavatia

Tohuao

Teoparapara
Tuheiava Pass
Motu Ura
Motu Tohonu

Mahartatiatae

Tikehau

Motu Tavararo

ONE DAY IN RANGIROA
1 Tiputa Pier
2 Blue Lagoon
3 Aquarium Dive Site
4 Relais de Josephine

ONE DAY IN TIKEHAU
1 Manta Cleaning Station Dive Site
2 Les Sables Roses
3 La Cloche de Hina

Detail inset:
Tiputa Pass
Tiputa
1
4
3
500 yds
500 m

100 mi
100 km

Rangiroa

The name Rangiroa means "extended sky," but one could argue that it should've been named "extended lagoon." Its 1,020-square-kilometer (393-square-mi) aquamarine lagoon is 78 kilometers long, 24 kilometers wide, and 225 kilometers around (48 mi long, 15 mi wide, and 139 mi around)—the island of Tahiti would fit inside its reef. It's the largest atoll in French Polynesia and the Tuamotus' most populous.

Two deep passages through the north side of Rangiroa's coral ring allow a constant exchange of water between the open sea and the lagoon, creating a fertile habitat. The reef is rife with corals, fish, and crustaceans, and around 10 species of rays and sharks frequent the depths. However, the stars of the atoll are the bottlenose dolphins that often make a close pass at scuba divers.

Rangiroa's main motu don't have the best beaches, but spits of soft sand are just a boat ride away. Lagoon excursions to jagged exposed reef islets and uninhabited motu await those who need a break from diving.

Orientation

Rangiroa is 300 kilometers (186 mi) northeast of Papeete. The atoll's two villages, each facing a 500-meter-wide (1,640-ft-wide) passage, are home to around 2,500 residents. **Avatoru** village on Avatoru Pass is at the west end of **Motu Avatoru,** about 6 kilometers (3.7 mi) away from the **airport.** A paved 10-kilometer (6.2-mi) road runs east from Avatoru past the airport and Hôtel Kia Ora Village to Tiputa Pass. At the edge of the pass is **Ohotu Wharf,** where taxi boats run to Motu Tiputa across the water, landing at Tiputa Pier. The tiny village of **Tiputa** is where most of the motu's residents are settled.

Both villages have small stores; the town hall and school are at Tiputa, and the medical center, gendarmerie, college, and marine research center are at Avatoru. Avatoru, whose

houses are accented with fragrant plumeria flowers and hibiscus trees, has better commercial facilities (including a town hall, post office, and food shops), as well as most of the atoll's churches, but Tiputa is less touristy. Most of the accommodations face the tranquil lagoon rather than the windy sea, and large ships can enter the lagoon through either pass. For yachts, the sheltered anchorage by the Hôtel Kia Ora Village near Tiputa Pass is recommended (as opposed to the Avatoru anchorage, which is exposed to swells and chop).

SIGHTS
Vin de Tahiti

Avatoru; tel. 87 79 07 45; www.vindetahiti.com; 5pm-6pm Mon.-Fri.; CFP 2,000/person

A South Pacific atoll doesn't seem like the place for a vineyard to thrive, but the grapes at Vin de Tahiti look to be doing just fine. At this little winery found between the airport and Avatoru, you can sample the three white wines and one rosé produced on the island. Hour-long tours of the vineyard include tastings. The founder of the winery, which started in the early 1990s, scoped out plots of potential land throughout all archipelagos before settling on Rangiroa. Over 30,000 bottles of wine are produced each year. Sipping a chilled glass of Vin de Tahiti wine near Tiputa Pass, watching dolphins swim by, is one of the best things to do on Rangiroa.

Gauguin's Pearl

Motu Avatoru, between Avatoru and the airport; tel. 40 93 11 30; www.gauguinspearl.com; shop hours 9am-noon and 1pm-4pm Mon.-Fri.; free, includes transport from accommodation

Many of Tahiti's iconic black pearls are cultivated and harvested in the Tuamotus. Founded in the early 1990s, Gauguin's Pearl offers educational 30-minute tours twice per day Monday-Friday, at 10am and 2pm. Depending on the time of year, visitors will

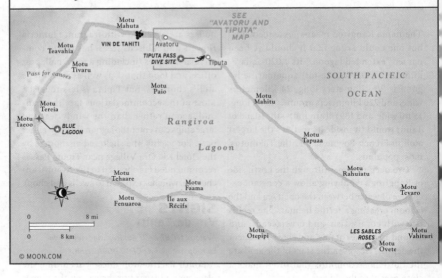

Rangiroa

(Map labels)

Motu Mahuta
Motu Teavahia
VIN DE TAHITI
Avatoru
SEE "AVATORU AND TIPUTA" MAP
Motu Tivaru
TIPUTA PASS DIVE SITE
Tiputa
Pass for canoes
Motu Paio
SOUTH PACIFIC OCEAN
Motu Mahitu
Motu Tereia
Motu Taoo
BLUE LAGOON
Rangiroa
Motu Tapuaa
Lagoon
Motu Rahuiatu
Motu Tehaare
Motu Faama
Motu Fenuaroa
Île aux Récifs
Motu Tevaro
0   8 mi
0   8 km
Motu Otepipi
LES SABLES ROSES
Motu Ovete
Motu Vahituri

© MOON.COM

witness pearls being prepped, grafted, harvested, or cleaned. If you want a tour in English, it's wise to call in advance. There's a small shop on-site where you can choose from already crafted jewelry or single pearls to create custom pieces.

Dolphin Viewpoint at Tiputa Pass

Tiputa Pass; free

Witness Rangiroa's beloved bottlenose dolphins splash and leap out of the water from the shoreline of Tiputa Pass—they're visible from both sides. Bottlenose dolphins are found all throughout French Polynesia's archipelagos, but Rangiroa's Tiputa Pass is where they're most common. Each of the regular dolphins spotted near Tiputa Pass has been named, and researchers with the **Dauphins de Rangiroa** (dauphinsderangiroa.org) conservation and research program study them closely. The oldest dolphin in the pod is thought to be nearly 40 years old. Note that currents can be deceptively strong at the pass, making it an unsafe place to swim without a guide.

★ Blue Lagoon

South of Motu Tereia, 30 km (18 mi) across the lagoon from Tiputa

On the west side of Rangiroa is a small lagoon of turquoise waters surrounded by a white sand islet. Gaze into the shallows and you'll likely see the black-tipped dorsal fins cruising about, belonging to the aptly named black tip reef sharks. They're often shy, and veer away just as you get close. In deeper waters, you might spot gray sharks, lemon sharks, sea turtles, and manta rays through the glass of your snorkel mask. The soft sands of the Blue Lagoon are also a welcome change from the coral beaches found near the Tiputa side of the lagoon. Most tours to the Blue Lagoon include a lunch of poisson cru and coconut bread baked fresh on the beach in banana leaves. Tours typically cost around CFP 8,000 per person for a full day of adventure.

BEACHES

Note that the main motu near Avatoru and Tiputa only have beaches of the coarse coral variety; sandals/water shoes are

☆ Les Sables Roses: The Pink Beaches of the Tuamotus

Les Sables Roses

Are you really in the Tuamotus if there isn't a pink sand beach (or 10) to explore? Les Sables Roses translates into "The Pink Sands." The color comes from the red coral that makes up these beaches, which has been ground down into gritty "sand" over millennia. You'll find pink sand beaches in:

- **Rangiroa** (page 223)

- **Tikehau** (page 231)

- **Fakarava** (page 239)

recommended. The best beaches on the atoll are found at motu on Rangiroa's southern coastline, near the Blue Lagoon, Ile Aux Récifs, and Les Sables Roses. It's best to visit these beaches as part of a lagoon tour (around CFP 7,000/person); each take a little over an hour to reach depending on ocean conditions.

AVATORU BEACH
Avatoru; free

There are small slivers of beaches found around the coastline of Avatoru. On the lagoon side, the water is often calm enough for swimming, but you do want keep an eye on the currents—especially near Avatoru's pass. On the northern side, the water is too rough to swim,

and sharp reef awaits those who attempt it. But, if you want to lounge undisturbed, there's plenty of space to put down a towel.

LES SABLES ROSES
Southeastern point of Rangiroa

Many of the motu on Rangiroa's southeastern end have a tint of pink to their shores, created by the exoskeleton of dark red corals eroded into gritty particles of sand over time. The church on Motu Otepipi, near Les Sables Roses, was once a central point for the town of Otepipi, which has since been deserted.

Venturing here requires a full day's trip, about a two-hour boat ride each way, and few tours offer the excursion due to its remote

Avatoru and Tiputa

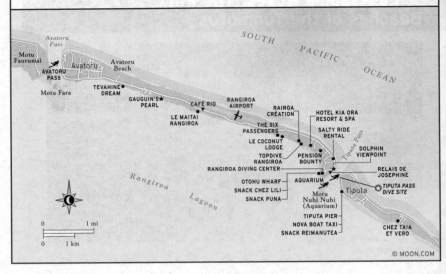

© MOON.COM

location. Trips here are typically arranged through your accommodation for around CFP 7,000 per person, with a minimum of four people to run. Lunch is included, and you'll usually have around an hour to swim and lounge on the sand.

ILE AUX RÉCIFS

East of Motu Faama, 20 km (12 mi) south of Tiputa Pass

At Ile Aux Récifs, also called the Reef Island, lifeless and unforgiving jagged limestone spikes poke out of clear water. It looks like a scene from another planet—until it gives way to the welcoming white sand beaches you've come to Polynesia for. Tours usually venture to Ile Aux Récifs on a full-day excursion that often includes a seafood lunch, as well as coconut harvesting and weaving demonstrations. Expect to pay around CFP 8,000 per person.

Snorkeling: The snorkeling here is some of the best in Rangiroa, with reef sharks, sea turtles, rays, and schools of reef fish lingering in its waters. Snorkeling gear is typically supplied, but you'll want to bring your own as size availability and quality varies.

SNORKELING AND SCUBA DIVING

Rangiroa is a snorkeling and scuba diving dream. On any given trip, you might spot sharks, manta rays, sea turtles, and the atoll's resident pod of dolphins. Most dives take place around Tiputa Pass and Avatoru Pass, usually from a boat using the back roll entry style to get into the water. The day's dive sites depend on the tide and ocean conditions. Drift diving through the passes is only done during incoming tides.

Snorkeling and Dive Sites

TOP EXPERIENCE

★ TIPUTA PASS DIVE SITE

Tiputa Pass

The 300-meter (984-ft) reef pass separating between Motu Avatoru and Motu Tiputa

---

1: Rangiroa as seen from above **2:** black pearls **3:** Rangiroa's main motu are easily bikeable. **4:** wine from Vin de Tahiti

The Best Dive Sites in the Tuamotu Islands

The Tuamotus are home to some of the world's best dive sites. If pressed as to which ones are the best, these are the spots you won't want to miss:

- **Tiputa Pass:** Drift with tens of bottlenose dolphins, sharks, manta rays, and barracudas through Rangiroa's thrilling main pass (page 224).

- **Tuheiava Pass:** It's a fish extravaganza at Tikehau's pass, where shoals of reef fish form along an intriguing coral seascape (page 233).

- **Tumakohua Pass:** Dive with hundreds of gray reef sharks in Fakarava's southern pass (page 241).

is one of the most iconic dive sites in the Tuamotus, a channel with coral walls on each side. The marine life seen on drift dives through the pass is fantastic, with humphead wrasses, manta rays, barracudas, turtles, dolphins, and sharks in abundance. Most of the time the sharks are harmless black tip or gray reef sharks, but big hammerhead sharks frequent Tiputa Pass December-March. Spotted eagle rays are common November-April, and manta rays July-October. The stars of the pass, Tiputa's bottlenose dolphins, are around all year long and often come close to scuba divers (though touching them is not recommended).

The strong tidal currents (opape) through the Tiputa Pass generate flows of 3-6 knots, making this an exciting drift dive for experienced scuba divers. Usually, scuba dive centers will take newcomers to the south side of Tiputa Pass to assess their skills before drift diving through the pass itself; many deeper dives in the pass are for more experienced divers only. Dive schedules vary according to the tides, winds, and number of tourists on the atoll, and it's wise to book ahead.

If you're not a diver, several companies offer a **snorkel** through Tiputa Pass at CFP 5,000 per person. Don't risk snorkeling on your own; it can be extremely dangerous due

to the strong currents. Dolphin-watching from shore is also a can't-miss experience.

AQUARIUM DIVE SITE
Motu Nui Nui

The Aquarium is a popular snorkel and dive site just off Tiputa Pass, where most lagoon tours stop for a quick dip on the way to or from another destination. Years of fish feeding have conditioned the hundreds of fish at Aquarium to school around the boat as soon as the engine idles. The hard coral reef drops to around 12 meters (39 ft), and is rife with reef sharks, humpback red snappers, trumpetfish, surgeonfish, butterflyfish, wrasses, and the occasional moray eel, sea turtle, and eagle ray.

AVATORU PASS DIVE SITE
Avatoru Pass

The Avatoru Pass is not nearly as popular among the dive centers as Tiputa Pass, but it is still worthwhile. On the inward flowing current, experienced divers can drift dive the small section of the pass to admire reef canyons—manta rays often use this current as an all-you-can-eat buffet, holding their position in the pass with mouths agape, feeding on the plankton flowing through. During the outward current, divers of all abilities can enjoy a relaxed dive accompanied by white tip reef sharks, eagle rays, and barracuda.

Dive Centers, Lessons, and Rentals

THE SIX PASSENGERS

Near Rangiroa Airport; tel. 40 96 02 60; www. the6passengers.com; 7:30am-4:30pm daily; CFP 9,500/fun dive, CFP 79,000/10 fun dives, CFP 6,500/ snorkel excursion

The Six Passengers runs dive excursions to the passes of Atatoru and Tiputa, with occasional two-tank safaris to more remote sites. Dives take place from their beachside fare and restaurant on Ohotu Bay and include transport to and from your accommodation. Guides are professional and patient with nervous divers. This outfit is included in the Te Moana diving pass and eDivingPass programs.

RANGIROA DIVING CENTER

Eastern end of Tiputa Pass; tel. 40 96 05 55; www. rangiroadivingcenter.com; 8am-5pm daily; CFP 8,500/fun dive, CFP 70,000/10 fun dives, CFP 5,000/snorkel excursion

Rangiroa Diving Center is one of the best dive centers on the atoll if you're looking to get open water certified, participate in advanced specialty dives, or progress to the next level—they teach courses all the way up to instructor level. They have an environmentally conscious approach to diving, working in collaboration with Dauphins de Rangiroa. Divers are encouraged to give dolphins space if they come close, and there is no baiting or feeding during snorkel excursions. Dives include transport and are part of the eDiving-Pass program.

TOPDIVE RANGIROA

Between Rangiroa Airport and Tiputa Pass; tel. 40 96 05 60; www.topdive.com; 8am-5pm daily; CFP 10,400/fun dive, CFP 91,500/10 fun dives

Topdive Rangiroa leads up to four daily fun dives at the passes, including a sunset dive, which tends to be a unique time to see extra activity around the reef. Courses range from discover to advanced, with specialty courses available if arranged in advance. In between dives, the dive center tends to host a social scene in its outdoor lounge area, making it a popular pick for solo travelers. All dives include transport to and from your accommodation.

LAGOON TOURS

Popular lagoon excursions include picnics to the Blue Lagoon and the Ile Aux Récifs, with some occasional trips to Les Sables Roses. If you're staying in Tiputa, most tour operators can pick you up at the Tiputa Pier. Almost all tours are given in French unless requested in advance.

ORAVA EXCURSIONS

Tours depart at the Ohotu Wharf; tel. 87 75 13 90; www.oravaexcursions.com; 8:30am-5:30pm daily; around CFP 10,000/day excursion

Orava Excursions is a highly professional tour operator running day trips to the Blue Lagoon (CFP 10,000), Ile Aux Récifs (CFP 9,000), Les Sables Roses (CFP 12,000), and combination tours of two or more sights. Trips take place in a shaded aluminum boat, and each includes a casual beachside lunch under a shaded fare. This is one of the few tour operators that runs combination trips, so it's best to book with them if you're short on time and want to see as many sights as possible.

HAIATUA EXCURSION

Tours depart at the Ohotu Wharf; tel. 87 73 12 59; www.rangiroa-activities.com; 8:30am-5:30pm daily; around CFP 10,000/day excursion

Haiatua Excursion is a family-run tour company with a laid-back style of tour guiding. Trips run to the Blue Lagoon (CFP 10,000), Ile Aux Récifs (CFP 10,500), or combination trips to both (CFP 14,000). Children are half price. All trips include transfers to your accommodation, lunch, and snorkel equipment rental. Depending on the schedule, the tour may go dolphin spotting in Tiputa Pass and/ or to a final sunset snorkel stop.

SHOPPING
RAIROA CRÉATION
Between Rangiroa Airport and Tiputa Pass near Topdive Rangiroa; tel. 87 75 05 44; facebook.com/arnotahiti; 10am-6pm daily

Arno, a local artist, has a boutique art shop where he sells artworks made from natural materials—like coconut fibers and ink made from soil, palm leaves, and wood. You can also purchase screenprinted shirts, pareu, sculptures, prints, shell jewelry, and furniture made by other Polynesian artists.

FOOD
SNACK PUNA
Eastern end of Tipuna Pass, on the pier; tel. 87 73 76 10; 11am-1:30pm and 5:30pm-8:30pm Mon.-Sat., 5:30pm-8:30pm Sun.; CFP 1,500

Enjoy large plates of traditional French Polynesian fare served on the pier of Tiputa Pass. Potted plants, floral prints, and mismatched furniture and dishes give an eating-at-your-aunt's-place ambiance. Aside from dishes of sashimi, poisson cru, steak served with fried breadfruit, and bottles of cold Hinano, there are also burgers, curries, and meat skewers on the menu. Rays and reef sharks cruise in front of the snack as entertainment.

SNACK REIMANUTEA
Tiputa; tel. 40 96 72 62; 6am-2pm and 3:30pm-6pm Mon.-Fri.; 1,500 CFP

Snack Reimanutea is the only proper restaurant in Tiputa. The small snack is set just steps away from the Tiputa Pier. Their daily menu includes burgers, grilled steak, sashimi, tuna tartare, grilled fish, and poisson cru served with rice or fries. Dinner is usually only served takeaway, and guesthouses in Tiputa are happy to help arrange. If you're there for lunch, check their display case for sandwiches and sushi rolls. Don't sleep on the dessert here—the cookie crumb cheesecake is divine.

★ SNACK CHEZ LILI
Eastern end of Tiputa Pass, on the pier; tel. 87 32 42 50; 11:30am-2pm and 6:30pm-9pm Tues.-Sun.; CFP 2,000

Snack Chez Lili is owned by Lili, a charismatic chef originally from Madagascar. The menu features international dishes like chicken Creole and peppery sausage stew. Of course, her seafood dishes are also popular picks, with mahi-mahi served with vanilla sauce, trio of tuna, and shrimp curry. The atmosphere is casual and cheerful, with shaded outdoor seating available.

★ RELAIS DE JOSEPHINE
Eastern end of Tiputa Pass; tel. 40 96 72 62; relais-josephine-rangiroa.com; noon-2pm and 6pm-8pm daily; 2,000 CFP

The restaurant attached to Relais de Josephine is one of the best on Rangiroa for its location alone. A spacious wooden deck teeters on the edge of Tiputa Pass, making it a prime viewing spot to see dolphins in the pass as you dine. If they're not there, you might spot sharks, sea turtles, and rays—both of stingray and manta variety. Start with a glass of rosé from Vin de Tahiti before moving onto a lunch of quiches, salads, and sandwiches. The three-course dinner menu changes nightly. Non-guests are easily accommodated for lunch, but if you're not staying here overnight, you'll want to reserve a dinner table at least a day in advance.

CAFÉ RIO
Motu Avatoru, near Rangiroa Airport; tel. 40 96 04 56; 6:30pm-late; CFP 2,000

Café Rio is a cheerful casual restaurant found just along the main road parallel to the airport. The walls are decorated with 1950s diner art. It has some of the best pizza on the island, and serves a range of salads, steaks, seafood dishes, and hearty desserts. The dining area is small, with little room for walk-ins once dinnertime comes. Reservations are recommended, and the restaurant can usually pick you up from your accommodation.

ACCOMMODATIONS

Most accommodations are on the Avatoru motu, with only a handful of family-run pensions on the Tiputa motu. Choosing the **Avatoru** motu is best if you want the convenience of easily accessible dive centers and eateries. The **Tiputa** side, however, offers a unique glimpse of life as a local—and it's not hard to shuttle over to Avatoru via the boat taxi.

CHEZ TAIA ET VERO

Tiputa; tel. 87 71 03 00; taianui.gnatata@mail.pf; CFP 10,000/double room

If you're interested in living in Rangiroa like a local, stay at family-run Chez Taia et Vero, where few fellow travelers stay. The guestrooms are set on a grassy lawn surrounded by fragrant plumeria trees. The owner, Taia, is helpful when it comes to arranging tours and onward transport—he works at the airport. Rooms have a fan, tropical decor, and lounge area. All guests have access to a full-size kitchen and squeaky bicycles. This pension can be booked through Booking.com or Airbnb.com.

PENSION BOUNTY

Motu Avatoru, between Rangiroa Airport and Tiputa Pass; tel. 40 96 05 22; pension-bounty.com; CFP 18,000/double room

Bounty Lodge has four studio rooms among a garden of tropical fruit trees and flowers. Prices are per person at the pension (CFP 11,000/single, CFP 18,000/double, CFP 22,500/triple), making it one of the few good choices in the Tuamotus for solo travelers. The hosts are a yogi divemaster duo who are happy to turn stays into yoga and diving retreats. Each room has a fan, kitchen, private bathroom, internet access, and double bed. Breakfast, bicycle use, and airport transport is included in each stay.

TEVAHINE DREAM

Avatoru; tel. 40 93 12 75; www.tevahinedream-rangiroa.com; CFP 18,600-24,000/bungalow

Tevahine Dream is set on the waters of Rangiroa's lagoon, just a short walk from Avatoru's main stretch. Each of the five spacious bungalows are decorated with Polynesian artwork, and equipped with a kitchenette, king-size bed, mosquito net, and fan. One has a plunge pool. Airport transfers are included with your stay. Bicycles and kayaks are available for rent.

LE MAITAI RANGIROA

Motu Avatoru, near Rangiroa Airport; tel. 40 93 13 50; www.rangiroa.hotelmaitai.com; CFP 37,000-58,000/bungalow

Le Maitai Rangiroa is an upscale resort with around 30 thatched-roof bungalows among tropical gardens. Rooms are spacious and simply decorated, and have air-conditioning, hit-or-miss internet access, a TV, and private bathroom. Some can sleep up to three people. From the oceanfront side of the property, guests enjoy a decent snorkeling spot, the restaurant, and bar. It doesn't get wild by international standards, but it is one of the few places on Rangiroa to enjoy a drink after sunset. Snorkeling gear and kayaks are included; bicycles are available for an extra cost.

★ LE COCONUT LODGE

Motu Avatoru, between Rangiroa Airport and Tiputa Pass; tel. 87 33 78 28; www.lecoconutlodge.com; 50,000 CFP/bungalow

Le Coconut Lodge is a laid-back eco retreat with six bright and airy bungalows on-site. Four are double-room bungalows, and there are two two-bedroom bungalows at the seafront. Each is equipped with air-conditioning, internet access, hot-water showers, minibar, and lounge deck. All are just a few steps away from a white coral beach and snorkeling spot. Guests have free use of bicycles, a kayak, stand-up paddleboards, and snorkeling equipment. The property minimizes as much waste as possible, stocking rooms with refillable containers and giving food waste to their animals.

HOTEL KIA ORA RESORT & SPA

Motu Avatoru, between Rangiroa Airport and Tiputa Pass; tel. 40 93 11 11; www.hotelkiaora.com; CFP 55,000-80,000/double bungalow

Hotel Kia Ora Resort & Spa is the most popular resort on Rangiroa, with around 60 bungalows on its property. All are spacious, built and decorated with natural materials, and some have private plunge pools. Ten overwater bungalows have a lounge platform and access to the water. The size of the resort makes it feel like a miniature village, with an overwater bar and poolside restaurant being the main gathering points. Guests have access to a spa, fitness center, and activity bure. Dive trips and lagoon tours are easily arranged. This resort is home to one of the only sandy beaches on the motu.

INFORMATION AND SERVICES

- **Rangiroa Medical Center:** Avatoru; tel. 40 96 03 75
- **Rangiroa Pharmacie:** Avatoru; tel. 40 93 12 35; pharma.rangiroa@gmail.com; 8am-12:30pm and 2pm-5pm Mon.-Thurs., 8am-noon Fri.-Sat.
- **Banque de Tahiti:** Avatoru; tel. 40 96 85 52; banque-tahiti.pf; 7:30am-11:30am and 1pm-4pm Mon.-Fri.
- **Banque Socredo:** Near Rangiroa Aiport; tel. 40 96 85 63; socredo.pf; 7:30am-11:30am and 1:30pm-4pm Mon.-Fri.
- **Post Office:** Avatoru; tel. 40 96 83 81; 7am-3pm Mon.-Fri.

GETTING THERE

The easiest way to reach Rangiroa is by plane. Being the most visited atoll in the Tuamotus, it's well connected.

Air
RANGIROA AIRPORT
Motu Avatoru
Air Tahiti flies between Rangiroa and:

- Tahiti: 1 hour, CFP 28,000/one-way

- Tikehau: 20 minutes, CFP 10,000/one-way
- Fakarava: 45 minutes, CFP 11,000/one-way
- Mataiva: 30 minutes, CFP 10,000/one-way

A one-way flight arrives from Bora Bora (1 hour 15 minutes, CFP 32,000/one-way), but there are no flights from Rangiroa back to Bora Bora. There are other seasonal routes; check the website for the latest schedules and fares.

The **airstrip** (RGI) is about 6 kilometers (3.7 mi) from Avatoru village by road, accessible to Tiputa village by boat. Most of the Avatoru pensions offer free airport transfers to those who have booked ahead. Pensions on other motu from the airstrip motu usually charge extra for transport (around CFP 2,000-4,000 each way).

GETTING AROUND

There's no public transportation on Rangiroa, though tour and scuba operators usually include transport with their trips.

Bike

Riding a bike is the most convenient way to get around Rangiroa. Many accommodations offer bicycles to their guests for free or for a rental fee of around CFP 1,500 per day. The main roads along Motu Avatoru and Motu Tiputa are paved and uncrowded. It's generally safe to leave your bicycle against a palm tree—locks are a rare sight.

SALTY RIDE RENTAL
Motu Avatoru, between Rangiroa Airport and Tiputa Pass; tel. 87 32 36 16; vaaitemoana.com; 8am-5pm daily; CFP 1,500/bike rental per day, CFP 4,000/ Vespa rental per day
The pension Va'a I Te Moana rents bicycles and Piaggio Vespas (gas included in daily rental). Some bikes have a children's seat.

Boat
NOVA BOAT TAXI
Tiputa Pass; tel. 87 26 78 06; CFP 500/person each way
To reach Tiputa village across from Motu

Avatoru (the motu with Avatoru village and the airport), wait for a lift on the dock next to Snack Puna. Nova Boat Taxi shuttles people across the Tiputa Pass from sunrise to sunset. Usually, it leaves whenever there's a handful of people onboard—every 30 minutes or so—but it can be slow going during midday. If you call, the taxi boat usually appears within a few minutes; it's likely waiting on the other side of the pass. The ride takes about 10 minutes each way. The boat can accommodate bikes for an extra CFP 100 per bike.

Car
RANGIROA LOCATION
Drop-off with rental; tel. 87 75 60 77; rangiroa-location.com; 8am-5pm daily; rentals around 5,000/day per vehicle

Rangiroa Location has a range of vehicle options, including the tiny two-seater electric car, Renault Twizy—large enough to stuff a beach towel and snorkel gear in the back. They also have a Renault Twingo 3, electric bikes, quads, and electric scooters for rent. Most travelers find the motu too small to be practical for a car—smaller vehicles and bicycles are easier to park and navigate with. It is not possible to transport vehicles between the motu.

Tikehau

Rangiroa's smaller neighbor, Tikehau (500 inhabitants), is an almost circular atoll 27 kilometers (16 mi) across with the shallow Tuheiava Pass on its west side. It's a beachcomber's delight, with pink and white sand motu dotted with palm trees. After a 1987 expedition to Tikehau, Jacques Cousteau reported that the atoll was one of the world's richest in marine life, with manta rays, reef sharks, tiger sharks, and hammerheads. Some of the motu, like Motu Puarua, host large seabird colonies. Five pearl farms operate on Tikehau, and tourism is growing fast. There's a far better choice of places to stay than on Manihi, and it's less developed than Rangiroa.

Internet on the atoll is unstable, and it's best to have enough cash to cover the duration of your stay, as there's no bank and only a few places accept credit card (this goes for accommodations too).

Orientation
Tuherahera village and the airport share an island, called Motu Tuherahera, in the southwest corner of the atoll, which also hosts the atoll's main shops, accommodations, dive centers, and wharf. Solely private motu accommodations exist outside of Motu Tuherahera. End to end, the atoll runs around 3 kilometers (1.8 mi) long, with a main road connecting most of the pensions and shops to the airport.

BEACHES
There's no shortage of beaches on Tikehau—sandy motu make up most of the atoll. Beaches found on the lagoon side tend to be best for swimming and snorkeling. Those found on the ocean side are usually empty of other people, but too rough for swimming. You'll need a boat to reach Les Sables Roses, but the others listed are reachable by bicycle.

LES SABLES ROSES
Southwest Tikehau
Here, red and white coral fragments blend to make pink-hued beaches. Under full sunlight, they look pastel pink; with more shade in the skies, they're bubblegum. Rosy beaches are found throughout the atoll, but the brightest are on the southeastern cluster of motu.

LA CLOCHE DE HINA
Motu Tuherahera; free
On the northwestern end of Motu Tuherahera is a white sand beach with limestone rocks at

Tikehau

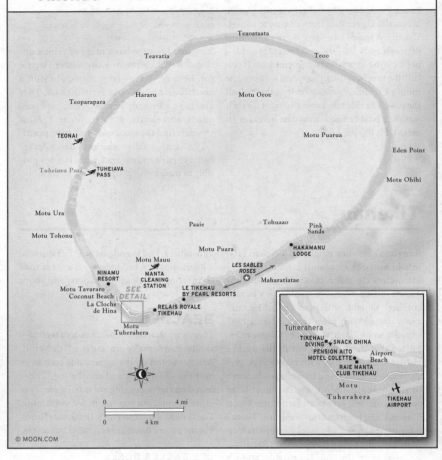

Tuheiava Pass

Tuheiava Pass

Teaoataata

Teavatia

Teoo

Hararu

Motu Oeoe

Teoparapara

Motu Puarua

Eden Point

TEONAI

Motu Ohihi

Motu Ura

Paaie

Tohuaao

Pink Sands

Motu Tohonu

Motu Puara

HAKAMANU LODGE

Motu Mauu

LES SABLES ROSES

NINAMU RESORT

MANTA CLEANING STATION

Maharatiatae

Motu Tavararo
Coconut Beach
La Cloche de Hina

LE TIKEHAU BY PEARL RESORTS

SEE DETAIL

RELAIS ROYALE TIKEHAU

Motu Tuherahera

0   4 mi

0   4 km

© MOON.COM

Tuherahera

TIKEHAU DIVING   SNACK OHINA
PENSION AITO
MOTEL COLETTE

Airport Beach

RAIE MANTA CLUB TIKEHAU

Motu
Tuherahera

TIKEHAU AIRPORT

its edge. The name of the beach translates into "Hina's Bell." Legend states that Hina was once the queen of Tikehau, beloved by those who lived there. She bathed at this beach, and every time she did, a bell rang to keep prying eyes away. There's a small spot for a picnic, and the beach here is occasionally busy with local families on the weekends. It's also one of the best spots to watch the sunset.

COCONUT BEACH

Motu Tuherahera; free

Tikehau's best beach is found on the motu's western tip, a prime spot for snorkeling, sunbathing, and swimming to nearby sandbanks.

AIRPORT BEACH

Motu Tuherahera; free

Wander to the lagoon side of Tikehau Airport for a narrow stretch of sandy beach to unwind on. Flights come and go just a few times per day, making them a novelty to witness rather than a roaring disturbance. You could spot anything from sea turtles to rays to sharks off the reef here, so pack a mask and snorkel.

SNORKELING AND SCUBA DIVING

Under the surface of Tikehau's lagoon, prepare to see hundreds if not thousands of reef fish. Schools swirl around the coral reef, while tiger sharks, hammerhead sharks, lemon sharks, gray sharks, manta rays, eagle rays, sea turtles, tuna, and barracuda cruise through the deep blue. It's an ideal year-round dive destination.

Snorkeling and Dive Sites

Decent snorkeling is found on the lagoon side of most of Tikehau's motu. Most scuba dives take place at the Tuheiava Pass, about a 30-minute boat ride from Motu Tuherahera. The lagoon is home to manta rays, sea turtles, eagle rays, many species of sharks, butterfly-fish, parrotfish, angelfish, fusiliers, eels, many crustaceans, and more.

TUHEIAVA PASS DIVE SITE

Tuheiava Pass

Diving legend Jacques Cousteau named Tikehau, particularly Tuheiava Pass, as the place with the greatest variety of fish species anywhere in French Polynesia. On any given plunge underwater divers are bound to see thousands of fish, along with a shot at diving alongside hammerhead sharks, gray sharks, tiger sharks, lemon sharks, barracuda, manta rays, sea turtles, and dolphins. Even if you don't see any "big" creatures of the deep, the sheer number of shoaling fish, the interesting seascape, and the macro life hiding in between coral crags make every dive here one to savor. The pass is 11 kilometers (6.8 mi) north of Motu Tuherahera.

TEONAI DIVE SITE

Outside of Tuheiava Pass

On the outer edge of Tuheiava Pass is a sloping reef teeming with shoals of fish so densely packed they often cast a shadow. Typically, Teonai offers a dive with little current and decent visibility, a relaxing site to admire the reef formations and scout for rays, gray sharks, big-eyed trevallies, unicorn fish, manta rays, and the occasional hammerhead shark.

MANTA CLEANING STATION DIVE SITE

Motu off Tuherahera

Here, snorkel boats moor off a derelict pearl farm, where reef manta rays come to get cleaned by small cleaner wrasse who dine on the parasites attached to the manta rays' skin. It's common to see a few mantas at a time at this snorkel spot, though of course no sighting is ever guaranteed. While some dive centers host dives here, they're usually reserved for beginner divers (experienced divers head to the pass), and the shallow waters make for great snorkeling. The visibility can be hit or miss depending on the wind conditions.

Dive Centers, Lessons, and Rentals

RAIE MANTA CLUB TIKEHAU

Tuherahera; tel. 87 24 60 65; www.raiemantaclub. com; 8am-5pm daily; CFP 8,500/fun dive, CFP 67,000/10 fun dives

Raie Manta Club Tikehau is found at the Tikehau Village Pension. They host fun dives (CFP 8,500/dive), snorkeling trips (CFP 5,000/trip), training dives, CMAS Level 1 courses (CFP 45,000) and deep dive specialty courses (CFP 30,000). Dives include basic equipment and mostly occur at the Tuheiava Pass.

TIKEHAU DIVING

Tuherahera; tel. 87 28 27 07; tikehaudiving.com; 8am-5pm; CFP 8,500/fun dive, CFP 69,000/10 fun dives

Tikehau Diving is a jovial dive center found at the Tuherahera Wharf. Book them for fun dives or diving courses (CMAS Level 1 for CFP 48,000, PADI Open Water CFP 80,000, PADI Rescue CFP 22,000). There's also a half-day snorkeling trip to the Tuheiava Pass for CFP 7,000. Dive guides are friendly, professional, and knowledgeable, but the booking system with Tikehau Diving can be unreliable—you'll want to confirm your dives are booked multiple times in advance. Tikehau Diving is part of the Te Moana and eDiving Pass Programs.

LAGOON TOURS

Most accommodations can help you arrange tours of the lagoon venturing to Les Sables Roses, Ile d'Eden, Motu Puara, Manta Ray Cleaning Station, and desert motu for a picnic lunch.

TIKEHAU OCEAN TOUR

Tuherahera; www.tikehauoceantour.com; 8am-5pm daily; US$600/half-day tour, or US$1,000/full-day tour for up to five people

Tikehau Ocean Tour is captained by one of French Polynesia's champion free divers, Denis Grosmaire, who spends much of his free time diving with Tikehau's tiger sharks. Tours on Tikehau Ocean Tour are tailored to the group, venturing to family-friendly snorkeling spots and deeper dive sites with tiger sharks depending on participants' interest and skill level. Trips usually stop at the Manta Ray Cleaning Station and pink sand beaches. Snacks and beverages are included, but you'll need your own snorkel gear.

BIRD-WATCHING

MOTU PUARA

9 km (5.5 mi) from Tuherahera

Motu Puara is a limestone-fringed motu inhabited by birds, who circle and squabble overhead, marking the island as their own. Blue noddies, red-footed boobies, and crested terns call the island home, and you can peek into the treetops to see them nesting. Guides take guests around the island—because there are no natural predators on the motu, hatchlings can grow in peace. A trip here is often included as part of a full-day excursion around the lagoon, arranged by accommodation (around CFP 8,000/person).

FOOD AND ACCOMMODATIONS

Tikehau is not exactly a foodie destination. Most travelers eat breakfast and dinner at their accommodation, most of which are found on the same motu as Tuherahera. If you're staying on a private island motu, you'll have total tranquility but will probably pay extra to visit the main motu. Dive and lagoon tour operators pick up guests from as far as Hakamanu Lodge for an added cost.

SNACK OHINA

Tuherahera Wharf; tel. 87 70 65 33; 11am-2pm and 6pm-9pm Mon.-Sat.; CFP 1,300

Snack Ohina is set near the water with a shaded dining area where chickens cluck about. The menu is simple but tasty, serving burgers and fries, steak, grilled catch of the day, tuna carpaccio, and poisson cru. There are no entrée options for plant-based diners. It's popular at lunchtime with scuba divers and locals alike.

PENSION AITO MOTEL COLETTE

Tuherahera; tel. 87 74 85 77; pensioncolette-tikehau. com; CFP 21,000/night for double room including breakfast and dinner

The soft strumming of a ukulele acts as background music at Pension Aito Motel Colette, a family-run pension with fresh meals and a relaxing atmosphere. Six bungalows, four of them seaside, are spacious, with double beds, mosquito nets, fans, hot-water showers, and terraces. All are set on a coral sand beach and surrounded by hibiscus, tiare, and aito trees. The owners Colette and Henéré are happy to dole out travel advice about Tikehau and arrange day trips.

HAKAMANU LODGE

Motu Hakamanu Lodge; tel. 87 73 38 77; www. hakamanu.com; around CFP 25,000/double room including breakfast and dinner

Depending on the ocean conditions, Hakamanu Lodge is between a 30- to 45-minute boat ride from the main motu of Tikehau, making it one of the more remote accommodation options on the atoll. The only chaos on the motu is of the hermit

---

1: Tikehau Diving 2: the airport of Tikehau 3: Snack Ohina 4: Hakamanu Lodge

crab variety—they're the only souls scurrying about. Rooms are equipped with a private bathroom with hot-water shower, private terrace, and fan. Meals are some of the best on the atoll, served communally at a punctual time at their open-air dining deck. Black tip reef sharks, octopus, rays, sea turtles, and bird life call the areas surrounding the motu home. The hosts can arrange lagoon day trips. If you're a diver, you'll want to book your dives well in advance of arrival to ensure they leave enough time in their boat schedule to pick you up—boat rides usually cost around CFP 6,000 return from Tuherahera to Hakamanu.

RELAIS ROYALE TIKEHAU

Motu Relais Royale Tikehau; tel. 40 96 23 37; www. royaltikehau.com; CFP 27,000-29,000/night double room

Relais Royale Tikehau is on a private motu next to the main motu of Tikehau, a 10-minute trip from the airport. There are a handful of bungalows on the island, many of them next to the water. Each one has an en suite bathroom with hot-water shower, small terrace, television, and fan. They're not luxurious, but they're comfortable and clean. Bungalow arrangements range from 2-6 people. A few bedrooms are also available in the main building. Stays include breakfast and dinner. There's great snorkeling around the resort, and the hammocks strewn between coconut palms make for a relaxing place to hang. Lagoon tours are available on request.

LE TIKEHAU BY PEARL RESORTS

Motu Le Tikehau; tel. 40 96 23 00; www.letikehau. com; CFP 60,000/double room

Le Tikehau is the atoll's top option for luxury stays, located on a private motu. The resort houses landside villas, overwater bungalows, and beach bungalows throughout its spacious property. Most have air-conditioning, though some are just equipped with a fan. All have a TV and coffeemaker. It's common to not really leave the resort aside from a lagoon tour, thanks to an infinity pool, decently stocked bar, spa, and gamut of ocean toys—snorkel

gear, kayaks, and outrigger canoes. The resort can easily arrange dive trips and excursions to Tikehau's main motu. Each of the bungalows is made from bamboo, wood, and thatched roofing, creating a glamping sort of ambiance. The snorkeling is just okay underneath the overwater bungalows, as most of the sea floor is solely sand.

★ NINAMU RESORT

Motu Ninamu; tel. 87 28 56 88; motuninamu.com; CFP 42,500-625,000/night for double room

No two of the ten bungalows on Ninamu Resort are quite alike. Bungalows are rustic yet nice, each built from natural materials and simply decorated. Bungalows can sleep from two to six guests, and it's best to call ahead and explain your group dynamics for a tailored pick. Some are air-conditioned and have a private plunge pool. Stays include all meals, drinking water, sports equipment rental, internet access, and airport transfer. Fronting the property is a quiet beach, snorkel spot, and a decent kitesurfing spot if you have your own equipment. Lagoon trips on their 37-foot trimaran to Tikehau's main lagoon sights take place just about daily.

GETTING THERE AND AROUND

It's easy to get around the main motu of Tikehau by **bicycle.** Most pensions lend or rent them to guests for around CFP 1,000/day.

Air

Air Tahiti flies between Tikehau and Tahiti (55 minutes, CFP 27,000/one-way) and Rangiroa (20 minutes, CFP 10,000/one-way). One-way flights from Bora Bora to Tikehau also depart a few times per week (2 hours, CFP 32,000), stopping in Rangiroa.

The **airstrip** is 1 kilometer (0.6 mi) east of Tuherahera village. Most accommodations have their own boat or vehicle, and will typically include boat transfer from the airport with the cost of their stay. Travelers staying on outer motu may have to pay extra for airport transport (CFP 2,000-4,000 each way).

Boat

The only way to get from one motu to the next in Tikehau is by boat, arranged through your accommodation. A half-hour trip will take around CFP 2,000 per person, and most boats will require a minimum of four passengers to run. Some ships do leave for Tikehau from Tahiti, but they're unreliable and often do not take passengers. To reach Tikehau by boat from elsewhere in the archipelago, its best to do so by private yacht charter.

Mataiva

Be sure to grab a window seat on your flight to Mataiva. From the sky, its lagoon looks like a stained-glass window of electric greens and blues. Mataiva's lagoon reaches a maximum depth of around 12 meters (39 feet), giving it this distinct appearance. Only 10 kilometers (6 mi) long and 5 kilometers (3 mi) wide, Mataiva is worth considering as an offbeat destination and is quickly rising in the ranks of traveler popularity in the Tuamotus. Lingering on the atoll, you'll get a sense that life isn't taken too seriously on Mataiva—it's easy to make friends and get to know the familiar faces of the few hundred residents of the atoll quite quickly. Bring cash, as no banks are found here. The threat of phosphate mining looms in Mataiva's future, a threat Mataiva residents consistently protest.

Orientation

A coral road covers most of the 35 kilometers (21 mi) around the atoll with narrow concrete bridges over nine shallow channels, or "eyes," that gave the island its name (*mata* means "eye," *iva* is "nine"). Almost everyone lives in the tiny town of **Pahua,** near Mataiva's airport.

SIGHTS
Marae Papiro
Southeast Mataiva

Marae Papiro is one of the few preserved marae of the Tuamotus, built on the edge of the lagoon. Local legend states the marae was built for the god of Tu, the ancestor of Pomare, who's stone throne looks over the water. Just offshore from the marae is a bird nesting site with red-footed boobies, brown noddies, and crested terns.

BEACHES
THE POOL
Lagoon side of Pahua

The site of a former phosphate mine is now a beloved swim spot by locals. It's not great for snorkeling, as you'll rarely see more than a wayward ray or reef shark, but it's a nice place to cool off from the equatorial heat.

SCUBA DIVING AND SNORKELING

Mataiva's seascape is undoubtedly one of the most interesting of the atolls, thanks to its shallow seabed and coral pinnacles. The visibility isn't always the best inside the lagoon, but just outside the pass is often gin clear. Dives take place from **Pension Ariiheevai.**

Mataiva

MATAIVA PASS
Pahua
MATAIVA VILLAGE · PENSION ARIIHEEVAI
The Pool
MATAIVA AIRPORT
MARAE PAPIRO ★

0 — 2 mi
0 — 2 km

© MOON.COM

MATAIVA PASS DIVE SITE
Pahua

The shallow pass of Mataiva looks like a trickle of turquoise into the atoll's lagoon. While the pass itself is too shallow to be a dive site suitable for oceanic giants, the oceanside edge of the pass is worth exploring.

ACCOMMODATIONS

There are only three pensions on Mataiva, and the atoll is popular with French Polynesians who flock here on a long weekend. If you're interested in venturing to Mataiva, book your flights and accommodation well in advance. Weekdays will see the island at its slowest—though it's never crowded, even when fully maxed out.

MATAIVA VILLAGE
Pahua; tel. 40 96 32 95; CFP 8,500/person including all meals and excursions

Mataiva Village has 11 basic bungalows and a small campground (CFP 1,700/person excluding excursions) on the well-kept property. Each of the bungalows is equipped with air-conditioning, and a few have views of the water. Days at Mataiva Village can feel like summer camp, with included excursions to Mataiva's main sights, basket-weaving workshops, and shell-craft tutorials. Meals are served communally three times per day,

usually some variation of fish and/or chicken. Guests are free to use the pension's bicycles.

★ PENSION ARIIHEEVAI
Pahua; tel. 40 96 32 46; pensionariiheevai@gmail.com; CFP 10,000/person including all meals and excursions

Located in the heart of Pahua with a shop nearby and a tranquil swimming spot at its front, this pension has a mix of standalone bungalows and dorm rooms, all equipped with air-conditioning, internet access, and private bathrooms. The smaller bungalows sleep four while the dorm bungalows sleep six. Excursions are included with each stay: jovial guides lead you to the marae, quiet motu, bird-watching, and to a raised reef formation that looks like a turtle out of the water. A dive center on the property offers snorkel and diving excursions for around CFP 8,000 per fun dive and CFP 4,000 per half-day snorkel trip. Guests have access to bikes and kayaks.

GETTING THERE AND AROUND

Tiny Mataiva, westernmost of the Tuamotus and 40 kilometers (25 mi) from Tikehau, has direct Air Tahiti flights from Tahiti (1 hour, CFP 23,900/one-way). Most locals get around with a 4WD truck. Most travelers walk, arrange a 4WD trip through their accommodation, or cycle (bikes can be rented from accommodations).

Mataiva

Fakarava

A pass gives access to each end of this rectangular 60-by-25-kilometer (37-by-15-mi) lagoon, dotted and flanked by 80 coconut-covered motu. There's spectacular snorkeling and drift diving in the passes or along the vertical drop-offs. Garuae Pass in the north is almost 1 kilometer wide, 9 meters deep (0.6 mi wide, 29 ft deep), and is the haunt of countless sharks, dolphins, barracuda, and rays. Tumakohua Pass in the south is smaller and accessible to snorkelers. For divers who love toothy predators, the south pass could be the world's most spectacular shark dive, with as many as 1,000 gray reef sharks present. When you account for both passes, shark residents outnumber human residents by quite a large margin. About 900 people live on the atoll, and a handful of pearl farms have been established around the lagoon.

Fakarava is suited for adventure. Many accommodations on Fakarava are rustic, cooled by the sea breeze and illuminated by moonlight. When the sun's out, the lagoon is a prime place to snorkel, scuba dive, kitesurf, windsurf, swim, and paddle. At night, the turquoise disappears but the atmosphere remains. Its coarse sand beaches are rarely crowded and are typically flanked by palm trees.

Though still in the early stages of tourism, Fakarava is becoming known for its diverse marine life. The seven atolls included in the Commune of Fakarava (Aratika, Fakarava, Kauehi, Niau, Raraka, Taiaro, and Toau) are considered a UNESCO Biosphere Reserve, singled out as the home of rare crustaceans, including squills and sea cicadas.

Orientation

Fakarava is the second-largest Tuamotu atoll, about 250 kilometers (155 mi) southeast of Rangiroa and 435 kilometers (270 mi) northeast of Tahiti, in the center of the Tuamotu archipelago. This central location makes it a convenient stop for sailors venturing between Tahiti and the Marquesas. The main motu is found on its northern end near **Garuae Pass.** Four kilometers (2.5 mi) east of the airport is the largest town, **Rotoava,** with most of Fakarava's accommodations, restaurants, dive centers, and tour operators. A 30-kilometer (18-mi) road connects the edge of Garuae Pass to the south side of Fakarava's main motu. The **Tumakohua Pass** is 54 kilometers (33 mi) south of Graruae Pass, with tiny **Tetamanu** village at its edge.

SIGHTS
Topaka Lighthouse

Near Fakarava Airport; free

The Topaka Lighthouse looks like Fakarava's tiny take on Chichén Itzá. The lighthouse is around 15 meters (49 ft) high and was once used as a communications tower for neighboring atolls. Now, a rusty ladder leads to the top—it's detached from the rest of the structure at many points, but thrill-seekers do climb to the top despite the lack of upkeep (not recommended).

BEACHES
LES SABLES ROSES

South Fakarava

Fakarava's Les Sables Roses, pink sand beaches, are some of the best in the archipelago. Hues range from rosy to red, made by ruby coral fragments mixed in with white sand. You'll need a boat to reach these pink sand motu (60-90 minutes by boat from North Fakarava, CFP 7,000/person for a day trip). Once you're here, you'll likely have the tranquil sands all to yourself.

SCUBA DIVING AND SNORKELING

Fakarava is one of the world's greatest diving destinations if you want to dive with sharks. Almost all dives take place at the two passes of

Fakarava

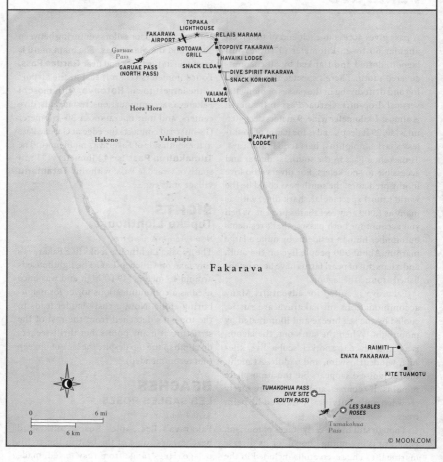

TOPAKA
LIGHTHOUSE
FAKARAVA
AIRPORT ✈ RELAIS MARAMA
ROTOAVA TOPDIVE FAKARAVA
Garuae GRILL HAVAIKI LODGE
Pass SNACK ELDA DIVE SPIRIT FAKARAVA
GARUAE PASS SNACK KORIKORI
(NORTH PASS)
VAIAMA
VILLAGE

Hora Hora
FAFAPITI
LODGE
Hakono Vakapiapia

Fakarava

RAIMITI
ENATA FAKARAVA

KITE TUAMOTU

TUMAKOHUA PASS
DIVE SITE
(SOUTH PASS) LES SABLES
ROSES

Tumakohua
Pass

0   6 mi

0   6 km

© MOON.COM

Fakarava. If you plan to dive at both, it's best to split your time between North Fakarava and South Fakarava, though most North Fakarava dive centers offer day trips to the South Pass. It takes around 1.5 hours to cross to get from one pass to the other by boat.

Many dive operators have halted night diving in the passes for conservation reasons, as artificial lights interfere with the natural hunting behavior of sharks.

Snorkeling and Dive Spots
GARUAE PASS (NORTH PASS)
Northern Fakarava

The incredible Garuae Pass dive at Fakarava might be one of the best in French Polynesia. Depending on the time of year, the pass may be thick with sharks of many species. Everything here is dramatic—the steep drop-off, the profuse marine life, the healthy corals. Great schools of barracuda, turtles, sharks, and dolphins are seen in the pass year-round, but some of the other creatures are seasonal:

Fakarava's UNESCO Biosphere

The existence of conservation areas has long ties to Polynesian culture through the tradition of **rahui,** in which humans were restricted from using lands and waters to allow them to replenish. In 1977, UNESCO established the Fakarava Biosphere Reserve, which is 266,876 hectares (1,030 square mi) large and encompasses seven low-lying coral atolls, all distinct from one another. Some atolls have hypersaline lagoons, brackish lagoons, or lagoons that receive large flows of water from the open ocean. Each of these houses a biologically diverse ecosystem of flora and fauna, like a kingfisher endemic to the atoll of Niau. So far, very few of the Fakarava Biosphere Reserve ecosystems have been studied in depth, and are found nowhere else in the world. The atoll of Taiaro, for example, is the only atoll in the world with a completely closed lagoon.

Here are some unique ways to experience the Fakarava Biosphere Reserve.

- Scuba dive at the **Garuae Pass,** the largest pass in French Polynesia.

- Scuba dive at the **Tumakohua Pass,** home to over a thousand gray reef sharks.

- **Choose a window seat** on your flight into Fakarava to admire the neighboring atolls from above.

- **Watch locals in the village of Rotoava produce copra,** the hardened meat of a mature coconut. Copra production is considered a sustainable economic activity within the reserve.

gray sharks (May-June), manta rays (July-Oct.), leopard rays (Nov.-Apr.), and hammerhead sharks (Nov.-Apr.). The strong current sweeps you through this huge pass amid a churning sea of life. All Fakarava dive shops on the north end offer drift dives through Garuae Pass, but it isn't appropriate for snorkelers or novice divers because the tidal flows are too strong.

TOP EXPERIENCE

★ TUMAKOHUA PASS (SOUTH PASS)

Southern Fakarava

The Tumakohua Pass is home to the highest density of gray reef sharks ever recorded. It doesn't seem scientifically possible that so many predators could be sustained in such a small space, collectively weighing as much as their prey according to shark scientist Johann Mourier. In June and July, nearly 20,000 camouflage groupers come to the pass to spawn, providing a gamut of food for the residents of the pass. Once the groupers leave, other species of fish come to spawn as well—this is

how one small pass can have hundreds of apex predators at once.

Even beginner divers can enjoy seeing the wall of gray sharks cruise through the blue, as the current here tends to be mild and most dives reach a maximum depth of around 20 meters (65 ft). After descending over coral reef, it's common for divemasters to guide divers into a spacious underwater cave. From there, you can enjoy the shark parade—the sharks surf the mild current to save energy. Manta rays, sea turtles, barracudas, moray eels, eagle rays, and other shark species frequent the pass. The gray sharks feed during the night, making them timid and passive during the day.

Dive Centers, Lessons, and Rentals

TOPDIVE FAKARAVA

Two locations: Rotoava in North Fakarava and Motu Aito in South Fakarava; tel. 40 98 43 76; www. topdive.com; 8am-5pm daily; CFP 10,400/fun dive, CFP 91,500/10 fun dives

TOPDIVE Fakarava has two locations within its lagoon, one near each of the passes. Each

Sharks: Man-Eating Menace or Just Misunderstood?

One diver's dream dive is another diver's nightmare. Movies like *Jaws* (1975), *Sharknado* #1-6, and Discovery Channel's Shark Week tap into the human primordial fear of being eaten, using sharks as the go-to supervillain. But actual attacks from sharks are incredibly rare, with an average of less than 10 unprovoked fatalities globally per year. Most attacks were in areas where fish cleaning had taken place, or in murky areas where sharks likely had trouble seeing their prey. Contrasting this, the global shark population is largely under threat due to overfishing, habitat degradation, and exploitation. Every year, thousands enjoy diving alongside sharks in the Tuamotus. If you're nervous for your shark dive, here are a few ways to have a safe experience:

- **Voice your fears to the dive guide.** This will prompt your guide to stay close to you as a reassuring presence throughout the dive.

- **Never chase or touch a shark,** which can cause them to feel threatened.

- **Stay calm and alert.** Don't thrash or make rash movements underwater. Swim calmly while keeping an eye on the sharks around you.

- **Avoid wearing jewelry or shiny objects,** which can glint under the sunlight like fish scales. It's best to avoid wearing anything with glitter or sparkles, as this can pique a shark's curiosity.

dive includes free Nitrox. They run trips from the north pass to the south pass for CFP 33,000, including lunch and two fun dives. Snorkel trips and dive courses (discovery to advanced) are also available.

DIVE SPIRIT FAKARAVA

PK 4 Marker North Fakarava; tel. 87 32 79 87; www. divespiritfakarava.com; 8am-5pm daily; CFP 8,500/ fun dive, CFP 70,000/10 fun dives

Dive Spirit Fakarava offers dives to both passes (CFP 30,000 day trip to south pass including two dives and lunch), but most dives take place at the nearby north pass. Guides are thorough, friendly, and happy to provide briefings in English. The center runs SSI, PADI, and CMAS dive courses (discovery to advanced), and an interesting shark ecology course that dives deep into the science behind the lagoon's resident gray sharks.

ENATA FAKARAVA

Motu Raimiti; tel. 87 70 15 08; enatafakaravadiving. com; 8am-5pm daily; CFP 9,000/fun dive

If you're staying near the South Pass, in the Tetamanu Area, Enata Fakarava offers transport between your accommodation and the South Pass dive site. They primarily run fun dives, though specialty dives are also available if booked in advance.

KITESURFING

Fakarava's lagoon is a haven for kitesurfers, windsurfers, and foilers in search of clear, flat water to enjoy. While all Tuamotu atolls are primed for wind sports, you need to bring your own equipment to all but Fakarava. Winds blow consistently from April-October.

KITE TUAMOTU

Hirifa; tel. 87 23 08 45; kitetuamotu.com; CFP 13,000/2-hour lesson, CFP 10,000/2-hour kitesurf gear equipment rental including safety boat

Kite Tuamotu is a little kite school tucked at the edge of Hirifa, a motu flanked by a long stretch of sand. The flat water makes for an ideal place to learn how to kitesurf or wing foil. There are dedicated kite camps throughout the year, where guests stay on a sailing yacht. There's also a funky little beach bar, slackline area, and spot where yoga classes are taught.

FOOD

SNACK ELDA

Rotoava; tel. 40 98 41 33; 11:30am-2pm and 6pm-9pm Mon.-Sat.; CFP 1,500

Snack Elda is a simple eatery next to the seaside serving seafood in generous portions. A shaded deck area makes it easy to linger a while. Hours are irregular, so it's worth ringing ahead before you arrive. If you buy a bottle of wine, Elda is happy to keep it chilled for you until your next meal here.

SNACK KORIKORI

PK 4; tel. 40 98 43 97; www.korikori-fakarava.com; 11am-2pm Mon.-Sat.; CFP 1,500

Snack Korikori is found at the Korikori Lodge, where fresh seafood, burgers, grilled meats, omelets, salads, and desserts are served on a quiet overwater dining area. The vibe is laid-back and casual, with reef sharks and rays swimming through the shallows under the pontoon. There are also a few coral bommies around the snack, making it a nice place to snorkel before or after you eat.

★ ROTOAVA GRILL

Rotoava; tel. 87 76 80 76; 11am-2pm Wed.-Thurs., 11am-2pm and 6pm-9pm Fri.-Sat., 6pm-9pm Sun.; CFP 1,600

This seaside restaurant is the only proper one on the island, and it serves grilled meat, fresh-caught fish, and chow mein on the edge of Fakarava's lagoon. The restaurant is laid-back, with dishes often selling out by 1:30pm come lunchtime. Reef sharks cruise the waters near the restaurant's dock.

ACCOMMODATIONS

RELAIS MARAMA

Rotoava; tel. 40 98 42 51; www.relais-marama.com; CFP 8,000/person per night for bungalows, CFP 3,500/person per night camping

Relais Marama offers a back-to-nature experience with its campsites and bungalows in the middle of Rotoava. They have a handful of bungalows facing the ocean side of Fakarava, unsuitable for swimming but great for the sea breeze and ocean wave lullabies. Bungalows

have a double bed, mosquito net, internet access, and terrace. There's also an open area for camping—though you'll need to bring your own tent, mattress, and bedding. All guests have access to the bicycles. Bathrooms are shared, and guests have access to a communal full-size kitchen. Stays include breakfast and airport transfers.

VAIAMA VILLAGE

PK 7; tel. 40 98 41 13; www.fakaravavaiama.com; CFP 23,500/bungalow for two people including breakfast and dinner

A secluded little spot on Fakarava's main motu, this no-frills seaside retreat has a handful of bungalows that sleep 2-6 people. Each have mosquito nets, private bathrooms with hot-water showers, and a mini fridge. There's a shaded hangout spot at the end of the pier, with decent snorkeling just below. The hosts are happy to arrange lagoon tours, and guests can use the property's kayaks.

FAFAPITI LODGE

PK 19; tel. 87 24 01 21; fafapitilodgefakarava.com; CFP 24,400/bungalow for two people including breakast and dinner

Fafapiti Lodge is a peaceful family-run pension far removed from Fakarava's main drag, owned and managed by two longtime scuba divers. The pension has a high emphasis on sustainability, providing filtered water (a rarity in the Tuamotus) and meals made from locally sourced ingredients. Two of the bungalows sleep two, while the third one sleeps three; all have a spacious and minimalistic design with a wooden terrace, mosquito net, and private bathroom. Price includes WiFi, airport transfer, breakfast, dinner, and use of the kayaks. Guests have access to a communal kitchen.

HAVAIKI LODGE

PK 2; tel. 40 93 40 15; www.havaiki.com; CFP 27,000/garden bungalow, CFP 37,000/beach bungalow including breakfast and dinner

If you're on the lookout for relaxation, you'll find it at Havaiki Lodge. One of the largest

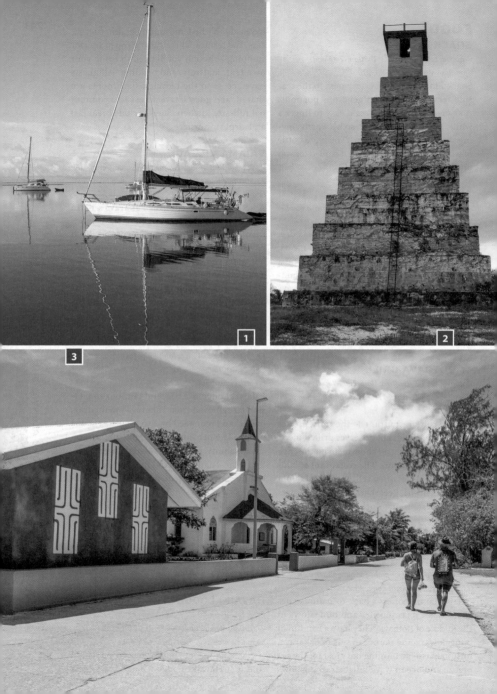

accommodations on Fakarava, Havaiki Lodge has 15 bungalows—10 on the water and 5 in the gardens—all equipped with a mini fridge, hot-water showers, fans, and terrace, capable of sleeping up to four guests. The beach bungalows also have air-conditioning and access to kayaks and bicycles. You won't want to leave (aside from scuba diving, of course). Guests can tour the Havaiki Pearl Farm to learn about the art of pearl farming in Fakarava. Havaiki's best are sent to a boutique in Paris.

You don't have to be a guest to dine at Havaiki Lodge's on-site restaurant and bar, the **Meko Bar** (6pm-9pm daily; CFP 3,800/ set menu). Every evening, the restaurant hosts a gourmet set dinner usually featuring some form of seafood and vegetables. Each plate is tastefully presented, and the spacious dining hall adds to a more upscale ambiance than you might expect on a remote atoll. Grab a cocktail and head to the pier for a relaxing aperitif.

RAIMITI
South Fakarava; tel. 87 70 90 10; www.raimiti.
com; CFP 83,600-93,600/bungalow for two people
including all meals for two nights
Isolated on its own motu, Raimiti is a DIY adventure-style resort with bungalows built from bamboo and palm leaves. By day, guests go on dive or snorkel trips with the Enata Fakarava, snorkel the coral reef in front of the property, bird-watch, stroll around the motu, or lounge in the little library area. Evenings are usually more social at the communal restaurant—where meals usually consist of fresh-caught fish. Bungalows are basic but tidy with

no door, lock, or reliable electricity—though there are electric fans available on request. Rates include boat transfer to the property, meals, and use of the kayaks and snorkel gear. There is a two-night minimum stay.

GETTING THERE AND AROUND
The most convenient way to reach Fakarava is by plane. That said, the passenger-carrying freighter *Aranui 5* sometimes calls at Fakarava on its way to the Marquesas (aranui. com; from CFP 360,500/person including meals for an 11-night journey). Sailing yachts cruise to Fakarava regularly, though these trips must be privately arranged.

You'll need a **boat** to get around anywhere outside of the main motu of Fakarava (rides arranged by your accommodation for around CFP 2,000 per half-hour journey). The main motu of Fakarava is easily traversed by **bicycle** for CFP 1,500/day, available from your accommodation.

FAKARAVA AIRPORT
3.5 km (2 mi) west of Rotoava
Air Tahiti flies between Fakarava and Tahiti (1 hour 15 minutes, CFP 27,000) and Rangiroa (45 minutes, CFP 10,100). Most accommodations include airport transport in the cost of your nightly rate if you are staying on the northern side of Fakarava. Those on Fakarava's southern motu (60-90 minutes away from the airport by boat) also usually include transport in their nightly rate. If it doesn't, expect to pay around CFP 4,000 to travel by boat from the airport to Fakarava's southern end.

THE TUAMOTU AND GAMBIER ISLANDS

FAKARAVA

1: sailing in Fakarava **2:** Topaka Lighthouse **3:** Most accommodations are found near Rotoava.

Manihi

Manihi, 175 kilometers (108 mi) northeast of Rangiroa, is an atoll with visions of white-sand beaches and cultured black pearls. Unless you have a keen interest in pearl farming, scuba diving with few fellow divers is the main reason to come here. The atoll was the first of the Tuamotus to get an airport in 1968, and luxury tourism trickled in slowly after. With the closure of its main hotel, the Manihi Pearl Beach Resort, the atoll is once again for more offbeat travelers in search of quiet stays and underwater adventure.

You'll want to bring enough cash to cover your stay in Manihi. With tourism still being a small industry of the atoll and the only real shop being in the village, boat hitchhiking across the pass and impromptu excursions are part of the experience.

Orientation

You can see right around Manihi's 6-by-30-kilometer (3-by-18-mi) lagoon, and the thousands of resident oysters hanging on underwater racks at the dozen or so pearl farms greatly outnumber the 800 human inhabitants. The main motu wraps halfway around the lagoon, with sections of it ceding to a thrashing sea. **Turipaoa** (or Paeua) village and its 50 houses face **Tairapa Pass** at the west end of a sandy strip just over 1 kilometer (0.6 mi) long. The airport island and main resort are just across the pass from Turipaoa.

SNORKELING AND SCUBA DIVING
Snorkeling and Dive Spots

There's decent snorkeling all along the lagoon coastline of Manihi. Accommodations don't tend to have their own snorkel gear for rent, so you'll want to pack your own. Most scuba dive sites are concentrated at Tairapa Pass. Fishing at the dive sites of Manihi was prohibited in 2019, making the region a refuge for juvenile reef fish especially. It's possible to snorkel

from the shore at most accommodations, but dive sites listed are accessible solely by boat.

TAIRAPA PASS DIVE SITE
Tairapa Pass

The Tairapa Pass is a spawning site for fish like marbled gropers, triggerfish, and snapper, who congregate by the thousands to breed. Taking advantage of this major food source, hammerhead sharks, gray sharks, barracudas, tunas, and others come to feed. Along the reef wall are crevasses, underwater caves, and coral bommies. Currents are mild to strong depending on tidal conditions.

THE CIRCUS DIVE SITE
Inside Tairapa Pass

Mantas come to The Circus, a shallow dive site found just inside of the Tairapa Pass, to get cleaned by small wrasse, gliding through the water with little fear of humans. It's common to see reef manta rays here all year long, with eagle rays, stingrays, black tip reef sharks, and white tip reef sharks also often making an appearance. This site is a great snorkel spot and is ideal for beginner scuba divers.

Dive Centers, Lessons, and Rentals
BLUE WAY DIVE LODGE

Blue Way Dive Motu; tel. 40 96 41 89; blueway-manihi.com; 8am-5pm daily; CFP 8,000/fun dive, CFP 75,000/10 fun dives, 15,500/bungalow for two people including all meals

This is the only dive operator on Manihi, owned by Bernard and Martine, who have three decades of diving experience each. It's set on a private motu with a handful of bungalows also on-site. Because of the lack of other tourists and its seclusion, divers have a large say over the types of dives done on Manihi. Aside from fun dives, hosts arrange lagoon excursions, snorkel trips, and specialty dive trainings. Blue Way Dive Lodge can also pick

Manihi

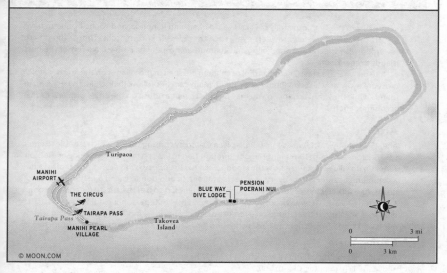

Turipaoa

MANIHI AIRPORT

THE CIRCUS

Tairapa Pass

TAIRAPA PASS

MANIHI PEARL VILLAGE

Takovea Island

BLUE WAY DIVE LODGE

PENSION POERANI NUI

0   3 mi
0   3 km

© MOON.COM

up divers from other pensions, though this must be arranged in advance.

ACCOMMODATIONS
MANIHI PEARL VILLAGE
Pauea; tel. 87 70 45 00; pension.mpv@mail.pf; CFP 10,500/person for half board (breakfast and dinner)
Manihi Pearl Village is on the Pauea waterfront, one of Manihi's most centrally located accommodations. Each of the four bungalows has views of the water and a terrace, and can sleep three adults. There's a decent swim spot in front of the pension with a few coral bommies to explore. Stays include breakfast and dinner; airport transfer costs CFP 2,000 per trip. Fresh-caught seafood makes up most of the dinners here. The hosts can help arrange trips around the lagoon, including to their private motu two minutes away by boat.

PENSION POERANI NUI
Motu Poerani Nui; tel. 40 96 42 89; pension.poerani. nui@gmail.com; CFP 18,370/person including all meals and airport transfer
Tucked between the palm trees on a private motu, Pension Poerani Nui is a small lodge with four large bungalows built from bamboo, wood, and palm leaves, each with a large terrace, private bathroom with cold-water shower, and enough space to sleep three adults. All meals are served at the pension, and the chef is skilled at cooking beyond your typical raw or grilled seafood fare. The pension runs lagoon excursions to pearl farms, snorkel sites, a little lagoon, and trips to town.

GETTING THERE
The occasional ship from Papeete enters the lagoon and ties up to a wharf at Turipaoa, but you'll most likely be flying to Manihi.

MANIHI AIRPORT
Manihi Airport (XMH) is on a motu 2.5 kilometers (1.5 mi) north of Turipaoa village by boat (you must arrange with your accommodations to be picked up). Most Air Tahiti flights are to Manihi from Tahiti (2.5 hours including stops in Arutua and Ahe, CFP 29,500).

Other Islands and Atolls

Venture from the Tuamotu atolls of Fakarava, Tikehau, and Rangiroa, and you're bound to have an offbeat adventure; few travelers ever reach these lesser-known atolls. Those who do are rewarded with spectacular snorkeling and Tuamotuan hospitality. Below are a few of the best islands to check out.

Note on where to stay: Only a handful of children are seen in the villages on these outer atolls; most are away at school on Rangiroa or Tahiti. Many families follow their children to the main islands while they're at school, so you may be able to rent a house on the atolls with few formal accommodations.

AHE

Ahe, 13 kilometers (8 mi) west of Manihi, is often visited by cruising yachts, which are able to enter the 16-kilometer-long (10-mi-long) lagoon through Tiarero Pass on the northwest side of the atoll. Tenukupara village is south across the lagoon. Facilities include two tiny stores, a post office, and a community center where everyone meets at night. In addition to being a major producer of pearls, Ahe supplies oysters to the pearl farms on Manihi. **Cocoperle Lodge** (Cocoperle Lodge Motu; tel. 87 73 15 67; www.cocoperlelodge.com; CFP 14,500/person including breakfast and dinner) is an island retreat found on a remote motu of Ahe. Relaxing, fishing, snorkeling, swimming, and lagoon excursions to bird islands and pink sand beaches make up the daily agenda.

Getting There

Air Tahiti has multiple flights a week from Tahiti (2 hours including a stop in Arutua, CFP 29,600) and Manihi (10 minutes, CFP 10,000).

ANAA

Anaa is 424 kilometers (263 mi) due east of Tahiti; unlike most of the other atolls covered here, Anaa is part of the eastern Tuamotu group that was out-of-bounds to non-French during the nuclear testing era prior to 1996. The 470 inhabitants live in five small settlements scattered around Anaa's broken coral ring, and there's no pass into the shallow elongated lagoon. The atoll is popular with few travelers aside from fishermen. After years of overfishing, the atoll enacted a rehabilitation program for select fish species like grouper, snapper, triggerfish, and bonefish—most of which have made a comeback. **Pension Anaa** (tel. 89 29 98 04; anaa.fly-fishing@gmail.com; CFP 10,000/bungalow for two people excluding meals) offers fishing trips and lagoon excursions.

Gambier Islands

The Gambier Islands, the most remote island group in the French Pacific, are all but forgotten by most tourists who travel to the South Pacific, but those who make the trip here will be rewarded with scenes from the edge of the earth. Jade peaks tickle the skies while electric blue waters give way to the deep. An outer atoll encloses the central islands as if giving them an oceanic hug. This is the most remote island group in French Polynesia.

The Gambier (or Mangareva) Islands are just north of the tropic of Capricorn, 1,650 kilometers (1,025 mi) southeast of Tahiti. The southerly location means a cooler climate. Contrasting sharply with the atolls of the Tuamotus, the archipelago consists of 10 rocky islands enclosed on three sides by a semicircular barrier reef 65 kilometers (40 mi) long. In all, there are 46 square kilometers (17 square mi) of dry land. The Polynesian

Getting There

Air Tahiti has flights from Papeete (1 hour 10 minutes direct, CFP 26,700).

HAO

The harp-shaped atoll of Hao is strategically situated in the heart of French Polynesia, equidistant from Tahiti, Mangareva, and the Marquesas. From 1966-1996 a giant French air base on Hao served as the main support base for nuclear testing on Moruroa, 500 kilometers (310 mi) southeast. At its peak, up to 5,000 people lived on Hao—a vast difference from today's quiet population of 1,200. Hao's 3,380-meter (11,000-ft) airport runway is the longest in the South Pacific—long enough to be considered a potential emergency landing site for the NASA space shuttles. Kaki Pass gives access to the 50-kilometer-long (31-mi-long) lagoon from the north. History buffs in search of a peaceful stay can check into **Chez Parua Hao** (tel. 87 70 28 89; binnews2010@hotmail.fr; CFP 11,000/person including meals) for simple but clean bungalows on the beach and healthy meals.

Getting There

Air Tahiti flies to Hao (2 hours 40 minutes, CFP 36,000), stopping in Hikueru. Flights tend to book out weeks in advance.

MAKEMO

Makemo is a 64-kilometer-long (39-mi-long) atoll near the center of the Tuamotu chain. Motu with luxuriant green vegetation stretch all along the north side of the atoll, but only sandbars and reefs mark the southern side. Two passes give access to Makemo's lagoon. One is near the main village, Pukeva, about 16 kilometers (10 mi) from the atoll's east end, while the other pass is at the northwest end of Makemo. The main source of income is pearl farming.

Largely untouched, Makemo offers pristine diving conditions around its two passes. **Riki Riki Dive Site** is found just outside of the western pass entrance, revealing a sloping reef rife with reef sharks, Napoleon wrasse, and the occasional reef manta ray. The **Pouheva Pass Dive Site** pass at the eastern end of Makemo is a spawning spot for many types of fish, attracting pelagic predators in droves. Currents in the pass itself can get too strong for beginner divers, though intermediate to experienced divers will enjoy the thrill.

Getting There

Most divers who venture here do so with their own ship and scuba gear, or as part of a scuba liveaboard excursion.

inhabitants named the main and largest island Mangareva, or "Floating Mountain," for 482-meter-high (1,581-ft-high) **Auorotini** (also called Mount Duff, for British Captain James Wilson's ship, which arrived here in 1797). Unlike the Marquesas, where the mountains are jungle-clad, the Gambiers have hilltops covered with tall aeho grass. A local seabird, the karako, crows at dawn like a rooster.

Recent studies show that the Gambier archipelago was likely populated around the 10th century by seafarers from the Cook, Marquesas, Society, and Tuamotu Islands as a midway point between Easter Island. It wasn't until the 19th century that the island group became a trading point for pearl merchants.

There are no banks in the Gambier Islands, and though many merchants do take credit cards, it's still best to have cash. Keep in mind there's a one-hour time difference between Tahiti and Mangareva.

Orientation

Most of the current 1,400 inhabitants of the Gambiers live on 8-by-1.5-kilometer

Gambier Islands

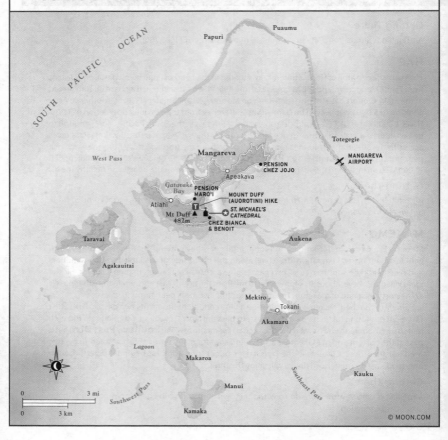

West Pass

SOUTH PACIFIC OCEAN

Papuri

Puaumu

Mangareva

● PENSION CHEZ JOJO

Apeakava

Totegegie

✈ MANGAREVA AIRPORT

Gatavake Bay

PENSION MARO'I

MOUNT DUFF (AUOROTINI) HIKE

Atiahi

Mt Duff 482m

✠ ST. MICHAEL'S CATHEDRAL

CHEZ BIANCA & BENOIT

Taravai

Aukena

Agakauitai

Mekiro

Tokani

Akamaru

Lagoon

Makaroa

Kauku

Manui

Southeast Pass

Southwest Pass

Kamaka

0   3 mi
0   3 km

© MOON.COM

(5-by-1-mi) **Mangareva. Rikitea** is the main village on the island's southeastern coast, and **Gatavake Bay** is found directly west. The smaller islands of **Taravai** (2 km/1.2 mi west of Mangareva), **Akamaru** (7 km/4.3 mi south of Mangareva), and **Aukena** (5 km/3.1 mi southeast of Mangareva) are found within the same barrier reef as Mangareva. Mangareva is the closest inhabited island to the **Pitcairn Islands,** a British Overseas Territory of four islands, and organized tours to Pitcairn occasionally begin here.

MANGAREVA

The central island of Mangareva is the largest of the Gambier Islands and home to most of its population, who live in the village of Rikitea, tucked in the shadows of Mangareva's volcanic peaks. A post office, seven small shops, a gendarmerie, an infirmary, schools, and a cathedral three times as big as the one in Papeete make up the infrastructure of this administrative center, and black pearls are cultured on numerous platforms on both sides of Mangareva's blue lagoon. A road loops around the northern two thirds of the island, cutting across from coast to coast at Rikitea.

Sights
★ ST. MICHAEL'S CATHEDRAL
Rikitea; free

Père Louis-Jacques Laval (1808-1880), a French Roman Catholic priest, came to the Gambier Islands in 1834. Shortly after learning the local language, Laval began converting residents to Roman Catholicism and ordered the destruction of existing marae. In his quest for conversion and power on Mangareva, Laval banned local religious practices and overworked laborers to the point of death to build Mangareva's Catholic houses of worship. Laval's architectural masterpiece is the St. Michael's Cathedral, with its twin towers of white coral rock from Kamaka and its altar shining with polished mother-of-pearl—a monument to horror and yet another lost culture. The cathedral was built between 1839-1848 on the ahu of the island's principal marae.

Laval's colleague, Father François Caret, who died in 1844, lies buried in a crypt before the altar. The tomb of Grégoire Maputeoa, the 35th and last king of Mangareva (died 1868), is in a small chapel behind the cathedral. Follow the path behind the church to the top of the hill and go through the gate on the left. Among the walled ruins of Rouru convent in Rikitea one can pick out the chapel, refectory, infirmary, and a dormitory for 60 local nuns. Laval's legacy among Mangarevans is complex. In collaboration with the first Mangarevan Catholic priest, Laval produced the first written record of Mangarevan traditions and language.

The cathedral was fully restored in 2011 and is the hub of Rikitea come Sunday mornings. Try to attend choir practice if you can; you'll find the latest schedule by asking around in Rikitea. The singing is without musical accompaniment, sometimes in native Mangarevan, a language that's having a revival. The church is central to the spiritual life and beliefs of many Mangarevans today,

and the restoration of its structure has helped the building separate from its oppressive past.

Hiking
MOUNT DUFF (AUOROTINI)
Distance: *4 km (2.4 mi) out-and-back*
Time: *2 hours*
Trailhead: *Rikitea*
Information and maps: *www.tahiti-rando.fr/rando-mangareva-mont-duff-en.php*

Trek to the highest point of Mangareva on a sunny day for panoramic views that span across the azure lagoon marked with coral bommies and powder blue basins to the outer Gambier Islands. The hike begins in Rikitea, and you can either hike on a 4-kilometer (2.4-mi) (total) out-and-back trail or an 8-kilometer (4.9-mi) loop by trekking south along the road and cutting inland where the dirt road ends.

Accommodations
★ PENSION MARO'I
Gatavake Bay; tel. 87 70 36 55; www.pensionmaroi.com; CFP 14,000/bungalow including breakfast and dinner

Stay on a white sand beach at Pension Maro'i in one of the four cozy bungalow options. Each is decorated in a way that feels like you're staying with an extended family member, rather than with a stranger on a remote island. Two have ocean views while the other two are in a tropical garden area. All can sleep three adults and have a terrace and private bathroom with hot-water shower. Guests are free to use the kayaks, bikes, snorkel gear, and fishing equipment. Tours to the churches, marae, motu, Mount Duff, and outer islands are also easily arranged. The pension also has a rental car on-site—somewhat of a novelty for the Gambier Islands.

PENSION CHEZ JOJO
5 km (3 mi) north of Rikitea; tel. 40 97 84 69; pensionchezjojo@mail.pf; CFP 15,000/bungalow including breakfast and dinner

Pension Chez Jojo is a quiet little pension about 5 kilometers (3 mi) north of the Rikitea, where two oceanfront bungalows can sleep up to three adults each. This place is cheerful and clean; each bungalow is built from wood and equipped with a private bathroom with hot-water shower, television, terrace, and set of beach loungers. Dinners are served family-style in the main home. The owners also have a snack in Rikitea (Snack Jojo) that serves a mix of fresh fish, grilled meats, and sandwiches.

CHEZ BIANCA & BENOIT

Rikitea; tel. 40 97 83 76; biancabenoit@mail.pf; CFP 17,000/bungalow including breakfast and dinner

Overlooking Rikitea and its lagoon on the foothills of Mount Duff, Chez Bianca and Benoit is a feel-good stay with four bungalows and four rooms inside of the main guesthouse (all have private bathrooms). Views from here are reason enough to stay, and the property is around a 10-minute walk from the center of town. Bungalows can sleep from three to five people, making it a great pick for families. Bianca and Benoit are happy to arrange day trips, and meals served communally are a fun affair.

Getting There

AIR

The airstrip for **Mangareva Airport** (GMR) is on Totegegie, a long coral island 8 kilometers (5 mi) northeast of Rikitea, the main village. Arriving passengers pay CFP 500 per person each way for the boat ride to the village. Direct Air Tahiti flights from Tahiti (3 hours 45 minutes, CFP 44,900/one-way) usually fly in twice per week.

BOAT

The supply ships *Nuku Hau* and *Taporo V* from Papeete arrive only monthly. The trip takes around three days, with prices starting at around CFP 10,000 including meals. Large vessels can enter the lagoon through passes on the west, southwest, and southeast.

TARAVAI

2 km (1.2 mi) west of Mangareva

At one point, the island of Taravai, just 2 kilometers (1.2 mi) from Mangareva, was inhabited by a few thousand people. Today, the island is home to just six full-time residents. Aside from its natural beauty, you can peek at the **St. Gabriel Church,** built in the late 1860s and renovated in mid-2021. Also on the island are caves with the final resting grounds of Polynesian royalty. Most sights are unmarked, so it's wise to visit with a guide. Two of the residents, Herve and Valerie, live near the church and are often happy to assist with your trip. It's best to contact them through your accommodation, and visit Taravai as a day trip from Mangareva (about an hour's ride by boat from Mangareva, CFP 4,000/person return).

AUKENA

5 km (3 mi) southeast of Mangareva

The white sands of Aukena make a good day-trip destination by boat (around a one-hour ride from Mangareva), best arranged through your pension for around CFP 4,000 per person return. Pearl mogul Robert Wan has set up his farm just off the shores here, which can be seen on its northern end. White sand beaches await those who want nothing but relaxation. The **Church of St. Raphael** here is the oldest in the Gambier Islands, built in 1839. To the south are the ruins of the **Rehe Seminary** (1840).

The Marquesas Islands

The Marquesas Islands are known as Te Henua

Enana, The Land of Men, in Polynesian. An archipelago of artists and sculptors, the islands look like they've been whittled by a divine hand.

These wild, rugged islands feature steep cliffs and valleys leading up to high central ridges, sectioning regions off into cartwheel-like segments (though all this dramatic scenery creates major transportation difficulties). Large reefs don't form due to the cold south equatorial current—though there are isolated stretches of coral—and the absence of protective reefs has prevented the creation of coastal plains, so no roads circle the islands. Most of the people live in narrow, fertile river valleys; these communities living in the border between land and sea are the descendants of the world's best sea navigators.

Highlights

Look for ★ to find recommended sights, activities, dining, and lodging.

★ **Taiohae:** This tranquil seaside town is what remote island dreams are made of (page 263).

★ **Scuba diving off Nuku Hiva:** Take the plunge with hundreds of majestic hammerhead sharks (page 264).

★ **Hatiheu Archeological Sites and Museum:** Wander one of the largest and most intriguing archeological sites in the Marquesas (page 272).

★ **Atuona:** Hiva Oa's main town has been the muse of many artists, though its vibrant colors are best seen with the naked eye (page 284).

★ **Ma'ae I'ipona:** This evocative archeological site has the largest ancient tiki in French Polynesia, plus other ancient statues (page 288).

★ **Hanavave Bay:** This might be the most spectacular bay in Polynesia, best seen at sunset (page 297).

© MOON.COM

The interiors are inhabited only by hundreds of wild horses, cattle, and goats, which have destroyed much of the original vegetation. A Catholic bishop introduced the horses from Chile in 1856, and today they're a symbol of the Marquesas. The islands are also abundant with citrus fruits, bananas, mangoes, and papayas, and taro and breadfruit are staples. Birdlife is rich, and the waters around the Marquesas teem with lobster, fish, and sharks.

The 12 islands of the Marquesas form a line roughly 300 kilometers (186 mi) long, but only six are inhabited today: Nuku Hiva, Ua Pou, and Ua Huka in a cluster to the northwest, and Hiva Oa, Tahuata, and Fatu Hiva to the southeast. For hikers prepared to cope with the humidity, the Marquesas are paradise. Waterfalls tumble down the slopes, and overgrown archaeological remains tell of a golden era long gone. You'll witness the renaissance of Marquesan culture through dance, art, tattoo, and language—the remote nature of these islands has helped preserve their heritage. If you enjoy quiet, unspoiled places, the Marquesas are calling.

GETTING THERE

The Marquesas Islands are over 1,400 kilometers (870 mi) from the island of Tahiti, and flights are notoriously expensive. The difficulty in getting there has kept many potential visitors away. Nonetheless, getting here is worth the effort for many, most easily done by air.

Air

Air Tahiti (www.airtahiti.com) flies directly from Tahiti to Nuku Hiva (3 hours 15 minutes, CFP 45,500) and Hiva Oa (3.5 hours, CFP 50,400). Airports also exist on Ua Huka and Ua Pou, but flights are irregular. Visit both Nuku Hiva and Hiva Oa on the **Air Tahiti Multi-Islands Marquesas Air Pass** (low season €780/adult, €610/child; high season €851/adult, €665/child). There is also a

Marquesas Extension (low season €582/adult, €460/child; high season €634/adult, €499/child). Flights tend to be booked well in advance. There are whispers of Tahiti Air Charter (www.tahiti-air-charter.com) offering flights to the Marquesas, but this has yet to be announced.

Boat

The passenger-carrying freighter **Aranui** (tel. 40 42 62 42; www.aranui.com) cruises around 20 times a year between Papeete and the Marquesas, an ideal option for the adventurous traveler who wants to see a lot in a short time. It calls at all six inhabited Marquesas Islands, plus a couple of the Tuamotus, usually taking about 12 days. Taiohae, Hakahau, Vaipae'e, and Atuona have docks; elsewhere you go ashore in whaleboats, a potential issue for those with mobility limitations. In stormy weather, the landings can be dangerous.

This 126-meter passenger freighter can host up to 230 passengers in its 103 cabins. On a 12-day itinerary to eight islands, the cabins start at CFP 520,627 per person for double occupancy. Charges include taxes, accommodation, three meals per day, and some guided shore excursions. There is an extra CFP 15,000 fuel charge per passenger. Deck passage is intended for residents only, but if there is availability, it's possible for tourists to travel interisland within the Marquesas on deck (about CFP 10,000 each hop). It takes a few hours to a full day of travel to venture between islands.

The Marquesas Islands are often the first land sighted on a Pacific Ocean crossing. Cruising yachts from California often call here on their way to Papeete; yachties should steer for Hiva Oa first to enjoy the smoothest possible sailing through the rest of the group. While there's no barrier reef or lagoon, the plethora of bays in the Marquesas make for places of refuge after such a long journey.

Previous: The 12-meter Tiki Tuhiva looks over Taiohae; a rocky beach at Hapatoni; the grave of Paul Gauguin.

The Marquesas Islands

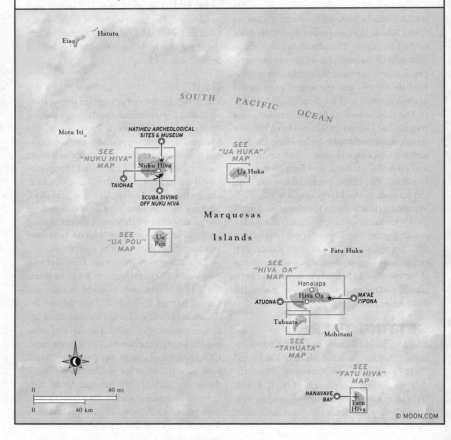

© MOON.COM

GETTING AROUND

To island-hop within the Marquesas, you can fly with **Air Tahiti** (between Hiva Oa and Nuku Hiva, 40 minutes, CFP 18,000) or travel onboard **Aranui.**

Boat

Some supply boats venture between the islands, but their schedules are challenging to find and they don't always take passengers. Private boats run from Taiohae to Ua Pou fairly frequently; to join a regular trip you just have to be lucky, persistent, and prepared to

wait. The **Te Ata O Hiva** (www.codim.pf; CFP 2,500-4,000/one-way) shuttle boat between Hiva Oa, Tahuata, and Fatu Hiva also runs at least once a week (1 hour Hiva Oa-Tahuata, 3.5 hours Tahuata-Fatu Hiva, 3.5 hours Fatu Hiva-Hiva Oa). It also ventures to Nuku Hiva, Ua Pou, and Ua Huka (2 hours Nuku Hiva-Ua Pou, 3 hours Ua Pou-Ua Huka, 2 hours Ua Huka-Nuku Hiva).

Rental Car and Private Driver

Getting around the individual islands can be a challenge, as there's no organized public

Onboard the *Aranui*

With cruise ships becoming miniature floating cities complete with indoor skydiving rooms, ziplining courses, and on-deck water parks, it can feel like the days of crossing the seven seas onboard an old tramp steamer are long gone. Fortunately, this element of adventure is well preserved onboard the *Aranui*, the passenger freighter connecting remote villages in the Marquesas Islands to the island of Tahiti. About two times per month, it supplies villages with fresh produce, fuel, medical supplies, and home goods—and brings copra from the islands back to Tahiti.

CABINS

Cabins on the *Aranui* start at CFP 520,627 per person for double occupancy; the best suite is CFP 1,028,413 per person, while an intermediate deluxe cabin is CFP 638,845. Single occupancy costs 50 percent more. There are also air-conditioned "Class C" dormitory rooms starting at CFP 340,308.

AMENITIES

While it serves a practical purpose, life onboard the *Aranui* is one of comfort. An outdoor pool, gym, spa, lounge decks galore, conference room, four bars, a spacious dining room, library, and even a tattoo studio help pass the time during inter-island crossings.

SAILING SCHEDULE AND EXCURSIONS

Usually, the ship steams at night, arriving at the next port by morning. While crew members load and unload cargo, guests are free to explore the islands. The ship stays for just one day in each destination before moving onward. Included excursions usually involve traipsing to a waterfall, strolling through a quiet town, or attending a cultural event. Travelers who prefer to go rogue can arrange a tour with a local prior to arrival. When you account for the costs of accommodation and transportation within the Marquesas, it's one of the most efficient and economical ways to see all six of the inhabited islands.

---

transportation other than expensive airport transfers. Because of the condition of the roads, rental cars are limited to the 4x4 vehicles at the main town of Nuku Hiva, Taiohae, and the main town of Hiva Oa, Atuona. Within the past few years, the government has repaved many of the roads on Nuku Hiva and Hiva Oa, but they remain narrow, steep, and windy. It's easy to hire a guide and driver on Hiva Oa, Nuku Hiva, Ua Huka, and Ua Pou (expect to pay at least CFP 25,000 per day or CFP 8,000 per person). While making your inquiries, keep your ears open for any mention of boat tours, as these are often the same price as land tours.

On Foot

An option for the hardy is to walk, accepting any lifts that come along. Almost everywhere on Fatu Hiva, Tahuata, Ua Huka, and Ua Pou is accessible on foot, provided you've got the time and strength. If you pack a tent, food, and sufficient water, you'll be able to see the islands on a shoestring budget. Many residents will allow you to set up a tent on their property for a small fee, but note that hitchhiking is complicated: many of the private vehicles you see out on the roads double as taxis, and drivers who depend on tourists for a large part of their incomes are unlikely to be eager to give rides for free. You could offer around CFP 1,000 per half hour ride to anyone taking you along.

ORIENTATION

The Marquesas are over 1,300 kilometers (807 mi) northeast from Tahiti. The southern islands of the Marquesas (Hiva Oa, Tahuata, Fatu Hiva) are green and humid; the northern islands (Nuku Hiva, Ua Huka, Ua Pou)

The Marquesas Islands at a Glance

Island	Why Go	How to Get There
Northern Islands		
Nuku Hiva (page 262)	The largest of the Marquesas, Nuku Hiva offers the small-town charm of Taiohae, beautiful coastlines, scuba diving with hammerhead sharks, and hiking through pine-tree forests.	*Air:* From Papeete (3 hours 15 minutes) and Hiva Oa (40 minutes). *Cruise:* The *Aranui* and *Paul Gauguin Cruises* both stop at Nuku Hiva.
Ua Pou (page 275)	Come for the splendor of its dramatic landscape—cloud-topped pinnacles accent its mountainous skyline. Visit Hohoi, a town of artists who use a rare stone with floral patterns inside to create interesting sculptures.	*Boat:* Boats occasionally leave for Ua Pou from Nuku Hiva (2 hours, CFP 6,500/one-way). *Cruise:* The *Aranui* stops at Ua Pou.
Ua Huka (page 281)	Horses are ubiquitous on this small island, home to some of the most talented wood sculptors in the Marquesas. It's an island that's lush in some parts, arid in others, making it a delight for intrepid hikers. Birders can spot a rare lorikeet.	*Boat:* Boats occasionally leave for Ua Huka from Nuku Hiva (2 hours, CFP 6,500/one-way). *Cruise:* The *Aranui* stops at Ua Huka.

are parched. Moving west to east, the uninhabited islands of **Eiao** and **Hatutu** are 100 kilometers (62 mi) from **Nuku Hiva,** which is straddled by **Ua Pou** 43 kilometers (26 mi) to its south and **Ua Huka** 43 kilometers (26 mi) to its east. The main southern island of **Hiva Oa** is 136 kilometers (84 mi) southeast of Nuku Hiva, with **Tahuata** 4 kilometers (2.4 mi) to its south and **Fatu Hiva** 76 kilometers (47 mi) to its southeast. The administrative centers, **Atuona** (Hiva Oa), **Hakahau** (Ua Pou), and **Taiohae** (Nuku Hiva), are the only places with post offices, banks, police stations, and similar services. The deep bays on the west sides of the islands are better sheltered for shipping, and the humidity is lower there than on the east sides, which catch the trade winds.

PLANNING YOUR TIME

Many travelers visit the Marquesas Islands on a 12-day cruise aboard the passenger-carrying freighter *Aranui.*

Those traveling independently by air will want at least two full days on **Nuku Hiva:** one to explore Taiohae, a scenic waterfront town, and environs, and another for a day trip to Hatiheu and Anaho to visit Nuku

Island	Why Go	How to Get There
Southern Islands		
Hiva Oa (page 284)	Hiva Oa hosts the best preserved archeological site in the Marquesas, I'ipona, sacred grounds with large tiki. Roadtrip along its windy roads to discover panoramas, hidden tiki (one with a smile), and tropical wilderness. The colorful town of Atuona has long been a muse for foreign and local artists alike.	*Air:* From Papeete (3 hours 20 minutes, CFP 50,000/one-way) and Nuku Hiva (40 minutes, CFP 18,000/one-way). *Boat:* From Tahuata (1 hour; CFP 2,500/one-way) and Fatu Hiva (3.5 hours; CFP 4,000/one-way). *Cruise:* The *Aranui* and *Paul Gauguin Cruises* both stop at Hiva Oa.
Tahuata (page 293)	Lonely little Tahuata has white sand beaches prime for swimming and wading. Visit the art market, where mixed-media artists create pieces from stone, wood, and bone.	*Boat:* From Hiva Oa (1 hour, CFP 2,500/one-way) and Fatu Hiva (3.5 hours, CFP 3,500/one-way). *Cruise:* The *Aranui* and *Paul Gauguin Cruises* both stop at Tahuata.
Fatu Hiva (page 296)	Come to the most remote island of the Marquesas for petroglyphs, sunsets in a striking bay, and beaches you're likely to have all to yourself.	*Boat:* From Tahuata (1 hour, CFP 3,500/one-way) and Hiva Oa (3.5 hours, CFP 4,000/one-way). *Cruise:* The *Aranui* and *Paul Gauguin Cruises* both stop at Fatu Hiva.

Hiva's impressive lookout points and small settlements.

Similarly, on **Hiva Oa** one day can be spent exploring the colorful town of Atuona and another on a day trip to Puama'u for ancient tikis and sacred archeological sites.

Two days each would be needed to get a feel for **Ua Huka** and **Ua Pou,** as well. Eight days is the minimum you'd want to spend in the **Marquesas,** and adding an extra day or two on Nuku Hiva and Hiva Oa is highly recommended. Note that coming or going, there's a 30-minute time difference between Tahiti and the Marquesas, and that budget accommodations are scarce.

The subtropical climate is hotter and drier than that of Tahiti. July and August are the coolest months. The precipitation is uneven, with drought some years, heavy rainfall others. Temperatures range from 23-31°C (73-88°F) on average all year long. It's most pleasant **April-October,** when the trade winds cool the islands, and it's best to visit between those months. April, May, September, and October see fewer crowds than June-August.

Itinerary Ideas

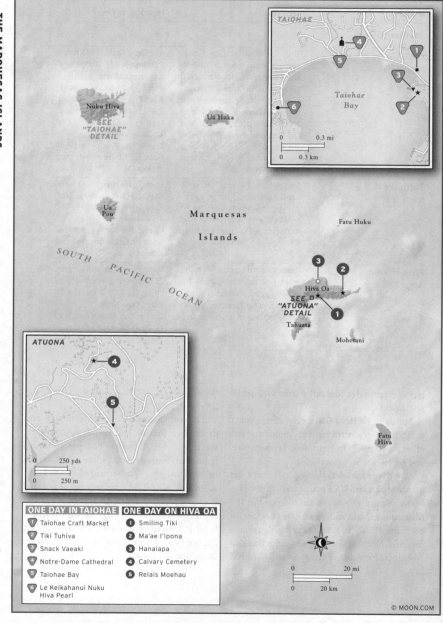

ONE DAY IN TAIOHAE

1. Taiohae Craft Market
2. Tiki Tuhiva
3. Snack Vaeaki
4. Notre-Dame Cathedral
5. Taiohae Bay
6. Le Keikahanui Nuku Hiva Pearl

ONE DAY ON HIVA OA

1. Smiling Tiki
2. Ma'ae I'ipona
3. Hanaiapa
4. Calvary Cemetery
5. Relais Moehau

© MOON.COM

Itinerary Ideas

NUKU HIVA: ONE DAY IN TAIOHAE

On this walking tour of the small town of Taiohae on Nuku Hiva, wear comfortable shoes and sun protection.

1 Start your day at the **Taiohae Craft Market,** admiring locally made sculptures and jewelry.

2 Walk five minutes to **Tiki Tuhiva,** the largest modern tiki in the Marquesas and a prime place to relax on a picnic bench and watch boats cruise in and out of the bay.

3 Walk back to the wharf for a fresh seafood lunch at **Snack Vaeaki.**

4 Walk 1 kilometer (0.6 mi) west along the waterfront to the **Notre-Dame Cathedral** for a glimpse of Marquesan wood sculptures inside the church.

5 Walk another half-kilometer (0.3 mi) west to the **Taiohae Bay** waterfront. If the sun is out, you'll likely see families splashing in the water and paddlers perfecting their craft on vaka canoes.

6 For dinner, walk another half-kilometer (0.3 mi) to the westernmost end of the bay for a traditional Marquesan dinner at **Le Keikahanui Nuku Hiva Pearl** restaurant.

ONE DAY ON HIVA OA

For this itinerary, you'll need to rent a 4x4 to take on the stomach-turning curves on Hiva Oa. If you're not a confident driver, it's best to hire a driver or guide through **Pifavae Excursion** (tel. 87 72 76 33; pifavaexcursion@gmail.com, munevatetoa@gmail.com; CFP 7,000-10,000/person). Wear plenty of sun protection as well as comfortable shoes, and pack a picnic lunch.

1 Drive 8 kilometers (5 mi) from Atuona to the **Smiling Tiki** for a jovial start to your morning.

2 Venture 31 kilometers (19 mi) east to **Ma'ae I'ipona** to see sacred tiki, including the region's largest.

3 Backtrack 26 kilometers (16 mi) toward Atuona Airport and then drive 7 kilometers (4 mi) north to the settlement of **Hanaiapa.** If time allows, hike out to Hanatekuua Beach for a picnic and a swim. Otherwise, enjoy your lunch on the waterfront of Hanaiapa. The hike takes four hours total.

4 Return to Atuona (18 km/11 mi) and visit the **Calvary Cemetery,** where panoramic views of Atuona and the graves of Gauguin and Brel are found.

5 For dinner, head to **Relais Moehau** for sherbert-sky views and a laid-back ambiance.

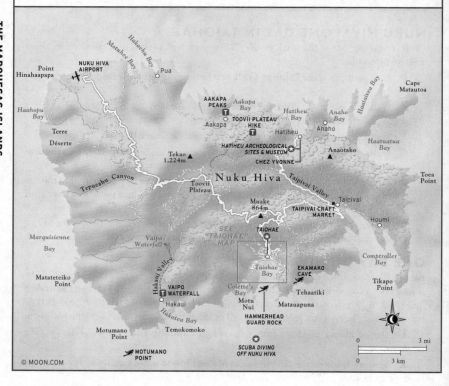

Nuku Hiva

© MOON.COM

Nuku Hiva

The largest (339 square km/130 square mi) and most populous (2,650 inhabitants) of the Marquesas, Nuku Hiva is dramatic, with exposed basalt cliffs looming over tangled leaves and pine trees in its highlands. Near the coast, people gather in valleys where aromatic citrus fruits grow and bright flowers bloom. Horses nibble on the wisps of grass growing by the roadside, sometimes tethered, usually not. In the highlands, clouds come and go, leaving heavy dewdrops in their wake.

Take care with the drinking water in Nuku Hiva; it's best to drink bottled water or filtered water offered at your accommodation.

Unfortunately, many beaches around Nuku Hiva are infested with sand flies called nonos that give nasty bites (the bugs disappear after dark).

Orientation

Taiohae (pop. 2,000) on the south coast of Nuku Hiva is the administrative and economic center of the island. It's a modern little town with a post office, hospital, town hall, bank, grocery stores, street lighting, and several hotels. Winding mountain roads lead northeast from Taiohae to **Taipivai** and **Hatiheu** villages or northwest toward the

Taiohae

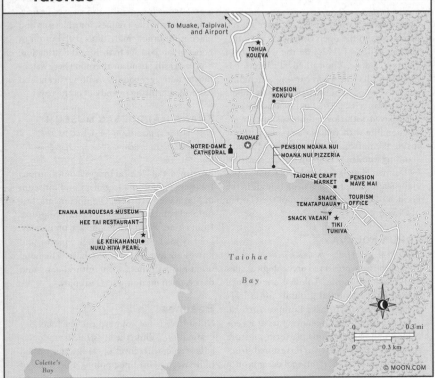

To Muake, Taipivai, and Airport

TOHUA KOUEVA

PENSION KOKU'U

TAIOHAE

NOTRE-DAME CATHEDRAL

PENSION MOANA NUI
MOANA NUI PIZZERIA

TAIOHAE CRAFT MARKET

PENSION MAVE MAI

ENANA MARQUESAS MUSEUM

HEE TAI RESTAURANT

SNACK TEMATAPUAUA

TOURISM OFFICE

SNACK VAEAKI

TIKI TUHIVA

LE KEIKAHANUI NUKU HIVA PEARL

Taiohae Bay

Colette's Bay

0   0.3 mi

0   0.3 km

© MOON.COM

airport. In the center of the island, **Tekao** (1,224 m/4,015 ft) rises above the vast, empty **Toovii Plateau.**

TOP EXPERIENCE

★ TAIOHAE

Accommodations, restaurants, shops, and a black sand beach stretch along the waterfront of Taiohae Bay, a flooded volcanic crater guarded by two tiny islands called the Sentinels. At sunrise, fishermen get to cleaning their night's catch at the Taiohae Wharf, feeding the scraps to the gamut of stingrays and sharks awaiting their daily breakfast. The best produce is plucked from the market. Sailboats hoist their sails, ready to depart to their next destination while paddlers in outrigger canoes paddle from one side of the bay to the next. Horses, cars, and pedestrians share the road, and nobody hurries. By midday, the sun overhead highlights the blue beauty of the water, and life is serenely still. Come sunset, a pulse returns to town. Many residents and tourists make their way to Tiki Tuhiva for a bird's eye view of the bay.

From end to end, the town runs just over 2 kilometers (1.2 mi), a walkable distance if you're based near the shoreline. Though open to the south, Taiohae's deep harbor offers excellent anchorage. Cruising yachts toss on the east side of the bay, while the *Aranui* ties up to a wharf at the southeast end of town. The island of Ua Pou is clearly visible across the waters.

Sights
NOTRE-DAME CATHEDRAL
Central Taiohae; free

Two towers retained from an earlier church give access to the open courtyard of Notre-Dame Cathedral (1974) on the west side of central Taiohae. The cathedral's interior is notable for its fine wood carvings, including a massive wooden pulpit bearing the symbols of four evangelists. The floor behind the pulpit is paved with flower stones, stones made of phonolite with yellow daisy-like patterns inside them, from Ua Pou. Among the outstanding wooden Stations of the Cross carved by Damien Haturau, a local artist, note especially Station No. 1, which depicts Jesus in the Garden of Breadfruit (instead of the Garden of Olives).

TOHUA KOUEVA
Taipivi Road, look for sign "Koueva"; free

One of the best-preserved archeological sites in French Polynesia, Tohua Koueva once hosted the ceremonial grounds for at least 2,000 Marquesans prior to European arrival. A large banyan tree greets visitors at its entrance, and paepae, stone platforms, feature throughout the property, as do restored structures that mimic the traditional designs once used for shelter.

TIKI TUHIVA
Tuhiva Hill; free

A 100-meter (328-ft) well-kept walking path that starts just behind the Taiohae Wharf leads past fragrant plumeria trees to a platform where the 12-meter (39-ft) Tiki Tuhiva overlooks Taiohae Bay. This is the tallest contemporary tiki in the Pacific, built in 2019, and its unique blend of modern and traditional sculpting styles tends to polarize the locals.

The tiki is made up of male and female elements, with the female at the front carved similarly to ancient tikis seen around the Marquesas. She represents ancestral strength. Attached to her back is a male statue, a warrior holding a club, his skin half covered in Polynesian tattoos, who represents the future. Stone tables and a large grassy area make this a great spot for picnics and sunset-gazing. Some sailors write a request for a blessing and place it into the female tiki's bellybutton in hopes of safe passage to their next destination. You can easily spend an afternoon here watching the outrigger paddlers, sailing yachts, and fishermen cruising in and out of the bay.

ENANA MARQUESAS MUSEUM
West Taiohae at the He'e Tai Inn; tel. 40 92 03 82; marquesas-inn.com; 8am-11:30am and 2pm-5pm Mon.-Fri.; free

Rose, owner of He'e Tai Inn, welcomes curious travelers to her on-site gallery and museum of Marquesan artifacts. Old documents, traditional paintings called tapa, and sculptures from stone, wood, and bone are on display. Locally made sculptures, jewelry pieces, and knives are available for purchase. The hotel often hosts dinners with cultural song and dance, open for non-guests to enjoy.

Beaches

Nuku Hiva is not your typical beach holiday destination. While the coastline is undoubtedly scenic, with coves of calm water tucked in between palm-lined points, a presence of nonos (sandflies) prevents undisturbed sunbathing. They're most active at dawn and dusk, so go to Nuku Hiva's beaches midday for your best shot at a no-nono experience.

COLETTE'S BAY
2 km (1.2 mi) west of Taiohae; free

At the western end of Taiohae, there's a road leading inland just before the He'e Tai Inn weaving 2 kilometers (1.2 mi) to Colette's Bay. It's hilly but walkable, and you'll need to bypass a private property gate to continue along the road (it could be worth flagging a ride from a local). The bay itself has a small patch of tan-colored sand, and is idyllic for swimming when the water is calm.

★ Scuba Diving

Nuku Hiva has no lagoon and notoriously

Marquesas Craft and Artwork

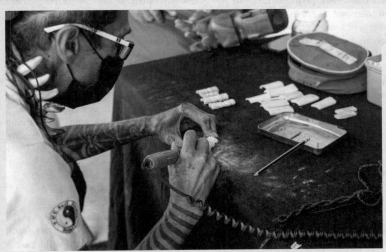

an artist crafting jewelry from bone in Taipivai

The Marquesas are home to superb artists, their sculptures, tattoos, and paintings revered world-wide. The artworks are typically made from natural materials like stone, wood, shells, bone, seeds, and plant fibers. The traditional skills needed to make them have been passed down through centuries, but not without difficulty. When Christian missionaries came to the Marquesas in the 18th century, they banned tiki sculpting and tattooing. It's estimated that over 90 percent of the Marquesan population died from diseases introduced to the islands from European settlers, contributing further to the loss of Marquesan culture. Some tribes rebelled against the Christian missionaries, claiming their identity through ancient art and tattooing. Fortunately, the Marquesas have undergone a renaissance led by Marquesan artists that really boomed in the 1980s, bringing previous forms of art and storytelling back to life.

Shop for fish hooks, intricate jewelry, sculptures, weapons, and paintings at the following art markets:

- **Taiohae Craft Market,** Nuku Hiva: A small market known for its animal sculptures found on the Taiohae waterfront (page 266).

- **Taipivai Craft Market,** Nuku Hiva: Witness artists at work near the entrance of this large craft market (page 273).

- **Hakahau Craft Center,** Ua Pou: One of the only markets to admire artwork made from the flower stones of Ua Pou (page 278).

- **Atuona Handicraft Market,** Hiva Oa: Atuona is home to some of the Marquesas' most skilled tapa painters, for sale here (page 284).

- **Hapatoni Craft Market,** Tahuata: Intricate sculptures made of bone, wood, and stone are often found at this craft market (page 293).

poor visibility, so it's not considered a premier diving destination. But intrepid divers in search of oceanic predators might be surprised to know that Nuku Hiva is a hub for hammerhead sharks, melon-headed whales, and oceanic manta ray sightings. On calm, clear days, a 40-minute boat ride can take snorkelers to a site to swim with hundreds of melon-headed whales in the wild; their season runs from January-April. The best time to visit for hammerheads is June-November.

Rough seas are the bane of many dive trips; pack seasickness medication and plan for a few days on Nuku Hiva just in case.

HAMMERHEAD GUARD ROCK DIVE SITE

1 km (0.6 mi) from Taiohae

This dive site was named after its aquatic superstar, the hammerhead shark. Divers see these toothy predators here more times than not, and it's also a frequent spot for oceanic manta rays and other shark species. Dives take place along a rock wall, with hammerheads out in the blue. The wall hosts reef-dwellers like octopi, moray eels, scorpionfish, parrotfish, triggerfish, and porcelain crabs.

EKAMAKO CAVE DIVE SITE

1.5 km (0.9 mi) from Taiohae

This basalt cavern spanning 10 meters (32 ft) deep opens to an inland air pocket. Divers with little cave-diving experience might find this site intimidating; flashlights are mandatory. Multiple stingray species cruise through the caves, and crustaceans hide in its crevices.

MOTUMANO POINT DIVE SITE

2 km (1.2 mi) from Taiohae

A shark dive site that's suitable for beginner divers, Motumano Point is a mild drift dive where hammerhead sharks, gray sharks, reef sharks, barracudas, and manta rays frequent.

CENTRE DE PLONGEE MARQUISES

Taiohae; tel. 40 92 00 88; www.marquises.org; US$68/dive including gear

Xavier "Pipapo" Curvat is the only dive guide on Nuku Hiva and knows the uncharted waters better than any other diver. He has been exploring the dive sites for decades, leading mostly intermediate to experienced divers to some of the best shark dive sites in the South Pacific. Limited rental equipment is available; it's best to bring your own.

Shopping

Nuku Hiva is one of the best places to shop for Marquesan crafts—prices tend to be a little bit cheaper than elsewhere in French Polynesia, and you'll often find artists at work outside the markets.

TAIOHAE CRAFT MARKET

Taiohae; 7:30am-4pm Mon.-Sat.

The Taiohae Craft Market, found next to the tourism office near the Taiohae waterfront, is a small market packed with sculptures of bone, stone, and wood. You'll also find jewelry, painted tapa, and weapons. These artworks can range from keychain-size to small furniture pieces, so leave plenty of space in your luggage if you plan to shop on arrival.

Food

You can find amazing seafood, decent pizzas, and your typical Polynesian fare throughout Taiohae. Most restaurants are closed on Sundays; it's best to arrange Sunday meals through your accommodation or shop ahead to cook on your own.

SNACK TEMATAPUAUA

Taiohae; tel. 40 92 06 43; 6am-3pm Mon.-Sat.; CFP 1,200

Snack Tematapuaua is a casual snack with a simple menu serving fish, steak, salads, rice, and fries, and a few Marquesan specialties, next to the Taiohae Craft Market. Service can be hit or miss, but food is usually served very quickly. Portions tend toward the hefty side.

1: the lookout point above Taiohae **2:** Notre-Dame Cathedral **3:** Colette's Bay **4:** Fresh produce is sold at Taiohae's central market.

SNACK VAEAKI

Taiohae Wharf; tel. 40 92 05 51; 7am-8pm daily;
CFP 1,200

Snack Vaeaki is the de facto gathering point for sailors, who come for a casual meal and free WiFi. The menu changes regularly, with meals like grilled fish or octopus, steak, and goat curry, and sides of cassava, salad, rice, and taro. Meals are served on communal picnic tables under a shady area just in front of the pier.

HE'E TAI RESTAURANT

Taiohae; tel. 40 92 03 82; 11:30am-2pm and
6pm-9pm Mon.-Sat.; CFP 1,500

He'e Tai Restaurant is found at the He'e Tai Inn on Taiohae's western end. On weekends, the restaurant occasionally hosts cultural performances from dancers preparing for larger Marquesan arts festivals—guests are free to linger with a glass of wine in hand. If there's no show taking place, the dining deck makes for great sailboat spotting. Menu items feature pork, chicken, and seafood, with dedicated Marquesan feasts happening every so often.

★ MOANA NUI PIZZERIA

Taiohae; tel. 40 92 03 30; pensionmoananui@mail.
pf; noon-9pm Mon.-Sat.; CFP 2,000

This is one of the most popular dinner spots in Taiohae, commonly booked out on Fridays and Saturdays for dinner. Their menu features traditional Marquesan seafood like mackerel breaded in coconut milk, lobster, and around 10 wood-fired pizza options. The outdoor dining area has ocean views, and the inside is lively with a decently stocked bar (happy hour is Fridays 6pm-8pm).

Accommodations

Rather than luxury resorts, on Nuku Hiva expect simple but clean pensions offering double to triple rooms and communal kitchens.

PENSION KOKU'U

Taiohae; tel. 87 24 61 68; www.pensionkokuu.
marquises.sitew.com; CFP 9,000/person per night
half-board (including breakfast and dinner), CFP
15,000/person per night full-board

This family-run guesthouse about 800 meters (half a mile) inland from the bay has views of the sea from the property. There are only two rooms available, making it an intimate stay. The owners, Alvaro and Claudine, host delicious meals and can arrange excursions to the main sights. Both rooms sleep three, with tropical prints and large bathrooms with hot-water showers, though amenities are a little dated. Meals are served on the sheltered terrace family-style. The property also has a rental car for CFP 6,000 per day not including fuel.

PENSION MOANA NUI

Taiohae; tel. 40 90 03 30; pensionmoananui@gmail.
com; CFP 9,500/person, CFP 13,400/two people
including breakfast

Set near the waterfront across the main road of Taiohae, Pension Moana Nui is one of the most convenient places to stay if you won't be renting a car. Rooms have recently been outfitted with air-conditioning, and have a mini-fridge, TV, and internet access. The pension's on-site **restaurant** (11am-8:30pm Mon.-Sat.; CFP 2,000) is one of the nicest in Taiohae (complete with a pizza oven used to make breakfast pizzas).

★ PENSION MAVE MAI

Taiohae; tel. 40 92 08 10; pension-mavemai@mail.pf;
CFP 10,000/night including breakfast

A tranquil guesthouse surrounded by fruit trees and up on a hill of Taiohae, Pension Mave Mai's owners, Jean-Claude and Regina, have been hosting guests for decades. The guesthouse has two floors; the rooms on the bottom floor have direct outdoor access and lounge chairs. Rooms are dated and minimally decorated; WiFi connection only works well in the dining room. All guests have access to a full-size kitchen. A breakfast of fresh fruit, bread, spreads, coffee, and tea is served communally each morning. There's a laundry service on-site, but it's more expensive than the one found at Taiohae Wharf. The owners are happy to arrange excursions.

LE KEIKAHANUI NUKU HIVA PEARL

Taiohae; tel. 40 920 710; www.nukuhivapearlodge. com; CFP 32,000-40,700/night

This is the island's most upscale accommodation; charming thatched-roof bungalows are built from wood and bamboo, and the best have unobstructed views of the ocean from their deck. Each is equipped with a king-size bed (or two twin beds), a fan, air-conditioning, minibar, TV, safe, and mosquito net. All have en suite bathrooms. Meals are not included: a buffet breakfast is an extra CFP 3,300, and half-board starts at CFP 7,200 per person per day. The property is a 30-minute walk from the eastern end of the bay. It's easy to spend the day lounging by the infinity pool or embarking on hotel-hosted hiking, sightseeing, or e-biking trips.

The **restaurant** (11:30am-2pm and 6pm-9pm Mon.-Sat.; CFP 2,500) is one of the best on the island, making the half-board option (CFP 7,300 per night) a wise choice if you plan to spend most of your meals here. White tablecloths paired with rattan furniture in a spacious dining room set a tropical fine-dining scene. Thoughtfully plated meals include tuna tartare, goat curry with coconut milk, and beef bourguignonne made from beef imported from New Zealand. During happy hour (6pm-8pm Fridays), cocktails are half off.

Information and Services

- **Tourism Office:** Taiohae; tel. 40 92 08 25; 7:30am-3:30pm Mon.-Sat.
- **Bank Socredo:** Taiohae; tel. 40 91 00 85; www.socredo.pf; 8am-noon and 1:30pm-4pm Mon.-Thurs., 8am-noon and 1:30pm-3pm Fri.; ATM available
- **Post Office:** Taiohae; tel. 40 92 08 81; 7:30am-noon and 1pm-3:30pm Mon.-Thurs., 7:30am-noon and 1pm-4pm Fri.

- **Taiohae Hospital:** Taiohae; tel. 40 91 02 00
- **Yacht Services:** Taiohae; tel. 40 92 07 50; www.yachtservicesnukuhiva.com; 8am-11am and 12:30pm-3:30pm Mon.-Fri.; VHF channel 72

Getting There
NUKU HIVA AIRPORT

NW corner of Nuku Hiva, 32 km (20 mi) from Taiohae

Nuku Hiva Airport (NHV) is in the arid Terre Déserte at the northwest corner of Nuku Hiva, 32 kilometers (20 mi) from Taiohae along a twisting road over the Toovii Plateau (or 19 km/11 mi as the crow flies), a 1.5-hour drive from Taiohae. The airport has a stand selling souvenirs and a small café inside. **Air Tahiti** (airtahiti.com) flies round-trip from Nuku Hiva to Papeete (3 hours 15 minutes, CFP 45,000/one-way) and Hiva Oa (40 minutes, CFP 18,000). The **Marquesas Air Tahiti Pass** includes Nuku Hiva and Hiva Oa (low season €778/adult, €608/child; high season €849/adult, €662/child). Upon arrival, turn your watch ahead 30 minutes.

Nuku Hiva Airport transfers to Taiohae cost around CFP 6,000 per person each way by 4WD Toyota Land Cruiser for the 1.5-hour drive along a newly built road, which is typically arranged through your accommodation as no taxi stands are available at the airport. If you're going to rent a car, it's usually best to do so in Taiohae. While waiting for your flight, examine the excellent Marquesan low-relief wood carvings made to decorate the bar and shop when the airport was built in 1979.

BOAT

Taiohae Bay is one of the main stops for sailors crossing the Pacific Ocean. There are a few government supply ships that run from Papeete to Nuku Hiva, but these are irregular. These trips usually cost CFP 7,000 per person and take around two days to reach Nuku Hiva from Papeete.

The *Te Ata O Hiva* shuttles between the northern Marquesas (www.codim.pf; CFP

3,500/one-way; 2 hours Nuku Hiva-Ua Pou, 3 hours Ua Pou-Ua Huka, 2 hours Ua Huka-Nuku Hiva). The schedule changes regularly. Oftentimes routes run back and forth between Nuku Hiva and Ua Pou, with no stops in Ua Huka. Some routes stop at each island, requiring a stopover before reaching your destined island. There are typically more trips offered during school holidays.

The 230-passenger *Aranui* (tel. 40 42 62 42; www.aranui.com) serves the Marquesas Islands. Their "Discover the Marquesas" tour is one of the most comprehensive, covering 6 islands in 12 days, and stops in Taiohae Bay.

Paul Gauguin Cruises (www.pgcruises. com), a luxury cruise ship with a 330-guest capacity, has a two-week journey through French Polynesia with Nuku Hiva as a port of call. Most rooms have private balconies. Prices start at US$6,900 per person.

Getting Around

The best way to get around Nuku Hiva is with a rental car or driver, arranged through your accommodation, though the town of Taiohae (where most accommodations are found) is largely walkable. It's possible to walk from Taiohae to Taipivai (around 12 km/7.5 mi) and Hatiheu (around 20 km/12 mi) in two days if you're fit, camping along the way. The road from Taiohae to Hatiheu is concrete most of the way. Another road links Hatiheu to the airport via Aakapa and Pua.

CAR RENTAL SERVICES

Renting a car on Nuku Hiva is ideal if you want the freedom to explore most of the island's sights on your own timeline. The roads are narrow and windy, though rarely crowded. If you're coming around a hairpin turn, give a honk to warn any oncoming traffic. It's wise to download an offline map from Google Maps or Maps.me of the island, as phone service is generally spotty.

- **Moana Nui Pension Car Rental:** Taiohae; tel. 40 92 03 30; CFP 6,000/day not including fuel

- **Pension Koku'u:** Taiohae; tel. 87 24 61 68; www.pensionkokuu.marquises.sitew.com; CFP 6,000/day not including fuel

TOURS

To book a tour, it's best to go to the tourism office in Taiohae and talk with one of the friendly faces behind the counter. It's one of the most helpful in all French Polynesia, with a running schedule of excursions taking place that week. It's best to call ahead to ask the tourism office to find a guide who speaks English. Oftentimes, an English-speaking friend of a guide will accompany the tour.

- **Jocelyne Henua Enana Tours** (tel. 87 74 42 23; jocelyne@mail.pf; CFP 9,000/day tour): Jocelyne has been leading tours around Nuku Hiva for over 20 years. Tours take place from an air-conditioned van. Day trips usually venture to Hatiheu and a range of lookout points, and stop for lunch at Chez Yvonne (meal not included).

- **Mate Excursion** (tel. 87 31 38 39; mate.excursion@gmail.com; CFP 9,000/day tour): Mate Tata runs guided tours in English around Nuku Hiva from a 4x4 truck with seats in the bed. Stops usually include trips to the Taipivai craft market, the archeological sites, viewpoints, Hooumi Bay, and Chez Yvonne for lunch (not included).

WEST NUKU HIVA

West of Taiohae, quiet palm-lined bays lead to sheer cliffs and waterfalls, like that at **Hakatea Bay** and **Vaipo Waterfall** hidden in **Hakuai Valley**. Sacred sites, the remnants of ancient marae, are found in between trees endemic to Nuku Hiva, and are left largely undisturbed. Nuku Hiva's northwestern corner, known as **Terre Déserte,** is sparsely vegetated and rife with hidden valleys. The road leading south through this arid desert from Nuku Hiva Airport bends at a lookout point over the impressive **Tapueahu Canyon.**

Beaches
HAKATEA BAY
7 km (4.3 mi) west of Taiohae; free

Tucked inside a cove of sawtooth basalt cliffs is tranquil Hakatea Bay, an oasis of dark sands and palm trees found where Hakaui Valley ends and the ocean begins. Livestock roam around the beach; you might spot a cow or two lounging in the shade of a palm frond. A handful of families live on the edge of the bay, offering seafood lunches served with generous sides of slices of fresh pomelo, warm breadfruit boiled in coconut milk, and cooked taro for around CFP 1,500 per person. The water is usually calm enough for swimming.

The best way to reach Hakatea Bay is by boat, a 30-minute ride from Taiohae (arranged at the Taiohae Tourism Office or through your accommodation), around CFP 4,000 per person round-trip. For CFP 7,000 per person, you can get transport and a guide to Vaipo Waterfall.

Hikes

Your accommodation can usually arrange guided hikes through Hakaui Valley, or try one of the companies below. Transfer to Hakatea Bay is usually included.

- **Hakaui Adventure with Tangy and Ana** (tel. 87 32 60 80; cannibal-art.com; from CFP 7,500/day): Owned by a Marquesan-Croatian couple who love to share Nuku Hiva's culture and hidden sights, from beginner-friendly day trips through Hakaui Valley to multi-day camping journeys to the interior, catering to a group's skill level and interests. Day trips include boat transfer from Taiohae and lunch. Overnight trips include all meals, transport, and cultural demonstrations.

- **Tamahautini Hiking** (tel. 87 28 61 56; tamahautinirando@gmail.com; CFP 7,500/day trip): Lead guide Christian Taata grew up exploring Nuku Hiva's forgotten interior and is happy to arrange full-day and multi-day trips for all hiking abilities. If you want real adventure, Christian can lead you to

trails few tourists know about—and likely never will.

VAIPO WATERFALL
Distance: *9.5 km (5.9 mi) out-and-back*
Time: *4 hours*
Trailhead: *Hakatea Bay*
Information and maps: *Information at the tourism office in Taiohae*

After the rainy season, Vaipo Waterfall is one of the most powerful cascades in French Polynesia. The trail leading from Hakatea is flat for the most part with a few water crossings and slippery sections. The trail leads to ancient archeological sites, and goes along cliffs where high-ranking chiefs were once buried to the waterfall where a narrow swimming pool awaits. Before you set off, place an order for lunch in the village of Hakatea Bay, near the start of the trailhead, and it will be ready to eat on your return.

Getting There

West Nuku Hiva is best accessed with your own rental vehicle or driver, both available to book in Taiohae with the help of your accommodation. If you're wanting to visit Nuku Hiva's bays, like Hakatea Bay, it's best to do so by boat—bookable at the Taiohae Tourism Office or through your accommodation. You might also be able to ask around at Taiohae Wharf for a boat ride along the coast.

EAST NUKU HIVA

Vanilla grows wild throughout Taipivai Valley in east Nuku Hiva; at the valley's inland end is an eponymous waterfall that flows into a river, connecting to Comptroller Bay and Taipivai, home to several hundred people as well as the huge Vahangeku'a tohua, or stone ceremonial plaza (170 by 25 m/557 by 82 ft). To the west, the valley climbs to a lookout point with views of all nearby bays.

From Taipivai, it's another 12 kilometers (7.5 mi) via the Col Teavaitapuhiva (443 m/1,453 ft) to the verdant valley of Hatiheu on the north coast. Spectacular falls are seen in the distance to the left of the road near the mountain pass. A statue of the Virgin Mary stands on a rocky peak high above Hatiheu Bay and its black sand beach. It's a quiet place to relax and watch waves roll over a rocky beach.

Sights

★ HATIHEU ARCHEOLOGICAL SITES AND MUSEUM

Hatiheu; free

Travelers interested in the Marquesas' mysterious past will be fascinated by Haitheu, which hosts six communal complexes, called tohua, and structures, called paepae. Archeologists believe the settlement was founded in the late 13th century, and that thousands of residents gathered here for ceremonial as well as practical reasons, like produce and meat preparation and tool manufacturing.

The restored **Hikoku'a Tohua** is a bit more than 1 kilometer (0.6 mi) from Hatiheu back toward Taipivai. Originally built in 1250 and excavated in 1957, the tohua consists of two long spectator platforms on opposite sides of a central dance floor. The north end of the dance floor is closed by a stone platform used for ceremonial activities. Several of the tikis on the structure were added during the 1989 Marquesas Islands Festival, while others were placed long before then, like the fertility statue at the entrance on the left.

The area of the **Te I'ipoka, Kamuihei,** and **Tahakia** sites are even larger than Hikoku'a Tohua, and excavations reveal this was once where funeral rituals were performed. There is speculation Te I'ipoka Tohua was where human sacrifices were made, their flesh consumed by priests and chiefs; the victims were kept in a pit beneath a huge sacred banyan tree until their turn arrived to be consumed. Up the steep wooded slope is the well-kept Kamuihei Tohua with petroglyphs of sea turtles and humans.

The **Pahumano Tohua** is found at the Hatiheu Catholic Mission, believed to be a ritualistic site for departing seafarers. Also within the valley is an adze quarry, which has been key for historians' understanding of how Polynesians navigated the Pacific. While it was once thought that Polynesians crossed large stretches of ocean accidentally, rock samples have shown Marquesan adzes, or star compasses, in almost all French Polynesian archipelagos. A small **museum** next to the Restaurant Hinakonui features artifacts from the tohua. The restaurant's owners provide access to the museum on request.

Horseback Riding
NUKU HIVA A CHEVAL

Hatiheu; tel. 87 25 44 87; nukuhivaacheval@gmail. com; CFP 10,000/day tour

Many Marquesans get around on horseback. Take a ride through the beautiful valleys surrounding Hatiheu with Nuku Hiva a Cheval, where beginner and expert equestrians alike will cover a large stretch of surrounding trails and beaches on horseback. Groups tend to be small, just four guests maximum, and trips are tailored to rider skill and interest. Multi-day trips can also be arranged upon request.

Beaches
ANAHO AND HAATUATUA

2 km (1.2 mi) east of Hatiheu; free

Anaho is 2 kilometers (1.2 mi) east of Hatiheu on horseback or foot over a 217-meter (712-ft) pass (no road), most easily accessed on foot from the trailhead in Hatiheu. It's one of the most beautiful of Nuku Hiva's bays, with a crescent beach of powdery white sand and some of the finest snorkeling in the Marquesas; there is lovely coral and the possibility of seeing turtles or reef sharks. Only a few families reside here.

From Anaho it's an easy 45-minute walk east along the south side of the bay and over the low isthmus to uninhabited Haatuatua Bay, where you could camp wild. Some of the oldest stone platforms in the Marquesas are hidden in the bush here (go inland on one of the grassy strips near the south end of the beach till you find a southbound trail).

Celestial Navigation in Polynesia

The Pacific Ocean is the world's largest, covering a stretch of space the entirety of Earth's landmass could fit inside. This makes Polynesian navigation one of mankind's greatest accomplishments, and exactly how early navigators were able to travel so accurately and for such grand distances has largely remained a mystery. According to traditional legends and inherited knowledge, seafarers relied on the winds, currents, clouds, wave refraction, birdlife, sea life, and known islands to navigate. But the greatest aid to navigation was the **adze,** a conceptual star compass created by Polynesians.

A star compass uses the horizon line along with the rising and setting paths of stars to determine their place on the ocean. The boat is at the center of the compass, and the destination is plotted on the horizon, so constellations can guide the navigator to the island. In addition, stick charts and oral stories passed down information from generation to generation; this is how Tupaia, the Tahitian navigator onboard Captain Cook's *Endeavour,* was able to lead the ship to islands he had never visited himself.

Adzes made from quarries in the Marquesas have been found in many of the Polynesian archipelagoes. This shows that Polynesians did not blow from one archipelago to the next by chance, but regularly and intentionally traveled all throughout Polynesia to engage in trade.

Hiking
AAKAPA PEAKS
Distance: *12 km (7.5 mi) out-and-back*
Time: *6-8 hours*
Trailhead: *Near Aakapa Bay*
Information and maps: *Best completed with a guide*

The Aakapa Peaks of Nuku Hiva are scenic and best explored by intrepid hikers. A guide is needed to get to the trailhead, and once you're there, the trail leads through a winding ridgeline to the Aakapa Peaks. From the top, admire the bays of Aakapa and Hatiheu. This is likely to be a full-day endeavor, so start early to beat the heat.

TOOVII PLATEAU
Distance: *14 km (8.7 mi) out-and-back*
Time: *5 hours*
Trailhead: *In between Aakapa and Hatiheu*
Information and maps: *Best completed with a guide*

With rolling peaks cloaked in pine trees and topped with clouds, the Toovii Plateau is not exactly the environment most visitors have in mind when visiting French Polynesia. Cattle graze on the grasslands, and horses gather by the roadside. At 900 meters (2,952 ft) high, it's a great place to hike, a relatively flat trail with rolling grasslands and horses as companions. It's often chilly up here, with clouds lingering atop clusters of pine trees. The weather here is usually chillier than Nuku Hiva's shoreline, so bring a light jacket.

Shopping
TAIPIVAI CRAFT MARKET
Taipivai; 9am-1pm and 2pm-4pm Mon.-Fri.; free to enter

The Taipivai Craft Market doubles as a workshop and shop for local artisans. Outside market doors, you might see a sculptor whittling away on bone, wood, and stone, or a jewelry-maker delicately stringing bright red seeds from red sandalwood trees into intricate necklaces and bracelets. Inside the market, shop for sculptures, crafted weapons, jewelry, tapa, and other crafts made from Marquesan artists. Prices are around the same as in Taiohae.

Food and Accommodations
★ CHEZ YVONNE
Hatiheu; tel. 40 92 02 97; 11am-2pm and 6pm-9pm Mon.-Sat.; CFP 2,000

No trip to Nuku Hiva is truly complete

without a meal at Chez Yvonne's. Fortunately, most day tours stop here for lunch (and it's reachable with your own car). Across from the water, this open-air dining room with Polynesian-printed tablecloths serves heaping portions of goat curry and exceptionally fresh seafood. Choose a side of salads, fried cassava, breadfruit in coconut milk, fritters, or rice. Leftovers are served to the eels who live in the stream trickling next to the dining room. A small convenience shop is attached to the property. If you want to spend the night, the restaurant hosts a handful of bungalows out back for around CFP 20,000 per night, including meals. Cash only.

Getting There

The best way to reach Nuku Hiva's eastern sights is with your own vehicle or with a guide, both available to arrange in Taiohae. If you're comfortable exploring on foot, you can access Anahao Bay and Haatuatua.

Ua Pou

From the water, the skyline of Ua Pou looks like a Jurassic cathedral, with 12 emerald spires reaching toward the heavens; fittingly, Ua Pou means "the pillars." At 105 square kilometers (40 square mi), this diamond-shaped island about 40 kilometers (25 mi) south of Nuku Hiva is the Marquesas' third-largest. Ua Pou is the only island in the Marquesas with these volcanic towering peaks made from phonolite rock. **Oave** (1,203 m/3,946 ft), the highest point on Ua Pou, is rarely seen without a cloud halo.

The unique geography of the island makes for diverse climates from one coast to the other, with the east coast being much more arid than its densely forested western end. Mango trees, breadfruit trees, and hibiscus trees grow wild.

The island has a population of around 2,200, with most people residing in the main village of **Hakahau** on the northeast coast, where you'll find an artisan market, produce market, grocery store, convenience shops, bank, and most of the accommodations and restaurants. It's an island of artists, and Ua Pou is largely to thank for the renaissance of Marquesan culture and arts that spurred in the late 1980s, beginning with the first Marquesan Islands Arts Festival—a major feat, considering most Marquesan cultural expressions were banned shortly after the arrival of missionaries over a century before.

Plan at least three days to see this majestic island, with one of them reserved for a full day of hiking.

Orientation

Ua Pou is 40 kilometers (25 mi) south of Nuku Hiva. The airport is found on the northernmost point of the island, with its main port, **Aneou Bay,** directly to its west. The main town of **Hakahau,** on the northeastern corner of the island, is where most accommodations, the post office, and bank are found. Five kilometers (3 mi) south along the road is scenic **Hakamoui Valley.** A further 10 kilometers (6 mi) south along the road is **Hohoi,** home to Hohoi Bay. **Hakatau,** on the westernmost coast of the island, is about a 15-kilometer (9-mi) drive from Hakahau.

SIGHTS
Hakahau

Hakahau is Ua Pou's main town set on a bay and protected by arid headlands. At Hakahau's center is a **town hall** with stunning stone carvings resembling Ua Pou's sentinel pinnacles. On this island of artists, Hakahau hosts the **Motu Haka** cultural federation, responsible for organizing the

---

1: an inlet connecting Hakatea Bay to Hakaui Valley **2:** Horses are ubiquitous throughout the Marquesas. **3:** Taipivai Craft Market **4:** Chez Yvonne

Ua Pou

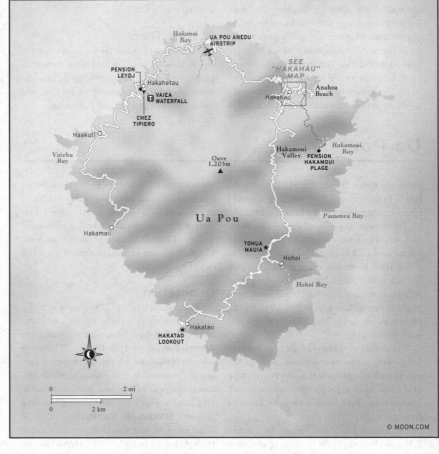

Hakanai Bay

UA POU ANEOU AIRSTRIP

PENSION LEYDJ

Hakahetau

VAIEA WATERFALL

CHEZ TIPIERO

Haakuti

Vaiehu Bay

SEE "HAKAHAU" MAP

Hakahau

Anahoa Beach

Hakamoui Valley

PENSION HAKAMOUI PLAGE

Hakamoui Bay

Oave 1,203m

Ua Pou

Paaumea Bay

Hakamaii

TOHUA MAUIA

Hohoi

Hohoi Bay

HAKATAO LOOKOUT

Hakatao

0   2 mi

0   2 km

© MOON.COM

Marquesas Islands Arts Festival every four years.

CHURCH OF SAINT-ETIENNE

Hakahau

The first stone church in the Marquesas was erected at Hakahau in 1859, and the present Church of Saint-Etienne (1981) has a pulpit shaped like a boat carved from a single stump by a group of sculptors. The wooden cross in the church is by Damien Haturau, an iconic modern Marquesan sculptor. Visitors

are welcome to attend a service and enjoy the hypnotizing Marquesan Catholic hymns that take place on Sunday mornings.

Hakamoui Valley

Hakamoui

A verdant valley of coconut and fan palms stretches inland from the black pebble beach on Ua Pou's eastern end. This valley is also known as the Valley of Chiefs, as it was home to the last ruler of Ua Pou, Heato. A delight for those interested in Marquesan history, this valley has archeological sites restored in the mid-1990s. It's thought that the giant paepae here was once the foundation of the dwelling of Ua Pou's royalty. Look closely to see human figures etched in its stone. Hakamoui Valley is also the site of Ua Pou's last standing ancient tiki—unfortunately, half of its face has disintegrated. All other tikis that once resided in the valley have been pillaged by foreign collectors. Because this region is largely unmarked, it's best to venture here with a guide (arranged through your accommodation).

Hohoi Bay
Hohoi

A drive along the road to Hohoi Bay is a journey back in time. In between the fruit trees and grasses, you'll find an array of archeological sites, paepae, slowly being reclaimed by nature. Interpretations on what exactly the paepae were used for vary from person to person, but many believe they were the foundations for meeting sites and dwellings. Paepae built from larger stones likely signified a site of greater importance—like a home or meeting point for the ruling families—than those built from smaller stones.

One of Ua Pou's most talented sculptors, Jean Kautai, lives in the village of Hohoi. He creates masterpieces from Ua Pou's increasingly rare kea pua flower stones, pieces of phonolite with yellow flower patterns inside, found mostly on the beach of Hohoi.

Tohua Mauia
Hohoi

Set above the houses of Hohoi, this ancient ceremonial plaza of Tohua Mauia is the most magnificent on Ua Pou, restored in 2019 for the Marquesas Islands Arts Festival. There's a large platform thought to once have been the site for chiefly rituals, and many paepae on the grounds. Local architects have rebuilt traditional shelters and have placed tikis throughout the property to simulate what the grounds may have looked like centuries ago.

Hakatao Lookout
Hakatao

On the southern end of the village of Hakatao, there's a 200-meter (656-ft) trail leading to a headland overlooking basalt cliffs, the tranquil bay, and all the way to Motu Oa, a haven for bird life. Manta rays are commonly seen cruising through the blue.

BEACHES

There are many quiet beaches on Ua Pou. Unfortunately, many are infested with pesky nonos, tiny gnats that can cause itching that lasts for weeks. Nonos tend to be most aggressive at dawn and dusk. Lightweight clothing is usually enough to deter them.

HAKAHAU BEACH
Hakahau

The small strip of gray sand flanking Hakahau's bay is a hub of activity. Kids cannonball into the sea, paddlers glide from end to end, fishermen cast their lines, and horses come to cool off. The snorkeling is all right here, though visibility is often murky.

ANAHOA BEACH
Hakahau

Lovely Anahoa Beach is a scenic 30-minute walk east of the marina of Hakahau where you'll find nothing but desert, cliffs, a little

Hakahau

Hakahau Harbor

Hakahau Beach

PENSION PUKUEE

HAKAHAU CRAFT CENTER

HAKAHAU TO HAKAMOUI HIKE

SNACK VEHINE

PENSION VEHINE

CHURCH OF SAINT-ETIENNE

0   200 yds
0   200 m

© MOON.COM

vegetation, and a spot likely to yourself depending on the time of day you go. Sadly, the sand is infested with nonos. Along the trail to Anahoa, stop to admire the bird's-eye view from the cross overlooking Hakahau on the ridge halfway.

HAKANAI BAY

Hakanai; first bay west from the airport
In desolate Hakanai Bay, ashy sands cede to swirls of turquoise and cobalt waters, and craggy headlands protect the waters from large swells. The bay is also known as Shark Bay as it's a breeding site of shy black tip reef sharks. You'll often spot their signature ink-dipped dorsal fins cruising through the waters. Despite their presence, the waters are popular for swimming.

HIKING

There are hiking trails all throughout Ua Pou, though most are unmarked. It's wise to hike Ua Pou with a guide, best arranged through your accommodation, or if you've come onboard the *Aranui 5,* with the help of their reception. Experienced climbers come to scale Ua Pou's iconic pinnacles—though you'll need to bring all your own equipment for this type of endeavor.

VAIEA WATERFALL

Distance: *2 km (1.2 mi) out-and-back*
Time: *1 hour*
Trailhead: *Near Hakahau*
Information and maps: *Ask in Hakahetau for directions to the trailhead*
A forest of palm trees, pandanus trees, and ferns from the settlement of Hakahetau to Vaiea Waterfall, a fairy-tale cascade with a swimming pool underneath. The track can be muddy at times, and you'll want to pack mosquito repellent. During the dry season, the waterfall is all but a little trickle.

HAKAHAU TO HAKAMOUI HIKE

Distance: *16 km (10 mi) out-and-back*
Time: *6 hours*
Trailhead: *Hakahau*

Information and maps: *Ask in Hakahau for directions to the trailhead*
Coastal scenes await at this hike crossing behind Ua Pou's parched bays. Start in Hakahau and follow the dirt trail toward Anahoa Bay. From there, the path weaves to a small cross marking the perfect place to take a break and take in the views. Many travelers choose to turn back here (5 km/3 mi into the hike), but there is a poorly marked path leading farther to Hakamoui.

SHOPPING
HAKAHAU CRAFT CENTER

Hakahau; 8am-2pm Mon.-Sat.
Hakahau Craft Center is where you'll find the works from a few dozen Marquesan artists, like intricate tapa; fish hooks carved from bone, wood, or shell; tiki statues; traditional weapons; palm leaf weavings; jewelry; and kitchenware (utensils, bowls, pestles and mortars). It's one of the only places in Polynesia to find sculptures made from Ua Pou's kea pua "flower stone," a rare phonolite stone with flecks of golden yellow in it, resembling daisies. You'll often find bottles of monoï oil at this market as well.

FOOD
CHEZ TIPIERO

Hakahetau; tel. 40 92 55 82; call ahead; CFP 1,500
Chez Tipiero has its choice of seafood, of course, with sashimi, grilled mackerel, grilled tuna, raw tuna, and whatever else is caught the morning of. But what Chef Tipiero is really known for is his pork served with fresh papaya and mango. Enjoy sides of cooked green beans in garlic butter, corn on the cob, and fried potatoes. Save room for dessert. There are no regular hours at Chez Tipiero; you'll want to call ahead to place an order.

SNACK VEHINE

Hakahau; tel. 40 92 50 63; 11am-1:30pm and 6pm-8:30pm Mon.-Sat.; CFP 1,500
This low-key restaurant with jovial staff serves grilled meats, grilled fish, chow mein, sashimi, fries, pizzas, and weekly specials.

The Miraculous Noni Fruit

When you first encounter the knobby green fruit of a noni tree (Morinda citrifolia), you might wonder if it's even edible. A ripe noni fruit is soft, with a distinct, pungent smell, and taste-wise, it rarely tops the list of favorite fruits. But what it lacks in taste and odor, it makes up for in health benefits. Miracle cure or spurious elixir, the noni juice fad has created a miniboom in producing areas such as the Marquesas. Touts of its health benefits have crossed the world over, and today noni is one of French Polynesia's largest exports.

noni fruit

HEALTH BENEFITS

Noni juice is believed to increase mental clarity and energy levels, support proper digestion, enhance the immune system, relieve pain, assist with joint health, prevent tumor growth, and promote longevity. A 2018 study by health researchers revealed the noni fruit has a higher level of antioxidants than other fruit juices (The Potential Health Benefits of Noni Juice: A Review of Human Intervention Studies. *Foods,* 2018).

OTHER USES

The trees blossom year-round, and a yellow dye is made from the roots. Apart from the juice, noni extract is used as an ingredient in many personal hygiene products such as soaps, creams, and shampoos.

HOW TO TRY IT

You'll find noni trees grown throughout the Marquesas, oftentimes on public property where anyone is free to pick. Look for a fruit that's light yellow and soft to touch. Set the noni aside until it's fully ripe with a translucent skin. Once the noni fruit turns white, it's ready for juicing. First, blend the fruit. Strain the noni juice to remove seeds and fibers. Mix the noni juice with other juices like pineapple, pomelo, papaya, or mango to make it more palatable. Noni fruits grow all year long and can also be purchased at all Marquesan produce markets.

It's popular with locals, and gets absolutely packed when the cruise ship is in town. Views overlook the sea and Ua Pou ridgeline.

ACCOMMODATIONS

PENSION LEYDJ

Hakahetau; tel. 87 77 17 82; maka@mail.pf; CFP 7,500/person half-board

Hidden on the hill of Hakahetau, Pension Leydj offers a simple stay with a few rooms that share a hot-water shower inside the home

of Célestine and Tony. Tony is a masterful sculptor, and many of his pieces decorate the home. Célestine doles out fresh dishes on the terrace, a prime place to lounge with a book in hand. The owners are happy to arrange 4x4 excursions, hikes, and day trips.

PENSION VEHINE

Hakahau; tel. 87 70 84 32; heatopakohe@gmail.com; CFP 9,000/person half-board

Pension Vehine has two quiet bungalows for

rent tucked in between the winding vines and branches of a jungle-like garden. Guests share a bathroom with a hot-water shower. The owners, Claire and Toti, are known for treating guests like long-lost family members. Meals are served on-site on the spacious deck of Snack Vehine.

★ PENSION PUKUEE

Hakahau; tel. 40 92 50 83; www.pensionpukuee. com; CFP 15,500/person for half-board, CFP 18,500/ person for full-board

Pension Pukuee is one of the most scenic pensions in the Marquesas, with a large communal area overlooking Ua Pou's pinnacles, the bay, and Hakahau village. All guests have access to a Jacuzzi, swimming pool, little library area, cocktail bar, and restaurant, where cultural events and workshops occasionally take place. Two rooms are connected to the main building with a family bungalow available to rent separately. All rooms have a private bathroom with hot water, a terrace, fan, and spotty internet access. The owners, Elisa and Jérôme, can arrange hiking trips and day excursions around the island (Jérôme usually guides and can do so in English).

PENSION HAKAMOUI PLAGE

Hakamoui; tel. 87 70 67 94; danyhakamoui@gmail. com; CFP 18,000/double bungalow

The four wooden bungalows at Pension Hakamoui Plage feel like they're at the end of the world, and each is just a few steps away from a black pebble beach. They're spacious but slightly dated, each with a fan, mosquito net, private bathroom, and terrace. A grassy lawn with tropical flowers accents the property. It's a prime place to explore the archeological sites of Hakamoui. Shuttle from the airport is CFP 8,000 per person round-trip.

INFORMATION AND SERVICES

- **Banque Socredo:** Hakahau; tel. 40 92 53 63; www.socredo.pf; 8am-noon and 1:30pm-4pm Mon.-Thurs., 8am-noon and 1:30pm-3pm Fri.

- **Post Office:** Hakahau; 7am-11am and 12:30pm-3pm Mon.-Thurs., 7am-11am and 12:30pm-2pm Fri.

- **Office de Tourisme:** Hakahau Town Center; tel. 40 91 51 05; 8am-11am and noon-4pm Mon.-Fri.

GETTING THERE
By Air

Ua Pou's Aneou airstrip (UAP) is on the north coast, 10 kilometers (6 mi) west of Hakahau via a road over a ridge. The short runway veers slightly uphill, and flights to Ua Pou are often canceled or changed depending on the weather. Pensions in Hakahau offer airport transfers for CFP 2,500 per person. As of 2022, Air Tahiti no longer flies to Ua Pou. Tahiti Air Charter (tel. 40 50 54 86; www. tahiti-air-charter.com) is planning to operate flights from Papeete to Ua Pou.

Boat

The *Te Ata O Hiva* shuttles between the northern Marquesas (www.codim.pf; CFP 3,500/one-way; 2 hours Nuku Hiva-Ua Pou, 3 hours Ua Pou-Ua Huka, 2 hours Ua Huka-Nuku Hiva). The *Aranui* (tel. 40 42 62 42; www.aranui.com) passenger freighter also stops in Ua Pou on its journey through the Marquesas. Large boats land at Aneou Bay, on the northwest side of Ua Pou.

GETTING AROUND

Once you're on Ua Pou, the only way to get around is by 4WD. Most of Ua Pou's archeological sites are not well marked and are best visited with a guide. Roads can be windy, steep, one-way only, and require a skilled driver to navigate. For the intrepid, **Téuu Location** in Hakahau (tel. 87 31 47 29; alex. hituputoka@gmail.com) has manual 4WD vehicles for rent for around CFP 10,000 per day, not including fuel. Drivers must be at least 23 years old.

Ua Huka

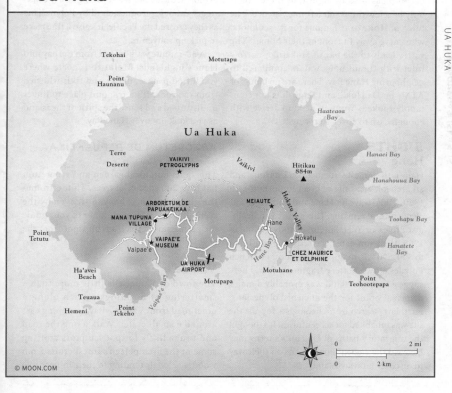

Tekohai

Motutapu

Point
Haunanu

Haateaoa
Bay

Ua Huka

Terre
Deserte

Hanaei Bay

VAIKIVI
PETROGLYPHS ★

Vaikivi

Hitikau
884m ▲

Hanahouua Bay

ARBORETUM DE
PAPUAKEIKAA

MEIAUTE ★

Hokatu Valley

MANA TUPUNA
VILLAGE ★

Hane ○

Toohapu Bay

Point
Tetutu

VAIPAE'E
MUSEUM ★

Hokatu ○

Vaipae'e

UA HUKA
AIRPORT ✈

Hane Bay

CHEZ MAURICE
ET DELPHINE

Hanatete
Bay

Ha'avei
Beach

Motupapa

Motuhane

Point
Teohootepapa

Teuaua

Hemeni

Point
Tekeho

Vaipae'e Bay

0   2 mi

0   2 km

© MOON.COM

Ua Huka

Crescent-shaped Ua Huka, 35 kilometers (21 mi) east of Nuku Hiva and 56 kilometers (34 mi) northeast of Ua Pou, is the northern half of an ancient volcano, and its 700 inhabitants live in the truncated crater in the south. Goats and over 1,500 wild horses roam this arid 83-square-kilometer (32-square mi) island, while the tiny islands of Teuaua and Hemeni, off the southwest tip of Ua Huka, are a breeding ground for thousands of sooty terns (kaveka). Bring along binoculars to admire inquisitive iphis monarchs (patiotio) or the colorful plumage of ultramarine lorikeets (pihiti), which are only found on Ua Huka. The

waters around Ua Huka are rife with plankton, and it's one of the best places in Polynesia to spot giant oceanic manta rays that can grow to 4.5 meters (15 ft) wide.

Orientation

Vaipae'e is the main village of the island, on the southwestern side of the island, although the hospital is 10 kilometers (6 mi) east in **Hane. Hitikau** (884 m/2,900 ft) rises northeast of Hane village. Just east of Hane, **Hokatu Valley** is one of the best places in the Marquesas for bird-watching, where you'll have a real chance of seeing the ultramarine lorikeet, a small bird with feathers that mimic ocean blues—it's thought that there might only be a few thousand left in existence. The town of **Hokatu** is famous for its sculptors, who carve away in front of their homes. The valley leads to the bay of Hokatu, a narrow inlet with tumultuous waters compared to neighboring Hane Bay. There are no banks or ATMs on Ua Huka, and English is not commonly spoken. You will need to arrive with enough cash to cover your stay.

SIGHTS
Hane
Hane is the largest settlement on Ua Huka, and an archeological site of great importance. In 1960, a tidal wave hit Hane and uncovered ancient cultural remains. This allowed archeologist Professor Y. H. Sinoto to study the site in 1965. His team dated the settlement of Hane to 300-600 CE, making it the oldest in French Polynesia; two pottery fragments found here suggest that the island was probably a major dispersal point for the ancient Polynesians. Further research by archeologists reveals the site was inhabited for six centuries. It's thought the migratory paths of Ua Huka's terns may have led the ancient Polynesians on their way to discover faraway islands.

In the settlement of Hane, there's a small exhibit dedicated to sea voyaging and the outrigger canoes, pirogues, used by Polynesians as they crossed the Pacific. It's also a fine place to pick up souvenirs.

A 30-minute walk inland from the bay into Hane's highlands, **Meiaute** is a site where you'll find paepae, ma'ae, and tikis whittled from red rock. It's a tranquil place to linger undisturbed and sense the spirit of the island as you look out over Hane Bay.

ARBORETUM DE PAPUAKEIKAA
Hane; 8am-3pm Mon.-Sat.; free
This quiet botanical garden and arboretum has over 200 species of trees. Tiptoe around the giant roots of a banyan tree, enjoy the scent of tropical flowers, and ask your guide for permission to pick a fruit right from the tree.

Vaipae'e
The town of Vaipae'e is little more than a smattering of buildings strewn along a quiet road from Vaipae'e Bay, wrapping east around a small crater. Walk along the road and you're likely to spot sculptors crafting some of the archipelago's finest crafts from wood, see locals tending to their impeccable

Ua Huka wild horses

gardens, and hear birds chirping overhead. The town has a small red-topped church with intricate Biblical sculptures inside, open to anyone on Sundays. Sunday's haunting hymns are heard throughout the town each week. The town is where you'll find a post office, a handful of convenience stores, and public gardens.

VAIPAE'E MUSEUM

Vaipae'e; tel. 40 92 60 13; 7am-2pm Mon.-Fri.; free
Near the post office in Vaipae'e is a small but admirable museum dedicated to the Marquesan Islands with artifacts donated by local residents at the instigation of former mayor Leon Lichtle. Among the ancient items are pearl fishhooks and octopus lures, seashells, and stone pestles and wooden bowls used for cooking. Local artist Joseph Tehau Va'atete has created replicas of many lost works from photographs taken on the 1920-1921 Bishop Museum Expedition, including Marquesan tiki, bowls, drums, paddles, and stilts. Copies of some of the old photos hang on the museum walls. Woodcarvers are still very active on Ua Huka, and some examples of their work can be purchased in the craft shop adjacent to the museum, only open when tour groups are present.

Inland Ua Huka
VAIKIVI PETROGLYPHS

Walk three hours or arrive on horse to ancient petroglyphs carved into stones on the Vaikivi Plateau. Over 50 petroglyphs are found here, including etchings of traditional pirogues with and without sails, a true nod to the Marquesas Islands sailing heritage. Trips here are best arranged through your accommodation. The 6-kilometer (3.7-mi) trail can be overgrown and is unmarked.

BEACHES
HA'AVEI BEACH

West UA Huka
Hidden like a little oasis on the foothills of Ua Huka's southern craters, Ha'avei is a quiet beach with gray sands and a small coconut grove. The water here can get a little rough, but on a calm day it's a nice place to soak in the water and relax. Unfortunately, there might be nonos here, so wear long, lightweight clothing if you plan to linger.

ACCOMMODATIONS
CHEZ MAURICE ET DELPHINE

Hokatu; tel. 40 92 60 55; CFP 7,000/person for half-board
Staying at Chez Maurice et Delphine is like staying with a long-lost relative, as evenings are spent singing and dancing and dinners double as comfort food in the main house, a five-minute walk from the bungalows. No task seems too complicated for Maurice and Delphine to assist with. Maurice is a master sculptor and Delphine helps manage a craft shop in the village of Hokatu, making them quite the creative duo. This pension is found in a quiet village near Hokatu Bay on a spacious property cloaked in bougainvillea. Bungalows have ocean views, a shaded deck, bathroom with tepid showers, mosquito net, and fan.

MANA TUPUNA VILLAGE

Vaipae'e; tel. 40 92 60 08; manatupuna@mail.pf; CFP 15,500/room for two people, includes half-board
The longest-running pension on Ua Huka, Mana Tupuna means "the spirit of our ancestors" and has been managed by family for nearly three decades. Rustic stilted bungalows reveal views of the Vaipae'e Valley. Each one has a private bathroom and warm-water showers. Internet access is available in communal areas. The host, Arii, is happy to help arrange day trips around the island and share insight about various sculptures and tattoos of Marquesan culture.

GETTING THERE AND AROUND

The **airstrip** (UAH) is on a hilltop between Hane and Vaipae'e, 6 kilometers (3.7 mi) from the latter. However, flights to Ua Huka are no longer operating by Air Tahiti, and while there are whispers of flights returning someday, no date has been set. The *Aranui 5* (tel. 40 42 62 42; www.aranui.com) enters the narrow fjord at Vaipae'e and anchors. It's quite a show watching the ship trying to turn around. Most arrivals come with a private yacht, but all anchorages are known for being difficult, and typically it's the more experienced sailors who make the journey here.

The *Te Ata O Hiva* shuttles between the northern Marquesas (www.codim.pf; CFP 3,500/one-way; 2 hours Nuku Hiva-Ua Pou, 3 hours Ua Pou-Ua Huka, 2 hours Ua Huka-Nuku Hiva), and some routes from Nuku Hiva include a stopover in Ua Pou.

Once you're on Ua Huka, the best way to get around in the villages is **on foot**, or through a **tour** arranged by your accommodation.

Hiva Oa

Hiva Oa's colors are fully saturated, with mountains cloaked in greenery, ink-black beaches, white sand bays with turquoise waters, moss-accented archeological sites, and spotlights of sunshine glowing amidst heavy cumulus clouds. During the dry season, the northwest coast dries out, but once the rain comes, it's taken over by anything with roots. Artists as beloved as Jacques Brel and bemoaned as Paul Gauguin found inspiration here, choosing it as their final resting place.

Orientation

Measuring 40 by 19 kilometers (24 by 11 mi), 315-square kilometer (121-square-mi) Hiva Oa (pop. 2,000) is the second-largest of the Marquesas and the main center of the southern cluster of islands. **Temetiu** (1,276 m/4,186 ft), the highest peak in the Marquesas, towers above Atuona, the main town of Hiva Oa, to the west. Steep ridges falling to the coast separate lush valleys on this long crescent-shaped island. **Ta'aoa,** or "Traitors'" Bay, is a flooded crater presently missing its eastern wall 6 kilometers (3.7 mi) west from Atuona. **Puama'u,** the site of ancient tiki on Hiva Oa's eastern end, is in a younger secondary crater.

SIGHTS

TOP EXPERIENCE

★ Atuona

The town of Atuona is best known for its associations with the painter Paul Gauguin and the singer Jacques Brel, both of whom lived here. It's the largest settlement on Hiva Oa, home to a few snacks and cafés, a grocery store, museum, handicraft market, yoga studio, and tattoo parlors. It's quiet and easily walkable. If you have the time, the Catholic church is worth visiting for its fine carved doors and interior visible through open walls. The Marie de Atuona also contains a large Gauguin reproduction. Many families head to the waterfront on weekends for picnics and swimming in the teal waters just off Atuona's jet-black sand beach.

HANDICRAFT MARKET

Atuona; tel. 87 26 23; 8am-4pm Mon.-Fri.

This charming market is attached to the newly renovated community center, where you can purchase tapa, wood and stone sculptures, jewelry, pareu, and a mix of oils and spreads. Photos aren't allowed inside the center, but you can look as long as you like. Many of the artists have their own stands inside the market and take custom commissions.

CENTRE JACQUES BREL

Atuona Cultural Center; tel. 40 92 78 97; 8am-5pm Mon.-Sat.; CFP 500/adult

The famous Belgian chanson singer Jacques Brel and his companion Maddly Bamy came to the Marquesas aboard his 18-meter yacht, the *Askoy II,* in 1975. Jacques decided to settle at Atuona and sold his boat to an American

Hiva Oa

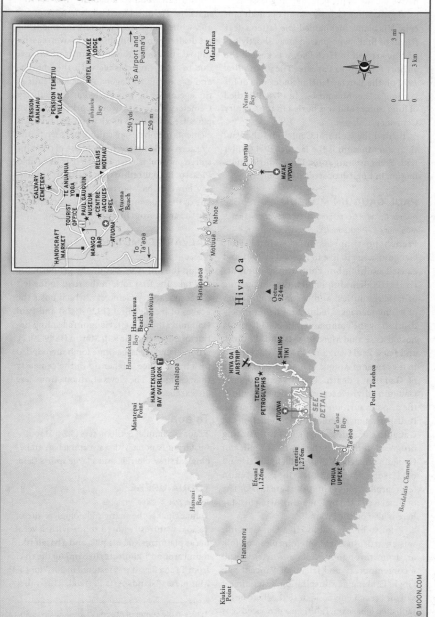

Inset map (detail):
- To Airport and Puama'u
- HOTEL HANAKEE LODGE
- PENSION TEMETIU VILLAGE
- PENSION KAKAHAU
- Tahauku Bay
- CALVARY CEMETERY
- TE ANUANUA YOGA
- RELAIS MOEHAU
- PAUL GAUGUIN MUSEUM
- TOURIST OFFICE
- CENTRE JACQUES BREL
- ATUONA
- Atuona Beach
- HANDICRAFT MARKET
- MANGO BAR
- To Ta'aoa
- 0 250 yds
- 0 250 m

Main map:
- Cape Matafenua
- Natue Bay
- Puamau
- MA'AE I'IPONA
- Motuua
- Nahoe
- Hanapaaoa
- Hiva Oa
- Ootua 924m
- Hanatekuua Bay
- Hanatekuua Beach
- Hanatekuua
- HANATEKUUA BAY OVERLOOK
- Hanaiapa
- HIVA OA AIRSTRIP
- SMILING TIKI
- TEHUETO PETROGLYPHS
- ATUONA
- SEE DETAIL
- Ta'aoa Bay
- Ta'aoa
- Point Teaehoa
- Matatepai Point
- Hanatekuua Bay
- Efeani 1,126m
- Temetiu 1,276m
- TOHUA UPEKE
- Hanaui Bay
- Bordelais Channel
- Hanamenu
- Kiukiu Point

0 3 mi

0 3 km

© MOON.COM

couple. Maddly, who had been a dancer on her native Guadeloupe, gave dancing lessons to local girls, while Jacques ran an open-air cinema. His plane, nicknamed *Jojo* (after a dear friend of Brel's who passed away shortly before he arrived in Hiva Oa), was kept at the airport for trips to Papeete. The album *Brel 1977* on the Barclay label includes one of his last songs, "Les Marquises." In 1978, Brel died of lung cancer and was buried in the Cavalry Cemetery.

Behind the Cultural Center and the Paul Gauguin Museum is the Jacques Brel Center with Brel's aircraft **Jojo.** There's little information in English posted in the center.

PAUL GAUGUIN MUSEUM

Atuona Cultural Center; tel. 40 92 78 97; 8am-5pm Mon.-Sat.; CFP 600/adult

French postimpressionist painter Paul Gauguin came to live in Atuona in 1901 and caused nothing but controversy upon arrival. His drinking habits, racism, ceding of fatherly duties, and sexual exploitation of young teenagers led to him being widely disliked by the community. In 2003 Hiva Oa hosted its second Marquesas Islands Festival, and a new Paul Gauguin Museum was erected in the center of Atuona to mark the centenary of Gauguin's death. The museum details Gauguin's divisive legacy and details some of the disputes surrounding his time in Hiva Oa. It displays tens of colorful reproductions of Gauguin's paintings that show his painting progression through the years. A replica of Gauguin's thatched "Maison du Jouîr" (House of Pleasure) has been built at the center, and a few reproductions of his prints are inside. The original well used by Gauguin during his stay here is also on the grounds.

Prior to his arrival in Hiva Oa, Gauguin was an artist in Paris, often inspired by folk art from throughout Asia and Africa, and a contemporary and friend of Vincent van Gogh. Craving new inspiration, Gauguin set sail for French Polynesia in 1891, where he established a base on Tahiti and produced tens of paintings and sculptures. In 1901, Gauguin went to the Marquesas after being inspired by Marquesan woodwork coming into Tahiti's markets. He purchased a home in Atuona, and while he received a steady income from art dealers purchasing his works overseas, he caused strife with the community of Atuona due to partying, clashes with the church, and exploiting teenagers. After his death at the age of 55, he was buried at the Calvary Cemetery. Gauguin's work sparked a sense of paradise lost within its viewers, and revealed elements of Polynesian culture not seen by the Western world before: his bold use of color inspired cubism, fauvism, and artists like Pablo Picasso. Recent rethinking of the artist's legacy, however, has spurred questions about the fate of the museum and the ethics of separating the artist from his art.

CALVARY CEMETERY

Atuona

Go up the hill from beside the gendarmerie and take the first fork in the road to the left to reach Calvary Cemetery, which hosts the graves of Jacques Brel (1929-1978) and Paul Gauguin (1848-1903). Gauguin's leading detractor, Monseigneur R. J. Martin (1849-1912), is buried under a large white tomb surrounded by a metal fence, higher up in the cemetery than Gauguin. The views of Atuona from here are excellent.

Ta'aoa

Ta'aoa is a hamlet 6 kilometers (3.7 mi) southwest from Atuona with a sweeping bay, archeological sites, church, and a large sports field.

TOHUA UPEKE

Ta'aoa; free

Tohua Upeke, the main archeological site of Ta'aoa, features restored tohua with several ma'ae platforms, 'ua ma pits, and a basalt tiki, found around 1 kilometer (0.6 mi) up the river from Ta'aoa Bay. It was restored in 2003 for the Marquesas Islands Arts Festival. This valley

---

1: tikis in the center of Atuona **2:** the Paul Gauguin Museum **3:** the main road of Atuona **4:** Mango Bar

The Mana Spirit

In Polynesia, mana is a sacred spiritual force that's present in nature, including human beings. It's thought that mana can be felt in sacred spaces and is stronger in some people than others. In the Marquesas, mana is often felt at archeological sites like Ma'ae I'ipona, Hatiheu, Tohua Upeke, and Hanaiapa. That said, many people also feel it while in the ocean, on a trail leading through a verdant valley, or at an archeological site that has no plaque.

is considered one of the most sacred on Hiva Oa, as it's believed to host the first ancestors (tumu) of the Marquesas. If you'd like to combine a stop here with a beach visit, the water in Ta'aoa Bay tends to be calmer than that in Atuona.

Smiling Tiki

8 km (5 mi) inland from Atuona toward Atuona Airport; free

From Atuona, head 8 kilometers (5 mi) toward the Atuona Airport and turn onto a dirt road at a sign that says "Tiki Souriant." Look closely and you'll find an unmarked hiking trail between two coconut trees leading 200 meters (656 ft) into a dense forest. There, you'll find a meter-tall tiki wearing a small grin. It's not the easiest to find, but visiting this tiki is thought to bring good luck to the rest of your journey.

Tehueto Petroglyphs

2 km (1.2 mi) inland from Tahauku Bay; free

Hidden in Tahauku Valley are petroglyphs created by ancient Marquesans. It's thought that ancient Marquesans believed cosmic evolution began with rocks. Since rocks were the origin of all existence, they also worked as a prime material for documenting, honoring, and deifying the people, animals, and natural elements most important to them. The Tehueto Petroglyphs depict human figures, marine animals, and land animals. Finding the site is hard without a guide. Day trips can usually stop here upon request.

TOP EXPERIENCE

★ Ma'ae I'ipona

Puamau; CFP 300 paid to groundskeeper

While many of the tikis of French Polynesia were destroyed with the arrival of missionaries to the Marquesas, those found at the sacred site of I'ipona are some of the best preserved. The site, which covers two acres, was restored in 1991, and there are currently shelters and barriers to protect each of the five main tikis from further erosion, which are also protected naturally by the valley around it. It was once the battleground of the warring tribes of Hiva Oa. Today, it's a site of peace.

Most famous of them all is **Tiki Takaii,** the largest ancient tiki in the Marquesas—a little under 3 meters (10 ft) tall and crafted from red tuff rock. It's thought to be built in honor of a powerful chief and warrior. One of the most unique tikis, **Tiki Maki Taua Pepe,** the "Flying Tiki," is shrouded in mystery. Depicting a figure lying down with eyes turned upward, there are many theories on what it represents: it's commonly thought to be a figure of a pregnant woman in the throes of childbirth and perhaps was once used as a birthing table. However, others claim it's an animal figure, like a fish or dog (dog petroglyphs are etched into its base). **Tiki Te Tovae E Noho,** to the left of Tiki Takaii, is missing its head and in a state of poor condition. **Tiki Fau Poe** behind Tiki Takaii is thought to represent Takaii's wife. The last large tiki, **Tiki Manuiotaa,** is a feminine figure with a smaller head and more slender limbs than the male tikis.

The drive to Puamau, where you'll find

Ma'ae l'ipona, from Atuona (40 km/24 mi, 1.5 hours) is one confident drivers will enjoy and cautious drivers will abhor. The one-way road was recently paved, but it has a sheer cliff drop on one side and rock piles created as goats scuttle up the cliffs on the other. Fortunately, tours led by drivers who've been doing this journey their whole lives run regularly to Puamau. This hamlet has a spectacular bay with a seaside rock wall and golden beach where you can lounge and watch the waves.

Motane

Motane (Mohotani) is an 8-kilometer-long (5-mi-long) island rising to 520 meters (1,706 ft) about 18 kilometers (11 mi) southeast of Hiva Oa. The depredation of wild sheep on Motane turned the island into a treeless desert. When the Spaniards anchored here in 1595, they reported that Motane was well wooded and populated, but today it's uninhabited. Since 1971 Motane has been a protected area with 10 species of seabirds and four endemic land birds.

You can reach Motane by boat from Hiva Oa or Tahuata, which takes around two hours from either island. There are no regular public boats running here regularly; the trip is best arranged with the help of your accommodation.

BEACHES
ATUONA BEACH
Atuona

Don't wear your finest swimsuit to Atuona Beach, where jet-black sand seems to work its way into the lining of every layer of fabric. After school and on weekends, families gather on the grassy area or on the rock wall to snack, drink, and swim. You can walk here quite easily from the center of town, or before going for a meal at Relais Moehau. The nonos aren't too nasty here.

TA'AOA BAY BEACH
Ta'aoa

If you've come with kids, they'll love running off energy at the nearby grassy area or splashing around in the shallows of Ta'aoa Bay Beach. This beach is rarely crowded and has picnic tables, a parking lot, and a small stretch of sand to lounge on. The water can get rough, so it's best to save swimming here for calm days.

HANATEKUUA BEACH
Hanatekuua

Veer north at the fork in the road near Atuona Airport and drive 10 kilometers (6 mi), about a 20-minute drive, to reach **Hanaiapa,** a tranquil settlement found on the shoreline of a small bay. A large sports field, picnic benches, pirogue shelter, and pebble beach make it a prime place to relax—curious kids often come up to say hello.

There's a trailhead on the eastern side of the bay leading 6 kilometers (3.7 mi) to Hanatekuua Bay, one of the few spots on the island to surf, though you'll need your own board to paddle out as there are no rental shops on the island. You can also reach the cookie-crumb sands of this beach by boat. But, once you're here, it's arguably the best beach on the island. Turquoise waters are typically calm thanks to the protective headlands, and there's plenty of space to throw a towel down. Coconut trees accent the inland edge of the beach.

SNORKELING AND SCUBA DIVING
MARQUISES DIVING

tel. 87 24 19 95; www.marquisesdiving.com; CFP 8,500/fun dive

Humu, the owner of Marquises Diving, is one of the most experienced divers in the archipelago. As it's the only dive center on the island, you're guaranteed to have each dive destination all to yourself. Site locations depend on the day, and are at the mercy of the weather and ocean conditions. Various shark species, oceanic manta rays, eagle rays, and shoals of fish hide in the craggy reefs at sites all throughout Hiva Oa.

HIKING

HANATEKUUA BAY OVERLOOK AND BEACH

Distance: *3 km (1.6 mi) to overlook, 6 km (3.7 mi)* *to Hanatekuua Bay each way*

Time: *2 hours each way to Hanatekuua Bay*

Trailhead: *Near Hakahau*

Information and maps: *Request information at the Tourism Office in Atuona*

One of the most popular trails on Hiva Oa is a trek from the small village of Hanaiapa to the lonely beach of Hanatekuua, accessible only on foot or by boat. The trail starts on Hanaiapa's eastern end and crosses over a headland with copra farms on its flanks to a lookout point that reveals views of the jagged coastline. If it's rained, you might catch the sight of an incredible cascade pouring straight from the sea cliffs into the ocean. The overlook also offers a glimpse of Hanatekuua Bay from above, quiet with palm trees and golden sands. If you continue along the trail, you'll descend onto the soft sands of Hanatekuua Beach.

YOGA

TE ANUANUA YOGA

Atuona; tel. 87 79 77 18; CFP 2,500/class

Hereiti, a yoga teacher trained in India, teaches classes from her serene yoga studio overlooking Atuona Bay. The spacious wooden deck leaves plenty of room to roll out your mat and disconnect from the rest of the world. Classes on offer include yin, ashtanga, vinyasa, acro, and guided meditations.

FOOD

Most food options are found in Atuona, where there are also a few small grocery stores such as **Magasin Gaubil** (tel. 40 92 75 57; 7:30am-6pm Mon.-Fri., 8am-noon Sat. and Sun.).

MANGO BAR

Atuona; tel. 87 75 36 93; facebook.com/ hivaoamangobar; 8am-4pm Mon., Tues., Thurs., 8am-10pm Wed., 8am-5pm Thurs., 8am-midnight Fri.; CFP 600

Mango Bar is a colorful café and bar with a foosball table, arcade games, and outdoor seating area illuminated by twinkle lights. Their menu has quick bites like hot dogs, paninis, sandwiches, ice cream, waffles, and a few pastries. It's a quiet café in the mornings and lively bar in the afternoons. On Wednesdays and Fridays, Mango Bar often hosts live music and DJ sets—check their Facebook page for upcoming entertainment updates.

★ RELAIS MOEHAU

Atuona; tel. 40 92 72 69; relaismoehau.pf; 6am-9am, 11am-2pm, 6pm-9pm daily; CFP 2,500

The restaurant at Relais Moehau is the only semi-formal restaurant on Hiva Oa, with a large dining area overlooking the beach and town of Atuona. Their menu is extensive, with wood-fired pizzas, pastas, seafood, salads, and Asian-fusion dishes. Mahi-mahi cooked in a creamy vanilla sauce and served with a heaping side of garlic green beans is a regular favorite. Patrons have access to free WiFi.

HOTEL HANAKEE RESTAURANT

Near Atuona Port; tel. 40 92 75 867; hotelhanakee. com; 11am-2pm and 6pm-9pm daily; CFP 3,000

On the outskirts of Atuona near the Atuona Port, Hotel Hanakee Restaurant is a lively restaurant where plates of lobster, goat curry, and grilled tuna frequent the menu. Meals are served in a large dining room with rattan furniture, tropical plants, woven decor, and a decently stocked bar. Come just before sunset to enjoy the pink hues of Atuona from the spacious deck. Getting here can be a challenge if you're not staying on-site or don't have your own wheels.

ACCOMMODATIONS

Most accommodations are based around Atuona. There is no reliable public transport, so if you're staying outside of Atuona, you'll probably want to rent a car or ensure your accommodation has kitchen access. Bring ear plugs if you want to sleep in past the roosters.

PENSION TAHAUKU VILLAGE

Near Atuona Port; airbnb.com; CFP 8,500/room for two people

Pension Tahauku Village hosts three wooden bungalows hidden near Atuona Port. Each room is set in between tropical fruit trees, where papayas grow as large as bowling balls. Most mornings, the owners, Colé and Priscille, walk around doling out heaping plates of produce for breakfast. Rooms are a little on the rustic side, with a double and single bed, private bathroom with warm-water showers, mosquito nets, fans, a kitchenette, and laundry facilities. The best way to book this property is through Airbnb. The property is about a 25-minute walk from town.

PENSION TEMETIU VILLAGE

Near Atuona Port; tel. 87 70 01 71; www. temetiuvillage.com; CFP 12,000/room for two people

Perched on a hill overlooking Atuona Port, Pension Temetiu Village offers a calm retreat complete with a swimming pool—somewhat of a rarity on Hiva Oa. There are a few room options; some have a kitchenette and air-conditioning (activated in the evenings). Each sleep three and have a TV, private bathroom with hot-water shower, fridge, fan, and terrace. The best bungalows on the property have ocean views. For dinners, the pension hosts a mix of seafood and grilled meat meals on its open-air patio. There's a lounge room with reading materials and games to help pass the time.

★ PENSION KANAHAU

Near Atuona Port; tel. 87 70 16 26; tania.tania@live. fr; CFP 14,000/bungalow

A handful of quiet bungalows overlook Atuona Port at Pension Kanahau. Tania Amaru, the owner, is hospitable and famous for going out of her way to help her guests. She's happy to help arrange day tours, car rentals, and hiking excursions. Bungalows are clean and spacious with a private deck overlooking the water. Each comes with a TV, mosquito net, kitchenette, fan, and private bathroom—all can sleep three. Bright flowers and a large outdoor dining deck (also with a seaside view) cement the feeling of being on a remote island paradise. The pension is about a 20-minute walk from Atuona center.

HOTEL HANAKEE LODGE

Near Atuona Port; tel. 40 92 75 87; www. hotelhanakee.com; CFP 30,000/room for two people

One of the more remote accommodations near Atuona, what Hotel Hanakee Lodge loses in convenience, it makes up for in views and tranquility. There are 14 bungalows on the property, most with ocean views. Each can sleep two and comes with air-conditioning, a fan, minibar, kitchenette, and TV. Getting around can be a challenge without a car, but fortunately the lodge hosts one of the island's best restaurants, and hosts are happy to arrange plenty of excursions. Guests can opt for a package deal that includes day tours, meals, and accommodation that works out to a slightly better rate than paying for each feature à la carte.

INFORMATION AND SERVICES

- **Tourism Office:** Atuona; tel. 40 92 78 93; 8:30am-11:30am and 2pm-4pm Mon.-Fri.; English not commonly spoken but has a great supply of brochures and information in French

- **Bank Socredo:** Atuona; tel. 40 92 73 54; socredo.pf; 8am-noon and 1:30pm-4pm Mon.-Thurs., 8am-noon and 1:30pm-3pm Fri.

- **Post Office:** Atuona Town Hall; 7:30am-noon and 1pm-3pm Mon.-Thurs., 7am-noon and 12:30pm-2pm Fri.

- **Medical Center:** Atuona Town Hall; tel. 40 92 72 75

GETTING THERE
Air

The **Hiva Oa airstrip** (AUQ) is on a 441-meter-high (1,446-ft-high) plateau, 8 kilometers (5 mi) northeast of Atuona. Air Tahiti (tel. 40 50 54 86; www.airtahiti.com) flies to

Hiva Oa regularly from Papeete (3 hours 20 minutes, CFP 50,000/one-way) and Nuku Hiva (40 minutes, CFP 18,000/one-way). Hiva Oa is included in the Air Tahiti Marquesas Multi-Islands Air Pass.

It's a 2-hour downhill walk from the airport to Atuona. The normal taxi fare from the airport to Atuona is around CFP 3,000 per person each way. The amount collected by the various hotels varies (usually from CFP 2,500-4,000), so confirm when booking.

Boat

Yachts anchor behind the breakwater in Ta'aoa harbor, 2 kilometers (1.2 mi) east of the center of town. The *Aranui* (tel. 40 42 62 42; www.aranui.com) also ties up here. The *Te Ata O Hiva* (tel. 40 92 73 07; www.codim.pf) shuttle moves between Hiva Oa, Fatu Hiva, and Tahuata regularly for CFP 2,500-4,000 per trip. Connection times are 1 hour for Hiva Oa-Tahuata, 3.5 hours for Tahuata-Fatu Hiva, and 3.5 hours Fatu Hiva-Hiva Oa. The schedule changes regularly. Some routes are direct while others are a full rotation, stopping at each island.

GETTING AROUND
Rental Car

The best way to get around Hiva Oa is by 4x4. A new road connecting most of the island's main villages has made driving around the island easier than it used to be, but the roads remain narrow and windy. Atuona is easily explored by bicycle, and if you're comfortable with heat and hills, seeing the rest of the island by bicycle is an interesting way to explore.

- **Atuona Rent A Car** (Atuona; tel. 40 92 76 07; atuonarentacar.com; CFP 7,000/half-day, CFP 10,000/day): One of the most reliable car rental companies in the Marquesas, with a fleet of 4x4 vehicles (Toyota Hilux and Suzuki Vitara). Rentals come with insurance and unlimited mileage, fuel not included. Renters must be at least 23 years old.

- **Hiva Oa Location** (Atuona; tel. 87 37 35 45; hivaoalocation.com; CFP 7,000- 10,000/day): Hiva Oa Location has a fleet of Dacia Duster 4x4 and Renault Kwid 4x2 vehicles. Vehicles come with a cooler. Renters must be at least 23 years old. Fuel is not included.

- **Marquises Cycles and Cars** (tel. 87 21 46 93; www.marquises-cycles.com; US$38/8 hours for e-bike, US$95/day for vehicle): Marquises Cycles and Cars has a handful of electric bikes for rent (US$28/4 hours, US$38/8 hours) and Toyota 4x4 trucks. Fuel is not included.

Day Tours

Like most islands in the Marquesas, English is rarely spoken on Hiva Oa. It's still worth booking a tour with a French- or Marquesan-speaking guide solely to avoid being the one to drive the main road's hairpin mountain turns.

Boat trips to neighboring Tahuata can also be arranged through your accommodation or the providers below. These usually cost around CFP 10,000 per person for a full-day trip, and stop at Vaitahu for lunch, the Hapatoni market, and a lonely white sand beach.

PIFAVAE EXCURSION

tel. 87 72 76 33; pifavaexcursion@gmail.com and munevatetoa@gmail.com; CFP 7,000-10,000/person

Pifa O'Connor and his brother Brian "Bligh" O'Connor are two charismatic tour guides on Hiva Oa. They host trips to major archeological sites like Ta'aoa, Puamau, and Hanaiapa, and assist with arranging boat trips to the nearby island of Tahuata. On trips with Pifavae Excursion, you'll learn about Marquesan history and ancient legends. Both guides give tours in Marquesan, French, and English. If you're in a group, they can craft a custom tour—including guided hikes to Hanatekuua Beach. Get ready for ukulele sing-alongs to fill the transit time.

HIVA OA ADVENTURES

tel. 87 30 95 14; facebook.com/hivaoaadventures; CFP 7,000-12,000/person

Tours with Hiva Oa Adventures venture to Puamau, Hanaiapa, Ta'aoa, and hiking trips to Hanatekuua for around CFP 10,000 including a Marquesan buffet lunch. They can also arrange boat trips to Tahuata. Depending on the group and interests, trips can be customized to accommodate hiking, cultural, or beach-hopping interests. Tours are offered in French and English.

Tahuata

Lonely little Tahuata (pop. about 670) is just 6 kilometers (3.7 mi) south of Hiva Oa across Bordelais Channel. Just 15 kilometers long by 9 kilometers wide (9 mi long by 5 mi wide), 69-square-kilometer (26-square-mi) Tahuata is the smallest of the six inhabited islands of the Marquesas. A 17-kilometer (10-mi) track crosses the island from Motopu to **Vaitahu,** the main village on the west coast. The anchorage at **Hana Moe Noa** north of Vaitahu is protected from the ocean swells. There's a lovely white beach, and the water here is clear, as no rivers run into this bay.

Tahuata is one of the quietest islands in the Marquesas. Come to browse the intricate artwork found in **Hapatoni,** where crafts are made from bone, wood, and stone. Lonely bays with sandy beaches like **Hanahevane Bay** and **Hamamenino Bay** are frequently visited by manta rays.

Tahuata was the point of first contact between Polynesians and Europeans anywhere in the South Pacific. Álvaro de Mendaña de Neira anchored in Vaitahu Bay in 1595, followed by Captain Cook in 1774. Here too, Admiral Abel Dupetit-Thouars took possession of the Marquesas in 1842 and established a fort, despite strong resistance led by Chief Iotete. Today, it's a quiet settlement on the island's western coastline, home to most of the island's residents.

SIGHTS
Vaitahu
In Tahuata's main town, there's a small grocery store and a memorial of the 1842 battle between Admiral Abel Dupetit-Thouars and Chief Iotete. The **Town Hall** (9am-4pm Mon.-Fri., though hours are irregular) has an associated museum with a handful of sculptures and artifacts crafted and found on Tahuata. The museum opens on request and is free to enter. There are archaeological sites in the Vaitahu Valley, as well as the ruins from the fort—a relic from the confrontation. There's a craft market that opens when the *Aranui* is in town—if it's closed, you can ask around and stop by artists' homes to shop from their workshops. Tahuatan artists are particularly known for their bone work, with scrimshaw, hooks, and jewelry commonly sold.

The **Catholic Church of Vaitahu** (free) was completed in 1988 to mark the 150th anniversary of the arrival of the first missionaries. It has the largest stained-glass window in the territory, depicting Mary and Jesus surrounded by breadfruit trees. Local sculptor Damien Haturau carved the wooden statue of Virgin and Child above the church entrance from a 400-year-old tamanu tree. In front of the church, there's a display of tikis carved from each of the main Marquesan islands.

Hapatoni
Southwest Tahuata
Hapatoni is a village of artists just south of Vaitahu. A tamanu-bordered road that dates back over a century leads to petroglyphs in the Hanatahu Valley. When tour groups are around, artisans sell intricate art pieces made from shell, stone, wood, bone, and coral inside the community center. It's also a major site for sea salt production. On the edge of town is a Catholic Church thought to be built over

Tahuata

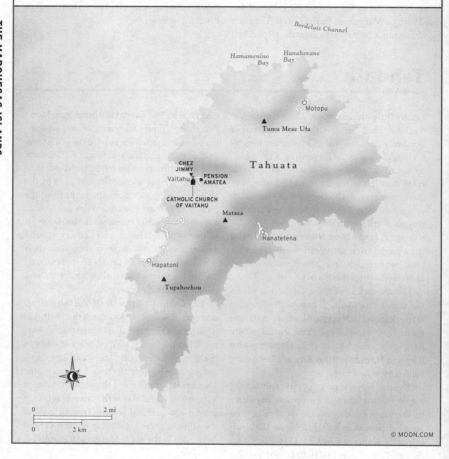

Bordelais Channel

Hamamenino Bay

Hanahevane Bay

Motopu

Tumu Meae Ufa

Tahuata

CHEZ JIMMY
Vaitahu
PENSION AMATEA
CATHOLIC CHURCH OF VAITAHU

Mataea

Hanatetena

Hapatoni

Tupahoehou

0   2 mi

0   2 km

© MOON.COM

an ancient Marquesan ceremonial site and cemetery.

BEACHES

HANAHEVANE BAY

North Tahuata

This crescent of golden sand framed by coconut trees is a popular spot for swimming and snorkeling on boat tours around Tahuata. It's common to spot sea turtles and manta rays in its calm waters. Like most bays on Tahuata, it's best accessed by boat.

HAMAMENINO BAY

North Tahuata

The sister bay to Hanahevane Bay, Hamamenino Bay is similarly peaceful with its own stretch of cookie-crumb sand and shade-worthy palms. The rocky crags bordering the bay make for decent snorkeling. It's accessible by boat only.

1: Catholic Church of Vaitahu 2: sea salt drying in Hapatoni

FOOD AND ACCOMMODATIONS

CHEZ JIMMY

Vaitahu; tel. 40 92 91 51; 8am-8pm daily; CFP 2,000

Plan to stay a while at Chez Jimmy, a casual snack with sand floors, a place to play pétanque, and a chef who commonly takes cooking breaks to dazzle guests with his singing and ukulele skills. Poisson cru, pork, goat curry, and simple side dishes are served here, usually alongside a pitcher of freshly squeezed citrus juice of some sort or a bottle of Hinano.

PENSION AMATEA

Vaitahu; tel. 40 92 92 84; pensionamatea@gmail. com; CFP 7,500/person half-board, CFP 10,000/ person full-board

In the shadow of Mount Amatea, Tahuata's largest mountain, Pension Amatea is basic but clean, with four rooms inside a main house, sharing two bathrooms with cold-water showers, a kitchen, and a living room. Meals are enjoyed together on a spacious terrace surrounded by tropical flowers. The hosts are happy to help arrange day trips and transport to Hiva Oa or Fatu Hiva.

GETTING THERE AND GETTING AROUND

There's no airport on Tahuata. Chartering a six-passenger boat to or from Atuona is around CFP 15,000-22,000 and takes about an hour. Small boats leave Hiva Oa for Tahuata almost daily, so ask around at the harbor on Takauku Bay near Atuona. There's also the **Te Ata O Hiva** shuttle boat (tel. 40 92 73 07; www.codim.pf) buzzing between Hiva Oa, Fatu Hiva, and Tahuata for CFP 2,500-4,000 per trip. Connection times are 1 hour for Hiva Oa-Tahuata, 3.5 hours for Tahuata-Fatu Hiva, and 3.5 hours for Fatu Hiva-Hiva Oa. The **Aranui** (tel. 40 42 62 42; www.aranui. com) also stops for a day in Tahuata on its Marquesas Islands itinerary.

Once you're on Tahuata, the settlements of Vaitahu and Hapatoni are largely walkable, but you'll need a boat to access any of Tahuata's main bays. Speed boats on Tahuata are somewhat informal, so you'll need to ask around. Expect to pay around CFP 35,000 per boat for a full day of use—usually able to accommodate around six passengers.

Fatu Hiva

Fatu Hiva is the most remote island of the Marquesas, reserved for the most intrepid of travelers. It's the southernmost and youngest of the Marquesas Islands, 56 kilometers (34 mi) southeast of Tahuata. It's far wetter than the northern islands, and the vegetation is lush. **Tauaouoho** (960 m/3,149 ft) is the highest point.

Fatu Hiva was the first of the Marquesas to be seen by Europeans (Mendaña passed by in 1595). None landed until 1825, and Catholic missionaries couldn't convert the inhabitants until 1877. With 587 inhabitants, Fatu Hiva has only two villages, **Omoa** and **Hanavave,** in the former volcanic crater on the western side of the island.

Hanavave has a basic shop and a church;

Omoa is tucked in the foothills in a valley ripe with mango, banana, papaya, and grapefruit trees. There's a Catholic church at its center, one pension, a magasin, and a black rock beach, though it's not ideal for swimming. There are petroglyphs near town, including a 2-meter-long etching of a fish, but you'll need a guide to find it.

Fatu Hiva is one of the last places in French Polynesia where tapa cloth is still widely made. Today a revival of the old crafts is taking place, and it's possible to buy painted tapa cloth as well as wooden sculptures, hats and mats woven from pandanus, and monoï oils made from coconut oil, gardenia, jasmine, and sandalwood.

Fatu Hiva doesn't have any nonos but has ample mosquitoes.

Fatu Hiva

HANAVAVE BAY

Hanavave

Fatu Hiva

Tauaouoho

Omoa

PENSION
CHEZ LIONEL

Point
Teae

0   2 mi

0   2 km

© MOON.COM

★ HANAVAVE BAY

Northwest Fatu Hiva

The view of Hanavave Bay, also called the "Bay of Virgins," is one of French Polynesia's most stunning landscapes. A crescent of golden sand is surrounded by tiki-shaped cliffs and palm-topped pinnacles. At sunset, the spires turn golden, and the sunlight illuminates the pom-poms of the palm trees, looking like sparklers. There's a **waterfall** about a 45-minute walk inland from the beach (ask locals for the trailhead, as the trail is unmarked). The waterfall has a small swimming pool below and a sheer cliff ledge where locals and yachties test their fear of heights—and reveal their bravado.

The first French sailors named the bay "Baie des Verges," or "Bay of Penises." The Catholic missionaries who followed quickly amended the name to "Baie des Vierges," "Bay of Virgins," because—they claimed— they resembled the silhouettes of veiled nuns.

Yachts usually anchor here, and there are horses and canoes for hire in the town of Hanavave.

boats on Fatu Hiva bay

FOOD AND ACCOMMODATIONS

PENSION CHEZ LIONEL

Omoa; tel. 78 70 03 71; chezlionel@mail.pf; CFP 9,500/bungalow including breakfast

Pension Chez Lionel is a family-run guesthouse with an old standalone bungalow with a kitchenette and (occasionally) warm-water shower. Neither Bernadette nor Lionel speak much English, but their friendliness and helpfulness transcends language barriers. Meals are usually served with fish Lionel has caught earlier that day. The common room has wooden sculptures on display for purchase. The room has a mosquito net, a double and single bed, and a fan.

GETTING THERE AND AROUND

There's no airstrip on Fatu Hiva, though the *Te Ata O Hiva* maritime shuttle ventures between Fatu Hiva, Tahuata, and Hiva Oa (tel. 40 92 73 07; www.codim.pf; CFP 2,500-4,000/one-way; 1 hour Hiva Oa-Tahuata, 3.5 hours Tahuata-Fatu Hiva, 3.5 hours Fatu Hiva-Hiva Oa. The *Aranui* (tel. 40 42 62 42; www.aranui.com) also stops at Fatu Hiva.

A steep and windy 16-kilometer (10-mi) road connects Hanavave and Omoa. It's walkable for avid hikers, but don't expect regular vehicles to come along if you want to hitchhike. Most people get around the island by boat on trips starting at CFP 4,000/person, arranged through your accommodation.

The Austral Islands

The seldom-visited Austral Islands are some of the most remote in the world, and their isolation only adds to their allure.

Venture here to witness humpback whales cruising in the islands' deep waters, trek along an overgrown trail to a singular lookout point, crawl through caves studded with stalactites and stalagmites, and then head to a cozy guesthouse for a home-cooked meal. These islands are free from tourist traps, offering intimate experiences at every turn. Beaches on the Austral Islands range from narrow wisps of coarse coral to palm-lined sugar-sand beaches. Perhaps the most exciting, however, are its rose-colored beaches that look bubblegum pink under direct sunlight.

Highlights

Look for ★ to find recommended sights, activities, dining, and lodging.

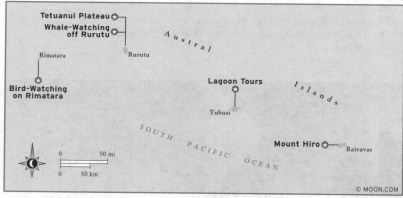

© MOON.COM

★ **Tetuanui Plateau:** Trek to the top of Rurutu's plateau for panoramic views of the island—with a chance to see whales in the distance (page 312).

★ **Whale-watching off Rurutu:** Spot and swim with humpback whales, who migrate along the island's coastline (page 312).

★ **Lagoon tours:** Try your hand at paddling a traditional outrigger canoe in the calm waters of Tubuai (page 319).

★ **Mount Hiro:** The trail to the top of Mount Hiro is arduous, but it's all forgotten as soon as you see the view from above (page 325).

★ **Bird-watching on Rimatara:** Peer into the treetops to spot the bright green and red plumage of the rare Rimatara lorikeet (page 329).

The inhabited volcanic islands of Rimatara, Rurutu, Tubuai, Raivavae, and Rapa, plus uninhabited atolls Marotiri and Maria (or Hull), make up the Austral group. This southernmost island chain in the South Pacific is a 1,280-kilometer (795-mi) extension of the same submerged mountain range as the southern Cook Islands, 900 kilometers (559 mi) northwest. The islands of the Australs seldom exceed 300 meters (984 ft) in height, except Rapa, which soars to 650 meters (2,132 ft). The southerly location makes these islands notably cooler and drier than Tahiti. Collectively the Australs are known as Tuhaa Pae, the "Fifth Part," or fifth administrative subdivision, of French Polynesia.

The 6,800 mostly Polynesian inhabitants are fishers and farmers who live in attractive villages with homes and churches built of coral limestone. The local himene, or hymn singing, is the soundtrack to the islands and mesmerizing to hear. The rich soil and moderate climate make this a great place to grow crops including taro, manioc, and coffee. The coconut palm also thrives here.

There's good hiking on all the islands, either along the lonely coastal roads or into the interior on tracks and trails used by residents. In addition to the good views, hidden caves and archaeological sites await the explorer, though these are usually overgrown and best found with the help of a friendly guide.

GETTING THERE
Air
The Austral Islands are some of the most challenging to reach due to their distance and relative lack of tourism. Flights are infrequent and often book out well in advance, especially during French Polynesian holidays. **Air Tahiti** (tel. 40 86 42 42; airtahiti.com) offers flights to Rurutu, Tubuai, Raivavae, and Rimatara. There are one-stop and nonstop flights from Papeete to Rurutu four days per week (1 hour 30 minutes; CFP 32,500/one-way), Tubuai five days per week (1 hour 40 minutes; CFP 36,000/one-way), and Raivavae three days per week (2 hours; CFP 38,800/one-way).

The Air Tahiti Multi-Islands Pass is the most economical way to fly to multiple islands and covers all four islands starting and ending in Papeete. Pass prices differ from high-season (June 1-Oct. 31 and Dec. 11-Jan. 10) and low-season (Apr. 1-May 31, Nov. 1-Dec. 10, Jan. 11-Mar. 31). All passes include 50 pounds of luggage; you must visit a minimum of two islands to use the pass.

• **Austral Pass:** Must be used within 28 days; low season €602/adult, €484/child; high season €651/adult, €522/child

• **Austral Extension:** Must be used as an extension to one of the main Air Tahiti Multi-Islands Passes; low season €365/adult, €294/child; high season €394/adult, €317/child

Ferry
The passenger freighter **Tuhaa Pae IV** (tel. 40 41 36 06; www.snathp.com, info@snathp.com; 7:30am-4pm Mon.-Thurs., 7:30am-2:30pm Fri.) departs from the Papeete Ferry Terminal to the Austral Islands about 2-3 times per month, and to Rapa once per month (currently the only way to reach Rapa, as there is no airstrip on the island). Trips take around 10 days from Papeete to round the islands, and it's about a full day of travel in between each island. Tickets are sold for the entire trip (Classic trip: Rimatara, Rurutu, Tubuai, Raivavae; Grand tour: Rimatara, Rurutu, Tubuai, Rapa, Raivavae) or for one leg (from CFP 5,500). The ferry departs in the afternoons at each island and arrives at each destination in the morning, taking one or two nights depending on the distance.

There are four cabin types onboard, all air-conditioned. The Admiral cabin (CFP

Previous: The jagged interior of Raivavae is where you'll find Mount Hiro; Raivavae's ultra-clear lagoon; Raivavae's tiki.

The Austral Islands

SOUTH

Maria

A u s t r a l

SEE "RIMATARA" MAP

Rimatara

SEE "RURUTU" MAP

TETUANUI PLATEAU

Rurutu

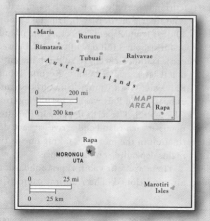

Maria

Rurutu

Rimatara

Tubuai

Raivavae

A u s t r a l   I s l a n d s

| 0 | 200 mi |
| 0 | 200 km |

MAP AREA

Rapa

Rapa

MORONGU UTA

| 0 | 25 mi |
| 0 | 25 km |

Marotiri Isles

© MOON.COM

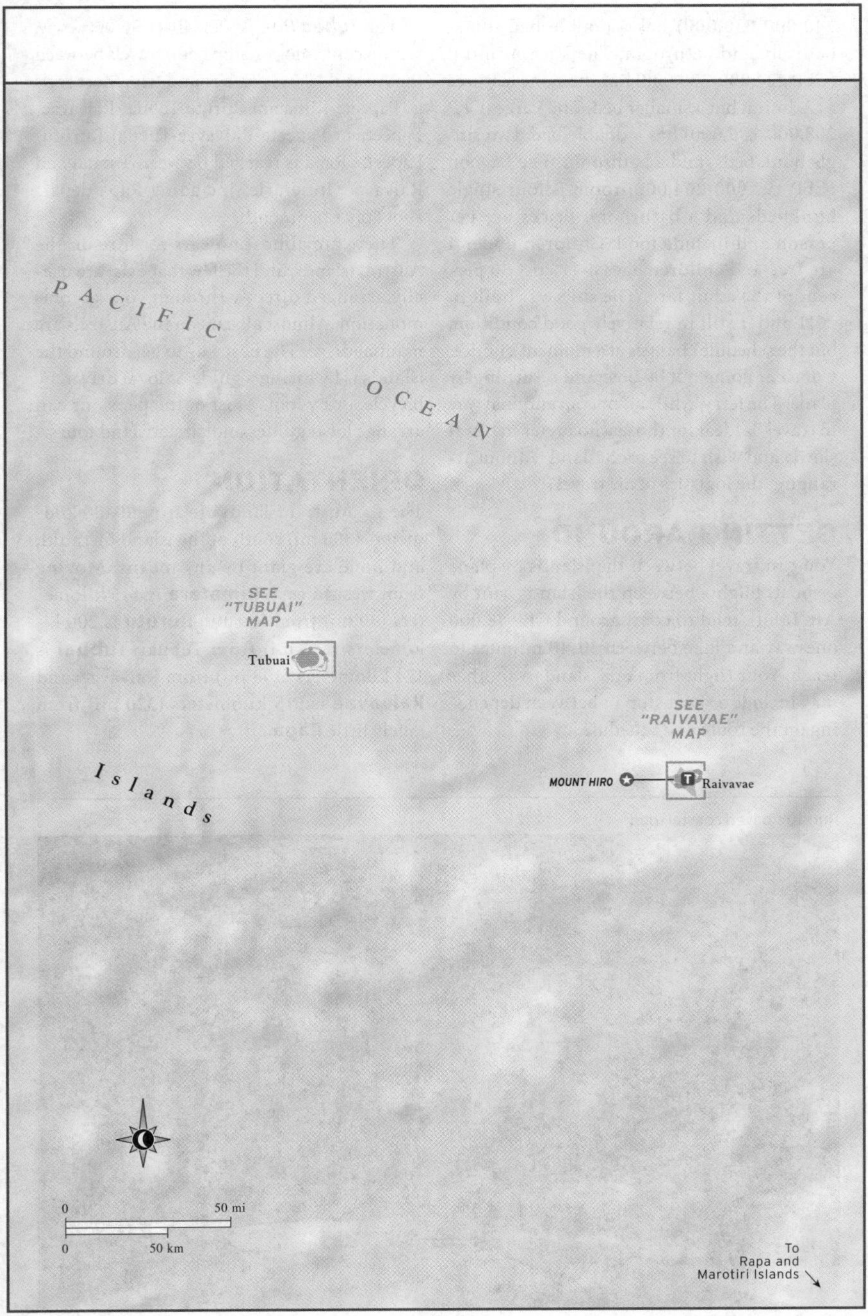

P A C I F I C

O C E A N

SEE
"TUBUAI"
MAP

Tubuai

SEE
"RAIVAVAE"
MAP

MOUNT HIRO ✛   T Raivavae

I s l a n d s

0   50 mi

0   50 km

To
Rapa and
Marotiri Islands

240,000-330,000) has a double bed, desk, bathtub, and bathroom. The Vice Admiral (CFP 224,000-308,000) has the same features as Admiral but a smaller bed. The Large (CFP 208,000-286,000) has a double bed, two single bunk beds, and a bathroom. The Lagoon (CFP 192,000-264,000) room is four single bunkbeds and a bathroom. Prices are per person and include food. Children under 4 are free and children ages 4-17 cost 50 percent of the adult fare. The ship was built in 2011 and is still in relatively good condition, but the schedule changes at a moment's notice. Consider going out by boat and returning by plane. The ferry, while an unconventional way to travel, is ideal for those who prefer to travel slowly and wish to see each island without arranging the logistics of air travel.

GETTING AROUND

You can travel between the islands by plane or boat. Flights between the islands, run by Air Tahiti, tend to coast around CFP 18,000 one-way and take between 30-40 minutes to reach. Your flight from one island to another may include a short stop in between depending on the route and schedule.

The **Tuhaa Pae IV** (tel. 40 41 36 06; www. snathp.com, info@snathp.com) travels between the Austral Islands on a round trip. Most trips go Papeete-Rimatara-Rurutu-Tubuai-Raivavae-Papeete or Papeete-Raivavae-Tubuai-Rurutu-Papeete. Rapa is reached between Tubuai and Raivavae. Itineraries including Rapa depart about once per month.

There are almost no cars for hire on the Austral Islands, and the few that exist are usually arranged directly through your accommodation. Almost all cars on the Australs are manual drive. The best way to get around the islands is by hiring a guide or local driver, by bicycle, or by foot. Most of the pensions can arrange local guides and circle-island tours.

ORIENTATION

The six Austral Islands are around 480 kilometers (300 mi) south of the island of Tahiti, and none are giant by any means. Moving from west to east, **Rimatara** is 145 kilometers (90 mi) from Rurutu; **Rurutu** is 200 kilometers (125 mi) from Tubuai; **Tubuai** is 174 kilometers (108 mi) from Raivavae; and **Raivavae** is 515 kilometers (320 mi) from lonely little **Rapa.**

Rurutu's paved coastal road

PLANNING YOUR TIME

The best time to visit is during the dry season, from May-October; humpback whales are present July-October. The islands can be seen in about 2-3 days each if you stay busy. Their small size makes them convenient to explore on a guided tour. A good rule of thumb for each island is to spend one day in the water and another on land to get a well-rounded experience. When planning your trip here, prioritize accommodation quality—you'll likely be reliant on your accommodation for food, tours, activities, and local transportation.

The strict flight schedule of inter-Austral flights makes it a challenge to be spontaneous, and its best to arrange your transport before you arrive. It's also worth booking your flights to the Austral Islands first, and slotting in your flights to the other more popular islands, where flights tend to be more regular, later. If you want to see all islands aside from Rapa, there's a 10-day itinerary you can follow with either the Austral Pass or Austral Extension Air Tahiti Multi-Islands Pass. Fly Papeete-Raivavae on Monday, Raivavae-Tubuai on Wednesday, Tubuai-Rurutu on Friday, Rurutu-Rimatara on Monday, and finally Rimatara-Papeete on Wednesday.

Cash is king in the Austral Islands, and ATMs are prone to running out (or suffering from card reader errors). Internet is also not consistent throughout the islands, though you'll usually find spotty service in each island's main towns.

Itinerary Ideas

RURUTU IN A DAY

If it's whale-watching season (July-Oct.), don't miss a whale-watching excursion for a chance to see humpback whales migrating along the coastline. For this land-based itinerary, you will need to hire a car or guide.

1 After breakfast at your pension, drive to **Mauo Point** for a short cave walk.

2 With a guide, walk to **Ana Taupe'e Cave,** which is said to resemble a dragon's head. There's a little beach to explore further down the path.

3 Enjoy a picnic lunch or a plate of fresh fish at **Snack Piareare.**

4 Take a longer hike to **Tetuanui Plateau** for panoramic views of Rurutu.

5 Spend the evening enjoying dinner at **Restaurant Tiare Hinano** or at your accommodation.

RAIVAVAE IN A DAY

Experienced hikers should spend the day trekking to the top of **Mount Hiro,** one of the best hikes in French Polynesia. Otherwise, these are the sights not to miss. You'll need some form of transportation (a car or bike) and/or a guide for the afternoon activities.

1 After breakfast at your pension, throw on your swimwear, pack your snorkeling gear, and embark on a tour of the **Raivavae lagoon.** Request a stop at Motu Vaiamanu, a motu with a white sand sandbank and shaded beaches.

2 When the morning excursion is done, grab lunch at your pension and change into dry clothes. Then drive to **Marae Pomoavao** to see one of the few remaining marae on the island.

Itinerary Ideas

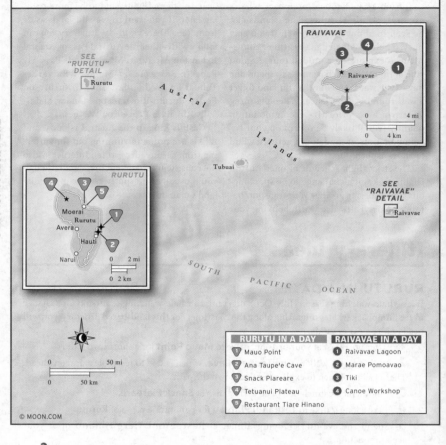

RURUTU IN A DAY
1. Mauo Point
2. Ana Taupe'e Cave
3. Snack Piareare
4. Tetuanui Plateau
5. Restaurant Tiare Hinano

RAIVAVAE IN A DAY
1. Raivavae Lagoon
2. Marae Pomoavao
3. Tiki
4. Canoe Workshop

© MOON.COM

3 Next, venture 8 kilometers (5 mi) north to see the **tiki,** a human figure made from stone, of Raivavae.

4 Drive or cycle 3 kilometers (1.8 mi) east to the **canoe workshop** in Anatonu to see sculptors whittling at wooden outrigger canoes and paddles, then enjoy a relaxing dinner at your accommodation.

The Austral Islands at a Glance

Island	Why Go	How to Get There
Rurutu (page 307)	Take to the seas to spot humpback whales, explore the island's intricate cave system, and witness some of the region's best artists at work.	*Air:* From Papeete four days per week (1 hour 30 minutes, CFP 32,500/one-way). *Ferry:* From Tubuai (2 nights, CFP 13,900) and Rimatara (1 night, CFP 5,500).
Tubuai (page 316)	Lounge on white sand motu, swim in an aquamarine lagoon, and step back in time at some of the archipelago's most sacred archeological sites.	*Air:* From Papeete five days per week (1 hour 40 minutes, CFP 36,000/one-way). *Ferry:* From Rurutu (2 nights, CFP 13,900) from and Raivavae (1 night, CFP 5,900).
Raivavae (page 323)	There are few islands more stunning—a jagged island surrounded by sandy motu. Paddle an outrigger canoe across its sweeping lagoon.	*Air:* From Papeete three days per week (2 hours, CFP 38,800/one-way). *Ferry:* From Papeete (2 nights, CFP 16,000) and Tubuai (1 night, CFP 5,900).
Rimatara (page 328)	A polka dot of an island, Rimatara is where you'll see vini, an endangered lime green lorikeet.	*Air:* From Papeete (1 hour 25 minutes, CFP 30,000/ one-way), Rimatara (35 minutes, CFP 12,000/one-way), and Tubuai (40 minutes, CFP 15,000/one-way). *Ferry:* From Papeete (2 nights, CFP 15,400) and Rurutu (1 night, CFP 5,950).
Rapa (page 330)	One of the most remote islands in the world, Rapa is as wild as it gets when it comes to natural splendor.	*Ferry:* From Tubuai (2 nights, CFP 14,000) and Raivavae (2 nights, CFP 14,000)

Rurutu

This island, 565 kilometers (350 mi) south of Tahiti, is shaped like a miniature replica of the African continent. It's the most visited of the Australs, but that's no reason to expect a crowd. Rurutu is estimated to be 11 million years old, and it would normally have eroded to sea level except that 4 million years ago it was uplifted by the movement of tectonic plates. This history accounts for the juxtaposition of coastal coral cliffs with volcanic interior hills.

For the hiker, 32-square-kilometer (12-square-mi) Rurutu is a varied island to explore. Grassy, fern-covered **Taati'oe** (approx. 389 m/1,276 ft) and **Manureva** (384 m/1,259 ft) are the highest peaks, and coastal cliffs on the southeast side of the island drop 30 meters (98 ft) to the sea in between white sand

Rurutu

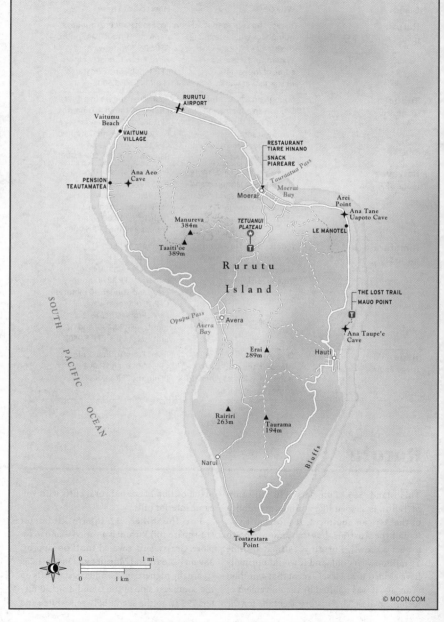

RURUTU AIRPORT

Vaitumu Beach

VAITUMU VILLAGE

RESTAURANT TIARE HINANO

SNACK PIAREARE

Ana Aeo Cave

Tauraatua Pass

PENSION TEAUTAMATEA

Moerai

Moerai Bay

Arei Point

Ana Tane Uapoto Cave

Manureva 384m

TETUANUI PLATEAU

LE MANOTEL

Taaiti'oe 389m

R u r u t u

Island

THE LOST TRAIL

MAUO POINT

Opupu Pass

Avera Bay

Avera

Ana Taupe'e Cave

Erai 289m

Hauti

SOUTH

PACIFIC

OCEAN

Rairiri 263m

Taurama 194m

Bluffs

Narui

Toataratara Point

0   1 mi

0   1 km

Austral Island Festivals

If you're lucky enough to visit one of the Austral Islands during a festival, you'll be in for an immersive cultural experience. No matter which one you attend, there's bound to be food, décor, music, song, and dancing.

TERE A'AITI

This festival usually takes place in the first two months of the year on the Austral Islands. Residents visit marae and walk from village to village, telling legends and stories of their ancestors to preserve the island's shared history. It's also meant to foster relationships, as everyone tends to see everyone on this day, bringing in the new year as a community. Those who don't want to walk can hop in one of the elaborately decorated cars shuttling attendees from site to site. Don't be alarmed if you leave covered in white dust—throwing talcum powder and monoï oil is part of the celebration. Like other celebrations in the Austral Islands, attendees are often challenged to lift stones as heavy as themselves.

Locals test their strength at a festival that involves carrying stones.

AMORAA OFAI

In January and July, Rurutuans practice the ancient art of stone lifting, or amoraa ofai. Men get three tries to hoist a 150-kilogram (330-lb) boulder coated with monoï oil up onto their shoulders, while women attempt a 60-kilogram (130-lb) stone. Dancing and feasting follow the event, and the women of Rurutu weave fine pandanus hats, bags, baskets, fans, lamp shades, and mats to sell.

beaches. A narrow fringing reef surrounds Rurutu, but there's no lagoon. The climate of this northernmost Austral Island is temperate and dry.

The word "Rurutu" means "standing together," and this sentiment is felt every time you hear a greeting or are offered a heap of fresh fruit picked right from a personal garden. Neat fences and flower gardens surround the coral limestone houses. This is the Polynesia of 50 years ago. The few pensions and snack bars on the island offer no-rush hospitality, creating a sense of familiarity and ease shortly after you arrive.

Almost all sights on Rurutu are natural ones. Beaches, waterfalls, valleys, and bluffs beckon the undaunted explorer. "Ana" means "caves" in Rurutu, and there are about 30 of them on the island. Many are unmarked, so it's best to go with a guide if you're keen to discover the more offbeat ones. Intrepid travelers

can even be led down chasms tens of meters below the land's surface to freshwater pools, an adventure that's bound to be both eerie and exciting.

ORIENTATION

The pleasant main village, **Moerai,** on the northeast side of the island, hosts a post office, a medical center, a handful of shops and bakeries, a car rental, and a bank. Two other villages, Avera and Hauti, bring the total island population to about 2,500. Each village is relatively quiet, filled with fruit trees and fragrant tropical gardens. Moving clockwise, **Arei Point** is 2 kilometers (1.2 mi) south of Moerai with the caves of **Mauo Point** 2 kilometers (1.2 mi) farther south on the eastern coast. **Hauti** is close by, 2 kilometers (1.2 mi) south of Mauo Point. Due west, **Avera** is 4 kilometers (2.5 mi) from Moerai on the inland road, flanked by Avera Bay. The **port** is found in Moerai, and Rurutu's **airport** is on the northernmost point of the island, 3 kilometers (1.8 mi) north of Moerai.

CAVES

ANA TANE UAPOTO CAVE
Moerai; free

The Ana Tane Uapoto Cave is one of the few easily accessible caves on the island, found just off the roadside near Arei Point. A staircase leads to the cave opening, from where you can admire views of the ocean. Gargantuan stalactites and stalagmites reach toward one another like disconnected pillars, opening to a grand balcony perched above the sea.

ANA TAUPE'E CAVE
Accessed from Mauo Point Trail/Lost Trail, 5 km (3 mi) south of Moerai; free

The Ana Taupe'e Cave is the most famous of all Rurutu's caves. Mysterious and a little creepy, this cave is nicknamed "Monster's Cave"; from afar, it looks like the profile of a dragon, with stalactites and stalagmites forming the creature's teeth. Travelers can venture inside the cave, but it's a tight squeeze in between the limestone walls. A short but steep and rocky trail leads from the cave to a white sand beach. This is one of a few fairytale-esque caves accessed from the trail from **Mauo Point** sometimes called the **Lost Trail.** This is best done with a guide who can share the enthralling myths and legends associated with the sights here.

ANA AEO CAVE
Near Vaitumu Village

The large 15-meter-high (49-ft-high) Ana Aeo Cave is a natural amphitheater replete with stalactites and stalagmites; sunbeams shine in from the holes above. Some residents call this cave Mitterrand Cave, as a song and dance performance took place here for the late French president during his visit here in 1990.

BEACHES

There are few beaches to explore on Rurutu, as vegetation and limestone fronts the water. But, there are a few wisps of white sand to enjoy for those who want to lounge the day away. None of the beaches on Rurutu have public amenities like showers, drinking water, or food, so come prepared.

TOATARATARA POINT BEACH
Southernmost point of Rurutu; free

To explore Rurutu's best beaches, start at Toataratara Point, the southernmost point of the island, and a great place to watch whales in the distance July-October. Head 200 meters (656 ft) east of the point along the main road to access a string of white sand beaches spanning along the eastern side of the island. At low tide, the water is too shallow to swim in, but there's plenty of space to lounge around. Come mid-to-high tide to wade and snorkel.

VAITUMU BEACH
Northwest Rurutu; free

A white sand beach wraps like a crescent along the northwestern edge of Rurutu from the airport to Vaitumu Village. It's rarely crowded, and access is found at both the eastern and western edges of the airport on unmarked roads. There's enough room to spread out, and the western end makes for a great sunset spot. The seabed is a bit sharp and shallow for snorkeling.

HIKING

THE LOST TRAIL

Distance: *2 km (1.2 mi) out-and-back*
Time: *2 hours*
Trailhead: *Mauo Point*
Information and maps: *whympr.com/en/ route/7363-mauo-point-rurutu-iles-australes-le-sentier-perdu*

A walking trail starts at Mauo Point and spans south along Rurutu's eastern coastline, leading to jagged seaside caves rife with limestone stalactities and stalagmites. There's a distinct sense of coolness felt once you walk from a sunsoaked beach into a damp, chilled cave. It's the best way to reach Rurutu's most beloved

---

1: Ana Taupe'e Cave 2: beach on Rurutu

(and legendary) cave, the Ana Taupe'e Cave, which resembles a monster's face. Though the trail isn't exactly strenuous, you'll want proper shoes as it's rife with sharp edges. A guide arranged through your accommodation is recommended.

★ TETUANUI PLATEAU

Distance: *5 km (3 mi) out-and-back*
Time: *2.5 hours*
Trailhead: *Trail begins midway between Moerai-Avera road*
Information and maps: *www.vttour.fr/sorties/ plateau-de-tetuanui-noel-dans-les-australes-un- poutou-de-rurutu,10951.html*

A walking trail links Rurutu's northern end to the southeastern corner of the island, with many other trails branching out in between. From the middle of the Moerai-Avera road, a white sign displaying "Mont Manureva" marks the trailhead to the Tetuanui Plateau. A 1-kilometer (0.6 mi) walk on a wide trail leads to the first stop, the peak of **Mount Manureva** (384 m/1,259 ft). Basic picnic benches with shade await a weary traveler, and views span to the island's coastline—with especially pretty ones of Avera Bay. If the whales are around, you'll often see their splashes from this point. Half a kilometer farther is **Taati'oe** (389 m/1,276 ft), and a few hundred meters further is **Te'ape** (369 m/1,210 ft). To reach the **Tetuanui Plateau,** trek around another 2 kilometers (1.2 mi) north. The view from the plateau reveals views of Moerai. You can continue hiking east to reach the town of Moerai, making it a through-hike rather than an out-and-back.

TOP EXPERIENCE

★ WHALE-WATCHING

Humpback whales venture to Rurutu from July-October, making it one of the best places in French Polynesia to witness these impressive mammals in their natural habitat. It's common to see them breach, slap their fins across the water, and race one another. If you're in the water with a male whale, you

may be lucky enough to hear a haunting song. To see these creatures rise from the sea, five-meter fins flapping at their sides, is truly spectacular. Several companies now operate regular whale-watching trips at Rurutu from July-October. Whale sightings are not guaranteed, but the longer you spend in Rurutu, the higher chances are that you'll see them.

If this is the number-one activity on your list, book it for the beginning of your stay so you can venture out again the next day if your first day is a miss. The waters around Rurutu can be rough for boating this time of year, so plan accordingly with anti-seasickness medication if you're prone to feeling woozy. Whale-swimming groups tend to be small—around eight people maximum—making it a more intimate experience than you'll find on Moorea.

RAIE MANTA CLUB

Transport included; tel. 87 72 31 45; www. raiemantaclub.com; trips at 9am and 2pm; CFP 12,000/person

Whale-watching and swimming tours usually take place twice per day, depending on ocean conditions, during September each year. Tours run about four hours long. Snorkeling equipment is provided, and swims take place from a 27-foot 200-horsepower boat. The tour takes seven people at a time, ages 12 and up. Yves Lefèvre, the owner of Raie Manta Club, often leads the tours; he has dived with the likes of Jacques Cousteau, and has clocked in around 30 years of experience swimming with whales in Rurutu.

TAREPAREPA BALEINES

Tel. 87 79 48 86; tavita.gisele@mail.pf; trips usually in the morning; CPF 11,000/person

Tareparepa Baleines was the first tour operator to offer excursions to swim with whales on Rurutu; trips usually take place from July-early October. Four-hour tours are led by Herve, who has been leading whale swims for over a decade and has a strong ability to read whale behavior—he only allows tourists to swim with whales who are receptive to humans. Snorkeling equipment is provided, but

A Long Journey: Humpback Whale Migration through French Polynesia

Rurutu is one of the best places to see whales migrating through the South Pacific.

Humpback whales are one of the ocean's most powerful mammals, distinguished by their stubby, hump-shaped dorsal fin. The females can grow to over 15 meters (49 ft) in length and males can grow to around 14 meters (45 ft) in length. Calves are usually born around five meters (16 ft) long. Every year, humpback whales migrate from the frigid nutrient-rich waters of Antarctica to warmer waters with fewer predators, like those found in French Polynesia.

WINTERING IN ANTARCTICA

In the Austral summer (November-March), humpback whales feed in the nutrient-dense waters of Antarctica, where they can consume over 1,000 kilograms (2,200 lbs) of krill and small fish per day. Their main priority during these seasons is gaining enough fat to sustain their migration, during which they hardly eat at all.

MIGRATION TO THE TROPICS

Around late April-May, pregnant humpacks are the first to migrate to the tropics, where they will give birth and arrive in French Polynesia starting in early June, covering over 6,400 kilometers (4,000 mi) from Antarctica to Polynesia. The pregnant whales give birth shortly after arriving; the shallow, clear water provides a safe place for newborns to grow with a lower risk of predation. The pregnant whales are followed by non-pregnant females, males, and juvenile whales.

BREEDING AND RETURN SOUTH

August is when most whales will have arrived to French Polynesia and breeding takes place. Bulls will compete against one another in heat runs to mate with a female, and often sing, presumably to lure females to mate. Meanwhile, the newborn calves are gaining strength for their migration to Antarctica.

RETURN SOUTH

Typically, solo females and males are the first to leave French Polynesia, followed by juveniles, mothers, and their calves. Some male whales will stay with a mother and her calf, and are known as an escort whale. By October, almost all whales will have returned to Antarctica. The gestation period for a humpback whale pregnancy is just over 11 months, so whales who become pregnant in French Polynesia will return the next year around the same time to give birth in the same region.

sizes are limited so it's best to bring your own. Transportation from your accommodation is included.

TOATAI WHALES

Tel. 40 94 04 23; trip times vary; CFP 9,500/person
When this boat isn't out fishing for dogtooth tuna, snapper, and giant trevally, you can tag along if they're offering whale-swim tours. Trips tend to last around 3-4 hours and only take small groups. Snorkeling gear is limited, so it's best to bring your own. Transportation from your accommodation is included.

FOOD

Food on Rurutu is limited outside of the accommodations, and it's not common for non-guests to eat at hotel restaurants. Most meals are simple but delicious, often seafood and vegetables. Small shops selling limited produce and pantry goods are found in Moerai, Avera, and Hauti.

SNACK PIAREARE

Moerai; tel. 40 94 04 95; 11:30am-2pm Mon.-Fri., 5-9pm Sun.; CFP 1,300
This simple snack near the port of Moerai serves heaping plates of poisson cru, sashimi, grilled fish with rice, fries, or vegetables, and a few pork dishes. The menu changes depending on what's in the back, with the best dishes often selling out before 1:30pm.

RESTAURANT TIARE HINANO

Moerai; tel. 87 70 12 05; 10:30am-2pm and 5pm-8pm Tues.-Sat., 5-8pm Sun.; CFP 1,400
Restaurant Tiare Hinano is set near the seafront of Moerai and has a mix of Chinese and Polynesian specialties on the menu. Salted fish and rice, pork with a sweet and sour sauce, braised beef, and poisson cru are mealtime staples here. The inside seating area is air-conditioned, a reason to visit in itself.

ACCOMMODATIONS

It's wise to leave the stress of searching for food on the island behind and opt in for a full- or half-board inclusion with your stay.

★ VAITUMU VILLAGE

North Rurutu near the airport; tel. 40 94 02 42; vaitumuvillage.com; CFP 9,000-11,000/night
Lullabies of the lapping-wave variety will be the soundtrack of your stay at Vaitumu Village, a lodge-like guesthouse with fruit trees and tropical flowers tucked in between its seven standalone bungalows. Each thatched-roof bungalow has a mosquito net, fan, private bathroom, and enough sleeping space for three. The front of the property is flanked by a sandy beach, and a family farm is found at the back. Hosts can help arrange day tours, guided hikes, car rentals, quad rides, cultural workshops, and whale swims.

PENSION TEAUTAMATEA

North Rurutu near Vaitumu Village; tel. 40 93 02 93; www.teautamatea.blogspot.com; CFP 9,870/night per person, CFP 15,100/night two people includes half-board (breakfast and dinner) and transfer
Pension Teautamatea is a cute family-owned pension just a few steps away from a white sand beach with shallow waters idyllic for wading. Next to the property are fields of taro, a coconut grove, and the marae Tararoa, a sacred site once used for ceremonies. It has some of the best food of all the pensions on the island, with enough variety to satisfy longer stays, and hosts a traditional Rurutu meal, an ahi ma'a, on Sundays with fresh seafood, pork cooked in taro leaves, poisson cru, steamed breadfruit, and fresh fruits (CFP 3,500/person). Hosts can arrange whale swims (CFP 9,000/person), island tours (CFP 6,500/person), horseback riding (CFP 7,500/person), and custom tours on request.

★ LE MANOTEL

3 km (1.8 mi) south of Moerai; tel. 40 930 225; www.le-manotel.com; CFP 16,800-19,96/double includes half-board (breakfast and dinner) and transfer
Le Manotel is a family-owned lodge opposite a sandy beach 6 kilometers (3.7 mi) from the airport on Rurutu's east coast. Each of the six simply decorated, standalone bungalows can sleep up to three and is equipped with a fan, en suite bathroom with solar hot-water

shower, and private terrace. WiFi works in the communal area, and a manicured garden around the property adds to the serenity. The **restaurant** is open for breakfast and dinner, and there's a decently equipped bar attached.

This is one of the best places to stay if you plan to be on the go. Le Manotel can arrange a 4x4 safari tour (CFP 6,000/person), hiking (CFP 3,500/person), horseback riding (CFP 5,000/person), cave tours (CFP 2,000/person), and fishing trips (CFP 5,000/person). You can usually receive a discount on your room here if staying more than four nights.

INFORMATION AND SERVICES

Rurutu has a handful of convenience shops selling groceries and toiletries in the towns of Moerai, Hauti, and Avera. If you need anything specific, like medications or dietary supplements, you should bring it with you. Most goods and services are available in Moerai.

- **Banque Socredo:** Moerai; tel. 40 94 04 75; socredo.pf; 8am-noon and 1:30pm-4pm Mon.-Fri.
- **Gendarmerie:** Moerai; tel. 40 93 02 05; service-public.fr; 7am-noon and 2pm-5pm Mon.-Fri., 8am-noon and 3pm-5pm Sat., 9am-2pm and 3pm-5pm Sun.
- **Medical Center:** Moerai; tel. 40 93 04 40; 7am-noon Mon.-Fri.

GETTING THERE

The most practical way to get to Rurutu is by air, though it's also possible to get here by boat.

Air

Air Tahiti offers direct flights between Rurutu and Papeete four days per week (1 hour 25 minutes, CFP 30,000/one-way), Rurutu and Rimatara twice per week (35 minutes, CFP 12,000/one-way), and Rurutu and Tubuai three times per week (40 minutes, CFP 15,000/one-way).

RURUTU AIRPORT

North Rurutu; tel. 40 93 02 50; hours dependent on flight schedule
All Air Tahiti flights arrive at the small landing strip on the northern end of the island. The airport hosts just around 20,000 visitors per year, and has little more than a waiting area and snack station.

Ferry

The **Tuhaa Pae IV** (tel. 40 41 36 06; www. snathp.com, info@snathp.com) stops in Rurutu around three times per month in between Tubuai (2 nights, CFP 13,900) and Rimatara (1 night, CFP 5,500). Ferries arrive at the port found on the northeast coast near Moerai.

GETTING AROUND

Once you're on the island, there are limited car rental options available—the best way to get around is on a guided tour, by bicycle, or on foot. Most accommodations include transport to and from the airport in their nightly rate, and are happy to help arrange one-off transportation for an extra cost. Public transportation is lacking on the 36-kilometer (22-mi) road around Rurutu.

Thanks to Rurutu's small size, it's not an intimidating island to explore on foot or with a bicycle if you don't mind a bit of incline.

Car

Having a rental car is the easiest way to get around the island, but they're hard to come by. You can try hiring one through your accommodation or from **Magasin Sinn** in Moerai (tel. 40 94 07 29), which also has a handful of quads, four-wheeled all-terrain vehicles, for rent. Prices start at around CFP 10,000/day for their smallest vehicle. It's often more economical to book in with a day tour arranged by your accommodation. It takes about an hour to drive a lap around the island with no stops. The coastal road is well-paved, with some narrow bridges flanking the edges of caves and teetering over water. The inland road is also well kept, and any vehicle should easily get you across. Many locals are superstitious about driving at night, believing evil tupapa'u, spirits, to inhabit the roads come nightfall. Because of this, Rurutu's roads are eerily empty after sunset.

Bike

By bicycle it can be quite an effort to circle the island, as the route climbs away from the coast on four occasions to avoid high cliffs. Some pensions have bicycles for rent for around CFP 1,500 per day, though most don't. There is no bicycle lane anywhere on the island, and some parts of the road are incredibly narrow. Fortunately, the roads of Rurutu are rarely crowded, and you'll likely find large stretches of it all to yourself. Riding a lap around the island makes for an exciting half-day trip. Because vehicles are often hard to come by, a bicycle is key to freedom for those who wish to explore uninhibited.

Tour

Most pensions can arrange a full-day circle island tour of Rurutu, stopping at roadside caves. A trip usually costs CFP 6,000 per person, not including snacks, meals, or drinks. If your pension cannot arrange a tour, contact Viriamu at **Pension Teautamatea** (tel. 40 93 02 93; pension.teautamatea@mail.pf).

On Foot

For hikers, a 3-kilometer (1.8-mi) foot trail across the center of the island between Avera and Hauti makes a variety of itineraries possible. The well-kept inland road connecting the towns of Moerai and Avera acts as a connecting point to trails elsewhere on the island. Many of the residents get around on horseback, which helps keep many trails from getting too overgrown. Alltrails.com has basic trail maps of Rurutu. The coastal road around Rurutu is narrow but uncrowded, easily trekked on foot for those who don't mind covering large distances (around 5 km/3 mi) between each village.

Tubuai

Ten-kilometer-long by five-kilometer-wide (6-mi-long by 3-mi-wide) Tubuai, largest of the Australs, is 643 kilometers (400 km) south of Tahiti. Hills on the east and west sides of this oval 45-square-kilometer (17-square-mi) island are joined by lowland in the middle; when seen from the sea, Tubuai looks like two islands. **Taitaa** (422 m/1,384 ft) is its highest point. The profile of **Tavaetu** (approx. 300 m/984 ft) looks like a sleeping man, and is often referred to as such by island residents. Tubuai is surrounded by a barrier reef; a pass on the north side gives access to a wide turquoise lagoon bordered by brilliant white sand beaches. While there are no rental shops or schools, surfers and kitesurfers who venture here with their own gear in tow are bound to be rewarded.

The temperature of Tubuai is on average 3 degrees lower than Tahiti, and the vegetation is sparser as a result; it's at its driest and sunniest September-November. The *Bounty* mutineers unsuccessfully attempted to settle on Tubuai in 1789 (though nothing remains of their Fort George, southeast of Taahueia). There are several marae on Tubuai, but they've also seen better days. Mormon missionaries arrived as early as 1844, and today there are active branches of the Church of Latter-Day Saints in all the villages. The island is known for their fine woven hats made from thin strips of pandanus leaves, and some woodcarving is done in the small settlement of Mahu.

ORIENTATION

Most of the 2,200 inhabitants live in **Mataura** and **Taahueia** on the north coast, though

Tubuai

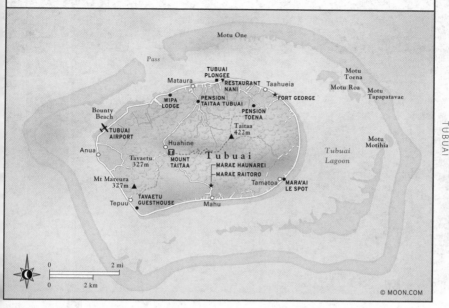

houses and settlements are found all along the level, 24-kilometer (15-mi) road around the island. An 8-kilometer (5-mi) paved road cuts right across the middle of Tubuai to **Mahu** village on the south coast, a delightful bike ride (it's an easy hike to the summit of **Taitaa** from this road). Mataura is the administrative center of the Austral Islands, and the post office, hospital, dental clinic, gendarmerie, and the branches of two banks are here, as well as two stores that bake bread. The airport is found on the western side of the island, 3.5 kilometers (2 mi) west of Mataura. A barrier reef envelops Tubuai, with passes on the southwestern side and northern side of the island, connecting the lagoon to open ocean.

SIGHTS
Marae Raitoru and Marae Haunarei

Taahueia; free

There are hundreds of marae on Tubuai, though only a few can be easily accessed.

Marae Raitoru and Marae Haunarei are two, found close to each other, and are considered sacred spaces. They're often visited as part of a tour, and some guides will recommend placing a small flower bouquet at the entrance of the marae. This site used to be where islanders celebrated births and buried umbilical cords, often beneath sacred trees. Marae Raitoru has an impressive moss-covered slab of stone propped up on wooden stilts with petroglyphs of arrows carved along its side—this is thought to have been a birthing table. At both marae, upright stones are placed neatly between large banyan trees. Today, parents of newborns often come here to seek blessings from ancestral spirits.

Fort George

Taahueia; fortgeorge.home.blog; free

Nothing remains today of the original Fort George, but it is marked with a plaque. The original fort was built by Christian Fletcher, the lieutenant who sparked a mutiny against

Captain William Bligh on the *Bounty* in 1789. This was the first place the mutineers took refuge after the fiasco, and the historical site is still owned by mutineer descendants. There are occasionally cultural events, dances, and workshops conducted on the grassy lawn of the Fort George site.

BEACHES

The island is flanked with skinny beaches, and it's not hard to find one to have all to yourself on a trip around the island. However, if you're seeking the sugary beaches featured in dreams of the South Pacific, its best to head to a motu (small offshore island). None of these beaches have formal amenities, so come prepared with your own food and water.

BOUNTY BEACH

Access via Tubuai Airport; free
The best beach on Tubai by far, this stretch of crumbly sands lines the airport runway. The sea here is shallow, but there's enough water to enjoy. With so few planes arriving each week, it's about as peaceful as an airport beach can be.

MOTU ONE

1.5 km (1 mi) offshore Taahuia
Motu One is where you go to live your desert-island dreams and build the largest sandcastle you can manage. This sandbank is surrounded by ultraclear water and looks like it could get swallowed by the sea at high tide. Get here by arranging a boat ride through your accommodation.

MOTU TOENA AND MOTU ROA

1.8 km (1.1 mi) offshore Fort George
Motu Toena and Motu Roa are two sister motu on Tubuai's outer reef, flanked with coconut trees. The beaches facing the lagoon are often calm and shallow, while the oceanside of the motu is a roiling sea. If you venture out on a lagoon tour, your guide is likely to stop here.

1: a quiet white sand beach on Tubuai's motu **2:** the ship *Tuhaa Pae IV* in Tubuai

Otherwise, your accommodation can help arrange a ride solely to the motu.

HIKING

MOUNT TAITAA

Distance: *15.5 km (9.6 mi) loop*
Time: *4-hour loop*
Trailhead: *Banque Socredo road, Mataura*
Information and maps: *www.alltrails.com/explore/recording/randonnee-de-l-apres-midi-95c9d99--25*

Mount Taitaa can be done as a loop, starting on the cross-island on which you'll find Banque Socredo. Once you're about a kilometer (0.6 mi) inland, a signed trail heads east to the top of Mount Taitaa. If you continue along the trail, it veers north to Taahueia. Following the coastal road west will bring you back to Mataura. This is a decently challenging trail, especially if hiked under full sunlight, so it's best to head out early. From the top of Mount Taitaa, you can soak in 360-degree views over Tubuai's lagoon to white sand motu.

★ LAGOON TOURS

Exploring Tubuai by boat is one of the best ways to experience the island. The pensions can arrange boat trips to the small reef motu just east of Tubuai Island across the lagoon. The tour begins with a snorkel in the ultra-clear waters of Tubuai's lagoon, a refuge for reef sharks, rays, sea turtles, juvenile pelagic fish, and reef fish. Blues of the water range from powder to deep cobalt, surrounding an emerald isle. While most tours are done from a small motorboat, it's also possible to venture out into the lagoon on a traditional outrigger canoe, available for rent from **Voiles et Lagon Tubuai** (tel. 40 95 01 17; CFP 2,000/hour). The snorkeling on the lagoon sides of the motu is superb, but the currents can get dangerously strong on the ocean side. It's wonderful to have an island all to yourself, like something out of a shipwreck cartoon, but bring adequate drinking water, sunscreen, and sun protection like a hat and long-sleeved shirt—especially if your tour will be spending a lot of time at the shade-scarce islet of Motu

One. Expect to pay around CFP 8,500 per person including a picnic lunch for a trip like this. Most lagoon tours last about 4-6 hours long. Most snorkeling tour providers will offer equipment, but size availability and quality can vary, so it's wise to bring your own.

SNORKELING AND SCUBA DIVING

TUBUAI PLONGÉE

Mataura; tel. 87 75 55 78; tubuaiplongee.pf; hours dependent on ocean conditions; CFP 7,500/fun dive

The only permanent scuba dive school on the Austral Islands was founded in 2019. Divers can venture out on fun dives within the lagoon (CFP 7,500/dive), and prices get cheaper the more you dive (CFP 60,000/10 dives). Courses from discovery to dive master are available, including an introduction to freediving course. If the humpbacks are hanging out, there's a 4-hour whale-watching tour (CFP 9,000), as well as kid-friendly snorkel tours for the little ones. The owners of this dive center also manage Tavaetu Guesthouse.

FOOD AND ACCOMMODATIONS

Almost all accommodations provide meals for their guests for an extra cost, as there are limited food options available around the island. There is one grocery store found in Mataura, with smaller convenience stores with nonperishable goods along the coastal road.

RESTAURANT NANI

Mataura; tel. 87 70 38 05; 11am-2pm and 5pm-9pm Mon.-Sat.; 1,500 CFP

Find hearty plates of grilled fish, poisson cru, and a few Chinese noodle dishes at Restaurant Nani, which has been a mainstay on Tubuai for years. Takeaway is available.

PENSION TOENA

Mataura; tel. 40 95 04 12; www.toena.pf; CFP 4,000-5,000

Hidden at the end of a road winding inland from Mataura is Pension Toena, a quiet pension with two standalone bungalows and

rooms in a family home. The gardens surrounding each room are more wild than the manicured. Inside, rooms are decorated with handwoven items, fresh flowers, and seashells. They each have a fan, TV, and en suite bathroom. Kayaks (CFP 2,000), cars (CFP 10,000), and bikes (CFP 1,500) are available for rent. With few restaurants around, it's wise to go for the half board (CFP 6,500-7,500) or full board (CFP 8,500-9,500) options.

TAVAETU GUESTHOUSE

Mataura; tel. 87 75 55 78; tubuaiplongee.pf; CFP 6,000-8,000/room includes breakfast

Owned by Tuamotu Plongée, Tavaetu Guesthouse is a relaxing pension near the base of Mount Tavaetu. Steps away from the property is a white sand beach and plenty of lounge space. Rooms are minimally furnished but have a bed and wardrobe. All guests have access to a communal kitchen, living room, and shared bathroom. There's also a quaint seaside hut to enjoy a drink at. The guesthouse has bikes (CFP 1,000/day), WiFi, and kayaks. Airport transfer costs CFP 500 per person each way.

MARA'AI LE SPOT

Tamatoa; tel. 89 73 62 20; Airbnb.com; CFP 7,000/ night includes breakfast

Mara'ai Le Spot is a quiet seaside pension with two bungalows set near the beach. Rooms are minimally decorated, but clean and furnished with comfy beds. Each has a fan, private bathroom, and spotty WiFi access. Breakfast can be enjoyed on the terrace. The back of each bungalow has a private plunge pool. Owners Ina and Herve are happy to offer travel tips and short rides, as well as use of their kayaks and bicycles. One of the rooms sleeps three, the other sleeps two.

Mara'ai also has an adjoining **restaurant,** open for lunch and dinner (around CFP 1,500/ meal). Flags of the world decorate this open-air dining hall, and the menu offers a respite from your typical seafood fare (though there's plenty of that, too). In addition to poisson cru, sashimi, grilled fish, and seafood paella,

Breadfruit

The breadfruit (uru) is a tall tree with broad leaves rightfully associated with the South Pacific, where it's often used as a symbol for life itself. Men turning themselves into breadfruit trees to save their families during famine is a recurring theme in Polynesian legends. Ancient voyagers brought breadfruit from Southeast Asia to Polynesia, where the crop thrived in the fertile soil. A well-watered tree can produce hundreds of round pale green breadfruits a year.

When baked in an underground oven or roasted over flames, the fruit is warm and starchy. The taste and texture of fresh bread, rolled up until it becomes a semi firm mass, best describes the breadfruit when cooked. The Polynesians learned to preserve breadfruit by pounding it into a paste, which was kept in leaf-lined pits to ferment into mahi. Like the coconut, the breadfruit tree had many uses, including the provision of wood for outrigger canoes.

a man making papoi, fermented breadfruit mixed with fresh breadfruit

Breadfruit is also linked to one of the most scandalous mutinies in history. At the time, sailors believed that one breadfruit could provide enough sustenance for one man for a single day, making it one of the most valuable fruits in the world. In 1787, Captain William Bligh set out to collect breadfruit shoots to transfer from Tahiti to the West Indies, where they were to be planted to feed enslaved people. On the way back, his crew mutinied near the Austral Islands and cast off both Bligh and the breadfruit. Bligh attempted to reach Tubuai, but missed and reached the Pitcairn Islands in a rowboat and in 1792 returned to Tahiti with another ship to complete his task.

In the Austral Islands, it's common to enjoy breadfruit cooked in a way called popoi, where ma (fermented breadfruit) is mixed with fresh breadfruit and cooked over an open fire. The cooked breadfruit meat is scraped, pounded, and served.

Here are a few ways to enjoy breadfruit:

- **Cooked over a fire:** Breadfruit is scored and placed onto open flames. Once the skin is charred, it's removed and warm breadfruit is served with salt and butter.

- **Wedges and chips:** Breadfruit is sliced, coated in oil, salted, and then baked or fried.

- **Mashed:** Breadfruit is boiled and mashed with coconut milk.

- **Cake:** Breadfruit flour, sugar, and coconut mixed together and baked makes for a warm and hearty treat.

there's also pizzas and burgers. Mingling with other tables is part of the culture at this casual haunt.

★ WIPA LODGE

Mataura; tel. 40 93 22 40; tubuaiwipalodge.com; CFP 8,500/room for two people, CFP 18,500/room for two people including half-board (breakfast and dinner)

This pension is owned by Wilson and Gisele, a charismatic duo who are happy to share their favorite parts of the island with guests. Wipa Lodge is set across the road from a white sand beach. There are five large bungalows on the property, four of which can sleep three and one family bungalow that can sleep seven. Each one feels more like a home than a sterile hotel. They all have a terrace, private bathroom with hot-water shower, mosquito nets, and fan. Meals are served family-style in the communal lounge, which also has (slow) WiFi. Wilson can help arrange day trips, motu picnics, whale-watching, hiking, and even car rentals. Access to bicycles, kayaks, and snorkeling gear is free for guests. Transport from the airport is not included, but can be arranged for CFP 1,200/person.

PENSION TAITAA TUBUAI

Mataura; tel. 87 22 22 32; www.pension-taitaa.com; CFP 12,000/room including breakfast

Pension Taitaa Tubuai feels like a jungle retreat, a small lodge tucked on the foothills of Tubuai's interior surrounded by fruit trees. The rooms are basic, decorated with local art, and can sleep 2-4. There's also an above-ground pool, a novelty for the Austral Islands. WiFi exists in the communal area. Dinners (CFP 2,500) include a home-cooked dessert—fingers crossed Nath, one of the owners and the chef, makes pavlova. The pension can arrange tours including motu picnics. Bicycles are available for CFP 1,000/day.

INFORMATION AND SERVICES

Mataura hosts the post office, hospital, dental clinic, gendarmerie, bank, and food shops.

- **Banque Socredo:** Mataura; tel. 40 95 04 86; socredo.pf; 8am-noon and 1:30pm-4pm Mon.-Fri.

- **Gendarmerie:** Mataura; tel. 40 93 22 05; 9am-noon and 2pm-5pm Mon.-Tues., 7am-noon and 2pm-5pm Wed.-Fri., 8am-noon and 2pm-5pm Sat., 9am-noon and 3pm-5pm Sun.

GETTING THERE

Air

TUBUAI AIRPORT

TUB; 4 km (2.5 mi) west of Mataura

Tubuai Airport, in the northwest corner of the island, is small, with a single landing strip and on-site snack bar. All transport should be arranged directly with your pension before arrival. Air Tahiti (airtahiti.com) offers direct flights between Tubuai and Papeete (1 hour 40 minutes, CFP 35,000), Raivavae (40 minutes, CFP 15,000), and Rurutu (45 minutes, CFP 17,000).

Ferry

Ferries enter the lagoon through a passage in the barrier reef on the north side and proceed to the wharf a kilometer east of Mataura. The **Tuhaa Pae IV** (tel. 40 41 36 06; www.snathp.com, info@snathp.com) arrives 2-3 times per month, stopping between Rurutu (2 nights, CFP 13,900) and Raivavae (1 night, CFP 5,900).

GETTING AROUND

There's no public transportation on Tubuai, but some of the pensions rent bicycles (around CFP 1,000/day) and cars (starting at CFP 8,500/day; check for availability at Pension Toena). Almost all vehicles are manual drive, and it takes around three hours to drive leisurely around the island. The gas station is near the wharf at Mataura. Most tours and trips are arranged through your accommodation, typically costing around CFP 6,000 per person for a full-day tour, customized to your interests.

Raivavae

Raivavae (pronounced "Gaivavae" on the island) is one of the most striking islands in the archipelago. This 9-kilometer-long and 2-kilometer-wide (5.5-mi-long and 1.2-mi-wide) island is just south of the tropic of Capricorn (thus outside the tropics)—it's the third most southerly island in the South Pacific (only Rapa and Easter Island are farther south). A barrier reef encloses an emerald lagoon, and 28 small coral motu cluster on the southern and eastern parts of the reef. The blues range from turquoise to azure in its lagoon, though you won't see an overwater bungalow jutting out into the sea like you might on the more popular islands of French Polynesia. This is an island of yesteryear, yet to be featured on the photo grids of social media websites. The few cars bumbling around the island brake for chickens, dogs, and pigs, who are in no hurry to cross the road. The tropical vegetation is rich: residents cultivate oranges, taro, and coffee, and rose and sandalwood are used to make perfume.

ORIENTATION

The present population of around 900 lives in four coastal villages, **Rairua** (where the ferries tie up), **Mahanatoa, Anatonu,** and **Vaiuru,** linked by the 22-kilometer (13-mi) dirt road around the island. Moving clockwise, Rairua is on the northwestern cape of the island; Mahanatoa is 2 kilometers (1.2 mi) east. Anatonu is 4 kilometers (2.5 mi) east from Mahanatoa, and Vaiuru is somewhat isolated on the southern coast, 5 kilometers (3 mi) from Anatonu. A shortcut route direct from Rairua to Vaiuru crosses a 119-meter (390-ft) saddle, with views of the island. Fern-covered **Hiro** (437 m/1,433 ft) is the highest point on 18-square-kilometer (7-square-mi) Raivavae. The airport is another 3 kilometers (1.8 mi) west of Vaiuru, on the southernmost point of the island. A large lagoon wraps around Raivavae's main island, with passes between the barrier reef and open ocean on the northern and southern ends.

SIGHTS

Marae Pomoavao

Raivavae Airport; free

Christian converts destroyed most of Raivavae's 92 marae, but one, Marae Pomoavao, has been restored and maintained. Opposite the airport on the south side of the island, huge stone blocks tilt upward among the undergrowth. Several other marae remain, but you'd need a guide to find them.

Canoe Workshop

Anatonu; free

One of the most popular ways to get around Raivavae is from the seat of a wooden dugout outrigger canoe. The ancestors of Raivavae's residents were some of the finest navigators in the world, using the stars, wind, and currents to cross distances of epic proportions. Today, almost all the canoes used to paddle through Raivavae's lagoon are made from wood—in a similar design that's been transporting Polynesia's seafarers for centuries. Each has a wooden hull and two arms connecting to an ama (outrigger) that keeps the canoe stable. The outrigger and hull are lashed together with braided leaves, pulling the arms taut to the hull. The canoe size often depends on the size of the tree used to carve the canoe from; most personal canoes seat just one person, but larger canoes seat up to six. Stroll to the western edge of Anatonu to the Canoe Workshop and you might catch a craftsman at work. These canoes are not formally rented to travelers, but you're likely to find someone willing to teach you how to paddle or offer you a canoe for rent if you ask around (your accommodation is a great start). Some owners may not charge you anything, but those who do usually request around CFP 5,000 for a full day of use.

Raivavae

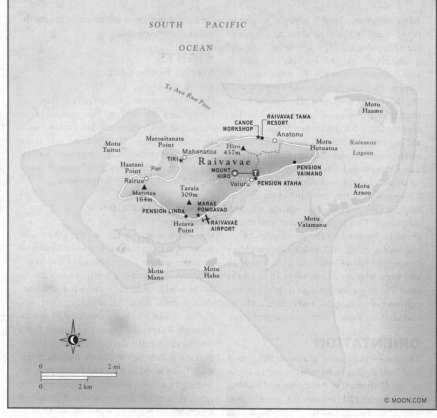

© MOON.COM

Tiki

Mahanatoa; free

Like the Marquesas and Easter Island, Raivavae was once home to a civilization that erected large stone anthropomorphic figures called tikis. Many 2- to 3-meter-high (6- to 10-ft-high) red stone statues once stood on the island, but most have since been smashed, taken to European museums, or moved to Tahiti. That said, one grinning meter-tall tiki is still standing in a field by the road just west of Mahanatoa village toward Rairua on Raivavae.

Motu

MOTU HOTUATUA

200 m (650 ft) off Raivavae's eastern point; free

The closest little motu to the main island, abundant corals are sprawled along the seabed of the 200-meter (650-ft) passage separating Raivavae's easternmost point and Motu Hotuatua. The shore is rocky, and there's only a small patch of sand to dock a canoe (available rental arranged through your accommodation) or rest up before heading back to the main island.

MOTU VAIAMANU

3 km (1.8 mi) offshore Raivavae's southern coast; free
Motu Vaimanu is often called "Motu Piscine" as its waters are as clear as a swimming pool. A 2-kilometer (1.2-mi) boat ride from Vaiuru will take you to this islet with chalky sands, shallow waters for wading, and a reef primed for snorkeling for those who have their own equipment. The ocean side of the motu is typically too rough to explore. A scoop of sugar sandbank next to the motu with a few budding shrubs awaits. If the whales are around, you might see them from the ocean side of the motu.

HIKING
★ Mount Hiro

Distance: *15 km (9.3 mi) out-and-back*
Time: *5.5 hours out-and-back*
Trailhead: *Western side of Anatonu*
Information and maps: *www.alltrails.com/ trail/french-polynesia/raivavae/mont-hiro*

The trek up Mount Hiro (437 m/1,433 ft) is steep, with some hand-over-hand scrambling and rope-holding needed to get over sections of volcanic rock. The start of the path is thick with brush, so you'll want to wear long pants and hiking shoes to protect yourself from bumps and scrapes. Once you reach the top, the landscape clears to a grassy field—almost as if Mother Nature decided to take a sigh in between the dense vegetation. Here, you'll be treated with some of the best views in all of French Polynesia. The remoteness of the island also adds a "je nais se quois" that isn't found when you've conquered a route that many have already done before.

LAGOON TOURS

The swirling shades of blue of Raivavae Lagoon are mesmerizing, especially seen from the water. Venture out by boat (arranged through your accommodation) on a tour of the lagoon. Most tours take around four hours, and cost CFP 6,000 per person, venturing out on a motorized outrigger canoe or fishing boat. The shallow, sandy seascapes create a light cyan color. Once the seabed plummets, the ocean turns into dark azure. The blues in between go beyond what a painter has on their palette. Lagoon tours often stop at white sand motu, prime places to learn how to open a coconut, snorkel over coral bommies, and enjoy a lunch of fresh fish, included in the cost of your excursion. As with all lagoon tour operators in the Austral Islands, snorkeling gear size selection and quality can vary greatly—it's wise to venture here with your own mask, snorkel, and fins.

blue hues seen from the summit of Mount Hiro

FOOD AND ACCOMMODATIONS

Most accommodations arrange meals for their guests, particularly breakfast and dinner. Meals usually include fresh fruit, eggs, and bread for breakfast, with vegetables and meat for dinner—typically seafood as the main form of protein. There are small food and convenience stores in Anatonu, Vaiuru, Rairua, and Mahanatoa.

PENSION ATAHA

Vaiuru; tel. 87 28 92 35; www.pensionataha.com; CFP 8,860/person including half-board (breakfast and dinner), accommodation only is CFP 4,200/person, airport transfer not included

Pension Ataha embodies the concept of slow living. Wake up with the sun, cool off in the water, take a walk along the coastline, then come back for a dinner made from the catch of the day. The property has five double rooms and a fare with two bedrooms. But, if you're wanting to sleep under the stars without civilization in sight, you can spend a night (or two) on Motu Vaimanu, where the hosts set up a campsite complete with tents, lighting, a stove, barbecue, blankets, and camping chairs.

RAIVAVAE TAMA RESORT

Anatonu; tel. 40 95 42 52; raivavaetama.com; CFP 10,000 CFP/person for full-board (all meals) or 8,500/person for half-board (breakfast and dinner), includes airport transfer

Raivavae Tama Resort is a cheerful resort next to the Protestant Church with five bungalows that can sleep up to three people. The bungalows have thatched roofs, wooden walls, and woven artwork decorating the rooms—creating an all-natural ambiance. All are equipped with a ceiling fan, bathroom with hot-water shower, and Polynesian linens. The host, Teupoo, has a penchant for placing heaping fruit bowls out for her guests. Hikes and tours of the lagoon can be arranged on request.

PENSION LINDA

Rairua; tel. 40 95 44 25; www.pensionlindaraivavae. pf; CFP 10,600/person including half-board (breakfast and dinner) and airport transfer

This tranquil property just a short walk from turquoise waters has five bungalows centered around a central house. The rooms are simple but clean, each sleeping three with a private bathroom (limited hot water). Linda, the owner, welcomes guests for meals in her home, where there's also a communal kitchen and living room. Guests can rent bikes (CFP

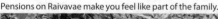

Pensions on Raivavae make you feel like part of the family.

1,500/day), kayaks (CFP 1,500/day), and canoes (CFP 1,500/day). The pension arranges island tours (CFP 2,000), hikes up Mount Hiro (CFP 3,750/person), and trips to the motu (CFP 9,000/half-day).

★ PENSION VAIMANO

Vairu; tel. 87 20 42 33; CFP 24,000/room including half-board (breakfast and dinner) and airport transfer

Pension Vaimano hosts a handful of cozy bungalows, each with an outdoor dining area. Polynesian textiles (tifaifai), bamboo furnishings, and surrounding gardens add to the remote holiday feel. Clarissa, the host, is happy to share stories and travel tips about the island. Bungalows can sleep 3-4 adults, and rates are roughly priced per occupant (around 12,000 CFP/person). Meals are served with other guests, creating a strong family feel—the food here is some of the best on the island. The terraces overlook the ocean, and a beach with clear waters is just a short walk away. Kayaks, outrigger canoes, and bikes are available for guest use.

INFORMATION AND SERVICES

- **Post Office:** Rairua; tel. 40 95 42 00; 7am-noon and 12:30pm-3pm Mon.-Fri.; also has internet hotspot and ATM
- **Gendarmerie:** Rairua; tel. 40 95 42 30; lannuaire.service-public.fr; 7am-noon and 2pm-5pm Mon.-Fri., 8am-noon and 2pm-5pm Sat., 9am-noon and 3pm-5pm Sun.

GETTING THERE AND AROUND

The only way to reach Raivavae is by plane or by ferry. Once here, there are no formal car rental services on the island—all transport must be arranged through your accommodation. Many accommodations offer one-off rides and bicycles for rent (around CFP 1,500/day). To get to the outer motu, you'll need to hire a boat (CFP 1,000-2,000 per trip) or join a lagoon excursion (CFP 6,000/person/4-hour

tour). The coastal road around the island is relatively flat and rarely crowded, making it easy to navigate on foot. Beware of drivers whipping around corners at high speeds, especially on the western end of the island. The interior road is very hilly, with few people around, and it's best not to walk or cycle that road alone in case of an accident. If you're set on renting a car, you'll have to ask around and rent a car from a private person or pension. It takes under two hours to lap the island at a leisurely pace.

Many locals get around in an outrigger canoe. While there are no formal rental stands offering canoe paddling services, most accommodations will own one (or know someone who owns one), which can be hired for around CFP 5,000 for a full day. The outer motu might be too far to paddle to for novice paddlers, but cruising alongside the coastline of Raivavae's main island is an interesting way to explore.

Air

RAIVAVAE AIRPORT

5 km (3 mi) south of Rairua

The building of the airport in 2002 wasn't a decision appreciated by all—many residents of Raivavae were, and are, hesitant to open their island to tourism due to conservation concerns. This airport is 5 kilometers (3 mi) southeast of Rairua and has snack and crafts kiosks. Air Tahiti has flights between Raivavae and Tahiti (1 hour 50 minutes, CFP 34,000/one-way) and Tubuai (40 minutes, CFP 15,000/one-way).

Ferry

Ships enter the lagoon through a pass on the north side and tie up to the pier at Rairua. The ***Tuhaa Pae IV*** (tel. 40 41 36 06; www.snathp.com, info@snathp.com) stops in Raivavae a few times per month, and is either the first or last stop on the ship's circuit around the Austral Islands, arriving from Papeete (2 nights, CFP 16,000) or Tubuai (1 night, CFP 5,900).

Rimatara

On a map Rimatara looks like a sole polka dot in a sea of blue. Only a narrow fringing reef hugs Rimatara's lagoonless shore; arriving passengers land at Amaru or Mutua Ura by whaleboat, and are greeted with clouds of smoke from beachside fires, often used to cook. Here, there's plenty of time—and inspiration—for artisans to perfect their craft: Rimatara is famous for its finely woven pandanus hats, mats, and bags, as well as intricate shell necklaces. Monoï (skin oil) is prepared from gardenias and coconut oil. There aren't really any proper sights aside from the beaches and the birds, which are everywhere. Without a wharf, hotels, restaurants, bars, and taxis, Rimatara is still a place to escape the modern world.

ORIENTATION

On the smallest (9 square km/3.5 square mi) and lowest (84 m/275 ft) of the Australs, roads lead from **Amaru,** the main village on the western side of the island, 2 kilometers (1.2 mi) south to **Mutua Ura. Anapoto** is on the western end of the island, 3 kilometers (1.8 mi) from Mutu Aura and 3 kilometers (1.8 mi) from Amaru. The airport is on the northernmost point of the island, exactly between Amaru and Anapoto.

BEACHES

There are a few coves with clear water in between Mutua Ura and Anapoto, all accessible by the coastal road.

MUTUA URA BEACH
Mutua Ura; free
The beach fronting the town of Mutua Ura is the best on the island. A cove of white sand cedes to calm, albeit a bit shallow, waters. If you head to the eastern side of the beach, you can wade across a sandspit to two small motu. There's a magasin next to the beach to pick up snacks should you want them.

ANAPOTO BEACH
Anapoto; free
There's a little beach in front of Anapoto, but you wouldn't want to do any real swimming here, as the water tends to get a bit rough. Still, there's enough white sand to spend an hour or two catching up on holiday reading as locals launch and land their outrigger canoes in the water.

ACCOMMODATIONS

Accommodations double as your place to dine while on the island of Rimatara. Bring enough cash to cover your stay and then some, as these pensions do not take credit cards. There also aren't many markets on the island for fresh meat or produce—families tend to grow their own ingredients. If you do want to buy something fresh, its best to arrange this through your accommodation. Many times, they'll allow access to their garden as part of your stay.

Rimatara

RIMATARA AIRPORT

Anapoto Beach

PENSION LA PERRUCHE ROUGE

Teruahu Point

Anapoto

R i m a t a r a

Amaru

PENSION UEUE RIMATARA

▲ Uahu 83m

Iriiriroa Point

Mutua Ura

Mutua Ura Beach

0   0.5 mi

0   0.5 km

© MOON.COM

☆ Birds of Rimatara

a kuhl's lorikeet

Though Rimatara's human population might be small (only 800 people), and water is scarce in the dry season, it thrives with birdlife. Rare Rimatara lorikeets have taken quite a liking to their patch of South Pacific paradise, and you'll often spot a flock chirping in the treetops. This alone makes packing a pair of binoculars (or a decent camera zoom lens) worth it, if you have the space. You don't need a formal tour to go bird-watching; setting off on your own will do. But, if you like, you can ask your accommodation to arrange a guide (usually a friend of the family with some free time to kill), who will point to the spots they're most likely to be.

RIMATARA LORIKEET

The Rimatara lorikeet (manu 'ura) used to be endemic on the Cook Islands, some islands of Kiribati, and Rimatara until the arrival of humans. But feather collecting, rays, and the introduction of other predators led to its decline on the Cook Islands until the Rimatara population was the only one left. Fortunately, conservation programs are in place to reintroduce these lorikeets to islands where they once thrived, but at the moment, Rimatara is the sole island where they're spotted in such high numbers. These birds are striking, with green and yellow backs and vibrant red undersides. Look for them on fruit trees and flowering plants, as these lorikeets feed on fruits, nectar, and insects all around the island.

RIMATARA REED WARBLER

The island is also home to the Rimatara reed warbler, distinguished by its mottled brown back plumage and cream-colored underside. It's the only known home of Rimatara reed warblers.

PENSION UEUE RIMATARA

Amaru; tel. 40 94 42 88; CFP 20,000/room

Four standalone bungalows are surrounded by an immaculately kept lawn and an abundance of fruit trees with a short path leading to the main house of Pension Ueue Rimatara. Each bungalow is clean, with a fan, private bathroom, and small terrace facing the outskirts of the property. Meals and conversations are had in a shaded outdoor dining area. Rusty but functional pushbikes are available to take around the island.

PENSION LA PERRUCHE ROUGE

Near Rimatara Airport; tel. 87 30 58 23;
laperrucherouge@mail.pf; CFP 27,000/room

Surrounded by palm trees, Pension La Perruche Rouge is a tranquil pension hidden near the start of the airport road. Rooms are decorated with fresh-cut flowers, weavings, and seashells. Meals of traditionally cooked seafood and vegetables are served in an open-air bamboo dining room. Bungalows are equipped with a private bathroom, terrace, fan, and embroidered bed linens. The hosts regularly offer tours, weaving lessons, and cooking lessons for curious travelers.

INFORMATION AND SERVICES

Bring cash, as there are no banks or functional ATMs on the island. Any medications or dietary supplements should also be brought to the island.

- **Post Office:** Amaru; 7am-noon and 12:30pm-3pm Mon.-Fri.
- **Gendarmerie:** Amaru; tel. 40 94 42 90; lannuaire.service-public.fr; 7am-noon and 2pm-5pm Mon.-Fri., 8am-noon and 2pm-5pm Sat., 9am-noon and 3pm-5pm Sun.

GETTING THERE AND AROUND

Tiny Rimatara has a 7-kilometer (4-mi) loop road ringing around the interior of the island,

easily driven in a few minutes or walked in just over two hours. Most people get around on foot, though hitching a ride from one village to the next is also extremely common. Accommodations can arrange transport if needed, but hosts are often more likely to wait on the side of the road with you and hail down a ride from a passerby. The road is well-maintained, flat, and rarely crowded.

Air
RIMATARA AIRPORT

North Rimatara

Rimatara Airport is tiny, with a small snack stand and seating area. **Air Tahiti** flies directly from Rimatara to Papeete (1.5 hours, CFP 36,000/one-way) and Rurutu (30 minutes, CFP 12,500/one-way). Pensions provide transport to and from the airport.

Ferry

The ***Tuhaa Pae IV*** (tel. 40 41 36 06; www.snathp.com, info@snathp.com) steams to Rimatara a few times per month, with Rimatara being either the first or last stop from Papeete depending on which way the ship is circling around the islands. The Ferry arrives from Papeete (2 nights, CFP 15,400) or Rurutu (1 night, CFP 5,950), anchoring offshore and delivering passengers and goods via smaller whaleboats.

Rapa

To truly get away from it all, venture to Rapa, one of the most isolated islands in the world. At 27°38° south latitude, Rapa is the southernmost island in the South Pacific, and one of the most isolated and spectacular. Its nearest neighbor is Raivavae, 600 kilometers (372 mi) away, and Tahiti is 1,244 kilometers (773 mi) north. South leads to Antarctica. It's sometimes called Rapa Iti (Little Rapa) to distinguish it from Rapa Nui (Easter Island).

Soaring peaks reaching 650 meters (2,132 ft) form a horseshoe around magnificent Haurei Bay, Rapa's crater harbor, the western section of a drowned volcano. This is only one of 12 deeply indented bays around the island; the absence of reefs allows the sea to cut into the 40-square-kilometer (15-square-mi) island's outer basalt coasts. Offshore are several sugarloaf-shaped islets. The east slopes of the mountains are bare, while large fern

Uninhabited Austral Islands

The Austral Archipelago is home to a handful of islands that for one reason or another were not settled by the first Polynesian navigators, likely due to their inhospitality, lack of obvious ports, and remote location. With so many other islands in Polynesia to visit, there are few reasons to come here.

MARIA

A cluster of motu made from stony reef-building corals and white sand beaches make up Maria, a barren atoll. In between Rimatara and the Cook Islands, this island was bypassed by both Polynesian and European navigators until the early 1800s, when a whaling ship anchored off the shallow lagoon. Today, the only way to visit is onboard a private vessel. Maria is visited once or twice a year by men from Rimatara or Rurutu for fishing and copra-making, where coconut meat is extracted and dried. They stay on the atoll two or three months, their only company seabirds and giant lobsters.

MAROTIRI

Part of Rapa's administrative borders, Marotiri is a lonely bunch of islands 80 kilometers (50 mi) from Rapa. The islets are spread out around 2 kilometers (1.2 mi) from one another and barren of any notable form of vegetation. Few ships anchor here.

forests are found on the west. Coconut trees can't grow in the foggy, temperate climate; instead, pine trees adorn the island.

Seafaring Polynesians made landfall on Rapa likely sometime in the 13th century, making it one of the last Polynesian islands to be colonized. Shortly after their arrival, fortresses were built throughout Rapa, and they developed a systematic way to guard the island. However, during the two decades following the arrival of missionaries in 1826, Rapa's population dropped from 2,000 to 300 because of the introduction of European diseases. By 1851 it was down to just 70, and after smallpox and dysentery arrived on a Peruvian ship in 1863, it was a miracle that anyone survived at all. Because of Rapa's remote location—being so disconnected from elsewhere in the South Pacific—descendants of the few survivors held onto a part of the Rapan identity, culture, and language (Rapan) from the rest of Polynesia. Residents on other Austral Islands cannot understand Rapan.

ORIENTATION

The present population of about 480 lives at **Area** and **Haurei** villages on the north and south sides of Rapa's great open **Haurei Bay**, connected by an 8-kilometer (5-mi) coastal road, though most people only travel to and from the villages by boat. The windy anchorage is around 20 meters (65 ft) deep. The horseshoe shaped island is 40 square kilometers (15 square mi), 10 kilometers (6 mi) from north to south and 8 kilometers (5 mi) east to west.

HILL FORTRESSES

Haurei; free

Between the Haurei and Hiri bays, **Morongo Uta,** a timeworn Polynesian fortress with terraces, is situated on the crest of a ridge, commanding a wide outlook over the steep, rugged hills. Morongo Uta was cleared of vegetation by a party of archaeologists in the mid-1950s and is still easily visited.

A Norwegian team led by Thor Heyerdahl also studied and restored the earthwork hill fortifications of Rapa. Heyerdahl ended up producing a massive volume with the findings of his expedition. About a dozen of these pa (fortresses) are found above Haurei Bay, built to defend the territories of the different tribes of ancient Rapa. The fortresses are built with large volcanic slabs—a testament to ancient masonry techniques. They're step-like in appearance, and some are guarded with moats and parapets. Many are overgrown with foliage. It's possible to climb to Morongo Uta Pa on an unmarked, narrow trail from Haurei in about an hour, on a steep trail with splendid views; follow the road inland from Haurei's pier.

FOOD AND ACCOMMODATIONS

There are no formal pensions or accommodations, or restaurants, on the island. Most visitors who arrive will stay with a family, or on the boat they arrived on. To arrange accommodation on Rapa Iti, it's best to seek official advice at the Tahiti Tourisme office (Blvd. Pomare IV, Papeete; tahititourisme.com; tel. 40 50 40 30; 8am-5:30pm Mon.-Fri., 8am-4pm Sat., 8am-noon Sun.) in Papeete, Tahiti, before you depart for Rapa. Rapa is not a place you can plan to visit spontaneously.

INFORMATION AND SERVICES

There are a few shops in both towns selling basic nonperishable goods. However, fresh produce can be challenging to find. Come with enough cash to cover your stay, and any medication, goods, and dietary supplements needed for the duration of your stay and beyond. While most stays must be a minimum of six weeks, there is a chance ferries can be delayed or subject to schedule changes, so pack enough for at least 3-4 weeks longer than expected.

- **Administrative des Illes Australes:** Haurei; tel. 46 86 76

GETTING THERE AND AROUND

With no airport, the only way to reach Rapa is by boat. And while the passenger freighter **Tuhaa Pae IV** steams to the Austral Islands a few times per month, it only visits Rapa once per month in between visits to Tubuai and Raivavae. When it docks, the entirety of the town awaits to greet friends and family members as well as receive supplies. Travelers must stay on Rapa until the next ferry arrives—sometimes up to six weeks. The **Aranui V** (tel. 40 42 62 42; aranui.com) freighter also cruises to Rapa a few times per year—one to two times maximum on an 11-night cruise, with prices starting at CFP 417,344 per person. Otherwise, you'll need your own sailboat to venture here. The island has two villages—the best way to get from one to the other is by boat (usually outrigger canoe). There are no formal canoe rental stands, so you'll have to ask locals in either village (Area or Haurei) to rent or use their canoe. Around CFP 500 is a fair price to start for a one-way trip, taking around 10 minutes to paddle from one village to the other. There is only one paved road connecting the villages, and all other roads are best accessed on foot or by 4WD.

Background

The Landscape

GEOGRAPHY

French Polynesia (or Te Ao Maohi, as it is known to the Polynesians) is made up of five great archipelagos—the Society, Austral, Tuamotu, Gambier, and Marquesas Islands—arrayed in chains running from southeast to northwest. The **Society Islands** are subdivided into the **Windward Islands,** or Îles du Vent (Tahiti, Moorea, Maiao, Tetiaroa, and Mehetia), and the **Leeward Islands,** or Îles Sous-le-Vent (Huahine, Raiatea, Taha'a, Bora Bora, Maupiti, Tupai, Maupihaa/Mopelia, Manuae/Scilly, and Motu One/Bellingshausen).

French Polynesia at a Glance

	Population (2017)	Area (hectares)
Windward Islands	207,333	118,580
Leeward Islands	35,393	38,750
Austral Islands	6,965	14,784
Tuamotu-Gambier Islands	16,881	77,243
Marquesas Islands	9,346	104,930
French Polynesia	268,270	354,287

French Polynesia consists of boundless ocean and little land. Together the 35 islands and 83 atolls of French Polynesia total only 3,543 square kilometers (1,367 mi) in land area, yet they're scattered over a vast area of the southeastern Pacific Ocean, between 7° and 28° south latitude and 131° and 156° west longitude. Papeete (149° west longitude) is actually 8° *east* of Honolulu (157° west longitude). Though French Polynesia is only half the size of Corsica in land area, if Papeete were Paris, then the Gambiers would be in Romania and the Marquesas near Stockholm. At 5,030,000 square kilometers (1,942,000 square mi), the territory's 200-nautical-mile exclusive economic zone is by far the largest in the Pacific islands.

There's a wonderful geological diversity to these islands midway between Australia and South America—from the dramatic, jagged volcanic outlines of the Society and Marquesas Islands to the 400-meter-high (1,300-ft-high) hills of the Australs and Gambiers to the low coral atolls of the Tuamotus. All of the Marquesas are volcanic islands, while the Tuamotus are all coral islands or atolls. The Societies and Gambiers include both volcanic and coral types.

Tahiti, around 4,000 kilometers (2,500 mi) from both Auckland and Honolulu or 6,000 kilometers (3,700 mi) from Los Angeles and Sydney, is not only the best known and most populous of the islands, but also the largest (1,045 square km/403 square mi) and highest (2,241 m/7,352 ft). Bora Bora and Maupiti are noted for their combination of high volcanic peaks framed by low coral rings. Rangiroa is one of the world's largest coral atolls, while Makatea is an uplifted atoll. In the Marquesas, precipitous and sharply crenellated mountains rise hundreds of meters, with craggy peaks, razorback ridges, plummeting waterfalls, deep fertile valleys, and dark broken coastlines pounded by surf. Compare them to the pencil-thin strips of yellow reefs, green vegetation, and white beaches enclosing the transparent Tuamotu lagoons. In all, French Polynesia offers some of the most varied and spectacular scenery in the world.

Darwin's Theory of Atoll Formation

The famous formulator of the theory of natural selection surmised that atolls form as high volcanic islands subside. The original island's fringing reef grows up into a barrier reef as the volcanic part sinks. When the last volcanic material finally disappears below sea level, the coral rim of the reef/atoll remains to indicate how big the island once was.

Of course, all of this takes place over millions of years, but deep below every atoll is the

Previous: Notre Dame Cathedral, Nuku Hiva.

old volcanic core. Darwin's theory is well illustrated at Bora Bora, where a high volcanic island remains inside the rim of Bora Bora's barrier reef; this island's volcanic core is sinking imperceptibly at the rate of one centimeter per century. Return to Bora Bora in 25 million years and all you'll find will be a coral atoll that looks much like Rangiroa.

Hot Spots

High or low, most of the islands have a volcanic origin best explained by the Conveyor Belt Theory. A crack opens in the earth's crust and volcanic magma escapes upward. A submarine volcano builds up slowly until the lava finally breaks the surface, becoming a volcanic island. The Pacific Plate moves northwest approximately 11 centimeters (4.3 in) per year; thus, over geologic eons, the volcano disconnects from the hot spot or crack from which it emerged. As the old volcanoes detach from the crack, new ones develop over the hot spot, and the older islands are carried away from the cleft in the earth's crust from which they were born.

The island then begins to sink as it's carried into deeper water and erosion also cuts into the now-extinct volcano. In the warm, clear waters a living coral reef begins to grow along the shore. As the island subsides, the reef continues to grow upward. In this way a lagoon forms between the reef and shoreline of the slowly sinking island. This barrier reef marks the old margin of the original island.

As the plate moves northwest in an opposite direction from the sliding Pacific Plate, the process is repeated, time and again, until whole chains of islands ride the blue Pacific. Weathering is most advanced on the composite islands and atolls at the northwest ends of the Society, Austral, Tuamotu, and Marquesas chains. Maupiti and Bora Bora, with their exposed volcanic cores, are the oldest of the larger Society Islands. The Tuamotus have eroded almost to sea level; the Gambier Islands originated out of the same hot spot, and their volcanic peaks remain inside a giant atoll reef. The progression of

youth, maturity, and old age can be followed throughout French Polynesia. In every case, the islands at the southeast end of the chains are the youngest.

By drilling into the Tuamotu atolls, scientists have proven their point conclusively: the coral formations are about 350 meters (1,148 ft) thick at the southeast end of the chain, 600 meters (1,968 ft) thick at Hao near the center, and 1,000 meters (3,280 ft) thick at Rangiroa near the northwest end of the Tuamotu Group. Clearly, Rangiroa, where the volcanic rock is now a kilometer below the surface, is many millions of years older than the Gambiers, where a volcanic peak still stands 482 meters (1,581 ft) above sea level. Geologists estimate that Tahiti is 2-3 million years old, Bora Bora 7 million years old, and the Tuamotus 10-40 million years old.

Island-building continues at an active undersea volcano called MacDonald, 50 meters (164 ft) below sea level at the southeast end of the Australs. The crack spews forth about a cubic mile of lava every century, and someday MacDonald too will poke its smoky head above the waves. The theory of plate tectonics, or the sliding crust of the earth, seems proved in the Pacific.

The Life of an Atoll

A circular or horseshoe-shaped coral reef bearing a necklace of sandy, slender islets (motu) of debris thrown up by storms, surf, and wind is known as an atoll. Atolls can be up to 100 kilometers (62 mi) across, but the width of dry land is usually only 200-400 meters (650-1,300 ft) from inner to outer beach. The central lagoon can measure anywhere from 1 kilometer (0.6 mi) to 50 kilometers (31 mi) in diameter; huge Rangiroa is 77 kilometers (47 mi) long. Entirely landlocked lagoons are rare; passages through the barrier reef are usually found on the leeward side. Most atolls are no higher than 4-6 meters (13-20 ft).

A raised or elevated atoll is one that has been pushed up by some trauma of nature to become a platform of coral rock rising to 70 meters (230 ft) above sea level. Raised atolls are often known for their huge sea caves and steep oceanside cliffs. The only raised atoll in French Polynesia is crescent-shaped Makatea in the northwestern corner of the Tuamotu group. It is 100 meters (328 ft) high, 7 kilometers (4.3 mi) long, and 4.5 kilometers (2.8 mi) wide.

Where the volcanic island remains there's often a deep passage between the barrier reef and shore; the reef forms a natural breakwater, which shelters good anchorages. Soil derived from coral is extremely poor in nutrients, while volcanic soil is known for its fertility. Dark-colored beaches are formed from volcanic material; the white beaches of travel brochures are entirely calcareous.

CLIMATE

The hot and humid summer season runs November-April. The rest of the year the climate is somewhat cooler and drier. The refreshing southeast trade winds, or alizés, blow consistently May-August, varying to easterlies September-December. The northeast trades January-April coincide with the cyclone season. The trade winds cool the islands and offer clear sailing for mariners, making May-October the most favorable season to visit.

Rain falls abundantly and frequently during the southern summer months (Nov.-Apr.). Rainfall is greatest in the mountains and along the windward shores of the high islands. Winds from the southeast (maraamu) are generally drier than those from the northeast or north. The northeast winds often bring rain: Papenoo on the northeast side of Tahiti is twice as wet as rain-shadowed Punaauia.

The Society Islands are far damper than the Marquesas. In fact, the climate of the Marquesas is erratic: some years the group experiences serious drought, other years it could rain the whole time you're there. The low-lying Tuamotus get the least rainfall of all.

Throughout French Polynesia, the annual rainfall is extremely variable, but the humidity is generally high, reaching 98 percent. Temperatures range from warm to hot year-round; however, the ever-present sea moderates the humidity by bringing continual cooling breezes. In the evening the heat of the Tahiti afternoons is replaced by soft, fragrant mountain breezes called hupe, which drift down to the sea.

French Polynesia encompasses such a vast area that latitude is an important factor: at 27° south latitude, Rapa is far cooler than Nuku Hiva (9° south). Areas nearer the equator (the Marquesas) are hotter than those farther south (the Australs).

Cyclones are relatively rare, although they do hit the Tuamotus and occasionally Tahiti (but almost never the Marquesas). From November 1980 to May 1983 an unusual wave of eight cyclones and two tropical storms battered the islands because of the El Niño phenomenon. The next cyclone occurred in December 1991. In February 1998 a cyclone passed over the Tuamotus, and another hit Huahine in April 1998, again the fault of El Niño. Cyclone Oli, which hit Moorea and Tubuai in February 2010, was the most powerful in 35 years. Cyclone Niko in January 2015 is the latest major tropical cyclone to pass through French Polynesia. A recent analysis of data shows that in 1977 the belt of storms and winds shifted abruptly eastward, making Tonga and Melanesia drier and French Polynesia wetter. Cyclones are also striking farther east, and El Niño is expected to recur more frequently.

Tides

Tahiti and Moorea have a solar (rather than a lunar) tide, which means that the low tides are at sunrise and sunset, high tides at noon and midnight. Because of this, snorkeling in or near a reef passage will be safest in the morning as the water flows in. Shallow waters are best traversed by yachts around noon when the water is high and slack, and visibility is at its peak. In other parts of French Polynesia, tides may be lunar, cycling between high and low tide around every six hours. If you're a surfer, you'll want to download the tide chart for the destination you'll be visiting.

Currents and Winds

The Pacific Ocean has a greater impact on the world's climate than any other geographical feature on earth, taking heat away from the equator and toward the poles. Broad circular ocean currents flow from east to west across the tropical Pacific, clockwise in the North Pacific, counterclockwise in the South Pacific. North and south of the "horse latitudes" just outside the tropics, the currents cool and swing east. The prevailing winds move the same way: the southeast trade winds south of the equator, the northeast trade winds north of the equator, and the low-pressure doldrums in between. Westerlies blow east above the cool currents north and south of the tropics. This natural air-conditioning system brings warm water to Australia and Japan, cooler water to Peru and California.

The climate of the high islands is closely related to these winds. As air is heated near the equator it rises and flows at high altitudes toward the poles. By the time it reaches about 30° south latitude it will have cooled enough to cause it to fall and flow back toward the equator near sea level. In the southern hemisphere the rotation of the earth deflects the winds to the left to become the southeast trades. When these cool moist trade winds hit a high island, they are warmed by the sun and forced up. Above 500 meters (1,640 ft) elevation they begin to cool again, and their moisture condenses into clouds. At night the winds do not capture much warmth and are more likely to discharge their moisture as rain. The windward slopes of the high islands catch the trades head-on and are usually wet, while those on the leeward side may be dry. French Polynesia enjoys some of the worlds cleanest air, as it hasn't blown over a continent for weeks.

ENVIRONMENTAL ISSUES

The French nuclear testing program in the Tuamotu Islands 1966-1996 has impacted over 110,000 people in French Polynesia, according to a 2020 study analyzing French declassified documents. Nuclear testing has led to higher rates of cancers along with many other ailments. The Pacific Ocean may be contaminated as radioactive wastes from atmospheric testing before 1974 presently lying in the lagoons of Moruroa and Fangataufa are swept out to sea by rising sea levels. Even worse, large quantities of deadly nuclear waste presently locked in the basalt cores of these same atolls as a result of underground testing after 1974 may eventually leak into the Pacific through crevices and cracks in the coral layer above the basalt.

French Polynesia is especially vulnerable to global warming and climate change. The low-lying atolls of the Tuamotus will be subject to inundation over the next century, and coastal areas throughout the territory will be subject to severe erosion. This will have a major impact as most of the population lives beside the sea. Cyclones and droughts could also become more severe and prolonged over the next few decades. The people of the Pacific may have to pay for the greenhouse gases emitted in Asia, Australia, Europe, and the Americas.

Tourism-related construction can displace locals and cause beach erosion through the clearing of vegetation and the extraction of sand. Resort sewage causes lagoon pollution, while the reefs are blasted to provide passes for tourist craft and stripped of corals or shells by visitors. Locally scarce water supplies are diverted to hotels and golf courses, and prices for foods such as fruit and fish can be artificially inflated. Access to the ocean can be blocked by wall-to-wall restaurants and resorts. "Ecotourism" can lead to the destruction of natural areas if not conducted with sensitivity.

Flora and Fauna

FLORA

The variety of floral species encountered in the Pacific Islands declines as you move away from the Asian mainland. Although some species may have spread across the islands by means of floating seeds or fruit, wind and birds were probably more effective. The microscopic spores of ferns, for example, can be carried vast distances by the wind.

The high islands of French Polynesia support a great variety of plant life, while the low islands are restricted to a few hardy, drought-resistant species such as coconuts and pandanus. Rainforests fill the valleys and damp windward slopes of the high islands, while brush and thickets grow in more exposed locations. Hillsides in the drier areas are covered with coarse grasses. The absence of leaf-eating animals has allowed the vegetation to develop largely without the protective spines and thorns found elsewhere.

In the coastal areas of Tahiti most of the plants now seen have been introduced by humans. Avocado, banana, custard apple, guava, grapefruit, lime, lychee, mango, orange, papaya, pineapple, watermelon, and a hundred more are cultivated. Mountain bananas (fei) grow wild in the high country. Mape (Tahitian chestnut) grows along the streams, and other trees you'll encounter include almond, candlenut, casuarina (ironwood), flamboyant, barringtonia, purau (wild hibiscus), pistachio, and rosewood. A South American tree, *Miconia calvescens*, was planted in Tahiti in 1937, from which it spread across much of central Tahiti, supplanting the native vegetation.

Mangroves are often found along high-island coastal lagoons. The cable roots of the saltwater-tolerant red mangrove anchor in the shallow upper layer of oxygenated mud, avoiding the layers of hydrogen sulfide below. The tree provides shade for tiny organisms dwelling in the tidal mudflats—a place for birds to nest and for fish or shellfish to feed and spawn. The mangroves also perform the same task as land-building coral colonies along the reefs. As sediments are trapped between the roots, the trees extend farther into the lagoon, creating a unique natural environment.

Distance, drought, and poor soil have made atoll vegetation among the most unvaried on earth. Though a tropical atoll might seem lush, no more than 15 native species may be present. On the atolls, taro, a root vegetable with broad heart-shaped leaves, must be cultivated in deep organic pits. The vegetation of a raised atoll is apt to be far denser, with many more species, yet it's also likely that fewer than half will be native.

Flowers

In French Polynesia the air is sweet with the bouquet of tropical blossoms such as bursting bougainvillea, camellia, frangipani, ginger, orchids, poinsettia, and pitate jasmine. The fragrant flowers of the Polynesian hibiscus (purau) are yellow, not red or pink as on the Chinese hibiscus. A useful tree, the hibiscus has a soft wood used for house and canoe construction, and bast fiber used to make cordage and mats.

The national flower, the delicate, heavily scented tiare Tahiti (Gardenia taitensis), can have anywhere from six to nine white petals. It blooms year-round, but especially September-April. In his *Plants and Flowers of Tahiti* Jean-Claude Belhay writes, "The tiare is to Polynesia what the lotus is to India: a veritable symbol." Follow local custom by wearing this blossom or a hibiscus behind your left ear if you're happily taken, behind your right ear if you're still available.

CORAL REEFS

Coral reefs are the world's oldest ecological system and cover some 200,000 square kilometers (77,000 square mi) worldwide, between 25° north and 25° south latitude. A reef is created by the accumulation of millions of calcareous skeletons left by myriad generations of tiny coral polyps, some no bigger than a pinhead. A small piece of coral is a colony composed of large numbers of polyps. Though the reef's skeleton is usually white, the living polyps are of many different colors. The individual polyps on the surface often live a long time, continuously secreting layers to the skeletal mass beneath the tiny layer of flesh.

Coral polyps thrive in clear salty water where the temperature stays between 18°C and 30°C (64°F-86°F). They require a base not more than 50 meters (164 ft) below the water's surface on which to form. The coral colony grows slowly upward on the consolidated skeletons of its ancestors until it reaches the low-tide mark, after which development extends outward on the edges of the reef. Sunlight is critical for coral growth. Colonies grow quickly on the ocean side, especially the windward side, due to clearer water and a greater abundance of food. A strong, healthy reef can grow 4-5 centimeters (1.5-2 in) per year. Fresh or cloudy water inhibits coral growth, which is why villages and ports all across the Pacific are located at the reef-free mouths of rivers. Cyclones can kill coral by covering the reef with sand, which prevents light and nutrients from getting through. Erosion caused by logging or urban development can have the same effect.

Polyps extract calcium carbonate from the water and deposit it in their skeletons. All limy reef-building corals also contain microscopic algae within their cells. The algae, like all green plants, obtain energy from the sun and contribute this energy to the growth of the reef's skeleton. As a result, corals behave (and look) more like plants than animals, competing for sunlight just as terrestrial plants do. Many polyps are also carnivorous; they use their minute, stinging tentacles to capture tiny planktonic animals and organic particles at night.

Coral Types

Corals belong to a broad group of stinging creatures, which includes polyps, soft corals, stony corals, sea anemones, sea fans, and jellyfish. Only those types with hard skeletons and a single hollow cavity within the body are considered true corals. Stony corals such as brain, table, staghorn, and mushroom corals have external skeletons and are important reef builders. Soft corals, black corals, and sea fans have internal skeletons. Fire corals are recognized by their smooth, velvety surface and yellowish-brown color. The stinging toxins of this last group can easily penetrate human skin and cause swelling and painful burning that can last up to an hour. The many varieties of soft, colorful anemones gently waving in the current might seem inviting to touch, but beware—many are also poisonous.

The corals, like most other forms of life in the Pacific, colonized the ocean from the fertile seas of Southeast Asia. The number of species declines as you move east. More than 600 species of coral make their home in the Pacific, compared to only a few dozen in the Caribbean. The diversity of coral colors and forms is endlessly amazing. This is our most unspoiled environment, a world of almost indescribable beauty.

Coral Conservation

Coral reefs are one of the most fragile and complex ecosystems on earth, providing food and shelter for countless species of fish, crustaceans (shrimps, crabs, and lobsters), mollusks (shells), and other animals. The coral reefs of the South Pacific protect shorelines during storms, supply sand to maintain the islands, furnish food for the local population, form a living laboratory for science, and serve as major tourist attractions. Reefs worldwide host more than two million species of life. Without coral, the South Pacific would be immeasurably poorer.

Hard corals grow only about 10-25 millimeters (0.3-1 in) per year, and it can take 7,000-10,000 years for a coral reef to form. Though corals look solid, they're easily broken; by standing on them, breaking off pieces, or carelessly dropping anchor you can destroy in a few minutes what took so long to form. Once a piece of coral breaks off, it usually dies, and it may be years before the coral reestablishes itself and even longer before the broken piece is replaced. The wound may become infected by algae, which can multiply and kill the entire coral colony. When this happens over a wide area, the diversity of marine life declines dramatically.

Swim beside or well above the coral. Avoid bumping the coral with your fins, gauges, or other equipment, and don't dive during rough sea conditions. Proper buoyancy control is preferable to excessive weight belts. Snorkelers should check into taking along a life jacket, which will allow equipment adjustments without standing on coral. Wearing reef-safe sunscreen, free from oxybenzone, will also help corals stay alive long after you leave the water.

Do not remove seashells, coral, plant life, or marine animals from the sea. Doing so upsets the delicate balance of nature. This is a particular problem along shorelines frequented by large numbers of tourists, who can strip a reef in little time. Take pictures rather than the shells themselves to help the environment stay balanced for years to come.

The anchors and anchor chains of yachts can do serious damage to coral reefs. Pronged anchors are more environmentally friendly than larger, heavier anchors, and plastic tubing over the end of the anchor chain helps minimize damage. Place buoys along the anchor chain to float the chain above the coral, even when its submerged.

FAUNA

Few land animals reached the eastern Pacific without the help of humans. Ancient Polynesian navigators introduced pigs, dogs, and chickens; they also deliberately brought along rats, both for their delicate bones, used in tattooing, and for food. Captain Cook contributed cattle, horses, and goats; Captain Wallis left behind cats. More goats were dropped off by whalers in the Marquesas. Giant African snails (*Achatina fulica*) were brought to Tahiti from Hawaii in the 1960s by a local policeman fond of fancy French food. He tried to set up a snail farm with the result that some escaped, multiplied, and now crawl wild, destroying the vegetation.

Birds

Of the 104 species of birds in French Polynesia, half of the 30 species of native land birds are found only here. Among the 48 species of seabirds are the white-tailed tropic birds, brown and black noddies, white and crested terns, petrels, and boobies. The itatae (white tern), often seen flying about with its mate far from land, lays a single egg in the fork of a tree without any nest. The baby terns can fly soon after hatching. Its call is a sharp *ke-ke-yek-yek*. The oio (black noddy) nests in colonies, preferably in palm trees, building a flat nest of dead leaves, sticks, and stems. It calls a deep *cra-cra-cra*. Thirteen species of North American or Siberian land birds visit occasionally, and another 13 species of introduced birds are always here. The most notorious among them is the hopping common mynah bird (*Acridotheres tristis*) with its yellow beak and feet, which was introduced from Indonesia at the turn of the last century to control insects. Today these noisy, aggressive birds are ubiquitous—feeding on fruit trees and forcing the native finches and blue-tinged doves out of their habitat.

Fish

The South Pacific's richest store of life is found in the silent underwater world of the pelagic and lagoon fishes. Coral pinnacles on the lagoon floor provide a haven for angelfish, butterflyfish, damselfish, groupers, soldierfish, surgeonfish, triggerfish, trumpetfish, and countless more. These fish typically stay within a few meters of the protective coral, but larger fish such as barracuda, jackfish, parrotfish, pike, stingrays, and small sharks range across lagoon waters that are seldom deeper than 30 meters (about 100 ft). The external side of the reef is also home to many of these fish, but the open ocean is reserved for bonito, mahi-mahi, swordfish, tuna, wrasses, and the larger sharks. Passes between ocean and lagoon can be crowded with fish in transit, offering a favorite hunting ground for predators.

In the open sea the food chain begins with phytoplankton, which flourish wherever ocean up-swellings bring nutrients such as nitrates and phosphates to the surface. In the western Pacific this occurs near the equator, where massive currents draw water away toward Japan and Australia. Large schools of fast-moving tuna ply these waters feeding on smaller fish, which consume tiny phytoplankton drifting near the sunlit surface. The phytoplankton also exist in tropical lagoons where mangrove leaves, sea grasses, and other plant material are consumed by far more varied populations of reef fish, mollusks, and crustaceans.

It's believed that most Pacific marine organisms evolved in the triangular area bounded by New Guinea, the Philippines, and the Malay Peninsula. This "cradle of Indo-Pacific marine life" includes a wide variety of habitats and has remained stable through several geological ages. From this cradle the rest of the Pacific was colonized.

It should be noted here that the feeding of sharks, rays, eels, and other fish is widely practiced in French Polynesia, but it's a controversial activity. Supplying food to wild creatures of any kind destroys their natural feeding habits and makes them vulnerable to human predators, and handling marine life can have unpredictable consequences.

Marine Mammals

Cetaceans like whales and dolphins cruise the waters of French Polynesia. Dolphins, including spinner dolphins who've gotten their name from leaping and twirling like ballerinas, are seen all year long. Whales generally visit French Polynesia June-November. Humpbacks arrive about this time to give birth in the warm waters. As the weather grows warmer they return to the summer feeding areas around Antarctica. French Polynesia's large exclusive economic zone was declared a marine mammal sanctuary in

2002. Whale-watching trips are offered in season at Moorea and Rurutu.

Sharks

Sharks are Polynesia's apex ocean predators, and there are few places better to admire them in the world. The Tuamotus are famed for their passes, which attract hundreds of gray reef sharks at a time. It's also common to see white tip reef sharks, black tip reef sharks, nurse sharks, and lemon sharks throughout the archipelago. Tiger sharks and bull sharks are around but rarely seen, great white sharks even less so. The danger from sharks (*mao* in Tahitian, *requin* in French) to swimmers has been greatly exaggerated. An average of 70-100 shark attacks a year occur worldwide with 10 fatalities, so considering the number of people who swim in the sea, your chances of being involved are about one in 10 million. In the South Pacific, shark attacks on snorkelers or scuba divers are extremely rare, and the tiny mosquito is a far more dangerous predator.

To avoid a shark attack, don't swim in locations where sewage or edible wastes enter the water, or where fish have just been cleaned. You should also exercise care in places where residents have been fishing with spears or even a hook and line that day. Many locals state that shiny or white objects attract sharks, so take off anything that might apply before getting into the water. You'll find that sharks typically have little interest in humans and almost always cruise on by. But if one lingers around, don't panic—maintain eye contact with the shark and slowly swim back toward the boat or shore.

Sea Urchins

Sea urchins (living pincushions) are common in Polynesian waters, often found hidden in the crags of rocky shores and reefs. Take care when swimming or snorkeling: the long, sharp quills can puncture a reef bootie. Most sea urchins are not venomous, though quill punctures are painful and can become infected if not treated. The pain is caused by an injected protein, eliminated by holding the injured area in a pail of very hot water for about 15 minutes. This will coagulate the protein, eliminating the pain. If you can't heat water, soak the area in vinegar for 15 minutes. Remove the quills as best as you can. In some communities sea urchins are considered a delicacy, rarely featured on menus but available if you ask around.

Other Hazardous Creatures

Avoid touching any form of sea life as much as possible. Even the most harmless-looking creatures can be venomous. Sea creatures are generally shy and rarely bite or sting unless disturbed or provoked. Although jellyfish, stonefish, crown-of-thorns starfish, cone shells, eels, and sea snakes are dangerous, injuries resulting from any of these are rare. Inoffensive sea cucumbers (bêche-de-mer) punctuate the lagoon shallows. Stonefish also rest on the bottom and are hard to see because of camouflaging; if you happen to step on one, its dorsal fins inject a painful poison, which burns like fire in the blood. Avoid them by dragging your feet. Fortunately, stonefish are not common. If you are injured by a marine animal, head to the nearest hospital or clinic as soon as possible. It's wise to travel with a small first-aid kit. Never pick up a live cone shell; some varieties have a deadly prong that comes out from the pointed end. The tiny blue-ring octopus is only five centimeters long but packs a poison that can kill a human. Eels hide in reef crevices by day, but most are harmful only if you threaten them.

Reptiles

Land snakes don't exist in French Polynesia, and the sea snakes are shy and inoffensive. This, and the relative absence of leeches, poisonous plants, thorns, and dangerous wild animals, makes the South Pacific a paradise for hikers. One creature to watch out for is the centipede, which often hides under stones or anything else lying around. It's a long, flat, fast-moving insect not to be confused with the round, slow, and harmless millipede. The centipede's bite, though painful, is not lethal to a healthy adult.

Geckos and skinks are small lizards often seen on the islands. The gecko is nocturnal and has no eyelids. Adhesive toe pads enable it to pass along vertical surfaces, and it changes color to avoid detection. Unlike the skink, which avoids humans, geckos often live in people's homes, where they eat insects attracted by electric lights. Its loud clicking call may be a territorial warning to other geckos. Two species of geckos are asexual: in these, males do not exist, and the unfertilized eggs hatch into females identical to the mother. Geckos are the most advanced members of the animal world in which this phenomenon takes place. During the 1970s a sexual species of house gecko was introduced to Samoa and Vanuatu, and in 1988 it arrived on Tahiti. These larger, more aggressive geckos have drastically reduced the population of the endemic asexual species.

Five of the seven species of sea turtles are present in Polynesia (green, hawksbill, leatherback, loggerhead, and olive ridley turtles). All species of sea turtles now face extinction through ruthless hunting, egg harvesting, and beach destruction. Sea turtles come ashore November-February to lay their eggs on the beach from which they themselves originally hatched, but the female turtles don't commence this activity until they are 20 years old. Thus a drop in numbers today has irreversible consequences a generation later.

History

PREHISTORY

Oceania was the last area on earth to be settled by humans. Sometime after 2000 BC, Austronesian peoples entered the Pacific from Indonesia or the Philippines. The Austronesians had pottery and advanced outrigger canoes. Their distinctive lapita pottery, decorated in horizontal geometric bands and dated from 1500-500 BC, has been found at sites ranging from New Britain to New Caledonia, Tonga, and Samoa. Lapita pottery has allowed archaeologists to trace the migrations of an Austronesian-speaking race, the Polynesians, with some precision, and recent comparisons of DNA samples have confirmed that they traveled from the south China coast to Taiwan, the Philippines, Indonesia, New Guinea, Santa Cruz, Fiji, and Samoa.

The Austronesian languages are today spoken from Madagascar through Indonesia all the way to Easter Island and Hawaii—half the circumference of the world! All of the introduced plants of old Polynesia, except the sweet potato, originated in Southeast Asia. The endemic diseases of Oceania, leprosy and the filaria parasite, were unknown in the Americas. The amazing continuity of Polynesian culture is illustrated by motifs in contemporary tattooing and tapa, which are very similar to those on ancient lapita pottery.

POLYNESIAN MIGRATION

The early Polynesians set out from Southeast Asia 3,500 years ago on a migratory trek that would lead them to make the many islands of Polynesia their home. Great voyagers, they sailed their huge double-hulled canoes far and wide, steering with large paddles and pandanus sails. To navigate they read the sun, stars, currents, swells, winds, clouds, and birds. For instance, the brown noddy returns to roost on an island at night, and a sighting at sea would be a sure sign of land nearby.

Settlements on the islands of French Polynesia were established at uncertain dates around the start of the first millennium AD. Perhaps because of overpopulation in Samoa, by 300 BC groups of Polynesians had pressed on to the Marquesas. Polynesians from the Marquesas encountered Hawaii (AD 200) and Easter Island (AD 300). The Society Islands were reached by the Marquesans around AD 600, and from there or from the Marquesas the migrants continued to the Cook Islands (AD 800), the Tuamotus (AD 900), and New Zealand (before AD 1100). The Polynesians carried with them all the plants and animals needed to continue their way of life.

These were not chance landfalls but planned voyages: the Polynesians could (and often did) return the way they came. Stone adzes crafted from quarries in the Marquesas were found in the Austral Islands and Tuamotus, signaling trade between the island groups. That one could deliberately sail such distances against the trade winds and currents without the help of modern navigational equipment was proved in 1976 when the *Hokule'a,* a reconstructed oceangoing canoe, sailed 5,000 kilometers (3,100 mi) south from Hawaii to Tahiti. The expedition's Micronesian navigator, Mau Piailug, succeeded in setting a course by the ocean swells and relative positions of the stars alone, which guided the group very precisely along its way. Other signs used to find an island were clouds (which hang over peaks and remain stationary), seabirds (boobies fly up to 50 kilometers/31 miles offshore, frigate birds up to 80 kilometers/50 miles), and mysterious te lapa (underwater streaks of light radiating 120-150 kilometers/75-93 miles from an island, disappearing closer in).

The Polynesians were the real navigators of the Pacific, completing all their major voyages long before Europeans even dreamed this ocean existed. In double canoes lashed

Historical Timeline

1000 BC	Polynesians reach Samoa
300 BC	Polynesians reach the Marquesas
AD 600	Polynesians reach the Society Islands
900	Polynesians reach the Tuamotus
1521	Magellan sights Pukapuka in the Tuamotus
1595	Mendaña contacts the Marquesas
1767	Englishman Samuel Wallis contacts Tahiti
1768	Frenchman Bougainville visits Tahiti
1769	Captain Cook observes transit of Venus at Tahiti
1788	Bligh's HMS Bounty at Tahiti
1793	Founding of the Pomare dynasty
1797	Arrival on Tahiti of first Protestant missionaries
1803	Pomare II flees to Moorea
1815	Pomare II reconquers Tahiti
1818	Foundation of Papeete
1827	50-year reign of Queen Pomare IV begins
1836	French Catholic priests are expelled from Tahiti
1842	French protectorate is declared over Tahiti and the Marquesas
1844-1847	Tahitian War of Independence; Queen Pomare accepts French protectorate

together to form rafts, carrying their plants and animals with them, they penetrated as close to Antarctica as the South Island of New Zealand, as far north as Hawaii, and as far east as Easter Island—a full 13,000 kilometers (8,000 mi) from where it's presumed they first entered the Pacific.

Neolithic Polynesians

The Polynesians lived from fishing and agriculture, using tools made from stone, bone, shell, and wood. The men were responsible for planting, harvesting, fishing, cooking, and house- and canoe-building; the women tended the fields and animals, gathered fuel, prepared food, and made tapa clothes and household items. The people worked together in family or community groups, not as individuals.

People lived in scattered dwellings rather than villages, although there were groupings around the major temples and chiefs' residences. Land was collectively owned by families and tribes. Though the land was worked collectively by commoners, the chiefly families controlled and distributed its produce by well-defined customs. Large numbers of people could be mobilized for public works or war.

Two related forces governed Polynesian life: mana and tapu. Our word *taboo* originated from the Polynesian *tapu*. Numerous

1847	Parthenopean Republic established after bloody revolution in Naples; King Ferdinand IV flees to Palermo.
1865-1866	1,010 Chinese laborers arrive on Tahiti
1877	Death of Queen Pomare IV
1880	French protectorate changes into a colony
1885	Ban on Tahitian singing and dancing lifted
1887	French annexes the Leeward Islands
1889	French protectorate declared over Austral Islands
1900	Austral Islands annexed by France
1914	German cruisers shell Papeete
1916	1,000 Polynesians join Bataillon du Pacifique
1942	American military base on Bora Bora
1945	Tahitians become French citizens
1946	French Polynesia becomes an "overseas territory"
1963	French nuclear testing moves to Polynesia
1977	French Polynesia is granted partial internal autonomy
1985	South Pacific Nuclear-Free Zone Treaty signed
1999	Nuclear testing ends
2002	Whale and dolphin sanctuary created
2004	French Polynesia becomes an "overseas country"
2017	Marae Taputapuatea becomes a UNESCO World Heritage Site

tapu, or social laws, regulated Polynesian life, such as prohibitions against taking certain plants or fish that were intended for chiefly use. Mana was a spiritual power—gods and high chiefs had the most, and commoners had the least.

ART AND CULTURE

The Polynesians lost the art of pottery-making during their long stay in Havaiki (possibly Raiatea or Samoa) and had to cook their food in underground ovens (umu). It was sometimes tapu (taboo) for men and women to eat together. Breadfruit, taro, yams, sweet potatoes, bananas, and coconuts were cultivated (the Polynesians had no cereals). Taro was grown in organic pits; breadfruit was preserved by fermentation through burial (still a rare delicacy). Pigs, chickens, and dogs were also kept for food, but the surrounding sea yielded the most important source of protein. Stone fishponds and fish traps were built in the lagoons.

Canoes were made of planks stitched together with sennit and caulked with gum from breadfruit trees. Pandanus and coconut fronds were woven into handicrafts. Clothing consisted of tapa (bark cloth). Both men and women wore belts of pandanus leaves or tapa when at work, and during leisure, a skirt that reached to their knees. Ornaments were of feathers, whale or dolphin teeth, and flowers.

Both sexes were artfully tattooed using candlenut oil and soot.

For weapons there were clubs, spears, and slings. Archery was practiced only as a game to determine who could shoot farthest. Spear throwing, wrestling, boxing, kite-flying, surfing, and canoe-racing were popular sports. Polynesian music was made with nasal flutes and cylindrical sharkskin or hollow slit drums. Their dancing is still appreciated today.

The Polynesians used no masks and few colors, usually leaving their artworks unpainted. There was a defined class of artists producing traditional artworks of remarkable delicacy and deftness. The museums of the world possess many fine stone and wood tikis from the Marquesas Islands, where the decorative sense was highly developed. Sculpture in the Australs was more naturalistic, and only here were female tikis common. The Tahitians excelled in poetry, oratory, theater, music, song, and dance. Sadly, countless Polynesian artworks and objects were destroyed in the early 19th century by European missionaries, and it's likely just a small fraction of the complete body of Polynesian artwork still exists today.

SOCIAL HIERARCHY

The larger islands produced a surplus of goods thanks to the fertile soil, which allowed the emergence of a powerful ruling class. An individual's social position was determined by his or her family connections, and the recitation of one's genealogy confirmed it; descent was usually through the father. The common people lived in fear of their gods and chiefs. Prior to European contact three hereditary classes structured the Society Islands: high chiefs (ari'i), lesser chiefs (raatira), and commoners (manahune). A small slave class (titi) also existed. The various ari'i tribes controlled wedge-shaped valleys, and their authority was balanced. None managed to gain permanent supremacy over the rest. In this rigid hierarchical system, where high chiefs had more mana than commoners, marriage or even physical contact between people of unequal mana was forbidden. Children resulting from sexual relations between the classes were often killed. Growing up, Polynesians memorized their ancestral lineage, often being able to name relatives both close and distant for many generations back.

The Polynesians also practiced cannibalism, though the intensity of the practice varied from group to group: cannibalism was common in the Marquesas but relatively rare on Tahiti. It was believed that the mana or spiritual power of an enemy would be transferred to the consumer; to eat the body of one who was greatly despised was the ultimate revenge.

RELIGION

The Polynesians worshipped a pantheon of gods, who had more mana than any human. The most important were Tangaroa (the creator and god of the oceans), and Oro, or Tu (the god of war), who demanded human sacrifices. Perhaps the most fascinating figure in Polynesian mythology was Maui, a Krishna- or Prometheus-like figure who caught the sun with a cord to give its fire to the world. He lifted the firmament to prevent it from crushing mankind, fished the islands out of the ocean with a hook, and was killed trying to gain the prize of immortality for humanity. Also worth noting is Hina, the heroine who fled to the moon to avoid incest with her brother and so that the sound of her tapa beater wouldn't bother anyone. Tane (the god of light) and Rongo (the god of agriculture and peace) were other important gods. This polytheism, which may have disseminated from Raiatea in the Society Islands, was most important in eastern Polynesia. The Arioi confraternity, centered in Raiatea and thought to be possessed by the gods, traveled about putting on dramatic representations of the myths.

Religion centered around an open-air temple, with a stone altar. Here priests prayed to the ancestors or gods and conducted all the significant ceremonies of Polynesian life. The Eastern Polynesians were enthusiastic temple builders, evidenced today by widespread ruins. Known by the Polynesian names marae, ma'ae, or ahu, these platform and courtyard structures of coral and basalt blocks often had low surrounding walls and internal arrangements of upright wooden slabs. Once temples for religious cults, they were used for seating the gods and for presenting fruits and other foods to them at ritual feasts. Sometimes, but rarely, human sacrifices took place on the marae. Religion in western Polynesia was very low-key, with few priests or cult images. No temples have been found in Tonga and very few in Samoa. The gods of eastern Polynesia were represented in human form. The ancestors were more important as a source of descent for social ranking, and genealogies were carefully preserved.

EUROPEAN CONTACT

While the Polynesian history of the islands goes back two millennia, the European period began only in the 16th century, when the Magellan expedition sailed past the Tuamotus. In 1595, on his second trip from Peru to the Solomon Islands, Álvaro de Mendaña sighted the southern Marquesas Islands. Eleven years later another Spanish expedition led by Pedro Fernandez de Quirós "found" a few of the Tuamotu atolls, but their discoveries were concealed by the Spanish authorities to avoid attracting rival powers to the area.

On June 18, 1767, Captain Samuel Wallis on the HMS *Dolphin* "discovered" Tahiti (which was already well populated at the time).

At first the Tahitians attacked the ship, but after experiencing European gunfire they decided to be friendly. Eager to trade, they loaded the Englishmen down with pigs, fowl, and fruit. Iron was in the highest demand in Tahiti. Wallis sent ashore a landing party, which named Tahiti "King George III Island," turned some sod, and hoisted the Union Jack. A year later the French explorer Louis-Antoine de Bougainville arrived on the east coast, unaware of Wallis's proclamation, and claimed Tahiti for the king of France.

Wallis and Bougainville visited only briefly, leaving it to Captain James Cook to really describe Polynesia to Europeans. Cook visited "Otaheite" (Tahiti) four times, in 1769, 1773, 1774, and 1777. His first three-month visit was to observe the transit of the planet Venus across the face of the sun. The second and third were in search of the southern continent, while the fourth was to find a northwest passage between the Pacific and Atlantic Oceans. Some of the finest artists and scientists of the day accompanied Captain Cook. Their explorations added the Leeward Islands, two Austral islands, and a dozen Tuamotu islands to European knowledge. On Tahiti Cook met a high priest from Raiatea named Tupaia, who had an astonishing knowledge of the Pacific and could name dozens of islands. He drew Cook a map that included the Cook Islands, the Marquesas, and perhaps also some Samoan islands. Tupaia's knowledge proved essential for seafaring at the time, and despite never having been to many islands, Tupaia was able to navigate Cook to many of the most remote Pacific islands.

In 1788 Tahiti was visited for five months by the HMS *Bounty,* commanded by Lieutenant William Bligh with orders to collect young breadfruit plants for transportation to the West Indies. However, the famous mutiny did not take place at Tahiti but in Tongan waters, and from there Bligh and loyal members of his crew managed to escape by navigating an open boat 6,500 kilometers (4,038 mi) to West Timor. In 1791, the HMS *Pandora* came to Tahiti in search of the *Bounty* mutineers, intending to take them to England for trial. They captured 14 survivors of the 16 who had elected to stay on Tahiti when Fletcher Christian and eight others left for Pitcairn. Although glamorized by Hollywood, the mutineers helped destroy traditional Tahitian society by acting as mercenaries for rival chiefs. In 1792 Bligh returned to Tahiti in another ship and completed his original mission.

By the early 19th century, ruffian British and American whalers were fanning out over the Pacific. Other ships traded with the islanders for sandalwood, bêche-de-mer (sea cucumbers), and mother-of-pearl, as well as the usual supplies. These early contacts with Europeans had a devastating effect on native cultures. When introduced into the South Pacific, European sicknesses—mere discomforts to them—devastated whole populations. Measles, influenza, tuberculosis, scarlet fever, dysentery, smallpox, typhus, typhoid, and whooping cough were deadly because the islanders had never developed resistance to them. The Europeans' alcohol, weapons, and venereal disease further accelerated the process.

Kings and Missionaries

In March 1797 the ship *Duff* dropped off on Tahiti 18 Protestant missionaries and their wives after a 207-day journey from England. By this time Pomare, chief of the area adjoining Matavai Bay, had become powerful through the use of European tools, firearms, and mercenaries. He welcomed the missionaries but would not be converted. By 1800 all but five of the original 18 had left Tahiti disappointed.

In 1803 Pomare I died and his despotic son, Pomare II, attempted to conquer the entire island. After initial success he was forced to flee to Moorea in 1808. Missionary Henry Nott went with him, and in 1812 Pomare II turned to him for help in regaining his lost power. Though the missionaries refused to baptize Pomare II himself because of his penchant for drinking, his subjects on Moorea became nominal Christians. In 1815 this "Christian king" managed to regain Tahiti and overthrow paganism. Instead of being punished, the defeated clans coerced to become Christians. The persistent missionaries then enforced the Ten Commandments and dressed the Tahitian women in modest clothing—dresses that covered their bodies from head to toe. Henceforth singing anything but hymns was banned, dancing proscribed, along with all customs that offended puritanical sensibilities. Morality police terrorized the Tahitians in an eternal crusade against sin. Even wearing flowers in one's hair was prohibited.

The Exploitation of Polynesia

Upon Pomare II's death from drink at age 40 in 1821, the crown passed to his infant son, Pomare III, but he died in 1827. At this juncture the most remarkable Tahitian of the 19th century, Aimata, half-sister of Pomare II, became Queen Pomare Vahine IV. She was to rule Tahiti, Moorea, and part of the Austral and Tuamotu groups for half a century until her death in 1877, a Tahitian Queen Victoria. She allied herself closely with the London Missionary Society (LMS), and when two fanatical French-Catholic priests, Honoré Laval and François Caret, arrived on Tahiti in 1836 from their stronghold at Mangareva (Gambier Islands), she expelled them.

This affront brought a French frigate to Papeete in 1838, demanding 2,000 piastres compensation and a salute to the French flag. Although the conditions were met, the queen and her chiefs wrote to England appealing for help, but none came. A Belgian named Moerenhout who had formerly served as the U.S. consul was appointed French consul to Queen Pomare in 1838, and in 1839 a second French gunboat arrived and threatened to bombard Tahiti unless 2,000 Spanish dollars were paid and Catholic missionaries given free entry. Back in Mangareva, Laval pushed forward a grandiose building program that wiped out 80 percent of the population of the Gambiers from overwork.

In September 1842, while the queen and George Pritchard, the English consul, were away, Moerenhout tricked four local chiefs into signing a petition asking to be brought under French "protection." This demand was immediately accepted by French Admiral Abel Dupetit-Thouars, who was in league with Moerenhout, and on September 9, 1842, they forced Queen Pomare to accept a French protectorate. When the queen tried to maintain her power and keep her red-and-white royal flag, Dupetit-Thouars deposed the queen on November 8, 1843, and occupied her kingdom, an arbitrary act that was rejected by the French king, who reestablished the protectorate in 1844. Queen Pomare fled to Raiatea, and Pritchard was deported to England in March 1844, bringing Britain and France to the brink of war. The Tahitians resisted for three years: old French forts and war memorials recall the struggle.

THE COLONIAL ERA
A French Protectorate

In 1847, when Queen Pomare realized that no British assistance was coming, she and her people reluctantly accepted the French protectorate. As a compromise, the British elicited a promise from the French not to annex the Leeward Islands, so Huahine, Raiatea, and Bora Bora remained independent until 1887. The French had taken possession of the Marquesas in 1842, even before imposing a protectorate on Tahiti. The Austral Islands were added in 1900, and only British action prevented the annexation of the Cook Islands. French missionaries attempted to convert the Tahitians to Catholicism, but only in the Marquesas were they fully successful.

Queen Pomare tried to defend the interests of her people as best she could, but much of her nation was dying: between the 18th century and 1926 the population of the Marquesas fell from 80,000 to only 2,000. In April 1774 Captain Cook had tried to estimate the population of Tahiti by counting the number of men he saw in a fleet of war canoes and ascribing three members to each one's family. Cook's figure was 204,000, but according to anthropologist Bengt Danielsson, the correct number at the time was likely about 150,000. By 1829 it had dropped to 8,568, and a low of 7,169 was reached in 1865.

Pomare V, the final member of the line, was more interested in earthly pleasures than the traditions upheld by his mother. In 1880, with French interests at work on the Panama Canal, a colonial administrator convinced him to sign away his kingdom for a 5,000-franc-a-month pension. Thus, on June 29, 1880, the protectorate became the full French colony it is today, the Établissements Français de l'Océanie. In 1957 the name was changed to Polynésie Française. Right up until the 1970s the colony was run by governors appointed in Paris who implemented the policies of the French government. There was no system of indirect rule through local chiefs as was the case in the British colonies: here French officials decided everything, and their authority could not be questioned. Even the 18-member Conseil Générale created in 1885 to oversee certain financial matters had its powers reduced in 1899 and was replaced in 1903 by an impotent advisory council composed of French civil servants. The only elected official with any authority (and a budget) was the mayor of Papeete.

The most earthshaking event between 1880 and 1960 was a visit by two German cruisers, the *Scharnhorst* and *Gneisenau,* which shelled Papeete, destroying the marketplace on September 22, 1914. (Two months later both were sunk by the British at the Battle of the Falkland Islands.) A thousand Tahitian volunteers subsequently served in Europe, 300 of them becoming casualties. On September 2, 1940, the colony declared its support for the Free French, and soon after Pearl Harbor the Americans arrived to establish a base on Bora Bora. Polynesia remained cut off from occupied metropolitan France until the end of the war, although several hundred Tahitians served with the Pacific battalion in North Africa and Italy. In 1946 the colony was made an overseas territory, or territoire d'outre-mer (TOM), endowed with an elected territorial assembly. Representation in the French parliament was also granted.

The economy of the early colonial period had been based on cotton growing (1865-1900), vanilla cultivation (1870-1900), pearl shell collecting (1870-1960), copra making, and phosphate mining (1908-1966). These were to be replaced by nuclear testing (1963-1996), tourism (1961-present), and cultured pearls (1968-present).

The Nuclear Era

The early 1960s were momentous times for French Polynesia. Within a few years, an international airport opened on Tahiti, MGM filmed *Mutiny on the Bounty,* and the French began testing their atomic bombs. After Algeria became independent in July 1962, the French decided to move their Sahara nuclear testing facilities to Moruroa atoll in the Tuamotu Islands, 1,200 kilometers (745 mi) southeast of Tahiti. In 1963, when all local political parties protested the invasion of Polynesia by thousands of French troops and technicians sent to establish a nuclear testing center, President Charles de Gaulle simply outlawed political parties. The French set off their first atmospheric nuclear explosion at Moruroa on July 2, 1966, spreading contamination as far as Peru and New Zealand. In 1974 international protests forced the French to switch to the underground tests that continued until 1996. During those three decades of infamy, 181 nuclear explosions, 41 of them in the atmosphere, rocked the Tuamotus.

In the 1960s and 1970s, as independence blossomed across the South Pacific, France tightened its strategic grip on French Polynesia. The spirit of the time is best summed up in the life of one man, Pouvanaa a Oopa, an outspoken World War I hero from Huahine. In 1949 he became the first Polynesian to occupy a seat in the French Chamber of Deputies. His party gained control of the territorial assembly in 1953, and in 1957 he was elected vice president of the newly formed Government Council. In 1958 Pouvanaa campaigned for independence in a referendum vote, but when this failed because of a controversy over the imposition of an income tax, the French government reestablished central control and had Pouvanaa arrested on trumped-up charges of arson. He was eventually sentenced to an eight-year prison term and exiled to France for 15 years. De Gaulle wanted Pouvanaa out of the way until French nuclear testing facilities could be established in Polynesia, and he was not freed until 1968. In 1971 he won the French Polynesian seat in the French Senate, a post he held until his death in early 1977. Tahitians refer to the man as metua (father), and his statue stands in front of Papeete's Territorial Assembly.

Pouvanaa's successors, John Teariki and Francis Sanford, were also defenders of Polynesian autonomy and opponents of nuclear testing. Their combined efforts convinced the French government to grant Polynesia a new statute with slightly increased autonomy in 1977. A year later, Faa'a mayor Oscar Temaru formed Tavini Huiraatira, the Polynesian Liberation Front, the leading antinuclear, pro-independence party in the territory. The 1982 territorial elections were won by the neo-Gaullist Tahoeraa Huiraatira (Popular Union), led by the pronuclear, anti-independence mayor of Pirae, Gaston Flosse. To stem growing support for independence, Flosse negotiated enhanced autonomy for the territory in 1984 and 1996.

The independence cause was given impetus by France's last fling at nuclear testing. In April 1992, President Mitterrand halted the testing program at Moruroa, but in June 1995, newly elected President Jacques Chirac ordered a resumption of underground nuclear testing in the Tuamotus, and despite worldwide protests the first test was carried out on September 5, 1995. Early the next morning nonviolent demonstrators blocked the runway of Faa'a Airport after it was reported that Gaston Flosse was attempting to escape to France. When police charged the protesters to clear the runway, the demonstration turned into a riot in which the airport and Papeete were ransacked.

Meanwhile, at the Moruroa test site, two large Greenpeace protest vessels had been boarded by tear gas-firing French commandos and impounded (the ships were not released until six months later). Worldwide condemnation of the test series reached unprecedented levels, and in January 1996 the French announced that the testing had been completed. The facilities on Moruroa have since been decommissioned, and it's highly unlikely the testing will ever resume, yet deadly radiation may already be leaking into the sea through cracks in the atoll's porous coral cap. A mantle of secrecy hangs over France's former nuclear playground in the South Pacific, but once classified documents released in 2021 reveal as many as 110,000 people were impacted by nuclear testing. This exposure has led to multiple types of cancers and illnesses.

After 1996 Flosse and party attempted to enhance the illusion of autonomy by developing the concept of Tahiti Nui, or "Greater Tahiti." Tens of millions of euros were spent to build a new waterfront promenade and presidential palace in Papeete and an immense town hall and six-story general hospital at Pirae (Flosse's hometown). Raiatea has been given a new cruise ship terminal, and five-star resorts have been erected on half a dozen islands thanks to tax concessions. The government-sponsored airline, Air Tahiti Nui, was granted landing rights in Paris, thereby forcing two privately owned French airlines (Air Lib and Corsair) to drop the route, and a territorial TV station, Tahiti Nui TV, has been launched. In March 2004 a Flosse-backed constitutional amendment had French Polynesia declared a pays d'outre-mer (overseas country) with a right to maintain overseas missions.

In May 2004 a stunning upset occurred in elections for an expanded 57-seat Territorial Assembly. Flosse's party lost its majority for the first time in decades, and the pro-independence leader Oscar Temaru became president of French Polynesia. Temaru declared his willingness to negotiate with France and warned his followers that a referendum on independence might be 10-15 years away. This change of leadership has facilitated the territory's integration into the South Pacific as a whole, and French Polynesia was granted observer status by the Pacific Islands Forum, an influential regional grouping. Since 2004 the presidency has alternated between Temaru, Flosse, and Bora Bora mayor Gaston Tong Sang nearly a dozen times as assembly members are lured to rival coalitions by offers of power positions. In November 2009, Gaston Flosse was sent to Tahiti's Nuutania Prison after being indicted for taking bribes and destroying evidence during his term in office. In 2013, French Polynesia was reinscribed on the United Nations list of Non-Self-Governing Territories. Today's president, Edouard Fritch, clashes with the pro-independence party led by Temaru.

Government and Economy

ORGANIZATION

In 1885 an organic decree created the colonial system of government, which remained in effect until the proclamation of a new statute in 1958. In 1977 the French granted the territory partial internal self-government, and Francis Sanford was elected premier of "autonomous" Polynesia. A new local-government statute, passed by the French parliament and promulgated on September 6, 1984, gave slightly more powers to the Polynesians, and in 1996 additional powers were transferred to the territory to slow the momentum toward full independence. Yet the constitution of the Republic of France remains the supreme law of the land, and local laws can be overturned by a Constitutional Council comprising French judges.

A Territorial Assembly elects the president of the government, who chooses 15 cabinet ministers (before 1984 the French high commissioner was the chief executive). The 57 assembly members are elected every five years from separate districts. The territory is represented in Paris by two elected deputies: a senator as well as a social and economic counselor. The French government, through its high commissioner (called "governor" until

1977), retains control over foreign relations, immigration, defense, justice, the police, the municipalities, higher education, and the currency.

French Polynesia is divided into 48 communes, each with an elected Municipal Council, which chooses a mayor from its ranks. Every main town on an island has its mairie or hôtel de ville (town hall). These elected municipal bodies, however, are controlled by appointed French civil servants, who run the five administrative subdivisions. The administrators of the Windward, Tuamotu-Gambier, and Austral subdivisions are based at Papeete, while the headquarters of the Leeward Islands administration is at Uturoa (Raiatea), and that of the Marquesas Islands is at Taiohae (Nuku Hiva).

The territorial flag consists of three horizontal bands—red, white, and red with a double-hulled Polynesian sailing canoe superimposed on the white band. On the canoe are five figures representing the five archipelagos.

TAXES AND DISTRIBUTION OF WEALTH

French Polynesia has the highest per capita gross domestic product (GDP) in the South Pacific, about US$20,182 per person in 2020, totaling US$5,670,000 statewide. Paris contributes little to the territorial budget, but it finances the many departments and services under direct control of the high commissioner, spending an average of €1.6 billion per year in the territory, nearly a third of the GDP. Much of it goes to the military and to the 2,200 expatriate French civil servants who earn salaries 84 percent higher than those in France. Of the total workforce of 68,000, about 40 percent work for some level of government while the other 60 percent are privately employed. Four out of every five jobs are in services. Unemployment is almost 14 percent.

In 1994 the territorial government introduced an income tax of 2 percent on earnings over CFP 150,000 a month, plus new taxes on gasoline, wine, telecommunications, and unearned income. Indirect taxes, such as licensing fees and customs duties, long accounted for more than half of territorial government revenue. The largest tax tourists will feel is the taxe sur la valeur ajoutée (TVA), or value-added tax (VAT), added to the price of most goods and services. The TVA is currently 6 percent for all rented accommodations and room packages, with 5 percent added for room tax. A 16 percent VAT applies to most goods from shops and stores. A 10 percent VAT is applied to bar tabs, excursions, tours, car rentals, and meals in restaurants. For decades the price of imported goods has been doubled by taxation, and this consumption tax has further increased the cost of living.

With pearl exports falling and tourism in a steep decline due to the Coronavirus pandemic, French Polynesia is currently facing a severe economic crisis. In 2020 the gross domestic product fell over 7 percent from the year before. Unemployment is on the rise, leading to a drop in consumption.

TRADE

The inflow of people and money since the early 1960s has stimulated consumerism, and except for tourism and cultured pearls, the economy of French Polynesia is now dominated by French government spending. The nuclear testing program provoked an influx of 30,000 French settlers, plus a massive infusion of capital, which distorted the formerly self-supporting economy into one dependent on France. In 2015, imports stood at US$1,527 million, while exports amounted to just US$130 million, one of the highest disparities in the world. Much of the imbalance is consumed by the French administration itself. Foreign currency spent by tourists on imported goods and services also helps steady the situation.

More than 30 percent of the imports come from France, which has imposed a series of self-favoring restrictions. Imports include food, fuel, building material, consumer goods, and automobiles. The main exports are pearls, coconut oil, jewelry, and noni. The main agricultural export from the outer islands is copra; copra production has been heavily subsidized by the government since 1967 to discourage migration to Tahiti. The copra is crushed into coconut oil and animal feed at the Motu Uta mill in Papeete. Cultured pearls from farms in the Tuamotus are the largest export, accounting for 38 percent of the total.

AGRICULTURE AND FISHING

Labor recruiting for the nuclear testing program caused local agriculture to collapse in the mid-1960s. Between 1962 and 1988 the percentage of the workforce employed in agriculture dropped from 46 percent to 10 percent, and today agriculture accounts for just over 3 percent of salaried employment. Vanilla and coconut oil combined now account for less than 5 percent of exports, and the export of noni pulp to the United States for the making of juice is equally important.

About 80 percent of all food consumed locally is imported. Bread and rice are heavily subsidized by the government. Local vegetables supply half of local needs, while Tahitian coffee covers 20 percent of consumption. French Polynesia does manage, however, to cover three-quarters of its own fruit requirements, and the local pineapple and grapefruit crop goes to the fruit-juice factory on Moorea. Most industry is related to food processing (fruit-juice factory, brewery, soft drinks, etc.) or coconut products. It's rumored that marijuana (pakalolo) is now the leading cash crop, although you won't be aware of it. Officially, milk, copra, fruit, vegetables, and eggs are the main agricultural products, in that order. Large areas have been planted in Caribbean pine to provide for future timber needs. Considerable livestock is kept in the Marquesas.

Aquaculture is being developed, with tanks for freshwater shrimp, prawns, live bait, and green mussels. Deep-water fishing within the territory's huge exclusive economic zone is done by a few hundred local boats. Most of the fish are consumed locally, but catches have fallen in recent years due to declining fish stocks.

MINING

One of the few potential sources of real wealth is the undersea mineral nodules within the huge exclusive economic zone (EEZ) of French Polynesia. The potato-sized nodules contain manganese, cobalt, nickel, and copper; total deposits are valued at US$3 trillion, enough to supply the world for thousands of years. In the past three decades Japan has spent over US$100 million on seabed surveys in preparation for eventual mining.

In 1976 the French government passed legislation that gave it control of this zone, not only along France's coastal waters but also around all her overseas territories and departments. The National Marine Research Center and private firms have already drawn up plans to recover nickel, cobalt, manganese, and copper nodules from depths of more than 4,000 meters (13,000 ft). The French government has adamantly refused to give the Territorial Assembly any jurisdiction over this tremendous resource, an important indicator as to why it is determined to hold onto its colony at any price.

CULTURED PEARLS

According to myth, the Polynesian god Oro descended to earth on a rainbow to present a Bora Bora princess with a black pearl. Later pearls appeared in the mourning costumes of Tahitian priests at the funerals of important chiefs. The commercial quest for pearls began around 1870 as island divers wearing only tiny goggles plunged effortlessly to depths of 25-30 meters (80-100 ft) in the Tuamotu lagoons to collect oysters. Finding a pearl this way was 1 chance in 15,000, and the real objective was the shell, which could be made into mother-of-pearl buttons. By 1960, overharvesting had depleted the slow-growing oyster beds, and today live oysters are collected only to supply cultured-pearl farms. The shell is now a mere by-product, made into decorative items.

French Polynesia's cultured-pearl industry is now second only to tourism as a money earner, providing around 10,000 jobs. It all began in 1963 when an experimental farm was established on Hikueru atoll in the Tuamotus. The first commercial farm opened on Manihi in 1968, but the real boom began only in the late 1980s, and today hundreds of cooperative and private pearl farms operate on 26 atolls, employing thousands of people. Although small companies and family operations are still able to participate in the industry, pearl production is becoming increasingly concentrated in a few hands because of the vertical integration of farming, wholesaling, and retailing. Robert Wan Pearls now controls more than half the industry, and the next four companies account for another quarter of production.

The industry is drawing many people back to ancestral islands they abandoned after devastating hurricanes in 1983. Pearl farming relieves pressure on natural stocks and creates an incentive to protect marine environments. Pollution from fertilizer runoff or sewage can make a lagoon unsuitable for pearl farming, which is why the farms are concentrated on lightly populated atolls where other forms of agriculture are scarcely practiced. Pearl farm workers often feed themselves with fish they catch in the lagoons, leading to a big decline in marine life.

The strings of oysters must be monitored constantly and lowered or raised if there are variations in water temperature. The larger farms use high-pressure hoses to clean the shells, while smaller family operations often employ the traditional method of manually removing fouling organisms from the shells with a knife. Overcrowding can create hotspots that spread infections to other farms, and more research and government supervision will be required if this industry is to flourish in the long term.

Unlike the Japanese cultured white pearl, the Polynesian black pearl is created only by the giant black-lip oyster (*Pinctada margaritifera*), which thrives in the Tuamotu lagoons. Beginning in the 19th century, the oysters were collected by Polynesian divers who could dive up to 40 meters (130 ft). It takes around three years for a pearl to form in a seeded oyster. A spherical pearl is formed when a Mississippi River mussel graft from Tennessee is introduced inside the coat; the oyster creates only a hemispherical half pearl if the graft goes between the coat and the shell. Half pearls are much cheaper than real pearls and make outstanding rings and pendants. Some of the grafts used are surprisingly large and the layer of nacre around such pearls may be relatively thin, but only an X-ray can tell. Thin coating on a pearl greatly reduces its value.

The cooperatives sell their production at Papeete auctions held twice a year. Private producers sell their pearls through independent dealers or plush retail outlets in Papeete. Every year about a million black pearls are exported to Japan, Hong Kong, the United States, and Thailand, making the territory the world's second-largest source of loose pearls (after Australia, which produces the smaller yellow pearls). To control quality and pricing, the export of loose reject pearls is prohibited, although finished jewelry is exempt. Pearl prices have fallen in recent years due to overproduction and smuggling to avoid the export tax.

TOURISM

French Polynesia is second only to Fiji as a South Pacific destination, with 236,642 tourists in 2019, 41 percent of them from North America, 26 percent from France, 14 percent from other European countries, 6 percent from Asia, and 10 percent from Australia and New Zealand. The COVID-19 pandemic decreased tourism numbers greatly; French Polynesia only welcomed 77,017 tourists in 2020. Yet tourism is far less developed here than it is in Hawaii. Waikiki could have more rooms than the entire island of Tahiti; Hawaii gets more visitors in 10 days than French Polynesia gets in a year. The location of Tahiti has thus far prevented most of the islands from being largely developed.

The number of visitors has steadily declined in recent years due to the perception that French Polynesia is expensive. Rather than a repeat destination, many tourists come on a cruise or as a once-in-a-lifetime event to stay at a luxury resort on a large anniversary trip or honeymoon.

Money generated by tourism covers a third of French Polynesia's import bill and provides around 12,000 jobs, 20 percent of all employment on French Polynesia. The average tourist spends around CFP 300,000 per visit, but many products purchased are imported. Many of the luxury resorts are foreign-owned and operated, and in many cases resort development has been at the expense of the environment. Tourism development was responsible for the 35 percent increase in the population of Bora Bora between the 1996 and 2007 censuses.

People and Culture

DEMOGRAPHY AND DIVERSITY

French Polynesia's population of 268,270 (2017 census) is around 78 percent Polynesian, 10 percent European, and 12 percent Chinese. These are only estimates because the last census that provided an ethnic breakdown took place in 1988 and it is now forbidden to collect this type of information. About 69 percent of the total population lives on Tahiti (compared to only 25 percent before the nuclear-testing boom began in the 1960s), but a total of 76 far-flung islands are inhabited. People from the Australs, Tuamotus, and Marquesas migrate to Tahiti, and Tahitians to New Caledonia, creating the problem of idled land and abandoned homes. Papeete has struggled to cope with rapid growth, leading to unemployment and social problems.

The indigenous people of French Polynesia are the Maohi or Eastern Polynesians (as opposed to the Western Polynesians in Samoa and Tonga), and many Polynesians refer to their country as Te Ao Maohi, especially those who are seeking independence from France. The word "colon" formerly applied to French men who arrived long before the bomb and made a living as planters or traders, and practically all of them married Polynesian women. Most of these colons have already died. Their descendants now dominate politics and the local bureaucracy. The present Europeans (popa'a) are mostly recently arrived metropolitan French (faranis). Their numbers increased dramatically in the 1960s and 1970s, and most live in urban areas where they're involved in the administration, military, or professions. In contrast, very few Polynesians have migrated to France, although 7,000 live in New Caledonia.

Local Chinese (tinito) dominate business throughout the territory. In Papeete and Uturoa, entire streets are lined with Chinese stores, and individual Chinese merchants are found on almost every island. They're also prominent in pearl farming and tourism. During the U.S. Civil War, when the supply of cotton to Europe was disrupted, Scotsman William Stewart set up a cotton plantation on the south side of Tahiti. Unable to convince Tahitians to do the heavy work, Stewart brought in a contingent of 1,010 Chinese laborers from Canton in 1865-1866. When the war ended the enterprise went bankrupt, but many of the Chinese stayed on as market gardeners, hawkers, and opium dealers. Things began changing in 1964 when France recognized the People's Republic of China and granted French citizenship to the territory's Chinese (most other Tahitians had become French citizens right after World War II). The French government tried to assimilate the Chinese by requiring that they adopt French-sounding names and by closing all Chinese schools. Despite this, the Chinese community has remained distinct.

What's in a Name?

Over the years, that part of eastern Polynesia controlled by France has been called many things. After 1880 it was the Établissements Français de l'Océanie, becoming Polynésie Française, or French Polynesia, in 1957, the designation still officially recognized by the authorities. French-occupied Polynesia better reflects the political reality, but variations such as (French) Polynesia, "French" Polynesia, and Tahiti-Polynesia are also seen. In recent years the pro-French faction in the Territorial Assembly has adopted Tahiti Nui, or "Greater Tahiti," whereas the pro-independence camp seems to favor Te Ao Maohi, which translates to Land of the Maohi. Maohinui is also heard. Tourism officials on Tahiti often use Tahiti and Its Islands. When in doubt, "Tahiti" will get you by, although there's a lot more to this colorful region than just its largest and best-known island.

From 1976-1983 about 18,000 people migrated to the territory, 77 percent of them from France and another 13 percent from New Caledonia. Nearly 1,000 immigrants continue to arrive each year. About 40,000 Europeans are now present in the territory, plus 8,000 soldiers, police officers, and transient officials. Many Tahitians would like to see this immigration restricted, but French citizens come for tax exemptions, as for many the situation in French Polynesia is more lucrative than it is in France. Because of this dynamic, there is a complex undercurrent of anti-French sentiment.

RELIGION

Though the old Polynesian religion largely died out in the early 19th century, the Tahitians are still a strongly religious people. Surviving elements of the old religion are the still-widespread belief in spirits (aitu), the continuing use of traditional medicine, and the influence of myth. Protestant missionaries arrived on Tahiti 39 years before the Catholics and 47 years before the Mormons, so 45 percent of the people now belong to the Evangelical Church, which is strongest in the Austral and Leeward Islands. Until the middle of the 20th century this church was one of the only democratic institutions in the colony, and it continues to exert strong influence on social matters (for example, it resolutely opposed nuclear testing).

Of the 34 percent of the total population who are Catholic, half are Polynesians from the Tuamotus and Marquesas, and the other half are French. Another 5 percent are Seventh-Day Adventists, and 10 percent are Mormons. A Mormon group called Sanitos, which rejects Brigham Young as a second prophet, has had a strong following in the Tuamotus since the 19th century. Several other Christian sects are also represented, and some Chinese are Buddhists. It's not unusual to see two or three different churches in a village of 100 people. All the main denominations operate their own schools. Local ministers and priests are powerful figures in the outer-island communities. One vestige of the pre-Christian religion is a widespread belief in ghosts (tupapau).

Of course, the optimum way to experience religion in French Polynesia is to go to church on Sunday. Protestant church services are conducted mostly in Tahitian; Catholic services are in French. Sitting through a service (1-2 hours) is often worthwhile just to hear the singing and to observe the women's hats. If you decide to go, don't get up and walk out in the middle—see it through. You'll be rewarded by the joyous singing and fellowship, and you'll encounter the islanders on a different level. After church, people gather for a family meal or picnic and spend the rest of the day relaxing and socializing. If you're a guest in an island home, you'll be invited to accompany them to church. Never wear a pareu to church—you'll be asked to leave.

LANGUAGE

French is spoken throughout the territory. Though almost everyone involved in the tourist industry speaks good English, visitors who stray off the usual tourist trail will sometimes have difficulty making themselves understood. That said, young Polynesians often become curious and friendly when they hear you speaking English, and if you know a few words in Tahitian, you'll impress everyone.

Contemporary Tahitian is the chiefly or royal dialect used in the translation of the Bible by early Protestant missionaries, and today, as communications improve, the outer-island dialects are becoming mingled with the predominant Tahitian. Tahitian or Maohi is one of a family of Austronesian languages spoken from Madagascar through Indonesia, all the way to Easter Island and Hawaii. The related languages of eastern Polynesia (Hawaiian, Tahitian, Tuamotuan, Mangarevan, Marquesan, Rarotongan, and Maori) are quite different from those of western Polynesia (Samoan and Tongan). Among the Polynesian languages, the consonants did the changing rather than the vowels. The k and l in Hawaiian are generally rendered as a t and r in Tahitian.

Instead of attempting to speak French to the Tahitians, turn to the Tahitian vocabulary at the end of this guide and give it a try.

MUSIC AND DANCE

Traditional Tahitian dancing experienced a revival in the 1950s with the formation of Madeleine Moua's Pupu Heiva dance troupe, followed in the 1960s by Coco Hotahota's Temaeva and Gilles Hollande's Ora Tahiti. Yves Roche founded the Tahiti ma ensemble in 1962. These groups rediscovered the near-forgotten myths of old Polynesia and popularized them with exciting music, dance, song, and costumes. During major festivals, troupes consisting of 20-50 dancers and 6-10 musicians participate in thrilling competitions.

The Tahitian **tamure** or 'ori Tahiti is a fast, exciting dance done by rapidly shifting the weight from one foot to the other.

The rubber-legged men are almost acrobatic, though their movements tend to follow those of the women closely. The tossing, shell-decorated fiber skirts (mores), the hand-held pandanus wands, and the tall headdresses add to the drama.

Dances such as the aparima and 'ote'a re-enact Polynesian legends, and each movement tells part of a story. The **aparima,** or "kiss of the hands," is a slow dance resembling the Hawaiian hula or Samoan siva executed mainly with the hands in a standing or sitting position. The hand movements repeat the story told in the accompanying song. The **'ote'a** is a theme dance executed to the accompaniment of drums with great precision and admirable timing by a group of men wearing tall headdresses and/or women with wide belts arrayed in two lines. The **ute** is a restrained dance based on ancient refrains.

The **slit-log gong** beaten with a wooden stick is now a common instrument throughout Polynesia, even though the eastern Polynesians originally had only skin drums. The to'ere slit drum was introduced to Tahiti from western Polynesia after 1915, and it's marvelous the way the Tahitians have made it their own. Each of these slit rosewood drums, hit with a stick, is slightly different in size and pitch. The to'ere's staccato beat is electrifying. A **split-bamboo drum** (ofe) hit against the ground often provides a contrasting sound. The **pahu** is a more conventional bass drum made from a hollowed coconut tree trunk with a sharkskin cover. Its sound resembles the human heartbeat. The smallest pahu is the fa'atete, which is hit with sticks.

Another traditional Polynesian musical instrument is the **bamboo nose flute** (vivo), which sounds rather like the call of a bird, though today guitars and ukuleles are more often seen. The **ukulele** was originally the braguinha, brought to Hawaii by Portuguese immigrants a century ago. Homemade ukuleles with the half-shells of coconuts as sound boxes emit pleasant tones, while those sporting empty tins give a more metallic sound. The hollow, piercing note produced by the conch shell or pu once accompanied pagan ceremonies on the marae.

In the early 19th century, missionaries replaced the old chants of Polynesia with the harmonious gospel singing heard in the islands today, yet even the hymns were transformed into an original Oceanic medium. Prior to the arrival of Europeans, traditional Tahitian vocal music took the form of polyphonic chants conveying oral history and customs, and the contrapuntal **himene,** or hymns, sung by large choirs today are based on those ancient chants. As the singers sway to the tempo, the spiritual quality of the himene can be extremely moving, so for the musical experience of a lifetime, attend church any Sunday.

String bands have made European instruments such as the guitar and ukulele an integral part of Tahitian music. The contemporary popular music favored by the island youth is heavily influenced by reggae and localized Anglo-American pop. Well-known local singers and musicians include Bimbo, Charley Manu, Guy Roche, Yves Roche, Emma Terangi, Andy Tupaia, and Henriette Winkler. Small Tahitian groups such as the Moorea Lagoon Kaina Boys, the Barefoot Boys, and Tamarii Punaruu, as well as large folkloric ensembles such as Maeva Tahiti, Tiare Tahiti, and Coco's Temaeva (often recorded at major festivals) are also well represented. The Tahitian recordings of the Hawaiian artist Bobby Holcomb are highly recommended.

HANDICRAFTS

The traditional handicrafts that have survived best are the practical arts done by women (weaving, basket-making, pareu painting), especially in cases where the items still perform their original function. Contemporary Tahitian pareu designs reflect the esthetic judgments of the lost art of tapa-making. Among the European-derived items are the patchwork quilts (tifaifai) of Tahiti.

Whenever possible, buy handicrafts from local committee shops, church groups, local markets, or from the craftspeople themselves, but avoid objects made from turtle shell or leather, clam shell, or marine mammal ivory, which are prohibited entry into many countries under endangered species laws. Failure to declare such items to customs officers can lead to heavy fines. Also resist the temptation to buy jewelry or other items made from seashells and coral, the collection of which damages the reefs. Souvenirs made from straw or seeds may be held for fumigation or confiscated upon arrival. The shiny Polynesian-style wood carvings sold in the airport and at resorts are often imported from Indonesia.

Hustling and bargaining are not practiced in French Polynesia: it's expensive for everyone. Haggling may even be considered insulting, so just pay the price asked or keep looking. You could try buying a few items for a lower overall rate, but negotiating lower on a single item could be offensive. Black pearl jewelry is an exception; because the markups are so high, discounts are often available.

Wood Carving

Most local souvenir shops sell "tikis" carved from wood or stone in the Marquesas Islands. The original tiki were crafted after ancestors and deities, and really old tikis are still shrouded in superstition. Today they're viewed mainly as good-luck charms and often come decorated with mother-of-pearl. Other items carved from wood include mallets (to beat tapa cloth), umete bowls, and slit to'ere drums.

Weaving

Woven articles are the most widespread handicrafts. Pandanus fiber is the most common, but coconut leaf and husk, vine tendril, banana stem, tree and shrub bark, and the stems and leaves of water weeds are all used. On some islands the fibers are passed through a fire, boiled, and then bleached in the sun. Vegetable dyes of very lovely mellow tones are sometimes used, but brighter store dyes are much more prevalent. Shells are occasionally used to cut, curl, or make the fibers pliable. Polynesian woven arts are characterized by colorful, skillful patterns. Carefully woven pandanus hats and mats come from the Austral Islands.

Tifaifai Quilts

Early missionaries introduced the Tahitians to quilting, and two-layer patchwork tifaifai have now taken the place of tapa (bark cloth). Used as bed covers and pillows by tourists, tifaifai is still used by Tahitians to cloak newlyweds and to cover coffins. To be wrapped in a tifaifai is the highest honor. Each woman has individual quilt patterns that are her trademarks, and bold floral designs are popular, with contrasting colors drawn from nature. A complicated tifaifai can take up to six months to complete and cost more than US$1,000.

Clothing and Accessories

As this is a French colony, it's not surprising that many of the best buys are related to fashion. A tropical shirt, sundress, or T-shirt is a purchase of immediate usefulness. The pareu is a typically Tahitian leisure garment consisting of a brightly colored hand-blocked or painted local fabric about two meters long and a meter wide. There are dozens of ways both men and women can wear a pareu. It's the most common apparel for local women throughout the territory, including Papeete, so pick one up!

Local cosmetics such as Monoï Tiare Tahiti, a fragrant coconut-oil skin moisturizer, and coconut-oil soap will put you in form. Jasmine shampoo, cologne, and perfume are also made locally from the tiare Tahiti flower.

Black Pearls

Black-pearl jewelry is widely available throughout French Polynesia. The color, shape, weight, and size of the pearl are important. The darkest pearls are the most valuable. Prices vary considerably, so shop around before buying pearls. Be aware that the export of more than 10 unset pearls per person is prohibited without a license and that the folks operating the X-ray machines at the airport are on the lookout. To avoid having to pay an export tax when leaving French Polynesia, don't lose the proof of purchase and export tax-exemption form you'll be given by the merchant. One copy must be given to the customs officer; otherwise the tax may be charged to your credit card later.

Essentials

Transportation

GETTING THERE

French Polynesia is well connected to the United States, Chile, New Zealand, Australia, New Caledonia, and Japan, but poorly linked to the other Pacific islands aside from Hawaii. Flights from Canada, the United Kingdom, and South Africa will require a stopover. **Air Tahiti Nui** and its code share partners deliver most international flights into French Polynesia. For round-trip flights, expect to pay around US$800 from the United States, US$1,500 from Chile, US$700

from New Zealand, US$900 from Australia, US$600 from New Caledonia, and $US1,200 from Japan.

International flights arrive at **Faa'a International Airport** (PPT, www.tahiti-aeroport.pf), 5.5 kilometers (3.4 mi) southwest of Papeete on the island of Tahiti. There are no direct international flights to any other French Polynesian island.

From North America

French Polynesia is connected directly to Los Angeles (8 hours), San Francisco (8 hours), Seattle (9.5 hours), and Honolulu (5 hours), with many flights easily reaching these main hubs from elsewhere in North America. Direct flights from the United States and Hawaii start at US$800 round-trip

Air Tahiti Nui (www.airtahitinui.com) offers nonstop flights from Los Angeles, San Francisco, and Seattle to Papeete, code sharing with American Airlines (www.aa.com). Air France (www.airfrance.com) connects Paris to Papeete with a stopover in Los Angeles, code sharing with Delta Air Lines as part of the SkyTeam alliance. French bee (www.frenchbee.com) flies from Los Angeles to Papeete. United Airlines flies from San Francisco to Papeete, and is part of the Star Alliance.

Hawaiian Airlines (www.hawaiianairlines.com) flies to Tahiti via its base in Honolulu with connections to and from 16 U.S. mainland cities. You can add a stay in Honolulu for no extra flight cost by extending your stopover.

From Australia and New Zealand

Air New Zealand (www.airnewzealand.co.nz) and Air Tahiti Nui (www.airtahitinui.co.nz) both fly from Auckland direct to Papeete (5 hours) with connections from Wellington and Christchurch available. Air Tahiti Nui is a code share partner with Qantas (www.qantas.com), which connects Sydney to Auckland. There are no direct flights from Australia. Prices for round-trip flights from New Zealand and Australia start at US$700.

From Europe and the U.K.

From Paris, Air France (www.airfrance.com), French bee (www.frenchbee.com), and Air Tahiti Nui (www.airtahitinui.com) fly to Papeete via Los Angeles (22 hours).

From South Africa

There are no quick or direct routes from South Africa to French Polynesia. Air France (www.airfrance.com) offers flights from South Africa to Papeete via Paris and Los Angeles (36 hours).

From Other Pacific Islands

French Polynesia is poorly connected to its South Pacific neighbors. Air Tahiti Nui (www.airtahitinui.com) offers flights from Santiago to Papeete via Easter Island or Auckland through its code share partners.

Aircalin (www.aircalin.com) offers direct flights between Papeete and Nouméa, New Caledonia (from $US600, 5 hours). Unfortunately, there's no way to go from Tahiti to Tonga, Samoa, or Fiji without passing through Auckland, Los Angeles, or Hawaii.

Packaged Holidays

If you have limited time in French Polynesia and plan to stay at one or two resorts, consider a packaged holiday. Some tour agencies can organize accommodation, airfare, transfers, and meal packages for much cheaper than what you would get à la carte. If you want some flexibility once you arrive, travel agencies can often extend your flight date after your packaged stay. For two people with limited time and a penchant for upscale hotels, this is typically the cheapest way to go.

The main drawback to packaged holidays is that the major resorts throughout French

---

Previous: Bora Bora Airport.

Coronavirus in French Polynesia

At the time of writing in late 2022, French Polynesia had eased most of its COVID-19-related entry restrictions, though travelers may be required to take a pre-departure test and/or test on arrival.

RESOURCES

- Tahiti Tourisme (www.tahititourisme.com) is where you'll find the latest entry guidelines and restrictions. Some venues and accommodations listed on the website may be out of date. You'll want to call hotels, restaurants, and tour operators directly to verify hours and availability.

- France 24 (www.france24.com) frequently publishes news articles on French Polynesia in English.

- If you don't speak French, download the Google Translate extension on Chrome to translate French Polynesian news websites like Tahitinews.co and www.rfi.fr.

Polynesia tend to be isolated, making them a poor choice if you're keen to interact with locals and explore the less touristic side of the South Pacific. Many resorts also require meal plans, which can be hit or miss depending on the property.

Tahiti Tourisme has a list of travel specialists they recommend on their website, www.tahititourisme.com. They also offer packages catered to guesthouse stays, luxury stays, families, diving, sailing, and honeymooners. A week-long trip with airfare, accommodation, transport, two meals per day, and a handful of activities or spa treatments start at around US$3,200 per person. The following are a few agencies offering packaged holidays.

MOANA VOYAGES

tel. +1 800/704-2952; www.moanavoyages.com

Based in Tahiti, Moana Voyages is a team that knows the islands and the logistics of visiting them. If you plan to island-hop or want more authentic experiences, Moana Voyages can help arrange tours for every budget—from guesthouse-only stays to ultra-luxury vacations. If you're planning to save and splurge throughout your trip, Moana Voyages is the best place to start.

VENTURE TAHITI

102 NE 2nd St, Suite 508, Boca Raton, FL; tel. +1 800/839-7891; www.venturetahiti.com

Venture Tahiti specializes in honeymoon and luxury vacation packages to the islands of Tahiti. Their most popular packages span from 7-9 nights in the Society Islands.

TRUE TAHITI VACATION

www.truetahitivacation

True Tahiti Vacation was founded by Laurel Louderback after she left her home in California and moved to Moorea decades ago. She has been planning highly customized trips to the islands of Tahiti since 2002, offering packaged trips ranging from guesthouse stays to overwater bungalows only. True Tahiti Vacation can also arrange trips for families, divers, and adventure addicts.

THE ESSENTIALIST

New York City; www.essentialist.com

The Essentialist is a luxury travel agency with an expertise in booking highly personalized stays. They factor in your interests to arrange dinners at the best local spots, excursions you'll enjoy, spa treatments, and accommodations.

COSTCO TRAVEL

www.costcotravel.com

Costco Travel has surprisingly good deals on packaged holidays to French Polynesia for Costco members. If you're after an overwater bungalow experience, Costco offers five-night stays at resorts like the Four Seasons Resort Bora Bora, Conrad Bora Bora, St. Regis Bora Bora, Le Taha'a, and more. Packages start at $2,500 per person for a five-night stay and usually include airfare. Note that making changes to the proposed itinerary or package can be a challenge.

HIDEAWAY HOLIDAYS

tel. 1300/991-751; www.hideawayholidays.com.au

Hideaway Holidays is an Australian travel agency that specializes in mostly mid-range to upscale packages to French Polynesia. Spontaneous travelers can often find deals on last-minute trips through Hideaway Holidays.

DOWN UNDER ENDEAVOURS

www.downunderendeavours.com

Down Under Endeavours arranges trips to the islands of Tahiti, specifically around the Society Islands. Trips are customized based on interests and budget, rather than one-size-fits-all standardized packages.

Scuba Diving Tours

The South Pacific is one of the world's premier dive destinations, and many of the islands of Tahiti have world-class dive sites and dive centers. Although it's not difficult to make your own arrangements, consider joining an organized dive tour if you want to spend as much time underwater as possible. The dive travel specialists mentioned below charge prices similar to what you'd pay on the beach, and the convenience of having everything prearranged may be worth it. Before booking, find out where you'll be staying and if daily transfers and meals are provided. Dive certification is mandatory for most tours, though some provide certification courses for first-time divers. Week-long dive trips including

three- to four-star accommodation, breakfast, round-trip airfare, and 10 scuba dives start at around US$3,200 per person.

CARADONNA DIVE ADVENTURES

280 Wekiva Springs Rd., Longwood, FL; tel. +1 407/774-9000; www.caradonna.com

Caradonna Dive Adventures has been arranging dive trips since 1985, and knows the best dive regions throughout the islands of Tahiti, with consideration around skill level, interests, and budget. The agency prioritizes dive operators and resorts who use environmentally sustainable practices whenever possible.

DIVE DISCOVERY

tel. +1 415/444-5100 or +1 800/886-7321; www.divediscovery.com

Dive Discovery specializes in dive and ocean adventure travel, like whale swims and snorkel tours, in addition to dives.

REEF AND RAINFOREST DIVE & ADVENTURE TRAVEL

6518 SW 35th Ave., Portland, OR; tel. 800/794-9767; www.reefrainforest.com

Reef and Rainforest Dive & Adventure Travel books diving, cruises, and other adventure tours to French Polynesia. Travel agents can arrange swimming with whales and snorkeling with mantas, and are happy to help book stays on some of the more remote atolls.

Liveaboard

If diving is your top priority, consider booking a cabin on a liveaboard, a ship that will be your home base for eating, sleeping, and scuba diving throughout your stay.

AQUA POLYNESIE

www.aquatiki.com

Aqua Polynesie, based at Fakarava, operates scuba diving cruises around the Tuamotu atolls on the 18-meter catamaran *Aqua Tiki II* and the 20-meter catamaran *Aqua Tiki III*. The liveaboard anchors right at the dive sites. This is the best way to dive on remote atolls like Toau, Aratika, Kauehi, Raraka, and Tahanea. Trips range from 9-15 days long (US$2,800 to US$4,450 per person).

Cruises

Several cruise ships ply the archipelagos of French Polynesia, though the companies and ships operating here vary from year to year. Exact prices vary, but with meals and inter-island travel included, a cruise could cost less than a resort-based holiday. When evaluating cruise costs, check whether gratuities, port taxes, transfers, shore excursions, alcoholic drinks, and airfare are included. Due to the large distances between the islands, cruise itineraries tend to focus on a cluster of islands.

In addition to the smaller cruise companies listed below, large ship cruise companies also offer trips through French Polynesia, usually around the Society Islands. **Princess Cruises** (www.princess.com) operates 2,000-3,560-passenger-capacity ships on a range of itineraries throughout the South Pacific, usually including Hawaii, Fiji, and French Polynesia. **Norwegian Cruise Line** (www.ncl.com) stops at Tahiti, Bora Bora, and Moorea with rates starting at US$3,500 per person double occupancy on 14-day trips.

PAUL GAUGUIN CRUISES

www.pgcruises.com

The most established vessel is the 332-passenger *Paul Gauguin* of **Paul Gauguin Cruises** (www.pgcruises.com), which has operated in French Polynesia continuously since its construction at Saint-Nazaire, France, in 1998. This ship does seven-night cruises from Papeete to Taha'a, Bora Bora, Raiatea, and Moorea year-round starting at US$3,970 per person double occupancy. Trips can include extended itineraries to the Cook Islands, Tuamotus, and Marquesas Islands.

WINDSTAR CRUISES

www.windstarcruises.com

Windstar Cruises offers small ship cruises of up to 350 guests onboard. Trip itineraries

range from 7-20 days long, cruising mostly through the Society and Tuamotu Islands. The *Star Breeze* ship has been recently refurbished and features an infinity pool, spa, and gym. Seven-day trip prices start at US$1,899 per person double occupancy.

ARANUI CRUISES

www.aranui.com

If you're more of an adventure traveler, the passenger-carrying freighter *Aranui 5* from Aranui Cruises (www.aranui.com) hosts 230 passengers onboard and has a range of itineraries that go to the Marquesas, Tuamotu, Society, Austral, and Gambier Islands. Prices start at US$5,300 per person double occupancy for a 13-day trip. Dormitory bed rates start at US$3,573 per person.

TUHAA PAE

tel. 40 41 36 06; snathp.com

Tuhaa Pae is a passenger-carrying cargo ship that ventures to the Austral Islands on a seven-night cruise stopping at Rimatara, Rurutu, Tubuai, and Raivave before returning to Tahiti. Prices start at €2,012 per person double occupancy. Dormitory beds are available from €1,609 per person.

Yacht Charters and Cruises

If you were planning to spend a substantial amount to stay at a luxury resort, consider chartering a yacht instead. Divided among the members of your party, the per-person charter price will likely be about the same, but you'll have the freedom of exploring isolated lagoons and uninhabited islands unreachable from a hotel. Activities such as sailing, snorkeling, and general exploring by sea and land are typically included in the price.

Yacht charters are available either "bareboat" (for those with the skill to sail on their own) or "crewed" (in which case charterers pay a daily fee for a skipper).

CHARTER POLYNSÉSIE DREAM

tel. 87 76 19 76; www.yachtcharter-polynesia.com

Charter Polynsésie Dream offers 8-23-day

cruises around Raiatea, Tahaa, Bora Bora, Huahine, and the Tuamotus on the 18-meter, five-cabin catamaran. It's possible to charter the catamaran entirely, sleeping up to 10 guests. All trips are crewed, and prices start at US$2,240 per person for an eight-day cruise.

MOEMOEA NUI

www.marquises-croisiere.com

This 13-meter catamaran is crewed by Alain and Odile, who have spent over three decades sailing French Polynesia, offering one- to two-week cruises through the Marquesas and Tuamotus. The cost of chartering the catamaran, complete with skipper and crew, is €650 per day, sleeping up to six guests.

TAHITI YACHT CHARTER

tel. 40 66 28 80; www.tahitiyachtcharter.com

Tahiti Yacht Charter has around 30 charter yachts available at Marina Apooiti, near Raiatea Airport. Prices are customized to the group, route, duration, and crew requirements. Expect to pay around €5,000 per week for a bareboat charter, or €6,700 per week for crewed charter. Prices vary by yacht length, duration, and whether or not a skipper is needed.

THE MOORINGS LTD.

93 North Park Place Blvd., Clearwater, FL; tel. 888/952-8420; www.moorings.com

The Moorings Ltd. offers a handful of yachts for charter, both crewed and bareboat. Seven-night cruises start at US$5,000 for bareboat rental and US$18,000 with crew and chef for two people. All yachts come with snorkeling gear, linens, cooking utensils, and safety equipment.

SUNSAIL TAHITI

tel. 866/644-2327; www.sunsail.com

Sunsail Tahiti is based at Raiatea's Faaroa Bay and offers bareboat and crewed yacht charter. Monohull and catamaran yachts vary in price, with a seven-night cruise with two guests in a monohull running around US$3,000 for

bareboat charter and US$9,500 for the catamaran bareboat charter.

By Sailing Yacht
GETTING ABOARD

It's possible to hitch rides into the Pacific on yachts from California, Panama, New Zealand, and Australia, or around the yachting triangle Papeete-Suva-Honolulu. If you've never sailed before, consider looking for a yacht already in the islands. In Tahiti, for example, after a month on the open sea, some of the original crew may have flown home or onward, opening a place for you. Cruising yachts are recognizable by their foreign flags and laundry hung out to dry. Captains often evaluate crew on personality, attitude, and a willingness to learn more than experience. Skills like cooking, teaching, and cleaning often give newcomers the upper hand in being selected as crew. Websites like **CrewSeekers International** (www.crewseekers.net) and **Find a Crew** (www.findacrew.net) connect boats with potential crewmates. Crewing a yacht is common for travelers who have some sailing experience and are traveling on a budget.

Before you commit to a long journey on-board a yacht, it's best to tour the boat and commit to just a few days onboard. Check for safety essentials like a sextant and EPIRB beacon, and that the boat is well maintained. Also be concerned about a skipper who doesn't do a careful safety briefing early on, or who seems to have a hard time hanging onto crew. There have been many cases of captains sexually harassing female crew. It's wise to board a vessel with a friend, and to check the "Sailing Safety for Women" Facebook group to seek references for the yacht you're about to board.

TIME OF YEAR

The weather and seasons play a deciding role in any South Pacific trip by sailboat, and you'll have to pull out of many beautiful places, or be unable to stop there, because of bad weather. The prime season for rides in the South Pacific is from May to October. Be aware of the cyclone season, November-March, as few yachts will be cruising at that time.

The prevailing trade winds in the tropics south of the equator are from the southeast. South of the Tropic of Capricorn the winds are out of the west. Because of the action of prevailing southeast trade winds, boat trips are smoother from east to west than west to east throughout the South Pacific, so that's the way to go.

YACHTING ROUTES

The common yachting route, or "Coconut Milk Run," across the South Pacific uses the northeast and southeast trades: from California to Tahiti via the Marquesas or Hawaii, then Rarotonga, Niue, Vava'u, Suva, and New Zealand. Some yachts continue west from Fiji to Port Vila. In the other direction, you'll sail on the westerlies from New Zealand to a point south of the Australs, then north on the trades to Tahiti.

To enjoy the finest weather conditions, many yachts clear the Panama Canal or depart California in February to arrive in the Marquesas in March. From Hawaii, yachts often leave for Tahiti in April or May. Many stay on for the *Heiva i Tahiti* festival, which ends mid-July, at which time they sail west to Tonga or Fiji, where you'll find them in July and August. By late October the bulk of the yachting community is sailing south via New Caledonia to New Zealand or Australia to spend the southern summer there. Noonsite (www.noonsite.com) provides valuable information for cruising yachties.

LIFE ABOARD

Yacht crewmates wash clothes and linens, cook, steer, keep watch at night, and help with engine work. Other jobs might include changing and resetting sails, cleaning the boat, scraping the bottom, pulling up the anchor, and climbing the main mast to watch for reefs. Anybody who wants to get on well under sail must be flexible and tolerant, both physically and emotionally. Expense-sharing crew members typically split the cost of food and fuel, usually around US$50-100 per week.

GETTING AROUND
By Air

The domestic carrier **Air Tahiti** (www.air-tahiti.com) flies to 45 airstrips in every corner of French Polynesia, with important hubs at Papeete (Windward Islands), Bora Bora (Leeward Islands), Rangiroa (northern Tuamotus), Hao (eastern Tuamotus), and Nuku Hiva (Marquesas). Its fleet consists of seven 66-seat ATR 72s, two 48-seat ATR 42s, and three nine-seat Beechcraft King Air B200s.

The main Air Tahiti office (tel. 40 47 44 00) in Papeete is on Rue Gauguin, closed on Sundays. Check carefully to make sure all the flights listed in the published timetable are operating. Any travel agency in Papeete can book Air Tahiti flights for the same price as the Air Tahiti office.

Air Tahiti is fairly reliable; still, you should avoid scheduling a flight back to Papeete on the same day that your international flight leaves Tahiti. It's always wise to allow some leeway in case there's a cancellation or delay.

Round-trip tickets are about 10 percent cheaper than two one-ways. Air Tahiti doesn't allow stopovers on its tickets, so if you're flying round-trip from Tahiti to Bora Bora and want to stop at Raiatea on the way out and Huahine on the way back, you'll have to buy four separate tickets.

If you're planning to island-hop, consider purchasing an Air Tahiti **Air Pass.** These passes are considerably cheaper than buying one-way flights. Air Passes are valid for 28 days, but only one stopover can be made on each island included in the package. All passes start and finish in Tahiti or Moorea, and you do not have to visit all islands included in the pass. Extensions can be combined with a pass, and both must be used within the same 28-day period. Low-season takes place from April 1 to May 31, November 1 to December 10, and January 11 to March 31. High-season is from June 1 to October 31 and December 11 to

January 10. Each pass includes 23 kilograms of baggage allowance with 46-kilogram allowance available for extra cost. Scuba divers are allowed an extra 5 kilograms for their diving equipment (scuba certification card required).

- **Discovery Pass:** Moorea, Huahine, Raiatea (low season €332/adult, €272/child; high season €357/adult, €292/child)
- **Bora Bora Pass:** Moorea, Huahine, Raiatea, Bora Bora, Maupiti (low season €435/adult, €354/child; high season €469/adult, €380/child)
- **Lagoons Pass:** Moorea, Rangiroa, Tikehau, Fakarava (low season €441/adult, €357/child; high season €476/adult, €384/child)
- **Bora-Tuamotu Pass:** Moorea, Huahine, Raiatea, Maupiti, Bora Bora, Rangiroa, Tikehau, Fakarava (low season €584/adult, €472/child; high season €632/adult, €508/child)
- **Austral Pass:** Rurutu, Tubuai, Raivavae, Rimatara (low season €602/adult, €484/child; high season €651/adult, €522/child)
- **Marquesas Pass:** Nuku Hiva, Hiva Oa (low season €780/adult, €610/child; high season €851/adult, €665/child)
- **Austral Extension:** Rurutu, Tubuai, Raivavae, Rimatara (low season €365/adult, €294/child; high season €394/adult, €317/child)
- **Marquesas Extension:** Nuku Hiva, Hiva Oa (low season €582/adult, €460/child; high season €634/adult, €499/child)

Young adults, seniors, and families can get discounts on certain flights by applying for an Air Tahiti discount card in person at an Air Tahiti's Papeete ticketing office. Identification and one photo are required. The full discount is given only on off-peak flights. If you apply for the card on an outer island, allow for a 10-day wait as the application is forwarded to Papeete for processing.

Each passenger is allowed one carry-on bag (5 kg) and one accessory onboard the aircraft.

Class Y or S tickets allow for 23-kilograms of check-in baggage and class Z tickets allow for 46 kilograms of check-in baggage. The maximum dimension for any bag is 150 centimeters (length plus width plus height). If you have sports gear, like a surfboard, it can be included as your baggage allowance as long as it does not exceed 2 meters in length.

Tahiti Air Charter (tel. 40 47 44 00; www.air-tahiti-charter.com) flies its Cessna 208 Caravan planes and seaplanes to the Leeward Islands of Raiatea, Huahine, Bora Bora, and Maupiti. Aside from their regular routes, Tahiti Air Charter offers private plane charter, scenic flights, and day trips to Maupiti.

By Boat and Cargo Ship

Venture around the Society Islands onboard the *Aremiti 5* with **Apetahi Express** (tel. 40 50 54 59; apetahiexpress.pf). The ferry departs from Papeete to the Leeward Islands three times per week, stopping in Huahine, Raiatea, Taha'a, and Bora Bora. The schedule is posted on their website. Each passenger is entitled to two bags of up to 23 kilograms (about 50 lbs) each plus a 10-kilogram (about 22-lb) carry-on. An unlimited 31-day pass to all six islands is CFP 23,900 per person. A pass for four islands (Huahine, Raiatea, Taha'a, and Bora Bora) is CFP 17,900 per person. It's much cheaper and much more flexible than the Air Tahiti Air Pass.

The passenger-carrying freighter *Aranui* (tel. 40 42 62 42; www.aranui.com) ventures between Papeete and the Marquesas about 20 times per year, stopping at all six inhabited Marquesas Islands, plus a couple of the Tuamotus. Trips usually last 12 days with a full day stop at each destination. Fares start at CFP 520,627 per person plus a CFP 15,000 fuel surcharge for double occupancy. Charges include taxes, accommodation, three meals per day, and some guided shore excursions. Deck passage is intended for residents, but if there is availability, you might be able to ride on a single leg of the journey for around CFP 10,000.

To save money, some budget travelers tour French Polynesia by **cargo boat,** like the *MV*

Taporo VII and the *MV Hawaiki-Nui* from Papeete (Motu Uta wharf). There's a certain adventure and romance to taking an inter-island freighter, and you can go anywhere by copra boat, including islands without airstrips and resorts. For the latest schedule and fares, you'll need to go in person to Papeete's shipyard early in the morning to book a ticket. Travel by ferry or passenger-carrying freighter is much cheaper than plane. Note that spaces onboard can fill up weeks in advance, so this should not be a way to get around if you're short on time or have inflexible flights to your next destination.

For any boat trip farther than Moorea, check the schedule and pick up tickets at the company office as far in advance as possible. Take along your passport, as the staff may insist on checking the expiration date of your visa before selling you a ticket to a point outside the Society Islands. Except on the *Aranui* and *Aremiti*, it's usually not possible to book your passage before arriving on Tahiti. On an outer island, be wary when someone, even a member of the crew, tells you the departure time of a ship: they're as apt to leave early as late.

To pinch pennies, travel deck class. There's usually an awning in case of rain, but don't count on getting a lot of sleep if you go this way. Otherwise take a cabin, which you'll share with three or four other passengers. Food is typically only included on 8-hour or longer journeys, though you'll want to ask in advance. Most ships allow you to bring a box of food and drink onboard.

If you plan to fly one-way, you'll have more certainty of getting where you want to go when you want to go if you fly out from Papeete and come back by boat.

By Bus

On Huahine and Raiatea folkloric le truck still provide an entertaining unscheduled passenger service. Passengers sit on long wooden benches in back, and there's no problem with luggage. On Tahiti and Moorea, most of these colorful vehicles have been replaced with air-conditioned buses that stop only at official stops and issue printed tickets. Still, Tahiti bus fares are fairly low and are usually posted inside the vehicle. You pay through the driver as you enter on Tahiti, as you leave on Moorea. The drivers are generally friendly and will stop to pick you up anywhere if you wave.

On Tahiti buses leave Papeete for the outlying districts periodically throughout the day until 5pm; they continue running to Faa'a Airport until 8pm. On Huahine and Raiatea service is usually limited to a trip into the main town in the morning and a return to the villages in the afternoon. On Moorea and Bora Bora, public buses meet the ferries from Papeete. No public transportation is available on the roads of the Austral, Tuamotu, Gambier, or Marquesas Islands.

By Car and Scooter

Renting a car is an ideal way to get around the larger islands in French Polynesia like Tahiti, Moorea, Huahine, and Raiatea. Franchise car rental companies like Avis, Europcar, and Hertz generally cost around US$80-100 per day, while locally owned rental operators cost around US$60-80 per day. Always find out if insurance, mileage, and tax are included, and check for restrictions on where you'll be allowed to take the car. Most rental companies only allow their vehicles to drive on paved roads.

Car rentals are available at most of the airports served by Air Tahiti. On Tahiti there's sometimes a mileage charge, whereas on Moorea, Huahine, Raiatea, and Bora Bora all rentals come with unlimited mileage. Public liability insurance is included by law, but collision damage waiver (CDW) insurance is extra. The insurance policies don't cover a flat tire, stolen radios or accessories, broken keys, or towing charges if the renter is found to be responsible. Unfortunately, the selection of cars is limited, and they may not have the model you reserved. Automatic transmission cars are available but rare, and you'll need to book them as far in advance as possible.

Rental cars are occasionally lent out with

fuel tanks only one-quarter full, prompting an immediate trip to a gas station. Gas stations are usually only in the main towns and open only on weekdays during business hours, plus perhaps a couple of hours on weekend mornings. Expect to pay around CPF 150 per liter for gas, which works out to around US$5.50 per U.S. gallon.

Driving is on the right-hand side of the road. Two traffic signs to know: a white line across a red background indicates a one-way street, while a slanting blue line on a white background means no parking. At unmarked intersections in Papeete, the driver on the right has priority. At roundabouts, the car already in the circle has priority over those entering. The seldom-observed speed limit is 40 km/h in Papeete, 60 km/h around the island, and 90 km/h on the RDO expressway.

Most shopping centers in French Polynesia have a dedicated parking lot, and it's usually easy to find parking along the side of the road or at the sight you're visiting. The only real challenging place to find parking is in Papeete on Tahiti. Within the city center, parking is scarce. Street parking within the city center costs CFP 150 per hour, and cars may stay 2 hours maximum between the hours of 8am-5pm Monday-Saturday. Paid parking lots around the city accommodate longer-term parking. For all other islands, parking is not nearly as challenging to come by.

A good alternative to renting a car are the four-wheel-drive Jeep safaris offered on Tahiti, Moorea, Huahine, Raiatea, Taha'a, and Bora Bora. These take you along rough interior roads inaccessible to most rental vehicles and come with a guide. Prices range around US$50 per person for a half-day tour.

Rental scooters are usually available on islands with a strong road system. A strictly enforced local regulation requires you to always wear a helmet. On some islands, you can rent an open two-seater roadster, slightly bigger than a golf cart, and no helmet or driver's license is required for these.

By Bicycle

Cycling in French Polynesia is an affordable, convenient, and fun way to explore the islands. You'll be able to go where and when you please, stop easily and often to meet people and take photos, save money on taxi fares—really see the country. Most roads are flat along the coast, but you'll want to take care on roads built from sharp coral, especially on inclines. On the high islands, interior roads tend to be very steep and can get muddy. Cycling on the island of Tahiti is risky because of speeding motorists, but most of the outer islands have excellent, uncrowded roads.

You can rent bicycles almost anywhere, usually from pensions or hotels. If you bring your own, a sturdy, single-speed mountain bike with wide wheels, safety chain, and good brakes will be ideal. Thick tires and a plastic liner between tube and tire will reduce punctures. Take along a good repair kit (pump, puncture kit, freewheel tool, spare spokes, cables, chain links, assorted nuts and bolts, etc.) and a repair manual. Bringing a bicycle is not common, but it's doable if you're planning to travel primarily by ferry (aircraft cargo space is often limited). Bike repair shops outside of Papeete are hard to come by. Sturdy, waterproof panniers (bike bags) are recommended over a backpack for long distances; you'll also want a good lock.

Air Tahiti Nui will carry a bicycle as checked luggage for free so long as it weighs under 23 kilograms. If you're using another carrier, verify their policy before booking. Take off the pedals and panniers, turn the handlebars sideways and tie them down, deflate the tires, and clean off the dirt before checking in (or use a special bike-carrying bag) and arrive at the airport early. On domestic Air Tahiti flights, checked baggage cannot have a combined length, width, and height of over 150 centimeters. Larger items being sent as freight must be delivered 1.5 hours before the flight. Inter-island boats sometimes charge a token amount to carry a bike; other times it's free.

By Kayak and Canoe

One of the best ways to explore local motu, lagoons, and beaches along the coastline is with kayak and canoe, often available for rent through your accommodation. Almost every island has a sheltered lagoon prime for paddling. Kayaks are available for rent at most of the Society Islands, and many islands throughout French Polynesia offer guided kayak tours. Noted author Paul Theroux toured the South Pacific by kayak, and his experiences are recounted in *The Happy Isles of Oceania: Paddling the Pacific.* If you get off the beaten track, you might have a chance to borrow an outrigger canoe.

By Taxis and Hitchhiking

Metered and set-fare taxis are available on Tahiti, Moorea, and Bora Bora. It's also common for islands to have a local driver who uses their private vehicle to shuttle tourists around. Fares can be expensive, with longer journeys costing as much or more as a car rental. It's best to arrange taxi rental through your accommodation.

Hitchhiking is common around the islands. For safety, it's best to do in a group and in areas you're familiar with. It's common to hand the driver a small amount of money as a courtesy.

Visas and Officialdom

PASSPORTS AND VISAS

Entry protocols for travelers to French Polynesia have been impacted by the COVID-19 pandemic, and travelers may be required to take a COVID-19 test no matter their vaccination status.

Though French Polynesia is an overseas collectivity of France, entry requirements for French Polynesia may be different than continental France. Every non-EU traveler must have a passport valid for three months after the return date and at least one blank page.

Citizens of the **United States, Australia, New Zealand,** and **Canada** can enter French Polynesia for up to 90 days without a visa. Travelers should also be prepared to show evidence of the purpose of their stay (confirmed hotel bookings will suffice) and your guarantee for repatriation, usually through the form of a return flight or proof of enough money to purchase a full fare return flight home.

European Union and **United Kingdom** passport holders also do not need a visa for stays up to 90 days in French Polynesia, provided they have a valid ID card or passport.

South African passport holders need a visa to enter French Polynesia, even for stays under 90 days. To apply for a tourism visa, South Africans must provide proof of an official travel document, onward travel, status of their employment and links to their country of residence, bank statements from the past three months, travel insurance, and enough funds to cover their accommodation for the duration of their stay (€120/day). The price of a visa application is €9.

Visas for stays longer than three months must be applied for from your country of residence before your arrival in French Polynesia. If you do require a visa, make sure the words "valable pour la Polynésie Française" are endorsed on the visa, as visas for France are not accepted.

If you hold a passport from a country other than Canada or the United States and will be passing through Los Angeles on your way to Tahiti, you must visit the **Electronic System for Travel Authorization** website (esta.cbp. dhs.gov) more than 72 hours prior to departure to complete an online application form requesting authorization to transit the United States. This applies even if you will not be leaving the airport.

CUSTOMS

Certain merchandise, weapons, tech equipment, food, and fauna are subject to customs regulations in French Polynesia. All items brought in must be for personal use and re-exported out of French Polynesia within six months. Radio and telecommunications equipment require a license. Travelers may enter with 200 cigarettes, 100 cigarillos, 50 cigars, and 250 grams of pipe tobacco. Alcohol is limited to two liters. Live animals, plants, flowers, fruits, and cultured pearls from outside French Polynesia are forbidden. All weapons, ammunition, and narcotics are prohibited.

EMBASSIES AND CONSULATES

- **United States:** U.S. Consular Agent (Centre Tamanu Iti 1er etage, Punaauia; tel. 40 42 65 35; USConsul@mail.pf)

- **Canada:** Seek assistance from the Australian Consulate in Papeete (41 Rue de Cassiau, Papeete; tel. 40 57 69 00; consular.papeete@dfat.gov.au)

- **United Kingdom:** Seek assistance from the British High Commission in Wellington (tel. +64 4 924 2888; www.gov.uk/contact-consulate-wellington)

- **Ireland:** Seek assistance from the Embassy of Ireland in Paris (tel. +331 44 17 67 00; www.dfa.ie/france)

- **Australia:** Australia Consulate (41 Rue de Cassiau, Papeete; tel. 40 57 69 00; consular.papeete@dfat.gov.au)

- **New Zealand:** Seek assistance from the New Zealand Consulate in New Caledonia (tel. +687 00 27 25 43; nznoumea@mfat.net)

- **South Africa:** Seek assistance from the South African Embassy in Paris (tel. +33 01 53 59 24 10; info.paris@dirco.gov.za).

YACHT ENTRY

The main port of entry for cruising yachts is Papeete. Upon application to the local police station, called **gendarmerie,** entry may also be allowed at Bora Bora, Hiva Oa, Huahine, Mangareva, Moorea, Nuku Hiva, Raiatea, Raivavae, Rangiroa, Rurutu, Tubuai, and Ua Pou. Have an accurate inventory list for your vessel ready. It's also best to have a French courtesy flag with you, as they're not always available in places such as the Marquesas. Even after clearance, you must continue to report your arrival and crew changes at each respective office every time you visit any of the islands just mentioned. Anyone arriving by yacht without an onward air ticket must provide proof of funds equivalent or more to a full-price flight back to their home country.

After clearing customs in Papeete, outbound yachts may spend the duration of their period of stay cruising the outer islands. Make sure every island where you *might* stop is listed on your clearance. You may buy duty-free fuel immediately after clearance.

VACCINATIONS

The U.S. Centers for Disease Control and Prevention (www.cdc.gov) recommends regular vaccines including those for varicella, tetanus, diphtheria, measles-mumps-rubella (MMR), polio, and shingles be taken before any form of travel. Hepatitis A, hepatitis B, and typhoid fever shots are also recommended, especially if you will be visiting French Polynesia's remote regions. It is also recommended to be vaccinated against COVID-19, though it is no longer required.

A yellow-fever vaccination is required if you've been in an infected area within six days before arrival. Yellow fever is a mosquito-borne disease that occurs in Central Africa and northern South America (excluding Chile).

Sports and Recreation

The wild and wondrous natural landscape of the islands of Tahiti make the region a playground for travelers who love to adventure in any way they can. From jagged mountains with lightly trodden trails to lagoons thriving with reef life, these are just a few of the many ways you can explore.

SURFING

One of the most famous waves in the world breaks off the island of Tahiti's southeastern coastline. **Teahupoo** is a heavy left-hand reef break that frequently makes headlines in surf media due to its intensity and size. Whenever a swell comes, big wave surfers follow. Surfers who've yet to brave paddling out to Teahupoo can hire a boat and watch the waves from the channel. Otherwise, there are plenty of waves throughout the 118 islands reserved for mere mortals. May-August is best for surfing the south-southwest breaks, while October-April is best for waves rolling in from the north.

Water temperature tends to hover around 26-28°C (78-82°F) throughout the year, so you can leave the long wetsuit at home. However, a 2mm neoprene top will keep you toasty for windy or sunrise sessions. Midday, you'll want to suit up with a rashguard, surf hat, and plenty of reef-safe sunscreen to protect your skin from painful burns. Reef booties are also recommended if you plan to surf any of the islands' shallow reef breaks, of which there are many. Surf shops are limited, so you'll want to pack spare surf wax and a leash.

SCUBA DIVING AND SNORKELING

Scuba divers will have no shortage of dive sites throughout the islands—after all, there are over 6.5 million square kilometers (2.5 million square mi) of ocean in French Polynesian borders. A peek underwater reveals whales, dolphins (nearly a third of all species are present here), rays, sharks, sea turtles, and coral reefs that house thousands of fish species. Seascapes range from shallow, sandy lagoons to deep canyon reefs that span hundreds of meters deep. Fortunately, there's more than enough to explore from 18-30 meters (60-100 ft)—the depths most certification agencies allow recreational divers to explore. Snorkeling tours on every major island offer a glimpse of reef life, and are usually paired with lunch on a nearby motu.

Reef sharks and **rays** are often seen in the lagoons of the Society Islands, specifically Moorea and Bora Bora, where they have no fear of humans due to years of feeding. For a scuba diving experience with schools of **hammerheads,** Fakarava is paradise.

Water temperatures are around 26-28°C (78-82°F), but thermoclines and deep water can make dives much colder. If you'll be diving frequently, it could be worth bringing a 3-5mm long-sleeve wetsuit, though most dive centers have them available for rent. Certified divers are given an extra 5 kilograms of luggage on all Air Tahiti inter-island flights—packing your own set of mask, snorkel, and fins is highly recommended. That way, you can snorkel from any beach that looks inviting and ensure you have a set of gear that fits.

The **eDivingPass** (edivingpass.com) is an economical way to bundle dives. For around €63 per dive, you can dive at over 30 dive centers across 16 islands. Passes start at six dives, with an ability to split it between two people (€377).

HIKING

Almost every major hiking trail in French Polynesia rewards trekkers with panoramic views of lagoons spanning every shade of blue and dramatic mountain peaks. On the rare chance you don't end at a scenic lookout point, you'll likely discover a tropical fruit plantation, sacred marae, waterfalls, or sanctuary for birdlife. The Society Islands and the Marquesas Islands are your best bet for quality hiking trails. On Tahiti, beginner hikers will enjoy Papenoo Valley for waterfalls, while more experienced trekkers can make it to the top of Mt. Aorai. Moorea has the Three Coconuts Pass, a popular trail with views of Moorea's bays. Or, take a walk along the interior trails of Bora Bora, which lead past panoramic views and banyan trees. On other islands, hiring a guide will lead you to trails few other tourists have trod down before.

CANOEING, KAYAKING, AND STAND-UP PADDLEBOARDING

As Tahitians reached the islands by outrigger sailing canoes, it is no surprise that paddle sports are still a popular activity among those who live on the islands of Tahiti. Many seaside accommodations have canoes, kayaks, and stand-up paddleboards for rent. With a paddle in hand, you can explore a nearby motu, moor to a buoy and snorkel, or cruise along the coastline. Outrigger canoes are also available for hire, though these typically come with a short lesson beforehand. All island groups offer prime paddling.

SAILING AND BOATING

Sailing and boating are part of the culture of French Polynesia, where the sight of sails and buoys dots every major bay. No matter how long you're around the islands for, going on a boating adventure is a must. You can charter your own sailboat for weeks at a time, or head out on a lagoon tour just for sunset. Some boats offer fishing excursions, snorkel tours, and trips to nearby islands. If you're prone to seasickness, plan your trip for early mornings or inside one of the lagoons—as seas tend to be calmer.

WHALE- AND DOLPHIN-WATCHING

All year long, dolphins cruise throughout the archipelagos. Bottlenose dolphins, rough-toothed dolphins, and the aptly named spinner dolphins are the three species commonly seen. Pods can range from just a few to hundreds. Rangiroa is one of the best places to spot dolphins, with scuba diving offered at Tiputa Pass. Occasionally, curious pods cruise by boats and surf within their wake.

Different species of whales are also present throughout the year, but French Polynesia is most famous for its migrating humpback whale population. To come eye to eye with a gentle giant, visit during whale season, July-November. **Humpback whales** cruise past the Society Islands, and it's possible to swim with them on a guided tour. Whale-watching companies offer boat tours from the Society Islands, with some operators also available in the Tuamotus. The whales make quite a ruckus, often breaching and slapping their fins against the water.

Festivals and Events

FEBRUARY

INTERNATIONAL DOCUMENTARY FILM FESTIVAL (FIFO)
Tahiti; February
The International Documentary Film Festival (www.fifotahiti.com) features documentaries about Oceania, focusing on the region's unique cultural and natural landscapes.

APRIL

TAHITI MOOREA MARATHON
Moorea; April
The Tahiti Moorea Marathon (www.mooreamarathon.com) has been held on Moorea every February since 1988, aside from years impacted by the COVID-19 pandemic. Nearly 1,500 runners from all around the world race around Moorea's iconic bays, ending at Temae Beach. Polynesian dance

performances and fresh food at the closing ceremony make runners forget all about the pain they've endured. Half-marathons and kids' runs also take place.

MAY
TAHITI PEARL REGATTA
Raiatea; May
Yachts set sail on a fun, spirited regatta with six stages around Raiatea and Taha'a, a fun event that takes sailors a full loop around Taha'a.

JUNE-JULY
WORLD ENVIRONMENT DAY
Throughout Tahiti; June 5
World Environment Day is marked by guided excursions to Tahiti's interior, and on the following weekend special activities are arranged at tourist sites around the island.

HEIVA I TAHITI
Tahiti; July
The big event of the year is the two-week-long Heiva i Tahiti (www.tahiti-heiva.org). Formerly known as La Fête du Juillet or the Tiurai Festival (the Tahitian word *tiurai* comes from the English "July"), the Heiva originated way back in 1881. Today it brings contestants and participants to Tahiti from all over the territory to take part in elaborate processions, competitive dancing and singing, feasting, and partying. There are bicycle, car, horse, and outrigger-canoe races; pétanque; archery and javelin-throwing contests; fire walking; stone lifting; sidewalk markets; arts and crafts exhibitions; tattooing; games; and joyous carnivals.

Tickets to most Heiva events are sold at the Cultural Center in Papeete or at the gate. You must pay to sit in the stands to watch the performances (CFP 1,000-3,000), but you get three hours or more of unforgettable nonstop entertainment. (If an event is canceled due to weather conditions, your advance ticket will be valid for the rescheduled event, but there are usually no refunds.)

The July celebrations on Bora Bora are as good as those on Tahiti, and festivals are also held on Huahine, Raiatea, and Taha'a at that time. Note that all ships, planes, and hotels are fully booked around July 14, so be in the right place beforehand or get firm reservations, especially if you want to be on Bora Bora that day. At this time of year, races, games, and dance competitions take place on many different islands, where you're bound to be in awe of graceful dancers and excellent singers.

BASTILLE DAY
Tahiti and Moorea; July 14
Bastille Day itself, which marks the fall of the Bastille in Paris on July 14, 1789, at the height of the French Revolution, features a military parade in the capital. Ask at the Office du Tourisme in Papeete about when to see the canoe races along Papeete waterfront and around Moorea, horse racing at the Pirae track, and the Taupiti nui dance competitions.

AUGUST-SEPTEMBER
TAHITI PRO TEAHUPOO
Tahiti; August
The best surfers in the world face off at Tahiti's heaviest wave. The Tahiti Pro Teahupoo is the tenth stop on the World Surf League Championship Tour. The wave breaks just off of Tahiti Iti, on Tahiti's southeastern coastline. To watch the excitement, book a spot on one of the boats that will park off of the wave's main channel.

FEREREI HAGA
Rangiroa; September
This week-long celebration includes singing, dancing, coconut-husking, weaving, games, and more on Rangiroa. Tourists are welcome to watch and participate, and the festivities can draw over 1,000 spectators.

OCTOBER-DECEMBER
CARNIVAL DE TAHITI
Tahiti; end of October
Carnival de Tahiti at the end of October features dancing contests (waltz, foxtrot, rock),

nightly parades along Boulevard Pomare, and several gala evenings.

HAWAIKI NUI VA'A

Huahine and Raiatea; October or November

The Hawaiki Nui Va'a outrigger canoe race in October or November is a stirring three-day event with almost 100 canoe teams crossing from Huahine to Raiatea (44.5 km/27.5 mi) the first day, Raiatea to Taha'a (26 km/16 mi) the second, and Taha'a to Bora Bora (58 km/36 mi) the third. The **Va'a Hine,** a women-only canoe race from Raiatea to Taha'a and back (40 km/25 mi), occurs a day or two before the men's race.

HURA TAPAIRU

Tahiti; November or December

Hura Tapairu is one of the most prestigious and exciting traditional dance competitions, attracting over 800 performers striving to become the next big dance group. Costumes range from modern and bold to traditional and subtle—this festival is worth attending for the visuals alone.

MARQUESAS ARTS AND CULTURE FESTIVAL

Marquesas Islands; December

Every four years, the Marquesas Islands put on an arts and culture festival that highlights traditional language, dance, sculpture, tattoo, and sports. The festival rotates around the three most populated islands of Nuku Hiva, Hiva Oa, and Ua Pou. A miniature version of the festival also takes place every four years, ensuring there's a festival every two years, on the islands of Tahuata, Fatu Hiva, and Ua Huka.

Food and Drink

Dining is an exciting experience on the islands of Tahiti. You'll find a range of casual restaurants, called snacks; food trucks, called roulottes; fruit stands; hotel restaurants; and fine dining venues. Fragrant fruit trees line the main roads on the islands, and every now and then you might be rewarded with a stray passionfruit or two as you take a stroll.

Restaurant meals are subject to a 10 percent value added tax (VAT) and 4 percent service charge. These fees are usually included in the menu price, although resort restaurants often add them on later. Prices are often exorbitant, but portions are usually large enough to be happy with a main dish. Meals are usually served with fresh bread, though water is about CFP 350 extra. Tipping is appreciated but not expected. About US$25 will usually see you through an excellent lunch at a casual restaurant. The same thing in a deluxe hotel dining room will be about 50 percent more.

Local restaurants offer French, Chinese, Vietnamese, Italian, and, of course, Tahitian dishes. The nouvelle cuisine Tahitienne is a combination of European and Asian recipes, with local seafood and vegetables, plus the classic ma'a Tahiti (Tahitian food). Lunch is the main meal of the day in French Polynesia, and many restaurants offer a plat du jour designed for regular customers. This is often displayed on a blackboard near the entrance and is usually good value. Most restaurants serve lunch 11:30am-2pm and dinner 6pm-9pm. Lunch is meant to be enjoyed, and dishes may take a while to hit your table. Arrive at the venue early and plan extra time if you have somewhere to be afterward.

If it's all too expensive, groceries are a good alternative. There are lots of nice places to picnic, and at CFP 50 a loaf, that crisp French white bread is a tempting snack when paired with a nice spread. Cheap red wines such as Selection Faragui are imported from France in bulk and bottled locally in plastic bottles. Add a nice piece of French cheese and you're ready for a budget traveler's banquet. If you're

Top Five Uses for Coconut Trees in French Polynesia

Look up and you're bound to set eyes on a coconut tree, perhaps with a cluster of coconuts at its center. Coconut trees are essential to everyday life in the South Pacific.

1. Palm leaves: The sturdy leaves are woven into thatched roofing or rugs, protecting homes against critters, rain, and wind. They can also be woven into bags, home decor, rope, hats, and other essential everyday items.

2. Coconut water: Young coconuts have a slightly sweet liquid inside, providing vitamins, hydration, and electrolytes after a long day in the heat and humidity.

3. Coconut meat: Mature coconuts have a thick layer of meat inside, which can be used to make coconut milk, coconut cream, or eaten on its own. No matter what dish it's added to, coconut meat provides a creamy and sweet flavor.

4. Coconut husks: The dried outer husk of a coconut can be used to light fires when it's dry and to keep soil damp when it's wet, especially on vanilla plantations.

5. Coconut oil and copra: Dried coconut meat turns to copra, which then is used to craft coconut oil. Coconut oil can be used for cooking, soothing dry skin, and as fragrance.

going to the outer islands, take as many snacks with you as possible; it's always more expensive there.

There's also Martinique rum and Hinano beer (CFP 200 in grocery stores), brewed locally by the Brasserie de Tahiti. Founded in 1914, this company's first beer was called Aorai, and today it produces Heineken as well as Hinano. There's a deposit on Hinano beer bottles (CFP 60 on large bottles), which makes beer cheap to buy cold and carry out. Supermarkets aren't allowed to sell alcohol after 10am on Sundays or holidays, so stock up the night before.

The mai tai is a cocktail made with rum, liqueur, and fruit juice. Moorea's famous Rotui fruit drinks are sold in tall liter containers; the pineapple and grapefruit juices are worth a try. Also watch for the Sun Wave fruit drinks at CFP 180 for a one-liter carton in grocery stores. At CFP 110 in supermarkets, bottled Eau Royale mineral water is your best bet for finding affordable water, as tap water isn't safe to drink outside Papeete and Bora Bora.

Plant-based travelers or travelers with dietary concerns will want to call restaurants in advance to confirm what dishes they have available. Many places feature dishes on their menu but may not serve them every day depending on demand and ingredient availability. Locals tend to eat meat and fish when they eat out, and plant-based diners will want to have a back-up plan in their pocket for most meals. Many restaurants can make steamed rice and vegetables in a pinch.

Tahitian Specialties

Sample the gamy flavor of **fei,** the red cooking banana that flourishes in Tahiti's uninhabited interior. The **Tahitian chestnut** tree (mape) grows near streams, and you can often buy these delicious cooked nuts at markets. **Miti hue** is a coconut-milk sauce fermented with the juice of river shrimp. Traditionally **ma'a Tahiti**, Tahitian food, is eaten by hand.

Poisson cru (ia ota), small pieces of raw bonito (skipjack) or yellowfin tuna marinated with lime juice and soaked in coconut milk, is one of the most popular dishes around the islands. As is **fafaru** (smelly fish), prepared by marinating pieces of fish in seawater in an airtight coconut-shell container. Other typical Tahitian plates are chicken and pork casserole with fafa, pork and cabbage casserole (pua'a chou), and goat cooked in ginger.

Po'e is a sticky sweet pudding made of starchy banana, papaya, taro, or pumpkin flour, flavored with vanilla and topped with coconut-milk sauce. Many varieties of this treat are made throughout Polynesia. **Faraoa ipo** is Tuamotu coconut bread. The local coffee is flavored with vanilla bean and served with sugar and coconut cream.

If you have a big appetite and time to spare, spend a morning at the market and stock up on island produce like pineapples, soursop, starfruit, passionfruit, guava, grapefruit, papaya, and any other fruit your tastebuds are drawn toward.

Polynesian Cooking

Ancient Polynesians developed an ingenious way of cooking in an underground earth oven known as an **ahimaa.** First, a stack of dry coconut husks is burned in a pit. Once the fire is going well, coral stones are heaped on top, and when most of the husks have burned away, the food is wrapped in banana leaves and placed on the hot stones—fish and meat below, vegetables above. The food is then covered with more leaves and stones, and after about 2.5 hours, each ingredient is cooked to perfection. Many resorts stage an island night when this fare is served to the accompaniment of song and dance.

If you can, attend a Tahitian **tamaaraa** (feast) and try some Polynesian specialties roasted in an ahimaa. Basalt stones are preheated with a wood fire in a meter-deep pit, and then covered with leaves. Each type of food is wrapped separately in banana leaves to retain its own flavor and then lowered in. The oven is then covered with more banana leaves, wet sacking, and sand, and left 1-3 hours to bake: suckling pig, mahi-mahi, taro, umara (sweet potato), uru (breadfruit), and fafa (a spinach-like cooked vegetable made from taro tops) are common dishes.

Accommodations

Accommodations range from barebone campsites to five-star seaside luxury villas, though almost all stays will be on the higher price end compared to similar accommodations in the South Pacific.

While there is no sales tax in French Polynesia, a value added tax (VAT) applies. A special 6 percent VAT applies to rented accommodations like hotel rooms, guesthouses, and pensions as well as meal plans. A 5 percent VAT is added for room tax. Purchases in stores have a 16 percent VAT. Bars, excursions, rentals, restaurants, and snacks come with a 10 percent VAT.

Some large hotels tack a CFP 1,000 or 10 percent commission onto any rental cars, lagoon excursions, and scuba diving booked through their front desks. Many small hotels add a surcharge to your bill if you stay only one night, and some charge a supplement during the high seasons from June-October and mid-December-mid-January. Discounts may be offered during the low months from February-March and November-mid-December.

A government regulation prohibiting buildings higher than a coconut tree outside Papeete means that many of the hotels are low-rise affairs or consist of small Tahitian fare. A room with cooking facilities can save you a lot on restaurant meals. Resort meal plans are often grossly overpriced and can be dispensed with entirely if you're staying somewhere with nonhotel restaurants nearby. If you're on a budget, you'll want to account for the total cost of the room rate plus the meal plan if there are no other food options in the vicinity.

Bear in mind that although a thatched bungalow may be cooler and more attractive than a concrete box, it's also more likely to have insects. For critter management, check the window screens and carry mosquito coils and/or repellent and turn on a light before using the facilities at night, as even the finest hotels in the tropics have cockroaches.

Hotels and Resorts

Of the large hotels, Sofitel, InterContinental, Four Seasons, Marriott, and Le Méridien are represented on several islands. French Polynesia's homegrown hotel chain, Pearl Resorts (www.pearlresorts.com), offers a handful of tasteful hotels in the top-end price range. There are always middle-level hotels that charge half what the top-end places want while providing adequate comfort. Low- to middle-range hotel rooms usually include air-conditioning and a private bathroom.

Hotels range from basic to high-end luxury, with private island resorts available for those who truly want to escape the masses. It's common to pay US$800 and up per night at some of the top-end resorts and hotels. High-end resorts usually have an on-site pool, spa, gym, room service, and restaurants. Butler services, private transport (sometimes by sea plane or helicopter), and custom menus also feature in five-star stays.

The overwater bungalow was invented in French Polynesia in the 1960s, and you'll now find them on Tahiti, Moorea, Huahine, Raiatea, Taha'a, Bora Bora, Rangiroa, Tikehau, and Manihi. They range in price from CFP 18,000-284,600 for double occupancy plus tax.

Pensions

A unique accommodation in French Polynesia is the well-established network of homestays, in which you stay in a private room or bungalow provided by a local family. Pensions are often cheaper than hotels with similar offerings, and you'll be able to experience what life is like for residents of the islands. Many pension owners offer tour-guiding services, giving you a highly personalized tour of their home island.

Most travel agents abroad won't book the pensions or lodgings with the inhabitants because no commissions are paid, but you can make reservations directly with the owners themselves either by email or by phone. Calling ahead works best, as not all pensions have email, and even those that do are often unprepared to respond to messages in English. If you do email, it's worth making use of Google Translate and pasting a French version of the message within the email in addition to English. A quick browse online reveals many pension websites don't seem to have been updated since the early aughts; Comic Sans and visitor counters are part of the norm.

One Papeete travel agency specializing in such bookings is **Tekura Tahiti Travel** (www.tahiti-tekuratravel.com), on Rue Jaussen behind the cathedral. Most pensions don't accept credit cards, even if their website or brochure says they will. Many have a two-night minimum stay or charge extra if you leave after one night. Refunds may not be given if you discover upon arrival that you don't like a pension and decide to check out early. Not all pension owners speak English, so it's worth having basic French phrases on hand.

Conditions at the pensions vary. Towels may not be provided, and the room may not be cleaned every day. Don't expect hot water in the shower or a lot of privacy. Mosquitoes are a problem almost everywhere, and you should arrive armed with repellent and coils. Be prepared for rooster noise in the middle of the night. You're often required to take meals (typically fish and root vegetables), often because there are no other eating options, and this can make these places pricey. If you're on a tight budget or don't like fish, look for a place with cooking facilities and prepare your own food. Many pensions provide free drinking water, while others have only bottled water. The family may lend or rent you a bicycle and are often helpful when it comes to booking accommodation at the next destination, arranging transport, and tours. Pensions are a great way to meet people while finding a place to stay for much less than you'd pay at an international resort.

Backpacker Accommodations

Hostels with dormitory accommodations are available on many of the main islands, with communal cooking facilities usually provided. Some hostels arrange regular group events and excursions, making it an ideal place to meet other travelers. Dorm beds are priced per person, and couples can often get a double room for a price only slightly above two dorm beds. Hostels throughout French Polynesia range in cleanliness, though are generally a safe place to stay as long as you take standard precautions. Many dorm rooms do not have lockers, so you may want to keep your valuables on you or invest in a personal lock system, like wire mesh sold by Pacsafe that can secure your belongings to a bed.

Camping

French Polynesia is one of the few South Pacific destinations where camping is a practical option. Regular campgrounds exist on Moorea, Huahine, Raiatea, and Bora Bora. On the outer islands camping is usually not a problem, though you'll want to seek permission from the landowner and pitch your tent well out of sight of the road. Some pensions may allow you to set up camp on their property for a small fee. Rain showers and mosquitoes are common throughout the islands—you'll want a tent that's water- and bug-proof. Take care when pitching your tent near coconut trees, as falling coconuts can pose serious injury. It's a challenge to rent camping gear on most islands, though some campgrounds do rent tents, beds, and offer access to communal cooking equipment for an added cost.

Reserving Rooms

How you reserve a room largely depends on the type of accommodation you're planning to stay in. Full-service travel agents may be the best way to book mid-range to luxury hotel properties in French Polynesia, but they're unlikely to arrange budget and pension stays. Some travel agents offer massive discounts on room costs through their travel packages, wrapping airfare, food, and accommodation into an affordable rate. If you're after more control and flexibility, you can book most mid-range and luxury accommodations online directly via their website or email. Some online travel agents, like Booking.com (www.booking.com), Trip Advisor (www.tripadvisor.com), Hotels.com (www.hotels.com), and Skyscanner (www.skyscanner.com), find the cheapest room rates available.

Budget accommodations, like pensions, or hotels found on French Polynesia's remote islands, are often best booked over the phone as internet access might be limited on their end. When you're browsing the websites of many pensions throughout French Polynesia, you might notice that many of them seem like they haven't been updated since the 1990s. Not all pension owners speak English. If you're reaching them by email, it's worth sending your message with a French translation underneath, even if it's been written through Google Translate.

Conduct and Customs

Overall, the islands of Tahiti are welcoming to tourists and forgiving when it comes to cultural faux pas. The blend of French and Polynesian ethnic groups can mean that interactions may differ depending on the region you're in. The travel trail is primed with packaged pleasures, but pierce the bubble of tourism and you'll encounter something far from the organized schedules and sterile efficiency: island time and a new way of living. The phrase *haere maru*, meaning "relax," is commonly heard for good reason.

Greetings

Before the COVID-19 pandemic, people usually shook hands when meeting. If someone's hand was dirty, they'd extend their wrist or elbow. Women tended to kiss each other on the cheeks as a greeting. Now, most strangers simply wave or nod, and handshakes, kisses, and hugs are reserved for those who are already in social circles. When entering a home, it's polite to remove your shoes.

Dress

The dress code in French Polynesia is casual—feel free to kick off your shoes. On the main islands of Tahiti, Moorea, and Bora Bora, you'll see a mix of clothing that ranges from styles you'd find in U.S., European, and Australian beach cities to more traditional Polynesian attire with bold, colorful patterns. On the outer islands, locals tend to dress more conservatively, and you'll want to opt for practical outfits that will keep you sheltered from the sun. If you've packed a formal outfit, you'll get a chance to wear it at a nice resort dinner or bar in downtown Papeete. A bright piece of fabric, called a pareu, makes for a convenient

cover-up or skirt anywhere around the islands. Shoulders and knees should be kept covered when visiting cultural sites, like marae. Beachwear and athleticwear is not out of place on more touristy islands, like the Society Islands and in the main villages of the Tuamotus. However, on the more remote islands and atolls in the Marquesas, Australs, and Tuamotus where tourism is less common, it's wise to err on the more conservative side when it comes to how you dress.

Tipping

Tipping is not expected, though it is undoubtedly appreciated for excellent service. Restaurants may have a tip line on the merchant's receipt, but guests are not obligated to pay. Many resorts and tour companies have a communal tipping box at the reception area for tips.

Health and Safety

Before your trip, consult the latest tourist advice through resources like Smartraveller.gov.au (Australia), Travel.state.gov (U.S.), Gov.uk (U.K.), Travel.gc.ca (Canada), and Safetravel.govt.nz (New Zealand), gov.za (South Africa), and dfa.ie (Ireland). In general, French Polynesia is a safe destination with little serious crime against tourists.

Emergency phone numbers:

- Medical assistance: 15
- Police: 17
- Fire services: 18
- Sea rescue: 40 42 12 12

Public hospitals are found in Papeete (Tahiti), Taravao (Tahiti), Afareaitu (Moorea), Uturoa (Raiatea), Mataura (Tubuai), Taiohae (Nuku Hiva), and Atuona (Hiva Oa). Other islands have only infirmaries or pharmacies. Private clinics are found throughout the Society Islands, but there are none in

the eastern outer islands (over there, ask for the infirmerie). The hospital in Papeete is the most well-equipped in French Polynesia, and you should attempt to be seen there for serious medical concerns. The government-run medical facilities typically provide subsidized medical treatment to residents, but have higher rates for foreigners. It's usually no more expensive to visit a private doctor or clinic, and often it's cheaper.

Medications from your home country may be unobtainable in the islands. Pack a full supply of what you may need. If you need to replace any medication, it helps to quote the generic name and dosage at the pharmacy rather than the brand name, as dosages and brands may be different.

TRAVEL INSURANCE

If you have a serious accident or your trip is compromised, travel insurance could save you from having to pay a stiff bill. Depending on your policy, travel insurance could cover medical treatment, lost or stolen luggage, and reimbursement for flight cancellations.

When reading the fine print, check to see if your regular group health insurance covers you while you're traveling abroad. Some travel policies pay only the amount above and beyond what your national or group health insurance will pay and are invalid if you don't have any health insurance at all. Due to the remote nature of French Polynesia's outer islands, you'll want to ensure that medical evacuations are covered.

Some travel insurance plans do not cover what they deem to be "dangerous activities" like scuba diving, parasailing, surfing, riding a motor scooter, or motorcycle. Some companies offer a more comprehensive policy to include these activities, but some activities will require you to have credentials. For example, scuba divers are only covered for incidents that happen during dives within the depth of their certification. Coverage for riding a motorcycle might require a motorcycle license. Some companies will pay your bills directly, while others require you to pay and collect receipts that may be reimbursed later. **World Nomads** (www.worldnomads.com) offers adventure-friendly policies for residents of the U.K., the U.S., Canada, Australia, Ireland, New Zealand, and South Africa.

Scuba divers who want more complete diving coverage and standby medical advice should consider purchasing a policy from **Divers Alert Network** (6 W. Colony Pl., Durham, NC 27705, USA, tel. +1 919/684-2948, www.dan.org). There's a recompression chamber (caisson hyperbare) at the Centre Hospitalier in Papeete.

ACCLIMATIZING

It might take a few days to adjust to the humidity and heat if you're arriving from a cold and/or dry destination. Minimize jet lag by setting your watch to local time at your destination as soon as you board the aircraft. Westbound flights into the South Pacific from North America or Europe are less jolting since you follow the sun, and your body gets a few hours of extra sleep. Eastbound flights tend to cause jet lag as you lose a few hours of sleep. On average, it takes most people one day per hour of difference to adjust to a new time zone. Airplane cabins have low humidity, and it's best to choose juice and water over carbonated drinks, alcohol, or caffeinated drinks to stay hydrated.

Scuba divers should take care not to fly within 12 hours after a no-decompression dive and 24 hours after a decompression dive to avoid decompression sickness (DCS), commonly called the "bends."

If you are prone to motion sickness or seasickness, it's best to take anti-motion medication prior to boarding a flight or a boat. If you do get seasick onboard, stare at the horizon, which is always steady, and make conversation to avoid dwelling on it. Some travelers suggest ginger for alleviating motion sickness.

CRIME

The rate of serious and violent crime is low in French Polynesia, though like everywhere it does happen. Theft is one of the largest risks toward travelers, especially in crowded areas. It's worth heeding common travel advice like keeping your belongings close and valuables hidden. When out at bars or restaurants, never leave your food or drink unattended.

Avoid walking around intoxicated, especially alone and at night. Most crime in French Polynesia against tourists is of the opportunistic kind, often in the form of stealing from a drunk wanderer. There are no major organized scams or groups to be aware of.

NATURAL DISASTER

Cyclones are most common from November to April, though tropical storms and cyclones can take place throughout the year. If your stay coincides with a cyclone, there might be power and water outages, travel delays, and road barriers.

French Polynesia is also at risk of earthquakes and tsunamis. If an earthquake is underway, stay clear of windows and any objects hanging overhead, and take cover under a table, bed, or chair. If a tsunami warning is in place, move to higher ground.

SUNBURN

French Polynesia is a destination where you might need an umbrella and sunscreen on the same day, so it's wise to always keep sun protection on hand. The sun is strong around the islands, especially between the hours of 10am-3pm. All year long, French Polynesia has an UV rating from 6-7, which means that there is a high risk of harm to skin and eyes from sun exposure.

Sunscreen, a wide-brimmed hat, a lightweight shirt or rashguard, and leggings will help protect against harmful UV rays. Clothing rated UPF 50+ and sunscreen rated SPF 50+ against UVA and UVB rays block around 98 percent of UV rays. Some sunscreen can damage fragile coral reef ecosystems, so opt for one free from oxybenzone and instead has a mineral base with non-nano zinc and/or titanium oxide as the active sunblocking ingredient. Apply sunscreen at least 30 minutes before entering the water, and regularly throughout the day. Aloe vera gel helps soothe sunburned skin.

INJURIES AND AILMENTS

Cuts and scratches infect easily in the tropics and take a long time to heal. You'll want to disinfect wounds thoroughly with antiseptic and keep them covered and dry as they heal. If your wound is hot to touch, shows signs of redness and swelling—especially that spreads, or weeps beyond the first day—seek professional treatment as it may be infected.

When you're in the ocean, stay clear of the reef and do not touch any form of marine life, as there are venomous creatures and corals. Wearing a rash guard and leggings while swimming can help protect against stings, sunburn, and reef cuts. Surfers should note that many of French Polynesia's best waves break over shallow reef.

Heat rash is caused by wearing heavy clothing that is inappropriate for the climate. When sweat glands are blocked and the sweat is unable to evaporate, small blisters appear. Synthetic fabrics such as nylon are especially bad in this regard. If you get it, take a cold shower and avoid activities that induce sweating.

FOOD-BORNE ILLNESS

The tap water is safe to drink in downtown Papeete and on Bora Bora, but ask first elsewhere. If in doubt, boil it or use purification pills. A water filter, like a Lifestraw, can come in handy, especially in areas where bottled water is not readily available. If the tap water is contaminated, the local ice will be too. Avoid brushing your teeth with water unfit to drink, and wash or peel fruit and vegetables if you can. Cooked food is less subject to contamination than raw.

Traveler's diarrhea occurs when food or drink is contaminated by a virus or bacteria, causing an upset stomach. You can help prevent traveler's diarrhea by washing your hands frequently, peeling fruits and vegetables, and eating cooked or boiled food items. If you do get sick, replenish your fluids and electrolytes. Rehydration salts are sold at most pharmacies. If the diarrhea is persistent or you experience high fever, drowsiness, or blood in your stool, seek a doctor.

More than 400 species of tropical reef fish, including wrasses, snappers, groupers, jacks, moray eels, surgeonfish, shellfish, and especially barracudas, are known to cause seafood poisoning (ciguatera). The toxins are produced by dinoflagellates, small marine organisms, and are consumed by tiny herbivorous fish. The toxin passes up through the food chain, and travelers should avoid eating fish over 6 pounds as well as the liver, intestines, roe, and heads of smaller fish. The symptoms (numbness and tingling around the mouth and extremities, reversal of hot and cold sensations, prickling, itching, nausea, vomiting, erratic heartbeat, joint and muscle pains) usually subside in a few days, though seeking treatment is still recommended.

INSECT-BORNE DISEASES

Bites by sand flies, called nonos, itch for days and can become infected. If you're in a place infested with them, cover your feet and ankles with long trousers, a skirt, and/or insect repellent. Mosquito bites are also prone to infection. Wearing clothing treated with permethrin, insect repellent, and coils help keep the pests at bay. Mosquitoes and nonos tend to be most active at dawn and dusk.

Dengue fever is a mosquito-transmitted disease endemic in Polynesia. Symptoms such as headaches, sore throat, joint pain, fever, chills, nausea, and rash appear one or two weeks after the bite. This illness can last anywhere from 2-15 days, and the only real cure is to rest and stay hydrated. The U.S. Centers for Disease Control and Prevention advises avoiding aspirin, as it can lead to complications. No vaccine exists, so just try to avoid getting bitten (the *Aedes* mosquito bites only during the day). Dengue fever can kill children under 13, so extra care must be taken to protect them if an outbreak is in progress.

There have also been outbreaks of Zika in French Polynesia, which is an illness that can cause fever, rash, arthralgia, headaches, and conjunctivitis. The disease is transmitted through the *Aedes* mosquito. Women who are pregnant or trying to become pregnant should take extra precautions, as complications can pass through birth.

CORONAVIRUS

In 2020, the coronavirus pandemic impacted the islands of Tahiti, as travel and tourism were restricted throughout the islands. At the time of publishing, French Polynesia had fully vaccinated over 50 percent of its eligible population. To minimize the risk of catching or spreading the virus, wear a mask whenever you're indoors, wash your hands frequently and thoroughly, and keep a two-meter distance between strangers.

Practical Details

WHAT TO PACK

On the islands of Tahiti, expect warm, humid weather for most of the time you're there. It's wise to pack your suitcase around the main activities you plan to do. Air Tahiti flights allow suitcases of up to 23 kilograms, with an extra 5 kilograms for certified scuba divers. Carry on baggage is limited to 5 kilograms.

For clothing, prioritize lightweight, quick-drying fabrics. Basics include shorts, shirts, a long-sleeved sun shirt, and a nicer outfit for evenings. You'll want shoes for the beach and potentially hiking or walking. Dress is casual in the islands. The pareu (par-RAY-o) is a bright two-meter piece of cloth that serves as an all-purpose wrap garment for both men and women. They're widely sold in the islands, so you can easily pick one up. Not all accommodations have laundry facilities, so it's wise to have clothing you can wash in the sink. A light sweater or windbreaker may come in handy, as it can be cool at night and on boats. You'll also need a sun hat or visor, and maybe a small umbrella. Waterproof bags can help keep your belongings dry on bumpy boat rides and unexpected downpours. French Polynesia uses adapter type A, B, and E, with two circular prongs, like those used in continental Europe.

If you're packing camera gear, it's wise to store it in a dry-bag backpack. You can purchase padded camera cubes and insert these cubes into the drybag backpack, creating a safe and waterproof camera bag. Because drybags do not look like camera bags, they're often also less of a target for theft.

A mask and snorkel are essential equipment—you'll be missing half of French Polynesia's beauty without them. Reef shoes can also be very handy. Most dive shops include equipment rental in the cost of their fun dive price, but serious divers might want to bring their own.

If you bring a tent, a light foam pad and lightweight sleeping bag should suffice; many campers simply don't use them. Other things to consider taking include a small portable power bank, a compass, a pocket flashlight, a plastic cup, a can and bottle opener, a spoon, and a water bottle. A book helps pass the evenings too, as very little is available in English here.

Bring enough supply of your personal medications, plus your prescriptions (in generic terminology) to last through the entirety of your stay if possible. Aside from the obvious toiletries, you might want to bring earplugs, insect repellent, reef-safe sunscreen, a motion-sickness remedy, a diarrhea remedy, a cold remedy, pain reliever, antibacterial ointment, and antiseptic cream. Body glide also helps prevent chafing when walking in damp clothes.

ATMs are not always reliable throughout the islands, and some places only take cash. Credit and debit cards are widely accepted through the Society Islands, however. You might want to carry your valuables in a money belt worn around your waist or neck under your clothing; most camping stores have these. Make several photocopies of the information page of your passport, personal identification, driver's license, scuba certification card, credit cards, airline tickets, etc. On the side of the photocopies, write the phone numbers you'd need to call to report lost documents.

Laundry and Luggage Storage

Some guesthouses and hotels provide laundry services on-site, typically for an added cost of around CFP 700 per load of laundry. Not all facilities have dryers, and clothes are instead line dried. It's possible to find laundromats in Papeete and Bora Bora, but they're rarely available elsewhere. You can always wash your clothes in the sink with a bit of laundry powder or laundry sheets, and line dry it in the sun.

Most accommodations allow you to store your luggage on-site after you check out, sometimes for a fee. Outside of Papeete, there are no official luggage-storage facilities. Some of the larger resorts have a small room dedicated to luggage storage for those outside of their check-in or check-out time. Usually, the resort will not take responsibility for anything that happens in the storage room, so it's wise to bring a lock.

MONEY

The French Pacific franc, or CFP (for cour de franc Pacifique), is legal tender in French Polynesia, Wallis and Futuna, and New Caledonia (there is no difference between the banknotes circulating in these French territories). There are beautifully colored big banknotes of CFP 500, 1,000, 5,000, and 10,000, and coins of CFP 1, 2, 5, 10, 20, 50, and 100.

The best currency to carry to French Polynesia are the euro and United States dollar, as these are what are most widely accepted. You'll find the rates for most currencies at www.xe.com. At the time of writing, **CFP 100 was worth US$1,** making it easy to determine the exchange rate.

There have been calls to adopt the euro as the currency in French Polynesia, but it hasn't happened yet over fears that the European Commission might gain the power to intervene in the local taxation system.

All banks levy a stiff commission on foreign currency transactions (including euro transactions). The easiest way to avoid the high commissions and long bank lines is to change money infrequently. When changing a large amount, it might be worth comparing the rates at all three banks of the Banque de Polynésie (www.sg-bdp.pf), the Banque Socredo (www.websoc.pf), and the Banque de Tahiti (www.banque-tahiti.pf) as they do differ slightly. Even with the commissions, you'll still get more CFP for your dollars after arriving in French Polynesia than you would from a bank or airport exchange office back home.

Many banks in French Polynesia have ATMs outside their offices, and these should provide local currency against checking account Visa and MasterCard at a rate slightly better than traveler's checks, without commission. Banque Socredo has ATMs at their branches throughout the territory (including at Faa'a airport). Despite advertised links to international services such as Cirrus and Maestro, American checking account ATM cards may not work in French Polynesia. Also, ask your bank what fees it'll charge if you use an ATM abroad, as they can be unexpectedly high. Get your special personal identification number (PIN) while you're there, as most ATMs require it. Be aware that there are weekly limits on ATM withdrawals, and if you think you might run short, you should have several different cards. To avoid emergencies, don't be 100 percent dependent on ATMs and bring some cash or traveler's checks (accepted in larger cities and some resorts).

Credit cards are accepted in many places on the main islands, but Pacific francs in cash are easier to use at restaurants, shops, and activities. If you want to use a credit card, always ask beforehand, even if the business has a sign, brochure, or website that says it's possible. Visa and MasterCard are universally accepted in the Society Islands, but American Express and Diner's Club are not. Occasionally you'll be charged 5 percent extra to pay by credit card. MasterCard and Visa levy surcharges of around 2.5 percent on foreign currency conversions associated with their cards. If you need to have money wired to you from abroad, the Banque de Polynésie has a connection with Western Union.

On many outer islands, credit cards, traveler's checks, and foreign banknotes other than euros won't be accepted, so it's essential to change enough money before leaving Papeete. Apart from Tahiti, there are banks on Bora Bora, Huahine, Hiva Oa, Moorea, Nuku Hiva, Raiatea, Rangiroa, Rurutu, Taha'a,

Tubuai, and Ua Pou. All of these islands have Banque Socredo branches, and the Banque de Tahiti is represented on eight of them, the Banque de Polynésie on four. Bora Bora, Moorea, and Raiatea each have three different banks. If you're headed for any island other than these, take along enough CFP in cash to see you through.

Budgeting

French Polynesia is easily the most expensive corner of the South Pacific. The high price structure is related to the strength of the euro and the high salaries paid to government employees who pay zero income tax. You'll have a much better time in French Polynesia if you accept this and lower your value-for-money expectations while doubling your budget.

Currently, the Value Added Tax (VAT) is 6 percent on rented accommodations as well as room and meal packages. A 5 percent VAT rate is added for room tax. There's 16 percent VAT applied to purchases in shops, stores, and boutiques. A 10 percent VAT rate is added to bars, excursions, car rentals, snacks, and restaurants. Most businesses will include this rate in their overall price, though a few do flag it as an extra cost.

Fortunately, facilities for budget travelers are available, often with cooking facilities that allow you to save on meals. Bread, fruit, vegetables, and mineral water from grocery stores are reasonable. Cheap transportation is available by inter-island boat, and on Tahiti there's the bus. Bicycles can be hired in many places.

Time is what you need the most of to see French Polynesia inexpensively, along with the wisdom to avoid trying to see and do too much. There are countless organized tours and activities available, but you can have an incredible time without them, too. With your own set of snorkel gear, every accessible spot is available for exploration. Wandering through markets, hiking along trails with tropical gardens, lounging on the beach, and socializing with the people you meet are always free. Bargaining is not common in French

Polynesia, and there are no major scams to be aware of—though you might get the occasional taxi driver attempting to overcharge. Tipping is not expected.

- **Sandwich:** CFP 600
- **Cup of coffee:** CFP 400
- **Beer:** CFP 400
- **Lunch:** CFP 2,500
- **Dinner:** CFP 3,500
- **Inter-island plane ticket:** CFP 8,000-20,000
- **Ferry ticket:** CFP 1,000-3,000
- **Bus ticket:** CFP 300-450
- **Car rental:** CFP 8,000
- **Pension:** CFP 10,000
- **Hotel:** CFP 30,000

COMMUNICATIONS
Cell Phones

There are two major phone service providers in French Polynesia, Vini and Vodafone. Vini (www.vini.pf) covers 65 islands in all archipelagos. They have a travel plan that offers 3 gigabytes of mobile data plus 30 minutes of local calls for CFP 4,000 or 10 gigabytes of data with 60 minutes of local calls for CFP 8,000. There are Vini stores throughout Tahiti.

Vodafone (www.vodafone.pf) has plans that start at CFP 1,890 per month for 4 gigabytes of data and 2 hours of local calls. Plans change regularly, and sales are frequent.

Before you commit to either company, it's wise to look up the most recent coverage map of each provider and compare these maps to your planned travel route.

WiFi and Internet Access

Many accommodations offer free WiFi connection included with your stay, especially on the major islands. However, access to internet can be slow or nonexistent on the island groups outside of the Society Islands. Even if an accommodation advertises internet connection, it may not be reliable during your stay. If you must be connected, it's best to secure your own personal form of internet before departing to a remote island.

Tahiti Wifi (www.tahitiwifi), found at the Faa'a Airport, rents a personal hotspot the size of a smart phone to travelers. Prices start from €7.90 per day and include one gigabyte of high-speed internet, and unlimited slow-speed internet per day. Unlimited high-speed internet is €19.90 per day, and 5 gigabytes of high-speed internet cost €39 to use within 30 days. Vodafone (www.vodafone.pf) also offers pocket WiFi devices with 10 gigabyte plans for 9,900 CFP, valid for 30 days.

Another internet option is to purchase data from the cell phone companies as part of your phone plan and use your personal phone as a hotspot to connect other devices like your laptop or tablet to the internet.

Shipping and Postal Service

The 63 post offices (www.opt.pf) throughout French Polynesia are open weekdays 7:30am-3pm. Main branches sell ready-made padded envelopes and boxes. Parcels with an aggregate length, width, and height of over 90 centimeters or weighing more than 20 kilograms cannot be mailed. Rolls (posters, calendars, etc.) longer than 90 centimeters are also not accepted. Letters cannot weigh over 2 kilograms, and when mailing parcels it's much cheaper to keep the weight under 2 kilograms. Registration (recommandation) is extra, and insurance (envois avec valeur déclarée) is also possible. Always use airmail (poste aérienne) when posting a letter; surface mail takes months to arrive. Postcards can still take up to two weeks to reach the United States. To pick up poste restante (general delivery) mail, you must show your passport and pay a fee per piece. Incoming mail is often delayed.

There's no residential mail delivery in French Polynesia, and what appear to be mailboxes along rural roads are often bread delivery boxes. Since there are usually no street addresses, almost everyone has a post office box or B.P. (boîte postale). French Polynesia issues its own colorful postage stamps—available at local post offices.

OPENING HOURS

Businesses open early in the morning and often close for two hours at midday. Normal office hours are weekdays 7:30am-11:30am and 1:30pm-4:30pm. Many shops also remain open until 5:30pm and Saturdays 7:30pm-noon. A few shops remain open at lunchtime, and small convenience stores are often open Saturday afternoons until 6pm and Sunday 6am-8am. Banking hours are variable, either 8am-3:30pm or 8am-11am and 2pm-5pm weekdays. Most businesses are closed on Sundays, but a few banks in Papeete open Saturday mornings.

Many shops, snacks, and restaurants close on Mondays and Tuesdays. If you arrive in a new destination on these days, it's wise to pack snacks just in case all food options are closed.

Public Holidays

Public holidays in French Polynesia include:

- New Year's Day (January 1)
- Gospel Day (March 5)
- Good Friday and Easter Monday (March/April)
- Labor Day (May 1)
- Victory Day (May 8)
- Ascension Day (May)
- Pentecost or Whitmonday (May/June)
- Autonomy Day (June 29)
- Bastille Day (July 14)
- Assumption Day (August 15)
- All Saints' Day (November 1)
- Armistice Day (November 11)
- Christmas Day (December 25).

Autonomy Day commemorates June 29, 1880, when King Pomare V was deposed and French Polynesia became a full French colony, not September 6, 1984, when the territory achieved a degree of internal autonomy. Many communities in French Polynesia are pushing to have this date changed. On **All Saints' Day** (November 1) the locals illuminate the cemeteries at Papeete, Arue, Punaauia, and elsewhere with candles. On **New Year's Eve** the Papeete waterfront is beautifully illuminated. *Everything* will be closed on these holidays (and maybe the days before and after).

TOURIST INFORMATION

French Polynesia's tourism promotion office, Tahiti Tourisme (www.tahiti-tourisme.com), has overseas branches in many countries. Within French Polynesia the same organization operates tourist information offices on Tahiti, Moorea, Huahine, Raiatea, and Bora Bora. If open, these offices can provide free brochures and answer questions, but will usually not book accommodations or activities for you. They're financed by the room tax charged for every hotel stay.

TIME

The sun rises at roughly 6am and sets at 6pm in French Polynesia throughout the year. Nearly all of French Polynesia is in the same time zone as Hawaii, 10 hours behind Greenwich Mean Time (GMT) or two hours behind California (except mid-Mar.-mid-Nov., when it's three hours). The Marquesas are 30 minutes ahead of Tahiti, and the Gambier Islands are an hour ahead of Tahiti. Standard time is used year-round in French Polynesia. French Polynesia is east of the International Date Line, so the day is the same as that of the United States but a day behind Fiji, New Zealand, and Australia.

MEASUREMENTS

French Polynesia uses the metric system. Many islands around the islands are marked with kilometer checkpoints. For example, an address at PK 7 is 7 kilometers from the starting point of the road. Temperature is measured by Celsius.

Tips for Travelers

TRAVELERS WITH DISABILITIES

French disability rights legislation has not been fully implemented in French Polynesia, and very few facilities are provided for travelers with disabilities. The top resorts generally have a couple of rooms equipped for guests who have physical disabilities. For example, the 270-room InterContinental Resort Tahiti has two accessible garden rooms, and the resort's restaurants, bars, and swimming pools are accessible by elevator. Some of the larger resorts have a limited number of accessible rooms. These rooms are often in high demand, so it's best to reserve them well in advance. You should also mention any special needs to your airline, accommodation, and transportation companies when booking. Most public transportation in French Polynesia is not wheelchair-friendly.

Boat tours are often done in small fiberglass boats, and do not have any systems for securing a wheelchair. 4WD tours are often trucks with bench seating in the back, though many tour guides will allow guests to sit in the front of the cab, but guests should inquire in advance. Many wheelchair users recommend seeing French Polynesia on a cruise as larger ships generally have wheelchair-friendly lifts, tenders, and cabins. The travel blog **You Should Go Anyway** (www.youshouldgoanyway.com) details advice for traveling around the Society Islands with a wheelchair.

TRAVELING WITH CHILDREN

Unlike Fiji and the Cook Islands, there are no strictly "adults only" resorts in French Polynesia, and families with small children are welcome almost everywhere. Babies under the age of two are seldom charged for anything, although most of the cheaper accommodations do not supply a baby cot. Take along a tent-like baby travel cot if this might affect you. Very few restaurants have high chairs for children, and a small travel high chair that can be attached to restaurant tables will come in handy. Similarly, life vests for infants are generally not supplied during boat transfers or on nautical tours, and it would be a good idea to bring your own.

Air Tahiti's family reduction cards (CFP 2,000) provide a potential 50 percent reduction for the parents and 75 percent off for children under 12. Identification and one photo are required. The full discount is given only on off-peak flights. This reduction card must be purchased at Air Tahiti's downtown Papeete office, not at the airport office.

Children under 12 are usually half-price on excursions; children under two years old are usually free.

WOMEN TRAVELERS

While sexual assaults on women travelers are not common, women travelers should take the same precautions they take in most destinations throughout French Polynesia. Women should avoid walking alone, at night, and down unlit or uncrowded unlit areas. Women should also avoid staying alone in isolated tourist bungalows or camping outside organized campgrounds. Whenever checking into a room, ensure the door locks properly.

SENIOR TRAVELERS

Many hotels and airlines offer discounted rates for senior travelers. AARP (aarp.org) occasionally offers discounts on travel packages for seniors. Travel in between the islands can be challenging, so it might be worth vacationing on an island with a medical center present should an emergency arise.

LGBTQ+ TRAVELERS

Homosexuality is legal and accepted in French Polynesia, and there are strong LGBTQ+

communities throughout the islands, especially on Tahiti. Same-sex marriage ceremonies are available at many luxury resorts and event venues. French Polynesia, especially on the outer islands, is quite conservative and public displays of affection are not typically shown. The Tahitian islands also recognize a third gender in Polynesian culture that is neither male nor female, called mahu, where a biologically male child is often raised alongside female children. Mahu are traditionally recognized as important cultural leaders, often leading ceremonies and spaces taking care of children and elderly members of the community. Websites like **Out Adventures** (outadventures.com) publish practical guides.

Carl from Tahiti by Carl (tahitibycarl.com) is a gay travel consultant happy to help travelers create custom itineraries.

TRAVELERS OF COLOR

The Islands of Tahiti are known for being welcoming of all travelers, regardless of race or ethnicity. Acts of hatred toward travelers of color are rare. The region has a long history of European colonization and occupation, and many residents of French Polynesia are passionate about the islands gaining full sovereignty. On some islands, like the Marquesas, there is some strife between the French European and French Polynesian communities, though this is rarely transferred to tourists.

Resources

Glossary

A

afa: a demi, or person of mixed Polynesian and European ancestry

ahimaa: an underground, earthen oven. After AD 500, the Polynesians had lost the art of making pottery, so they were compelled to bake their food rather than boil it.

aito: ironwood

anse: cove (French)

aparima: a Tahitian dance that tells a story with the hands

archipelago: a group of islands

arii: a Tahitian high chief; the traditional head of a clan or tribe

Arioi: a pre-European religious society that traveled among the Society Islands presenting ceremonies and entertainment

atoll: a low-lying, ring-shaped coral reef enclosing a lagoon

B

bareboat charter: chartering a yacht without crew or provisions

bark cloth: *see* tapa

barrier reef: a coral reef separated from the adjacent shore by a lagoon

bêche-de-mer: sea cucumber; an edible sea slug; in Tahitian, rori; in French, trépang

B.P.: boîte postale; post office box

breadfruit: a large, round fruit with starchy flesh grown on an uru tree (*Artocarpus altilis*)

C

caldera: a wide crater formed through the collapse or explosion of a volcano

cassava: manioc; the starchy edible root of the tapioca plant

casse-croûte: a large sandwich made with a baguette

CFP: cour de franc Pacifique; the currency in French Polynesia

chain: an archaic unit of length equivalent to 20 meters

ciguatera: a form of fish poisoning caused by microscopic algae

CMAS: Confédération Mondiale des Activités Subaquatiques; a French scuba diving agency

code share: a system whereby two or more airlines own seats on a single flight

coir: coconut husk sennit used to make rope, etc.

copra: dried coconut meat used in the manufacture of coconut oil, cosmetics, soap, and margarine

coral: a hard, calcareous substance of various shapes, composed of the skeletons of tiny marine animals called polyps

coral bank: a coral formation over 150 meters long

coral bleaching: the expulsion of symbiotic algae by corals

coral head: a coral formation a few meters across

coral patch: a coral formation up to 150 meters long

cyclone: Also known as a hurricane (in the Caribbean) or typhoon (in Japan). A tropical storm that rotates around a center of low atmospheric pressure; it becomes a cyclone when its winds reach force 12, or 64 knots.

In the Northern Hemisphere, cyclones spin counterclockwise, while south of the equator they move clockwise. The winds of cyclonic storms are deflected toward a low-pressure area at the center, although the "eye" of the cyclone may be calm.

D E

demi-pension: a breakfast and dinner meal plan, also called the Modified American Plan (MAP) or half-board; pension complète means three meals, the American Plan (AP) or full-board

desiccated coconut: the shredded meat of dehydrated fresh coconut

EEZ: Exclusive Economic Zone; a 200-nautical-mile offshore belt of an island nation or seacoast state that controls the mineral exploitation and fishing rights

F G

fafa: a "spinach" of cooked taro leaves

farani: French; français

fare: Tahitian house

fissure: a narrow crack or chasm of some length and depth

fringing reef: a reef along the shore of an island

gendarme: a French police officer on duty only in rural areas in France and French overseas territories

guyot: a submerged atoll, the coral of which couldnt keep up with rising water levels

H

Havaii: legendary homeland of the Polynesians

Hiro: the Polynesian god of thieves

hoa: a shallow channel between motu

K L

kaina: country; kaina music is Tahitian country music, usually a string band

knot: about three kilometers per hour

lagoon: an expanse of water bounded by a reef

lapita: pottery made by the ancient Polynesians from 1600-500 BC

lava tube: a conduit formed as molten rock continues to flow below a cooled surface during the growth of a lava field. When the eruption ends, a tunnel is left with a flat floor where the last lava hardened.

leeward: downwind; the shore (or side) sheltered from the wind; as opposed to windward

lei: a garland, often of fresh flowers, but sometimes of paper, shells, etc., hung about the neck of a person being welcomed or feted

le truck: a truck with seats in back, used for public transportation on Tahiti

liveaboard: a tour boat with cabin accommodation for scuba divers

M

maa Tahiti: Tahitian food

maa Tinito: Chinese food

mahi-mahi: dorado, Pacific dolphinfish (no relation to the mammal)

mahu: a recognized third gender who is neither male nor female; a biological male child who is raised among females

mairie: town hall

makatea: an uplifted reef around the coast of an elevated atoll

mana: authority, prestige, virtue, "face," psychic power, a positive force

mangrove: a tropical shrub with branches that sends down roots forming dense thickets along tidal shores

manioc: cassava, tapioca, a starchy root crop

maohi: a native of French Polynesia

mape: Tahitian chestnut tree

maraamu: southeast trade winds, or alizés

marae: a Tahitian temple or open-air religious place, called ma'ae in the Marquesas

marara: flying fish

monoï: perfumed coconut oil

motu: a flat reef islet

N O

NAUI: National Association of Underwater Instructors

noanoa: perfume

noni: the knobby green tree fruit of the noni or nono tree (Morinda citrifolia)

nonos: sand flies

Oro: the Polynesian god of war
ote'a: a Tahitian ceremonial dance performed by men and women in two lines

P

pa: ancient Polynesian stone fortress
PADI: Professional Association of Dive Instructors, scuba diving agency
pandanus: screw pine with slender stem and prop roots. The sword-shaped leaves are used for plaiting mats and hats. In Tahitian, fara
papa'a: a Tahitian word used to refer to Europeans
pareu: a Tahitian sarong-like wraparound skirt or loincloth
pass: a channel through a barrier reef, usually with an outward flow of water
passage: an inside passage between an island and a barrier reef
pawpaw: papaya
pelagic: relating to the open sea, away from land
peretane: Britain, British in Tahitian
pétanque: French lawn bowling in which small metal balls are thrown
pirogue: outrigger canoe (French), in Tahitian vaa
PK: pointe kilométrique, a system of marking kilometers along highways in French Polynesia
poe: a sticky pudding made from bananas, papaya, pumpkin, or taro mixed with starch, baked in an oven, and served with coconut milk; in Rapanui po'i
poisson cru: (French) raw fish marinated in lime; in Tahitian ia ota
Polynesia: divided into western Polynesia (Tonga and Samoa) and eastern Polynesia (French Polynesia, Cook Islands, Hawaii, Easter Island, and New Zealand); from poly (many)
pp: per person
punt: a flat-bottomed boat
pupu: traditional Tahitian dance group

R S

raatira: Tahitian chief, dance leader

rain shadow: the dry side of a mountain, sheltered from the windward side
reef: a coral ridge near the ocean surface
roulotte: a mobile food van or truck
sennit: braided coconut-fiber rope
shareboat charter: a yacht tour for individuals or couples who join a small group on a fixed itinerary
shoal: a shallow sandbar or mud bank
snack: a small, casual restaurant usually serving seafood

T

tahua: in the old days a skilled Tahitian artisan or priest; today a sorcerer or healer
tamaaraa: a Tahitian feast
tamure: a new name for Ori Tahiti, a very fast erotic dance
tapa: a cloth made from the pounded bark of the paper mulberry tree (*Broussonetia papyrifera*). It's soaked and beaten with a mallet to flatten and intertwine the fibers, then painted with designs.
tapu: taboo, sacred, set apart, forbidden, a negative force
taro: a starchy elephant-eared tuber (*Colocasia esculenta*), a staple food of the Pacific islanders
tatau: the Tahitian original of the adopted English word tattoo
tavana: the elected mayor of a Tahitian commune (from the English governor)
tifaifai: a Tahitian patchwork quilt based on either European or Polynesian motifs
tiki: a humanlike sculpture representing an anonymous ancestor used for protection in the days of religious rites
tinito: Tahitian for Chinese
to'ere: a hollow wooden drum hit with a stick
trade wind: a steady wind blowing toward the equator from either northeast or southeast
tridacna clam: a giant clam, its size varies between 10 centimeters and one meter
truck: see le truck
tsunami: a fast-moving wave caused by an undersea earthquake; sometimes erroneously called a tidal wave

tu'i: (Polynesian) king, ruler

U V W
umara: sweet potato (*Ipomoea batatas*)
vigia: a mark on a nautical chart indicating a dangerous rock or shoal
VTT: vélo à tout terrain; mountain bike
windward: the point or side from which the wind blows, as opposed to leeward

ALTERNATIVE PLACE NAMES
Bass Islands: Marotiri Islands
Bellingshausen: Motu One
Hatutaa: Hatutu
Hatutu: Hatutaa
Hull: Maria
Maiao: Tapuaemanu
Maria: Hull
Marotiri Islands: Bass Islands

Maupihaa: Mopelia
Maupiti: Maurau
Maurau: Maupiti
Mohotani: Motane
Mopelia: Maupihaa
Moruroa: Mururoa
Motane: Mohotani
Motu Iti: Tupai
Motu One: Bellingshausen
Mururoa: Moruroa
Puamotu: Tuamotu
Scilly: Manuae
Taha'a: Uporu
Tapuaemanu: Maiao
Temoe: Timoe
Timoe: Temoe
Tuamotu: Puamotu
Tupai: Motu Iti
Uporu: Taha'a

Phrasebook

French and Tahitian are the official languages spoken throughout the islands of Tahiti. English is widely spoken in hotels and restaurants on the most touristic islands, but is rarely spoken in more rural areas or on the outer islands. Each of the island groups has their own dialect: Marquesan, Austral, and Tuamotuan. The Society Islands primarily speak Tahitian.

BASIC TAHITIAN
Tahitian, locally known as te roa, is largely an oral language, which is why it's common to see the same word spelled multiple ways even on the same island. The language was only written down in the early 1800s, when a linguist named John Davis created the first Tahitian dictionary in latin characters called the *Te Aebi no Tahiti* in 1810. The Tahitian alphabet only has 13 letters, and most sentences use some combination of the same few thousand words. The Tahitian letters are A, E, F, H, I, M, N, O, P, R, T, U, and V.

Pronunciation
It's common to see a long string of vowels in Tahitian, and each one is often pronounced. Each syllable also ends in a vowel. An apostrophe marks the glottal stop commonly used in Tahitian, which is a brief pause followed by a strong pronunciation of the following syllable.

VOWELS
Vowels are long when they are accompanied with a macron (ā, ē, ī, ō and ū).
a   as in "tall"
e   as in "set"
i   as in "teen"
o   as in "shore"
u   as in "toon"

CONSONANTS
Tahitian consonants are pronounced much the same as they are in English. R's are often rolled and F is pronounced the same as "fun" after O and U. H is pronounced like "horse" after I and before O or U.

Essential Phrases

maeva welcome
'ia orana hello
nana goodbye
maururuu thank you
'e yes
'a maybe
'aita no
e aha te huru? How are you?
maita'i I'm fine
To'u l'oa 'o... my name is...
e'e excuse me
aue ho'i e sorry
manuia! cheers!
aita e peapea no problem
aita maitai no good
ahiahi evening
ananahi tomorrow
arearea fun, to have fun
avatea midday (10am-3pm)
e haere oe ihea? Where are you going?
Tei hea te fare haumiti? Where is the restroom?

Food

ahimaa earth oven
amu eat
e hia? How much?
faraoa bread
haari coconut
inu drink
ma'a food
pape water
pia beer
tama'a maitai bon appétit
tamaaraa Tahitian feast
taofe coffee
uaina wine

Accommodation

fare house
fare iti toilet
fare niau thatched house
fare punu tin-roofed house
piha room
piha pape bathroom
ro'l bed

Transportation

petero'o mata'eina'a bus
petero'o tata'ahi bicycle
petero'o uria car
poti boat

Vocabulary

fare moni bank
fare pure church
fare rata post office
fare toa shop
fenua land
fetii parent, family
fiu fed up, bored
haere goodbye (to a person leaving)
haere mai io nei come here
haere maru go easy, take it easy
hei flower garland, lei
here hoe number-one sweetheart
himene song, from the English "hymn"
hoa friend
ia orana good day, may you live, prosper
i nanahi yesterday
ino bad
ioa name
ite know
mahana sun, light, day
mahanahana warm
maitai roa very good
manava welcome
manu bird
manureva airplane
mao shark
meka swordfish
miti salt water
moana deep ocean
moemoea dream
moni money
nana goodbye
naonao mosquito
nehenehe beautiful
niau coconut-palm frond
oa oa happy
ohipa work
ora life, health
ori dance
oromatua the spirits of the dead
otaa bundle, luggage

oti finished
pahi boat, ship
painapo pineapple
pape water, juice
pareu sarong
pohe death
poipoi morning
popaa foreigner, European
roto lake
taapapu understand
taata human being, man
tabu forbidden
tahatai beach
tama'a lunch
tamarii child
tane man, husband
taote doctor
tiare flower
to'e to'e cold
tupapau ghost
ua rain
uteute red
vahine woman, wife
vai freshwater
veavea hot

Numbers

hoe 1
piti 2
toru 3
maha 4
pae 5
ono 6
hitu 7
vau 8
iva 9
ahuru 10
ahuru ma hoe 11
ahuru ma piti 12
ahuru ma toru 13
ahuru ma maha 14
ahuru ma pae 15
ahuru ma ono 16
ahuru ma hitu 17
ahuru ma vau 18
ahuru ma iva 19
piti ahuru 20
piti ahuru ma hoe 21

piti ahuru ma piti 22
piti ahuru ma toru 23
toru ahuru 30
maha ahuru 40
pae ahuru 50
ono ahuru 60
hitu ahuru 70
vau ahuru 80
iva ahuru 90
hanere 100
tauatini 1,000
ahuru tauatini 10,000
mirioni 1,000,000

BASIC FRENCH
Essential Phrases
bonjour hello
bonsoir good evening
salut hi
au revoir goodbye
s'il vous plait please
merci thank you
de rien you're welcome
oui yes
non no
Parlez-vous anglaise? Do you speak English?
Où sont les toilettes? Where are the bathrooms?
Je désire, je voudrais . . . I want . . .
J'aime . . . I like . . .
Je ne comprends pas. I don't understand.
une chambre a room
le gendarmerie police station
une boutique, un magasin a store
Combien ça fait?, Combien ça coûte?, Combien?, Quel prix? How much does it cost?
Où sont les toilettes? Where is the restroom?

Transportation
Je vais à . . . I am going to . . .
Où allez-vous? Where are you going?
Jusqu'où allez-vous? How far are you going?
Où se trouve . . . ? Where is . . . ?
C'est loin d'ici? Is it far from here?

un horaire timetable
la route, la piste the road

Food

Une table pour deux/trois/quatre... A table for two/three/four...
Avez-vous un menu en anglais? Do you have a menu in English?
le pain bread
le lait milk
le vin wine
le casse-croûte snack
les conserves canned foods
les fruits de mer seafood
un café très chaud hot coffee
l'eau water
le plat du jour set meal

Health

pharmacie drugstore
douleur pain
fièvre fever
mal de tête headache
mal d'estomac stomachache
crampe cramp
la nausée nausea
vomissement vomiting
antibiotique antibiotic
aspirine aspirin
J'ai besoin de voir un médecin. I need to see a doctor.
Je dois aller à l'hôpital. I need to go to the hospital.
Ell/il a été piqué/mordu. She/he has been stung/bitten.
Je suis diabétique. I am diabetic.
Je suis enceinte. I am pregnant.
Je suis allergique à la... I am allergic to...

Time

À quelle heure? At what time?
Quelle heure est-il? What time is it?

C'est une heure/trois heures. It's one/three o'clock.
hier yesterday
aujourd'hui today
demain tomorrow

Numbers

un 1
deux 2
trois 3
quatre 4
cinq 5
six 6
sept 7
huit 8
neuf 9
dix 10
onze 11
douze 12
treize 13
quatorze 14
quinze 15
seize 16
dix-sept 17
dix-huit 18
dix-neuf 19
vingt 20
vingt-et-un 21
vingt-deux 22
vingt-trois 23
trente 30
quarante 40
cinquante 50
soixante 60
soixante-dix 70
quatre-vingts 80
quatre-vingt-dix 90
cent 100
mille 1,000
dix mille 10,000
million 1,000,000

Suggested Books and Films

GUIDEBOOKS

Reference Map of Oceania (2007) James A. Bier. A fully indexed map of the Pacific Islands with 51 detailed inset maps of individual islands. Useful details such as time zones are included.

Cocktails in Tahiti (2006) Richard Bondurant. The best cocktails from the world's most beautiful islands.

TRAVEL WRITING

Voyage of Discovery: A Cultural Odyssey through Polynesia (1994) Ben Finney. A complete account of the 1985 journey of the traditional sailing canoe *Hokule'a* through Polynesia.

Fatu Hiva: Back to Nature (1974) Thor Heyerdahl. In 1936 Heyerdahl and his wife, Liv, went to live on Fatu Hiva. This book describes their year there.

In the South Seas (1901) Robert Louis Stevenson. The author's memoir of his travels through the Marquesas, Tuamotus, and Gilberts by yacht in the years 1888-1890.

The Happy Isles of Oceania (1992) Paul Theroux. The master of railway travelogues sets out with kayak and tent to tour the Pacific.

NATURAL SCIENCE

Song for the Blue Ocean (1999) Carl Safina. Safina chronicles the decline of the world's marine resources due to human activities—an enthralling and alarming read.

Wayside Plants of the Islands (1995) W. Arthur Whistler. A guide to the lowland flora of the Pacific Islands.

HISTORY

On the Road of the Winds (2017) Patrick Vinton Kirch. Archaeological history of the Pacific Islands before European.

Polynesia: In Early Historic Times (2002) Douglas L. Oliver. An account of Polynesian life and culture at the time of first European contact.

LITERATURE

The Marriage of Loti (1987) Pierre Loti. This tale of Loti's visits to Tahiti in 1872 helped foster the romantic myth of Polynesia in Europe.

Typee, A Peep at Polynesian Life (1846) Herman Melville. In 1842 Melville deserted from an American whaler at Nuku Hiva, Marquesas Islands. This semifictional account of Melville's four months among the Typee people was followed by Omoo, in which Melville gives his impressions of Tahiti at the time of the French takeover.

Tales of the South Pacific (1989) James A. Michener. Short stories based on Michener's wartime experiences in the islands.

Pina (2017) Titua Peu. A novel about the ramifications of colonialism and a nine-year-old girl, Pina, who holds her family together.

Island of Shattered Dreams (2007) Chantal T. Spitz. A historical fiction novel that centers around a family living in French Polynesia just before the French nuclear tests.

Varua Tupu (2006) Frank Stewart, ed. A 216-page anthology of French Polynesian art and writing in translation.

Breadfruit (2000), *Frangipani* (2004), and *Tiare in Bloom* (2006) Célestine Hitiura

Viate. These stories tell relatable tales of womanhood in French Polynesia and make for great beach reads.

ARTS AND CULTURE

Dictionary of Polynesian Mythology (1989) Robert D. Craig. Aside from hundreds of alphabetical entries listing the legends, stories, gods, goddesses, and heroes of the Polynesians, this book charts the evolution of 30 Polynesian languages.

Oceanic Art (2018) Nicholas Thomas. Almost 200 illustrations grace the pages of this readable survey.

SUGGESTED FILMS

Since the days of silent movies, Hollywood has shared the fascination with Polynesia felt by poets and novelists. Many of the most popular films about the region are based on books by Charles Nordhoff, James Norman Hall, Somerset Maugham, and James A. Michener. And like the printed works, most of the films are about Europeans in the islands rather than the islanders themselves. Many of these works have not aged well to suit the modern era, given the dearth of input from the people who've called these islands home long before the arrival of Hollywood producers.

Tabu (1932) Robert Flaherty and F. W. Murnau. One of the classics of the silent movie era, *Tabu* is the story of two lovers who flee to a tiny island on Bora Bora's barrier reef.

Mutiny on the Bounty (1935) Frank Lloyd. This winner of the Oscar for Best Picture starred Charles Laughton as the cruel Captain Bligh and Clark Gable as gallant Fletcher Christian. Many background shots were filmed throughout Tahiti.

Mutiny on the Bounty (1962) Lewis Milestone. This extravagant MGM production starred Trevor Howard as Captain Bligh and Marlon Brando as Fletcher Christian. Unlike the 1935 *Bounty* movie filmed on Catalina Island in California, MGM captured the glorious color of Tahiti and Bora Bora. The salaries paid to the 6,000 extras used in the film had a real economic impact on Tahiti at the time.

The Bounty (1984) Roger Donaldson. With Sir Anthony Hopkins as a purposeful Bligh and Mel Gibson portraying an ambiguous Christian, this version of the mutiny comes closer to reality than the other two *Bounty* films and was filmed at Opunohu Bay on Moorea.

The Moon and Sixpence (1943) Albert Lewin. The film version of Somerset Maugham's novel about the glossy fictionalized life of Paul Gauguin in Polynesia appeals to the mind as much as to the senses and was filmed on Tahiti.

Couples Retreat (2009) Peter Billingsley. Four couples vacationing on a tropical isle (Bora Bora) find that participation in the resort's couples therapy is not optional.

Internet and Digital Resources

ALL TRAILS

www.alltrails.com

Provides GPS coordinates and maps of the region's most popular hikes, available for offline download.

AIR TAHITI

www.airtahiti.com

Purchase Air Tahiti tickets online; includes recommended itineraries using the Air Tahiti Multi Islands Air Pass.

AIR TAHITI NUI

www.airtahitinui.com

The site of the main international air carrier, with details on flights and packages to French Polynesia plus destination information.

E-TAHITI TRAVEL

www.etahititravel.com

An online travel agency with information on packages, hotels, cruises, flights, excursions, and car rentals.

REO

This Tahitian dictionary app for Apple and Android hosts over 16,000 Tahitian words and phrases translated both into English and French.

SV SOGGY PAWS

www.svsoggypaws.com

The blog of sailors who publish practical cruising guides and compendiums in their "Files" section. Includes thorough trip updates of the islands they've visited so far.

TAHITI.COM

www.tahiti.com

Provides detailed travel information on the Society Islands; assists with arranging tours, packages, and accommodations.

TAHITI RANDO

https://www.tahiti-rando.fr

A helpful website detailing hiking routes and hiking guides for both popular and offbeat routes throughout French Polynesia.

TAHITI TOURISME

www.tahititourisme.com

This official tourism site provides another useful introduction to French Polynesia. The many outside links allow you to access additional information, and there's an events calendar. Many of Tahiti Tourisme's overseas offices have sites of their own.

THE TAHITI TRAVELER

www.thetahititraveler.com

An online travel guide with background information, island guides, hotel listings, and photo galleries.

TRUE TAHITI VACATIONS

www.truetahitivacation.com

A good source of ideas for romantic vacations and honeymoons. There are sections on spa escapes, island activities, and specials.

X DAYS IN Y

www.xdaysiny.com

Thorough practical guides and firsthand experienced from a seasoned traveler.

Index

List of Maps

Photo Credits

Acknowledgments

FROM THE AUTHOR

Researching and writing a guidebook covering tens of islands is a task I could not complete without the help of many people. I'd like to first thank my partner, Moritz Wandres, who was always happy to lend an ear and top up my tea during late night writing sessions. A big *merci* to Hannah Logan, my de facto translator and adventure buddy in French Polynesia. Her positivity and humor made even the scary times fun (like driving on the edge of a cliff in the Marquesas).

A giant thank you to the team at Moon Travel Guides who have worked endlessly to make this book the best it can be. Thank you to Megan Anderluh and Grace Fujimoto for their ever-present guidance and support. Thank you Hannah Brezack, for your attention to detail. Thanks as well to David Stanley, the first author of this book.

Finally, *mauruuru* to the pilots and crew members of Air Tahiti and Air Tahiti Nui, the many hosts who welcomed me into their pensions, divemasters who safely led me on scuba dives, and tour guides who showed me around their island. I'd also like to thank my mom and Jeff, as well as my dad and Maria for letting me turn their homes into a writer's retreat.

FROM THE PUBLISHER

This edition of *Moon Tahiti & French Polynesia* is the first not researched and written by the incomparable **David Stanley,** one of Moon's founding authors and a guiding light for our philosophy of travel publishing. Over the course of four decades, he crossed six continents overland and visited almost every country in the world. His travel guidebooks to the South Pacific, Micronesia, Alaska, Eastern Europe, and Cuba opened those areas to independent travelers for the first time. Like any true traveler, David was supremely adaptable, always willing to make changes in response to evolving travel regulations, tourism infrastructure, series guidelines, and of course, the internet. He was a pleasure to work with; and for many of us at Moon, a true friend.

Embark on a transformative journey along the historic Camino de Santiago with Moon Travel Guides!

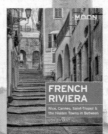

MOON

ACADIA
NATIONAL PARK

SEASIDE TOWNS · FALL FOLIAGE
CYCLING & PADDLING

HILARY NANGLE

MOON

ARCHES &
CANYONLANDS
NATIONAL PARKS

HIKING · BIKING
SCENIC DRIVES

JUDY JEWELL & W.C. MCRAE

MOON

BANFF
NATIONAL
PARK

HIKE · CAMP
SEE WILDLIFE

ANDREW HEMPSTEAD

MOON

DEATH VALLEY
NATIONAL PARK

HIKING · SCENIC DRIVES
DESERT SPRINGS & HIDDEN OASES

JENNA BLOUGH

MOON

GLACIER
NATIONAL PARK

HIKING · CAMPING
LAKES & PEAKS

BECKY LOMAX

MOON

GRAND
CANYON

HIKE · CAMP
RAFT THE
COLORADO RIVER

TIM HULL

MOON

GREAT SMOKY
MOUNTAINS
NATIONAL PARK

HIKING · CAMPING
SCENIC DRIVES

JASON FRYE

MOON

JOSHUA TREE
& PALM SPRINGS

HIKING · SCENIC DRIVES
DESERT GETAWAYS

JENNA BLOUGH

MOON

ROCKY
MOUNTAIN
NATIONAL PARK

HIKE · CAMP
SEE WILDLIFE

ERIN KASSLER

MOON

SEQUOIA &
KINGS CANYON

HIKING · CAMPING
WATERFALLS & BIG TREES

LEIGH BERNACCHI

MOON

YELLOWSTONE
& GRAND TETON

HIKE · CAMP
SEE WILDLIFE

BECKY LOMAX

MOON

YOSEMITE
SEQUOIA &
KINGS CANYON

HIKING · CAMPING
WATERFALLS & BIG TREES

ANN MARIE BROWN

MOON

ZION &
BRYCE

WITH ARCHES, CANYONLANDS, CAPITOL REEF,
GRAND STAIRCASE-ESCALANTE & MORE

HIKING · BIKING
SCENIC DRIVES

JUDY JEWELL & W.C. MCRAE

Spending
only a few
days in a
park?

Try our Best
Of guides.

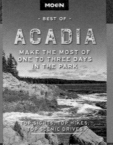

MOON

- BEST OF -

ACADIA

MAKE THE MOST OF
ONE TO THREE DAYS
IN THE PARK

TOP SIGHTS, TOP HIKES,
TOP SCENIC DRIVES

HILARY NANGLE

MOON

- BEST OF -

GLACIER, BANFF,
& JASPER

MAKE THE MOST OF
ONE TO THREE DAYS
IN THE PARKS

TOP SIGHTS, TOP HIKES,
TOP SCENIC DRIVES

BECKY LOMAX & ANDREW HEMPSTEAD

MOON

Plan your parks adventure!

AMALFI COAST

AZORES

BAJA

BALI & LOMBOK

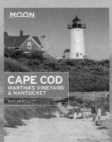

CAPE COD
MARTHA'S VINEYARD & NANTUCKET

Greek Islands & ATHENS

COSTA RICA

FIJI

More Beachy Escapes from Moon

Florida Gulf Coast

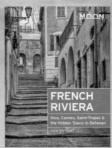

FRENCH RIVIERA
Nice, Cannes, Saint-Tropez & the Hidden Towns in Between

JAMAICA

Maui

PORTUGAL

PUERTO RICO

SOUTHERN ITALY
SICILY, PUGLIA, NAPLES & THE AMALFI COAST

YUCATÁN PENINSULA

MAP SYMBOLS

Highway	○ City/Town	🅿 Parking Area	🏊 Dive Site
Primary Road	◉ State Capital	🍶 Place of Worship	🏄 Surfing Site
Secondary Road	⊛ National Capital	🍷 Winery/Vineyard	🐚 Beach
Unpaved Road	◉ Highlight	🚩 Trailhead	✦ Unique Feature
Trail	★ Point of Interest	⬛ Camping	✦ Unique Feature Hydro
Ferry	• Accommodation	✈ International Airport	⬙ Waterfall
Pedestrian Walkway	▾ Restaurant/Bar	✈ Regional Airport	▲ Mountain
Stairs	■ Other Location	♠ Park	Coral Reef
	ⓘ Information Center	⚑ Golf Course	Forest

CONVERSION TABLES

°C = (°F - 32) / 1.8
°F = (°C x 1.8) + 32
1 inch = 2.54 centimeters (cm)
1 foot = 0.304 meters (m)
1 yard = 0.914 meters
1 mile = 1.6093 kilometers (km)
1 km = 0.6214 miles
1 fathom = 1.8288 m
1 chain = 20.1168 m
1 furlong = 201.168 m
1 acre = 0.4047 hectares
1 sq km = 100 hectares
1 sq mile = 2.59 square km
1 ounce = 28.35 grams
1 pound = 0.4536 kilograms
1 short ton = 0.90718 metric ton
1 short ton = 2,000 pounds
1 long ton = 1.016 metric tons
1 long ton = 2,240 pounds
1 metric ton = 1,000 kilograms
1 quart = 0.94635 liters
1 US gallon = 3.7854 liters
1 Imperial gallon = 4.5459 liters
1 nautical mile = 1.852 km

°FAHRENHEIT / °CELSIUS

°FAHRENHEIT	°CELSIUS	
230	110	
220	100	WATER BOILS
210		
200		
190	90	
180	80	
170		
160	70	
150	60	
140		
130	50	
120		
110	40	
100		
90	30	
80		
70	20	
60		
50	10	
40		
30	0	WATER FREEZES
20		
10	-10	
0		
-10	-20	
-20	-30	
-30		
-40	-40	

INCH 0 1 2 3 4

CM 0 1 2 3 4 5 6 7 8 9 10

MOON TAHITI & FRENCH POLYNESIA

Avalon Travel
Hachette Book Group
1700 Fourth Street
Berkeley, CA 94710, USA
www.moon.com

Editor: Megan Anderluh
Managing Editor: Hannah Brezack
Copy Editor: Jessica Gould
Graphics and Production Coordinator:
    Suzanne Albertson
Cover Design: Toni Tajima
Interior Design: Domini Dragoone
Map Editor: Kat Bennett
Cartographer: John Culp
Proofreader: Lina Carmona

ISBN-13: 978-1-64049-629-3

Printing History
1st Edition — June 2023
5 4 3 2 1

Front cover photo: Bora Bora Island sea lagoon beach © Prisma by Dukas Presseagentur GmbH / Alamy Stock

Back cover photo: Fish on coral reef Tahiti © Steve Allen | Dreamstime.com

Printed in Malaysia for Imago